Lecture Notes in Computer Science 13607

More information about this series at https://link.springer.com/bookseries/558

Jolita Ralyté · Sharma Chakravarthy ·
Mukesh Mohania · Manfred A. Jeusfeld ·
Kamalakar Karlapalem (Eds.)

Conceptual Modeling

41st International Conference, ER 2022
Hyderabad, India, October 17–20, 2022
Proceedings

Editors
Jolita Ralyté 🆔
University of Geneva
Carouge, Switzerland

Sharma Chakravarthy 🆔
The University of Texas at Arlington
Arlington, TX, USA

Mukesh Mohania 🆔
IIIT Delhi
New Delhi, India

Manfred A. Jeusfeld 🆔
University of Skövde
Skövde, Sweden

Kamalakar Karlapalem 🆔
International Institute of Information
Technology Gachibowli
Hyderabad, India

ISSN 0302-9743   ISSN 1611-3349 (electronic)
Lecture Notes in Computer Science
ISBN 978-3-031-17994-5   ISBN 978-3-031-17995-2 (eBook)
https://doi.org/10.1007/978-3-031-17995-2

This Springer imprint is published by the registered company Springer Nature Switzerland AG
The registered company address is: Gewerbestrasse 11, 6330 Cham, Switzerland

Preface

We are pleased to welcome you to the proceedings of the 41st edition of the International Conference on Conceptual Modeling (ER 2022), which took place during October 17–20, 2022. Originally, the conference was planned to take place in the beautiful city of Hyderabad, India, but due to the uncertain COVID-19 situation it was finally held virtually.

The ER conference series aims to bring together researchers and practitioners building foundations of conceptual modeling and/or applying conceptual modeling in a wide range of software engineering fields. Conceptual modeling has never been more important in this age of uncertainty. As individuals, organizations, and nations face new and unexpected challenges, software and data must be developed that can cope with and help address this new uncertainty in an ever-faster changing world. Conceptual modeling can be used to describe, understand, and cope with increasing levels of uncertainty in our world. Conference topics of interest include the theories of concepts and ontologies underlying conceptual modeling, modeling languages, methods and tools for developing and communicating conceptual models, and techniques for transforming conceptual models into effective implementations.

This year, ER 2022 chose as an overall theme "Conceptual Modeling to Support Big Data Analytics and AI". Big data analytics demands modeling complex data in a variety of models and accommodating the 5V's (Volume, Velocity, Variety, Value, and Veracity). Can the conceptual modeling community seize the opportunity to meet the needs of big data analytics? Conceptual modeling helps deep understanding of data and knowledge that is the backbone of AI systems. The modern data-driven AI systems have less representation schemes for the input data and the output. Techniques that aid the conceptual understanding of data movement through deep learning models help to develop and apply these learning models.

A total of 82 papers were submitted to the main track of the conference. Each paper went through a thorough review process and received at least three reviews from members of the Program Committee. The papers with no clear decision were discussed online. The discussions were moderated by senior Program Committee members who helped us with the final selection by providing recommendations and writing meta-reviews. We are deeply grateful to all the members of the Program Committee for their competence and fairness. The results of the review process allowed us to accept 19 high-quality full papers and 11 short papers which are included in this volume.

In addition to the paper presentations organized in eight sessions, the conference program included four inspiring keynote talks: "Conceptual Modelling in the Age of Artificial Intelligence and Quantum Computing", by Wolfgang Maaß from the Saarland University, Germany; "In an Increasingly Digital World, You Have to Put the People First", by Bas van Gils from Strategy Alliance, The Netherlands, and Antwerp Management School, Belgium; "Modeling and Software", by Pankaj Jalote from IIIT-Delhi, India; and "Threat Intelligence Modeling Using Graphs", by Ashish Kundu from

Cisco Research, USA. We thank the speakers for sharing their knowledge, research achievements, and practice insights.

Besides the main track, ER 2022 hosted a Doctoral Symposium, where PhD students could present their research projects and receive advice from advanced academics, and a Forum, Demo and Poster track, allowing researchers to present novel and innovative outcomes regarding conceptual modeling.

Finally, the conference program also included five interesting tutorials and a panel on "New Frontiers for Conceptual Modeling". We thank the presenters for transmitting their knowledge and expertise to the ER community.

Overall, organizing ER 2022 was a great pleasure, since we had an exceptional Organizing Committee. We thank all the chairs for their engagement and contribution.

We also thank Springer for their assistance in the production of the conference proceedings and EasyChair for providing an efficient conference management system. Special thanks to our sponsors and to the ER Steering Committee.

October 2022

Jolita Ralyté
Sharma Chakravarthy
Mukesh Mohania
Manfred A. Jeusfeld
Kamalakar Karlapalem

Organization

General Chairs

Kamalakar Karlapalem   IIIT Hyderabad, India
Manfred A. Jeusfeld   University of Skövde, Sweden

Program Committee Chairs

Sharma Chakravarthy   University of Texas at Arlington, USA
Mukesh Mohania   IIIT Delhi, India
Jolita Ralyté   University of Geneva, Switzerland

Workshop Chairs

Renata Guizzardi   University of Twente, The Netherlands
Bernd Neumayr   Johannes Kepler University Linz, Austria

Tutorial Chairs

Hans-Georg Fill   University of Fribourg, Switzerland
Vinay Vkulkarni   Tata Consultancy Services, India

Panel Chairs

Vikram Goyal   IIIT Delhi, India
Carson Woo   University of British Columbia, Canada

Forum, Demo and Posters Chairs

Sebastian Link   University of Auckland, New Zealand
Iris Reinhartz-Berger   University of Haifa, Israel
Jelena Zdravkovic   Stockholm University, Sweden

Doctoral Symposium Chairs

Dominik Bork   TU Wien, Austria
Srinath Srinivasa   IIIT Bangalore, India

Sponsoring and Industry Chairs

Aditya Ghose	University of Wollongong, Australia
Henderik A. Proper	LIST, Luxembourg

Publicity Chairs

Judith Michael	RWTH Aachen University, Germany
Marcela Ruiz	Zurich University of Applied Sciences, Switzerland

Local Organizing Chair

P. Radha Krishna	National Institute of Technology Warangal, India

Web Co-chairs

Sangharatna Godboley	National Institute of Technology Warangal, India
Syed Juned Ali	TU Wien, Austria

Steering Committee

Peter P. Chen	Louisiana State University, USA
Isabelle Comyn-Wattiau	ESSEC and CNAM, France
Karen Davis	Miami University, USA
Ulrich Frank	Universität Duisburg-Essen, Germany
Aditya Ghose	University of Wollongong, Australia
Giancarlo Guizzardi	Free University of Bozen-Bolzano, Italy, and University of Twente, The Netherlands
Jennifer Horkoff	University of Gothenburg, Sweden
Matthias Jarke	RWTH Aachen University, Germany
Paul Johannesson	KTH Royal Institute of Technology, Sweden
Gerti Kappel	TU Wien, Austria
Alberto Laender	Universidade Federal de Minas Gerais, Brazil
Stephen W. Liddle	Brigham Young University, USA
Tok Wang Ling	National University of Singapore, Singapore
Hui Ma	Victoria University of Wellington, New Zealand
Heinrich C. Mayr	Alpen-Adria-Universität Klagenfurt, Austria
Antoni Olivé	Universitat Politècnica de Catalunya, Spain
José Palazzo Moreira de Oliveira	Universidade Federal do Rio Grande do Sul, Brazil
Jeffrey Parsons	Memorial University of Newfoundland, Canada
Oscar Pastor	Universidad Politécnica de Valencia, Spain

Sudha Ram	University of Arizona, USA
Motoshi Saeki	Tokyo Institute of Technology, Japan
Peretz Shoval	Ben-Gurion University, Israel
Vítor E. Silva Souza	Federal University of Espírito Santo, Brazil
Il-Yeol Song	Drexel University, USA
Veda C. Storey	Georgia State University, USA
Juan Carlos Trujillo	University of Alicante, Spain
Yair Wand	University of British Columbia, Canada
Carson Woo	University of British Columbia, Canada
Eric Yu	University of Toronto, Canada

Senior Program Committee

Jacky Akoka	CNAM, France
Paolo Atzeni	Università Roma Tre, Italy
Stefano Ceri	Politecnico di Milano, Italy
Isabelle Comyn-Wattiau	ESSEC and CNAM, France
Karen Davis	Miami University, USA
Gill Dobbie	University of Auckland, New Zealand
Xavier Franch	Universitat Politècnica de Catalunya, Spain
Ulrich Frank	Universität Duisburg-Essen, Germany
Aditya Ghose	University of Wollongong, Australia
Giancarlo Guizzardi	Free University of Bozen-Bolzano, Italy, and University of Twente, The Netherlands
Jennifer Horkoff	University of Gothenburg, Sweden
Matthias Jarke	RWTH Aachen University, Germany
Paul Johannesson	KTH Royal Institute of Technology, Sweden
Alberto Laender	Universidade Federal de Minas Gerais, Brazil
Stephen W. Liddle	Brigham Young University, USA
Sebastian Link	University of Auckland, New Zealand
Heinrich C. Mayr	Alpen-Adria-Universität Klagenfurt, Austria
John Mylopoulos	University of Toronto, Canada
Antoni Olivé	Universitat Politècnica de Catalunya, Spain
Oscar Pastor	Universidad Politécnica de Valencia, Spain
Jeffrey Parsons	Memorial University of Newfoundland, Canada
Colette Rolland	Université Paris 1 Panthéon-Sorbonne, France
Motoshi Saeki	Tokyo Institute of Technology, Japan
Peretz Shoval	Ben-Gurion University, Israel
Pnina Soffer	University of Haifa, Israel
Veda C. Storey	Georgia State University, USA
Juan-Carlos Trujillo	University of Alicante, Spain
Carson Woo	University of British Columbia, Canada
Eric Yu	University of Toronto, Canada

Program Committee

Mara Abel	Universidade Federal do Rio Grande do Sul, Brazil
João Paulo Almeida	Federal University of Espirito Santo, Brazil
João Araujo	Universidade NOVA de Lisboa, Portugal
Fernanda Baião	PUC-Rio, Brazil
Wolf-Tilo Balke	TU Braunschweig, Germany
Ladjel Bellatreche	LIAS, ISAE-ENSMA, France
Devis Bianchini	University of Brescia, Italy
Sandro Bimonte	INRAE, France
Dominik Bork	TU Wien, Austria
Shawn Bowers	Gonzaga University, USA
Stephane Bressan	National University of Singapore, Singapore
Robert Andrei Buchmann	Babeș-Bolyai University of Cluj Napoca, Romania
Cinzia Cappiello	Politecnico di Milano, Italy
Luca Cernuzzi	Universidad Católica, Paraguay
Suphamit Chittayasothorn	King Mongkut's Institute of Technology Ladkrabang, Thailand
Tony Clark	Aston University, UK
Dolors Costal	Universitat Politècnica de Catalunya, Spain
Fabiano Dalpiaz	Utrecht University, The Netherlands
Sergio de Cesare	University of Westminster, UK
Johann Eder	Alpen Adria Universität Klagenfurt, Austria
Vadim Ermolayev	Zaporizhzhia National University, Ukraine
Rik Eshuis	Eindhoven University of Technology, The Netherlands
Hans-Georg Fill	University of Fribourg, Switzerland
Frederik Gailly	Ghent University, Belgium
Yunjun Gao	Zhejiang University, China
Faiez Gargouri	Institut Supérieur d'Informatique et de Multimédia de Sfax, Tunisia
Aurona Gerber	University of Pretoria, South Africa
Mohamed Gharzouli	Constantine 2 University, Algeria
Asif Qumer Gill	University of Technology Sydney, Australia
Cesar Gonzalez-Perez	Incipit CSIC, Spain
Georg Grossmann	University of South Australia, Australia
Esther Guerra	Universidad Autónoma de Madrid, Spain
Renata Guizzardi	University of Twente, The Netherlands
Simon Hacks	University of Southern Denmark, Denmark
Sven Hartmann	Clausthal University of Technology, Germany
Martin Henkel	Stockholm University, Sweden

Shareeful Islam	Anglia Ruskin University, UK
Ivan Jureta	University of Namur, Belgium
Marite Kirikova	Riga Technical University, Latvia
Agnes Koschmider	Kiel University, Germany
Vinay Kulkarni	Tata Consultancy Services Research, India
Hui Luo	RMIT University, Australia
Hui Ma	Victoria University of Wellington, New Zealand
Wolfgang Maass	Saarland University, Germany
Beatriz Marín	Universidad Politécnica de València, Spain
Wolfgang Mayer	University of South Australia, Australia
Massimo Mecella	Sapienza University of Rome, Italy
Judith Michael	RWTH Aachen University, Germany
Haralambos Mouratidis	University of Essex, UK
Nanjangud Narendra	Ericsson Research, India
Selmin Nurcan	Université Paris 1 Panthéon-Sorbonne, France
Shawn Ogunsey	Bentley University, USA
Andreas L. Opdahl	University of Bergen, Norway
Jose M. Parente De Oliveira	Aeronautics Institute of Technology, Brazil
Barbara Pernici	Politecnico di Milano, Italy
Geert Poels	Ghent University, Belgium
Christoph Quix	Fraunhofer FIT, Germany
Manfred Reichert	University of Ulm, Germany
Hajo A. Reijers	Utrecht University, The Netherlands
Iris Reinhartz-Berger	University of Haifa, Israel
Manuel Resinas	University of Seville, Spain
Genaina Rodrigues	University of Brasilia, Brazil
Marcela Ruiz	Zurich University of Applied Sciences, Switzerland
Sourav S. Bhowmick	Nanyang Technological University, Singapore
Shazia Sadiq	University of Queensland, Australia
Melike Sah	Near East University, Cyprus
Jie Shao	University of Science and Technology of China, China
Vítor E. Silva Souza	Universidade Federal do Espírito Santo, Brazil
Samira Si-Said Cherfi	CNAM, France
Stefan Strecker	University of Hagen, Germany
Markus Stumptner	University of South Australia, Australia
Arnon Sturm	Ben-Gurion University, Israel
Angelo Susi	Fondazione Bruno Kessler – ICT Irst, Italy
David Taniar	Monash University, Australia
Ernest Teniente	Universitat Politècnica de Catalunya, Spain
Victoria Torres	Universitat Politècnica de València, Spain

Panos Vassiliadis	University of Ioannina, Greece
Gottfried Vossen	ERCIS, Germany
Chaokun Wang	Tsinghua University, China
Xiaoli Wang	Xiamen University, China
Yves Wautelet	Katholieke Universiteit Leuven, Belgium
Hans Weigand	Tilburg University, The Netherlands
Manuel Wimmer	Johannes Kepler University Linz, Austria
Robert Wrembel	Poznan University of Technology, Poland
Apostolos Zarras	University of Ioannina, Greece
Jelena Zdravkovic	Stockholm University, Sweden
Xiangmin Zhou	RMIT University, Australia
Xuan Zhou	Renmin University of China, China

Additional Reviewers

Doyinsola Afolabi
Syed Juned Ali
Carlo Alberto Bono
Sissi Chan
Simon Curty
Karamjit Kaur
Jens Lechtenbörger
Yunkai Lou
Fabian Muff

Sreedhar Reddy
Gabriel Rodrigues
Kristina Rosenthal
Matt Selway
Vladimir A. Shekhovtsov
Gengyuan Shi
Sagar Sunkle
Benjamin Ternes
Yorck Zisgen

Abstracts of Invited Keynotes

Conceptual Modelling in the Age of Artificial Intelligence and Quantum Computing

Wolfgang Maass [1,2]

[1] Saarland University, Germany
[2] German Research Center for Artificial Intelligence (DFKI), Germany
wolfgang.maass@dfki.de

Keynote Abstract

Models are not true, but some are useful. Models are either used as mental constructs by individuals or they are used by groups as social constructs. Conceptual modeling has always focused on socially constructed, explicit representations that are useful for gaining shared understanding of an affair or even for designing and implementing technical systems, most of all information systems.

For mental representations of individuals, the working hypothesis of neuroscience is that mental representations are embossed into neural structures and ultimately into electric signals. Socially constructed conceptual models require explication by representations governed by some shared conceptual-modelling grammar (Wand & Weber 2001), i.e., they become social reality by information in a medium.

Different phases of conceptual modeling have been conducted in the past decades. Initially, conceptual models were fully controlled and "closed" representations, e.g., frames. This was followed by a phase of conceptual models that are unrestricted ("open") for capturing the richness of human knowledge in general, most of all ontologies. Statistical models and machine learning models often lack direct connections to individual knowledge and socially constructed knowledge but emerge from data alone. The underlying assumption is that data is taken directly from reality and is therefore objective. Recent discussions on biases and distortions of data raise the question of the social construction of data as well. Current research on explainability and interpretability tries to build bridges between both fields. Hybrid models are an attempt in this direction by trying to merge socially constructed conceptual models with machine learning models. The success of machine learning models has initiated chip design research to develop dedicated chips that can directly support AI processing. This might have repercussions on preferred designs of information systems and machine learning models. Even more advanced are quantum computing and quantum information theory when transforming data representations into quantum representations that are accessible by quantum computing algorithms.

In this talk, common aspects between all these fields are discussed and some thoughts on research questions will be presented. A focus will be laid on the interplay between conceptual modeling and machine learning models but also some connections to advanced chip designs and quantum computing are given.

In an Increasingly Digital World, You Have to Put the People First

Bas van Gils[1,2]

[1] Strategy Alliance, Amersfoort, The Netherlands
[2] Antwerp Management School, Antwerp, Belgium
bas.vangils@strategy-alliance.com

Keynote Abstract

Digital transformation is a key trend in which data plays a crucial role. As a result of the ongoing digital transformation, in line with the *law of requisite variety*, I see increased complexity and variety that helps in dealing with the challenges of today. Complexity is not bad in and of itself, as long as we have enough understanding of the organization in order to manage it effectively, and even use it to our advantage.

Three real-world cases show that organizations struggle with data/data management. Key questions in this are: (1) Do we know our data well enough in order to use it? (2) How do we balance "grip on data" with "value creation"? I will argue that effective use of models can help answer these questions. This is not a new position: several scholars have made this claim in the past as well. Very few organizations appear to have a mature modeling capability, leading to high cost, low agility, and hindering digital transformation. It is entering to ponder how this state of affairs came to be: why is modeling such an under valued skill in light of the fact that both scientific theories as well as heuristic frameworks emphasize it so strongly? Going a step further: why is "theory" such a dirty word in most organizations, up to the point where considering the use of heuristics-based frameworks is already cause for raised eyebrows and serious discussions?

There is no silver bullet that will improve the status quo: if there was, we would have found it by now. I will propose a strategy that combines a fast cycle (learning by doing) and a slow cycle (build the capability, re-learn the value of theory/models) to move forward. This generic approach can only be successful when tailored to the specific situation in an organization. Last but not least, I will argue that training and experimentation are key enablers: don't wait to educate people when they are in the field but start already during their university education.

Modeling and Software

Pankaj Jalote

IIIT-Delhi, Okhla, New Delhi, India
jalote@iiitd.ac.in

Keynote Abstract

No complex system can be built without effective modeling. And software systems are complex. Hence, modeling is necessary for building software systems, and a range of models are used for different tasks in the software development process – each playing an important role for that task. The nature and use of models in building a system, however, depends on the nature of the system also – if the system being developed is "hardware" which is costly to change, more rigorous and detailed modeling becomes necessary. If the system being developed is "software" which is easy to change and the cost of change is not high, modeling can be at higher levels of abstraction helping develop the software solution, rather than guiding the development of the details of the system. In other words, for software it is often desirable to have a gap between models and the final solution, and while models guide the development of the solution, it may be acceptable to have the final solution diverge from the model. In such situations, reverse engineering models from the solution can also be useful. Detailed modeling is more appropriate for application domains where errors and changes in the solution are much more expensive. In such cases, domain specific modeling can be useful which may lead to executable models. However, if models are to be executable, then the modeling language becomes another programming language at a higher level of abstraction and needs to compete in other programming languages for that domain.

Threat Intelligence Modeling Using Graphs

Ashish Kundu ⓘ

Head of Cybersecurity Research, Cisco Research, San Jose, CA, USA
ashishkundu@gmail.com

Keynote Abstract

Security attacks form a system of specific flow of computation and data by one or multiple threats. Attacks follow a set of steps in a sequence. Threats work together as threat groups. Holistic 360-degree defenses against APTs often interconnect multiple threat intelligence computation and defense mechanisms. Each of these processes have a graph structure inherent to their execution. Graphs can be used to model spatio-temporal dimensions and flows of different facets of security as well as privacy. In our previous work, we have studied the use of graphs for modeling security lifecycle, attacks, attack surface as well as defense modeling. Moreover, we have also modeled threat intelligence as a system of graphs and using graph analytics and graph deep learning in order to predict, infer, extract features and information for assuring holistic security. Such work has been developed in the context of autonomous cars, AI, cloud and edge computing. In this talk, we will also explore how to use NLP and NLU on how to automatically construct such graph models for specific systems under protection/attack.

Contents

Foundations of Conceptual Modeling

A FAIR Model Catalog
for Ontology-Driven Conceptual Modeling
Research

Pedro Paulo F. Barcelos[1]([✉]), Tiago Prince Sales[1], Mattia Fumagalli[1],
Claudenir M. Fonseca[1], Isadora Valle Sousa[1], Elena Romanenko[1],
Joshua Kritz[2], and Giancarlo Guizzardi[1,2]

[1] Conceptual and Cognitive Modeling Research Group (CORE),
Free University of Bozen -Bolzano, Bolzano, Italy
{pfavatobarcelos,tprincesales,mfumagalli,cmoraisfonseca,ivallesousa,
eromanenko}@unibz.it
[2] University of Twente, Enschede, The Netherlands
{j.kritz,g.guizzardi}@utwente.nl

Abstract. Conceptual models are artifacts representing conceptualizations of particular domains. Hence, multi-domain model catalogs serve as empirical sources of knowledge and insights about specific domains, about the use of a modeling language's constructs, as well as about the patterns and anti-patterns recurrent in the models of that language cross-cutting different domains. However, to support domain and language learning, model reuse, knowledge discovery for humans, and reliable automated processing and analysis by machines, these catalogs must be built following generally accepted quality requirements for scientific data management. Especially, all scientific (meta)data—including models—should be created using the FAIR principles (Findability, Accessibility, Interoperability, and Reusability). In this paper, we report on the construction of a FAIR model catalog for Ontology-Driven Conceptual Modeling research, a trending paradigm lying at the intersection of conceptual modeling and ontology engineering in which the Unified Foundational Ontology (UFO) and OntoUML emerged among the most adopted technologies. In this initial release, the catalog includes over a hundred models, developed in a variety of contexts and domains. The paper also discusses the research implications for (ontology-driven) conceptual modeling of such a resource.

Keywords: Ontology · Ontouml · Data catalog · Fair · Linked data

1   Introduction

Conceptual models are concrete artifacts representing conceptualizations of particular domains. Ontology-Driven Conceptual Modeling (ODCM) is a trending paradigm that lies at the intersection of conceptual modeling and ontology

J. Ralyté et al. (Eds.): ER 2022, LNCS 13607, pp. 3–17, 2022.
https://doi.org/10.1007/978-3-031-17995-2_1

engineering. ODCM is frequently about the use of foundational ontologies, i.e., axiomatic ontological theories (in the philosophical sense) to improve conceptual models, modeling languages, and tools [26].

In this context, the Unified Foundational Ontology (UFO) and the UFO-based conceptual modeling language OntoUML [5,8,12,13] have emerged among the most used approaches in the field [26]. Over the years, UFO and OntoUML have been adopted by research, industrial, and governmental institutions worldwide to create ODCM models in different domains [13,26]. In this context, conceptual models are created either by directly extending UFO's categories (e.g., having the type *Agent* specializing the UFO type *Object*, or having the type *Action* specializing the UFO type *Event*) or, more frequently, by using OntoUML stereotypes for classes and relations—which also reflect UFO's ontological distinctions (e.g., decorating the type *Action* with the ≪ event ≫ stereotype).

Multi-domain model catalogs serve as sources of empirical knowledge and insights about: (i) how specific domains are modeled (ii) the use of a modeling language's constructs, and (iii) domain-independent patterns that emerge from the use of a language. However, to support domain and language learning, model reuse, knowledge discovery for humans, and reliable automated processing and analysis by machines, these repositories must be built following generally accepted quality requirements for scientific data management. In particular, all scientific (meta)data—including models—must be created using the FAIR principles, which are: **F**indability, **A**ccessibility, **I**nteroperability, and **R**eusability [27].

In this paper, we report on the construction of an ODCM catalog, henceforth termed the **OntoUML/UFO Catalog**. This is, to the best of our knowledge, the first FAIR catalog of ontology-driven conceptual models. It is a structured, collaborative, and open-source catalog that contains UFO-grounded models—the vast majority of which are represented in OntoUML [5,8,12].

The OntoUML/UFO Catalog has two goals. First, we want to provide curated structured data to support empirical research in OntoUML/UFO, specifically, and on conceptual modeling in general. For example, this can provide high-quality data on *why*, *where*, and *how* these approaches are used, which can enable researchers to understand the evolution of the language and its foundations. It can also serve as a repository for patterns and anti-patterns detection [20], as well as a benchmark against which, e.g., language transformation models [2] and complexity management techniques [11,19] can be assessed. Additionally, it can support novice modelers who want to learn ODCM in OntoUML/UFO, as well as advanced users who want to reuse existing models as *seed models* [3].

The first catalog release offers a diverse collection of 127 models obtained from academic and industrial sources, created by modelers with varying modeling skills, for a range of domains, and for different purposes. These models are available in the JavaScript Object Notation (JSON) and Turtle machine-readable formats, and are accessible via permanent Uniform Resource Identifiers (URIs).

The rest of this paper is organized as follows. Section 2 discusses the process we followed and the tools we have used to create the catalog. Section 3 presents the catalog's structure and introduces the vocabularies we used to build it. Section 4 briefly discusses some statistics on the current release of the catalog. Section 5 evaluates the catalog with relation to the FAIR principles. Section 6 elaborates on the importance of the catalog for the community and on the different research endeavors it facilitates or enables. Section 7 positions our work with relation to other catalogs and datasets available to the modeling community. Finally, Sect. 8 makes some final considerations and discusses future works.

2   Methods and Materials

The OntoUML/UFO Catalog was conceived to be open and easily accessible to all members of the modeling community, to allow collaborative work, and to be easily maintainable. These are important requirements in this context, since we envision a continuous growth of the catalog in years to come. To reach these goals, we created a GitHub repository for hosting the catalog and associated it with a permanent URL[1].

The first activity for the catalog creation was the definition of a set of governance rules, an activity done by a team of OntoUML and Linked Data specialists. To be accepted into the catalog, a dataset submission had to comply with these rules. For example, a basic rule regarded what exactly constituted a submission: a *dataset submission* should include three files: the UFO-based/OntoUML model itself, a file with the model's metadata information, and the model's associated bibliography (when available). The catalog rules are formalized and made available for contributors on its GitHub's wiki page.

Once these rules were established, we could then populate the catalog. We encouraged the participation of the conceptual modeling and ontology engineering communities through public invitations for collaboration. Researchers were asked to submit their models to the catalog. Intending to familiarize them with the catalog structure and content, we also requested their cooperation for the migration of existing data to the catalog. Seventeen experienced modelers contributed to this activity.

To cover as many models as possible and to reduce the chances of receiving duplicates, we elaborated a list of all OntoUML/UFO-based models that we could find in a broad non-systematic literature search and in personal databases (e.g., OntoUML/UFO-based models developed by students during academic courses)—the final list contained more than 300 models.

After collecting these models, our collaborators began the data migration phase, which comprised adapting the original models to the catalog standards. The collaborators obtained images of OntoUML/UFO-based models from papers and technical reports and manually rebuilt them on the latest version (v16.3) of the Visual Paradigm (VP) modeling editor[2] using the ontouml-vp-plugin[3]. This

---

[1] https://purl.org/ontouml-models.

[2] Despite being a commercial tool, VP (https://www.visual-paradigm.com/) has a free community version that could be used by our contributors.

[3] Downloadable from https://purl.org/ontouml-vp.

plugin is an extension to VP that offers several important modeling services [6]. For example, it allows the use of OntoUML constructs (stereotypes for classes, associations, and attributes) when building UML class diagrams, and supports syntax verification, model serialization in JSON and Web Ontology Language (OWL), as well as model modularization and abstraction. Models already available in editable format were imported into VP.

We provided instructions to modelers to harmonize systematically their design decisions, including a Frequent Asked Questions (FAQ) page in the GitHub catalog's wiki for specifying topics that could lead to inconsistencies. As we want the migrated models to be as truthful as possible to the original ones, collaborators were advised not to reinterpret the model to be submitted and, e.g., they were asked to: preserve the original OntoUML stereotypes used, keep syntactical errors, maintain the original diagram layout as much as possible, and preserve the original terminology used in the model.

Files containing BibTeX references and, especially, rich metadata (see discussion in Sect. 3) for the submitted datasets were produced. As these files are fundamental parts of a dataset submission, the rules on how they should be produced were also detailed in the catalog's wiki.

To ensure the catalog's consistency, every new submission was subject to peer evaluation by the catalog curators (a team of OntoUML/UFO experts). The evaluation included a manual analysis of the files composing the dataset, checking for errors, and verifying their compliance with the defined catalog's governance rules. Once approved, the dataset was included in the catalog, where complementary files associated with it were derived. By the end of this process, the submitted dataset was then included in the catalog.

3   Catalog Structure

Following the recommendations for implementing the FAIR principles [15], the OntoUML/UFO *catalog schema* (see Fig. 1) reuses classes and properties from the following vocabularies:

- Data Catalog Vocabulary (DCAT)[4]
- Dublin Core Terms (DCT)[5]
- Simple Knowledge Organization System (SKOS)[6]
- Metadata for Ontology Description and Publication (MOD)[7]
- Friend of a Friend (FOAF)[8]

The catalog (dcat:Catalog) is maintained by a community of users (foaf:Agent), composed of a set of models (instances of mod:SemanticArtefact), which are described by the following metadata (asterisks show mandatory items):

---

[4] https://www.w3.org/TR/vocab-dcat-2/.
[5] https://www.dublincore.org/specifications/dublin-core/dcmi-terms/.
[6] https://www.w3.org/TR/skos-reference/.
[7] https://w3id.org/mod/2.0.
[8] http://xmlns.com/foaf/0.1.

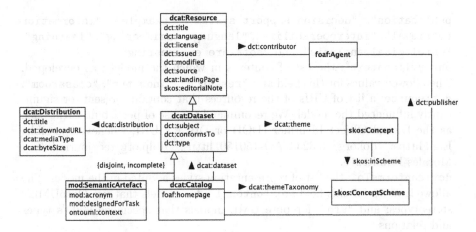

Fig. 1. The OntoUML/UFO Catalog schema in a UML class diagram representation.

- `dct:title`*: the name of the model. E.g., `"Common Ontology of Value and Risk"`, `"Reference Ontology of Trust"`.
- `mod:acronym`: the acronym one can use to refer to the model. E.g., `"RDBS-O"`, `"COVER"`, `"ROT"`.
- `dct:issued`: the year when the model was first published. E.g., 2022.
- `dct:modified`: the year of the most recent publication of the model (in a scientific publication, a technical report, a website, etc.). E.g., 2018.
- `dct:contributor`: a list of URIs of people who contributed to the development of the model. If possible, we recommend using a contributor's persistent URI from DBLP (e.g., https://dblp.org/pid/96/8280) or ORCID (e.g., https://orcid.org/0000-0003-2736-7817).
- `dct:subject`*: a list of strings that identify the domains covered by the model. E.g., `"robotic"`, `"technology"`, `"services"`, `"risk"`.
- `dcat:theme`*: the central theme of the model according to the Library of Congress Classification (LCC) system.[9] E.g., `"Class S - Agriculture"`, `"Class T - Technology"`. LCC is available as a `skos:ConceptScheme` and each of its classes as instances of `skos:Concept`.
- `skos:editorialNote`: general notes on the model documentation process. E.g., `"The ontology was originally designed in Portuguese"`.
- `dct:type`*: the list of types in which the model can have categories. Since OntoUML and UFO are frequently used for building `core` and `domain` ontologies, these are among the allowed values for this field (the other allowed value is `application`).
- `dct:language`*: the language in which the lexical labels of the model are written (using the IANA Language Sub Tag Registry[10]). E.g., `"en"`, `"pt"`.
- `mod:designedForTask`*: the list of goals that motivated the development of the model. The allowed values are `"conceptual clarification"`, `"data`

---

[9] https://www.loc.gov/catdir/cpso/lcco/.
[10] https://www.iana.org/assignments/language-subtag-registry/.

publication", "decision support system", "example", "information
retrieval", "interoperability", "language engineering", "learning",
"ontological analysis", and "software engineering".

- ontouml:context*: the list of contexts in which the model was developed.
  The allowed values for this field are: "research", "industry", "classroom".
- dct:source: a list of URIs of the resources that contain, present, or significantly influenced the model. We recommend the use of persistent URIs, such
  as the Digital Object Identifier (DOI) or DBLP's URI, whenever possible.
  E.g., https://doi.org/10.3233/AO-150150, https://dblp.org/rec/journals/ao/
  Morales-Ramirez15.
- dct:conformsTo*: the list of representation styles adopted in the model. The
  allowed values for this field are: "ontouml", for models that use OntoUML's
  stereotypes; and "ufo", for pure UML models that specialize UFO's types
  and relations.
- dcat:landingPage: a URL of a web page to gain access to the ontology,
  its distributions and/or additional information. E.g., https://www.model-a-
  platform.com.
- dct:license: a URI of the model's license. E.g., https://creativecommons.
  org/licenses/by/4.0/.

Each model, after being added to the catalog, is available via three distributions (dcat:Distribution), namely a JSON distribution, a Turtle distribution,
and a distribution in the format of the modeling tool used to represent the model.
Each distribution is described by a dcat:title and a dcat:downloadURL.

A GitHub repository hosts the whole catalog. Its root directory has: (a) a
catalog.ttl file[11] that is the file encoding the catalog itself—i.e., the aggregated data of all datasets that are part of the catalog; (b) a metadata.ttl file,
which provides (in a triple-based format) all the catalog's metadata listed above,
and which aggregates all metadata from its composing datasets; and (c) a list
of folders—the datasets, each one including all the information related to an
OntoUML/UFO-based model. We structured the dataset folders as from Fig. 2,
namely:

- ontology.vpp: the Visual Paradigm project of the model;
- ontology.json: contains the JSON serialization of the model exported via
  the ontouml-vp-plugin;
- ontology.ttl: uses the OntoUML Metamodel in OWL[12] to map the model's
  data. This is a vocabulary designed to support the serialization and exchange
  of OntoUML models in compliance with the ontouml-schema[13], which is a
  specification of how to serialize OntoUML models as JSON objects [6]. This
  file provides a specific URI for all data from the model[14], and its publication
  allows anyone to access and manipulate all the model's instances;

---

[11] https://purl.org/ontouml-models/catalog.
[12] https://purl.org/ontouml-models/vocabulary.
[13] https://purl.org/ontouml-schema.
[14] These URIs are generated according to the following template:
https://purl.org/ontouml-models/<folder name>.

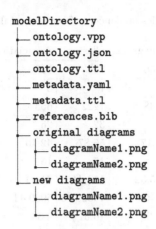

```
modelDirectory
├── ontology.vpp
├── ontology.json
├── ontology.ttl
├── metadata.yaml
├── metadata.ttl
├── references.bib
├── original diagrams
│   ├── diagramName1.png
│   └── diagramName2.png
└── new diagrams
    ├── diagramName1.png
    └── diagramName2.png
```

Fig. 2. Folder structure for each model in the catalog.

- `metadata.yaml`: contains the model's metadata;
- `metadata.ttl`: is an Resource Description Framework (RDF)-based version in Turtle syntax of `metadata.yaml`.
- `references.bib`: contains the BibTeX citation data for each publication about the model (this file is not required for unpublished models).
- `original diagrams/`: is a folder containing images in PNG format of the diagrams created by the authors of the model.
- `new diagrams/`: is a folder containing images in PNG format of all diagrams rebuilt on Visual Paradigm (keeping the names matching the original ones).

Note that the `vpp`, `yaml`, and `bib` files are the ones provided by the collaborators. In contrast, the OntoUML plugin for Visual Paradigm automatically generates the `json` file for each model. The `png` files hosted in the `new diagrams` folder are automatically generated; the same occurs for all the `ttl` files.

4   Catalog Statistics

4.1   Statistics on the Models

Table 1 presents some basic statistics in the current state of the catalog, considering the number of diagrams, classes, domain associations, and generalizations relations. These statistics give us an idea of the dimension of the models there included. In its current version, the catalog has 127 models, which have 656 diagrams, 7223 classes, 5392 associations, and 5474 generalizations. The size of the represented models varies, ranging from simple models with only 7 classes or models with no domain association (e.g., models that are mere taxonomies) to large and complex models with more than a thousand classes. While mean and median values show us the medium size of the models in the catalog, the mode value indicates that most of these models are small. The standard variation,

Table 1. Statistics on concepts from the catalog ontologies

	Diagrams	Classes	Associations	Generalizations
Sum	656	7223	5392	5474
Minimum	1	7	0	0
Maximum	138	1222	655	1119
Median	2	32	26	19
Mean	5,17	56.87	42.46	43.1
Mode	1	18	15	2
Standard Deviation	15.52	118.44	71.34	115.47
Sample Variance	240.84	14028.79	5089.44	13332.43
Standard Error	1.38	10.51	6.33	10.25

sample variance, and standard error values indicate that the catalog comprises models of varied sizes. This is a positive feature, demonstrating that the catalog collects a heterogeneous model sample, which can be useful for supporting different empirical analyzes.

4.2 Statistics on the Metadata

The 127 models included in the catalog have been created between 2005 to 2022 (coded in the `issued` metadata field). The models represent 161 different domains (`subject` metadata), being the most frequent ones *software engineering*, with 6 occurrences, followed by *finance* and *safety* with 5 occurrences each, and *value, economics*, and *education* with 4 occurrences each. Regarding the metadata field `conformsTo`, 115 (90,6%) of these models are represented using OntoUML stereotypes, and 18 (14,2%) of them directly extending UFO. Note that the sum of these values is over 127 because this field can assume multiple values—the same happens to the metadata fields `language`, `type`, `designedForTask`, and `context`. The metadata `theme` (which codes a library classification) can assume only one value, and therefore, the sum of its occurrences must be equal to the number of datasets that are in the catalog.

Considering the field `language`, the catalog has 119 (93,7%) models that use lexical terms in English (`en`), followed by Brazilian Portuguese (`pt-br`) with 10 (7,9%) occurrences, and Dutch (`nl`) with a single item (0,8%). Considering the `type` of these models, 112 (88,2%) of them are classified as domain ontologies, 12 (9,4%) as core ontologies, and 6 (4,7%) as application ontologies. Regarding their `context`, 94 (74,0%) models were created within a *research* environment, 28 (22,0%) within a *classroom* environment, and 7 (5,5%) within an *industry* setting. In terms of their purposes(`designedForTask` property), we have representatives in all the ten available classifications categories, distributed as follows: 85 (66,9%) *conceptual clarification*, 23 (18,1%) *learning*, 20 (15,7%) *interoperability*, 13 (10,2%) *software engineering*, 9 (7,1%) *ontological analysis*, 3 (2,4%)

decision support system, 3 (2,4%) *example,* 2 (1,6%) *information retrieval,* 2 (1,6%) *data publication,* and 2 (1,6%) *language engineering.*

Finally, regarding the library classification of the domains represented in these models (`theme`), of the 21 possible LCC classes, we have exemplars of 13 of them, distributed this way: 44 (34,6%) of *Social Sciences (Class H)*; 36 (28,3%) of *Technology (Class T)*; 8 (6,3%) of *Science (Class Q)*; 7 (5,5%) of *Medicine (Class R)*; 6 (4,7%) of *Geography, Anthropology, and Recreation (Class G)*; 6 (4,7%) of *Education (Class L)*; 5 (3,9%) of *Philosophy, Psychology, Religion (Class B)*; 5 (3,9%) of *Political Science (Class J)*; 4 (3,1%) of *Law (Class K)*; 3 (2,4%) of *Agriculture (Class S)*; 1 (0,8%) of *Music (Class M)*; 1 (0,8%) of *Military Science (Class U)*; and 1 (0,8%) of *Bibliography, Library Science, and General Information Resources (Class Z)*.

5   FAIRness Evaluation

In this section, we discuss how our catalog complies with the FAIR principles for scientific data management put forth by Jacobsen *et al.* [15].

Findable. The first FAIR principle refers to the importance of making (meta)data easily findable to both humans and computers. To accomplish this, the following more specific requirements are laid out [15]: (F1) the (meta)data must have "a globally unique and persistent identifier" (F2) the data must be "described with rich metadata" (F3) the metadata "clearly and explicitly include the identifier of the data they describe", and (F4) (meta)data must be registered/indexed in a searchable resource. The catalog uses persistent identifiers for all its resources (F1). Our data is described with rich metadata accessible to users (F2) and correctly referencing identifiers (F3). Finally, all (meta)data is hosted on a public GitHub repository, guaranteeing that they are indexed and findable by web search tools (F4).

Accessible. The second principle, accessibility, regards authentication and authorization. It requires that (A1) the (meta)data must be retrievable by their identifier using a standardized communications protocol that is open, free, universally implementable, and that allows authentication and authorization procedures, where necessary. It also requires that the (A2) metadata must be "accessible, even when the data are no longer available". We hosted the catalog in a public GitHub repository. Thus, all its resources are accessible to anyone with a browser and an internet connection (A1). We store data and metadata about each model in different files in our catalog (e.g., the `ontology.ttl` and `metadata.ttl` files in a model directory). Thus, even if an author removes their ontology from our catalog, its metadata will remain there (A2).

Interoperable. An important principle, in which ontology-driven conceptual models play an essential role [9], is interoperability. This principle states that the data should be able to integrate with other data, applications, or workflows. To achieve this goal (I1) the (meta)data must "use a formal, accessible, shared, and broadly applicable language for knowledge representation" (I2) the (meta)data must "use vocabularies that follow FAIR principles", and (I3) also must "include qualified references to other (meta)data".

The datasets in the catalog are available using open, free, and standardized semantic web and syntax definition languages, such as JSON and RDF-based languages (I1). The catalog's metadata is described using FAIR vocabularies, such as DCAT, DCT, SKOS, and MOD. Our custom vocabulary, built to describe the models in our catalog, is also FAIR compliant, being accessible via a permanent URI, specified in RDF/OWL, hosted on its own GitHub repository, and with a clear license for reuse. Our metadata reuses identifiers from other data providers, such as the DBLP's author identifier, DOI, and LCC, thus paving the way for the integration with additional datasets (I3).

Finally, the interoperability of the models comprising the catalog is facilitated by having each of these models grounded on a foundational ontology (UFO), i.e., by having the domain concepts and relations in these models explicit connected to UFO's basic ontological categories.

Reusable. The last principle addresses data reuse, requiring that (meta)data should be structured and well-described, enabling them to be replicated or combined. More specifically (R1) the (meta)data must be "richly described with a plurality of accurate and relevant attributes" (R1.1) it must be "released with a clear and accessible data usage license" (R1.2) the (meta)data must be "associated with detailed provenance", and (R1.3) must "meet domain-relevant community standards". Our catalog metadata is extensive in the description of each piece of metadata, containing all relevant attributes for understanding each model, like name, source, modeler, and domain (R1). Moreover, the catalog registers the usage license for the included models (R1.1), each model in the catalog has its original source presented (publications, files, and diagrams) (R1.2), and for the whole catalog we used well-established vocabularies when defining the metadata standards (R1.3).

6   Relevance for Research

This catalog paves the way for research in the areas of ontology engineering, software design, and conceptual modeling, but also in the areas of machine learning, and, more precisely, relational learning, where the focus is to address prediction or information induction tasks by reusing knowledge encoded in a graph-structured format. We grouped some main usage examples as follows.

Algorithm Evaluation. An obstacle often found by OntoUML developers is how to evaluate their algorithms' effectiveness and performance. By lacking a reliable dataset for testing, authors most of the time rely on toy examples use-cases, or on unrealistic scoped domains. Most of the time, when testing on already published models, modelers must manually rebuild these models from their image files to produce a machine-readable version of the model. Using this catalog, interested users can find a significant amount of reliable data (since all input on the catalog is peer-reviewed) already in the desired format, thus creating a beneficial scenario for testing algorithms. To cite just two examples, algorithms that would directly benefit from this catalog include those for automated clustering [11] and abstraction of conceptual models [19].

Language Evolution. For over fifteen years, the OntoUML research community has contributed to the development of the modeling language and to the evolution of its foundational ontology, UFO. By observing how OntoUML has been used over the years, by several groups, and in a variety of domains, one can derive fruitful empirical observations about the language. Previous works have already observed several diverse ways in which people systematically bent the syntax of the language, triggering its designers to evolve the language [12]. These *systematic subversions* refer to recurrent model fragments appearing in models produced by different users that albeit grammatically incorrect signal (to a language's creation) a design limitation of the language. The observation and analysis of these subversions in OntoUML have already been used as input to evolve UFO's theory of relations [5] and its theory of types [12]. Being a structured source of models' data in a machine-readable format, the OntoUML/UFO Catalog can be queried, and its data can be used for the identification of these subversions for further analysis.

Language Design and Evaluation. "How much language is enough?". With this question in mind, Muehlen and Recker analyzed Business Process Modeling Notation (BPMN) models using mathematical and statistical techniques and, among other findings, discovered that less than 20% of BPMN's vocabulary is regularly used—a piece of information that has implications for the entire language ecosystem and community [16]. Researchers can perform an equal analysis of OntoUML using our catalog. Such an analysis could benefit the OntoUML community by helping teachers and students to create improved pedagogical strategies. The results of such analyzes could also drive future researchers' efforts, allowing them to focus on the most used language concepts. Examples of these include [22], which proposes ontology-based rules for designing the concrete syntax of visual modeling languages, and [10], which proposed a canvas for ontology modeling. Both approaches aimed to address subsets of OntoUML/UFO categories. With this catalog, such design choices can be evidence-based.

Empirical Discovery of Modeling (Anti-)Patterns. A straightforward way to exploit the catalog is to use its information to understand how people use OntoUML in practice. This involves the empirical discovery of patterns or anti-patterns [20], as good or bad modeling practices, which can be used to evolve OntoUML or by modelers that need to create new models. Note that, since OntoUML is a profile for UML class diagrams, the catalog offers an opportunity for researchers interested in the discovery patterns in that language as well.

Application Development. The availability of OntoUML models encoded in a uniform and processable format supports the development of new model engineering techniques and the improvement of existing ones. For instance, through an analysis of how people create diagrams (i.e., what are the cognitive steps in model construction), new editing and automatic layout services could be devised. Many datasets (or parts of them) may be used directly to design database schemes for working applications of related domains, i.e., high-quality models there included can serve as *seed models* [3] for future developments.

New Source of Information for Machine Learning Set-Ups. Recently, machine learning approaches have taken advantage of graph-structured data to address specific tasks [17]. In this context, the catalog offers ODCM data that can be easily exploited and assessed in different scenarios and domains. The combination of domain-level and top-level knowledge, which is structural in OntoUML, represents an added information that is crucial sometimes. For instance, exploiting background knowledge with top-level information is recognized to be of remarkable significance for cross-domain transfer learning tasks [1,7]. Similarly, having a large catalog with domain data related to top-level data may significantly improve tasks in which schemes must be matched according to a reference standard [23]. It can also provide training data for ontology matching tasks leveraging on data annotated with categories coming from foundational ontologies—a still unexplored approach to ontology matching [24]. Finally, our catalog can be exploited as a training set for machine learning prediction tasks, where the goal is to predict the correct foundational category of a given class, thus providing automated support to build new models and define their scope.

7   Related Work

Our contribution here builds primarily on the large amount of work in recent years on the generation of repositories for maintaining and reusing knowledge resources, such as ontologies, conceptual models, and vocabularies. Based on an analysis of the collected data and their organization, we identified some initiatives that are close to ours, which we discuss in the sequel. Considering the different scope, we excluded from this section domain-specific catalogs and catalogs for artifacts different from models or ontologies (e.g., design patterns catalogs).

In the past, some of us have made a first attempt to gather and organize OntoUML models [20]. This effort gathered 54 models, most of which were (or will eventually be) included in the catalog presented here. This repository of models—which is no longer available or maintained—was created with the specific goal of supporting the empirical discovery of ontological anti-patterns [20]. Differently from the catalog described in this paper, that repository was not built in compliance with the principles represented in FAIR, or with the goal of fostering open and collaborative community participation.

The *Linked Open Vocabularies (LOV)* [25] is a platform that provides access to a catalog of OWL vocabularies. Starting in 2011, LOV is now hosted by the *Open Knowledge Foundation*, and it currently offers almost eight hundred vocabularies. LOV is based on some quality requirements, including URI stability and availability on the web. It relies on standard formats and publication best practices, quality metadata, and documentation. As a distinctive feature, LOV shows indicators that are not provided by other catalogs, such as the interconnections between vocabularies, the versioning history along with past and current editors (individual or organization). LOV is a catalog of vocabularies and/or lightweight ontologies, i.e., semantic web models focused on web-based information sharing and computability issues. Ours, in contrast, focuses on ontology-driven conceptual models, i.e., models focused on expressivity and domain appropriateness, and capturing the result of ontological analyzes [8].

An example of a repository of ontologies as logical specifications is Onto-Hub [4], which collects over 20.000 specifications organized in almost 150 repositories. Most of the ontologies there are also lightweight models. We can say the same for the LOV-inspired Linked Open Vocabularies for the Internet of Things (LOV4IoT) [14], a domain-specific repository. In this sense, it is similar to the BioPortal [21], which includes almost 1.000 in the life sciences. In contrast to these other approaches, the OWL models in BioPortal usually are based on the Basic Formal Ontology (BFO) foundational ontology and, in principle, have a similar focus (e.g., with relation to domain appropriateness) to the ones in our catalog. However, despite their firm grounding, these models are subject to OWL's expressivity limitations and, hence, leave out unrepresented many important ontological nuances (e.g., related to modality, multi-level structures). Additionally, since these ontologies are rendered as textual (sentential) logical specifications, they do not provide data for supporting the study of diagrammatic/visual aspects of domain representations (e.g., model layout, visual patterns and anti-patterns).

Last, another initiative comparable to ours is the one by G. Robles *et al.* [18], who built an extensive catalog of UML models. Their approach was to gather UML models automatically from sparse GitHub projects and put them into a reference hub. The output is a catalog with over 93.000 UML diagrams from over 24.000 projects. Their catalog is clearly much larger than ours, but our goals are also different. First, in scope, they include any UML models, while we focused on ODCM models. Second, their emphasis is on quantity, while striving for a minimal quality threshold for the models and for the homogeneity of the data. All our models are available in the same formats and are described with rich and linked metadata, making our catalog much easier to reuse and analyze.

8   Final Considerations

In this paper, we presented the first FAIR Model Catalog for Ontology-Driven Conceptual Modeling Research. We provide a structured, collaborative, and open-source catalog of ODCM models designed with the OntoUML language (or by extending the UFO ontology). This resource shall support the conceptual modeling and ontology engineering communities with many important empirical tasks. These include language design, understanding, and evolution; machine-learning research over model data; testing model manipulation (e.g., code generation, mining, modularization, abstraction); and model reuse.

The catalog currently contains 127 models, but we expect it to grow, especially considering the UFO and OntoUML relevance to the ODCM field and considering that the catalog is open to receive contributions from the community. Instructions on how to collaborate are available on the repository's GitHub page. We have identified many models that still have to be rebuilt in the Visual Paradigm to be included in the catalog. Given that this is a laborious task, we intend to investigate ways in which this process can be at least partially automated (e.g., by automating the normalization of data, partially generating models from figures). Additionally, we intend to create a service in the OntoUML plugin for modelers to submit their models directly to the catalog.

Inspired by the LOV initiative (which claims to be a high-quality catalog of reusable vocabularies), we envisage the creation of a Linked Open OntoUML Models (LOOM). Differently from LOV, LOOM would organize the space of ontologically well-founded domain models, i.e., a space of conceptual models grounded on a foundational ontology and, thus, having deeper ontological semantics by design.

Even though our catalog is restricted to UFO/OntoUML conceptual models, its metadata schema could be easily adapted to accommodate models built following other foundational ontologies. Nonetheless, to the best of our knowledge, UFO is the only mainstream foundational ontology [26] that has an ODCM language that is explicitly associated to it, i.e., in a technical sense: (i) having the modeling primitives of the language directly reflecting the distinctions of the ontology; (ii) having the grammatical constraints of the language explicit representing the axiomatization of the ontology.

Finally, as previously discussed, the models are included in this catalog in their original form, i.e., preserving the original modeling choices made by their creators. This is important to study how the language is actually used in practice, what are the most common modeling errors and anti-patterns, how different users subvert the grammatical rules of the language signaling possible evolution trends, etc. However, as a direct consequence, the catalog shall contain models that are of a variety of quality levels, including models bearing syntactic, semantic, and pragmatic problems. This hinders the potential (re)use of these models (e.g., as Seed Models or reusable modeling components). As future work, we intend to address this issue by investigating methodological and computational mechanisms for assessing some quality aspects of these models (e.g., with relation to syntactical correctness, presence of anti-patterns, visual pragmatics, among others).

Acknowledgements. We would like to thank Accenture Israel Cybersecurity Labs for supporting this work, as well as Ítalo Oliveira, Thomas Derave, Tim van Ee, Cristiano Silva, and Lucas Maddalena for their contributions to the catalog. We especially thank András Komáromi for his contribution and inspiring passion for modeling in OntoUML.

References

1. Al-Halah, Z., Stiefelhagen, R.: How to transfer? Zero-shot object recognition via hierarchical transfer of semantic attributes. In: WACV, pp. 837–843 (2015)
2. Barcelos, P.P.F., et al.: An automated transformation from OntoUML to OWL and SWRL. In: Seminar on Ontology Research in Brazil, vol. 1041 (2013)
3. Blaha, M.: Patterns of Data Modeling, vol. 1. CRC Press (2010)

4. Codescu, M., et al.: Ontohub: a semantic repository engine for heterogeneous ontologies. Appl. Ontol. **12**(3–4), 275–298 (2017)
5. Fonseca, C.M., et al.: Relations in ontology-driven conceptual modeling. In: Conceptual Modeling. ER 2019, vol. 11788, pp. 28–42 (2019)
6. Fonseca, C.M., et al.: Ontology-driven conceptual modeling as a service. In: JOWO 2021. The Joint Ontology Workshops, vol. 2969 (2021)
7. Fumagalli, M., et al.: Ontology-driven cross-domain transfer learning. In: Formal Ontology in Information Systems, vol. 330, pp. 249–263 (2020)
8. Guizzardi, G.: Ontological foundations for structural conceptual models (2005)
9. Guizzardi, G.: Ontology, ontologies and the "I" of FAIR. Data Intell. 2(1–2) (2020)
10. Guizzardi, G., Sales, T.P.: "As simple as possible but not simpler": towards an ontology model canvas. In: Proceedings of the Joint Ontology Workshops (2017)
11. Guizzardi, G., et al.: Automated conceptual model clustering: a relator-centric approach. Softw. Syst. Model (2021)
12. Guizzardi, G., et al.: Types and taxonomic structures in conceptual modeling: a novel ontological theory and engineering support. Data Knowl. Eng. **134**, 101891 (2021)
13. Guizzardi, G., et al.: UFO: unified foundational ontology. Appl. Ontology **17**(1), 167–210 (2022)
14. Gyrard, A., et al.: LOV4IoT: a second life for ontology-based domain knowledge to build semantic web of things applications. In: IEEE FiCloud (2016)
15. Jacobsen, A., et al.: FAIR principles: interpretations and implementation considerations. Data Intell. **2**(1–2), 10–29 (2020)
16. Muehlen, M., Recker, J.: How much language is enough? Theoretical and practical use of the business process modeling notation. In: CAiSE 2008, pp. 465–479 (2008)
17. Nickel, M., et al.: A review of relational machine learning for knowledge graphs. Proc. IEEE **104**(1), 11–33 (2016)
18. Robles, G., et al.: An extensive dataset of UML models in GitHub. In: 14th International Conference on Mining Software Repositories, pp. 519–522 (2017)
19. Romanenko, E., et al.: Abstracting ontology-driven conceptual models: objects, aspects, events, and their parts. In: RCIS (2022)
20. Sales, T.P., Guizzardi, G.: Ontological anti-patterns: empirically uncovered error-prone structures in ontology-driven conceptual models. DKE **99**, 72–104 (2015)
21. Salvadores, M., et al.: Bioportal as a dataset of linked biomedical ontologies and terminologies in RDF. Semantic Web **4**, 277–284 (2013)
22. da Silva Teixeira, M.D.G.: An ontology-based process for domain-specific visual language design. Ph.D. thesis, Ghent University (2017)
23. Sleeman, J., Finin, T., Joshi, A.: Entity type recognition for heterogeneous semantic graphs. AI Mag. **36**(1), 75–86 (2015)
24. Trojan, C., et al.: Foundational ontologies meet ontology matching: a survey. Semant. Web (2021)
25. Vandenbussche, P., et al.: Linked open vocabularies (LOV): a gateway to reusable semantic vocabularies on the web. Semant. Web **8**(3), 437–452 (2017)
26. Verdonck, M., Gailly, F.: Insights on the use and application of ontology and conceptual modeling languages in ontology-driven conceptual modeling. In: ER (2016)
27. Wilkinson, M.D., et al.: The FAIR Guiding Principles for scientific data management and stewardship. Sci. Data **3**(1) (2016)

Incorporating Types of Types
in Ontology-Driven Conceptual Modeling

Claudenir M. Fonseca[1](✉), Giancarlo Guizzardi[1,2], João Paulo A. Almeida[3],
Tiago Prince Sales[1], and Daniele Porello[4]

[1] Conceptual and Cognitive Modeling Research Group,
Free University of Bozen-Bolzano, Bolzano, Italy
{cmoraisfonseca,gguizzardi,tprincesales}@unibz.it
[2] Services and Cybersecurity Group, University of Twente,
Enschede, The Netherlands
[3] Ontology and Conceptual Modeling Research Group,
Federal University of Espírito Santo, Vitória, Brazil
jpalmeida@ieee.org
[4] University of Genoa, Genoa, Italy
daniele.porello@unige.it

Abstract. The Unified Foundational Ontology (UFO) has been used to
provide foundations for the major conceptual modeling constructs. So
far, UFO has reflected a view in which domain entities are fundamentally divided into those that collect invariants of the domain (i.e., types)
and those entities that manifest those invariants (i.e., instances), following
the conventional two-level classification scheme. This paper extends UFO
with support for multi-level classification schemes, in which some entities
accumulate both type-like and instance-like characteristics. This requires
an ontological interpretation and a formal theory of types of types. This
theory is employed to engineer new constructs and constraints into the
OntoUML language, and to develop computational support for the formal
verification of constraint violation over multi-level conceptual models.

Keywords: Ontology-driven conceptual modeling · Multi-level
modeling · High-order types · UFO · OntoUML

1 Introduction

The Unified Foundational Ontology (UFO) has been used to provide foundations for the major conceptual modeling constructs [19,23]. This ontology has
led to the OntoUML Ontology-Driven Conceptual Modeling language [19,21], a
UML class diagram profile reflecting the ontological micro-theories comprising
UFO. Despite the increasing adoption [36] and successful application [23] of this
language to address problems in a variety of areas, so far, UFO's foundations
to OntoUML have reflected a view in which domain entities are fundamentally
divided into those that collect invariants of the domain (i.e., types) and the

J. Ralyté et al. (Eds.): ER 2022, LNCS 13607, pp. 18–34, 2022.
https://doi.org/10.1007/978-3-031-17995-2_2

entities that manifest those invariants (i.e., instances). However, in a multitude of domains, entities that accumulate both type-like and instance-like characteristics play a central role. For example, in biological taxonomy, the type *Canis familiaris* collects the properties manifested in individual dogs (e.g., *having fur, being quadrupeds*) while manifesting itself properties of the type Species (e.g., *having a certain biological origin, having an expected lifespan*). In other words, in this domain, we are concerned not only with types of individuals (i.e., *first-order* types), but also with types of types (i.e., *high-order* types). Models that extend the traditional two-level scheme by accommodating types that are themselves instances of other (high-order) types are called multi-level models [5].

This paper extends UFO and then OntoUML with support for multi-level modeling, including an ontological interpretation and formal model of high-order types. By leveraging a formal theory called MLT (Multi-Level Theory) [9], we incorporate a micro-theory of high-order types in UFO. This theory is then employed to engineer new constructs and constraints into the OntoUML language and to develop computational support for the formal verification of constraint violation over these models. We position our work with respect to competing approaches present in the literature and demonstrate how our contributions answer an existing demand in conceptual modeling for ontologically sound and semantically precise support for types of types.

A distinctive feature of our approach is that, by considering types as *endurants*, we can account for qualitative changes that these types may undergo in time [20]. This means that the UFO ontological categories applicable to types of individual endurants (such as kinds, phases, roles, etc.) [22] also apply to types of types. For instance, in biology, this allows us to account for high-order types such as Endangered Species or Extinct Species as *phases*, as the very same species can instantiate these types in different situations. Treating types as endurants also allows us to account for temporal properties of their existence: this is particularly important for types such as social roles, artifactual types, and nominal kinds in general [35]. For example, consider the numerous crime types defined in most penal codes; these come into existence at determinate times as a result of the exercise of legislative institutional power. The same move also allows us to account for contingent or accidental properties of high-order types: for example, an animal species may be characterized by a changing population size; a car model may be characterized by a recommended sales price.

Empirical evidence for high-order types shows their relevance: a study of Wikidata in 2016 encountered over 17,000 classes involved in multi-level taxonomies [6]. That study already indicated the importance of rules to detect problematic usage of high-order types in that knowledge base, which was corroborated by an updated study in 2021 [12]. The latter found over 5 million problematic statements in Wikidata that could have been avoided with automated rules. The inconsistencies found over the years reveal that modelers struggle to represent high-order types adequately [6,12]. In OntoUML, there are 123 documented occurrences of high-order types across 19 ontologies in a dataset of 113 ontologies.[1] This count considers classes explicitly labeled as types (e.g., Person Type) and those decorated with various *ad hoc* stereotypes (e.g., «type», «powertype», and «high-order type»). This indicates that modelers *subvert* [23] the modeling language in order to capture somehow types of types even when support for them is not explicitly part of the language, a phenomenon that has also been observed in OntoUML with event types [2] and with reified properties [22].

The remainder of this paper is structured as follows: Sect. 2 presents the UFO and OntoUML background, discussing why the current status lacks full support for high-order types; Sect. 3 introduces high-order types explicitly in UFO; Sect. 4 presents the corresponding OntoUML extension; Sect. 5 discusses related work and Sect. 6 presents our final considerations.

2   Background and Motivation

OntoUML is an ontology-driven conceptual modeling (ODCM) language that focus on the representation of types of object-like entities termed *endurants*, and their type-level relations. In UFO, *endurant types* (Fig. 1) are types of entities that exist in time and that can undergo changes while keeping their identity. Endurants encompass (i) *existentially independent* objects such as a person, an organization, or a car, whose types are called Substantial Types and (ii) *existentially dependent* aspects of objects, such as Paul's height, or John's employment at Big Tech Inc., whose types are called Moment Types. The *existential dependence* relation tying moments to their bearers is called *inherence*.

Moment types are further classified into types of intrinsic (internal) moments, Quality Type and Intrinsic Mode Type, and types of extrinsic (relational) moments, Relator Type and Extrinsic Mode Type. Quality types classify aspects of endurants that can be mapped to some quality space, such as a person's height, or a car's color; intrinsic mode types, on the other hand, classify internal aspects of endurants that are not conceptualized in terms of a quality space, such as one's ability to speak English; extrinsic mode types classify relational aspects that simultaneously inhere on a unique endurant and *externally depend* on another. Extrinsic modes ground unilateral relations such as *John loves Mary*; finally, relator types classify relational aspects of endurants that inhere in the sum of all endurants it involves, such as John's employment at Big Tech Inc., which is the sum of aspects of John as the employee as well as aspects of Big Tech Inc. as the employer.

The aforementioned classification forms a taxonomy of endurant types based on the ontological nature of their instances. On top of that, endurant types in UFO are also classified according to orthogonal characteristics of how they apply to their instances. Sortals are endurant types that provide a uniform *principle of identity* for their instances, i.e., a principle capturing what are properties that two instances of that type must have in common in other for them to be the same. In particular, the identity principle informs which changes an endurant may undergo while preserving its identity. A sortal can either directly provide

---

[1] Dataset available at https://purl.org/ontouml-models/git.

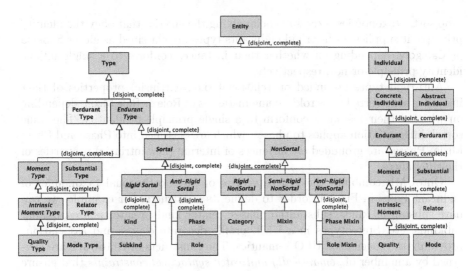

Fig. 1. UFO's original taxonomy of endurant types.

the identity principle for its instances, or inherit that principle provided by another sortal. Non-sortal types, on the other hand, classify endurants that follow distinct identity principles, being also referred to as *dispersive types* [19]. Non-sortals aggregate properties that are common to different sortals. Therefore, while Computer, Mobile Phone, and Tablet are examples of sortals following distinct identity principles (i.e., their identity principles are clearly based on distinct sets of properties), Electronic Device is an example of non-sortal that aggregates properties that are common to the instances of each of these three sortals, among others.

Sortals and non-sortals are further differentiated according to their rigidity. Rigid types necessarily classify (in the modal sense) endurants, i.e., a rigid type classifies its instances as long as they exist. Anti-rigid types, in contrast, classify their instances contingently, having their instances moving in and out of their extension without ceasing to exist, i.e., while maintaining their identities. For example, Person is typically conceived as a rigid type as, in most conceptualizations, it classifies its instances at all times. In contrast, Student and Teenager only classify persons manifesting certain (accidental) properties, namely *holding an enrollment at an educational institution* and *having an age between thirteen and nineteen years old*. It is also possible that types necessarily classify some of its instances but not others, being referred as semi-rigid types. An example of semi-rigid type is Insured Item which accounts for domains in which some entities are necessarily insured (e.g., cars), while others are not (e.g., bikes, cellphones). UFO only accounts for semi-rigid types among non-sortals, which are called Mixins.

All sortal types sharing the same identity principle inherit it from a unique sortal a common *ultimate sortal*, or Kind. For this reason, kinds rigid types sitting atop sortal taxonomies, *necessarily* classifying the entities that obey the identity principle it supplies. Other rigid endurants types are classified as either Subkind or Category, depending on whether their instances conform to a single unique identity principle or not, respectively.

Anti-rigid types grounded on relational (i.e., extrinsic) properties of their instances are referred to as roles, being instances of Role or Role Mixin, depending on whether their instances conform to a single principle of identity. The same sortal differentiation applies to phases, which are classified into Phase and Phase Mixin. Phases are grounded on variances of internal (i.e., intrinsic) properties of their instances.

OntoUML combines the leaf categories of these orthogonal taxonomies of endurant types in Fig. 1 in order to define its constructs. For example, we can have substantial kinds, substantial phases, relator kinds, relator phases, quality subkinds, etc. Stereotypes in a UML profile decorate classes and associations providing the specialized UFO semantics. The constructs of OntoUML are governed by a number of *semantically-motivated syntactical constraints* that ensure that any valid OntoUML model represents a sound conceptualization in terms of UFO. These constraints are implemented in tools that automatically detect errors in a conceptual model [22]. For example, a specific constraint rules out a model in which a phase is specialized by a subkind; this model would be unsound by definition, as an anti-rigid type (e.g., a phase) cannot be a supertype of a rigid type (e.g., a subkind). For a detailed account of the various rules derived from the UFO taxonomy of endurant types, we refer the reader to [22].

An example of an OntoUML model in the shipping domain is shown in Fig. 2. This model considers that a Ship can go through different phases (Docked Ship, On Route, Decommissioned), can be of different subkinds (Panama-class Ship, or Suez-class Ship). The use of the «kind» stereotype indicates that ships and persons are substantials. Ships are characterized here by «quality» Size, instances of which are qualities inhering in a particular ship and representing its length, weight and hull draft. The model also exemplifies the Assignment of a ship to a Person contingently playing the role of Captain. The stereotype «relator» indicates Assignment is a relator kind. Since relators are endurants, they can also be classified using the taxonomy of endurant types [22]. Here, assignment relators are classified into Temporary and Permanent assignment, which are considered to be phases, reflecting a domain rule that a temporary assignment may become permanent (e.g., after a certain duration).

Note that all types in Fig. 2 capture invariants applicable to individuals: substantials (persons, ships), their qualities (ships' sizes) and relators (assignments). However, we may also be interested in capturing various domain-specific aspects of types themselves. For example, consider when *ship types themselves* become relevant for modeling aspects of this domain. Some ship types (such as Panama-class Ship, or Suez-class Ship) are *created by* regulations, are *applicable to* certain canals (Panama, Suez), and establish a *maximum size* for the ships that instantiate these classes. Persons may be *licensed to captain* specific *ship types*; we may be interested in knowing the current *number of ships* of a certain *ship type* that are on route, whether a *ship type* is *under production* or *discontinued*, etc. Further, we can anticipate in this domain that the model is not exhaustive with respect to ship types; thus, the focus shifts to invariant aspects of ship types, that we may have in the future (not unlike particular ships and persons, these do not have to be 'hard-coded' in the model). Thus, we need to introduce the notion of Ship Type in our model, itself a high-order type (or metatype) as its instances are types. However, the UFO taxonomy shown in Fig. 1 and reflected in OntoUML does not confer to *types* the same possibilities that are conferred to endurant individuals. In the following sections, we refactor the UFO taxonomy shown earlier in order to ascribe full endurant status to types, later revisiting OntoUML's stereotypes and rules to support high-order types. We also incorporate the MLT theory [1,10] as a microtheory of UFO in order to account for multi-level phenomena (such as the notion of type *order*).

3   Extending UFO with High-Order Domain Endurant Types

In order to accommodate high-order types in UFO's domain of inquiry, we rely on a notion of instantiation (iof for short) that breaks away with the two-level divide and admits that types may classify not only individuals, but other types as well. Hence, we incorporate into UFO the notion of instantiation provided by MLT, where iof is a primitive relation that holds between an instance e and a type t in a world w where t classifies e (a1). UFO entities can thus be divided into those that can possibly have instances (in a modal sense) (a2) and those that cannot (a3), i.e., between types and individuals (see Fig. 4).

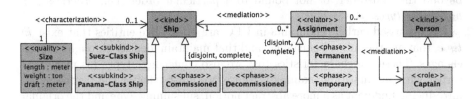

Fig. 2. Example OntoUML model in the domain of maritime ships.

a1 $\text{iof}(e, t, w) \rightarrow \text{entity}(e) \wedge \text{type}(t) \wedge \text{world}(w)$
a2 $\text{type}(t) \leftrightarrow \text{entity}(t) \wedge \exists e, w\,(\text{iof}(e, t, w))$
a3 $\text{individual}(i) \leftrightarrow \text{entity}(t) \wedge \neg\text{type}(i)$

This basic distinction of entities allows for the characterization of three fundamental classification schemes: (i) the two-level scheme, which include individuals and types of individuals, also referred to as *first-order types*; (ii) the strictly stratified scheme, which extends the two-level scheme by including *second-order types* (i.e., types of first-order types), *third-order types* (i.e., types of second-order types), and so on; and (iii) the non-stratified schemes, where types' extensions span across the boundaries of any particular order. For example, consider the entities in the domain represented schematically in Fig. 3 where all dashed arrows represent iof relations. At the lowest level of classification, we have two individuals (particular animals) Chilly Willy, instantiating Emperor Penguin, and Lassie, instantiating Dog and Collie. These five entities fit the two-level scheme of individuals and first-order types. Moving higher in the multi-level classification scheme, Species and Breed are examples of types classifying first-order types, i.e., second-order types, where the former classifies Emperor Penguin and Dog, while the latter classifies Collie. Likewise, the instantiation chain continues with Taxonomic Rank, a third-order type, classifying Species and Breed. All of these types are instances of Biological Concept. The latter (with instantiation spanning across various levels indicated by red dashed arrows) is an example of an *orderless type*.

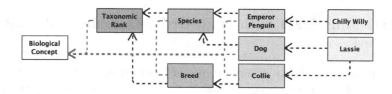

Fig. 3. Multi-level classification in the biology domain.

Note that the adopted characterization of types allows the stratified scheme to extend with no upper boundary, accounting for instantiation chains as long as necessary for any particular domain. Moreover, we refer to the types sitting beyond the first-order, or not bound to a particular order (i.e., orderless), as *high-order types*.

As discussed earlier, endurants in UFO are object-like entities that exist *in time*, that are the subject of change, and that maintain identity throughout such changes. These are characteristics that we also confer here types (as motivated earlier with the maritime example). Hence, we must refactor the taxonomy by introducing Endurant as a more abstract notion, subsuming Type and the original notion of Endurant, now adequately renamed Endurant Individual, see Fig. 4.

In multi-level models, a set of relations that we refer here as *structural relations*, characterize how types are related in terms of their intensions, i.e., the properties they collect about their instances. The most fundamental of these is the specialization relation, which we differentiate here between specialization (a4) and proper specialization (a5). A type t_1 specializes a type t_2 iff every possible instance of the former is necessarily instance the latter; t_1 specializes t_2 iff t_1's intension includes t_2's. Since every type includes its own intension, specializes is a reflexive relation. The proper specialization relation, on the other hand, characterizes the specialization between two different types. Specialization relations, proper or otherwise, can only hold when the specialized type (or *supertype*) is an orderless type or an ordered type of the same order (or level) as the specializing one (or *subtype*) [1].

a4 $specializes(t_1, t_2) \leftrightarrow type(t_1) \land type(t_2) \land \forall e, w \, (iof(e, t_1, w) \rightarrow iof(e, t_2, w))$

a5 $properSpecializes(t_1, t_2) \leftrightarrow specializes(t_1, t_2) \land (t_1 \neq t_2)$

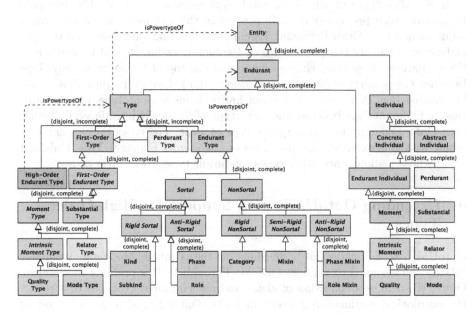

Fig. 4. UFO extension for high-order endurant types.

Other two structural relations emerge from the *powertype* variants as defined by Cardelli [7] and Odell [30]. These are structural relations that hold from a type of a higher order to a *base type* of the order immediately below (or between two orderless types). In UFO, a type t_1 is powertype of a base type t_2 iff every specialization of the latter is an instance of the former (a6), following Cardelli's notion. From Odell's notion, a type t_1 categorizes a base type t_2 iff every instance of the former is a proper specialization of the latter. In other words, the instances of a (Cardelli) powertype are all those whose intensions include a base type's intension; in turn, the instances of a categorizer (following Odell) are those types whose intensions include not only a base type's intension, but also some further restrictions defined in that categorizer.

a6 $isPowertypeOf(t_1, t_2) \leftrightarrow type(t_1) \land type(t_2) \land \forall t_3, w \, (specializes(t_3, t_2) \leftrightarrow iof(t_3, t_1, w))$

a7 $categorizes(t_1, t_2) \leftrightarrow type(t_1) \land type(t_2) \land \forall t_3, w \, (iof(t_3, t_1, w) \rightarrow properSpecializes(t_3, t_2))$

In the original UFO taxonomy of Fig. 1, every type in the taxonomy Individual, with the exceptions of Concrete Individual and Abstract Individual, has a power-type in the taxonomy of Type: Type is the powertype of Individual, Endurant Type is the powertype of Endurant, an so on. Moreover, the taxonomy of the types in the taxonomy of Individual are first-order types, while the types of the taxonomy of Type are second-order types.

With the extension of Fig. 4 this is no longer the case as the taxonomy of Type classifies types of any order (and Type is thus orderless). The mirrored taxonomies seen previously are still present in this extension, given the proper adjustments: First-Order Perdurant Type, First-Order Endurant Type, and the specializations of it are the powertypes of Perdurant, Endurant, and its specializations. However, important changes emerge at the top of UFO's taxonomy. Type becomes the powertype of Entity (following MLT) since every type that classifies entities (i.e., every specialization of Entity) is instance of Type. For the same reason, Endurant Type becomes the powertype of the newly introduced Endurant. High-Order Endurant Type is the powertype of Type. The types that we can now admit with this extension are instances of High-Order Endurant Type: endurant types whose instances are other types (endurant types themselves or not).

4   Extending OntoUML with Support for High-Order Types

OntoUML is a *lightweight extension* of the Unified Modeling Language (UML) [29] designed to support ODCM. Through UML's profiling mechanism, OntoUML defines a collection of class- and association stereotypes that reflect the ontological distinctions present in UFO. OntoUML also defines a set of *semantically-motivated syntactical constraints* that govern how the language's constructs can be employed and ensures that every syntactically correct model represents a sound UFO-based ontology. The OntoUML profile presented here is implemented as in a UML CASE tool which includes the automated verification of syntactical constraints in users' models[2].

4.1   Stereotypes and Tagged Values

Figure 5 presents the extended OntoUML profile, enabling the representation of high-order endurant types (we use the term 'classes' here following UML convention). Stereotypes of endurant classes are used in a model to position them under the two orthogonal taxonomies of Endurant Type of UFO (cf. Fig. 4). One of these taxonomies settles the sortality, rigidity and external dependence of types, and the other settles the ontological nature of a type's instances (i.e., whether the instances of a type are objects, relators, modes qualities or other types). This is achieved by three complementary design choices: (i) through the representation of the variations in sortality, rigidity and external dependence as stereotypes (concrete class stereotypes in gray in the diagram, namely, «subkind», «role», «phase», «category», «mixin», «roleMixin», «phaseMixin»); (ii) through the differentiation of kinds (i.e., ultimate sortals) based on unique ontological natures

---

[2] The OntoUML plugin for Visual Paradigm is available at https://purl.org/krdb-core/ontouml-plugin.

(the concrete stereotypes: «type» for high-order kinds, «kind» for substantial kinds, «relator» for relator kinds, «quality» for quality kinds and «mode» for mode kinds); and (iii) through the use of the restrictedTo *tagged value* that determines the possible ontological natures of the entities present in the extension of the decorated class (type, object – as a synonym for substantial –, relator, mode and quality). The latter tagged value is automatically derived when a class specializes an ultimate sortal, as the ultimate sortal settles the ontological nature of its instances. A suggested color scheme reflects these ontological natures, and is adopted in the examples in this paper (classes of types in purple, of objects in red, of relators in green and of intrisic moments in blue). The stereotypes in white reflect the taxonomic structure of UFO, they are abstract, and as such they are not directly available to the modeler.

Generalization sets may be used to indicate which higher-order types are instantiated in subclasses in line with plain UML. The «instantiation» stereotype is used to provide specialized semantics to an association between a higher-order type and a base type following [8], a solution which, differently from plain UML, can cater for the cases in which no explicit specializations of the base type are provided. When the higher-order type is tagged isPowertype=true, it is a Cardelli powertype of the base type; otherwise, it is a categorizer of the base type. An order tagged value is also included (an is typed UnlimitedNatural to allow for orderless types).

4.2   Revisiting the Ship Domain with the Extended Profile

We now revisit the maritime ship example with the OntoUML diagram shown in Fig. 6. We introduce a Ship Type powertype (of order 2) for Ship, with a number of specializations: Licensed Ship Type is the role played by ship types in the context of a Captain License, ship types can be Discontinued (obsolete) or

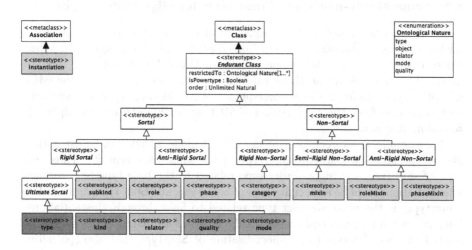

Fig. 5. OntoUML profile for high-order domain types.

Current, a subkind of Ship Type, namely, Ship Class by Size classifies ship types using maximum size for those classes. The generalization set annotation indicates that Suez-Class Ship and Panama-Class Ship are instances of Ship Class by Size, and thus can be related to a Canal (e.g., the Panama Canal, the Suez Canal) through the establishment of Canal Restrictions that determine the admissible ship classes for that canal. (The orders of subclasses are inherited from their superclasses and can be omitted here since order is defined for Ship Type.)

The attribute fleet of Ship Type corresponds to the number of ships that instantiate the type, and is an example of 'resultant property' [20]. The attributes of Ship Class by Size are examples of the so-called regularity attributes [9,20], and should be accompanied by OCL constraints relating a ship type's max length, max weight and max draft to a ship's length, weight and draft. These attributes are given values as static features of the instances of Ship Class by Size.

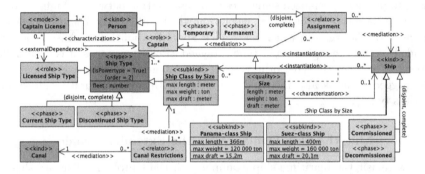

Fig. 6. Example including high-order types in the maritime domain.

4.3   Semantically-motivated Constraints for High-Order Types

Here, we discuss a number of consequences of the theory introduced in Sect. 3 for the various combinations of modeling constructs involving high-order types. These rules can be detected automatically in OntoUML models and rule out unsound models. Some of these rules are direct consequences of the MLT microtheory, some are a direct consequence of considering types as endurants, and some arise from the combination of MLT with UFO constraints applicable to endurant types.

For example, as a direct consequence of MLT alone, a higher-order categorizer always specializes a Cardelli powertype of the same base type [9]. Thus, any type of ship (i.e., any higher-order type related to the base type Ship through «instantiation») will be a specialization of Ship Type, and Ship Type, as a Cardelli powertype, is the most abstract type related to Ship through «instantiation». Further, as a direct consequence of MLT, classes of a different order cannot be related by specialization (so, a specialization of ShipType that also specializes

Ship can be ruled out automatically[3]). Likewise, «instantiation» can only relate entities of adjacent orders. See [1] for other rules that can be inferred from MLT, including those involving orderless types. Further rules arising from MLT alone govern the interaction between high-order types and the UML semantics of isCovering and isDisjoint metaproperties of generalization sets [8].

As a straightforward consequence of considering types as endurants is that all constraints applicable to endurant types in OntoUML [22] also apply to high-order types. Hence, anti-rigid (high-order) types cannot specialize rigid (high-order) types, (high-order) non-sortals cannot specialize (high-order) sortals, each (high-order) sortal specializes a unique (high-order) kind, and (high-order) kinds are the most abstract (high-order) sortals in a taxonomy. Further, since every kind is disjoint, classes stereotyped «type», «kind», «relator», «quality» and «mode» cannot specialize each other and must not have common subclasses.

Rules that arise from the combination of MLT with UFO govern the way that previously existing OntoUML stereotypes can be used with the introduced «type» stereotype. For example, consider that a Cardelli powertype imposes a single requirement for its instances: that they specialize the base type, i.e., that they include the intension of the base type in their intension. Since types cannot change their intension while maintaining their identity [9, 20], *any Cardelli powertype must be rigid*, thus classes with isPowerType set to true must be stereotyped «category», «type» or «subkind». (Note that this does not make the *instances* of a Cardelli powertype—e.g., Comissioned, Decomissioned—themselves rigid!)

4.4   Rules Involving UFO Classes in OntoUML

Including support for high-order types in OntoUML opens up the possibility to represent certain UFO categories themselves in OntoUML. This allow us to settle the ontological categories of instances of high-order types that are not represented explicitly in a model. For example, in the biological taxonomy domain, all instances of Species are kinds, all instances of Breed are subkinds. For specific species or breeds included in the model, stereotypes reveal the applicable ontological categories. However, general statements about species and breeds can be made by Species specializing UFO Kind and Breed specializing UFO Subkind.

In this case, certain rules are applicable for types related by «instantiation», depending on the stereotype of the base type following the analysis in [10]:

- If the *base type is anti-rigid* (i.e., stereotyped «phase», «role», «phaseMixin» or «roleMixin»), the high-order type (whether a Cardelli or an Odell powertype) will specialize UFO Anti-Rigid Type[4]; its instances will be stereotyped «phase», «role», «phaseMixin» or «roleMixin» when modeled as the base type's specializations.

---

[3] This kind of error may appear simple to prevent, however, there is overwhelming empirical evidence that it occurs very often in practice, see [6,12].

[4] This class was omitted from Fig. 1, but is a supertype of Anti-Rigid Sortal and Anti-Rigid NonSortal, more specifically, their disjoint union.

– If the *base type is a sortal* (i.e., stereotyped «kind», «relator», «mode», «quality», «kind», «type», «phase» or «role»), the high-order type will specialize UFO Sortal or one of its subcategories *except* for UFO Kind (because the base type already supplies a principle of identity). Its instances, when explicitly modeled as specializations of the base type, will thus either be stereotyped «subkind», «phase» or «role».
– More specifically, *if the base type is a sortal stereotyped «role» or «phase»*, the high-order type will either specialize UFO Phase or Role, and its instances when explicitly modeled will thus either be stereotyped «phase» or «role» accordingly.

Rules can also be formulated in the other 'direction', i.e., rules that apply depending on which UFO type is specialized by the higher-order type that is related to a base type through «instantiation»:

– If *the higher-order type specializes UFO NonSortal*, then its base type must be a non-sortal (i.e., stereotyped «mixin», «phaseMixin» or «roleMixin»).
– If *the higher-order type specializes UFO Rigid Type*, its base type must be rigid.
– More specifically, *if it specializes UFO Kind*, its base type must be a «category» or a semi-rigid «mixin». A powertype that specializes UFO Kind cannot be an overlapping categorizer of a base type, i.e., cannot have an upper bound cardinality higher than one in the association end attached to it in an association stereotype «instantiation». This is because all kinds are pairwise disjoint and thus no overlap in kinds is admissible.

5   Related Work

Multi-level modeling has been an active area of research, with many approaches developed and studied in the last two decades [4,5,9,11,15,24,25,28], but with roots in the 1990s [3,14,30,33] and 1980s [7]. In this paper, we have incorporated into UFO a key tenet of the multi-level modeling literature: the recognition of entities that are simultaneously types and instances ('clabjects' [3]), leading to the iterated application of instantiation across an arbitrary number of classification levels.

The use of UFO as a foundation allowed us to address the ontological nature of types, an aspect which is not addressed explicitly in the aforementioned approaches, which are neutral as concerns ontological choices (in the sense discussed in [17,18]). We have proposed an ontological interpretation for types as endurants, which means that the various distinctions for endurant types in UFO also apply to high-order domain types. Note that, none of the related efforts in the multi-level modeling literature incorporates modeling guidelines considering the metaproperties of rigidity and sortality. At the time of writing, OntoUML is the only conceptual modeling language to leverage these metaproperties to multi-level taxonomies. The OntoUML plugin is capable of checking the semantically-motivated rules automatically, some of which are direct consequences of MLT, and some of which arise from the combination of MLT with UFO.

Beyond the literature on multi-level modeling, the conceptualization of types of types has also received some attention in the ontology literature. BORO (tracing back to [32]), e.g., is an extensional 4D ontology that uses the concept of *power class* to refer to the class whose instances are all specializations of a class (similar to [7]). Because of the ontological choices of BORO, power classes are not subject to change, which is a key difference to our approach. Types of types are also incorporated into the Cyc ontology [13], including some support for order stratification similar to MLT's which we have incorporated in OntoUML. However, differently from the work reported here, Cyc does not address the various modal aspects of types. Other foundational ontologies, such as BFO [31] and TUpper [16] are defined within traditional two-level schemas and hence do not cater to the representation of domain ontologies with types of types.

The same can be said in general of DOLCE [26], although recent work with this foundational ontology has explored the issue of *concept change* in time with a focus on designed product types [34]. In this work, objects instantiate *concepts* (i.e., domain types) when they manifest the properties collected in that concept [34]. Concepts may change the properties they collect arbitrarily (throughout the design process). In their own words, they "are totally liberal with respect to how concepts can change through time". Because of this, the instantiation relation depends not only on the state of the object being classified but also on the state of the concept. The same can be said of [27] when addressing the notion of *concept drift*. While this intricacy may be required in the domains the authors intended to address, it poses a significant challenge to conceptual modeling as fundamental structural relations like specialization become time-dependent. Here, instead, we consider intensions to be essential (part of the high-order kind), and hence changing a type's intension would amount to the creation of a new type (not identical but historically related to the previous one).

6   Conclusion

This paper proposes an extension of UFO based on a formal multi-level theory dubbed MLT [1,9]. This extension is motivated by empirical evidence supporting the demand for high-order types in ODCM [6,12]. Particularly to OntoUML, a recently developed dataset (See footnote 1) has indicated several ontologies that systematically subvert the language's syntax and rules to capture multi-level features present in subject domains.

The proposed extension revisits the UFO taxonomy by employing MLT's characterization of multi-level schemes in place of UFO's original two-level characterization. Further, we perform an ontological analysis of the concept of Type, proposing an account of *types as endurants*. This analysis incorporates in UFO a preliminary analysis of higher-order types some of us conducted earlier [20], which makes the case for the ontological soundness of this particular interpretation of *types as endurants*, and details the advantages of this interpretation over competing approaches. By formalizing in UFO this interpretation, the ontology is now able to admit types as entities that *exist in time* and that undergo changes without changing their identities. This account also enables the classification of types of types (i.e., high-order types) based on the same modal features originally recognized in endurant types: (i) sortal high-order types, in contrast to non-sortal types, classify entities conforming to a unique identity principle which it either provides or inherits from another high-order type; (ii) rigid high-order type necessarily classify (in the modal sense) their instances, as opposed to anti-rigid and semi-rigid types. Moreover, (high-order) phases are anti-rigid high-order types based on intrinsic properties of their instances, whilst anti-rigid high-order types based on relational properties are classified as (high-order) roles.

The syntactic constraints we have defined for the profile stem directly from independently developed axiomatizations of UFO [22] and MLT [1,8,9]. The result is a rich set of rules that prevent common mistakes in multi-level models and also those involving incorrect combinations of metaproperties. The latter case motivated early ontology-driven approaches such as OntoClean and was originally incorporated in UFO's taxonomy of substantials [19], and recently extended for the taxonomy of endurants [22]. A full formalization of the overall combined theory is a subject of ongoing work.

Acknowledgements. This research is partly funded by Brazilian funding agencies CNPq (313687/2020–0 and 407235/2017–5), CAPES (23038.028816/2016–41) and FAPES (281/2021).

References

1. Almeida, J.P.A., Fonseca, C.M., Carvalho, V.A.: A comprehensive formal theory for multi-level conceptual modeling. In: Mayr, H.C., Guizzardi, G., Ma, H., Pastor, O. (eds.) ER 2017. LNCS, vol. 10650, pp. 280–294. Springer, Cham (2017). https://doi.org/10.1007/978-3-319-69904-2_23
2. Almeida, J.P.A., Falbo, R.A., Guizzardi, G.: Events as entities in ontology-driven conceptual modeling. In: Laender, A.H.F., Pernici, B., Lim, E.-P., de Oliveira, J.P.M. (eds.) ER 2019. LNCS, vol. 11788, pp. 469–483. Springer, Cham (2019). https://doi.org/10.1007/978-3-030-33223-5_39
3. Atkinson, C.: Meta-modelling for distributed object environments. In: Proceedings First International Enterprise Distributed Object Computing Workshop, pp. 90–101 (1997)
4. Atkinson, C., Gerbig, R.: Melanie: multi-level modeling and ontology engineering environment. In: Proceedings of the 2nd International Master Class on Model-Driven Engineering: Modeling Wizards, pp. 1–2 (2012)
5. Atkinson, C., Kühne, T.: The essence of multilevel metamodeling. In: Gogolla, M., Kobryn, C. (eds.) UML 2001. LNCS, vol. 2185, pp. 19–33. Springer, Heidelberg (2001). https://doi.org/10.1007/3-540-45441-1_3
6. Brasileiro, F., Almeida, J.P.A., Carvalho, V.A., Guizzardi, G.: Applying a multi-level modeling theory to assess taxonomic hierarchies in Wikidata. In: Proceedings of the 25th International Conference Companion on World Wide Web, pp. 975–980. WWW 2016 Companion (2016)
7. Cardelli, L.: Structural subtyping and the notion of power type. In: Proceedings of the 15th ACM SIGPLAN-SIGACT Symposium on Principles of Programming Languages, pp. 70–79 (1988)

8. Carvalho, V.A., Almeida, J.P.A., Guizzardi, G.: Using a well-founded multi-level theory to support the analysis and representation of the powertype pattern in conceptual modeling. In: Nurcan, S., Soffer, P., Bajec, M., Eder, J. (eds.) CAiSE 2016. LNCS, vol. 9694, pp. 309–324. Springer, Cham (2016). https://doi.org/10.1007/978-3-319-39696-5_19
9. Carvalho, V.A., Almeida, J.P.A.: Toward a well-founded theory for multi-level conceptual modeling. Softw. Syst. Model. **17**(1), 205–231 (2018)
10. Carvalho, V.A., Almeida, J.P.A., Fonseca, C.M., Guizzardi, G.: Multi-level ontology-based conceptual modeling. Data Knowl. Eng. **109**, 3–24 (2017)
11. Clark, T., Gonzalez-Perez, C., Henderson-Sellers, B.: A foundation for multi-level modelling. In: Proceedings of the MULTI 2014 Co-located with ACM/IEEE MoDELS 2014. CEUR Workshop Proceedings, vol. 1286, pp. 43–52. CEUR-WS.org (2014)
12. Dadalto, A.A., Almeida, J.P.A., Fonseca, C.M., Guizzardi, G.: Type or individual? evidence of large-scale conceptual disarray in wikidata. In: Ghose, A., Horkoff, J., Silva Souza, V.E., Parsons, J., Evermann, J. (eds.) ER 2021. LNCS, vol. 13011, pp. 367–377. Springer, Cham (2021). https://doi.org/10.1007/978-3-030-89022-3_29
13. Foxvog, D.: Instances of instances modeled via higher-order classes. Found. Aspects Ontol. **9–2005**, 46–54 (2005)
14. Goldstein, R.C., Storey, V.C.: Materialization. IEEE Trans. Knowl. Data Eng. **6**(5), 835–842 (1994). https://doi.org/10.1109/69.317711
15. Gonzalez-Perez, C., Henderson-Sellers, B.: A powertype-based metamodelling framework. Softw. Syst. Model. **5**(1), 72–90 (2006)
16. Grüninger, M., Ru, Y., Thai, J.: TUpper: a top level ontology within standards. Appl. Ontol. **17**(1), 143–165 (2022). https://doi.org/10.3233/ao-220263
17. Guarino, N.: The ontological level. In: 16th International Wittgenstein Symposium, pp. 443–456. Hölder-Pichler-Tempsky (1993)
18. Guarino, N.: The ontological level: revisiting 30 years of knowledge representation. In: Borgida, A.T., Chaudhri, V.K., Giorgini, P., Yu, E.S. (eds.) Conceptual Modeling: Foundations and Applications. LNCS, vol. 5600, pp. 52–67. Springer, Heidelberg (2009). https://doi.org/10.1007/978-3-642-02463-4_4
19. Guizzardi, G.: Ontological foundations for structural conceptual models. TI/CTIT (2005)
20. Guizzardi, G., Almeida, J.P.A., Guarino, N., Carvalho, V.A.: Towards an ontological analysis of powertypes. In: Joint Ontology Workshops (JOWO), vol. 1517. CEUR-WS.org (2015)
21. Guizzardi, G., Wagner, G., Guarino, N., van Sinderen, M.: An ontologically well-founded profile for UML conceptual models. In: Proceedings of the 16th International CAiSE Conference, pp. 112–126 (2004)
22. Guizzardi, G., Fonseca, C.M., Benevides, A.B., Almeida, J.P.A., Porello, D., Sales, T.P.: Endurant types in ontology-driven conceptual modeling: towards OntoUML 2.0. In: Trujillo, J.C., et al. (eds.) ER 2018. LNCS, vol. 11157, pp. 136–150. Springer, Cham (2018). https://doi.org/10.1007/978-3-030-00847-5_12
23. Guizzardi, G., et al.: Towards ontological foundations for conceptual modeling: the Unified Foundational Ontology (UFO) story. Appl. Ontol. **10**(3–4), 259–271 (2015)
24. Jeusfeld, M.A., Neumayr, B.: DeepTelos: multi-level modeling with most general instances. In: Comyn-Wattiau, I., Tanaka, K., Song, I.-Y., Yamamoto, S., Saeki, M. (eds.) ER 2016. LNCS, vol. 9974, pp. 198–211. Springer, Cham (2016). https://doi.org/10.1007/978-3-319-46397-1_15

25. de Lara, J., Guerra, E.: Deep meta-modelling with METADEPTH. In: Vitek, J. (ed.) TOOLS 2010. LNCS, vol. 6141, pp. 1–20. Springer, Heidelberg (2010). https://doi.org/10.1007/978-3-642-13953-6_1

26. Masolo, C., Borgo, S., Gangemi, A., Guarino, N., Oltramari, A.: WonderWeb Deliverable D18. Tech. rep, CNR (2003)

27. Masolo, C., Sanfilippo, E.M., Lamé, M., Pittet, P.: Modeling concept drift for historical research in the digital humanities. In: CEUR Workshop Proceedings, vol. 2518. CEUR-WS.org, JOWO (2019)

28. Neumayr, B., Grün, K., Schrefl, M.: Multi-level domain modeling with m-objects and m-relationships. In: CRPIT, vol. 96, pp. 107–116. Australian Computer Society, APCCM (2009)

29. Object Management Group: Unified Modeling Language (UML) Version 2.5.1. Tech. rep. (2017). www.omg.org/spec/UML/2.5.1

30. Odell, J.: Power types. J. Object-Oriented Program. $7(2)$, 8–12 (1994)

31. Otte, J.N., Beverley, J., Ruttenberg, A.: BFO: Basic formal ontology. Appl. Ontol. $\mathbf{17}$, 17–43 (2022)

32. Partridge, C.: Business objects: re-engineering for re-use. Butterworth-Heinemann (1996)

33. Pirotte, A., Zimányi, E., Massart, D., Yakusheva, T.: Materialization: A powerful and ubiquitous abstraction pattern. In: 20th International Conference on Very Large Data Bases, pp. 630–641. Morgan Kaufmann (1994)

34. Sanfilippo, E.M., Masolo, C., Porello, D.: Design knowledge representation: an ontological perspective. In: Proceedings of the AIDE 2015, vol. 1473. CEUR-WS.org (2015)

35. Schwartz, S.P.: Natural kinds and nominal kinds. Mind $\mathbf{89}$(354), 182–195 (1980)

36. Verdonck, M., Gailly, F.: Insights on the use and application of ontology and conceptual modeling languages in ontology-driven conceptual modeling. In: Comyn-Wattiau, I., Tanaka, K., Song, I.-Y., Yamamoto, S., Saeki, M. (eds.) ER 2016. LNCS, vol. 9974, pp. 83–97. Springer, Cham (2016). https://doi.org/10.1007/978-3-319-46397-1_7

Rethinking Model Representation - A Taxonomy of Advanced Information Visualization in Conceptual Modeling

Giuliano De Carlo[1], Philip Langer[2], and Dominik Bork[1]✉ iD

[1] TU Wien, Business Informatics Group, Favoritenstrasse 9-11, 1040 Vienna, Austria
dominik.bork@tuwien.ac.at
[2] Eclipsesource, Vienna, Austria

Abstract. Conceptual modeling is an integral part of computer science research and is widely adopted in industrial practices, e.g., business process and enterprise architecture management. Providing adequate and usable modeling tools is necessary for the efficient adoption of modeling languages. Meta-modeling platforms provide a rich set of functionalities and are mature in realizing state-of-the-art modeling tools. However, despite their maturity and stability, most of these platforms did not yet leverage the full extent of functionalities and the ease of exploitation and integration enabled by web technologies. Current web technologies now enable much richer, advanced opportunities for visualizing and interacting with conceptual models. However, a structured and comprehensive overview of possible information visualization techniques linked to conceptual models and modeling tools is lacking. This paper aims to fill this gap by presenting a taxonomy of advanced information visualization, albeit its generic nature, applicable to conceptual modeling. We believe this taxonomy greatly benefits researchers by providing a standard frame to position their works and for method and tool engineers to spark innovation.

Keywords: Information visualization · Human computer interaction · Taxonomy · Conceptual modeling · Modeling tools · Notation

1 Introduction

Technology usage forms an essential part of our private and professional lives. Having access to the right tools and the knowledge to use them correctly can save time and effort. The connection between the user of a tool and the tool itself is usually its user interface and the supported interactions that come with it. While the functionalities of a tool also play a significant role, without a graphical user interface that is well designed, tools are often labeled as not very useful for a user [26]. This is especially important in the field of conceptual modeling, where information visualization makes up a central aspect that directly influences the comprehensiveness of models and the usability and ease of use

J. Ralyté et al. (Eds.): ER 2022, LNCS 13607, pp. 35–51, 2022.
https://doi.org/10.1007/978-3-031-17995-2_3

of modeling tools [9,23]. Tool development is therefore denoted as an essential part of enterprise modeling [23] and modeling business information systems [9] research. However, past research primarily focused on the development of new and the evaluation [4,22] and improvement of existing modeling languages [5].

Today, a wide range of different modeling tools are available. Most of these tools are mature and established applications that have been actively worked on over a relatively long period. Because of their age, their functionalities are often built on older technology stacks, i.e., not compatible with state-of-the-art platforms built on web technologies. Although the results produced with such tools are still unsurpassed, the functionality, especially concerning the user interfaces and the information visualization, often lacks advanced techniques like zooming. The usage of such techniques, we believe, could speed up the model development process. It could also improve usability and ease of use of the tools and comprehension of conceptual models by humans. Web technologies have been heavily used and improved over the previous years and offer a wide range of great functionalities, which is why they are the perfect fit to develop such advanced techniques. Compared to platforms used in most traditional modeling tools, web technologies provide a future-proof, feature-rich, robust, and efficient foundation for state-of-the-art visualization and interaction techniques.

Only very few research can be found focusing user interface design for modeling tools [27] and visualization techniques used in conceptual modeling have barely evolved in the last years [13,14]. A structured and comprehensive overview of information visualization techniques with an emphasis on conceptual modeling and modeling tools is lacking. This paper aims to fill this gap by presenting a generic taxonomy of advanced information visualization that is also applicable to conceptual modeling. According to Tory and Moeller [29], visualization taxonomies can: (*i*) *guide people* outside the core community by classifying existing works and pointing them to possible, current visualizations, and (*ii*) *guide research* by enabling researchers to position their contributions within a well-defined classification scheme, and by establishing a structured foundation for progressing the field in different dimensions. We believe that our advanced visualization taxonomy for conceptual model representation will activate a rethinking in the conceptual modeling and modeling tool communities. This rethinking might question state of the art in conceptual model representation and, hopefully, steer the focus of research toward novel and advanced visualizations. We also demonstrate the broad spectrum of advanced visualization techniques with the proposed taxonomy, which have not yet found wide adoption in current modeling tools. With the flexibility of web technologies, introducing them in modern tools becomes increasingly accessible and supports users to more efficiently comprehend and interact with conceptual models. Thus, we hope that the proposed taxonomy sparks innovation in future modeling tool development.

In the remainder of this paper, Sect. 2 briefly reports on related information visualization taxonomies. The applied research method is then presented in Sect. 3. The taxonomy for advanced information visualization in conceptual modeling is presented in Sect. 4 and consecutively evaluated in Sect. 5. Eventually, Sect. 7 concludes the paper and provides some directions for future research.

2 Related Approaches

Information visualization is a long-lasting topic in academia. We, therefore, first look at existing taxonomies that could provide valuable input for the development of our taxonomy. Although we could not find an existing taxonomy that perfectly fits our scope, the subsequently described works partly align with our goal. We briefly introduce these taxonomies' core dimensions and categories before excerpting the relevant ones for our scope. Shneiderman [24] proposes a task by data type taxonomy with seven data types for applications with advanced graphical user interfaces. These tasks are: *Overview, Zoom, Filter, Details-on-demand, Relate, History,* and *Extract.* The data-types are: *1-dimensional, 2-dimensional, 3-dimensional, temporal, multi-dimensional, tree,* and *network.* The relevant tasks within the scope of our study are mainly Overview, Zoom, Filter, and Details-on-demand. Moreover, shapes and forms of conceptual models can be classified as 2-dimensional concerning the data type. Silva and Catarci [25] categorize temporal-data features by *visualization* and *interaction* features. Visualization features describe visual techniques of a system, as in their example, Snapshot View or Multiple Calendars. Interaction features are categorized very similarly to Shneiderman's categories mentioned above.

Tory et al. [29] categorize visualization techniques based on their design model instead of their data. The authors propose to categorize design models into two higher level groups: *discrete* and *continuous.* Continuous models assume that data can be interpolated, and discrete models assume that they cannot. Data can often be visualized in multiple ways, and therefore it is possible to present the same data with continuous models and discrete models.

Cockburn et al. [7] categorize graphical user interfaces into four categories: *overview-plus-detail, zooming, focus-plus-context,* and *cue-based.* Overview-plus-detail represents the spatial separation of information. It splits up information into two separate views: overview-view and detail-view. Zooming represents the temporal separation of information. It allows magnification and demagnification of information. Focus-plus-context seamlessly combines a focused representation of information within its context. Cue-based techniques change how an object is displayed and rendered and are often combined with search criteria or off-screen elements.

3 Taxonomy Development Research Method

Nickerson et al. [20] propose a development method to create taxonomies for information systems. They define a taxonomy as a set of n dimensions $D_i(i = 1, ..., n)$ each consisting of $k_i(k_i \geqslant 2)$ *mutually exclusive* and *collectively exhaustive* characteristics $C_{ij}(j = 1, ..., k_i)$ such that each object under consideration has one and only one C_{ij} for each D_i. To create a valid taxonomy, Nickerson et al. propose an iterative approach that is applied until all ending conditions are met. One iteration can either consist of an *empirical-to-conceptual* step, or a *conceptual-to-empirical* step. Which one to choose depends on the researcher's knowledge and the available data. An empirical-to-conceptual iteration should be chosen when there are many objects available, and the researcher is familiar with them. It consists of looking at these objects and identifying characteristics based on their qualities. A conceptual-to-empirical iteration should be chosen when there are few objects and the researcher has a broad understanding and knowledge base of the relevant domain. Instead of primarily looking at objects, the researcher will identify characteristics merely based on her knowledge.

3.1 Problem Identification and Motivation

Kundisch et al. [19] recently updated the taxonomy development method proposed by Nickerson et al. They argue that most past taxonomies possess inconsistent adoption of existing methods and a non-transparent reporting of relevant design decisions. To overcome this limitation, they present an extended taxonomy design process (ETDP) and give examples of well-written taxonomies for each step in their process. The additional steps in their ETDP focus mainly on problem identification, motivation, and taxonomy evaluation. More accurately, they add three initial steps which should be conducted before the taxonomy is designed and developed. These steps consist of specifying: *i*) the *observed phenomenon*, *ii*) the *target user group(s)*, and *iii*) the *intended purpose* of the taxonomy, which also influences the *ex-post* evaluation of the taxonomy.

The phenomena observed in this research are visualization and interaction features applicable to conceptual modeling. We are interested in concrete examples and theoretical concepts of features that allow users to modify underlying data by utilizing graphical user interface interaction methods. The target user groups are conceptual modeling researchers, method engineers, and developers of modeling tools interested in realizing advanced model visualization and interaction features. Our taxonomy is supposed to help identify defining characteristics of such features and provide aid during the conceptualization and integration of them into new methods or tools. Furthermore, our taxonomy should give a basic understanding of the opportunities and limitations of the existing features, which should establish a foundation for designing new features.

3.2 Solution Objectives

Two essential qualities of a valid taxonomy were already mentioned: mutually exclusiveness and collectively exhaustiveness. This means that every object has to have precisely one characteristic in each taxonomy dimension. These two qualities form two of ten objective ending conditions (cf. [19, 20]), which, together with five subjective ending conditions, are used to determine when a taxonomy is considered complete. Consequently, these ending conditions need to be applied during the iterative application of either an *empirical-to-conceptual* or *conceptual-to-empirical* step until the ending conditions are met.

Subjective and objective ending conditions are essential to determine when the iterative process can be stopped, and the taxonomy holds enough characteristics to classify the phenomenon it is supposed to describe. For this reason,

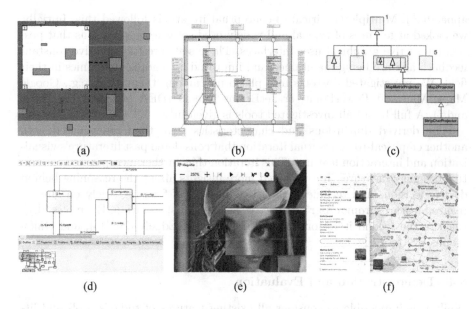

(a)   (b)   (c)

(d)   (e)   (f)

Fig. 1. Examples of survey results: **a)** Off-screen elements are shown with their orthographic direction, the color shows the distance, and markers indicate the number of off-screen elements in that direction [30]; **b)** Off-screen elements are represented as proxies on the border of the focused view [10].; **c)** Onion graph visualization by [18]. Blue elements are focused whereas yellow elements are not focused. Nodes 3 and 5 represent individual classes while Nodes 2 and 4 represent multiple generalizations; **d)** A minimap in the Eclipse IDE. The main view shows only a part of a class diagram. The minimap in the bottom left shows the entire diagram with a much smaller zoom factor. The blue square provides orientation inside the main view; **e)** The Windows 10 Magnifier app magnifies parts of the view while hiding others; **f)** Google Maps' search results at the left act as a proxy. Clicking on one, zooms and scrolls the map to the corresponding position. (Color figure online)

they are both used as an *ex-ante* evaluation. Subjective ending conditions are, e.g., **Robustness:** Do the dimensions and characteristics enable differentiation among objects sufficient to be of interest? And **Comprehensiveness:** Can all objects or a (random) sample of objects within the domain of interest be classified? Are all dimensions of the objects of interest identified? Objective ending conditions are, e.g., All objects or a representative sample of objects have been examined while no new dimensions or characteristics were added in the last iteration, and no dimensions or characteristics were merged or split in the previous iteration. For the sake of brevity, we refer the interested reader to the literature proposing the well-established ending conditions in great detail [19, 20].

3.3 Design and Development

The first iteration for developing this taxonomy was a conceptual-to-empirical one. We thereby looked at taxonomies and related literature (see this paper's appendix[1]). Multiple empirical-to-conceptual iterations followed this. Initially, we looked at features of typical and widely used software applications that possess interactive graphical user interfaces. These software tools receive constant feedback and are being maintained and improved by leading companies in their field. We investigated 46 tools and platforms; among them were, e.g., Google Maps, Microsoft PowerPoint, or JetBrains IntelliJ IDEA (e.g., see Fig. 1d, e, and f). A full list of all investigated tools is given in[1].

The derived dimensions and characteristics were then re-evaluated with another empirical-to-conceptual iteration that considered past literature's visualization and interaction features. This iteration thus further incorporated conceptual designs of features and provided more insights about the reasoning behind design decisions and technical conditions instead of focusing solely on already realized features from a user perspective as in the first iteration. Examples identified in the second iteration are City Lights [30], EdgeRadar [15], and Onion graphs [18] (see Fig. 1).

3.4   Demonstration and Evaluation

While it is impossible to consider all existing features of today's tools and literature, the sample of features was expanded until all subjective and objective ending conditions were met. It is to note that, ideally, this taxonomy should only be used to categorize concrete examples of features in the end. We realized that conceptual designs of features could often be interpreted and implemented in many different ways during the development. E.g., the concept of a magnifying glass feature can be implemented in a separate and independent view or by magnifying the current view. In the first case, it would be classified as an overview-plus-detail interface, but in the second case, it would be classified under focus-plus-context. When classifying conceptual designs of features that have not been implemented yet, one must be aware that it may include a subjective bias. Often, it is not immediately obvious how such features operate, which is why it is even more important to describe them accurately.

After the description of the first steps of the extended taxonomy design process in this section, we will, in the following section, present the final taxonomy for advanced information visualization in conceptual modeling. Eventually, the comprehensive evaluation of the final taxonomy is reported in Sect. 5.

4   Taxonomy

For our taxonomy, three meta-characteristics emerged which provide the structure of the following sections: **Presentation**, **Interaction**, and **Data**.

---

[1] https://www.dropbox.com/s/1oudgdyb0xqi6ns/taxonomy_appendix_0_3.pdf?dl=0.

4.1   Presentation

This dimension mainly describes if and how a feature utilizes one or multiple views, it describes the dependency between views, and how views represent information.

Presentation/Interface Type: The first dimension mainly describes how a feature uses the available space, represents information to the user, and generally, how a user can interact with it. This dimension consists of four categories, which are based on Cockburn et al.'s work [7]: *overview-plus-detail, zooming, focus-plus-context,* and *cue-based.* This categorization is thus not new and can be found recurring when browsing the information visualization literature.

Overview-Plus-Detail: This interface scheme is used in many applications nowadays. It splits the information space into two physically separated views; one shows information at an overview level, and the other shows similar or even the same information in greater detail. Although they are physically separated, the two views do semantically depend on each other, and actions in one view are usually immediately reflected inside the other view. The essential characteristic of the dependency between both views is that they are usually not spatially dependent on each other. If one or even both views were to be moved to a different location, no issues would arise.

An overview-plus-detail interface usually has two primary purposes. Firstly, it should give the user a better feeling about what subset of information they are currently looking at in relation to the entire information space. Secondly, they should give the user an easy way of navigating the information space by letting the user interact with the overview interface. Usually, they operate on the x- and y-axis and utilize interaction methods such as panning or scrolling. Operation on the z-axis is seen less often and mostly overlaps with the zooming category introduced later.

A good example is shown in Fig. 1d. An excerpt of a UML diagram is shown in detail on the center view, while in the bottom left corner, an overview is displayed, which shows the entire diagram. Actions like panning or zooming inside one view are directly reflected inside the other view. The overview interface does not always have to show the same type of information as the detail-view; it may also provide a completely different type of data, e.g., spatial data. An example of this is the scrollbar. Scrollbars can be seen as the overview interface that gives one-dimensional information about what the other view displays in relation to the entire information space. E.g., the Sublime Text 3 editor widened the vertical scrollbar to show spatial information and additional information concerning syntax highlighting. Another good example is Microsoft PowerPoint, where the overview view on the left shows a miniature version of the slide that is currently displayed inside the detail view along with the following and preceding slides.

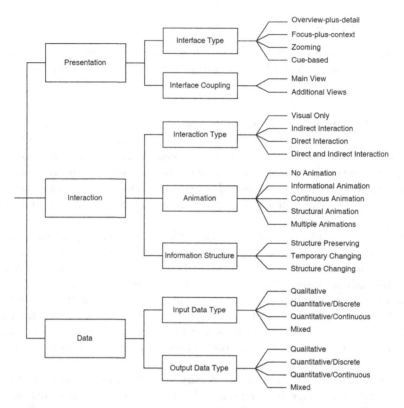

Fig. 2. Advanced information visualization in conceptual modeling taxonomy.

Focus-Plus-Context: This scheme lets a user see specific parts of the information space in more or full detail while also getting an overview of the information around it (distortion of the information space). Unlike overview-plus-detail, both parts (overview and detail) are displayed *inside the same view* which is often accomplished by distorting the information space to fit the user's needs. The focus of the information that the user is interested in is shown in greater detail. At the same time, information around it, the context, is preserved and made visible to the user but in lesser detail.

The level of distortion that is applied differs from implementation to implementation. It goes from no/infinite distortion, e.g., by using the Windows 10 Magnifier app (Fig. 1e), to distortion that affects the entire view, as seen, e.g., in Google Street View. The distortion aspect is an essential feature of focus-plus-context interfaces, differentiating this category's components from others. Without distortion, as with the Windows 10 Magnifier app, a feature can often be categorized as a basic zooming feature or an overview-plus-detail feature instead.

An advantage of having only one view instead of two or more is that the user does not have to switch between multiple views and can rather keep focusing on the same view. In a field study conducted by Baudisch et al. [2], who compared overview-plus-detail, focus-plus-context, and zooming-plus-panning, all chosen tasks could be performed faster on the focus-plus-context interface by a margin of 21–36%. They attribute the differences to the context switches that do not have to be made on a focus-plus-context interface and the consistent scale that the focus-plus-context interface offers.

Zooming: Zooming utilizes the temporal separation of the information space. It is similar to overview-plus-detail with the difference that only one view is provided instead of two or more. Another difference is that the user has to utilize interaction methods (e.g., button click, CTRL+mousewheel, or CTRL+"+"), mainly the zooming method, to change the size in which information is displayed. This represents basic zooming which can be further advanced by combining it with other techniques such as fisheye zoom [1,12,21] or semantic zoom [10,11].

A precondition to making zoomable interfaces possible is to have information that can be magnified and de-magnified. The magnification process can be categorized into *continuous* and *discrete zooming*. Continuous zooming occurs when the subject does not have a countable amount of zoom levels. The simplest form of magnification is to increase the subject's size. This can be done on every subject with some visual representation. Since there is no clear separation of zoom levels, and the subject can theoretically be rendered in any size, this can be considered continuous zooming. An example of discrete zooming takes place in Google Maps (see Fig. 1f). With Google Maps, users can change the presented level of detail by zooming in and out of predefined zoom levels (i.e., discrete). Notably, during the zooming in one zoom level, Google Maps applies continuous zooming by increasing/decreasing the size of the presented elements.

Cue-Based: Cue-based techniques often show alternative graphical representations of objects on the stage to give cues that lead to other information in the information space. These alternative representations, often in the form of simple labels, can then be used to, e.g., navigate to the actual object or notify the user that the object exists. Examples of cue-based techniques are the visualization of off-screen objects with interaction functionality as seen in Figs. 1a and b. Cue-based techniques are also often used in combination with search criteria. An example is the clickable search results presented to the users of Google Maps (see Fig. 1f). Clicking on them pans and zooms the map to the position of the search result.

Presentation/Interface Coupling: This category distinguishes features that require **additional views** from those operating inside the **main view**. This is an essential aspect as it impacts how a user uses the feature and how to implement a feature. From an implementation perspective, having to add another view can become complicated because, depending on the size and significance of the implemented feature, new space has to be found on the user interface, and, instead of managing just one view, multiple views have to be managed and kept consistent [3]. From the user's perspective, additional views mean multiple separated points of interest. Switching between them demands a focus switch in our brains, which requires a mental effort that can quickly become exhausting.

As Baudisch et al. and Hornbak et al. [2,16] showed, tasks could be performed faster on focus-plus-context interfaces (one-view) than on overview-plus-detail (two views). Contrarily, Thabet et al. [28] analyzed the positive effect of automated consistency management in multiple views.

4.2   Interaction

This dimension focuses on the characteristics of a feature that the user directly interacts with. The attributes in this dimension significantly impact how a feature is being used by the target group and, therefore, its usability. It should give insight into critical user-related aspects of a feature and help make design-related decisions. Unlike the first dimension **Presentation**, which is mainly based on previous literature, this dimension was conducted by looking at different tools and our experiences made during software development.

Interaction/Interaction Type: This characterization distinguishes the kinds of interaction that a feature offers. While this category can be further extended by going more into detail and considering all kinds of interaction types and events, this taxonomy remains on a more abstract level with only four main categorizations: *visual only*, *indirect interaction*, *direct interaction*, and *direct and indirect interaction* to also account for the subjective goal of *Conciseness* [20].

Visual Only: Features which do not give a user the ability to interact with it, i.e., features that only add visual benefits. An example of a visual-only feature is a grid system that helps users position elements but does not provide direct interaction possibilities.

Direct Interaction: Features that add new interaction possibilities. They are usually intentionally performed by a user, and their primary purpose is to manipulate feature-specific data directly. An example of this is the *Peek Definition* feature in conventional IDEs like IntelliJ and VS Code, where programmers can directly interact with a function/method inside the code by triggering a specific context menu on that feature. This interaction process is specific to the feature, and the context menu would have no use if this feature did not exist.

Indirect Interaction: Actions of a feature with indirect interactions can usually be triggered by performing interactions that are not part of the feature itself. Actions controlled by indirect interactions are usually triggered either concurrently alongside actions of other features or as a side effect of such. An example of an indirect interaction feature is the ruler visible in many text or diagram editors that provides basic functionality to related elements on the stage, e.g., a spatial position.

Direct and Indirect Interaction: Some features utilize direct and indirect interactions. An example of such would be the basic scrollbar commonly known from text editors like Notepad and Word. A direct interaction would be to click and move the scrollbar. An indirect interaction would be to move the position of the current viewport by different means (e.g., with the mouse wheel). This would indirectly automatically trigger the scrollbar to move as well.

Interaction/Animation: This categorization gives an overview of the types of animations a feature uses. Animations are essential in visualizing even complex changes to the users intuitively and understandably. The proper use of animations prevents users from getting confused about these changes and increases their sense of orientation (cf. [6]). Here, it is crucial to understand the difference between a separate animation played alongside a feature and its functionality. In this category, animations are considered visual techniques that physically move graphical objects and are triggered by the user but not directly controlled by them. Most of the time, they are played right after the user's interaction has finished.

No Animation: Features that do not utilize animations in any form, like adjusting the physical positioning of visual objects through basic scrollbars.

Informational Animation: Animations, which give the user additional information (often in the form of text) but do not directly interfere with elements on the stage. An example of this is given by Igarashi and Hinckley in [17]: "..., when the user presses the mouse button, a pink slider appears." Another example would be a small label that is transitioned in and out during a zooming interaction, showing the current zoom level. This could be done with discrete zoom levels (as is done by yEd[2]) or with continuous zooming actions which show the current zoom level relative to a base value.

Continuous Animation: Animations, that take existing elements on the stage and change, in a continuous process, the way they are represented. The characteristic of this kind of animation is that no additional information is added or removed. Examples are a simple magnification of an element (see Fig. 1e) or by clicking on a proxy element (e.g., $+/-$ symbols).

Structural Animation: This type of animation is used when the structure of elements or the stage is changed. Unlike continuous animations, new information is added, old is removed, or existing is changed. This new information could, e.g., be entire elements or just properties of elements. An example of such an animation is the already mentioned *Peek Definition* feature.

Multiple Animations: Some features utilize multiple animations independently from each other in different areas of an application. For such cases, we decided to include a *Multiple Animations* categorization, which consists of features that utilize a combination of informational, continuous, and/or structural animations. An example would be the already mentioned feature Speed-dependent automatic zooming [17]. It does utilize not only an informational animation in the form of a pink slider but also a continuous animation: "When the user releases the mouse button, an animated transition gradually returns the document to the original base scale." [17, p. 142]

Interaction/Information Structure: Many tools, especially modeling tools, give the user the option to adjust the structure of the information space. The user can personalize the information space by adjusting the position of objects inside it. Positions are saved, and objects are positioned at the previously defined position upon re-opening a file. Not having to recreate the mental map of the information space every time a file is opened saves a lot of the user's time and effort. Because of that, this characteristic is precious and should not be carelessly taken away. The larger an information space is, the more time a user requires to get used to a new structure, and therefore, the more critical it is to keep the structure intact.

Nevertheless, preserving the structure is not always easily possible. E.g., problems can arise when dealing with the typical "expand/collapse" functionality. An expanded element may become too large, pushing other elements out of the way. Another common cause for a change in the information structure is the automatic process of rearranging elements. Some modeling tools offer a "center all elements" functionality, which automatically adjusts and centers the position of all elements. Such functionality can be a dangerous game, and finding a good algorithm that prevents the user from having to recreate the mental map of their workspace is a challenging task. For that reason, it is often the best solution to stay away from implementing features that frequently change the layout of a user's workspace.

Structure Preserving: This category includes all features that do not change the structure at all. The critical point of features in this category is that users do not have to recreate the mental map of their workspace. An example for such a feature is the semantic zoom in yEd[2] that adds/removes information but preserves the structure.

Structure Changing: Features in this category adjust the structure to the point that causes users to recreate their mental map. An example is the grouping feature in yEd. Unlike their semantic zooming implementation, closing or opening groups automatically adjusts the structure. When opening a group, the position of elements inside the group is adjusted. When closing a group, the position of elements outside the group is changed to utilize the previously occupied space.

Temporary Changing: Features of this category temporally adjust the structure. Often, features visually change the structure, only for a limited amount of time, to execute a specific functionality (e.g., the *Peek Definition* feature).

---

[2] yEd [online], https://www.yworks.com/products/yed, last visited: 26.04.2022.

4.3 Data

This dimension describes the feature-specific data used by a feature and can be distinguished from the tool-specific data. Just like the previous dimension, this one is also based on inspection of different tools and software development experiences. If we use the scrollbar of a PDF reader software as an example, the tool-specific data would be the PDF itself, and the feature-specific data would be the x- and y-coordinates of the viewport. The scrollbar feature does not manipulate the PDF at all. Instead, it moves the viewport to different locations by changing its coordinates. Unlike the tool-specific data, the feature-specific data is often independent of the tool itself, which helps to keep this taxonomy more abstract.

Data can be split into input data that is read by a feature to perform an action and output data modified or returned by an action of a feature. Both sub-dimensions, **Data/Input Data Type** and **Data/Output Data Type**, consist of the same characteristics: *Qualitative, Quantitative/Discrete, Quantitative/Continuous*, and *Mixed*.

Qualitative data is semi-structured data, such as labels, attributes, or entire domain model elements. Quantitative data can be counted or measured and is expressed as numbers. Furthermore, quantitative data exists in two variations, i.e., *quantitative/discrete* and *quantitative/continuous*. Quantitative/discrete data is countable and can only take specific values. Quantitative/continuous data, on the other hand, is measurable and can be split into smaller parts.

Similar to the *Interaction/Animation/Multiple Animations* categorization, some features operate with multiple different sets of data. E.g., the visualization of off-screen elements (Fig. 1a and b) work with information about position, color, and size of off-screen elements. Such features should be classified as *Mixed*. It is ideal for a feature to work with continuous data most of the time. This is because continuous data reflect user interactions more directly and responsively. It is easier to follow continuously rendered changes than discretely rendered ones. This is also reflected in [8].

5 Evaluation

In the following, we report on the application of two widely used taxonomy evaluation techniques in our ex-post evaluation, i.e., *Illustrative scenario with real-world objects* and *Illustrative scenario with existing research* [19]. We classified 33 features that were also used during the iterative steps of the taxonomy design. Features of existing commercial tools represented real-world objects while visualization features of past literature represented existing research. Table 1 exemplifies the classification of features. The complete classification can be found in the online appendix[1]. In the future, we plan to use this taxonomy to classify academic prototypes presented at tool and demo tracks and also have external tool developers use and evaluate it. In a first step, we classified two prototypes

Table 1. Selected features classified with the taxonomy.

Category	Minimap[a]	Magnifying App[b]	Search Results[c]	Zooming [17]
Interface Type	overview-plus-detail	focus-plus-context	cue-based	zooming
Interface Coupling	additional views	main view	additional views	main view
Interaction Type	direct + indirect	direct	direct	indirect
Animations	no animation	continuous	continuous	multiple (continuous + informational)
Information Structure	structure preserving	structure preserving	structure preserving	temporary changing
Input Data Type	quantitative/ discrete	quantitative/ discrete	qualitative	quantitative/ continuous
Output Data Type	quantitative/ discrete	quantitative/ discrete	qualitative	quantitative/ continuous

[a]Eclipse IDE [b]Windows 10 [c]JetBrains IntelliJ IDEA, Google Maps

featuring advanced interaction techniques in a state-of-the-art modeling environment (Eclipse GLSP) that we developed in a separate work. The taxonomy greatly supported the design of a concept for these prototypes.

6 Challenges and Limitations

The main challenge during the conceptualization of the characteristics for this taxonomy was to keep the mutual exclusivity intact. Some features were too complex or had too many functionalities to only have one characteristic in a single dimension. For that reason, we created extra categories that combine multiple other characteristics, e.g., *Interaction/Animation/Multiple Animations*. A feature with animations of multiple types can then be placed under this category. Here, in some cases it may also help to split up a feature into sub-features and categorize each sub-feature individually.

During some of the empirical-to-conceptual iterations, it was not always clear under which of Cockburn et al. [7] interface types a feature should be placed. Some features have characteristics of multiple interface types and could therefore be assigned to multiple categories. We felt that especially the *overview-plus-detail* and *focus-plus-context* category could often be used interchangeably. To mitigate this issue, we added the additional constraint of spatial dependency to the *focus-plus-context* type. We further limited our scope mainly to existing and widely used tools. While this provides a good foundation for categorization of established features, it lacks relevance with respect to prototypical tools originating from research.

Another limitation might be the number of characteristics of this taxonomy. There might be a need for additional characteristics in the dimension *Interaction*. Similarly, to how some user interactions are followed by animations, they could also trigger other functionalities such as, e.g., audio playback. This is just a theoretical example as we could not find features that rely on audio playback. According to Nickerson et al. [20] there is no agreed upon maximum for what represents an appropriate number of dimensions or characteristics. Nevertheless, with their proposed subjective ending condition *concise*, they suggest having a limited number to keep the taxonomy comprehensive and easy to apply. Besides *Interaction*, we also considered the characteristics of the *Presentation/Interface Type* dimension problematic at times. As already mentioned above, classification in this dimension was not always easy, and, although we were able to place all our observed features into one of the proposed interface types, we did get the impression that this space is not fully covered yet and new types will come up in the future, leading to potential extensions of the taxonomy.

7 Conclusions

We presented a taxonomy of advanced information visualization with applications to conceptual modeling. The taxonomy structures visualization features along the three higher-level dimensions *Presentation*, *Interface*, and *Data* and further seven lower-level dimensions, each of which with specific characteristics. We evaluated the taxonomy with ex-ante and ex-post taxonomy evaluation methods by relating it to existing research and by applying our taxonomy to real-world objects[1]. This taxonomy combines established categorizations with new and original ones. From a scientific viewpoint, we contribute a novel taxonomy with an expressivity in classifying visualization features lacking in past literature. The presented taxonomy can facilitate a new feature's ideation and conceptualization phases from a practical viewpoint. The taxonomy can push method engineers and tool developers toward rethinking model representation and designing and implementing advanced information visualization features. We thus hope that the proposed taxonomy sparks innovation in future conceptual modeling research.

References

1. Bartram, L., Ho, A., Dill, J., Henigman, F.: The continuous zoom: a constrained fisheye technique for viewing and navigating large information spaces. In: Proceedings of the 8th Annual ACM Symposium on User Interface and Software Technology, pp. 207–215 (1995)
2. Baudisch, P., Good, N., Bellotti, V., Schraedley, P.: Keeping things in context: a comparative evaluation of focus plus context screens, overviews, and zooming. In: SIGCHI conference on Human factors in computing systems, pp. 259–266 (2002)
3. Bork, D., Buchmann, R., Karagiannis, D.: Preserving multi-view consistency in diagrammatic knowledge representation. In: Zhang, S., Wirsing, M., Zhang, Z. (eds.) KSEM 2015. LNCS (LNAI), vol. 9403, pp. 177–182. Springer, Cham (2015). https://doi.org/10.1007/978-3-319-25159-2_16
4. Bork, D., Karagiannis, D., Pittl, B.: Systematic analysis and evaluation of visual conceptual modeling language notations. In: 2018 12th International Conference on Research Challenges in Information Science (RCIS), pp. 1–11. IEEE (2018)

5. Bork, D., Roelens, B.: A technique for evaluating and improving the semantic transparency of modeling language notations. Softw. Syst. Model. **20**(4), 939–963 (2021)
6. Card, S.K., Robertson, G.G., Mackinlay, J.D.: The information visualizer, an information workspace. In: Conference on Human Factors in Computing Systems, pp. 181–186 (1991)
7. Cockburn, A., Karlson, A., Bederson, B.B.: A review of overview+ detail, zooming, and focus+ context interfaces. ACM Comput. Surv. **41**(1), 1–31 (2008)
8. Cockburn, A., Savage, J.: Comparing speed-dependent automatic zooming with traditional scroll, pan and zoom methods. In: Neill, E., Palanque, P., Johnson, P. (eds.) PC XVII—DS, pp. 87–102. Springer, London (2004). https://doi.org/10.1007/978-1-4471-3754-2_6
9. Frank, U., Strecker, S., Fettke, P., Vom Brocke, J., Becker, J., Sinz, E.: The research field modeling business information systems. Bus. Inf. Syst. Eng. **6**(1), 39–43 (2014)
10. Frisch, M., Dachselt, R.: Visualizing offscreen elements of node-link diagrams. Inf. Vis. **12**(2), 133–162 (2013)
11. Frisch, M., Dachselt, R., Brückmann, T.: Towards seamless semantic zooming techniques for UML diagrams. In: 4th ACM Symposium on Software Visualization, pp. 207–208 (2008)
12. Furnas, G.W.: Generalized fisheye views. ACM Sigchi Bull. **17**(4), 16–23 (1986)
13. Gulden, J.: Recommendations for data visualizations based on gestalt patterns. In: Li, G., Yu, Y. (eds.) International Conference on Enterprise Systems, pp. 168–177 (2016)
14. Gulden, J., Reijers, H.A., Grabis, J., Sandkuhl, K.: Toward advanced visualization techniques for conceptual modeling. In: CAiSE Forum, pp. 33–40. CiteSeer (2015)
15. Gustafson, S.G., Irani, P.P.: Comparing visualizations for tracking off-screen moving targets. In: Extended Abstracts on Human Factors in Computing Systems, pp. 2399–2404 (2007)
16. Hornbæk, K., Bederson, B.B., Plaisant, C.: Navigation patterns and usability of zoomable user interfaces with and without an overview. ACM Trans. Comput. Hum. Interact. (TOCHI) **9**(4), 362–389 (2002)
17. Igarashi, T., Hinckley, K.: Speed-dependent automatic zooming for browsing large documents. In: ACM Symposium on User Interface Software and Technology, pp. 139–148 (2000)
18. Kagdi, H., Maletic, J.I.: Onion graphs for focus+ context views of UML class diagrams. In: International Workshop on Visualizing Software for Understanding and Analysis, pp. 80–87 (2007)
19. Kundisch, D., Muntermann, J., Oberländer, A.M., Rau, D., Röglinger, M., Schoormann, T., Szopinski, D.: An update for taxonomy designers: methodological guidance from information systems research. Bus. Inf. Syst. Eng. **63** (2021). https://doi.org/10.1007/s12599-021-00723-x
20. Nickerson, R.C., Varshney, U., Muntermann, J.: A method for taxonomy development and its application in information systems. Eur. J. Inf. Syst. **22**(3), 336–359 (2013)
21. Reinhard, T., Meier, S., Glinz, M.: An improved fisheye zoom algorithm for visualizing and editing hierarchical models. In: Second International Workshop on Requirements Engineering Visualization (REV 2007), p. 9. IEEE (2007)
22. Roelens, B., Bork, D.: An evaluation of the intuitiveness of the PGA modeling language notation. In: Nurcan, S., Reinhartz-Berger, I., Soffer, P., Zdravkovic, J. (eds.) BPMDS/EMMSAD -2020. LNBIP, vol. 387, pp. 395–410. Springer, Cham (2020). https://doi.org/10.1007/978-3-030-49418-6_27

23. Sandkuhl, K., et al.: From expert discipline to common practice: a vision and research agenda for extending the reach of enterprise modeling. Bus. Inf. Syst. Eng. **60**(1), 69–80 (2018)
24. Shneiderman, B.: The eyes have it: A task by data type taxonomy for information visualizations. In: The Craft of Information Visualization, pp. 364–371. Elsevier (2003)
25. Silva, S.F., Catarci, T.: Visualization of linear time-oriented data: a survey. In: First International Conference on web information systems engineering, vol. 1, pp. 310–319. IEEE (2000)
26. Stone, D., Jarrett, C., Woodroffe, M., Minocha, S.: User interface design and evaluation. Elsevier (2005)
27. Ternes, B., Rosenthal, K., Strecker, S.: User interface design research for modeling tools: a literature study. Enterp. Model. Inf. Syst. Architect. (EMISAJ) **16**, 1–4 (2021)
28. Thabet, R., Bork, D., Boufaied, A., Lamine, E., Korbaa, O., Pingaud, H.: Risk-aware business process management using multi-view modeling: method and tool. Requir. Eng. **26**(3), 371–397 (2021)
29. Tory, M., Moller, T.: Rethinking visualization: a high-level taxonomy. In: IEEE Symposium on Information Visualization, pp. 151–158. IEEE (2004)
30. Zellweger, P.T., Mackinlay, J.D., Good, L., Stefik, M., Baudisch, P.: City lights: contextual views in minimal space. In: CHI2003 Extended Abstracts on Human Factors in Computing Systems, pp. 838–839 (2003)

Pattern Discovery in Conceptual Models Using Frequent Itemset Mining

Mattia Fumagalli[1]([⊠]), Tiago Prince Sales[1], and Giancarlo Guizzardi[1,2]

[1] Conceptual and Cognitive Modeling Research Group (CORE),
Free University of Bozen-Bolzano, Bolzano, Italy
{mattia.fumagalli,tiago.princesales,giancarlo.guizzardi}@unibz.it
[2] Services and Cybersecurity Group,
University of Twente, Enschede, The Netherlands

Abstract. Patterns are recurrent structures that provide key insights for Conceptual Modeling. Typically, patterns emerge from the repeated modeling practice in a given field. However, their discovery, if performed manually, is a slow and highly laborious task and, hence, it usually takes years for pattern catalogs to emerge in new domains. For this reason, the field would greatly benefit from the creation of automated data-driven techniques for the empirical discovery of patterns. In this paper, we propose a highly automated interactive approach for the discovery of patterns from conceptual model catalogs. The approach combines graph manipulation and Frequent Itemset Mining techniques. We also advance a computational tool implementing our proposal, which is then validated in an experiment with a dataset of 105 UML models.

Keywords: Modeling patterns · Pattern discovery · Itemset mining

1 Introduction

For a while now, patterns have been widely used by the modeling community for a range of different purposes, including to understand how languages are used in practice [3,8]. Their popularity is evinced, among other factors, by the growing number of pattern catalogs[1] for different modeling languages. Pattern discovery, however, if performed manually, is highly laborious and, hence, it usually takes years for pattern catalogs to emerge. First, because of the sheer size of data to be analyzed. Second, searching for patterns consists of cognitively demanding steps, such as partitioning models into smaller fragments, calculating the frequency of candidate patterns, and filtering out constructs of interest (e.g. when one is looking for taxonomic structures in domain models).

In this paper we propose a highly-automated interactive approach for the empirical discovery of patterns from conceptual model catalogs. In particular,

---

[1] E.g. https://github.com/wilmerkrisp/patterns, http://www.bpmpatterns.org.

This work was supported by Accenture Israel Cybersecurity Labs.

J. Ralyté et al. (Eds.): ER 2022, LNCS 13607, pp. 52–62, 2022.
https://doi.org/10.1007/978-3-031-17995-2_4

we focus on the discovery of *recurrent modeling structures* that can be defined by a fixed combination of the constructs of a language. Our approach, developed using the *Design Science Methodology* [7], aims at supporting language designers throughout all activities of the pattern discovery process, namely: *i) input data preparation*, when the input conceptual models data are manipulated to feed the mining process; *ii) mining process customization*, when the parameters for the mining process are provided; *iii) pattern mining*, the actual mining process; and *iv) output assessment*, when the user assess the discovered patterns. For this purpose, we combine *graph manipulation* techniques with the *Frequent Itemset Mining* algorithm [1].

We implemented our approach in a proof-of-concept application, which was validated according to a set of requirements gathered from expert language designers about *what* our approach should do, as well as *how* it should do it. We tested these criteria using a catalog of 105 domain models [2] specified in OntoUML [5], a pattern-based well-founded extension of *UML Class Diagrams*.

The remainder of this paper is structured as follows. Section 2 lists the requirements that drove the design of our approach. Section 3 describes the pattern discovery method embedded in our approach. In Sect. 4, we report on the experiments we conducted to validate our solution. Then, in Sect. 5, we position our contribution with respect to the state of the art. Finally, in Sect. 6, we reflect on our results and discuss some future work.

2   Requirements

Following the Design Science methodology [7], we grounded the design of our approach on a preliminary *problem identification* activity. In this phase, we interviewed five senior researchers who developed conceptual modeling languages. We asked them, in open-ended interviews, about: *i) the relevance of an approach for facilitating the empirical discovery of structural patterns in conceptual models* and *ii) what is required to facilitate this discovery process*. From their feedback, we defined the following requirements:

- **Interest (R1)**: the approach should be able to discover *subjectively interesting* patterns. Here, the notion of "subjectively interesting" is inspired by the work from Silberschatz and Tuzhilin [14], where a pattern is ranked as interesting by a user if: *a)* it is considered *exploitable* for modeling activities, *b)* it contradicts some user's expectations.
- **Customization (R2)**: the approach should support the manipulation of input models so that one can look for a particular type of pattern. For instance, from class diagrams, one should be able to filter out everything but classes and generalizations to look for taxonomic patterns.
- **Comprehension (R3)**: the approach should support the assessment and analysis of the output patterns by generating human-readable visualizations and providing their *absolute frequency* (i.e. how many times the pattern occurs in all models of the catalog) and their *model frequency* (i.e. how many models in the catalog have at least one occurrence of the pattern).

- **Reliability (R4)**: the approach should accurately calculate the absolute and model frequencies for all the patterns it finds. More precisely, the ratio between the number of occurrences retrieved by the approach and the number of actual occurrences should be at least 0.5.
- **Performance (R5)**: the processing and mining steps should *happen* in a reasonable amount of time, even with a *large* set of models. By "a reasonable amount of time" we mean an amount that would not discourage language designers to interact with such a tool, and naturally, that is lower than the time it would take for them to produce the same outputs manually. For now, we are assuming a threshold of 5 min to mine patterns from 100 models. By "large set of models", we mean between 100 and 10000 models, as we do not expect model catalogs to be much bigger than that.
- **Compatibility (R6)**: the approach should be generic enough such that it works with any conceptual modeling language.

3   Discovering Frequent Patterns

We represent our approach as a workflow composed of 7 main tasks, whose inputs, outputs, and dependencies are combined as from Fig. 1 below.

The first task is *Filtering (0)*, where the user can select what language constructs to filter out from the models. For instance, in the case of OntoUML, one may want to look for patterns only involving classes decorated with certain stereotypes, or involving only classes, generalizations, and generalization sets.

The *Abstraction (1)* task allows the user to input a set of transformation functions to be applied to the models, by which certain constructs can be abstracted into more general constructs. For instance, in ArchiMate, business processes, business functions, and business collaborations may be abstracted into business internal behavior elements. This step allows users to look for more general patterns that apply to several types of constructs.

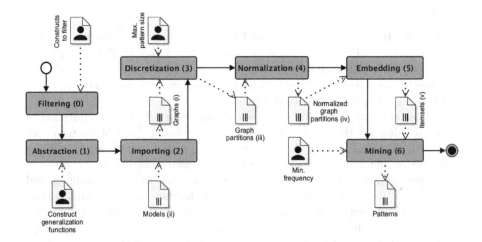

Fig. 1. The frequent patterns discovery workflow.

The *Importing (2)* task consists of taking a set of conceptual models M encoded in a given language (e.g., UML or BPMN) and transforming each model $m_i \in M$ into a graph g_j. This may seem trivial at a first glance, after all, conceptual models are basically graphs. That, however, is not always the case. Consider, for instance, the transformation of UML class diagrams into graphs. The simple solution is transforming classes into nodes and generalizations and associations into edges. Still, if we want to convert, generalization sets, association classes, generalizations between associations, cardinalities, and several other constructs, that no longer works. This task is language-dependent and requires an *ad hoc* transformation for each source conceptual modeling language.

Discretization (3) takes each graph g_j and splits it into graph partitions gp_k that represent subsets of the input conceptual model m_i. We do this by repeatedly executing the *Kernighan Lin Bisection Algorithm* [9], which splits a graph into two balanced bisections[2], until we obtain graph partitions with at most N nodes–a threshold value provided by the user. Note, however, that we lose some edges in the bisection process. To counter this effect, after generating our graph partitions, we restore some removed edges back to them. A removed edge e_l is restored to a partition gp_k if gp_k contains at least one of the two nodes connected by e_l. If one such node is not part of gp_k, it is also restored to it. This discretization task is completely language-independent.

Through the *Normalization (4)* task, the graph partitions are relabeled and indexed to enable the detection of patterns across them. The relabeling of the graph partition occurs by firstly associating both a label and an index to each node, where, originally, the node corresponds to an *id* and the label corresponds to the language construct associated with that node. Once the relabeling is applied, the index of the nodes with the same label is normalized (from 0 to n). Normalization is also a language-independent task.

Embedding (5), still a language-independent task, converts normalized graph partitions into item sets. Here each graph edge is transformed into an item, thus enabling to mine all the information encoded by the node and the edge labels. Notice that this allows accounting for the rich amount of information encoded by conceptual models. For instance, an item can easily represent nodes and edges labels, association source and target cardinalities, and edges directionality.

Figure 2 provides an example of how a conceptual model '.*i*' is converted through the steps described so far. The importing step produces the graph shown by '.*ii*'. The discretization task produces the partitions shown by '.*iii*'. The normalization task produces the normalized partitions '.*iv*' and the embedding returns the set of item sets represented by '.*v*'.

Notice that each column of the item set table '.*v*' represents an item i_j, namely a graph edge with the standardized nodes. Each record represents an input partition graph. I_1, for instance, encodes the left-side graph in of Fig. 2.'.*iii*' and I_2 encodes the graph on the right side. The index of the labels was standardized from "0" to "3" for the larger partition and from "0" to "2" for the

---

[2] The bisections are balanced in terms of the number of nodes and edges.

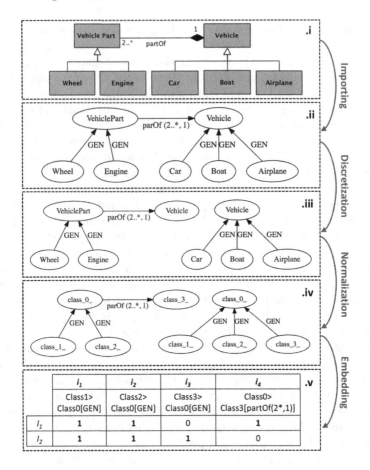

Fig. 2. From *importing* to *embedding*: *.i* input conceptual model, *.ii* transformed graph, *.iii* graph partitions, *.iv* normalized graph partitions, *.v* set of item sets.

smaller one, thus enabling the detection of recurrent items across the item sets. For instance, in '.v' both i_1 and i_2 occur in both I_1 and I_2.

The *Mining (6)* task represents the final part of the workflow and is aimed at *a)* generating the candidate patterns and *b)* making the output accessible to the user for the final assessment. This task allows for another interaction with the user, who can select the frequency threshold for the output patterns (e.g., filter out patterns that occur less than 30 times) or some *ad hoc* parameters of the mining algorithm (e.g., avoid sub-patterns with the same frequency). The output of the mining task will then consist of a *1)* list of the discovered patterns in a format that eases the final assessment[3]; *2)* a set of frequency measures, for each output pattern, namely: *2.1)* the *absolute frequency*, calculated as the number of pattern occurrences over the total number of item sets generated through

---

[3] Example at https://purl.org/mining-cm-patterns/pattern-example.

embedding; *2.2)* the *model frequency*, calculated as the number of pattern occurrences over the number of conceptual models used as inputs of the whole process. For instance, given 5 models we can have a pattern occurring with an absolute frequency of '10', but the model frequency cannot be more than '5'.

4 Evaluation

To evaluate our approach, we implemented it as a Python command-line application[4] in which the user can interactively set up the process, manipulate the data, and assess the output of the mining algorithm. The implementation is built on top of two main packages, namely *NetworkX* and *PrefixSpan*. NetworkX is a comprehensive, open-source, graph analytics and processing toolkit, independently developed and maintained by a large and lively community of developers. PrefixSpan is a very simple yet flexible implementation of the homonymous algorithm. With this application, we evaluated our requirements by running the following two experiments.

4.1 Experiment 1

This experiment assesses our solution w.r.t. **R1**, **R2**, **R3**, and **R4**.

(i) Data. As input data, we used **105** models from a catalog of *OntoUML* models [2], a pattern-based language that extends *UML Class Diagrams* [5].

(ii) Setup. For the validation, we used, as "litmus test", 6 common OntoUML patterns, which were previously manually identified by the designers of the language within multiple example models, retained to be useful for building OntoUML models [6,13]. The selected patterns are represented in Fig. 3.

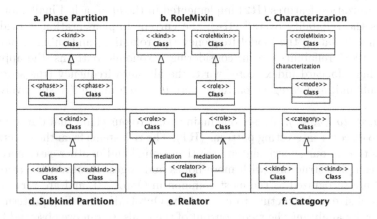

Fig. 3. OntoUML modeling patterns examples [13].

---

[4] Source code is available at https://purl.org/krdb-core/mining-cm.

We run the application **6** times and we checked whether the proposed solution is able to discover the pre-identified interesting patterns (**R1**). Moreover, we checked the role of the customization steps in supporting the discovery process (**R2**) and the level of comprehensibility of the outcome (**R3**). For each trial, we selected different parameters. In the first three trials, we just customized the number of nodes allowed in the graph partition, selecting *12*, *8*, and *4* as reference sizes. The partition size parameters were selected based on the average number of classes in OntoUML patterns. In the last three trials, we reused the same partition parameters by filtering out stereotypes and edge types that are not used in the pattern. Finally, we queried the input models to count the real-existing number of occurrences for each pattern and we compared the results with the occurrences found by our application. The level of reliability (**R4**) was then simply calculated through an application of the *Jaccard index* $J(A, B) = \frac{|(A \cap B)|}{|(A \cup B)|}$ [4,16], where A is the set of manually found pattern occurrences and B is the set of occurrences for the same pattern found by the process.

(iii) Results. Figure 4 resumes the output data of experiment 1. The first observation is that the approach is able to find the patterns we selected beforehand (**R1**), which are clearly mapped into the output pattern graphs (**R3**). All the discovered patterns (with examples of more complex patterns as well) can be found at our git repository[5]. Secondly, it can be noticed that the partition parameters have an impact on the reliability of the process. This seems to be dependent on the structure of the pattern. For instance, in the case of hierarchical patterns, such as phase, subkind, and category patterns (see Fig. 3), the discovery better performs with larger graphs; differently, in the case of patterns that are not characterized by a taxonomical structure, the behavior seems opposite (see roleMixin, relator and characterization patterns). Moreover, in the trials where the user interacts with the application to filter out information, the reliability significantly improves in most of the cases, thus demonstrating the key role of the customization features (**R2**) implemented in the approach. Finally, for what concerns the reliability overall (**R4**), the current implementation is evidently better in calculating the model frequency (for roleMixin and subkind patterns we have 100% reliability). Still, considering taxonomic patterns, the approach returns high Jaccard index scores w.r.t. the absolute frequency (the scores for phase, subkind, and category patterns were *0.91*, *0.9* and *0.7*, respectively).

(iv) Threats to Validity. We see one main threat to our claim that our approach is able to discover interesting patterns (**R1**). The risk stems from the selection of patterns that in our experiment are relatively small and in other cases may have a more complex structure, with more nodes and edges. However, the examples we used are recognized as the most common in OntoUML and are very similar in terms of size and structure to most of the OntoUML modeling patterns [13]. Moreover, by analysing the whole output of the trials we ran, we observed bigger

---

[5] https://purl.org/mining-cm-patterns/experiment.

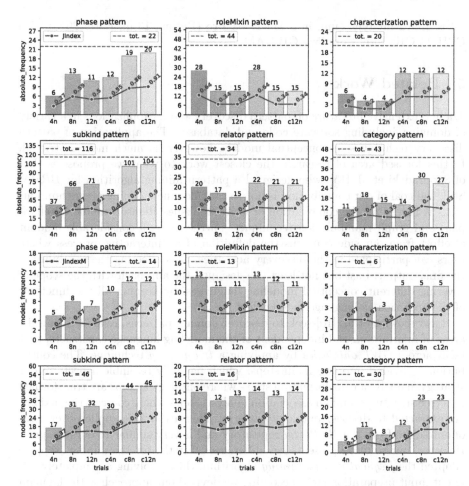

Fig. 4. Trial 1 results. Each chart shows the data for a pattern. Bars represent found occurrences no.; the first six charts refer to *absolute frequency* data, while the last six refer to *model frequency* data. The red line in each chart is the total number of occurrences found with the queries. The blue and purple lines represent the *jaccard index* for the *absolute frequency* and the *model frequency*, respectively. (Color figure online)

but less frequent patterns than those presented in Fig. 3, thus suggesting that the approach can discover more complex structures.

4.2   Experiment 2

The second experiment asseses our approach w.r.t. **R5**. Information about *(i) Data, (ii) Setup, (iii) Results* and *(iv) Threats to validity* can be found in our git repository[6]. In a nutshell, processing and mining the 105 models in our catalog

---

[6] https://purl.org/mining-cm-patterns/performance.

takes approximately 2 min in a MacBook Pro (Retina, 13-in. Early 2015) with CPU 2,7 GHz Intel Core i5, 8 GB RAM.

5   Related Work

There is extensive literature on pattern discovery and its applications in a variety of domains, including software code and databases. The application of pattern discovery techniques in conceptual models, however, is much more restricted. In this focused area of research, the closest work to what we propose is that of Skouradaki et al. [15], who designed a pattern mining algorithm for *BPMN*. Still, the goal of our contribution is not to provide a new mining algorithm. Our focus is indeed on the combination of well-established itemset mining (PrefixSpan) and graph manipulation techniques. Furthermore, a considerable amount of effort from our side concerns the definition of an interactive process where users can participate in the discovery activities, thus affecting the reliability of the final output. Last but not least, we designed the approach with the scope of covering different conceptual modeling languages, by keeping all the functions of the approach as language-independent.

Ławrynowicz et al. [10] seek to discover domain patterns, related to specific areas of information and independent of the modeling language constructs, that recur across *OWL ontologies* by applying a *tree-mining* technique. The contribution is divided into two main steps, which partially resemble aspects of our strategy, namely: a transformation step - where ontology axioms are transformed into tree structures; and an association analysis step - where co-occurring axioms are extracted to discover ontology patterns. This research is applied over a set of ontologies from the *BioPortal* repository and is very similar to ours in spirit. However, our solution presents key differences. Firstly, for the mining step, we adopted the *frequent itemset mining* algorithm, thus involving a completely different input preparation step. Secondly, we devised our approach with the main goal of discovering *structural modeling patterns*, namely patterns defined simply by the combination of constructs of a modeling language. In [10] the discovered patterns concern primarily domain-specific information that may recur within or across ontologies (e.g., what are the recurrent properties of the class "person"). Again, the interaction capabilities we proposed are out of their scope.

In the same direction, Lee et al. [11] seek to discover domain patterns across and within ontologies. However, to address this challenge, two different steps are adopted: a step where sub-graphs are extracted through candidate generation and chunking processes; a step where *frequent sub-graphs mining* [12] is adopted. This work also focuses on domain-specific patterns and one of its priorities is to allow the processing of large-scale knowledge graphs. Moreover, no account of how to handle an interactive discovery process is provided.

Unlike the above-presented approaches, our goal is mainly to offer an interactive tool for pattern discovery. Our approach finds recurrent modeling structures, which do not represent necessarily examples of good or bad modeling practices. Finally, one key aspect of our solution is to apply *frequent itemset mining*. This technique enables us to mine information (e.g., cardinalities, edge labels, class labels vs. stereotypes) that, with more orthodox approaches (e.g., *frequent subgraph mining* [12]), which are mostly aimed at mining unlabeled undirected graphs, could not be fully exploited.

6   Final Considerations

This paper presents an interactive approach for automating the empirical discovery of modeling patterns in conceptual models by combining graph manipulation techniques and frequent itemset mining. By doing so, we move towards automating the construction of pattern catalogs for modeling languages and we create a mechanism for helping language designers to create higher-granularity primitives in their languages, i.e., modeling patterns that can become part of the grammar and tools of that language [6].

Based on the encouraging results from our evaluation with 105 OntoUML models, we envision a series of next steps. First, we will test, in collaboration with language designers, if our approach can find unexpected patterns in OntoUML. Second, we are going to extend the set of constructs to be encoded in the input graphs (e.g., *generalization sets*). Third, we will test our approach with models encoded in different modeling languages, such as BPMN and ArchiMate (**R6**).

References

1. Agrawal, et al.: Mining association rules between sets of items in large databases. In: ACM SIGMOD International Conference on Management of Data, pp. 207–216 (1993)
2. Barcelos, P.P.F., et al.: A FAIR model catalog for ontology-driven conceptual modeling research. In: Conceptual Modeling, ER 2022 (2022)
3. Gangemi, A., Presutti, V.: Ontology design patterns. In: Staab, S., Studer, R. (eds.) Handbook on Ontologies. IHIS, pp. 221–243. Springer, Heidelberg (2009). https://doi.org/10.1007/978-3-540-92673-3_10
4. García-Vico, et al.: A big data approach for the extraction of fuzzy emerging patterns. Cogn. Comput. **11**(3), 400–417 (2019)
5. Guizzardi, et al.: Types and taxonomic structures in conceptual modeling: a novel ontological theory and engineering support. Data Knowl. Eng. **134**, 101891 (2021)
6. Guizzardi, G.: Ontological patterns, anti-patterns and pattern languages for next-generation conceptual modeling. In: ER 2014, vol. 8824, pp. 13–27 (2014)
7. Hevner, A.R., March, S.T., Park, J., Ram, S.: Design science in information systems research. Manag. Inf. Syst. Quart. 28(1), 75–105 (2004)
8. Hitzler, P., Gangemi, A., Janowicz, K.: Ontology engineering with ontology design patterns: foundations and applications, vol. 25. IOS Press (2016)
9. Kernighan, B.W., Lin, S.: An efficient heuristic procedure for partitioning graphs. Bell Syst. Tech. J. **49**(2), 291–307 (1970)
10. Ławrynowicz, A., Potoniec, J., Robaczyk, M., Tudorache, T.: Discovery of emerging design patterns in ontologies using tree mining. Semant. web **9**(4), 517–544 (2018)
11. Lee, K., Jung, H., Hong, J.S., Kim, W.: Learning knowledge using frequent subgraph mining from ontology graph data. Appl. Sci. **11**(3), 932 (2021)

12. Ramraj, T., Prabhakar, R.: Frequent subgraph mining algorithms-a survey. Procedia Comput. Sci. **47**, 197–204 (2015)
13. Ruy, F.B., et al.: From reference ontologies to ontology patterns and back. Data Knowl. Eng. **109**, 41–69 (2017)
14. Silberschatz, A., Tuzhilin, A.: On subjective measures of interestingness in knowledge discovery. In: KDD, vol. 95, pp. 275–281 (1995)
15. Skouradaki, M., Andrikopoulos, V., Kopp, O., Leymann, F.: RoSE: reoccurring structures detection in BPMN 2.0 process model collections. In: Debruyne, C., et al. (eds.) OTM 2016. LNCS, vol. 10033, pp. 263–281. Springer, Cham (2016). https://doi.org/10.1007/978-3-319-48472-3_15
16. Tan, P., et al.: Selecting the right interestingness measure for association patterns. In: International Conference on Knowledge Discovery and Data Mining, pp. 32–41 (2002)

Ontologies and their Applications

Legal Power-Subjection Relations: Ontological Analysis and Modeling Pattern

Cristine Griffo[1]([✉]), Tiago Prince Sales[1], Giancarlo Guizzardi[1,2],
and João Paulo A. Almeida[2]

[1] Free University of Bozen-Bolzano, Bolzano, Italy
{cristine.griffo,tiago.princesales,gguizzardi}@unibz.it
[2] Federal University of Espírito Santo, Vitoria, Brazil
jpalmeida@ieee.org

Abstract. The development of dependable information systems in legal contexts requires a precise understanding of the subtleties of the underlying legal phenomena. According to a modern understanding in philosophy of law, much of these phenomena are relational in nature. In this paper, we employ a theoretically well-grounded legal core ontology (UFO-L) to conduct an ontological analysis focused on a fundamental legal relation, namely, the power-subjection relation. We show that in certain cases, power-subjection relations are primitive, i.e., by means of institutional acts, other legal relations can be generated from them. Examples include relations of rights and duties, permissions and non-rights, liberties, secondary power-subjection, etc. As a contribution to the practice of conceptual modeling, and leveraging on the result of our analysis, we propose a conceptual modeling pattern, which is then applied to model a real-world case in tax law.

Keywords: Ontology design pattern · Legal power · Legal relations · UFO · UFO-L

1 Introduction

The development of dependable information systems in critical contexts and applications requires a precise understanding of the subtleties of the domain at hand. In these contexts, *Ontology-Driven Conceptual Modeling*, i.e., the practice of conceptual modeling driven by formal ontological analysis [25], has been increasingly adopted. In some situations, the phenomena being analyzed crosscut several specific classes of applications. For example, an analysis of the general notion of *Service Contract* [9] can be captured in general reference models called *Core Ontologies* [10,11]. From these ontology, a number of *Ontology Design Patterns* can be systematically extracted [10]. Finally, these patterns are reusable higher-granularity modeling primitives that can then be employed to create conceptual models in specific domains (e.g., healthcare service contracts, telecommunication service contracts, etc.) [11].

J. Ralyté et al. (Eds.): ER 2022, LNCS 13607, pp. 65–81, 2022.
https://doi.org/10.1007/978-3-031-17995-2_5

The legal domain is an example of such a critical domain. Over the years, a multitude of authors have contributed to the ontological analysis of different legal notions (e.g., [5,8,30,47,51]). In particular, some of us have proposed a *Legal Core Ontology* termed UFO-L [20], which was developed by extending the foundational ontology UFO (Unified Foundational Ontology) [27], and by incorporating the theory of constitutional rights proposed by the German philosopher of law Robert Alexy [1]. The latter offers an original perspective on the law by conceiving it in terms of legal relations. Besides its appropriateness for understanding legal cases (e.g., analyzing judicial decision-making [22]), this perspective turned to be particularly fruitful for conceptual modeling of information systems [20] (given the central role of relations in their design).

In the past, from UFO-L, some of us have manage to extract a catalog of ontology design patterns addressing different legal relations. These include the *Unprotected Liberty Pattern*, the *Right-Duty to an Action Relator pattern*, and the *Right-Duty to an Omission Pattern* [19,20]. Other authors, have proposed ontology patterns to address notions such as *complaint behavior* [39], *personal data* [37,38], *norm* and *case* [14,15], as well as and some legal relations, such as "rights and obligations relationships" [37]. What has been missing from the literature is an ontological analysis (and, hence, a corresponding modeling pattern) addressing *Power-Subjection Relations*.

Generally speaking, power-subjection relations abound [13,50], and different notions of *power* can be connected to different outcomes of their exercise. For example, power-subjection relations based on *utilitarian power* will result in some performance-reward contingency; if based on *coercive power* will result on imposing conduct on others by means of fear; if based on *charismatic power*, will result on negligence of personal interests due to personal admiration of the charismatic-power holder; if based on *normative power* will result in the subjection-holder's belief that the social institution has the "right" to govern/submit his/her behavior [13]. It is in this latter type, i.e., *Legal Power-Subjection relations* that we are interested here.

In contrast to the other aforementioned types of legal relations, power-subjection relations are in a sense "reflexive", since they bestow legal agents with the capacity of creating other legal relations. For example, the law makes certain individuals (playing a certain legal role) capable of joining people in matrimony. This capacity is not a natural ability, but an artificial one constructed by legal norms. When they are exercised, they generate new legal relations with new legal positions of conduct or derivative powers. In contrast, legal relations such as right-duty, permission-no-right, and liberties [21] are related to the performance or abstention of actions of conduct, which, in general, demand only natural (or otherwise preexisting) abilities. This means that the legal positions of conduct only regulate the action or omission that was already possible, e.g., by virtue of natural capacity, such as expressing an opinion, entering a building, etc. As Alexy points out, power is more than permission to act and more than natural ability to act [1]. Suitably understanding this specific nature of this relations is fundamental, e.g., for correctly representing (and monitoring) certain computational contracts [21,45] as bearers of legal powers have the capacity of changing the contract itself (often unilaterally).

The contributions of this paper are two-fold: firstly, we present of an ontological analysis of Legal Power-Subjection Relations based on UFO-L; secondly, we leverage on this analysis to propose an ontology design pattern for modeling this type of relation. The pattern is then employed to analyze and model a case study in Brazilian tax law.

The remainder of the paper is structured as follows: Sect. 2 briefly reviews the notion of power in the relevant literature with a particular focus on legal powers; Sect. 3 presents the contributions of the paper, namely, our ontological analysis the resulting ontology design pattern; Sect. 4 presents our case study; Sect. 5 positions our contributions w.r.t. related work; finally, Sect. 6 presents some final considerations.

2   On (Legal) Powers

The question of *what is power* has had significant attention in law [1,31,33] and social psychology [13,50]. Several works in the field of computer science have also addressed this notion, among which we highlight the works on *normative positions* [44], *powers and permissions* in security systems [12] and norm-governed computational societies [3]. There are also works focused on logical formalization of *power* or *institutional power*, for instance, [6,7,16,17,32,42].

The concept of legal power[1] [1], or legal competence [33,34,48,49], or institutional power [32], has been intensively discussed by legal [28,29,31,35] as well as computer science scholars, e.g., Sartor [41] as well as Governatori and Rotolo [18] distinguish different types of power: enabling-power, potestative right, and declarative power; Boella *et al.* [5], by proposing an action-based ontology of legal relations, introduce the idea of *recursion* from *power*. Differently from what was proposed in [5], we understand that exercising power not only creates duties and obligations, but it may also create other power-subjection legal relations in a recursive manner.

We focus here on the notion of legal power as proposed by Alexy [1], who extends Hohfeld's concept of power [31]. For Hohfeld, a power relation involves a power holder and the subjection holder (a *dyadic relation*) as correlative notions. Alexy goes one step further and makes it a triadic relation by also reifying the object of the relation (referent)[2]. Moreover, they both understand power as a legal position able to alter a legal situation [1]. The exercise of a power is a performance of an *institutional act* [1,43]. In general, legal relations are

---

[1] In both legal and computer science literature, *power* appears as a synonym to legal capacity, legal competence, competence norm, constitutive norm, etc. Here, we use the terms 'legal power', 'legal ability', 'legal capacity', and 'power' interchangeably.

[2] The object of the relation can be an *action* or an *omission* performed by the power holder.

founded on the occurrence of legal events, but certain legal events (e.g., signing of contracts, breaking laws, paying taxes, etc.) can create, extinguish and change legal relations.

UFO-L is a core ontology grounded on the *Unified Foundational Ontology (UFO)* [26], which employs UFO's *theory of relations* [23] to model legal positions (e.g., rights, duties, liabilities, etc.) from this relational perspective advocated by Hohfeld and Alexy. In the next section, we present an ontological analysis of the legal power-subjection relation in the context of UFO-L, and use it to propose our modeling pattern.

3   The UFO-L Power-Subjection Relator Pattern

3.1   Power and Subjection in UFO-L

UFO's theory of relation is founded on the central notion of a *relator* [23,26]. A relator is a bundle of objectified relational properties (called *relational aspects*) that, by being existentially dependent on a number of relata, connects them. For example, Marriages, Enrollments, Employments and Presidential Mandates are relators. On one hand, they are object-like entities having properties and a life-cycle of their own; on the other hand, they are the so-called *truthmakers* of relations and inducers of role-playing, in the sense, for example, in which the marriage between John and Mary makes true the proposition "John and Mary are married" but also that John is a Husband and Mary is a Wife in the situations where that relator exists.

UFO-L [20,21] extends this notion by proposing the notion of *legal relator* as similarly reifying *legal relations*. On one perspective, legal relators are classified according to legal nature as: *Right-Duty relators, NoRight-Permission relators, Unprotected Liberty relators*, etc.; on an orthogonal (mereological) perspective, legal relators are classified as *Simple Legal Relator* or *Complex Legal Relator*. Simple legal relators are composed of *Legal Aspects* (or legal positions) *(e.g., Right, Duty, NoRight to an Omission, Permission to Act)*, and complex legal relators are composed of simple legal relators [21].

Legal aspects are linked to *legal roles* played by *legal agents* by means of a type of a relation of *inherence* (a type of *existential dependence* represented here by relation of *characterization*) and connected to the other legal agent, participant of the same relation, by means of a relation of *external dependence* (*externally depends on*). For instance, suppose a legal relation between employee and employer. The employee's right of salary payment (as against employer) correlates with the employer's duty to pay the employee's salary. An UFO-L pattern addressing this case is the *Right-Duty to an Action pattern* [19]. The employee's right is externally dependent on the Employer *as Duty Holder* and, conversely, the employer's duty is externally dependent on the Employee *as Right Holder*.

Legal Powers are special types of *Legal Aspects*. Their exercise occur by means of *institutional acts* [1], whose types (and consequent situations) are explicitly prescribed in *Legal Normative Descriptions* or *Legal Norms* [21]. Moreover, their correlative legal aspects are *Legal Subjections*. Thus, legal Power-Subjection relations, if simple, are composed of correlative power-subjection pairs (inhering in opposing agents); if complex, they are composed of simplex power-subjection relations.

Legal Relations created, altered or extinguished by a legal power-subjection relation are called *Derived Legal Relations*. Thus, *Legal Power-Subjection Relations* are divided in two groups: *Original Legal Power-Subjection Relations* and *Derived Legal Power-Subjection Relations*. *Legal Events* ground both these relations. *Original Legal Power-Subjection Relations* are those that were introduced by original constituent powers. For example, in the Brazilian constitution, an original constituent power gives Brazilian municipalities the power to impose taxes on their subjects (citizens, organizations); on the other hand, derived power-subjection relations are those that are created by some other legal power-subjection relation (with the exception of an original constituent power). For example, the municipal law approved by the Vitória City Council and sanctioned by the mayor of Vitória gives the municipality of Vitória the power to levy the urban property tax (IPTU). This local law defines a legal power-subjection relation derived from the original power to institute taxes prescribed by Brazilian constitution. *Derived* Legal Relations require additional *founding events* [24,26], which are *historically dependent*[3] on the legal events founding the relations are derived from. For example, when the consumer clicks the "I Agree" button to contract some Internet service, they agree with the terms of that service, including the clause in which the service provider can unilaterally change the contract terms with or without the consumer's consent. In cases that the service provider changes any clause without the need for consumer consent, the event that will provide the basis for the new legal positions will be the publishing of the modified agreement (historically dependent on the original event). In cases that consumer consent is required for those changes to be applicable, the new founding event will be the clicking of the "I consent" button, which is also historically dependent on the event grounding the relation of agreement.

3.2 The Legal Power-Subjection Relator Pattern

In this section, we leverage on UFO-L's ontological analysis of the power-subjection relations to proposed a reusable modeling pattern. The proposed pattern is: (1) constituted by pattern name, pattern code, rationale, guidelines for the use, a list of competence questions (Table 1); (2) represented in UFO-based conceptual modeling language OntoUML (Fig. 1); (3) enriched by axioms (Table 2) regulating the pattern, and by a list of verification criteria to check

---

[3] 'An event b depends historically on a whenever: (i) a (or one of its parts) brings about the situation that triggers b (or one of its parts); (ii) a (or one of its parts) brings about a situation that is necessary-but not sufficient-to trigger b (or one of its parts); (iii) a (or one of its parts) brings about a situation that is necessary-and more than sufficient-to trigger b (or one of its parts); or, (iv) b depends historically on an event z that depends historically on a.' [2].

whether the modeling situation at hand can be appropriately addressed by the pattern (Table 3). Figure 1 shows the *Legal Power-Subjection Relator* pattern (henceforth identified as *P7-PS-LR* in UFO-L's pattern catalog).

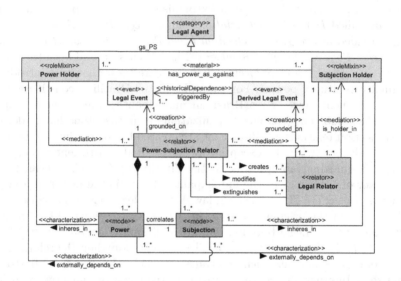

Fig. 1. Legal Power-Subjection Relator Pattern

Rationale. A Legal Power-Subjection Relator is established between Power Holder and Subjection Holder. The Legal Relator is composed of a pair of legal positions: Legal Power, which is inherent in the Power Holder and externally dependent on the Subjection Holder; and Legal Subjection, which is inherent in the Subjection Holder and externally dependent on the Power Holder. By means of an institutional act in a power-subjection relation, the Power Holder creates, modifies, or extinguishes legal positions held by the Subjection Holder.

Guidelines for the Use. This pattern must be used in potestative relations (competence, legal capacity, legal power) with some changing of legal position of Subjection Holder. The action must be conducted by a Power Holder and it needs to be an institutional act, i.e., it must be prescribed by law. The competence questions shown in Table 1 guide the modeler in applying the proposed pattern. The modeler must be able to answer these questions to know if the power-subjection pattern is the adequate pattern for the representation of the relations to be modeled, or rather, the built ontology must be able to answer the questions according to the proposed pattern. For example, for CQ2, the legal roles found and represented must be Power Holder and Subjection Holder, otherwise, the pattern was applied incorrectly and it is necessary to check in the UFO-L patterns catalog a more adequate pattern for the relation to be represented. In this sense, the restrictions presented in Table 2 will also help the modeler in this task and the applicability issues (Table 3) will help in checking existing aspects of this pattern.

Table 1. Competence questions

CQ1: What are the types of agents involved in the legal relation?
CQ2: What categories of legal roles are involved?
CQ3: What are the legal positions composing the legal relations?
CQ4: Who are the bearers of each existing legal position in the legal relations?
CQ5: Which legal position Subjection Holder holds in the derived legal relation?
CQ6: Which events are the basis of each legal relation?
CQ7: Which institutional act is performed by the Power Holder?
CQ8: What kind of association exists between the legal power-subjection relator and the derived legal relator (creates, alters or extinguishes)?
CQ9: Which Legal Object (e.g. Legal Normative Description or Legal Norm) prescribes the institutional act performed?
CQ10: Who are the role players in the derived legal relation?
CQ11: What event is the basis of the derived legal relation?
CQ12: What is the action/omission of the derived legal relation?
CQ13: What is the Legal Object (e.g. Legal Normative Description or Legal Norm) that legally defines the derived legal relation?

A *Power-Subjection Relator* is composed of two types of *Legal Aspects*: *Power* and *Subjection*. The legal *Power-Subjection* relator mediates disjoint legal agents, who play legal roles (represented here *Legal RoleMixins*, given that they may be played by agents of different kinds).[4] The legal relation between Power Holder and Subjection Holder is a *material relation* called *has power as against*, which connects Power Holders to Subjection Holders. Power inheres in Power Holder and is externally dependent on Subjection Holder. On the other hand, Subjection inheres in Subjection Holder and is externally dependent on Power Holder. This implies that it is only meaningful to talk about power in a relational context. Thus, at the other end of the relation is the correlative position called *subjection*. The converse relation (omitted from the diagram) can be understood as *being subject to*: an agent is subject to another agent who, in turn, has power over that one.

Power Holder has the power to create, alter or extinguish legal relations in which Subjection Holder participates. It means that Power Holder has the legal ability to change the Subjection-Holder's legal reality. This change is possible because the legal power is performed as an action prescribed by law (i.e., an institutional act) . In addition, Power-Subjection relators are grounded on *Legal Events*, for instance, the publishing of a law conferring powers to an entity to institute taxes. This kind of event brings about situations, which can activate other dispositions (including other legal aspects) of individuals [4].

---

[4] UFO-L patterns employs UFO's notions of rolemixin, agent, category, mode, event, material relation, and relator. For details, one should refer to [4,26,40].

Table 2. PSLR: axioms

A1. A Legal Power-Subjection Relator is a relator composed of legal positions called Legal Power and Legal Subjection, which are *essential* and *inseparable* parts of the legal relator [26].
A2. Every exercise of legal power changes the legal reality but not every act that alters the legal reality is an exercise of legal power.
A3. Every action performed by Power Holder in the context of legal power-subjection relation is an institutional act prescribed by an institutional agent in a Legal Object (Legal Normative Description or Legal Norm).
A4. Every act of legal power exercised by a Power Holder towards a Subjection Holder is a permissible action (There is no prohibition on the action) but not every permissible action is an action of legal power.
A5. A material relation "has a legal power as against" holds between agents A and B iff there is a conversing relation "is legally subject towards" holding between them.
A6. Every Power Holder has the power of creating, modifying or extinguishing at least one legal relation in which Legal Agent as Subjection-Holder is holder of another legal position

Table 3. Questions to determine applicability of the pattern

V1. Does the act performed by the Power Holder change the legal situation of Subjection Holder (i.e. creates, modifies or extinguishes legal positions hold by the Legal Agent who is the Subjection-Holder in the legal power-subjection relation)?
V2. Is the Power-Holder's act prescribed by any Legal Normative Description or Legal Norm?
V3. Is the type of the derived legal relation identifiable?
V4. Are the founding legal events (original legal event and derived legal event) of the modeled relations also modeled?

4   Case Study: Legal Power in Brazilian Tax Law

Motivation. The purpose of this case study is applying the pattern to model a case in covering Brazilian constitutional norms as well as a local tax law. Tax law was selected for containing legal power-subjection relations that are generally known to law experts and laypeople alike.

Description. Brazilian tax law is regulated by the Federal Constitution, the National Tax Code, and state or municipal laws. The case analyzed here is the urban property tax (*aka* IPTU) collected by municipalities and the Federal District. There must be a law promulgated by these entities, which is in accordance with the norm of power prescribed by the Federal Constitution. The selected municipality is the municipality of Vitória in the state of Espírito Santo, Brazil and the Act no. 4,476/1997 governs the tax on urban property (IPTU) in Vitória.

Techniques and Methods. We first identified the articles that regulate taxes and are contained in the Brazilian Federal Constitution (CRFB/1988), the National Tax Code (CTN), and applicable municipal law (Act no. 4,476/1997); we then used the competence questions summarized in Table 1 to scope the legal relations therein. As result, the following aspects of legal scope were identified: material (real states), temporal (January 1st of each year), jurisdictional/territorial (municipality of Vitória, Espírito Santo State, Brazil), quantitative (progressive rate on property market value), and subjective (taxpayers/owners own real states in Vitória; collector/municipality) aspects. Furthermore, the P7-PS-LR pattern was instantiated to model the legal relations of power-subjection at hand. Finally, the set of verification criteria summarized in Table 3 were checked confirming that the pattern applied was the correct one.

Materials. (1) **CRFB1988**. *Article 145. The Union, the states, the Federal District, and the municipalities may institute the following tributes: I - taxes; (...) (...) Article 156. The municipalities shall have the competence to institute taxes on: (...) I - urban buildings and urban land property; (...)*; (2) **CTN**. *Art. 32. The tax, which is the competence of the Municipalities, on urban land and property has as a triggering event the ownership, useful domain or possession of immovable property by nature or by physical accession, as defined in civil law, located in the urban area of the Municipality.(...)*; (3) **Law n. 4.476/1997**. *Art.1 The Tax on Urban Property and Territorial Property has as a triggering event the property, useful domain or possession of urban immovable property. (...) Art.2 The triggering event is considered to have occurred on the first day of January of each year (...) Art.6 Taxpayer is the owner, holder of the useful domain or possessor of the property in any capacity. (...) Art. 7 The basis for calculating the tax is the market value of the property, as set out in this law. (...) Art. 9 The tax rates, differentiated according to the use and progressive according to the market value of the properties, observing the respective value range, (...)*

Ontological Analysis. The promulgation of the Brazilian Constitution gives municipalities the power to institute tax norms (Arts. 145 and 156). The exercise of this power by means of an institutional act disposes municipalities in a new relation of Power-Subjection (Fig. 2). In this case, the municipal Act no. 4,476/1997 creates the power for the Municipality of Vitória (*as Power Holder*) to levy IPTU tax against taxpayers (*as Subjection Holder*). The ontological choice made for municipalities and taxpayers refers to the ontological nature of each. In fact, the Municipality of Vitória is an instance of Municipality, which provides a principle of identity to its instances; on the other hand, taxpayers may be of different types, i.e., natural persons or juristic persons (e.g. companies, universities), which one providing different principles of identity to their instances.

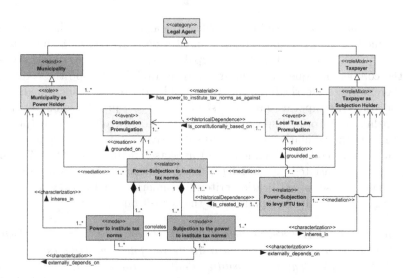

Fig. 2. Derived legal power-subjection for municipality to levy IPTU tax

This power to levy IPTU tax is manifested only in the applicable legal circumstances. The law is explicit with respect to those circumstances by defining hypotheses of tax incidence, i.e., defining *Situation types*, whose instances can trigger [4] certain *Events*, such as the assessment of the tax credit by the municipality. For example, *Being owner of land or buildings in the territory of Vitória in January 1st of each year* (a situation type) has instances that trigger events that will lead to obligations to pay. In other words, an urban property owner eventually becomes taxpayer when the situation "being an immovable property owner in January 1st, in Vitória, Espírito Santo State, Brazil" obtains. When this situation effectively occurs in the world, in a certain time and space with the taxpayer and tax collector roles clearly and uniquely identified, the *legal situation/fact* subsumes to the legal norm, i.e., the hypothesis of tax incidence is true in a specific instance. For example, Maria owns an apartment in Vitória. In January 1st, 2021, the municipality of Vitória verified the group of ownerships in which the IPTU tax is levied on, generating the IPTU tax credits in its favor *(municipality of Vitória as Creditor/Right holder)* (Fig. 3). Now, Maria as an apartment's owner will be notified about her IPTU tax duty. After the *Assessment of IPTU Credit-Debit* (Fig. 4), the municipality officially notifies taxpayers. The taxpayer notification is the event that creates the valid duty of the taxpayer to pay IPTU tax in a right-duty relation. According to the legislation, the obligation to pay exists only when taxpayers have been notified. In our example, Maria ought to pay the IPTU tax to the municipality of Vitória after receiving the notification of the obligation to pay the IPTU tax (Fig. 5).

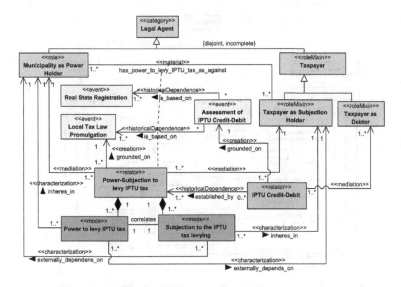

Fig. 3. Legal power-subjection pattern applied to tax law

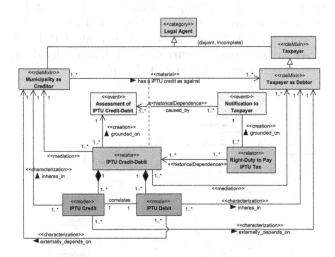

Fig. 4. IPTU credit-debit

There is a chain of *historical dependence* relations connecting the events that create these legal relations: *Local Tax Law Promulgation* (event E_2) is founded on the Federal Constitution, and, therefore, *Constitution Promulgation* (event E_1) must be prior to event E_2. Also, the *Assessment of IPTU Tax Credit-Debit* (event E_3) must be done by means of a valid law (event E_2) and, therefore, E_3

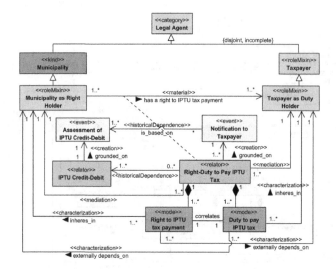

Fig. 5. Right-duty to an action pattern applied to tax law

historically depends on event E_2 and, by transitivity, on event E_1. Following this line of reasoning, the event of "Notification (of IPTU tax) to Taxpayer" (event E_4) can only occur if the event of "Assessment of IPTU Tax Credit-Debit" (event E_3) has previously occurred, which historically depends on the event "Real Estate Registration" (event E_5) (Fig. 6).

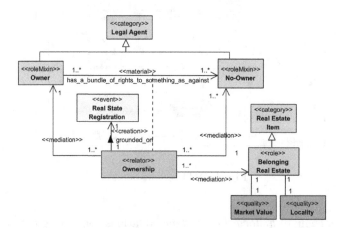

Fig. 6. Ownership of real estate

5   Related Work

There are approaches in the literature that explicitly consider powers. For example:

- In the same line of our work, the RuleML initiative planned to differentiate the concept of legal power from the concept of permission, by introducing "empowering rules".[5] Nevertheless, powers and correlative subjections have not been incorporated in LegalRuleML to the present date (a related notion of constitutive rule is included in that specification instead) [36];
- Symboleo [45] is a formal specification language for contracts, in which contracts consist of collections of obligations and powers. Since the contract domain ontology behind the Symboleo language was based on UFO-L, the concept of power is similarly defined as *"the right of a party to create, change, suspend or extinguish legal positions (...)"*. Differently from the pattern proposed here, the correlated position of power (subjection) is not explicit in Symboleo. Representation of the correlative legal positions is relevant for analyzing violations of powers and duties. For example, in the analysis of a concrete case, if Mary does not submit herself to the power of municipality of Vitória to levy the IPTU tax, the municipality can by coercion subject Mary to that power, imposing administrative sanctions or initiating legal actions against her. In UFO-L, with the use of legal relator pattern, it is possible to indicate, at the instance level, who violates a legal power-subjection relation;
- Similarly to Symboleo, Nòmos2 [46] defines power as legal capability to produce changes "in the legal system towards another subject". The latter acquires the corresponding *liability* but not explicit the correlated legal position;
- In contrast, in FIBO[6], *legal power* is reduced to *legal capacity* defined as *"the capability to carry out certain actions or to have certain rights together with the resources to do so"*. This definition overlaps to the definition of legal permission proposed in UFO-L, since permission is a legal position hold by a subject who performs an action or an omission towards someone [21].

6   Final Considerations

In this paper, we present the *Legal Power-Subjection Relator* pattern, a new pattern to be included in the UFO-L pattern catalog [19,20]. This pattern is mainly composed of Power Holder and Subjection Holder, a set of roles played by Legal Agents in the context of legal relations. Differently to the other types of legal relations presented in previous works, this type of legal relation shows that the action holder alters, creates, or extinguishes legal positions of the subjection holder by means of institutional actions.

---

[5] http://ruleml.org/policy/.
[6] https://spec.edmcouncil.org/fibo/ontology/FND/Law/LegalCapacity/.

In order to demonstrate the applicability of the proposed pattern, the legal power to levy taxes was modeled as well the derived legal relations. By using the pattern, we were able to reveal a number of aspects of the case at hand. For instance, it is possible to represent the levying of the property tax over Mary's properties while she is under 65 years old (in the case that the property tax law grants *immunity* from tax to owners over 65 years of age), or the application of bundle of legal permissions in emergency situations for a group of owner's properties without bringing inconsistency to the legal system. The proper modeling of these situations is only possible with the triadic representation of legal relations (i.e. the explicit representation of the parties and the object at hand). In other words, these cannot be properly modeled if the representations of these correlative roles (e.g., *subjection holder*, in this case the taxpayer) are not explicit. For instance, if restricted by monadic deontic operators, one would typically represent the first case as follows: $\neg S(x)$ (where $\neg S$ is the "not subject to the payment of" and x is the IPTU tax). In the same legal system, there would be $\neg S(x)$ for taxpayers aged 65 or over and $S(x)$ for taxpayers aged under 65. This representation does not make explicit the instances of tax-exempt taxpayers and the instances of taxpayers, which may result in inconsistencies. The same occurs in the case of legal permissions in emergency situations.

Regarding future work, we plan to extend our ontological analysis and modeling by: addressing violations of power-subjection relations by applying types of powers and non-powers; conducting a systematic comparison with other types of legal relations, in particular, rights-duties and permissions-no-rights relations. Another relevant study is to investigate some approaches to model meta-powers (powers that establish powers). Finally, in line with [20], we intend to conduct empirical studies to assess the usability of the proposed patterns by legal experts.

There are some questions raised and still open. The first one is whether the pattern proposed here for legal powers can somehow be applied to other types of power (e.g. in autonomous systems). At first, we are inclined to say that yes, it is possible to apply in systems other than legal systems. However, it is necessary to develop some works to conclude that it is applicable in other systems.

The second question is if there is the possibility to distinguish the Original and Derived legal power-subjection relations by means of intrinsic aspects. We have observed that several aspects of legal nature are only activated when their bears are related to others. In the case of original legal power-subjection relations, they are usually perceived in socio-political contexts depending on events to occur. This is an intriguing debate that can be addressed in future research.

Acknowledgements. This research is partly funded by Brazilian funding agencies CNPq (313687/2020-0) and FAPES (281/2021).

References

1. Alexy, R.: A Theory of Constitutional Rights. Oxford Univ. Press, Oxford (2009)
2. Almeida, J.P.A., Falbo, R.A., Guizzardi, G.: Events as entities in ontology-driven conceptual modeling. In: Laender, A.H.F., Pernici, B., Lim, E.-P., de Oliveira, J.P.M. (eds.) ER 2019. LNCS, vol. 11788, pp. 469–483. Springer, Cham (2019). https://doi.org/10.1007/978-3-030-33223-5_39
3. Artikis, A., Sergot, M., Pitt, J.: Specifying norm-governed computational societies. ACM Trans. Comput. Logic (TOCL) **10**(1), 1–42 (2009)
4. Benevides, A.B., et al.: Representing a reference foundational ontology of events in SROIQ. Appl. Ontol. **14**(3), 293–334 (2019)
5. Boella, G., Favali, L., Lesmo, L.: An Action-Based Ontology of Legal Relations. In: ICAIL 2001 (2001). https://doi.org/10.1145/383535.383566
6. Boella, G., Sauro, L., van der Torre, L.: Power and dependence relations in groups of agents. In: Proceedings of IAT 2004, pp. 246–252. IEEE (2004)
7. Boella, G., van der Torre, L.: The ontological properties of social roles in multi-agent systems: definitional dependence, powers and roles playing roles. Artif. Intell. Law **15**(3), 201–221 (2007). https://doi.org/10.1007/s10506-007-9030-8
8. Breuker, J., Hoekstra, R., et al.: Core concepts of law: taking common-sense seriously. In: Proceedings of Formal Ontologies in Information Systems (FOIS-2004), pp. 210–221 (2004)
9. Fabio, I. et al.: 'What exactly is a lockdown?': towards an ontology-based modeling of lockdown interventions during the COVID-19 pandemic. In: Proceedings of XIV Seminar on Ontology Research in Brazil (ONTOBRAS) and V Doctoral and Masters Consortium on Ontologies (WTDO). CEUR Workshop Proceedings, vol. 3050, pp. 151–165. CEUR-WS.org (2021). http://ceur-ws.org/Vol-3050/Paper12.pdf
10. de Almeida Falbo, R., Barcellos, M.P., Nardi, J.C., Guizzardi, G.: Organizing ontology design patterns as ontology pattern languages. In: Cimiano, P., Corcho, O., Presutti, V., Hollink, L., Rudolph, S. (eds.) ESWC 2013. LNCS, vol. 7882, pp. 61–75. Springer, Heidelberg (2013). https://doi.org/10.1007/978-3-642-38288-8_5
11. Falbo, R., et al.: An ontology pattern language for service modeling. In: Proceedings of the 31st Annual ACM Symposium on Applied Computing, pp. 321–326 (2016)
12. Firozabadi, B.S., Sergot, M.: Power and permission in security systems. In: Christianson, B., Crispo, B., Malcolm, J.A., Roe, M. (eds.) Security Protocols 1999. LNCS, vol. 1796, pp. 48–53. Springer, Heidelberg (2000). https://doi.org/10.1007/10720107_6
13. French, J.R., Raven, B., Cartwright, D.: The bases of social power. Classics Organ. Theory **7**, 311–320 (1959)
14. Gangemi, A.: Design patterns for legal ontology construction. In: LOAIT, pp. 65–85 (2007)
15. Gangemi, A.: Introducing pattern-based design for legal ontologies. In: Law, Ontologies and the Semantic Web, pp. 53–71. IOS Press (2009)
16. Gelati, J., Governatori, G., Rotolo, A., Sartor, G.: Declarative power, representation, and mandate: a formal analysis. In: Legal Knowledge and Information Systems. Jurix 2002: The 15th Annual Conference, pp. 41–52. IOS Press (2002)
17. Gelati, J., Rotolo, A., Sartor, G., Governatori, G.: Normative autonomy and normative co-ordination: Declarative power, representation, and mandate. Artif. Intell. Law **12**(1), 53–81 (2004)

18. Governatori, G., Rotolo, A.: Modelling contracts using RuleML. In: Gordon, T. (ed.) Jurix 2004 17th Annual Conference, pp. 141–150. IOS Press, Amsterdam (2004)
19. Griffo, C., Almeida, J.P.A., Guizzardi, G.: A pattern for the representation of legal relations in a legal core ontology. Front. Artif. Intell. Appl. **294**, 191–194 (2016)
20. Griffo, C., Almeida, J.P.A., Guizzardi, G.: Conceptual modeling of legal relations. In: Trujillo, J.C., et al. (eds.) ER 2018. LNCS, vol. 11157, pp. 169–183. Springer, Cham (2018). https://doi.org/10.1007/978-3-030-00847-5_14
21. Griffo, C., Almeida, J.P.A., Guizzardi, G., Nardi, J.: Service contract modeling in enterprise architecture: an ontology-based approach. Inf. Syst. (2019). https://doi.org/10.1016/j.is.2019.101454
22. Griffo, C., et al.: Legal theories and judicial decision-making: an ontological analysis. In: Formal Ontology in Information Systems: Proceedings of the 11th International Conference (FOIS 2020), vol. 330, p. 63. IOS Press (2020)
23. Guarino, N., Guizzardi, G.: "We need to discuss the *relationship*": revisiting relationships as modeling constructs. In: Zdravkovic, J., Kirikova, M., Johannesson, P. (eds.) CAiSE 2015. LNCS, vol. 9097, pp. 279–294. Springer, Cham (2015). https://doi.org/10.1007/978-3-319-19069-3_18
24. Guarino, N., Poli, R.: Formal ontology in conceptual analysis and knowledge representation. Int. J. Hum. Comput. Stud. **43**(5/6), 1–21 (1995)
25. Guizzardi, G.: Ontological patterns, anti-patterns and pattern languages for next-generation conceptual modeling. In: Yu, E., Dobbie, G., Jarke, M., Purao, S. (eds.) ER 2014. LNCS, vol. 8824, pp. 13–27. Springer, Cham (2014). https://doi.org/10.1007/978-3-319-12206-9_2
26. Guizzardi, G.: Ontological foundations for structural conceptual models. Ph.D. thesis, CTIT Ph.D. thesis series, Amsterdam (2005)
27. Guizzardi, G., Wagner, G.: Some applications of a unified foundational ontology in business modeling. In: Business Systems Analysis with Ontologies, pp. 345–367. IGI Global (2005)
28. Halpin, A.: The concept of a legal power. Oxford J. Legal Stud. **16**, 129 (1996)
29. Hart, H.L.A.: The Concept of Law. Oxford University Press, Oxford (1976)
30. Hoekstra, R., Breuker, J., Di Bello, M., Boer, A.: LKIF core: principled ontology development for the legal domain. In: Proceedings of 2009 Conference on Law, Ontologies and the Semantic Web: Channelling the Legal Information Flood, vol. 188, pp. 21–52. IOS Press (2009)
31. Hohfeld, W.N.: Some fundamental legal conceptions as applied in judicial reasoning. Yale Lj **23**, 16 (1913)
32. Jones, A.J., Sergot, M.: A formal characterisation of institutionalised power. Logic J. IGPL **4**(3), 427–443 (1996)
33. Lindahl, L.: Position and Change. A Study in Law and Logic, vol. 1–10. D. Reidel Publishing Cia, Boston (1977). https://doi.org/10.1093/philmat/s1-10.1.111
34. Lindahl, L., Reidhav, D.: Legal power: the basic definition. Ratio Juris **30**(2), 158–185 (2017)
35. MacCormick, N.: Norms, institutions, and institutional facts. Law Philos. **17**, 301–345 (1998)
36. Palmirani, M., Governatori, G., Athan, T., Boley, H., Paschke, A., Wyner, A.: LegalRuleML core specification version 1.0 (2017)
37. Palmirani, M., Martoni, M., Rossi, A., Bartolini, C., Robaldo, L.: Legal ontology for modelling GDPR concepts and norms. In: Legal Knowledge and Information Systems, pp. 91–100. IOS Press (2018)

38. Pandit, H.J., O'Sullivan, D., Lewis, D.: An ontology design pattern for describing personal data in privacy policies. In: WOP@ ISWC, pp. 29–39 (2018)
39. Santos, C., et al.: Complaint ontology pattern-CoP. Adv. Ontol. Des. Patterns **32**, 69–83 (2016)
40. Santos, P.S., Almeida, J.P.A., Guizzardi, G.: An ontology-based analysis and semantics for organizational structure modeling in the ARIS method. Inf. Syst. **38**(5), 690–708 (2013)
41. Sartor, G.: A teleological approach to legal dialogues. In: Pavlakos, G. (ed.) Law, Rights and Discourse: The legal Philosophy of Robert Alexy, pp. 249–274. Hart Publishing, London (2006). https://doi.org/10.5040/9781472563989.ch-012
42. Sartor, G.: Fundamental legal concepts: a formal and teleological characterisation. Artif. Intell. Law **14**(1–2), 101–142 (2006)
43. Searle, J.R.: The Construction of Social Reality. The Free Press, New York (1995)
44. Sergot, M.: Normative positions. Handb. Deontic Logic Normative Syst. **1**, 353–406 (2013)
45. Sharifi, S., Parvizimosaed, A., Amyot, D., Logrippo, L., Mylopoulos, J.: Symboleo: towards a specification language for legal contracts. In: 2020 RE Conference, pp. 364–369. IEEE (2020)
46. Siena, A., Perini, A., Susi, A., Mylopoulos, J.: A meta-model for modelling law-compliant requirements. In: Requirements Engineering and Law 2009 (2009)
47. Singh, M.P.: An ontology for commitments in multiagent systems. Artif. Intell. Law **7**(1), 97–113 (1999)
48. Spaak, T.: The concept of legal competence: an essay in conceptual analysis (1994)
49. Spaak, T.: Explicating the concept of legal competence. In: Hage, J.C., von der Pfordten, D. (eds.) Concepts in Law. Law and Philosophy Library, vol. 88, pp. 67–80. Springer, Dordrecht (2009). https://doi.org/10.1007/978-90-481-2982-9_5
50. Turner, J.C.: Explaining the nature of power: a three-process theory. Eur. J. Soc. Psychol. **35**(1), 1–22 (2005)
51. Valente, A., Breuker, J.: A Functional Ontology of Law. Artif. Intell. Law **7**, 341–361 (1994)

Atomically True Ontology Modelling: Residential Buildings

Atish Maganlal$^{(\boxtimes)}$ ⓘ and Duncan Coulter ⓘ

University of Johannesburg, JHB, Johannesburg, South Africa
{amaganlal,dcoulter}@uj.ac.za

Abstract. Creation of realistic residential buildings has been the topic of research in procedural content generation (PCG) for several years. Most PCG methods rely on analysing domain knowledge in the applicable setting and encoding that knowledge as configuration for the PCG methods used. While this technique does solve the immediate problem, it is often not portable, and extensions of a specific generation technique often requires reconfiguring when new or more detailed domain knowledge is attained. This paper presents a holistic ontological driven PCG technique that allows for varied PCG methods to be used and interchanged while having a stable platform for domain knowledge. The technique presented in the paper is an implementation of a PCG framework: atomically true ontology modelling (ATOM). Using ATOM for creating residential buildings allows for the definition of general concepts such as rooms and room types that can be then used to drive PCG methods to produce residential buildings in distinctive styles and environments.

Keywords: Procedural content generation · Building plans · Ontology development · Generative design

1 Introduction

When creating virtual environments, content in these environments is often created manually. Manual creation is time-consuming and requires expert knowledge in most cases but has the benefit of producing content to the specification required.

When working with creating virtual environments that mimic real world scenarios, often background elements are not given the same time and focus as the rest of the environments. For example, when creating a city environment, important buildings might have full interiors with all the required furnishings while other buildings in the scene contain little to no detail.

Procedural content generation (PCG) methods have been used to create these background elements to provide more realism to the scene. However, PCG methods are either primitive, offering basic components [4,7], or complex [9,21], requiring extensive configuration when used. Due to the extensive configuration

© The Author(s), under exclusive license to Springer Nature Switzerland AG 2022
J. Ralyté et al. (Eds.): ER 2022, LNCS 13607, pp. 82–91, 2022.
https://doi.org/10.1007/978-3-031-17995-2_6

these methods are not directly portable across different domains that deal with the same type of content.

Semantic methods [26,27] linking with PCG methods have been proposed but rely on primitive PCG methods that do not consider all the objects and relationships presented in the semantic model.

This paper expands on semantic methods. Knowledge is encoded in an ontology that is interpreted in a specific domain. Relevant parts of the ontology are used as needed. As the ontology grows, the interpretation can be updated as necessary. This paper will be focusing on the generation of residential buildings.

To fully explore the ontological approach presented in this paper a few key aspects will be discussed. In Sect. 2 current PCG methods as well as ontological modelling approaches are reviewed. Section 3 and Sect. 3.2 details the atomically true ontology modelling (ATOM) conceptual framework while Sect. 3.4 specifically details the residential building implementation. Finally, Sect. 4 shows the results of the paper. Thereafter, the paper is concluded.

2   Related Work

One of the long-term goals of PCG as outlined by the authors of [25] is multi-level, multi-content PCG. This goal details creation of entire virtual environments, in full detail for the target application. The authors further state that this goal is yet to be achieved. While the goal of the conceptual framework presented in the paper tackles this goal, this paper focuses mainly on the domain of residential buildings.

When looking at how current PCG methods try and achieve this goal in relation to building generation methods, there are two distinct approaches. Shape grammars and facade generation deal specifically with how a specific building looks, with less focus on the role of the building or rooms within. Knowledge and semantic based approaches use relationships between different components found in building plans to determine the layout of rooms within.

2.1   Shape Grammars and Facade Generation

Shape grammars [17,18,23,31] are a production system. Shape grammars operate with shapes, defining how shapes can be acted upon by different production rules. Application of these production rules produces sub-shapes that can also have production rules applied to them. Application of the rules result in either building envelopes, or buildings with rooms, although without specific purpose for the rooms.

Facade generation [5,18] provides a means to add more details to building envelopes generated with shape grammars. More advanced shape grammars [21] tie facade generation with shape grammars to better align the features of the building shape and facade details. Using ontologies and shape grammars was briefly explored in [6,10]. Interactive PCG was also briefly explored in [13,22].

2.2 Knowledge and Semantic Based PCG

In [27], the authors discuss how semantic information is more important in virtual environments such as video games and simulations. Key criteria for including semantic information are identified: object semantics, object relationships and world semantics. Usage of semantic data has been explored in the generation of floor plans [26], and furniture placement [15]. Expert knowledge can also be encoded into Bayesian networks [16]. In [28], the authors provide a framework for integrating existing PCG techniques with semantic information. While the framework presented by the authors does accomplish their desired goal, it only provides a means of generating geometry. It is not clear if the semantics used to generate the building are available after the conductor has executed a plan.

3 Holistic PCG Using ATOM

To understand the need for holistic PCG, issues with current research in the field of semantic PCG is discussed as well as current methods of sharing building or city information. Thereafter the overview of the ATOM framework is discussed.

3.1 Shortcomings of Current Research

When looking at the current research in the field of PCG techniques for generating residential buildings the focus of the research has been mostly of physical attributes and appearance as a final output. Semantic information has been used [1,3,14] to augment the final output or place furniture around a room but ultimately is just for visual appearance.

Data models exist for sharing 3D models of cities and buildings within. One of the most used data models for this purpose is city geography markup language (City GML) [11]. CityGML contains information about things that can exist in cities and the relationships between them. Some research has been conducted into complementing CityGML into an ontology [32].

Efforts to introduce more semantics into modelling have changed systems such as computer aided design (CAD) into building information modelling (BIM) and further integrated with geographic information system (GIS) into city information modelling (CIM) [24]. However, these advancements for tools for planning of cities and buildings are for expert users.

The ATOM conceptual framework seeks to cater for varied content types, other than 3D models or be confined to expert users.

3.2 ATOM Conceptual Framework

The atomically true ontology modelling (ATOM) conceptual framework takes inspiration from the previous PCG framework [28] as well as the product development process [29]. ATOM is a PCG framework that caters for varied content types as well as keeping semantic information available with the generated content. An ontology is developed as part of using ATOM in the implementation presented in the paper. However, existing ontologies or other semantic information can be used but will require some changes to accommodate the PCG components. The ATOM conceptual framework consists of several phases; an overview is shown in Fig. 1.

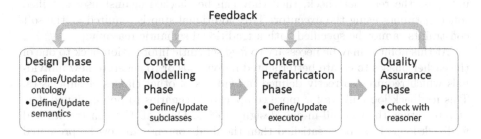

Fig. 1. Atomically true ontology modelling conceptual framework overview

In the **design phase**, classes of elements are defined. All classes in the ontology used in ATOM will be a subclass of **Procedural content**. **Procedural content** will have a property indicating which generator was used to create the content. The elements represented by the classes are the foundation of where knowledge is introduced into the framework and serves as an indication as to what elements are required to produce the content required. The classes are compiled into the ontology. If possible, world semantics, basic object properties, and object semantic relationships can be specified at during this phase. Additionally, each class is assigned a unique symbol, which is important for the ATOM grammar. The ATOM grammar is in more detail in Sect. 3.3.

In the **content modelling phase**, subclasses of design phase classes are defined. Properties for each element can be defined along with the relationship with the type of content generated. At this phase, restrictions on properties and classes can be defined. Other user constraints can also be specified that can tune the individual elements to desired parameters. Each subclass will have a unique symbol independent but related to the superclass symbol. In this phase elements can be obtained from static assets provided by the user, using PCG techniques that take in properties and constraints as input, or another ATOM grammar.

In the **content prefabrication phase**, the ontology from the content modelling phase is then integrated into the ATOM grammar. Since there can be multiple subclasses for a specific class, there can be multiple routes a production rule can take. These choices are managed by an executor. The executor is the next level for knowledge to be coded into the system. The executor is also responsible for creating individuals from the chosen subclasses. Individuals that are created from subclasses that rely on PCG techniques generate their elements using the semantic information found in the ontology. This semantic information is relayed via the executor to the individual.

In the **content prefabrication phase**, individuals generated can be combined into the final content required. However, consistency of the content still needs to take place. ATOM does not define its own reasoner, instead leveraging on existing semantic reasoners. An existing semantic reasoner is be used to determine if the knowledge and user constraints encoded in the ontologies are being upheld. If not, then either another set of individuals are created, or the executor needs to be tweaked to avoid issues with the reasoner. If the individuals pass the reasoner check, then they can be checked against user specified soft constraints using the executor. This additional step is required as the soft constraints cannot be specified with a traditional semantic reasoning.

At this point it may be necessary to feed semantic information back to one of the earlier phases to create better suited individuals or to generate new individuals which requires correctly defined individuals of other classes or subclasses. This feedback loop allows for more complicated scenarios to be developed iteratively rather than an all-in-one design process. Once all the constraints and feedback loops have been satisfied then the final content can now be presented to the end user. Semantic information is stored with the generated content so that when the content is consumed it has the required information available to be used correctly.

3.3 ATOM Grammar

The ATOM grammar is a production system, similar in concept to both L-Systems [19] and shape grammars. Symbols are used to define or identify something in the system. Production rules define how symbols are changed into other symbols. Terminal symbols are defined as a symbol that can have no production rule that can be applied, implying that there is no more generation that needs to take place. Non-terminal symbols can have one or more production rules applied that will eventually yield terminal symbols.

Symbols in the ATOM grammar define content that is represented by subclasses found in the ontology. The way in which the production rule is applied and how the subclass is chosen is coded into the executor. In the context of residential buildings, the executor can choose a specific type of room to generate based on the rooms that have already been generated or rooms that are still required to satisfy the semantic reasoner.

ATOM grammars can also be used in a hierarchical manner. Terminal symbols in the ATOM grammar can be replaced by another ATOM grammar that further defines the content of that terminal symbol. Using ATOM grammars in this way allows grammars to be reused in different contexts if the grammar is applicable to the context.

3.4 ATOM: Residential Buildings

In this subsection the ATOM conceptual framework is applied to the domain of residential buildings. Each phase of the framework is discussed in the context of residential buildings.

The **design phase** requires the basics to be specified using domain knowledge. By using A Pattern Language [2] in conjunction with observations made from the papers discussed in the Sect. 2, the residential building ontology was developed. A residential plot is associated with a specific street where the street belongs to a specific suburb. Both street and suburb are classes that hold metadata that is used to generate unique varied content. Residential plots consist of different areas. Social areas hold social rooms. Similarly service and private areas hold service rooms and private rooms, respectively. Along with the street, a plot number is stored. Areas can be connected to other areas, while rooms can be directly adjacent to other rooms.

In the **content modelling phase**, specific room subtypes are defined. These specific types of rooms are created to have concrete elements that can be combined into a residential building. Additionally, constraints for a residential plot are defined. Figure 2 shows a visual representation of the ontology after the modelling phase.

In the **content prefabrication phase**, the executor can now be defined. To generate individuals, the executor needs to fill all the required properties of a residential plot. PCG techniques can be used to create the needed properties for different classes. Generation of a residential plot using PCG techniques can be tuned using the knowledge available from earlier phases or specific knowledge acquired during this phase.

Finally, in the **quality assurance phase**, the individuals created by the executor can now be checked against the ontology and user constraints. Depending on the output of the reasoner the PCG techniques of the reasoner can be adjusted to obtain desired results. Furthermore, if the domain knowledge needs to be adjusted after the reasoner is successful then classes or constraints from the earlier phases can be changed to accommodate this new knowledge. For the current ontology, feedback was incorporated during the development process.

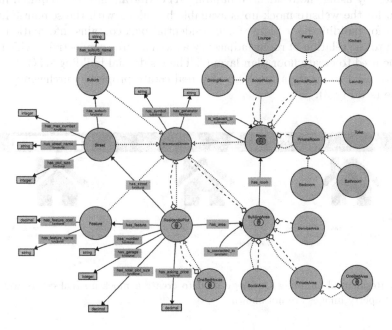

Fig. 2. Ontology after content modelling phase, visualised using WebVOWL [30]

4   Example of an ATOM Grammar

Using the ontology developed in the previous section, an ATOM grammar was defined for the executor to use. Several residential plots were generated in two suburbs with a few streets in each suburb. Although not the focus of residential buildings specifically, suburbs and streets allow houses that are close together to share common properties such as plot size, types of rooms or typical number of rooms of a type. One additional subclass was defined (**OneBedHouse**) to show additional end user constraints by creating specific subclasses.

The information for the generated individuals could be used to generate a floor plan. Room adjacency can be used for generating doorways or passages. Windows can be generated by looking at the perimeter wall of rooms. However, by using information from the street and suburb, extra context can be generated for the residential building. More recent suburbs would have more modern room structure and layout. Older streets can have run down buildings that can be generated. All these different aspects can be accomplished by modifying the executor to manage more PCG techniques.

4.1   Alternate Applications of the Residential Building ATOM Grammar

ATOM is presented as a framework that can do more than 3D geometry. By adjusting the view of the final end-user to that of a potential homeowner, a different use case of the ontology developed can be shown. Real estate property websites show key details of the property and not full details of the floor plan. However, by using the residential building ATOM grammar, the required information for the website mock-up is available but along with the semantic information for building floor plans. Each residential plot contains information pertaining to the relation of rooms adjacency as well as area connectivity which can then be used to create floor plan layouts. The residential building ATOM grammar was used to create a mock-up of a real estate property purchasing/rental website (see Fig. 3).

Fig. 3. Residential Building Ontology used to create a mock-up real estate website. Note: Property images are not shown.

The residential building ATOM grammar was implemented using Owlready2 [12] which combines the programming language Python with web ontology language (OWL). Using Owlready2 the executor was defined by creating the ontology directly in Python and then subsequently using PCG techniques to create individuals. Owlready2 provides access to a reasoner to check the individuals and ontology is consistent.

Mixing the ontology and programming concepts is non-trivial. However, since PCG techniques are implemented in various programming languages, a crossover between the two domains is inevitable.

4.2   Results

Since the discourse of related work was tailored specifically towards generating geometry, the focus on the comparison of results is to encapsulate other uses of residential buildings data. Using this different focus, however, does have the issue of directly comparable data.

Alternate generation techniques for creating content that do not specifically consider semantic information is deep neural networks. One such neural network is StyleGAN [8] which generates stylistic images using generative adversarial networks. **ThisRentalDoesNotExist** [20] is part of a family of websites that generate images to mimic some content. **ThisRentalDoesNotExist** specifically tries to mimic a rental website such as AirBNB. While StyleGAN focuses on images and style transfer it does try to address the problem of generating content. However, the results can only be used as-is, without any end-user input apart from the training data. A similar problem exists with the text that describes the generated rental. Apart from the training data, the end user has no way to tailor the specific content generated. The images generated and the text used to describe the rental are not related to each other.

5   Conclusion and Future Work

Creating holistic procedurally generated content for various environments has been a long-term goal of PCG. This paper presented the ATOM conceptual framework for combining PCG with semantic information to generate varied content that can be used in different circumstances. Existing PCG techniques can be integrated with the ATOM conceptual framework. An implementation of the framework is presented with the residential building ATOM grammar. This implementation highlights how the ATOM conceptual framework can be utilised to create content for a specific domain.

In future research, the framework will be expanded in several ways. One aspect is how content and related semantic individuals that have been created can be accessed and shared without being involved in the design process. Another avenue of focus is a more automated approach to the interaction of the executor and the semantic reasoner. Finally, regarding content generation, a content warehouse can provide specific types of static content that can be combined, and by changing the content warehouse, another stylistic variation of the content can be created.

References

1. Adão, T., Magalhães, L., Peres, E.: Ontology-based Procedural Modelling of Traversable Buildings Composed by Arbitrary Shapes. SCS, Springer, Cham (2016). https://doi.org/10.1007/978-3-319-42372-2
2. Alexander, C., Ishikawa, S., Silverstein, M.: A Pattern Language: Towns, Buildings, Construction, vol. 2. Oxford University Press, New York (1977)
3. Caneparo, L., Berta, M., Rolfo, D.: Semantic analysis and 3D generation of buildings and cities. Int. J. Des. Sci. Technol. 24(1), 1–37 (2020)
4. Dart, I.M., De Rossi, G., Togelius, J.: Speedrock: procedural rocks through grammars and evolution. In: Proceedings of the 2nd International Workshop on Procedural Content Generation in Games, p. 8. ACM (2011)
5. Finkenzeller, D.: Detailed building facades. IEEE Comput. Graphics Appl. 28(3), 58–66 (2008)
6. Grobler, F., Aksamija, A., Kim, H., Krishnamurti, R., Yue, K., Hickerson, C.: Ontologies and shape grammars: communication between knowledge-based and generative systems. In: Gero, J.S., Goel, A.K. (eds.) Design Computing and Cognition 2008, pp. 23–40. Springer, Dordrecht (2008). https://doi.org/10.1007/978-1-4020-8728-8_2
7. Interactive Data Visualization: Speedtree (2019). http://www.speedtree.com
8. Karras, T., Laine, S., Aila, T.: A style-based generator architecture for generative adversarial networks (2019)
9. Kelly, G., McCabe, H.: Citygen: an interactive system for procedural city generation. In: Fifth International Conference on Game Design and Technology, pp. 8–16 (2007)
10. Klerk, R.D, et al.: Ontologies and shape grammars-a relational overview towards semantic design systems (2016)
11. Kolbe, T.H., Gröger, G., Plümer, L.: CityGML: Interoperable access to 3D city models. In: van Oosterom, P., Zlatanova, S., Fendel, E.M. (eds.) Geo-information for Disaster Management, pp. 883–899. Springer, Heidelberg (2005). https://doi.org/10.1007/3-540-27468-5_63
12. Lamy, J.B.: Owlready: ontology-oriented programming in python with automatic classification and high level constructs for biomedical ontologies. Artif. Intell. Med. 80, 11–28 (2017)
13. Lipp, M., Wonka, P., Wimmer, M.: Interactive visual editing of grammars for procedural architecture. In: ACM Transactions on Graphics (TOG), vol. 27, p. 102. ACM (2008)
14. Liu, Y., Xu, C., Zhang, Q., Pan, Y.: The smart architect: scalable ontology-based modeling of ancient Chinese architectures. IEEE Intell. Syst. 23(1), 49–56 (2008)

15. Marson, F., Musse, S.R.: Automatic real-time generation of floor plans based on squarified treemaps algorithm. Int. J. Comput. Games Technol. **2010**, 7 (2010)
16. Merrell, P., Schkufza, E., Koltun, V.: Computer-generated residential building layouts. In: ACM Transactions on Graphics (TOG), vol. 29, p. 181. ACM (2010)
17. Müller, P., Wonka, P., Haegler, S., Ulmer, A., Van Gool, L.: Procedural modeling of buildings. ACM Trans. Graph. (TOG) **25**(3), 614–623 (2006)
18. Parish, Y.I., Müller, P.: Procedural modeling of cities. In: Proceedings of the 28th Annual Conference on Computer Graphics and Interactive Techniques, pp. 301–308. ACM (2001)
19. Prusinkiewicz, P., Lindenmayer, A.: The Algorithmic Beauty of Plants. Springer, New York (2012)
20. Schmidt, C.: This rental does not exist (2021). http://thisrentaldoesnotexist.com/about/
21. Schwarz, M., Müller, P.: Advanced procedural modeling of architecture. ACM Trans. Graph. **34**(4), 1071–10712 (2015). https://doi.org/10.1145/2766956
22. Smelik, R., Tutenel, T., de Kraker, K.J., Bidarra, R.: Integrating procedural generation and manual editing of virtual worlds. In: Proceedings of the 2010 Workshop on Procedural Content Generation in Games. PCGames 2010, pp. 2:1–2:8. ACM (2010). https://doi.org/10.1145/1814256.1814258
23. Stiny, G.: Introduction to shape and shape grammars. Environ. Plann. B. Plann. Des. **7**(3), 343–351 (1980)
24. Stojanovski, T.: City information modeling (CIM) and urbanism: blocks, connections, territories, people and situations. In: Simulation Series, vol. 45, pp. 86–93 (2013)
25. Togelius, J., et al.: Procedural content generation: Goals, challenges and actionable steps. Schloss Dagstuhl-Leibniz-Zentrum fuer Informatik (2013)
26. Tutenel, T., Bidarra, R., Smelik, R.M., De Kraker, K.J.: Rule-based layout solving and its application to procedural interior generation. In: CASA Workshop on 3D Advanced Media In Gaming and Simulation (2009)
27. Tutenel, T., Bidarra, R., Smelik, R.M., Kraker, K.J.D.: The role of semantics in games and simulations. Comput. Entertain. (CIE) **6**(4), 57 (2008)
28. Tutenel, T., Smelik, R.M., Lopes, R., De Kraker, K.J., Bidarra, R.: Generating consistent buildings: a semantic approach for integrating procedural techniques. IEEE Trans. Comput. Intell. AI Games **3**(3), 274–288 (2011)
29. Ulrich, K.T.: Product Design and Development. Tata McGraw-Hill Education, New York (2003)
30. Visual Data Web VOWL: Webvowl (2021). http://vowl.visualdataweb.org/webvowl.html
31. Wonka, P., Wimmer, M., Sillion, F., Ribarsky, W.: Instant architecture, vol. 22. ACM (2003)
32. Zalamea, O., Van Orshoven, J., Steenberghen, T.: From a citygml to an ontology-based approach to support preventive conservation of built cultural heritage. In: Proceedings of the 19th AGILE international conference on geographic information science (2016). https://doi.org/10.1007/978364234234-9

An Ontological Analysis of Digital Technology

Silvia Bogea Gomes[1,2](✉) ⓘ, Flavia Maria Santoro[3] ⓘ, and Miguel Mira da Silva[1] ⓘ

[1] Instituto Superior Tecnico, University of Lisbon, Lisbon, Portugal
silvia.bogea@inov.pt, mms@tecnico.ulisboa.pt
[2] INOV INESC Inovacao, Lisbon, Portugal
[3] Institute of Technology and Leadership, Sao Paulo, Brasil
flavia@inteli.edu.br

Abstract. In a growing number of industries, digitalization enables new value co-creation, leading to innovative changes in the economy and society. Digitalization arises from the Information Technology domain, blending and encapsulating digital technologies' transformational effects. Digital technologies are fundamental components for organizations to transform digitally; therefore, what is digital technology? It is a type of technology involving one or more digital objects whose components include one or more bitstrings. The Theory of Digital Objects proposes to capture digital objects' ontological complexity and understand how their identity and usage are bound up with a "dual nature" constituting physical form and social function. This paper presents an ontological analysis of this theory, grounded on the Unified Foundational Ontology (UFO), using OntoUML to identify the core components to answer what digital technology is. The analysis adds ontological clarity to the Theory of Digital Objects.

Keywords: Theory of digital objects · UFO · OntoUML · Digital Technology

1 Introduction

Organizations are increasingly confronted with the need to respond and adapt to changes creatively, to remain profitable and develop sustainable competitive advantages. Many will cease to exist unless they keep up with technological trends. In a growing number of industries, digitalization enables new value co-creation, leading to changes in the economy and society. Digitalization arises from the Information Technology (IT) environment, blending in and encapsulating digital technologies' transformational effects [1]. IT is a collective term for various technologies involved in the processing and transmission of information, including computing, telecommunications, and microelectronics [2].

IT has enabled human actors, Information Systems, and innovative products to interact via multiple digital channels. Since the 1990s, the Information Systems domain extended the concept of business transformation from IT-enabled to transformations where IT is part of core business [3]. Currently, Information Systems are making and shaping the physical reality from a digital version of reality. This ontological reversal has many implications for the role of humans and technology in society [4]. In a digital

J. Ralyté et al. (Eds.): ER 2022, LNCS 13607, pp. 92–101, 2022.
https://doi.org/10.1007/978-3-031-17995-2_7

world, human digital technology experiences can be mediated entirely or partially by four dimensions: time, place, artifacts, and actors [5].

Digital technology has been associated with trendy technologies, such as cloud, wearables, mobile devices, social media, business analytics, the Internet of things (IoT), and Artificial Intelligence (AI) [6–8]. The term digital technology was already used before the World Wide Web (better known as the Web) and the Internet. Everyday activities increasingly leverage digital technologies for personal and professional purposes, in organizational and non-organizational contexts. Digital technologies are fundamental components for organizations to digitally transform themselves. Literature has discussed the unique characteristics or properties of digital technologies: that offer opportunities to create new infrastructures, products, and business models, reshaping organizations [9]. Moreover, many efforts have been made to comprehensively understand digital technologies [4, 5, 10–15].

Faulkner and Runde's theory [15] provides a clear and complete explanation in ontological terms; thus, we took this theory as starting point and applied an ontological analysis grounded on the Unified Foundational Ontology (UFO) [16–18] and using OntoUML [19], to identify the *digital technology* core components, making explicit connections, disambiguating collapsed concepts, and clarifying underspecified aspects. In this context, we aim to answer the Research Question: *What is digital technology?*

The rest of the paper is structured as follows: Sect. 2 presents the literature review; Sect. 3 outlines the Theory of Digital Objects, Sect. 4 introduces the Unified Foundational Ontology (UFO) and OntoUML; Sect. 5 exhibits the unified digital technology conceptualization underlying the Theory of Digital Objects; Sect. 6 discusses the ontological analysis results; and Sect. 7 concludes the paper.

2 Literature Review

The core concepts related to digital technology theories, ontologies, or conceptual frameworks identified in a literature review were consolidated in Fig. 1.

Yoo [5] describes **digital artifacts** as everyday artifacts with embedded computing capabilities. Digital artifact is one of the four dimensions of human experiences through digital technology, the other three being: time, space, and actors. Furthermore, the layered modular architecture extends the modular architecture of physical products by incorporating four loosely coupled layers: the devices, networks, services, and contents created by digital technology [11]. Digital artifacts vary in the processes, they mediate and how they are qualified as objects. Hence why, for [10], a digital artifact is a quasi-object, considering it can exist in more than one similar but distinct implementation.

Digital artifacts differ from physical objects and other cultural records (e.g., art objects, paper-based files) by their non-digital constitution, along several dimensions [12]. These differences confer to the digital objects a distinctive functional profile. These authors subsume all digital technologies, devices, and digital cultural artifacts such as music, video, and image under the category of **digital objects**.

These theories provide a useful conceptual grid for studying social practices and identifying the peculiar generativity and instability that digital objects introduce - across various settings and situations. Digital artifacts such as files, images, and films or videos

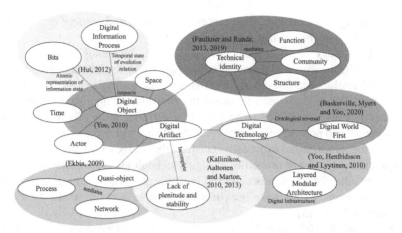

Fig. 1. The selected theories' main concepts.

are considered fluid and editable, often embedded in complex, distributed, and shifting digital environments [10, 12], although [13] argued that the term digital artifact is a mean of theorizing the mentioned incompleteness. They are objects, yet they lack the plenitude and stability afforded by traditional items and devices.

Digital objects are approached through the concept of "relations" with the material and the temporal relations, contrasting digital objects with natural objects (e.g., apples) and technical objects (e.g., hammers). They are abstract entities, such as information and data. As a technical object, a technical individual supports its inner structure functioning since it can adapt to an external milieu (i.e., a person's social environment) with its functioning. The main attributes that characterize the digital object are bits, digital information, and process. The related concepts are natural and technical objects [20].

Faulkner and Runde [14] state that a **technological object** is a type of object that is a structured continuant. Structured means it is composed of distinct parts and organized in some way. Continuant means it is fully present at every point the time during which it exists. Since the **technological objects** are not agents, they do not have practices like human agents, although they occupy social positions. They also are not self-reflexive and cannot exercise conscious choices. The identity of technological objects is defined with a focus on the immaterial status of digital artifacts, their reproducibility (meager marginal cost), recombinability, and non-rival nature, likewise the ways these attributes are implicated in the innovation of products and services [14, 15, 21, 22].

The **Theory of Digital Objects** [15] organizes an object's conception into two perspectives: the bearers of nonmaterial objects and the social positioning of digital objects. Digital objects are, therefore, distinct from other kinds of entities, such as events. The digital objects' identity and system functions flow from their social positioning in the communities where they arise [15]. They focus on bearers of nonmaterial technological objects, where digital objects *qua* objects, i.e., all digital objects, are objects.

Digital artifacts are reprogrammable and self-referential entities whose distinct functional makeup is closely tied to data homogenization (or digitization), critical in enabling digital artifacts to develop innovative properties [5, 11, 14, 15, 21, 22]. As digital artifacts diffuse, these properties become involved in making modular and multi-layered digital infrastructures, that instantiate the independence of services from devices and content from the underlying networks [11]. Such condition opens the potential for innovation, enabling the mixing of inputs/outputs across the traditional and usually fixed industry borders associated with standard physical products, and vertical integration. Furthermore, the classical view of an information system that represents and reflects physical reality is increasingly obsolete: digital technologies are now creating and shaping physical reality [4]. They call this phenomenon **ontological reversal**, where the digital version is created first and the physical version second (if needed).

We decided to use the Theory of Digital Objects from [15] since they present a clearer and more complete solution in ontological terms. In the next section, the terms highlighted in *italic* correspond to the theory entities [14, 15, 21, 22].

3 Theorizing Digital Objects

The Theory of Digital Objects [15] is centered around an object's conception, positioning, and identifying technological objects in a community, and surfacing the hidden assumptions about how technology implicates human activities. A technological object is any object with one or more uses assigned to it by the members of some (human) community. Moreover, technology is composed of technological objects.

An object can be categorized as either material or nonmaterial. *Material objects*, such as scanners and smartphones, refer to an object's physical mode of being. *Nonmaterial objects* have a non-physical existence, examples include articles, operating systems, software, and conceptual schemes.

A *material object* can be a bearer of a *nonmaterial object*. *Material bearers* are vital for practical engagement with *nonmaterial objects*: a *nonmaterial object* must be born on a *material object* to be accessed. For example, for a digital book to be read by a human being, it must be displayed on a suitable *material object*, like a tablet. Similarly, if that digital book needs to be archived, it must be held on an appropriate *material object*. The *nonmaterial object* is distinct from all these *material objects* owning particular attributes. For instance, where an object serves as a *material bearer* to archive a *nonmaterial object*, properties such as durability and portability are likely to be essential attributes of the *material object* concerned. The *hybrid* refers to objects that comprise both *material* and *nonmaterial objects* as component parts [15].

A *nonmaterial object* (e.g., a computer program) is born from (or contained within) some *syntactic object* (e.g., computer language). In this case, we can call any *syntactic object* in which a *nonmaterial object* is born (or contained) a *nonmaterial bearer* of that *nonmaterial object*. Faulkner and Runde [15] consider *syntactic objects* as the most important category of *nonmaterial objects* for their purposes; the *syntactic objects* consist of symbols arranged into well-formed expressions, i.e., these expressions adhere to the syntactical and semantic rules of the language in which they are couched. For example, manuals, and contracts are *syntactic objects* in natural language, while musical notation, Morse code, and mathematics are *syntactic objects* in artificial languages.

Any *syntactic* entity satisfies the two criteria for *nonmaterial* objecthood: it is an object and has a non-physical mode of being. In a *syntactic object* such as a novel, the component parts are letters and punctuation marks arranged to form words and sentences. *Syntactic objects* are ubiquitous in the digital world, and one type of them stands out as fundamental: the *bitstring* [15].

A *bitstring* is a type of *syntactic object* made up of bits, which are the 0s and 1s employed in a binary numbering system, where these bits are structured according to an appropriate file format to be readable by the computer hardware for which they are intended. *Bitstrings*, often called computer files, are one of the cornerstones of the digital revolution since the information stored and manipulated by computers, in general, is encoded in bitstrings. *Bitstrings* are divided into two categories: program files (PF) (e.g., operating systems, applications, browsers, smartphone apps, and games) and data files (DF) (e.g., documents, videos, and audio recordings) [15].

Digital objects are ones that component parts include one or more *bitstrings*. *Digital objects* are components' structured ensembles, themselves objects. As a type of object, *digital objects* inherit the objects' characteristics (*material* and *nonmaterial objects*). *Digital hybrids* acquire the physical mode of their material components. In general, *digital objects* have community-dependent aspects (e.g., the same platform can be used for e-learning and business meetings) rather than intrinsic aspects.

A *technological object* is any object that has one or more uses assigned to it by members of some human *community*, besides having a "dual nature" in that it is constituted of both the $<<$ *physical form* $>>$ and the $<<$ *social function* $>>$ [14]. Regarding the "dual nature", its physical form is crucial for the functions assigned to it. Those objects (e.g., a book) must generally possess the physical characteristics and capabilities required to perform the functions concerned. For their new forms (e.g., an e-book) or cases in which existing technological objects are used in a new way (e.g., phone as a smartphone), the group assigning the function may initially be very small, including no more than those responsible for the innovations concerned [21].

Furthermore, the context-dependent aspects, such as how the *digital objects* look (smartphones, banking apps) depend on their social positioning [15]. A *social position* is a specific status within a system, that locates its occupant as a system's component. Any *entity's social identity* is the entity's kind of object according to its occupied *social position*. *Social positions* typically exist independently of, and usually before, any individual occupant. The *technological object identity's* definition can be used to pinpoint *digital objects*. For example, the social networking personal profile's identity, a *technological object*, is a *digital object*, as it is assigned to a community (e.g., LinkedIn).

4   UFO and OntoUML

The Unified Foundational Ontology (UFO) [16–18] is an axiomatic formal theory based on contributions from Formal Ontology in Philosophy, Philosophical Logics, Cognitive Psychology, and Linguistics. It is the second-most used foundational ontology in conceptual modeling and the one with the fastest adoption rate [23].

OntoUML [19] is a language whose meta-model has been designed to comply with the ontological distinctions and axiomatization of UFO. It is among the most widely used languages in ontology-driven conceptual modeling, together with UML, (E)ER, OWL and BPMN. A brief explanation of a selected subset of the ontological distinctions set out by UFO is given below, together with how these distinctions are represented by the modelling primitives of OntoUML (as a UML profile). In this work, the terms highlighted in **bold** correspond to the UFO entities and those between «brackets» to OntoUML stereotypes.

UFO consists of three main modules: UFO-A theory synthesizes the Endurants (i.e.: objects, continuants); UFO-B comprises an ontology of Events (i.e.: events, processes, states); and UFO-C is an ontology of intentional and social entities, which is constructed on top of UFO-A and UFO-B, and addresses notions such as Beliefs, Desires, Intentions, Goals, Actions, Social Roles and Social Relators and others [19]. It starts by making a fundamental distinction between **endurants** and **events**. **Endurants** are entities that exist in time and can change qualitatively, while maintaining their identity. **Events**, in contrast, are entities that unfold in time, accumulating temporal parts (e.g., a football game, a speech). **Endurants** are further divided into **substantials** and **aspects**. **Substantials** are existentially independent entities such as apples, and a person.

Substantials can be either **agents** or **objects**. An **agent** is a substantial that creates actions, perceives events, and to which we can ascribe mental states (intentional moments). Agents can be physical (e.g., a person) or social (e.g., an organization). A human agent is a type of physical agent. An **object** is a substantial which is unable to perceive events or have intentional moments. Objects can also be further categorized into **physical** (e.g., a book, a car) and **social objects** (e.g., money, language) [18]. **Collectives** («Collective») of **agents** or **objects** (e.g., a project team, a deck of cards) have uniform structures and contain other Endurants as members («memberOf»).

5   Theory of Digital Objects in OntoUML

The ontological function of a conceptual model is to provide conceptual clarification and unambiguous communication [24]. The model should reconstruct the intended conceptualization (set of possible interpretations) and be explicit and transparent with its ontological semantics. Revealing the ontological semantics of an information artifact is a fundamental type of explanation for symbolic models (including conceptual models).

We present an ontological analysis of the conceptualization underlying the Theory of Digital Objects using OntoUML. The result of this analysis is captured in an integrated model, comprising the digital object and its technical identity (see Fig. 2). We applied the generally accepted color-coding scheme from OntoUML. Moreover, in the diagram, we highlighted the entities from UFO [16] and TDO (Theorizing Digital Objects) [15], starting the name of the class with "UFO:" or "TDO:" or both.

Faulkner and Runde [15] provide a framework that considers *material, nonmaterial,* and *hybrid objects* in a unified way, looking at digital phenomena and their potential. It informs the existing perspectives on theorizing *digital technology* per se and the relationship between people and *digital technology*. It considers the computation' role and how the *object's technical identity* and *object's functions* flow from their social positioning in the *communities* in which they arise. They [15] focus on the *digital objects'* conception and a *bearer* theory of how *material* and *nonmaterial objects* combine.

In UFO, Guizzardi et al. [18] consider an **object** as a substantial, not able to perceive **events** or have **intentional moments** that can be further categorized into **physical** and

social objects. According to Markosian [25], objects from different ontological categories, such as physical, non-physical, propositions, and universals, all exist in time; however, not all of them exist in space. The ones that exist in both time and space are the ones that count as *physical objects*. Markosian [25], like us, assumes that the expressions **physical object** (as defined in UFO) and *material object* (as defined in TDO) are synonymous. A *nonmaterial object* (TDO) can be a type of **social object** (UFO).

The organizational consequences of technology cannot be fully understood without a reference to this framework. For example, understanding the organizational consequences of blockchain requires knowing about the properties of (nonmaterial) data structures, cryptographic keys, consensus mechanism protocols, and the material infrastructure elements required to maintain a geographically distributed ledger.

The technical identity of a *technological object* within some *community* is constituted by its *function* and *structure*, which is beneficial to the community's interests. Structured means an object composed of several distinct parts (component parts), organized in some way. Since a *community* collectively assigns functions, those functions are never intrinsic to the objects concerned and are therefore always necessarily community relative. To sustain the *function* assigned to a *technological object*, it must generally possess the characteristics and capabilities required to perform it [22].

According to [14], *technical identities* might reside at different levels of abstraction, including nested *technical identities*. For example: networks monitoring iPhone applications are members of a broader class of iPhone applications, and those are themselves members of an even broader class of application software. An application such as Google Translate derives its identity, not only from the structures of the bitstrings comprising it, but also from the function assigned to those bitstrings, in this case, to translate text, documents, and websites from one language into another. *Technological objects* of a given *technical identity* often vary in the details of their structures. However, despite their diversity, people can still identify different **objects** as tokens of the same type of technological device. Thus, while Google Translate, Microsoft Translator, and their various competitors contrast somewhat in their structures, they share sufficient commonalities to be grouped as online translators.

It is also possible that similar or even identical **objects** may have contrasting functions assigned to them, to such an extent that the same object may have radically different technical identities in different communities. This is more likely to occur to intermediate products - further upstream in the manufacturing process -, for example, in the case of the gramophone turntable becoming a musical instrument in specific communities [21].

Modeling this theory in OntoUML demonstrated that *digital technologies* have the << participation >> of *digital objects* that are, in turn, **objects** characterized by some capabilities required to perform specific functions of this *technological object*. Finally, we answer (RQ1) *What is digital technology? Digital technology* is the technical identity of a *digital object*, its type of use assigned by a community, and its social functions. *Digital objects* are a type of *technological object* constituted by *component parts*, including one or more *bitstrings*. Bitstrings, a *nonmaterial object*, can be beared by a *material object* or remain as a *nonmaterial* bearer. A *nonmaterial* bearer can be one of the various kinds of *nonmaterial objects* corresponding to the diverse kinds of information employed in computing. A *digital object* has a *technical identity* mediated by its *structure* and *social function*.

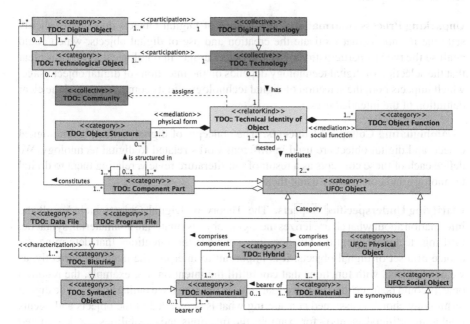

Fig. 2. Digital Object and their Technical Identity in OntoUML.

6 Discussion

The conception of digital objects and the novel "bearer" theory, of how material and nonmaterial objects combine, is part of the Theory of Digital Objects [15]. This theory considers the computation's role as the digital objects' identity and functions and their social positioning in the communities they arise from. However, focusing on the digital object alone can mask the complexity of the digital technological domain, when concepts have a rich semantic structure. The ontological unpacking provided a detailed analysis of the complex notions hidden within the digital object and was essential for acquiring a deep understanding of the domain. The ontological analysis aims to support the digital object's conceptual aspect to facilitate the technology's understanding. It leads to the following advantages:

Making Connections Explicit. The Theory of Digital Objects represents the concept of the resource from three perspectives of viewing resources: resource-based (i.e., material, physical, objects), knowledge-based (i.e., social worlds, social rules, relations), and service-dominant logic (i.e., operand as machinery, operant as competences). The different perspectives are relevant for distinguishing between distinct kinds of resources (especially the nonmaterial and fluid nature of certain types of resources). The problems these authors identified represent the weaknesses in conceptualizing digital technology in IS research. Grounding this theory in UFO and OntoUML makes those concepts and relationships explicit.

Unpacking Process Information. The Theory of Digital Objects does not explicitly state the intentions that motivate the creation and use of digital objects, which could confuse the type of participation of digital object usage. In ontological terms, it is clear that the selection of digital technology depends on the intentions of digital object usage, which impacts both the selection of digital technology and its components, and the clear definition of the intended uses.

Disambiguating Collapsed Concepts. The concepts of digital artifact, technological object, and digital object are used in different works related to digital technology. We define each of these concepts as a result of our literature review, relating them to digital technology and consistently using them.

Clarifying Underspecified Aspects. The Theory of Digital Objects includes all the information about what characterizes the digital objects (material, nonmaterial, syntactic, bitstring, technical identity) but does not consider the intentions that determine the choice of a set of digital objects. It is important to interpret the intention correctly, as we need objects with functions that can fulfill the intention. For example, the required objects could be more than just an e-learning software to have online classes. The digital technology choice is assigned considering what is demanded of the objects and agents (including artificial agents) - for example, the functions and capabilities - as determined by a community.

7   Conclusion

In this paper, we analyzed the Theory of Digital Objects, that offers an object-based definition of digital objects able to explain why digital objects are specifically digital, covering both hardware and nonmaterial objects. We conducted an ontological analysis to unpack and identify the core components of the Theory of Digital Objects. The results demonstrate the effectiveness of this conceptual model and the usefulness of unpacking a model to conceptualize digital technology. Future research will aggregate digital technology, its roles, and its impacts on Digital Transformation Ontology [1].

References

1. Gomes, S.B., Santoro, F.M., da Silva, M.M.: An ontology for BPM in digital transformation and innovation. Int. J. Inf. Syst. Model. Des. **11**, 52–77 (2020)
2. Nyamboga, C.M., Kemparaju, T.D.: Information technology in university libraries in Karnataka. Inf. Dev. **18**, 257–265 (2002)
3. Baiyere, A., Salmela, H., Tapanainen, T.: Digital transformation and the new logics of business process management. Eur. J. Inf. Syst. **29**, 238–259 (2020)

4. Baskerville, R.L., Myers, M.D., Yoo, Y.: Digital first: the ontological reversal and new challenges for information systems research. MIS Q. **44**, 509–523 (2020)
5. Yoo, Y.: Computing in everyday life: a call for research on experiential computing. MIS Q. Manag. Inf. Syst. **34**, 213–231 (2010)
6. Sedera, D., Lokuge, S.: Do we put all eggs in one basket? a polynomial regression study of digital technology configuration strategies. In: 40th International Conference on Information Systems, ICIS 2019 (2019)
7. Arbaiza, C.E.S.: Critical variables for success in the technology adoption process in the framework of digital transformation. In: ACM International Conference on Proceeding Series, pp. 109–113 (2018)
8. Berger, S., Bitzer, M., Häckel, B., Voit, C.: Approaching digital transformation - development of a multi-dimensional maturity model. In: ECIS 2020 Proceedings, pp. 1–18 (2020)
9. Drechsler, K., Gregory, R., Wagner, H.T., Tumbas, S.: At the crossroads between digital innovation and digital transformation. Commun. Assoc. Inf. Syst. **47**, 521–538 (2020). https://doi.org/10.17705/1CAIS.04723
10. Ekbia, H.R.: Digital artifacts as quasi-objects: qualification, mediation, and materiality. J. Am. Soc. Inf. Sci. Technol. **60**, 2554–2566 (2009)
11. Yoo, Y., Henfridsson, O., Lyytinen, K.: The new organizing logic of digital innovation: an agenda for information systems research. Inf. Syst. Res. **21**, 724–735 (2010)
12. Kallinikos, J., Aaltonen, A., Marton, A.: A theory of digital objects. First Monday **15**, 1–28 (2010)
13. Kallinikos, J., Aaltonen, A., Marton, A.: The ambivalent ontology of digital artifacts. MIS Q. **37**, 357–370 (2013)
14. Faulkner, P., Runde, J.: Technology objects, social positions and the tranformational model of social activity. MiS Quaterly. **37**, 803–818 (2013)
15. Faulkner, P., Runde, J.: Theorizing the digital object. MIS Q. **43**, 1278–1302 (2019)
16. Guizzardi, G.: Ontological foundations for structural conceptual models (2005)
17. Benevides, A.B., Bourguet, J.R., Guizzardi, G., Peñaloza, R., Almeida, J.P.A.: Representing a reference foundational ontology of events in SROIQ. Appl. Ontol. **14**, 293–334 (2019)
18. de Oliveira Bringuente, A.C., de Almeida Falbo, R., Guizzardi, G.: Using a foundational ontology for reengineering a software process ontology. J. Inf. Data Manag. **2**, 511 (2011)
19. Guizzardi, G., Wagner, G., Almeida, J.P.A., Guizzardi, R.S.S.: Towards ontological foundations for conceptual modeling: the unified foundational ontology (UFO) story. Appl. Ontol. **10**, 259–271 (2015)
20. Hui, Y.: What is a digital object? Metaphilosophy **43**, 380–395 (2012)
21. Faulkner, P., Runde, J.: On the identity of technological objects and user innovations in function. Acad. Manag. Rev. **34**, 442–462 (2009)
22. Faulkner, P., Runde, J.: The social, the material, and the ontology of non-material technological objects. In: European Group for Organizational Studies (EGOS) Colloquium, Gothenburg, pp. 1–34. Citeseer (2011)
23. Verdonck, M., Gailly, F.: Insights on the use and application of ontology and conceptual modeling languages in ontology-driven conceptual modeling. In: Comyn-Wattiau, I., Tanaka, K., Song, I.-Y., Yamamoto, S., Saeki, M. (eds.) ER 2016. LNCS, vol. 9974, pp. 83–97. Springer, Cham (2016). https://doi.org/10.1007/978-3-319-46397-1_7
24. Guizzardi, G., Bernasconi, A., Pastor, O., Storey, V.C.: Ontological unpacking as explanation: the case of the viral conceptual model. In: Ghose, A., Horkoff, J., Silva Souza, V.E., Parsons, J., Evermann, J. (eds.) ER 2021. LNCS, vol. 13011, pp. 356–366. Springer, Cham (2021). https://doi.org/10.1007/978-3-030-89022-3_28
25. Markosian, N.: What are physical objects? Philos. Phenomenol. Res. **61**, 375–395 (2000)

"All the Things that Come and Go, Stop and Say Hello": Towards an ontological account of how participants enter and exit events

Fabrício Henrique Rodrigues[1]([⊠])[iD], Joel Luís Carbonera[1][iD],
Lucas Valadares Vieira[1,2], and Mara Abel[1][iD]

[1] Informatics Institute, Federal University of Rio Grande Do Sul, Porto Alegre, Brazil
{fabricio.rodrigues,joel.carbonera,marabel}@inf.ufrgs.br,
lucasvaladares@petrobras.com.br
[2] Petrobras, Rio de Janeiro, Brazil

Abstract. This paper presents an ontological account for how participants enter or exit events, based on a view of events as delimited by systems. With that, we introduce the notions of *engaging* and *disengaging event* as the events through which (respectively) an object becomes or ceases to be a participant of a main, external event by becoming or ceasing to be a component of the system that delimits this external event. We argue that it is a general type of event with many practical examples, which reveals a contextual facet of events and may shed light on the notion of roles for events.

Keywords: Ontologies · Events · Processes · Occurrents · Systems · Roles · Context

1 Introduction

On 8 February 2021 the Spanish magazine *Sport* dedicated its cover story to the football match between Barcelona and Real Betis that happened the day before. It read: *"Messi changed the game with his entry in the 57th minute and led the comeback of a team that already has 6 consecutive victories"*.[1] The emphasis on reporting such a happening exemplifies an important fact: to make sense of the world we need to consider not only the objects that surround us, but also what happens to them, i.e., the events in which they are involved. In fact, it seems that a great part of our reality is fundamentally dependent on events (e.g., from chemical reactions to social gatherings). Hence, any attempt to make a faithful representation of reality should pay attention to this aspect.

Representing reality is the business of ontologies. In Computer Science, an ontology is the specification of a system of categories accounting for a certain

---

[1] twitter.com/BarcaTimes/status/1358557234486272000 (original in Spanish at sport.es/es/noticias/comunicacion/portada-hoy-11504710).

J. Ralyté et al. (Eds.): ER 2022, LNCS 13607, pp. 102–112, 2022.
https://doi.org/10.1007/978-3-031-17995-2_8

view of the world [8]. It not only includes categories for both the things that *are* in time (e.g., a person, a piece of rock, a machine), which are called *continuants*[2], but may also cover things that *happen* in time (e.g., a meeting, the erosion of a mountain, the manufacturing of a good), which we are called *events*[3]. Indeed, current ontologies offer rich support to model various aspects of events [12].

Nevertheless, taking a closer look on the mentioned magazine issue, we can notice that it reported not just any sort of event, but a rather noteworthy case: an event that affects the course of another event. In particular, it consisted in the entry of a participant (i.e., Lionel Messi) in an external, main event (i.e., the ongoing football match). There are many examples like this one (e.g., hiring a new professional to an ongoing project, replacing an equipment during an industrial process), which evidences a more general type of event. Moreover, it reveals a facet of the context of events, i.e., the way events affect one another by feeding or taking away participants, and helps to explain the issue of variation of participants along an event (e.g., the ways in which it happens). This may be useful for evaluating models according to the correctness of the distribution of participants along an event as well as for making inferences about implicit events. Even so, the nature of such sort of event does not seem to get much attention in current efforts regarding the ontology of events.

With that, in this paper we propose an ontological account for events through which participants enter and exit other events, based on a view of events as delimited by systems [13]. Sect. 2 recollects some background notions to convey the idea of this paper, Sect. 3 presents our proposal, Sect. 4 presents an example to illustrate it, and Sect. 5 brings our concluding remarks.

2   Background Notions

Continuants are things that continue to exist through time while maintaining their identity, being wholly present at any time point they are present [1]. *Objects* are continuants that are existentially independent of other entities (e.g., a person, a ball). *Individualized properties* are continuants that are existentially dependent on other continuants (e.g., the height of a person, the color of a ball, a contract imposing obligations between two people). We say that an individualized property *inheres* in the continuant(s) on which it depends, which are the bearer(s) of the property.

In this work, we regard a *situation* as an instantaneous, particular configuration of a part of reality that is understood as a whole [10,11]. It is determined by a snapshot at a given instant of a collection of one or more objects, i.e., a set of attributions referring to individualized properties (intrinsic and/or relational) inhering in such objects, and/or about formal relations among them. If a situation s is a snapshot of a collection of objects which includes the object o, we say that o is present at s and that s includes o.

---

[2] Sometimes also referred to as endurants.

[3] Sometimes also referred to as processes, perdurants, or occurrents.

Dispositions are individualized properties [2,10,14] that determine the behavior that their bearers will show under certain circumstances [14], corresponding to what we usually broadly refer to as capacities, tendencies, and so on [7,14]. As such, dispositions are characterized by exhibiting characteristic manifestations under some stimulus conditions [7]. We consider that the stimulus conditions for a disposition *d* inhering in an object *x* include some object *y* that is external to *x* and that bears some property that matches *d* [5, ch.4.3]. Also, there must be some relationship between *x* and *y* so that the matching properties can be exposed to each other [14][5, ch.4.3]. An example is the fragility of a piece of glass, i.e., the disposition to break in response to being struck [2]. In this case, the striking event brings about a situation that gathers the stimulus conditions for the fragility disposition (i.e., a hard object exerting pressure over the glass) that lead to its manifestation in the event of glass breaking.

We regard a (concrete) *system* as a complex object composed of a collection of at least two interrelated material components forming an integrated, unitary whole [3][6, p.4] . The components of a system are linked by what is called *connections*, i.e., relations through which (at least) one of the relata affects the behavior of the other, changing the way the object will behave given certain circumstances [6, p.6] [3], so that its behavior is different from that they would exhibit if they were not in such connection [3, p.55–56] (e.g., exerting pressure). Three main facets characterize a system: a definite composition (i.e., the collection of system's components), a definite immediate environment (i.e., the collection of entities that are connected to the system or its components, but that are not themselves components of the system), and a definite structure (i.e., the connections and other properties among system's components as well as between these and the environment) [6].

Events are broadly characterized as things that happen in time. An event is usually regarded as a transition among successive states of the world [4][6, p.22] or as a transformation of a portion of reality from a situation to another [10]. Events are also regarded as manifestations of dispositions of objects, such that, when we have a situation that gathers all the stimulus conditions needed to activate certain dispositions an event happens, bringing about another situation, which may also gather the stimulus conditions required for the manifestation of further dispositions, leading to another situation and so on [10].

Considering an event as a transformation of portion of reality, it remains the question of how to delimit such portion of reality. Regarding this, [13] proposes delimiting events using the notion of systems, restricting an event to a transition among situations that are snapshots of a single, invariant system over time. The idea goes as follows. For a disposition to be manifested, its bearer must stand in a relation with another object in a way that the stimulus conditions of the disposition are fulfilled. This relation clearly changes the behavior of the bearer of the disposition, since it would behave differently (i.e., not manifesting the disposition) if such a relation were not present - what characterizes the relation as a *connection*. In fact, any relation in which an object stands and that provides some of the stimulus conditions for the activation of one of its dispositions consists in a *dispositional connection* (i.e., a relationship that partially (or fully) fulfills the stimulus conditions of a disposition of one of its relata [13]).

Given that, whenever a disposition is manifested we necessarily have a system composed of at least two objects and a dispositional connection between them. Then, every event that is the manifestation of some disposition requires a system in order to happen. Its initial situation is a snapshot of a system with its components arranged in a way that activates certain of their dispositions. The situation the event brings about after that is another configuration of the same system that results from the manifestation of those dispositions. Therefore, for every disposition manifestation, there is a corresponding event consisting in a transition between snapshots of a system. Moreover, the resulting snapshot of the system may consist in an arrangement of its components in order to further activate their dispositions, which keeps the event going on. This recurrent correspondence between the manifestation of dispositions and the transition between snapshots of the system that activates them suggests the pervasive nature of this type of event, which were called *system-event* (i.e., an event whose course is composed of situations that are snapshots of a single system. [13]).

In a system-event, its participants maximally compose a system that persists during the happening of the event and whose connections are responsible for the manifestations of the dispositions that bring about the successive situations in the course of the event. Also, it is said that such a system delimits the event. Thus, being a participant of a system-event at an instant t consists in being, at t, a component of the system that delimits the event and vice versa.

3   How Participants Enter and Exit Events

Taking an event e delimited by a system sys, the participants of e at a given instant t are the components of sys at t. Hence, becoming or ceasing to be a participant of e is a matter of becoming or ceasing to be a component of sys. With that, the entry of a participant in e is an event itself, consisting in the transition from a situation in which an object does not qualify as a component of sys to a situation in which it qualifies (and the other way around for the exit of a participant). Let us call *main event* the event that gains and/or loses participants, *engaging event* and *disengaging event* the events through which a participant enters and leaves a main event (respectively), which we will broadly call *exchange events*.

An exchange event necessarily has a temporal overlap with its main event. The ending situation of an engaging event is tied to the same time point of the situation in which the new participant first appears in the course of the main event (e.g., the ending situation of a player's entry in a match temporally coincides with the first situation in the match that includes the player). Analogously, the initial situation of a disengaging event temporally coincides with the situation in which the leaving participant lastly appears in the main event.

Despite this temporal overlap, an exchange event cannot be part of its main event. This is so because at least one situation in the course of every exchange event necessarily includes an object that does not participate in the main event at the time (i.e., that is outside its delimiting system). Putting it another way, an exchange event and its main event are transformations of different portions of reality. Still, although such events are not mereologically related, there is a relation between them beyond a simple temporal overlap, which we explore now.

3.1 Engaging and Disengaging Events

We can think an exchange event in three levels of abstraction. The outermost one regards its distinctive feature, i.e., its relation with a main event. With that, an exchange event is the one that operates a variation in the participants during the happening of a main event. That is, it is by means of an exchange event that an object becomes or ceases to be a participant of a given system-invariant event. On an intermediate level, an exchange event is the entry/exit of a component into/from the system that delimits an ongoing main event. Finally, on the innermost level of abstraction, an exchange event is generally a local interaction involving objects inside and outside the system that delimits the main event, implying modifications in such a system.

For example, let us consider a party as an event system delimited by a complex system composed of all the guests, the musicians who are playing for people to dance, the reception staff, and so on. The entry of a guest in the party would be the guest's entry in such a system through an interaction with some of its components of the system, e.g., presenting a ticket to someone in the reception.

To illustrate this view in three levels of abstraction, Fig. 1 presents the an *engaging event* in which a participant *a* enters into an event *main*. In Fig. 1(A) we have what fundamentally happened: an event which we will call *aux*, consisting in the transition between situations *s-aux$_1$* and *s-aux$_2$*, happening during the time interval $[t_1,t_2]$. In *s-aux$_1$*, objects *a* and *b* stand in a dispositional connection of type *Q*, which fulfills the stimulus conditions to activate some dispositions inhering in *a* and *b*. Then the manifestation of such dispositions results in *s-aux$_2$*, with *a* and *b* standing in a dispositional connection of type *R*.

As depicted in Fig. 1(B), during the interval $[t_1,t_2]$, *b* was a component of a system *sys*, which consists in a collection of objects maximally connected by relations of type *R*. Thus, being a component of *sys* is a matter of being connected to another of its components through a relation of type *R*. At time t_1, the components of *sys* were the objects *b*, *c*, and *d*. Given the happening of *aux*, object *a* becomes connected to *b* through a relation of type *R* (situation *s-aux$_2$*). With that, *a* meets the requirements to be a component of *sys* from t_2 onwards.

Finally, in Fig. 1(C) we observe that *sys* was delimiting another event, which we will call main, consisting in the transition among the situations *s-main$_1$*, *s-main$_2$* and *s-main$_3$*, which are snapshots of *sys* during the interval $[t_1,t_3]$. As a component of *sys* in the interval $[t_2,t_3]$, *a* was present at situations *s-main$_2$* and *s-main$_3$*, being a participant of *main* during this interval.

Summing up, the event *aux* establishes a connection *R* between *a* and *b*, in virtue of which *a* became a component of *sys* and, as a consequence, *a* became a participant of *main*. Therefore, *aux* is an exchange event of *main*. That is, above

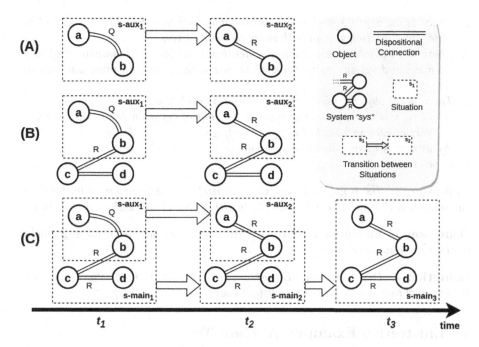

Fig. 1. The three levels of abstraction of an exchange event.

all, *aux* is the event in which *a* and *b* ceased to stand in a relation of type *Q* and acquired a relation of type *R*. The event *aux* just happened to modify *sys* because *b* was a component of such a system. Furthermore, *aux* just happened to affect the external event *main* for *sys* happened to delimit *main*.

With that, an exchange event is an independent event that, given the circumstances in which it happens, ends up affecting a parallel system-event. That is, it fundamentally is a plain event that contextually plays the role of exchange event in relation to some main system-event. This context is given by some relationship between the exchange event and its main event. Such a relationship is based on an overlap between the systems that delimit each of these events, which entails an overlap between situations in the course of both events.

Then, given a system-event *main* delimited by *sys-main* that happens during the interval i_{main}, an event *aux* delimited by *sys-aux* that happens during the interval i_{aux}, two distinct time points t_1 and t_2 that are both in i_{main} and i_{aux}, we can define the *engagingIn* and *disengagingFrom* relations as well as the *engaging* and *disengaging* events (definitions 1 to 4). In the following section we work upon an illustrative case of system-event presented in [13] to exemplify the use of engaging and disengaging events.

Definition 1. *engagingIn(aux,main)* $=_{def}$ *a binary relation between events* aux *and* main *such that*

1. *There is an object* a *that is a component of both* sys-main *and* sys-aux *at* t_1 *(and, thus, participates in both* main *and* aux *at* t_1);
2. *There is an object* b *(which may be identical to* a*) that is a component of both* sys-main *and* sys-aux *at* t_2 *(and, thus, participates in both* main *and* aux *at* t_2);
3. *There is an object* x *(distinct from* a *and* b*) such that*
   (a) *at* t_1, x *is a component of* sys-aux, *but not of* sys-main *(and thus, at* t_1, *it participates in* aux, *but not in* main*); and*
   (b) *at* t_2 x *is a component of* sys-main.
4. t_1 *precedes* t_2

Definition 2. *disengagingFrom(aux, main)* $=_{def}$ *a binary relation between* aux *and* main *that meets conditions (1) to (3) in def. 3, but with* t_2 *preceding* t_1.

Definition 3. *Engaging Event* $=_{def}$ *An event that stands in an* engagingIn *relation to some system-event.*

Definition 4. *Disengaging Event* $=_{def}$ *An event that stands in an* disengagingFrom *relation to some system-event.*

4   Illustrative Example: A Train Trip

Back to the news realm, let us take an excerpt of an article of *The New York Times* from 6 May 2021: *"From a peak of running more than 60 trains a day, Eurostar cut service during the pandemic to one daily round trip between London and Paris, and one on its London-Brussels and Amsterdam routes"*.[4]

In this excerpt, the term *trip* (or *train trip*) refers to an event in which a train departs from an origin station and travels towards a final destination station, carrying some passengers. Moreover, it is not simply a non-stop origin-to-end trip, with train stopping by intermediary stations along its route so that people can enter in and/or leave the train - that is, to allow events of *boarding* (i.e., a person getting on a train to travel somewhere[5]) and *deboarding* (i.e., a person leaving the train to quit the trip). With some simplification, we consider as the participants of a train trip the train, the train driver, and the passengers. Also for simplification, we consider that a person participates in a trip during the time s/he is onboard a train that has already departed from the origin, but does not participate in any trip while waiting at the station. Given that, we can regard a *train trip* as a transportation event, comprising changes in the spatial position of its participants, which are distributed along a route.

Hence, a *train trip* can be characterized as an event delimited by a system composed of a train, a driver, and some passengers. These components bear some properties that characterize the structure of the system. All of them bear a spatial position, whose value changes with the happening of the trip. Passengers

---

[4] www.nytimes.com/2021/05/06/business/eurostar-moves-to-double-its-london-paris-service-to-two-trains-a-day.html.

[5] collinsdictionary.com/dictionary/english/board.

and driver have the disposition of *transportability* (i.e., capability of being moved or conveyed from one place to another[6]), which is manifested in the trip. The stimulus conditions for manifesting this disposition include (1) the person being inside of a vehicle and (2) the vehicle being in movement. The driver also bears the disposition of *driving ability*, whose stimulus conditions include having access to the controls of the train. Finally, the train has dispositions complementary to those of the other components, such as its capacity to carry the objects that are inside it and its disposition to be driven.

The structure of the system includes the *contains* relation between the train and each person inside it. This relation qualifies as a dispositional connection for fulfilling the stimulus condition (1) for transportability, exposing it to the transporting capacity of the train. The structure also includes the *guided by* relation between the driver and the train, which means that the driver has access to the controls of the train. It is also a dispositional connection for fulfilling a stimulus condition for the driver's driving ability. The environment includes objects that are related to its components in some other way (e.g., stations).

With that, we have a system that unifies the course of the trip and establishes a closure with respect to what participates in the trip at any given instant, excluding other objects that interact with the participants, but that are not regarded as participants themselves (e.g., stations, traffic controllers). Besides that, it allows us to account for the possible variation of participants (e.g., passengers) during the event, which result from the events following described.

4.1 Boarding and Deboarding as Engaging and Disengaging Events

A *boarding* event is the transition between two situations: one including a station at which a train is stopped and a person waits, and another in which the person is inside the train stopped at the station. Thus, *boarding* is the event of ceasing a *waiting at* relation between a person and a station and establishing a *contains* relation between a train and the person, in virtue of which the person becomes a component of a system that is delimiting a trip, becoming a participant of such a trip. With that, *boarding* is an *engaging event* in respect to *train trip*. Analogously, *deboarding* is a *disengaging event* in respect to *train trip* since it ceases the *contains* relation that makes a person participate in the trip.

Figure 2 exemplifies the case of a *boarding* event. There is a train trip event happening as the transition among situations *s-trip$_1$* to *s-trip$_4$*. During the interval $[t_1,t_2]$, its participants are a train, a driver, and passengers p_1 and p_2. In the interval $[t_3,t_4]$, the trip also involves the passenger p_3. This variation in participants in the interval $[t_2,t_3]$ is the result of a parallel boarding event consisting in the transition between situations *s-boarding$_1$* to *s-boarding$_2$*, bound to times t_2 and t_3, respectively. This event involves the same train that participates in the trip, the station at which the train is stopped, and person p_3, who is waiting at the station in *s-boarding$_1$* and is inside the train in to *s-boarding$_2$*. We can see the overlap of the situations in the course of both events. The train participates

---

[6] wordnetweb.princeton.edu/perl/webwn?s=transportable.

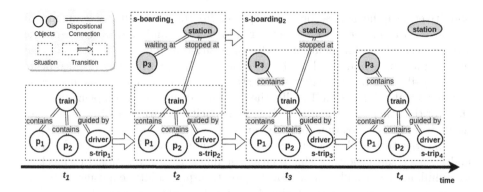

Fig. 2. The train trip main event and the boarding engaging event.

at both events during the interval $[t_2, t_3]$ (being present at the situations in the course of both events), while p_3 only participates in the boarding event at t_2 (being present at *s-boarding$_1$* but not at *s-trip$_2$*) and participates in both events at t_3 (being present at both *s-boarding$_2$* and *s-trip$_3$*).

5   Concluding Remarks

This work presented an ontological analysis of how participants take part in or leave events. It employed the view that an event is a transition among situations that are snapshots of a single system of connected components so that the participants in the event at an instant t are the components of such a system at t. With that, we proposed the notions of *engaging* and *disengaging events* as the events through which an object becomes or ceases to be a participant of another, external event by becoming or ceasing to be a component of the system that delimits this external event.

A noteworthy point of our work is that it brings to light a contextual facet of events. The notions of *engaging event* and *disengaging event* along with the *engagingIn* and *disengagingFrom* relations can be used to build a 'feeding' network of events, characterizing how events are linked in respect to the exchange of participants - which is not covered by subsumption, mereological, temporal, or successively causal relations. With that, our approach may help in modeling types of events characterized by the entry/exit of participants during its occurrence (e.g., manufacturing processes, with different tools being employed in different stages and new components being added to the unfinished product). It may also be useful for inferences about implicit events and relations between events.

Besides that, this work seems to shed some light on the notion of roles for events. It points out that certain types of events are not instantiated in virtue of what an event is on its own, but just in relation to its context - in particular, in relation to other events. E.g., a boarding event is in essence the event of a person

p entering in a train t that is stopped at a station s, which, however, happens in the special circumstance of t taking part on an ongoing trip. Suppose instead that we had t on display in an exposition of trains held at s and p enters t to take a look inside. It would still be exactly the same event of someone entering a train, but no longer a boarding event.

The idea of roles that an entity may play in relation to others is widely employed in applied ontology, but usually restricted to continuants, with just a few works mentioning the possibility of event roles [9, 12]. Thus, in this work we bring an analogous view by defining relations among events and types of event defined in terms of such relations, although still restricted to a specific aspect of events (i.e., the entry and exit of participants).

Acknowledgements. Research supported by CAPES (Funding Code 001), CNPq, and Project Petwin (financed by FINEP and LIBRA Consortium). The third author also thanks the support of Petrobras.

References

1. Arp, R., Smith, B., Spear, A.D.: Building Ontologies with Basic Formal Ontology. The MIT Press (2015)
2. Barton, A., Jansen, L., Ethier, J.F.: A taxonomy of disposition-parthood. In: Joint Ontology Workshops (JOWO 2017), vol. 2050. CEUR-WS (2017)
3. von Bertalanffy, L.: General Systems Theory Foundations, Development, Applications, Revised George Braziller, New York (1968)
4. Botti Benevides, A., Masolo, C.: States, events, and truth-makers. In: FOIS 2014, pp. 93–102. IOS Press, Amsterdam (2014)
5. Bunge, M.: Treatise on Basic Philosophy: Ontology I: The Furniture of the World, vol. 1. D. Reidel Publishing Company, Dordrecht (1977)
6. Bunge, M.: Treatise on Basic Philosophy: Ontology II: A World of Systems, vol. 4. D. Reidel Publishing Company, Dordrecht (1979)
7. Choi, S., Fara, M.: Dispositions. In: The Stanford Encyclopedia of Philosophy. Metaphysics Research Lab, Stanford University, Fall 2018 ed. (2018)
8. Guarino, N.: Formal Ontology and Information Systems. In: International Conference on Formal Ontology and Information Systems (FOIS'98), pp. 3–15 (1998)
9. Guarino, N., Baratella, R., Guizzardi, G.: Events, their names, and their synchronic structure. Appl. Ontol. **17**(2), 249–283 (2022)
10. Guizzardi, G., Wagner, G., de Almeida Falbo, R., Guizzardi, R.S.S., Almeida, J.P.A.: Towards ontological foundations for the conceptual modeling of events. In: Ng, W., Storey, V.C., Trujillo, J.C. (eds.) ER 2013. LNCS, vol. 8217, pp. 327–341. Springer, Heidelberg (2013). https://doi.org/10.1007/978-3-642-41924-9_27
11. Herre, H.: General formal ontology (GFO): a foundational ontology for conceptual modelling. In: Poli, R., Healy, M., Kameas, A. (eds) Theory and Applications of Ontology: Computer Applications. Springer, Dordrecht (2010). https://doi.org/10.1007/978-90-481-8847-5_14
12. Rodrigues, F.H., Abel, M.: What to consider about events: a survey on the ontology of occurrents. Appl. Ontol. **14**(4), 343–378 (2019)

13. Rodrigues, F.H., Carbonera, J.L., Vieira, L.V., Garcia, L.F., Abel, M.: What delimits an event: systems as invariant elements along events. In: ONTOBRAS 2021), vol. 3050, pp. 218–230. CEUR-RS (2021)
14. Röhl, J., Jansen, L.: Representing dispositions. J. of Biomed. Semantics **2**(4), S4 (2011)

Applications of Conceptual Modeling

Characterizing Fake News: A Conceptual Modeling-based Approach

Nicolas Belloir[1,2]([⊠]) [iD], Wassila Ouerdane[3] [iD], and Oscar Pastor[4] [iD]

[1] CREC St-Cyr, Académie Militaire de St-Cyr Coëtquidan, Guer, France
[2] IRISA, Vannes, France
nicolas.belloir@irisa.fr
[3] MICS, CentraleSupélec, Université Paris-Saclay, Gif sur Yvette, France
[4] PROS Research Group, Universitat Politècnica de València, Valencia, Spain

Abstract. For some time, and even more so now, Fake News has increasingly occupied the media and social space. How identify Fake News and conspiracy theories have become an extremely attractive research area. However, the lack of a solid and well-founded conceptual characterization of what exactly Fake News is and what are its main characteristics, makes it difficult to manage their understanding, identification, and detection. This research work advocates that conceptual modeling must plays a crucial role in characterizing Fake News content accurately. Only by delimiting what Fake News is will it be possible to understand and manage their different perspectives and dimensions, with the ultimate goal of developing a reliable framework for online Fake News detection, as much automated as possible. To contribute in that direction from a pure and practical conceptual modeling perspective, this paper proposes a precise conceptual model of Fake Newss, an essential element for any explainable Artificial Intelligence (XAI)-based approach that must be based on the shared understanding of the domain that only such an accurate conceptualization dimension can facilitate.

Keywords: Conceptual Modeling · Characterization · Fake News · Explainable Artificial Intelligence

1 Introduction

Conceptual modeling is a discipline that contributes rich and diverse results when applied to well-understand the conceptual support of a particular domain of interest. One domain especially interesting nowadays is the Fake News one. Although Fake News is not a new phenomenon [20], questions such as why it has emerged as a global topic of interest and why it is attracting increasingly more public attention are particularly relevant in our times. The leading cause is that fake news can be created and published online faster and cheaper when compared to traditional news media such as newspapers and television [18]. In addition, recent discussions of higher education's failure to teach students how to identify Fake News have appeared in leading newspapers [14].

J. Ralyté et al. (Eds.): ER 2022, LNCS 13607, pp. 115–129, 2022.
https://doi.org/10.1007/978-3-031-17995-2_9

Conceptual Modeling should play an essential role to understand and communicate what Fake News is. In a sound Information Conceptual Modeling context, a correct data management of Fake News must be supported by a precise conceptual characterization of "what" a Fake News is. This is where Conceptual Modeling becomes a crucial actor. If an information structure must represent a conceptualization, the entities that represent that conceptualization must be explicitly determined. Any information system intended to register information about Fake News must identify in detail what are the relevant entities that conceptually characterize the different dimensions that must be considered to treat Fake News data correctly. Ontologically speaking, a precise ontological commitment that involves a precise identification of the relevant entities that constitute the conceptualization must be stated. Our previous work [5] has focused on exploring what are the concepts that should be considered for achieving that purpose. In this paper we introduce the result of such an ontological analysis, by presenting a conceptual model of Fake News. This is the main contribution here addressed, by facing a fundamental question regarding the terminology and the ontology of Fake News: what constitutes and qualifies as Fake News?

To achieve that goal, in Sect. 2 we discuss the literature and show that the views on the concept of Fake News are not unified. In order to propose the conceptual model of FN, the Sect. 3 summarizes the key notions that need to be considered when the goal is to provide a robust conceptual characterization of the notion of FN. These key notions are derived from a previous work. As a consequence, a precise definition of Fake News is proposed, and a Fake News Conceptual Model is presented in Sect. 4. A discussion of the application of this conceptual model as an initial building block for an XAI approach is provided in Sect. 5. Concluding remarks and the list of used references complete the work.

2 Related Work

In recent years, different works were interested in studying and understanding the nature of information encompassed in Fake News. Indeed, to help online users identify valuable information, there has been extensive research on establishing practical and automatic frameworks for online Fake News detection [2,24,25].

An important element is to be able to identify very clearly what is a Fake News or what are the principal features characterizing it. However, what we can notice first in the literature is that the concept of Fake News is still ambiguous, and the frontier between the definition of Fake News and other related concepts, such as mis-information, des-information, hoax news, propaganda news, etc., is blurred. Indeed, as it is illustrated by some categorization examples [11,20,21], it is not always clear or precise how these different concepts are related, or how we can distinguish between theme. On the other hand, as we can see in Table 1, several definitions of Fake News have been proposed in the literature, most of which include falsehood and the news form as common factors. Even if it can be argued that there is some common intuition on what a Fake News is, what we can note is that it is difficult to have a consensus and a unified vision on what "exactly" -conceptually-speaking- a Fake News is.

Table 1. A sample of Fake News definitions

Definitions	Reference
Fake News is a news article that is intentionally and verifiably false	[18]
Fake News are intentionally false news published by a news outlet	[25]
Fabricated news articles that could be potentially or intentionally misleading for the readers	[15]
News articles that are intentionally and verifiably false, and could mislead readers	[1]
Fabricated information that mimics news media content in form but not in organisational process or intent	[12]
Fake News are fabricated stories presented as if they were originating from legitimate sources with an intention to deceive	[10]

A recent work has proposed a first step towards a characterization of Fake News [13]. It introduces a taxonomy of operational indicators in four domain (message, source, structure, and network) to distinguish seven types of online content under the label of "Fake News" (false news, polarized content, satire, etc.). The proposed characterization is of interest, but it is not based on a precise conceptual model, which is our contribution in this paper. As a representation that captures the conceptualization of a person's understanding of a domain, a conceptual model is the natural strategy for obtaining a reliable representation of the domain that is used by human users to support communication, discussion, negotiation, etc. In our context, it allows us to define a domain with specific and precise semantics. Moreover, the conceptual model will expose the relationships between the concepts composing the Fake News in a more informative and robust way, which will offer a reliable and practical means for the detection or even automatic generation of Fake News. In this line, [22] have proposed a conceptual model to examine the phenomenon of Fake News. Their model focuses on the relationship between the creator and the consumer of the information, and proposes a mechanism to determine the likelihood that users will share their Fake News with others. In contrast, in this paper, we are particularly interested in the conceptualization of the content of Fake News.

A further advantage of relying upon a conceptual model is its ability to facilitate building well-justified and explainable models for Fake News detection and generation, which, to date, have rarely been available. Works as [4] explores and integrates the use of ontologies (OWL-based) trying to detect fake news on social media by identifying contextual features for news articles. However, as it was emphasized by [23,25], despite the surge of works around the concept of Fake News, how one can automatically assess news authenticity in an *effective* and *explainable* manner is still an open issue, especially due to the lack of the precise conceptual characterization of the Fake News concept that this paper advocates.

Facilitating explainability and interpretability has been of great interest in artificial intelligence and machine learning research (see for instance [6,7]). Indeed, eXplainable Artificial Intelligence (XAI) is recognized as a major need for future applications. It aims to produce intelligent systems that enhance the confidence of users to understand the underlying reasoning and automations [3,9]. For Fake News context, to our knowledge, works involving explainability feature within Fake News detection methods are still at their beginning [17].

In this paper, we propose an original approach to contribute to understanding what is a Fake News. Our proposal is novel at different levels. First, we offer to characterize Fake News content by relying on a Conceptual Model. A conceptual understanding of Fake News will help us distinguish them better and rule them from real news. A well-grounded conceptual characterization would make feasible to go beyond what the classical approaches normally do, by opening the door to design a Fake News generation process fully guided by the Conceptual Model. More precisely, we follow the XAI-based process proposed by [19] to facilitate building well-justified and explainable models for Fake News generation. Our aim is to propose an approach that is understandable, trustable and manageable to humans, as suggested in [8]. More specifically, the different steps suggested by [19] are: (i) Get a shared understanding of the domain (ii) Understand the task and select the right scope (iii) Collect the right data and improve its quality (iv) Select AI techniques that deliver results (v) Generate good explanations, and (vi) Evolve the solution over time. Our contribution establishes the foundation of such a process by solving the first, essential step of getting a shared understanding of what a Fake News is by introducing a precise conceptual model of Fake News. From that sound conceptual basis, the rest of the proposed XAI process can be applied in a reliable way. The explainability with our approach is conceptually guided by the conceptual model which conforms the core of the contribution: to have an ontologically well-grounded definition of what a Fake News is, which is directly derived from the conceptual model.

3   Characterization of Fake News

We briefly present our definition of the concept of Fake News and a summary of the essential semantic elements to be considered in the characterization of the concept of fake news. Both have been proposed and discussed in a previous publication [5] and we invite the reader who wants more details to consult it.

Definition 1. (Fake News) *A Fake News is false but verifiable news composed of false facts based on real ones. Drafted in a way to trigger an emotional load, it aims to deceive its readers and influence their opinion through an implicit conclusion.*

Among the highlights that have been identified, one concerns the origin of fake news. Indeed, in the same way that a cyber-attack is rarely the work of a single person but rather that of an organized group or even a state service, Fake News is rarely created by an isolated person. However, identifying the chain of creation of a Fake News allows us to understand what objective it serves, and therefore to better understand and counter it. Thus, a conceptual model of Fake News must be able to take into account the entities that were involved in the creation of a Fake News and the different levels of decision-making involved. For example, at the moment Fake News target pro-Ukrainian political figures. This is part of an operational context aimed at manipulating pro-Ukrainian opinion and part of a strategic vision that seeks to justify the Ukrainian-Russian war.

Fake News is usually built on a distortion of reality. Representing this distortion is a second point of interest for the characterization of a fake news. Indeed, even if we can find fake news totally false, most of the time they are built by mixing true facts and false facts. This increases its credibility. The thinner the line between the two, the more real the fake news seems. Here, by fact, we mean the facts reported by the Fake News, and not facts that would be proven facts, that is to say facts that really happened. We call the latter real facts. The real facts can take different forms. For instance, real facts can come from a political statement, an event that occurred, or real data such as a photo or video. In the same way, different types of false facts exist. Here, what we call false facts are the elements of disinformation propagated by the fake news. Indeed, as mentioned earlier, false facts may not be based on any real element. This makes it less credible. Other times, the false fact may be constituted by distortion of real elements. Photos or videos can be altered, articles can be falsified. Finally, one can take them out of their context of real facts for example, or associate several real facts but independent of each other.

In order to reinforce the credibility of a Fake News, their authors often use an "authority". The latter can be of different nature but its objective is always to reinforce the realistic side of the Fake News by relying on a reassuring element. This authority can be of three types: internal, external or false. In the first two cases, the authority is real. For the first one, the authority can be a person or an entity in direct link with the subject carried by the Fake News. In the second case, it may be a reference to a historical authority whose word or deed is considered true and safe. Finally, in the last case, the authority may be totally invented or its field of competence may have nothing to do with the information carried by the Fake News.

Fake News is constructed to influence the opinion of its target by generating an emotional charge. The reaction of the target leads him to draw certain conclusions and to change his opinion on a subject. That is the objective. Identifying the latter and knowing who the Fake News is aimed at is therefore a challenge in order to try to counter it. Thus, in a conceptual model, three aspects need to be addressed: the target, its opinion on a topic and the way in which the Fake News will change it. It can seek to strengthen or weaken it. We talk about the goal of Fake News. The human mind can be seen as a two-tiered system. The first is instinctive, almost automatic. It reacts to perception, to emotion. The second is slower, more analytical. Fake News takes advantage of these two systems. It generates an emotion which makes the first system react. Then, in a second step, the second system analyzes the reaction to the emotion and to what generated it and draws conclusions. A Fake News must therefore be able to trigger an emotion. It does this by a catalyst mechanism. Then, the target of the Fake News reacts to this emotion and goes where the Fake News wants to take him. This is what we call an emotional load. Without it, the brain analyzes the fake news in an analytical way and not in an instinctive way. The emotional charge can therefore be seen as the necessary precondition for fake news to work. A conceptual model must therefore be able to capture this mechanism.

The conceptual model that we present is articulated using the three main dimensions of: (i) identification of the origin of the Fake News (the'attacker' dimension) (ii) the relationship between true and false fact (the'fact' dimension), and (iii) the target including opinion and reactive emotion (the'target' dimension). They all together vertebrate the conceptual model of Fake News that we present in the next section.

4   Conceptual Model

In this section, we present a Fake News conceptual model. It captures the main points of view identified through Sect. 3. The *Attacker sub-model* describes the context in which the Fake News is created. The *Target sub-model* allows designing the target population of the Fake News and the psychological effects generated by it. The *Fact sub-model* allows specifying the real fact on which a Fake News is based and the way it will be altered to produce the desired psychological effect.

To illustrate this section, we draw on an identified Fake News that was disseminated during the 2016 U.S. presidential campaign: it was published by a Donald Trump's supporter named Sean Hannity and stated that Trump helped 200 marines to come home after Iraq war as illustrated by the Fig. 1.

Fig. 1. Fake News stating that Donald Trump helped 200 Marines return to the US

4.1   Attacker Sub-model

The Fig. 2 is a part of the complete conceptual model describing the actors directly or indirectly involved in Fake News creation process. As mentioned above, it is common that the creation of a Fake News is the result of a structured disinformation campaign, in which we find a classic division into three levels of responsibility: strategic, operational and tactical. At the head of the organization is the Strategic Attacker managing the Information Warfare and commanding Campaign Leaders. These Campaign Leaders manage the Disinformation Campaigns and have the Fake News Creator under their command to feed these campaigns with Fake News. The latter are created to be conform within a Disinformation Campaign. This is represented by the Is a part of relationship. Moreover, a Disinformation Campaign can also re-use a Fake News for its own purposes. Indeed, some of them can become viral and some campaigns could grasp the opportunity to re-use them to fulfill their own goals. It is represented by the Re-uses relationship. Both Information Warfare and Disinformation Campaign can be characterized by the context in which they are conducted. The Fig. 3 illustrate how data are integrated into the different classes of the conceptual model.

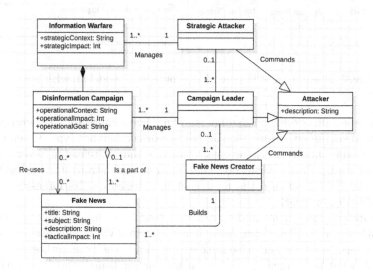

Fig. 2. Fake News attacker conceptual model

4.2 Fact Sub-model

This part of the model illustrated in Fig. 4 details the facts on which a Fake News relies. Figure 5 shows how data populate it.

Fake News is the key notion. The entire diagram is created around it. title of a Fake News consists of its headline and is described by a string. subject corresponds to the category of knowledge it refers to. description is a textual summary of the key ideas contained in. tacticalImpact is an integer evaluating the number of potential readers, expressing the size of the targeted population.

A Fake News relies on at least one Real Fact. Since the context is important to understand the Real Fact itself, it is modeled through the context attribute. The description attribute provides a textual description of the Real Fact. It is characterized by a value stored in an enumeration: DATA, STATEMENT, or EVENT. A Real Fact can also be illustrated by a Document, which can either be a PICTURE, a FIGURE or a VIDEO.

False Facts contains its own description. It can be specified in three categories: made-up event, deformation of the truth or combination of true events,

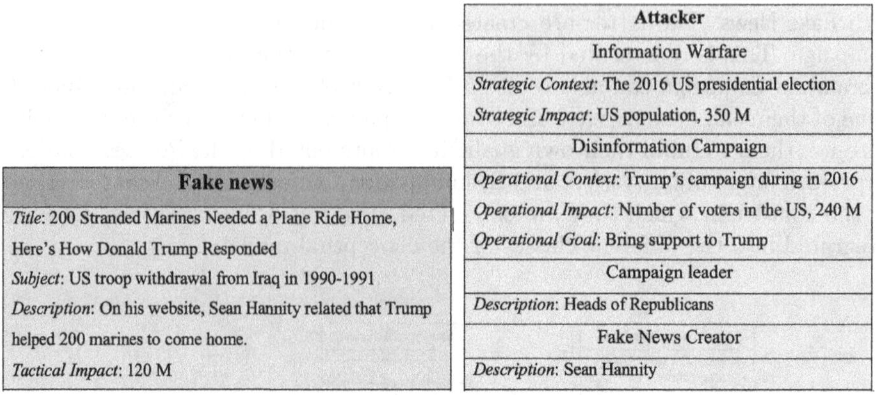

Attacker
Information Warfare
Strategic Context: The 2016 US presidential election
Strategic Impact: US population, 350 M
Disinformation Campaign
Operational Context: Trump's campaign during in 2016
Operational Impact: Number of voters in the US, 240 M
Operational Goal: Bring support to Trump
Campaign leader
Description: Heads of Republicans
Fake News Creator
Description: Sean Hannity

Fake news
Title: 200 Stranded Marines Needed a Plane Ride Home, Here's How Donald Trump Responded
Subject: US troop withdrawal from Iraq in 1990-1991
Description: On his website, Sean Hannity related that Trump helped 200 marines to come home.
Tactical Impact: 120 M

Fig. 3. Illustration of the use of the conceptual model attacker part

which are specializations of False Facts. Thus, False Facts are characterized as either eventDescription, deformationDescription or combinationType. When a false fact is a Combination of true events, it means that it refers to several unrelated Real Facts. Reality Distortion characterizes how strong the distortion is between the False Fact and the Real Fact it is based on. Its intensity can be LOW, MEDIUM or HIGH.

An Authority has a name and an expertise field. The three types of references to an authority discussed above make it possible to divide the concept into two simpler categories: true and false authorities. While the true authority did say or publish what is claimed to have been said or published, the false authority didn't. Thus, a Fake News can call upon an Authority, which can be either a True Authority, linked to a Real Fact, or a False Authority, linked to a False Fact. Both are specializations of Authority. In both cases, the Authority is characterized by a Credibility regarding the fact at hand. A False Authority also includes a Boolean attribute which models whether the Authority is a real entity or not.

4.3   Target Sub-model

Fake News target specific communities and aim at affecting as many people as possible. To do that, they use cognitive mechanisms. The part of the model illustrated in Fig. 6 deals with the target of the Fake News and the process through which it is influenced by the content, while Fig. 7 shows a data example instantiation.

A Target corresponds to the group of people that the Fake News intends to reach and influence. targetCharacteristics are their descriptions. They determine what makes them the Target. targetValues are ideas about which the readers will be especially sensitive about. An effective Fake News will twist these values to elaborate the Trigger Idea and maximize the Emotional Load. Fake News are spread through a media which can be either conventional, state-affiliated, alternative, or social. It is represented by Vector in the model. It also defines the

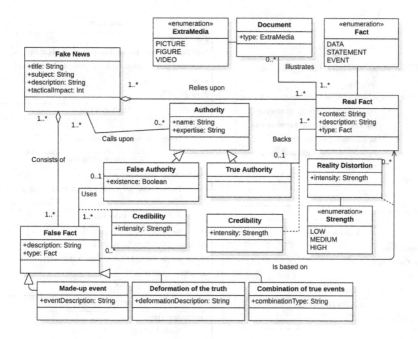

Fig. 4. Fake News fact conceptual model

Trust that the Target has in it. The latter is measured with an intensity: low, medium or high.

A Target expresses an Opinion about an opinionSubject. It is described with the opinionDescription and the type classifies the position: pro, anti, or neutral. This opinion depicts the target's original thinking before being influenced by the Fake News, i.e., changed or strengthened. Note that the manipulation of the Opinion starts with the Disinformation Campaign. The Goal of the Fake News can either be to WEAKEN or STRENGTHEN the opinion expressed by the target. Its action is determined by the Processed Information. Fake News contains Trigger Ideas which represent arguments in favor of the Processed Information. The latter is the mixing effect of an emotion and an information. It represents how the information is assimilated and understood by the target. It is directly responsible for influencing or changing the opinion of the target. Processed Information conveys an implicitConclusion through its Trigger Ideas. Fake News aims to influence opinions and lead the target to come to the desired conclusion. The emotional load enhances the phenomena. The trigger ignites an Emotional Load. Emotional load has a type which can be chosen among the eight standard emotions: JOY, TRUST, FEAR, SURPRISE, SADNESS, ANTICIPATION, ANGER and DISGUST. The intensity of the load is evaluated based on the Plutchik wheel [16].

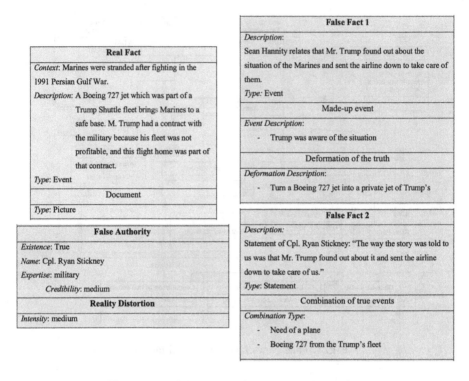

Fig. 5. Illustration of the use of the conceptual model fact part

5   Discussion

The focus of our proposal is a Conceptual Model for Fake News. Our next further work includes a n intensive validation process, that we have started to accomplish through a preliminary validation phase with ten existing Fake News (see Table 2). Results have been very positive: with the support of the conceptual model, we have been able to characterize all of them in detail, what reinforces Fake News communication and management, our main purpose.

For lack of space, we will not detail the study, but we refer the reader to this website: https://people.irisa.fr/Nicolas.Belloir/public/ER2022. Some relevant conclusions have been obtained. Concerning the attacker part of the model, it is sometimes tricky to formally identify the operational and strategic levels in which a Fake News operates. This is not surprising since one of the pillars of disinformation is to hide the initiators to make it more credible. However, they can often be guessed. Concerning the Facts part of the model, we note that the different types of False Facts appear equitably. We also note that the studied Fake News often play on the difference between correlation and causality, especially when a Fake News is built around several True Facts, which is not surprising. We also find an equal distribution of true and false authorities. Finally, if we look at the Target part, the emotional mechanisms are pretty easily identifiable,

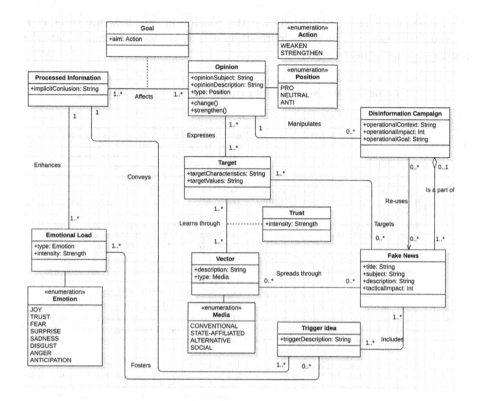

Fig. 6. Fake News target conceptual model

Trigger Idea		
Trigger description: participation of Trump during the Gulf War		
Emotional Load		
Type: Trust		
Intensity: High		

Vector		
Description: published on Sean Hannity's website		
Type: Alternative		
Trust		
Intensity: medium		

Target		
Target Characteristics: the US population		
Target Values: voters		
Opinion		
Opinion subject: Trump		
Opinion description: whether Trump is supported		
Type: Pro		
Processed Information		
Implicit conclusion: Trump helped soldiers to come back home then he is a hero		
Goal		
Aim: Strengthen		

Fig. 7. Illustration of the use of the conceptual model target part

as well as the objective of the Fake News. However, if this study shows us that we manage to characterize existing Fake News with our model, the number of studied examples remains limited, and the conclusions we draw are to be considered with reserve. A more in-depth study will be necessary to consolidate the results and in the near future.

Table 2. Fake News used for conceptual model evaluation

Num.	Fake News title	Description
1	Hillary has six months left	During the 2016 US presidential campaign, numerous rumours about Hillary Clinton's health were published. These rumours were posted after she fainted during the ceremony for the 9/11 victims in New York.
2	200 Stranded Marines Needed a Plane Ride Home, Here's How Donald Trump Responded	On his website, Sean Hannity related that Trump helped 200 marines to come home.
3	War Russia-NATO: An analyst from Pentagon foresees how it could end	An online article published in Ukraine claims that Russia could be easily defeated by NATO. The source is linked with Pentagon
4	Youngkin's false claim that McAuliffe 'opposes' election audits	Youngkin twitted a thread against his opponent Terry McAuliffe and claimed that the democrat was against audits.
5	Omar Holding Secret Fundraisers with Islamic groups tied to terror	Ilhan Omar was accused of having links with terrorists' groups during Minnesota Campaign
6	The Chinese President visits a mosque and asks Muslims to pray for the country to protect it from this disaster of Covid. It's now they discover Islam virtues!	The Chinese President asks Muslims to pray for the country to be protected against Covid-19
7	When did patient zero begin in US? [...]It might be the US army who brought the epidemic to Wuhan	The spokesperson of the Chinese Ministry of Foreign Affairs Lijian Zhao, insinuated in a tweet that the US Army actually brought Covid-19 to Wuhan. The fact that dead from Covid-19 might have been attributed to influenza is the proof that Covid-19 was in the US before the emergence in China.
8	Norway reclassifies Covid-19: No more dangerous than ordinary flue	The Norwegian Institute of Public Health, or NIPH, declared that Covid-19 had known several mutations and was now less dangerous. It is now no more dangerous than ordinary flue
9	Bill Gates backed polio vaccine disabled 47,000 kids	Bill Gates is accused of poisoning children in India with his polio vaccine
10	Here is what our brothers and sisters live every day all around the world because of the Gospel. Let us pray for our missionaries	Following the fall of Afghanistan, Christians are tortured and packaged in plastic bags until they die

We also used the conceptual model to create a Fake News. The advantage of relying on a conceptual model is that it allows associating a process that will enable to control the Fake News generation. Such a formalized process is still a challenge, but our conceptual model is the first step to make it possible because it increases the interpretability of the resulting Fake News.

Indeed, explainability and interpretatbility is recognized as a major feature for future intelligent systems in AI and Machine Learning research. Known under the name eXplainable Artificial Intelligence (XAI), the aim is to produce intelligent systems that enhance the confidence of users to understand the underlying reasoning and automations [9]. For Fake News context, to our knowledge, works involving explainability feature within Fake News detection methods are still at their beginning [17]. A promising line of work is to follow the XAI-based process proposed by [19] to facilitate building well-justified and explainable models for Fake News generation. The idea is to offer an approach that is understandable, trustable and manageable to humans, as suggested in [9]. The contribution of this paper establishes the foundation of such a process by solving the first, essential step of getting a shared understanding of what a Fake News is by introducing a precise conceptual model of Fake News. From that sound conceptual basis, the rest of the proposed XAI process can be applied in a reliable way. The explainability with our approach will be conceptually guided by the conceptual model which conforms the core of the contribution: to have an ontologically well-grounded definition of what a Fake News is, which is directly derived from the conceptual model.

6 Conclusion

This paper presents a conceptual model of Fake News allowing to identify and specify the relevant entities that conceptually characterize the different dimensions that must be considered in Fake News. We believe that this model will contribute significantly to improving tools for generating/detecting fake news. Under a sound conceptual modeling perspective, we argue that a correct Fake News management process will only be feasible if it is based on a precise conceptual modeling approach, as the one proposed in this paper. We have chosen to focus on the following main aspects: the production chain, the articulation around true and false facts, and the manipulation mechanism used by Fake News and based on emotions. We have confronted this conceptual model to up to ten different fake news in order to evaluate its conformity. The first results are encouraging. A larger study will be conducted in the near future in order to evaluate its scaling up. Moreover, the proposition addresses the first step of the XAI process proposed by [19], that it is crucial to make possible the full XAI-based process. The explainability with our approach is conceptually guided by the conceptual model which conforms the core of the contribution: to have an ontologically well-grounded definition of what a Fake News is, which is directly derived from the conceptual model. The next steps of the process are naturally our future work.

Acknowledgment. The authors would like to thank the final year engineering students of the Military Academy of St-Cyr Coëtquidan who worked on this project: Glenn Le Roux, Gaspard Croizat, Hugo Fouché, Émilien Frugier and Louis-Antoine Nicolazo De Barmon.

References

1. Allcott, H., Gentzkow, M.: Social media and fake news in the 2016 election. J. Econ. Perspect. **31**(2), 211–36 (2017)

2. Ansar, W., Goswami, S.: Combating the menace: a survey on characterization and detection of fake news from a data science perspective. Int. J. Inf. Manag. Data Insights **1**(2), 100052 (2021)
3. Arrieta, A.B., et al.: Explainable artificial intelligence (XAI): concepts, taxonomies, opportunities and challenges toward responsible AI. Inform. Fusion **58**, 82–115 (2020)
4. Bani-Hani, A., Adedugbe, O., Benkhelifa, E., Majdalawieh, M.: Fandet semantic model: an OWL ontology for context-based fake news detection on social media. In: Lahby, M., Pathan, A.-S.K., Maleh, Y., Yafooz, W.M.S. (eds.) Combating Fake News with Computational Intelligence Techniques. SCI, vol. 1001, pp. 91–125. Springer, Cham (2022). https://doi.org/10.1007/978-3-030-90087-8_5
5. Belloir, N., Ouerdane, W., Pastor, O., Frugier, E., de Barmon, L.A.: A conceptual characterization of fake news: a positioning paper. In: Guizzardi, R., (eds) Research Challenges in Information Science. RCIS 2022¡ Lecture Notes in Business Information Processing, vol. 446. Springer, Cham (2022). https://doi.org/10.1007/978-3-031-05760-1_41
6. Gilpin, L.H., Bau, D., Yuan, B.Z., Bajwa, A., Specter, M., Kagal, L.: Explaining explanations: an overview of interpretability of machine learning. In: IEEE 5th International Conference on Data Science and Advanced Analytics, pp. 80–89 (2018)
7. Guidotti, R., Monreale, A., Ruggieri, S., Turini, F., Giannotti, F., Pedreschi, D.: A survey of methods for explaining black box models. ACM Comput. Surv. (CSUR) **51**(5), 93 (2019)
8. Gunning, D.: Explainable artificial intelligence (XAI). In: DARPA 2 (2017)
9. Gunning, D., Stefik, M., Choi, J., Miller, T., Stumpf, S., Yang, G.: XAI: explainable artificial intelligence. Sci. Robot. **4**(37), 7120 (2019)
10. Katsaros, D., Stavropoulos, G., Papakostas, D.: Which machine learning paradigm for fake news detection? In: IEEE/WIC/ACM International Conference on Web Intelligence, pp. 383–387 (2019)
11. Kumar, S., Shah, N.: False information on web and social media: a survey (2018)
12. Lazer, D.M.J., et al.: The science of fake news. Science **359**(6380), 1094–1096 (2018)
13. Molina, M.D., Sundar, S.S., Le, T., Lee, D.: "Fake news" is not simply false information: a concept explication and taxonomy of online content. Am. Behav. Sci. **65**(2), 180–212 (2021)
14. Nadav, Z., Sam, W.: Op-ed: why can't a generation that grew up online spot the misinformation in front of them? Los Angeles Times, 6 November 2020 (2020). Available online: https://www.latimes.com/opinion/story/2020-11-06/colleges-students-recognizemisinformation Accessed on 11 January 2021
15. Pierri, F., Ceri, S.: False news on social media: a data-driven survey. SIGMOD Rec. **48**(2), 18–27 (2019)
16. Plutchik, R.: Emotion: Theory, Research, and Experience: Theories of Emotion, vol. 1 (1980)
17. Shu, K., Cui, L., Wang, S., Lee, D., Liu, H.: Defend: explainable fake news detection. In: Proceedings of the 25th ACM SIGKDD, pp. 395–405 (2019)
18. Shu, K., Sliva, A., Wang, S., Tang, J., Liu, H.: Fake news detection on social media: a data mining perspective. SIGKDD Explor. Newsl. **19**(1), 22–36 (2017)
19. Spreeuwenberg, S.: AIX: Artificial Intelligence Needs EXplanation: Why and How Transparency Increases the Success of AI Solutions. LibRT BV, Amsterdam (2019)
20. Tandoc, E., Lim, Z., Ling, R.: Defining "Fake news": a typology of scholarly definitions. Digit. J. **6**, 1–17 (2017)

21. Wang, C.: Fake news and related concepts: definitions and recent research development. Contemp. Manag. Res. **16**, 145–174 (2020)
22. Weiss, A.P., Alwan, A., Garcia, E.P., Kirakosian, A.T.: Toward a comprehensive model of fake news: a new approach to examine the creation and sharing of false information. Societies **11**(3), 82 (2021)
23. Zafarani, R., Zhou, X., Shu, K., Liu, H.: Fake news research: theories, detection strategies, and open problems. In: Proceedings of the 25th ACM SIGKDD, pp. 3207–3208. Association for Computing Machinery (2019)
24. Zhang, X., Ghorbani, A.: An overview of online fake news: characterization, detection, and discussion. Inf. Process. Manag. **57**(2), 102025 (2020)
25. Zhou, X., Zafarani, R.: A survey of fake news: fundamental theories, detection methods, and opportunities. ACM Comput. Surv. **53**(5), 1–40 (2020)

Modeling Lifelong Pathway Co-construction

Nicolas Ringuet[1,2]([✉]), Patrick Marcel[1][iD], Nicolas Labroche[1][iD],
Thomas Devogele[1], and Christophe Bortolaso[2]

[1] University of Tours, Tours, France
{nicolas.ringuet,patrick.marcel,nicolas.labroche,
thomas.devogele}@univ-tours.fr
[2] Berger-Levrault, Boulogne-Billancourt, France
{nicolas.ringuet,christophe.bortolaso}@berger-levrault.com

Abstract. While personal coach applications are now ubiquitous, personal lifelong pathway co-construction, although present in a wide range of situations (e-learning, healthcare, return to employment, home-care of elders, etc.) is largely overlooked. Modeling generic lifelong pathway co-construction is feasible since these situations share many properties. In this paper, we contribute with a model for the co-construction of lifelong pathways, backed by a literature survey of semantic trajectories, and applicable in a wide range of situations. The model supports the interactions between the two main actors, the advisee and the advisor, in the co-construction, and include the key specific aspects of lifelong pathway: the advisee's long-term goal, the evaluation of the advisee's multi-dimensional (educational, professional, financial, medical, etc.) trajectory, the guiding of the advisee via advices that influence the stages of the pathway. To illustrate the importance of this model, we detail its use in a guidance system, to help the advisor's work in guiding the advisee towards their goal.

Keywords: Semantic trajectories · Life trajectories · Lifelong pathway · Co-construction

1 Introduction

Capturing and modeling the coached evolution of a person according to several possibly independent dimensions is of prime importance in many real life situations. A typical context is that of healthcare, where diagnoses are established before doctors devise patient management and monitor their health over a potentially long period of time. In an e-learning context, the skills and knowledge acquisition states of learners in different courses are modeled and, based on prior evaluations of the learner, a personalized curriculum can be established under the guidance of a teaching staff. In the context of elderly home support,

Funded by ANRT CIFRE 2020/0731.

which concerns up to 15 million people aged 60 or more in France, it is expected to help maintaining independence, autonomy, mobility or cognitive abilities by preemptively taking action on these aspects with personalized training programs on the basis of a diagnosis of their medical and social conditions. Finally, in the context of job seekers assistance, which concerns 2.06 millions low resources beneficiaries in 2020 in France, one may want to model beneficiaries upon social, professional, medical or educational dimensions. The objective is then to provide the best combined support that improves their social integration or their financial situation based on prior analysis of beneficiaries' diplomas, past work experiences, social data on housing, family or health condition.

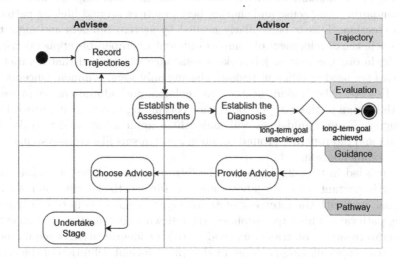

Fig. 1. Activity diagram for the co-construction of a lifelong pathway

Common to all these scenarios are: (i) the person whose evolution is under consideration, hereafter called the *advisee*, who has a *long term goal*, (ii) the entity in charge of supporting and helping advisees to reach their objectives, called the *advisor*, and (iii) a *diagnosis* that defines the actual situation of the advisee in terms of different dimensions (e.g., health, financial, professional, education, etc.) and the objectives for the advisee. As depicted in Fig. 1, an advisor represents the entity in charge of diagnosing and periodically monitoring the advisee's progresses based on undertaken actions on all dimensions over time, the latter forming the advisee's *life trajectory*. In this paper, we are interested in modeling a *lifelong pathway*, i.e. a set of stages made of tailored actions undertaken by an advisee and the underlying co-construction mechanism, participating in the evolution of this advisee's life trajectory. A life-long pathway involves several entities such as the advisee, the advisor or any other stakeholder involved in its *co-construction*, fulfilling the *objectives* and *long term goal* of the advisee.

As our experience with data of job seekers assistance suggests [4], there is need to support the advisor in the tedious exploration of all combinations of actions to offer to an advisee. This lifelong pathway model will be a corner stone in the development of an intelligent system that helps the advisor in the task of identifying relevant actions. For instance, this system could be a recommender system that would implements the activities in the guidance layer of Fig. 1. While a great deal of work has been done to model trajectories as geographical or semantically enriched entities (see Sect. 3 below), there is not yet, to the best of our knowledge, a generic model able to represent the richness necessary for the above mentioned situations.

Obviously, while the design of lifelong pathway co-construction applications can be conducted without such a model, formalizing guidelines with a conceptual modeling of the domain will drive further researches, and help the understanding, standardization, reuse and sharing best practices around lifelong pathways co-construction. This is particularly needed by system builders and algorithm designers in the development of complex different interoperable applications. For example, in our use case of job seekers assistance, we noticed that a variety of platforms are used in different regions, sharing only some common concepts and needs. However, the amount of data, technologies and administrative processes make the design of these applications time consuming and their interoperability challenging. Formal guidelines will make these applications easier to develop, maintain and interoperate around common mechanisms like cross-systems pathways recommendation.

As detailed in Sect. 2, this needs the introduction of different stakeholders, the most important being the advisee and the advisor, the specification of a long term goal, and with the intervene of an intelligent agent to help co-constructing lifelong pathways. This paper proposes the following contributions: (i) an extensive literature survey on trajectory models, (ii) the identification of requirements to set up a proper lifelong pathway model, (iii) a formal definition of the constituting blocs of a lifelong pathway, and (iv) a new model for lifelong pathways.

This paper is organized as follows. Section 2 details the requirements the model should satisfy. These requirements are used in Sect. 3 as drivers to survey the bibliography around trajectory modeling. Section 4 presents the model, and Sect. 5 focuses on its use for implementing a guidance system to facilitate the advisor's work. Finally, Sect. 6 concludes and draws perspectives.

2   Requirements

In this section, we give a set of requirements for the modeling of a system that supports the iterative co-construction of pathways based on an evaluative multidimensional and multi-granular profile of an advisee who has a long term goal.

The model should represent:

1. a **human trajectory**: the model should be tailored to the description of the evolution of a person mainly through semantic dimensions not focusing solely on the geographical perspective, and possibly during a long period of time.

2. a **long-term goal**: the pathway construction is driven by a long term goal (e.g., find a job, treat a disease) that will correspond to milestones in the pathway. These milestones enable the monitoring of the evolution of an advisee, for analytical purpose (e.g., urban study or demographic study) or for suggestion purpose (e.g., home support, job finding), via a diagnosis and can be defined as objectives.

3. **multidimensional** and **multi-granular factors**: the model should enable the comprehension of how the trajectory is impacted by internal and external factors, structured around various dimensions related to the use case (e.g., health, residence or education) and at different granularity levels (e.g., temporal, geographic or business related) to account for the difficulty to precisely characterize the data related to human situations,

4. pathway **co-constructors** and **influencers**: different stakeholders, with different objectives, participate and impact the construction of the pathway. The advisee, who has a long term goal, the advisor (either a person or a group of persons playing the role of a coach with their own objectives) and external stakeholders (services providers, financing institutions, etc.) have to conciliate their objectives and may express constraints that may bend the trajectory.

In the light of these requirements, we conducted a bibliography review of the modeling of trajectories. The result of this survey is reported in the next section.

3 Related Works

Modeling trajectories aims at capturing the movement of entities, especially through time and space.

The simplest way of modeling these movements is through the succession of spatio-temporal points arranged in sequences representing different stages of the trajectory of a moving entity. Different types of trajectory models were proposed in the literature, that first differ by their wealth level of description:

1. raw trajectories, as defined by Parent et al. [12] as: "a trajectory extracted from a raw movement track and containing only raw data (e.g., speed, direction) for its Begin-End interval referring to the first (Begin) and the last (End) positions of the object for the trajectory".

2. semantic trajectories, defined by Parent et al. [12] as: "a trajectory that has been enhanced with annotations and/or one or several complementary segmentation."

3. life trajectories, a concept stemming from sociology [11]. A life trajectory is defined by Hélardot [8] as: "an interweaving of multiple biographical lines that are more or less autonomous or dependent on each other: the educational path, the relationship to work and employment, family life, social life, health, the residential trajectory, the political itinerary, etc.".

As can be seen in Table 1, where works are ordered based on types of trajectories, modeling trajectories started with models adapted to raw, less complex movements, being then enriched giving rise to semantic trajectories. As we will see below, this category can be subdivided into two types of contributions, depending on the complexity of the concepts represented. The works can also be divided according to their generosity, which we qualify as metamodel in Table 1, this characteristic being important for our model, requiring to model various use cases. Recently in [11], more sophisticated models were proposed for life trajectories, that are closer to our objective. Note also that all existing models are adapted for either retrieval (i.e., simply retrieving data described with the model) or analysis (i.e., statistic computations over the represented data), i.e., exploiting past data. In the case of modeling lifelong pathway co-construction, in the presence of a long term goal, our final objective is to support the advisor's daily work in the co-construction of the pathway. In what follows, we describe in more details trajectory models from each type, each time assessing to which extent they satisfy the requirements of Sect. 2 for lifelong pathway co-construction.

Table 1. Main existing trajectory models based on their complexity (R: Raw trajectory, S: Semantics trajectory, L: Life trajectory), their moving entity (H: Human, A: Animal, G: Generic) and their exploitation (A: Analysis, R: Retrieval, G: Guidance, i.e., using the data to make recommendations)

Model	Complexity	Moving entity	Exploitation	Metamodel
[13]	R	A	R/A	✓
[6]	R	G	R/A	✓
[1]	S	A	R/A	✓
[2]	S	H	R	✓
[7]	S	H/A	R/A	✓
[5]	S	H	R/A	
[3]	S	H/A	R/A	
[10]	S	H	R/A	
[9]	S	H/A	R/A	✓
[11]	L	H	R/A	✓
[14]	L	H	R/A	
The present model	L	H	R/A/G	✓

3.1   From Geographical Trajectories to Life Trajectories

Raw Trajectories. The seminal proposal of Spaccapietra et al. introduced the concept of *stop* (period of activity) and *move* (moving period) to model geographic trajectories. This concept focuses on the spatio-temporal component of trajectories and is used by subsequent proposals [2,6]. Raw trajectories are well-fitted for applications that only consist in locating moving entities or conducting analyses on the spatio-temporal characteristics of a trajectory. However, most analysis applications require a certain semantic complexity but also a genericity allowing to answer different use cases. This leads to introduce more generic models and then models allowing a semantic enhancement defined by [12] as an *annotation* which is an additional data attached to the trajectory or to its subparts. These models therefore suffer from expressiveness mainly at the semantic level and do not meet our requirements, but have provided a basis that has been enriched subsequently.

Semantically Enriched Trajectories. The need to annotate trajectory segments and to model points of interest led to the introduction of new models [1,7]. In particular, Hu et al. [7] bring genericity with new formalisms and adapt to more applications by the level of abstraction they propose. Other more recent models propose an annotation of the trajectories, in particular by the annotation of POI, for example by means of transportation of an individual, an hotel opening hours, or the means of transportation of a trip. However, although these models meet our needs of genericity or the semantic dimension that is missing in raw trajectories, they do not satisfy our requirement of multidimensional or multi-granular factors.

Multidimensional and Multi-granular Models. More semantic is introduced with multidimensionality [3], where a semantic trajectory is composed of sub-trajectories, each covering a specific dimension of interest, and each characterized by a specific goal. However, although this model allows a multidimensional representation, it remains centered on the modeling of trajectories of moving objects and is not adapted to the modeling of non-geographical trajectories. Indeed, any sub-trajectory is a composition of geometry, and the concepts used are those of the movement in geographical space (such as speed, acceleration). It does not include the notion of multi-granularity either, where a specific trajectory can be hierarchically composed of different nested segments [5]. Other models include the notion of multidimensional representation to trajectory modeling [9,10] with the added ability to consider different levels of granularity. However, none of these models propose a modeling of the actors involved and only models geographical trajectories.

Life Trajectories. Models in this category represent a type of trajectory centered on the personal life of an individual, going beyond the geographical dimension at the core of other models. Modeling life trajectories was initiated by Marius Thériault et al. [14] to analyze professional, family and residential trajectories. Those dimensions are modeled by the concepts of *episodes*, a set of attributes that remain unchanged over a period of time, and *events* which alternate these attributes and serve as a transition between episodes. However, this model cannot be extended to models of trajectories for other use cases requiring other dimensions, attributes and events than those they initially proposed.

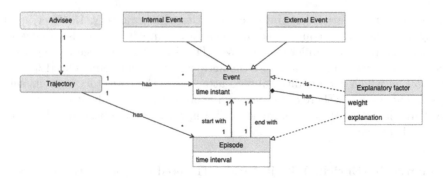

Fig. 2. Noël's life trajectory model [11]

Noël et al. [11] extend the model of [14], making it more generic, adding the concept of explanatory factor to enrich events, giving it the possibility to model different use cases. This allows to observe different points of view, representing different angles of analysis on an individual's life. Their model is presented in Fig. 2 and aligned with our notations, the individual at the center of the trajectory being qualified here as advisee. In the end, Noël et al.'s model meets most of our requirements by proposing a generic semantic model, allowing for multidimensional representation and different levels of granularity. On the other hand, the model does account for co-construction with various actors and does not include the concept of long-term goal.

3.2   The Need for a Model of Lifelong Pathways

Table 2 provides a summary of the aforementioned models based on the requirements of Sect. 2. We identify 3 main types of contributions. First, models tailored for a specific modeling need related to a particular use case, such as the analysis of bird trajectories [13]. Second, models that enrich trajectories with semantic related to point of interest of moving entity. These models provides either multidimensional representation [3], multi-granularity [5] or both [9,10]. Finally, the third category of models corresponds to more expressive models that can better capture trajectories not only related to geographical entities such as point of interest and moving entities, but more generally to any social dimension representation space related to a person as in [14] and extended by [11].

These models, however, are not expressive enough to represent a lifelong pathway. Notably, the concepts of short-term objectives and long-term goals are missing, even though a very straightforward notion of objective is introduced as a simple label on a segment in [3] (hence the bracketed tick in Table 2). Models of life trajectory [11,14] are natural candidates for the elaboration of our lifelong pathway model. They indeed have the potential to represent the multiple dimensions and the different granularities needed to describe human activity. However, these models miss two important aspects of our proposal: (i) the introduction of specific actors and stakeholders influencing the co-construction (a limit form

Table 2. Lifelong pathway requirements compliance. Stakeholders denotes advisors and advisee roles, co-constructors and influencers.

Model	Human trajectory	Long-term goal	Multi-dimensional	Multi-granularity	Multi-stakeholder
[13]					
[6]	✓				
[1]					
[2]					
[7]					
[5]				✓	
[3]		(✓)	✓		
[10]			✓	✓	
[9]			✓	✓	
[11]	✓		✓	✓	
[14]	✓			✓	(✓)
The present model	✓	✓	✓	✓	✓

is present in [14] hence the bracketed tick in Table 2), and (ii) the introduction of a concept of evaluation attached to long-term goals that can be derived into short-term objectives. In the case of modeling lifelong pathway co-construction, in the presence of a long term goal, our final objective is to support the advisor's daily work in the co-construction of the pathway. This is why the pathway model not only should describe the past life trajectory of the advisee, but also include concepts for representing guidance, i.e., the advisors' work in the co-construction of the potential future trajectory of the advisee. Indeed, not only do we need to model the past and present life of an advisee, but also to envision different future trajectories, embodied in the model under the concept of Advice. Advice represent possible future actions to be undertaken as stages of the advisee's pathway. The next section details how we extend the model of Noël and al. [11] to model lifelong pathways.

4   The Lifelong Pathway Model

This section introduces our model of lifelong pathway, first with a functional overview, then detailing the concepts.

4.1   Functional Overview

As explained above, we base our lifelong pathway model on that of life trajectory introduced by [14] and completed by [11], since this model already covers many of the requirements presented in Sect. 2, as explained in Sect. 3.

Figure 3 gives a functional overview of our model. It is composed of 4 components representing the four layers of Fig. 1. The *Trajectory* component encapsulates the model of Noel et al. [11]. This component is responsible for providing and updating the advisee profile, i.e., episodes of multidimensional trajectories. The *Evaluation* component is responsible for the assessment of the advisee by

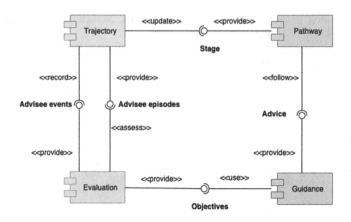

Fig. 3. Component diagram

analyzing the advisee's trajectory. This results in the generation of a set of objectives for the advisee. The *Guidance* component uses the objectives to provide advices to the advisee. Finally the *Pathway* component uses the advice that the advisee agrees with, to build a sequence of stages. These stages impact the advisee's trajectories, resulting in new episodes and events. Completion of the pathway, when the long term goal is reached, is determined by a final diagnosis.

4.2   Advice as the Essence of Co-construction

The class diagram of the model is given in Fig. 4. Note that the colors are used consistently with Fig. 1, 2 and 3. The model includes the two actors, the advisee and the advisor, who interact with the advisee's trajectories. Theses trajectories are modeled according to Noel's model of life trajectories, illustrated in Fig. 2. Remember from Fig. 1 that the first step of the global co-construction process is to establish an assessment. This assessment is based on the advisee's trajectories. A diagnosis is then established from which a long term goal and a set of objectives to reach it are defined. Advice to achieve the objectives are formulated by the advisor and validated by the advisee. Once validated, the advice are turned into stages of the lifelong pathway. These stages are undertook by the advisee, which updates their trajectories.

We now detail the concepts of the 4 components.

Trajectory. The *trajectory* component is at the core of our lifelong pathway model and is in charge of modeling an advisee profile in terms of multidimensional trajectories, using the model of [11]. As can be seen in Fig. 2, a trajectory describes a person from one point of view and the overall trajectory of the person is composed of different trajectories which are themselves composed of episodes. Events serve as transitions between episodes and have associated explanatory factors.

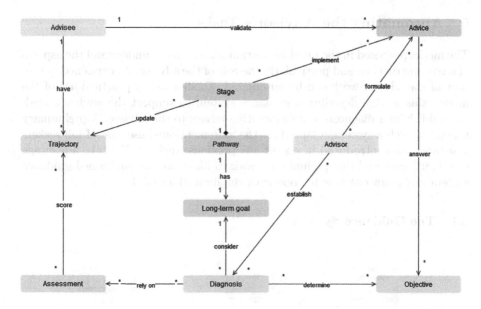

Fig. 4. The class diagram for lifelong pathway co-construction

Evaluation. The *evaluation* component models the assessment of the advisee using their trajectories (e.g., with numerical indicators on the different points of view). For each assessment, a diagnosis is determined by the advisor. Together with the advisee's long term goal, the diagnosis is used to derive a set of objectives for the advisee. Each stage towards the achievement of the long term goal updates the advisee trajectory upon completion and the latter can be submitted to a new assessment.

Guidance. The *guidance* component models the advice proposed to the advisee to achieve the objectives determined by the evaluation. This component is the essence of the co-construction, in the sense that advice are formulated by the advisor and validated by the advisee. Note that the Advisor entity models either one expert or a group of experts participating in the formulation of the advice. In this sense, implementing this concept should include contradiction resolution mechanisms. Also, while advice can be determined solely by human experts, it makes sense to automate part of the advisor's work by implementing a guidance system. For instance, this guidance system could resolve contradictions among experts, or suggest actions to undertake, as explained in Sect. 5 below.

Pathway. The *pathway* component models the evolution of the advisee towards their long-term goal. This long term goal is set by a diagnosis established by the advisor after the first assessment of the advisee's trajectories. A pathway is a sequence of stages, each composed of actions undertaken by the advisee following the advice formulated. Once a stage is closed, it is used to update the trajectories accordingly.

5   Automating the Advisor's Tasks

The model proposed in the previous section is essential to understand the aspects of a co-construction, and particularly the role of the advisor. As explained above, part of the advisor work can be automated. To showcase a practical use of the model, this section describes a guidance system to support the advisor's work of establishing a diagnosis and formulating advice to the advisee. A preliminary version of such a system, adapted for the aforementioned use case of job seekers assistance, was introduced in one of our previous work [4]. We take advantage of this use case and this preliminary work to illustrate the envisioned guidance system and point out how to cope with the limitations of [4].

5.1   The Guidance System

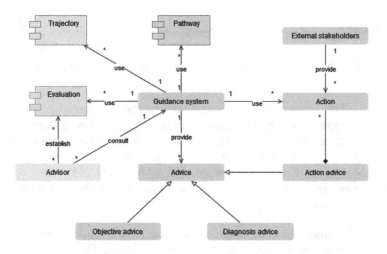

Fig. 5. The generic guidance system

A Generic Guidance System. The model for a generic guidance system is given in Fig. 5. The guidance system model formulates different type of Advice: either future actions to help the advisee in their pathway towards their goal (Action advice), or elements to help the advisor in the evaluation of the advisee and their pathway (Diagnosis advice or Objective advice). When suggesting Action advice, the system chooses among actions provided by external actors those that best match the objectives set for the advisee. This choice is made considering inputs from the Trajectory, Pathway and Evaluation components: e.g., pathways of former advisees similar to the current advisee, for whom the suggestions are made, or evaluations of former advisees for whom similar diagnoses were made. The same inputs may be used when suggesting Objective of Diagnosis advice: e.g., diagnosis can be established on the basis of diagnoses made for former advisees with similar trajectories and long term goals, or on the basis of undertaken stages failed by the advisee.

A Preliminary Guidance System for Job Seeker Advisees. A first guidance system was proposed in [4] in the context of job seeker assistance. For this system, only some key concepts necessary to the support of job seekers were identified. The system took the form of a recommender system, suggesting to job seekers (called beneficiaries in [4]) a personal pathway using a large set of actions pertaining to health, social or professional aspects. Technically speaking, [4] addresses the complex problem of recommending several items at once, also known as composite item recommendation. The produced so-called bundles of actions ensure the adequacy of actions with the beneficiary diagnosis (relevance of an action), complementarity between actions (distance between actions) and the feasibility of each action in the context of the beneficiary (cost measure attached to each action). As such, this preliminary work does not encompass all the concepts of the model described in Sect. 4. More precisely, the concepts used were those of advisee, actions (each action having a cost and each pair of actions a distance), diagnosis (represented by a set of features), pathway (modeled as a sequence of actions), and guidance. This guidance system generated recommendation under the form of a pathway of actions, in a collaborative fashion, based on the diagnoses and pathways of former beneficiaries. The model used in [4] is on many aspects consistent with the one presented here. For instance, consistently with Fig. 5 the guidance system of [4] uses the evaluation of the advisee to propose advice picked from the possible actions, based on the pathways and evaluations of former advisees. Propositions rely on the computations of cost for the actions and distance between actions defined in methods of the Action class, and relevance defined in a method of the Advisee class, etc. However, that model mixed different concepts and overlooked some others. For instance, the notions of diagnosis, assessment and objectives were not distinguished, which prevented the definitions of advice based on the objectives determined by different diagnoses. As another example, advisee's trajectories were defined only coarsely, which prevented to calculate fine-tuned distances between advisees' profiles.

Example 1. Consider an Advisee named Alice, whose long term goal is to find a full time job. Her trajectory shows that she lives in a small city, has a young kid and does not have a driving license. There is a first job offer in the city she lives in, but for which having a vehicle is necessary, and two jobs offers in a distant city, one which is close to a child care and another which corresponds more to her qualifications. If the notions of diagnosis, assessment and objectives are not distinguished, and trajectories are only coarsely defined, like in [4], only simple likelihoods based on the set of advisees can be expressed to make advice. In this case, the guidance system will suggest e.g., the application for a new degree, which is the most popular advice among former advisees, while other advice like registration to a bus service between the two cities, will be overlooked.

5.2 Taking Advantage of the Lifelong Pathway Co-construction Model

In the job seekers use case, the system of [4] recommends professional projects for the french solidarity income beneficiaries. It primarily predicts the relationship between the evaluation and the advisee's actions within the observed pathways to recommend complementary actions. As explained above, it does not take into account the advisee's long-term goal (e.g., being recruited for a precise job) or a finer notion of pathway of an advisee as a sequence of stages. Our lifelong pathway model explicits trajectories, pathways, diagnoses, and objectives attached to a long-term goal for each advisee, allowing to represent the history of what was proposed to each advisee and with what success in relation to their long-term goal. With this model, new guidance scenarios can be considered, leading to more accurate advice.

For example, instead of predicting for each action whether it should be added or not to an advisee's pathway, simple collaborative filtering techniques could be implemented. Leveraging pathway information, a user-item matrix can be constructed from the advisee-action relationship of the pathways and classical recommender system machinery can be deployed. To allow for direct bundle recommendations, the long-term goal, together with the more specific objectives that follow the evaluation, will help to determine a subset of other advisee pathways to pick relevant actions from. In this case, following the principles of nearest neighbors recommendation, this needs to devise new similarity measures between objectives, trajectories, pathways or long-term goals.

Guidance could also take advantage of the advisee-goal or advisee-diagnosis relationship. In this case, the advisor and the advisee do not directly agree on the actions to be taken but rather (i) on the selection of relevant objectives from a set of objectives that may be very large or (ii) on the definition of a new diagnosis to search for completely new objectives. Since the model now enables a rich description of advisees and actions provided by external stakeholders, determining the relevance of an action to an advisee can rely on more complex similarity measures based on different conceptual spaces representing the actions and pathways, trajectories made of episodes or events, evaluation and assessments. As in any guidance system, actors will only use the system if they trust it. This is the trendy problem of the explainability of any recommendation system [15]. One way to enforce trust in the system is to propose elements of discussion, or examples that justify why an advice was eventually made to an advisee. In this regard, our model provides access to examples (of other advisees and their pathways, trajectories, and long-term goals) or a rich description of actions, episodes, or events in the advisee's trajectory that could serve as an interpretable space on which a formal explanation can be learned.

Example 2. Continuing the scenario of Example 1, illustrated in Fig. 6, a guidance system implementing the co-construction model will formulate advice as follows. First, the trajectory of Alice is evaluated. From the assessment made, the system suggests a diagnosis where it appears that Alice mobility situation is critical and should be addressed first. The system can also formulate the objective of improving her mobility situation, and suggest action advice of getting a driving license to apply for the job in the city she lives in. Besides, with a fine description of the advisees' trajectories, the guidance system can base the advice on the similarity of Alice's trajectory with those of former advisees and suggest action advice of applying for the job in the distant city, using a bus service between the two cities and the child care of that city. This information stored in Alice's trajectory could eventually serve as an explanation why she applied for a job in a distant city.

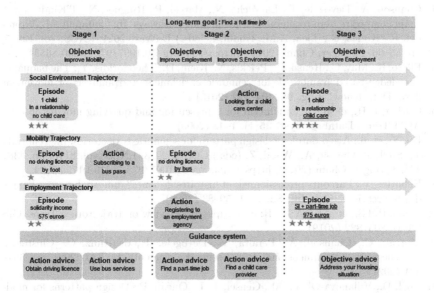

Fig. 6. Graphical depiction of Alice's pathway in Example 2, using the color code of the diagrams. The *pathway* consists of 3 *stages*, with 3 *trajectories* composed of *episodes*, each *assessed* in terms of criticity (green stars). The pathway evolves with the *actions* undertaken following the Guidance System suggestions. (Color figure online)

6   Conclusion

This paper proposes a better understanding of the concepts and mechanisms involved in the co-construction of lifelong pathways. We contribute with a generic model for the co-construction of lifelong pathways, backed by a literature survey of semantic trajectories. We also describe a guidance system to support the co-construction, leveraging the proposed model.

We are currently working on a generic guidance system implementing the co-construction model. We will experiment it in two contexts for which data are already available to us: the return to employment and the elderly support. As explained in Sect. 5, one key challenge will be to enforce the confidence that the advisee will have in the guidance system.

References

1. Andrienko, G., Andrienko, N., Heurich, M.: An event-based conceptual model for context-aware movement analysis. Int. J. Geogr. Inf. Sci. **25**(9), 1347–1370 (2011)
2. Baglioni, M., Macedo, J., Renso, C., Wachowicz, M.: An ontology-based approach for the semantic modelling and reasoning on trajectories. In: Song, I.-Y., et al. (eds.) ER 2008. LNCS, vol. 5232, pp. 344–353. Springer, Heidelberg (2008). https://doi.org/10.1007/978-3-540-87991-6_41
3. Bogorny, V., Renso, C., de Aquino, A.R., de Lucca Siqueira, F., Alvares, L.O.: CONSTAnT - a conceptual data model for semantic trajectories of moving objects. Trans. GIS **18**(1), 66–88 (2014)
4. Chanson, A., Devogele, T., Labroche, N., Marcel, P., Ringuet, N., T'Kindt, V.: A chain composite item recommender for lifelong pathways. In: Golfarelli, M., Wrembel, R., Kotsis, G., Tjoa, A.M., Khalil, I. (eds.) DaWaK 2021. LNCS, vol. 12925, pp. 55–66. Springer, Cham (2021). https://doi.org/10.1007/978-3-030-86534-4_5
5. Fileto, R., May, C., Renso, C., Pelekis, N., Klein, D., Theodoridis, Y.: The baquara^2 knowledge-based framework for semantic enrichment and analysis of movement data. Data Knowl. Eng. **98**, 104–122 (2015)
6. Güting, R.H., et al.: A foundation for representing and querying moving objects. ACM Trans. Database Syst. **25**(1), 1–42 (2000)
7. Hu, Y., et al.: A geo-ontology design pattern for semantic trajectories. In: Tenbrink, T., Stell, J., Galton, A., Wood, Z. (eds.) COSIT 2013. LNCS, vol. 8116, pp. 438–456. Springer, Cham (2013). https://doi.org/10.1007/978-3-319-01790-7_24
8. Hélardot, V.: Parcours professionnels et histoires de santé?: une analyse sous l'angle des bifurcations. Cah. Int. Sociol. **1**, 59–83 (2006)
9. Mello, R.d.S., et al.: MASTER: a multiple aspect view on trajectories. Trans. GIS **23**(4), 805–822 (2019)
10. Moreau, C., Chanson, A., Peralta, V., Devogele, T., de Runz, C.: Clustering sequences of multi-dimensional sets of semantic elements. In: SAC 2021, pp. 384–391 (2021)
11. Noël, D., Villanova-Oliver, M., Gensel, J., Le Quéau, P.: Design patterns for modelling life trajectories in the semantic web. In: Brosset, D., Claramunt, C., Li, X., Wang, T. (eds.) W2GIS 2017. LNCS, vol. 10181, pp. 51–65. Springer, Cham (2017). https://doi.org/10.1007/978-3-319-55998-8_4
12. Parent, C., et al.: Semantic trajectories modeling and analysis. ACM Comput. Surv. **45**(4):42:1–42:32 (2013)
13. Spaccapietra, S., Parent, C., Damiani, M.L., de Macedo, J.A., Porto, F., Vangenot, C.: A conceptual view on trajectories. Data Knowl. Eng. **65**(1), 126–146 (2008)
14. Thériault, M., Claramunt, C., Séguin, A.-M., Villeneuve, P.: Temporal GIS and statistical modelling of personal lifelines. In: Richardson, D.E., van Oosterom, P. (eds.) Advances in Spatial Data Handling, pp. 433–449. Springer, Heidelberg (2002). https://doi.org/10.1007/978-3-642-56094-1_32
15. Zhang, Y., Chen, X.: Explainable recommendation: a survey and new perspectives. **14**, 1–101 (2020)

LIREM: A Generic Framework for Effective Online Video Novelty Detection

Chengkun He[1,2], Xiangmin Zhou[1(✉)], and Chen Wang[2]

[1] RMIT University, Melbourne, Australia
{Chengkun.He,Xiangmin.Zhou}@rmit.edu.au
[2] CSIRO Data61, Sydney, Australia
chen.wang@data61.csiro.au

Abstract. Novelty detection in social video has drawn much attention of researchers and is applied to many tasks in real-world applications, such as e-commerce and e-learning. Existing methods cannot address this issue effectively, since most of them do not consider the quality of videos or the long-term information of online social videos. In this paper, we propose a general framework, Long-term Information REconstruction-based Model (LIREM), which cleans the video feature information and captures both short-term and long-term spatial-temporal information of video segments to detect novelty online. We first design a novel outlier detection method for feature cleaning to improve the learning performance. Then, an LSTM-Decoder model is constructed and applied to the cleaned video segments for predicting the reconstruction error of video features. Our experiments are conducted on three real datasets, and the experimental results demonstrate the performance of our model outperforms other novelty detection models.

Keywords: Feature cleaning · Novelty detection · Online social video

1 Introduction

Over the past decade, online social video platforms generate a huge amount of videos which have a far-reaching impact on people. Taking YouTube as an example, it has 2.3 billion users worldwide by 2021 and more than 500 h of video are uploaded to the platform every minute, as Statista[1] reported. Especially, with the popularization of personal mobile devices and 5G networks, online social video profoundly shapes our daily life [32]. Novelties have been very common in social video data as the unusual and new observations that do not occur regularly or are simply different from the others [22], which plays important role in user social activities. Accordingly, automatically detecting novelty in social online video has become a critical concern in many real-world fields, like e-business,

---

[1] https://www.statista.com/.

J. Ralyté et al. (Eds.): ER 2022, LNCS 13607, pp. 145–160, 2022.
https://doi.org/10.1007/978-3-031-17995-2_11

health, and food safety, public security, transportation, etc. For example, in e-business, a platform may recommend specific videos or influencers by detecting the novelties to social users for sales promotion. In public security, a platform may identify the talks that are related to people's safety or a critical event by detecting the video novelties.

Novelty detection aims to identify the unseen data to determine whether it is normal or novel (abnormal). Novelty detection task is often formulated as a form of anomaly detection problem. Many studies have been conducted on novelty detection and a large number of novelty detection techniques are widely utilized in real-world applications. In electronic IT security, network intrusion detection is conducted by anomaly detection which monitors the activity or behavior of a system, identifies attacks and generates alarms when attacks are occurring, so that actions can be taken to mitigate the consequences [14]. For industrial systems, anomaly detection is used to detect damage (deterioration), which is important for preventing further escalation and losses, maintaining the performance of the machine and reducing the repair cost [26]. In transportation, detecting abnormal trajectories [18] in a large-scale dataset could discover the unnecessary detours of drivers and inform passengers to protect their interests. Anomaly detection in image and video [16,17,19–21] draws much attention for surveillance in security. However, rare researchers pay attention to anomaly detection in online social videos.

In practice, there are two key challenges in novelty detection over such video streams. Considering the volume of online video streaming and potential mistakes of manual labeling, the quality of normal segments is quite important. The noises could lead to the degradation of algorithms and make samples less representative. Therefore, they need to be filtered properly. Another challenge is that for such video data, long-term temporal information needs to be considered. In real scenarios, an influencer in social videos often takes relevant actions over time, and traditional novel detection techniques only focus on short-term information, which could misjudge the novelty. Furthermore, according to the manual labeling, unseen action may not be the novel. Therefore, the model should be able to resort to the long-term information. To address these challenges, we propose a generic framework called Long-term Information REconstruction-based Model (LIREM) to detect novelty in online social videos. Specifically, we first propose a novel iterative outlier detection method for feature cleaning. Then we design an LSTM-Decoder model to capture long-term information and reconstruct the representation of segments. The reconstruction error is regarded as the novelty score. Our contributions in this paper are summarized as follows.

- We propose a novel framework LIREM that exploits iterative outlier detection-based feature cleaning and the long-term sequence features for novelty detection over social videos.
- We propose a new iterative outlier detection method that measures the discrimination for each segment in multiple scales and selects the outliers in an iterative manner for feature cleaning. The new method well excludes outliers in the feature space and improves the learning process.

- We design an LSTM-Decoder model that well integrates the LSTM model and decoder layers. With the LSTM-Decoder model, we can identify the long-term sequence information of videos and enlarge the difference between normal and novel segments, which enables more accurate novelty identification.
- We conduct extensive experiments over three real datasets to evaluate the effectiveness and efficiency of the proposed LIREM framework.

The rest of the paper is organized as follows. In Sect. 2, we review related work about outlier detection for feature cleaning and anomaly detection in video. Section 3 describes the proposed generic framework for novelty detection in online social video. The proposed iterative outlier detection and the LSTM-Decoder model are presented in detail. The experimental results are presented in Sect. 4 to demonstrate the effectiveness and efficiency of our framework. Finally, we draw a conclusion in Sect. 5.

2   Related Work

This section reviews the existing research highly related to this work, including the outlier detection methods for feature cleaning, and video anomaly detection.

2.1   Feature Cleaning

The idea of feature cleaning is to detect and remove outliers that are significantly different from other observations. To address this challenge, many outlier detection methods have been developed. DBSCAN [5] is a density-based clustering algorithm which focuses on finding neighbors by density on an "n-dimensional sphere" with radius ϵ. A cluster can be defined as the maximal set of 'density connected points' in the feature space. It runs efficiently and can effectively deal with noise. Unlike k-means, no cluster number k is required. The Local Outlier Factor (LOF) [1] algorithm is an unsupervised outlier detection method which computes the local density deviation of a given data point concerning its neighbors. It considers as outliers the samples that have a substantially lower density than their neighbors. One-Class Support Vector Machine (OCSVM) [24] is an unsupervised learning algorithm that is trained only on the normal data. It learns the boundaries of these points and is, therefore, able to classify points that lie outside the boundary as outliers. The iForest [15] evaluates outliers by building multiple isolation trees (iTrees). For each iTree, randomly sampled observations are iteratively split by selecting a feature dimension and a corresponding split value between the maximum and minimum values. This method has few parameters, which makes it fairly robust and easy to optimize. However, all these methods are not suitable for large-scale data which has high volume with high-dimensional features, since they require prior knowledge of the model or are sensitive to parameters, and their processing is computationally expensive.

2.2 Video Anomaly Detection

Anomaly detection in image and video has drawn much attention in recent years, and existing techniques can be mainly divided into two categories: metric-based methods [3,19–21] and learning-based methods [9,11,12,16–18,28,29]. Early works on anomaly detection in video rely on handcrafted appearance and motion features to represent normal events and then judge the target event by distance or density metrics, thus they are called metric-based methods. However, these methods need domain experts to identify low-level features like HOG and SIFT, and most of them have high time costs. Therefore, they can barely deal with a huge volume of high-speed online social video streams.

The neural networks have developed by leaps and bounds, and many learning-based methods have been conducted on anomaly detection in video. DARE [28] is an unsupervised method to learn reconstructions using an autoencoder. It reveals that when data is embedded into low-dimensional representations and then reconstructed by an autoencoder, the normalities tend to have smaller reconstruction errors than the anomalies. AnoGAN [23] is based on deep generative adversarial networks. By concurrently training a generative model and a discriminator, it enables the identification of anomalies on unseen data in an unsupervised manner. In work [17], Liu et al. propose a future frame prediction network for anomaly detection using U-Net as a basic prediction network. In the testing phase, if a frame agrees with its prediction, it potentially corresponds to a normal event. Otherwise, it is classified as an anomaly. In [30], Zenati et al. utilize modified GAN methods that learns an encoder during training to develop an anomaly detection method. However, these approaches only focus on short-term information using optimal flow or 3d-convolution layers, some of them even ignore the temporal information. This could bring false negative alarms triggered by short-term information. And this is a challenge for detecting novelty in online social video.

In addition, anomaly detection models trained in the supervised way have also been studied due to its high performance [12]. Liu et al. [16] propose a framework, MLEP to detect anomalies by enlarging the margin between normal and abnormal events, under a strong assumption that normal events can be well predicted. Work [25] solves the problem of labeled data shortage by transfer learning and proposed a video anomaly detection method that learns in a supervised learning manner. In work [31], Zhang et al. propose a weakly supervised anomaly detection method. Multi-instance learning (MIL) is introduced to utilize both normal and anomaly videos. Since the above studies trained the novelty or abnormal detection model in a supervised way, they suffer from several problems such as data imbalance and vulnerability to undefined novelty [12].

In this work, we take long-term information of online social video into consideration. First, we propose an iterative outlier detection for cleaning the feature space, then an LSTM-Decoder model is designed to overcome the disadvantages of the existing work.

3   LIREM Novelty Detection Framework

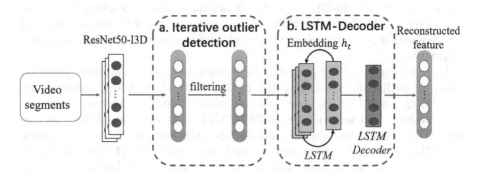

Fig. 1. Overview of the proposed framework.

In this section, we describe the proposed generic framework called LIREM for novelty detection in online social video. Given a video stream which can be divided into segments $V = \{v_1, v_2, \cdots, v_n\}$, and these segments are described as set $F = \{f_1, f_2, \cdots, f_n\}$, where f_i denotes feature of the segment i. Given incoming video segments V_q and a novelty scoring function $score$, the task of novelty detection returns a list of segments with top scores, S_{novel}. For any segment $v_i \notin S_{novel}$ and $v_j \in S_{novel}$, the following condition holds:

$$score(v_i) < score(v_j) \tag{1}$$

The proposed framework is shown in Fig. 1. It mainly contains two modules: (1) iterative outlier detection; (2) LSTM-Decoder. To detect novelty in online social video, both short-term and long-term information are important. After extracting features by ResNet50-I3D [2] which captures the short-term spatial-temporal information from video segments. Then these features are filtered by the proposed outlier detection method to improve the learning performance. After that, we design an LSTM-Decoder model where LSTM structures capture the long-term information and the decoder layer enlarges the reconstruction error of novel segments.

3.1   Iterative Outlier Detection

Feature Extraction. To capture the short-term information of online social video, video segments should be effectively represented. Due to the high volume of video streams, an efficient feature extraction method is also required. Besides, the temporal information should also be captured, since influencer behaviors are described by consecutive sequences of frames. Therefore, we need to divide the video into segments and find the proper representation of these segments. First, we divide the collected videos into segments by the sliding window strategy.

For each segment, the sliding window size is 64, which means it contains 64 frames. And the sliding window step is 25 because the FPS of the video is 25. During segmentation, proper transformations are adopted. After that, we utilize a pre-trained ResNet50-I3D model to extract the action recognition feature for each segment. The ResNet50-I3D model takes a sequence of frames as input and returns a vector as the representation which captures short-term spatio-temporal information.

Once all segments are presented by feature vectors, we can filter potential noises by outlier detection. Existing methods like DBSCAN [5], iForest [15], OCSVM [24], and LOF [1] have been conducted to address this issue. However, these methods have some problems: DBSCAN is sensitive to pre-defined parameters. iForest could lose the information when the feature is high-dimensional. OCSVM and LOF are time-consuming and memory-intensive for large datasets. Besides, none of the methods outperforms the others for all datasets. And this requires other operations to select proper methods. To address these challenges, we propose a new outlier detection method in an iterative manner. The key idea is to adaptively select outliers and optimize the selection strategy for a large feature set by using iterative measurement. The algorithm is shown in Fig. 2, and we describe the details below.

---

input: F: feature set of normal segments;
         M_{AE}: pretrained autoencoder;
         τ: weight for selecting outliers;
output: S: the set of excluded features.
1. $S \leftarrow \emptyset$; $F_0 \leftarrow F$;
2. for i from 1 to max_iter do:
3. $S_i \leftarrow \emptyset$;
4.   for $f \in F_{i-1}$ do:
5. $RE(f) = MSE(M_{AE}(f), f)$;
6. $AveRE = \frac{1}{|F_{i-1}|} \sum RE(f)$;
7.   for $f \in F_{i-1}$ do:
8.   if $\tau \cdot RE(f) \geq AveRE$:
9.   Put f into S_i;
10.   if $S_i \subseteq S$:
11.   Break;
12.   else:
13. $S = S \cup S_i$;
14. $F_i = F_{i-1} - S_i$;
15.   Fine-tune M_{AE} with F_i;
16. Return S.

Fig. 2. Interative outlier detection.

Given a pre-trained autoencoder model M_{AE}, feature set F, and weight τ, our method performs outlier detection with three steps in an iterative manner:

(1) compute RE for each feature and average RE (line 4–6); (2) select potential outliers (line 7–9); (3) update normal feature set and fine-tune the autoencoder model with it (line 10–15). We first initialize S to store the excluded features and put the feature set F as F_0 (line 1). In the i-th iteration, a set S_i is initialized for storing the excluded features. Then, we compute reconstruction error (RE) for each feature f by mean squared error (MSE), where $M_{AE}(f)$ means the reconstructed feature. Following that, the average RE value for the whole dataset F_{i-1} is computed (line 4–6). To distinguish noise in feature space, we set $\tau \in (0, 2]$ as the weight and select feature f whose RE is $\frac{1}{\tau}$ times larger than the average RE into S_i (line 7–9). If S_i is empty or every element in S_i has been selected in S, we end the processing by the early stop. Otherwise, S_i is added to S with removing duplicate elements (line 10–13). Based on S_i and F_{i-1}, we generate filtered normal feature set F_i and fine-tune the model M_{AE} with it. This makes outliers at different scales will be considered (line 14–15). After ending the whole loop, we return the final set S of excluded features (line 16). In the end, we exclude these features and generate a filtered feature set $F' = F - S$.

3.2 LSTM-Decoder Model

After cleaning the features by the iterative outlier detection, we need to train a model over the filtered data, and use the model for detecting the novelties from social video streams. As mentioned before, the behaviors of influencers are relevant over long periods. Hence, the ideal model should be able to capture the long-term temporal information of video sequences, while differentiating the normal video segments and novelties. In this work, we investigate existing deep neural networks for time series problems and decoder structures and select suitable ones to be integrated as a uniform model for this task.

For time series problems, many works have been conducted. Typical approaches include Long Short-Term Memory (LSTM) [10] and Bidirectional Encoder Representations from Transformers (BERT) [4]. LSTM is a well-known variant of recurrent neural network (RNN), which addresses the vanishing gradient problem and is capable of capturing long-term dependencies. BERT is designed for natural language processing (NLP), which performs great for processing text sequences in language generation tasks and natural language understanding tasks. Our novelty detection handles online streaming video data which contains a large amount of visual information with long-term dependencies. The ideal model needs to capture the characteristics of the visual feature and long-term temporal dependency information. In addition, efficient online processing is also demanded. To choose a better model to be integrated into our framework, we conduct preliminary experiments over the influencer dataset in Sect. 4 to compare the effectiveness and efficiency of the detection using these two models. To adapt BERT from NLP to general sequence processing, we abandon the tokenizer and modify the input as the feature sequence. With the same input sequences $seq \in R^{M \times q \times d}$, the AUROC score and the average time cost of the two models are reported in Table 1. According to the table, LSTM outperforms BERT in terms of AUROC. This could be caused by the difference between visual feature-based learning and text-based learning. Besides, some studies [6] also reveal that LSTM outperforms BERT on some tasks and datasets. For efficiency comparison, BERT takes much more time than LSTM. This is because BERT has a larger model complexity than LSTM. What's more, this also leads to the requirement of many resources to train or fine-tune. Therefore, we utilize LSTM structures to model the sequence of features and capture its long-term information.

In this work, we aim to generate the prediction of the next-time segment from a sequence of segments and enlarge the difference between normal and novel segments. From the view of seq2seq [27], RNN can be used as both encoder and decoder to generate an objective sequence from the input sequence. Thus, the LSTM modeling the sequence of segment features can be regarded as an encoder, and we also use another LSTM as the decoder. However, instead of generating a new sequence, we focus on the next segment of the input sequence. Hence, given the input sequence, we only take the last hidden states which are the most relevant to the next time segment as the input of the decoder and reconstruct a vector to represent the next time segment. With this processing, we reduce the computing cost of reconstruction while keeping the most relevant information.

Table 1. Comparison of average time cost.

Methods	LSTM	BERT
AUROC (%)	77.98	71.22
Time cost (ms)	9.4	67.3

Training Strategy. In this work, we first organize q consecutive features as an input sequence $s_t = [f_{t-q}, ..., f_{t-1}]$ to cover 250 frames according to the previous work [7]. For filtered feature set F', the set of feature sequences is $Seq = \{s_{t_1}, s_{t_2}, ..., s_{t_n}\}$. Besides, we collect all next-time segments of sequences as set $X = \{f_{t_1}, f_{t_2}, ..., f_{t_n}\}$. For each sequence s_t, we put it into LSTM and get a set of hidden states $\{h_i\}$ with corresponding cell states $\{C_i\}$, where $i = t - q, \cdots, t - 1$. As mentioned before, we only take the last hidden states (with the cell states) into consideration and this process is formulated as:

$$[h_t, C_t] = LSTM(s_t) \tag{2}$$

To train the LSTM decoder, we first initialize its states by the last states of the encoder $[g_0, C_0] \leftarrow [h_t, C_t]$, and a full-connection layer is added to generate prediction of next-time segment from the hidden state g_1. The representation of the next-time segment is computed by:

$$\hat{f}_t = De([h_t, C_t]) \tag{3}$$

For the given feature sequences Seq and corresponding next-time segments X, the prediction of X is calculated by:

$$\hat{X} = M(Seq, \theta) \tag{4}$$

M is the integrated model and θ is the set of parameters to be learned. To jointly optimize the LSTM and decoder networks and make the decoder layer reconstruct properly feature from the hidden state of LSTM structures, we formulate the objective function based on reconstruction error. We compute the L2 loss between the input features and the reconstructed features by MSE. The objective function is shown below:

$$L_M = MSE(\hat{X}, X) \qquad (5)$$

The model is optimized by minimizing the objective function. Specifically, we randomly initialize the states of LSTM and decoder layers and optimize the model with Adam [13] algorithm which is an effective and efficient optimization algorithm and is widely used in deep neural network training. The learning rate is set to 0.001 and adjusted with the epoch increasing.

Novelty Identification. With learned model $M(\cdot, \theta)$, given incoming feature sequence s_t and the corresponding feature f_t, the reconstructed feature $\hat{f}_t$ and reconstruction error can be computed by:

$$RE_t = ||\hat{f}_t - f_t||_2 \qquad (6)$$

where $\hat{f}_t = M(s_t, \theta)$. Different from the traditional reconstruction error-based measurement that normalizes the reconstruction error values into $(0, 1)$, we keep the values in the original space. Because it's impossible to find the minimal and maximal reconstruction errors on the streaming data in real online social video scenarios.

4   Experimental Evaluation

In this section, we will present the effectiveness and efficiency of the proposed framework on novelty detection in online social video.

4.1   Experimental Setup

Table 2. Overview of datasets.

Dataset	Duration	Description
Influencer	09:52	Influencer makes an introduction of products for promoting
Speech	10:06	Speaker makes a formal speech to express opinions
TED	10:15	Expert presents a talk at TED conference

As presented in Table 2, we conduct our experiments on a 30-hour video collection which is downloaded from bilibili[2]. And it contains three types of video:

---

[2] https://www.bilibili.com/.

influencer, speech, and TED talk. The influencer dataset contains videos mainly about an influencer promoting products. They would introduce some items in specific styles (actions, gestures, etc.). Speech videos are about a speaker making a formal speech, and their actions are quite limited. And TED talk dataset contains influential videos from expert speakers on education, business, science, tech, and creativity. Different from a formal speech, the speaker in the TED talk would interact with the audience by using more actions and gestures. For each type, we select about 10-hour videos to organize the dataset, and each video is resized to 480×480 with the 25 FPS. In experiments, we divide the datasets into training, validation, and testing parts by 3 : 1 : 1. Only the normal segments in the training part are used for model learning.

To label the novelties, 5 evaluators who majored in computer science are given these videos. After watching, they will report segments which they think are novel. Segments which are voted by more than 2 evaluators will finally be regarded as novelties.

4.2   Evaluation Methodology

We compare the proposed framework with three novelty detection methods: LTR [8], SCL [19] and VEC [29]. LTR [8] utilizes a fully convolutional feed-forward deep autoencoder-based approach to learn representation and classifier. SCL [19] is based on dictionary learning to learn the normal behaviors and used reconstruction error to measure anomalies. VEC [29] addressed novelty detection with a new learning paradigm, which trains deep neural networks to complete the erased patches of incomplete video events.

To estimate effectiveness, we report our results using the Area Under the Receiver Operating Characteristic curve (AUROC), following previous works on novelty or anomaly detection [8,19,29]. With the ROC curve, the sensitivity (true positive rate) and specificity (true negative rate) for all potential thresholds are incorporated in the AUROC score. The high AUROC score indicates that the model is good at distinguishing. To estimate the efficiency, we report the average time cost for detecting novelty on testing parts of the datasets.

The proposed framework is implemented using the Pytorch, a widely used deep learning library. The experiments are carried out using an Intel i5, 2.30 GHz processor machine with 4 GB NVIDIA GTX 1050Ti graphics card.

4.3   Effectiveness Evaluation

In this section, we first evaluate the effect of iterative outlier detection for cleaning feature space and find the optimal parameters for the algorithm. Then we study the effect of training epoch number based on reconstruction error. Finally, we compare the proposed model with the other three novelty detection approaches.

Effect of Iterative Outlier Detection. We evaluate the effect of the proposed iterative outlier detection algorithm with different triggering thresholds τ on original extracted features. The AUROC of novelty detection is reported by varying τ from 0 to 2, which controls the tolerance of outliers. With different τ, multiple sets of outliers are generated. When $\tau = 0$, no outlier is selected and the original feature set will not be filtered. Following that we conduct LSTM-Decoder model training on each filtered feature set. The results of novelty detection for three datasets are presented in Fig. 3.

For the influencer dataset (Fig. 3(a)), we observe that AUROC grows with the τ increasing at the beginning (τ is from 0 to 1.1). This demonstrates that the original feature set contains noises and outliers which weaken the model learning. Comparing with the no-filtering, where $\tau = 0$ and AUROC = 0.7459, the proposed iterative outlier detection method does improve the effectiveness (AUROC = 0.7798) of the model. On the other hand, a large τ leads to a loose condition for selecting outliers, where many features are excluded. This could misjudge the normal features, and the AUROC descends (τ is from 1.1 to 2.0). Similar observations are obtained on speech and TED datasets. Generally, the optimal AUROC is achieved when τ is around 1.0. Hence, we set τ to 1.0 and generate the filtered feature sets for the following experiments.

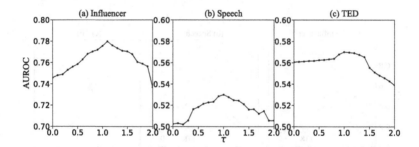

Fig. 3. Effect of τ.

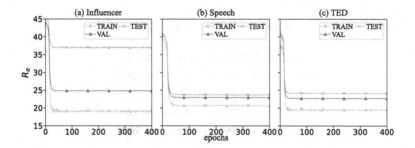

Fig. 4. Effect of epoch.

Effect of Epoch. To evaluate the effect of epoch, we report the average reconstruction error (RE) over epochs on three datasets. According to the tendency of RE, we can achieve a suitable epoch number for model convergence. Specifically, we compute RE for training, validation, and testing parts by the Eq. 6. It's worth noting that, the training part only contains features of normal segments. Correspondingly, only normal segments in the validation part and novel segments in the testing part are sampled to show the difference between normal and novel segments. Figure 4 shows the change of RE values over epochs. We have several observations: (1) The average RE for different parts are distinctive. For all datasets, RE of the training part converges after around 50 epochs, meanwhile, RE curves of validation and testing parts become stable. This indicates that the proposed model is able to capture the information which could be used for detecting novelties. (2) Besides, we get a large difference between validation and testing parts on the influencer dataset, while the difference is relatively small on speech and TED datasets. It is because influencer videos contain more discriminative action information than speech and TED videos. And this corresponds with the observation that influencers would like to use more actions and gestures, but the speaker in a speech or TED talk keeps few actions. In experiments, we set the maximal epoch number as 400 and report the best detecting performance.

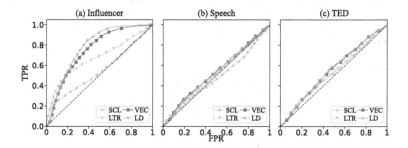

Fig. 5. ROC curves comparison.

Table 3. AUROC comparison.

Method	Influencer	Speech	TED
SCL	0.5469	0.4833	0.5282
LTR	0.6685	0.5104	0.5362
VEC	0.7478	**0.5362**	0.5559
LD	**0.7798**	0.5298	**0.5604**

Effectiveness Comparison. To further evaluate the performance of proposed method, we compare effectiveness of LSTM-Decoder (LD) method with three existing novelty detection methods, LTR [8], SCL [19] and VEC [29]. First, the ROC curves are presented in Fig. 5 (a)–(c). As we can see, the proposed LSTM-Decoder outperforms other methods on the influencer dataset and gets similar curves with VEC on speech and TED datasets. Specifically, SCL gets the worst performance on all datasets for it's based on traditional sparse coding and handcrafted representation. LTR utilizes fully convolutional networks and an autoencoder structure, which is able to capture more information. However, the convolutional network only captures short-term information by taking several frames as input. VEC gets better curves than LTR and SCL on all datasets. This is because VEC uses both appearance information and optical flow as the input of the model and trains the model in a novel learning paradigm. However, VEC builds on a designed spatio-temporal cube which also only considers short-term information. And this leads to the second best on influencer and TED datasets. In addition, all methods get limited AUROC on speech and TED datasets. It is because limited actions in speech and TED talk videos lead to the shortage of visual information, no matter short-term or long-term, for novelty detection. Therefore, all methods perform poorly, especially on the speech dataset. Furthermore, we report corresponding AUROC in Table 3. As observed before, LSTM-Decoder gets the best AUROC on influencer and TED datasets, which verifies the effect of long-term information. VEC gets slightly better AUROC on the speech dataset. This could be contributed by the complex structures of VEC. LTR is inferior to VEC and the traditional method SCL performances worst.

4.4 Efficiency Comparison

In this section, we report the average time cost for detecting novelty on testing data to present the efficiency comparison. As reported in Table 4, LTR costs the least time since it can be modeled in an end-to-end manner and the feature extraction is embedded in the whole model. For VEC and the proposed LSTM-Decoder, an independent neural network is used as a feature extractor. However, with the help of GPU, they can still process frames at a fast speed. As for SCL, it's a traditional sparse coding method, and handcrafted features need to be computed. Thus, it costs much more time than other methods. Due to the network structures, the proposed method gets second best in efficiency comparison, but it achieves better effectiveness performance than LTR. To conclude, the proposed method is efficiently acceptable for novelty detection in online social video.

Table 4. Time cost of different methods.

Method	SCL	LTR	VEC	LD
Time cost (ms)	102	18	52	32

5 Conclusion

In this paper, we design a generic framework, LIREM to explore novelty detection in online social video. We first propose a novel iterative outlier detection method to clean the feature space. Then, we model the features of video segments as sequences and design an LSTM-Decoder-based model to capture the long-term information for novelty detection. The experimental results show the effectiveness and efficiency of our proposed framework against baseline novelty detection methods.

References

1. Breunig, M.M., Kriegel, H., Ng, R.T., Sander, J.: LOF: identifying density-based local outliers. In: Proceedings of the 2000 ACM SIGMOD International Conference on Management of Data, pp. 93–104 (2000)
2. Carreira, J., Zisserman, A.: Quo vadis, action recognition? a new model and the kinetics dataset. In: 2017 IEEE Conference on Computer Vision and Pattern Recognition, CVPR 2017, pp. 4724–4733 (2017)
3. Cong, Y., Yuan, J., Liu, J.: Abnormal event detection in crowded scenes using sparse representation. Pattern Recognit. **46**, 1851–1864 (2013)
4. Devlin, J., Chang, M., Lee, K., Toutanova, K.: BERT: pre-training of deep bidirectional transformers for language understanding. CoRR abs/1810.04805 (2018)
5. Ester, M., Kriegel, H., Sander, J., Xu, X.: A density-based algorithm for discovering clusters in large spatial databases with noise. In: Proceedings of the Second International Conference on Knowledge Discovery and Data Mining (KDD-96), pp. 226–231 (1996)
6. Ezen-Can, A.: A comparison of LSTM and BERT for small corpus. CoRR abs/2009.05451 (2020)
7. Geest, R.D., Tuytelaars, T.: Modeling temporal structure with LSTM for online action detection. In: 2018 IEEE Winter Conference on Applications of Computer Vision, WACV 2018, pp. 1549–1557 (2018)
8. Hasan, M., Choi, J., Neumann, J., Roy-Chowdhury, A.K., Davis, L.S.: Learning temporal regularity in video sequences. In: 2016 IEEE Conference on Computer Vision and Pattern Recognition, CVPR 2016, pp. 733–742 (2016)
9. Hinami, R., Mei, T., Satoh, S.: Joint detection and recounting of abnormal events by learning deep generic knowledge. In: IEEE International Conference on Computer Vision, ICCV 2017, pp. 3639–3647 (2017)
10. Hochreiter, S., Schmidhuber, J.: Long short-term memory. Neural Comput. **9**, 1735–1780 (1997)
11. Ionescu, R.T., Khan, F.S., Georgescu, M., Shao, L.: Object-centric auto-encoders and dummy anomalies for abnormal event detection in video. In: IEEE Conference on Computer Vision and Pattern Recognition, CVPR 2019, pp. 7842–7851 (2019)

12. Kim, J., Cho, S.: Unsupervised novelty detection in video with adversarial autoencoder based on non-euclidean space. In: 15th International Conference on Signal-Image Technology & Internet-Based Systems, SITIS 2019, pp. 22–27 (2019)

13. Kingma, D.P., Ba, J.: Adam: A method for stochastic optimization. In: 3rd International Conference on Learning Representations, ICLR 2015 (2015)

14. Lee, J., Kim, J., Kim, I., Han, K.: Cyber threat detection based on artificial neural networks using event profiles. IEEE Access **7**, 165607–165626 (2019)

15. Liu, F.T., Ting, K.M., Zhou, Z.: Isolation forest. In: Proceedings of the 8th IEEE International Conference on Data Mining (ICDM 2008), 15–19 December 2008, Pisa, Italy, pp. 413–422 (2008)

16. Liu, W., Luo, W., Li, Z., Zhao, P., Gao, S.: Margin learning embedded prediction for video anomaly detection with A few anomalies. In: Proceedings of the Twenty-Eighth International Joint Conference on Artificial Intelligence, IJCAI 2019, pp. 3023–3030 (2019)

17. Liu, W., Luo, W., Lian, D., Gao, S.: Future frame prediction for anomaly detection - A new baseline. In: 2018 IEEE Conference on Computer Vision and Pattern Recognition, CVPR 2018, pp. 6536–6545 (2018)

18. Liu, Y., Zhao, K., Cong, G., Bao, Z.: Online anomalous trajectory detection with deep generative sequence modeling. In: 36th IEEE International Conference on Data Engineering, ICDE 2020,. pp. 949–960 (2020)

19. Lu, C., Shi, J., Jia, J.: Abnormal event detection at 150 FPS in MATLAB. In: IEEE International Conference on Computer Vision, ICCV 2013, pp. 2720–2727 (2013)

20. Mahadevan, V., Li, W., Bhalodia, V., Vasconcelos, N.: Anomaly detection in crowded scenes. In: The Twenty-Third IEEE Conference on Computer Vision and Pattern Recognition, CVPR 2010, pp. 1975–1981 (2010)

21. Mehran, R., Oyama, A., Shah, M.: Abnormal crowd behavior detection using social force model. In: 2009 IEEE Computer Society Conference on Computer Vision and Pattern Recognition (CVPR 2009), pp. 935–942 (2009)

22. Sabokrou, M., Khalooei, M., Fathy, M., Adeli, E.: Adversarially learned one-class classifier for novelty detection. In: 2018 IEEE Conference on Computer Vision and Pattern Recognition, CVPR 2018, pp. 3379–3388 (2018)

23. Schlegl, T., Seeböck, P., Waldstein, S.M., Schmidt-Erfurth, U., Langs, G.: Unsupervised anomaly detection with generative adversarial networks to guide marker discovery. In: Niethammer, M., Styner, M., Aylward, S., Zhu, H., Oguz, I., Yap, P.-T., Shen, D. (eds.) IPMI 2017. LNCS, vol. 10265, pp. 146–157. Springer, Cham (2017). https://doi.org/10.1007/978-3-319-59050-9_12

24. Schölkopf, B., Platt, J.C., Shawe-Taylor, J., Smola, A.J., Williamson, R.C.: Estimating the support of a high-dimensional distribution. Neural Comput. **13**, 1443–1471 (2001)

25. Shin, W., Cho, S.-B.: CCTV image sequence generation and modeling method for video anomaly detection using generative adversarial network. In: Yin, H., Camacho, D., Novais, P., Tallón-Ballesteros, A.J. (eds.) IDEAL 2018. LNCS, vol. 11314, pp. 457–467. Springer, Cham (2018). https://doi.org/10.1007/978-3-030-03493-1_48

26. Surace, C., Worden, K.: Novelty detection in a changing environment: A negative selection approach. Mech. Syst. Signal Process. **24**(4), 1114–1128 (2010)

27. Sutskever, I., Vinyals, O., Le, Q.V.: Sequence to sequence learning with neural networks. In: Advances in Neural Information Processing Systems 27: Annual Conference on Neural Information Processing Systems 2014, pp. 3104–3112 (2014)

28. Xia, Y., Cao, X., Wen, F., Hua, G., Sun, J.: Learning discriminative reconstructions for unsupervised outlier removal. In: 2015 IEEE International Conference on Computer Vision, ICCV 2015, pp. 1511–1519 (2015)
29. Yu, G., Wang, S., Cai, Z., Zhu, E., Xu, C., Yin, J., Kloft, M.: Cloze test helps: Effective video anomaly detection via learning to complete video events. In: MM '20: The 28th ACM International Conference on Multimedia, pp. 583–591 (2020)
30. Zenati, H., Foo, C.S., Lecouat, B., Manek, G., Chandrasekhar, V.R.: Efficient gan-based anomaly detection. In: International Conference on Learning Representation, pp. 1–13 (2018)
31. Zhang, J., Qing, L., Miao, J.: Temporal convolutional network with complementary inner bag loss for weakly supervised anomaly detection. In: 2019 IEEE International Conference on Image Processing, ICIP 2019, pp. 4030–4034 (2019)
32. Zhou, J., Pun, C.: Personal privacy protection via irrelevant faces tracking and pixelation in video live streaming. IEEE Trans. Inf. Forensics Secur. **16**, 1088–1103 (2021)

When IT Service Adoption Meets Behavioral Economics: Addressing Present Bias Challenges

Iris Reinhartz-Berger[1] (✉) ⓘ, Doron Kliger[2] ⓘ, Eliad Amsalem[2],
and Alan Hartman[1] ⓘ

[1] Information Systems Department, University of Haifa, Haifa, Israel
{iris,ahartman}@is.haifa.ac.il
[2] Economics Department, University of Haifa, Haifa, Israel
kliger@econ.haifa.ac.il, eamsal09@campus.haifa.ac.il

Abstract. In an ideal world, IT service adoption is derived from the value it gives to the different stakeholders. However, in the real world, human behavior may induce sub-optimal decision making that raises barriers to the optimal adoption of the service. In this paper, we focus on a specific and common behavioral phenomenon – *present bias* – people's tendency to prefer immediate gratification at the expense of future outcomes. We start by conceptualizing the considerations for selecting the economically-preferred IT service, from a list of alternatives. Then, we devise an approach for assessing the present values of the alternatives from the viewpoints of the various stakeholders. Lastly, we evaluate our approach using a case study of service adoption in a multinational technology enterprise.

Keywords: Behavioral economics · IT adoption · Present bias · Service value

1 Introduction

In an ideal world, service value is the core determinant of stakeholder decisions regarding the adoption of IT services. In real life, however, there are many barriers, hampering optimal practice of the decision-making process. The list of barriers confronted by the organization includes technological challenges (problems of security, insufficient infrastructure), organizational factors (management style, shortage of financial sources), barriers arising from the surrounding environment (incomplete knowledge of the market), and individual barriers (bounded knowledge, personal relations in the organization) [1]. A recent systematic review [6] suggest guidelines for IT adoption and ways to overcome adoption barriers. Specifically, it is suggested that "decision makers should adopt IT in a formalized manner; making IT planning and strategy necessary before implementing IT." While this review focuses on small and medium organizations, we find the material it presents relevant to large enterprises, as well. Many studies on technology adoption aim to understand, predict, and explain variables influencing adoption behavior at the individual, as well as at the organizational, level [18]. These studies have led to the development of conceptual models and frameworks aimed at understanding the relationship between barriers and adoption behavior.

J. Ralyté et al. (Eds.): ER 2022, LNCS 13607, pp. 161–175, 2022.
https://doi.org/10.1007/978-3-031-17995-2_12

In our research, we focus on real-world situations, where aspects of human behavior induce sub-optimal decision making. We list causes for such behavior and point to possible behavioral and economic interventions to improve the chances of adoption of the economically-preferred IT service, out of a list of alternative solutions. We concentrate on a specific prominent cause of sub-optimal behavior, namely – *present bias* – people's tendency to prefer immediate gratification at the expense of future outcomes. Having presented a root-cause analysis of human behavior, which results in convergence to economically-inferior solutions, we devise an approach that facilitates the selection of the preferred alternative. In particular, we shed light on the following questions: (i) What are the behavioral properties that hamper optimal decision making by the enterprise's stakeholders? and (ii) What remedies may be employed for improving the decision-making process and arriving at adoption of the economically-preferred solution?

Our main contribution is a conceptual model, accommodating the phenomenon of present bias, highlighting both behavioral and economic considerations, and assessing the present values of the alternatives from the viewpoints of the various stakeholders. We further present and discuss a case study based on a real IT service adoption scenario in a multinational technology enterprise, and demonstrate the potential of our approach to improve IT service adoption, through employing behavioral-economics principles and tools.

The rest of the paper is structured as follows. Section 2 presents the underlying conceptual model; Sect. 3 provides a root-cause analysis of economic behavior, yielding a behavioral model for improving service adoption; Sect. 4 presents some preliminary results and insights from our case study; Sect. 5 reviews the relevant literature; and Sect. 6 summarizes and highlights some future research directions.

2 The Underlying Conceptual Model

In our previous work [11], we developed a conceptual value-based service adoption model whose goal is to analyze IT service alternatives from IT and organizational perspectives. That version of the model referred only to core organizational and IT concepts and ignored economic and behavioral considerations. Figure 1 presents an extended version of that conceptual model (the extensions are marked in grey in the figure), and Table 1 summarizes the elements. Sections 2.1 and 2.2 explain the organizational and IT concepts, respectively, while Sect. 2.3 concentrates on the combination of concepts. In Sect. 3, we introduce a root-cause analysis of economic behavior on top of this extended value-based service adoption model.

Throughout this paper, we exemplify the concepts and considerations on a case study of a vehicle management IT service in a multinational technology enterprise. The case study is elaborated in Sect. 4 where we evaluate our approach. Here we describe some essential characteristics that help us demonstrate the approach. The operations team at the enterprise is responsible for managing the vehicle fleet, ordering new vehicles when needed, tracking toll payments, reviewing and validating invoices, pricing new vehicle models, and providing a catalog of available vehicles for the employees. Currently, the team manages the service with spreadsheets that require frequent manual updates and provide limited access to the information by the employees who receive and use the vehicles.

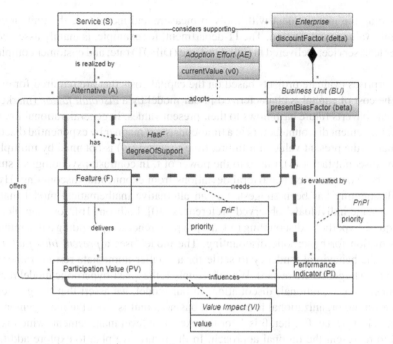

Fig. 1. The extended conceptual model (the extensions are marked in grey)

2.1 Organizational Concepts

An *enterprise*, a.k.a. Multi-Business Organization (MBO), is composed of *business units (BUs)*, each of which consists of a group of stakeholders with similar or mutual business goals. The business units are evaluated via *performance indicators (PIs)* – success measures of the enterprise or of particular business units of the enterprise [2].

The performance indicators may be weighted (i.e., prioritized) differently by the business units (e.g., ranging from irrelevant to very high priority). We denote this prioritization by *PriPI*. In our vehicle management case study, we refer to six stakeholder groups: the executive level management (management for short, acting strictly under an economic rationale); the IT department (in charge of selecting, implementing and maintaining the IT solutions); the corporate operations team (the business unit responsible for managing the vehicle fleet); the finance division (for auditing and controlling purposes); the payroll division (for salary calculations); and the employees in their role as service users[1]. The management evaluates operations in economic-value maximizing terms, such as Return on Investment (ROI) and Earnings per Share (EpS). The other units (i.e., stakeholder groups) are evaluated in terms related to their activities, which are aimed

---

[1] Although not a homogeneous business unit, the employees are the ones who receive and use the vehicles and thus an important stakeholder group with similar characteristics to a certain extent.

at providing the management with tools to measure and incentivize the units towards economic-value maximization. The IT department, for example, is mainly assessed via cost per lead/service; Delivered in Full, On Time (DiFOT) rate; and customer complaints [2].

Enterprises evaluate projects based on the capital costs that are required for execution. The cost of capital is characterized in our model by a *discount factor* (marked by δ), which converts future cash flows to their present values. In general, rational financial models implement discount factors in a time-consistent manner by exponential discounting. That is, the present value of a future, time-t reward (v_t) is obtained by multiplying it by the discount factor (δ), raised to the power of t. In contrast, psychological studies (cf. [8]) have documented behavioral deviations from exponential discounting. Hyperbolic discounting has been suggested as an alternative mathematical model that lies closer to some individuals' observed preferences [10]. Laibson [16], for example, proposed quasi-hyperbolic discounting (a.k.a. "β-δ preferences"), providing a discrete-time approximation for hyperbolic discounting. The model uses a *present bias factor* (β), which is the behavioral tendency to settle for a smaller immediate reward rather than waiting for a larger future reward. When β equals 1, the quasi-hyperbolic model reduces to exponential (i.e., rational) discounting. In our model, we assert that the greater the distance (in the organizational hierarchy) a business unit is from the management, the smaller is its β value. Further, β is 1 for the executive level management, which is presumed to represent the rational approach. In the future, we plan to explore additional factors which may have impact on β values.

2.2 IT-Related Concepts

We assume that the enterprise considers a set of services. The notion of service has different meanings in various disciplines, including service as behavior perspective, service as value co-creation, service as capability, service as application of competences and service as software [19]. Inspired by [18], we refer to a *service (S)* as a self-contained unit of software that performs a specific task for business units. A service can be realized by a set of *alternatives (A)*, each of which is a specific implementation of the service. An alternative has (or exhibits) a set of *features (F)* – prominent or distinctive user visible aspects, qualities, or characteristics [13]. An alternative may support a particular feature to a certain degree (represented in the model by *HasF*).

A service alternative offers a range of participation values, which are delivered by the features of the service alternatives. Like service, the term value is also heavily overloaded. Nevertheless, irrespective of the exact definition, two characteristics of value are discussed in [22]. First, value is goal-dependent, i.e. things have value to people because they allow them to achieve their goals. Second, value is ascribed to experiences (not objects) and is subjective in nature. Accordingly, we define *participation value (PV)* as a value that the participants may gain from using the service alternative [21]. Participation value comprises both economic value and less tangible values such as service quality, service equity, confidence benefits, or perceived sacrifice [9]. Participation value influences the performance indicators through value impact factors, represented in the model by the relation *VI*. For instance, efficiency contributes to ROI, EpS, DIfOt rate, and cost per lead/service; whereas usability contributes to quality index and DIfOt rate.

Table 1. A summary of elements (alphabetically ordered, grouped by type; attributes appear under their underlying concepts)

Name	Type	Abbr.	Description
(Service) Alternative	Concept	A	A specific implementation of a service
Business Unit	Concept	BU	A group of stakeholders with similar or mutual business goals
Business Unit.Present bias factor	Attribute	β	A factor reflecting the behavioral tendency to settle for a smaller immediate reward rather than to wait for a larger future reward
Enterprise	Concept	E	An organization that consists of several business units providing services to external or internal customers
Enterprise.Discount factor	Attribute	δ	A factor converting future cash flows to their present values
Feature	Concept	F	A prominent or distinctive user-visible aspect, quality, or characteristic of a service (alternative)
Participation Value	Concept	PV	The value which a participant gains from using a service alternative
Performance Indicator	Concept	PI	A success measure of the enterprise or any of its particular business units
Service	Concept	S	A self-contained unit of software that performs a specific task for business units
Adoption Effort	Relation	AE	A mapping $A \times BU \to \Re$, indicating the costs/efforts (V_0) of adopting a service alternative by a business unit
Delivers	Relation	Dlv	A mapping $F \times PV \to [0, 1]$, indicating the degree to which a feature delivers a participation value
Has	Relation	HasF	A mapping $A \times F \to [0, 1]$, indicating the degree to which a service alternative implements a feature
Influences	Relation	VI	A mapping $PV \times PI \to [0, 1]$, indicating the degree to which a participation value impacts a performance indicator
Is-evaluated-by	Relation	PriPI	A mapping $BU \times PI \to [0, 1]$, indicating how a business unit prioritizes its performance indicators
Needs	Relation	PriF	A mapping $BU \times F \to [0, 1]$, indicating how a business unit prioritizes a feature of the service alternatives

Returning to our case study, we consider three service alternatives: (A1) retaining the current solution (spreadsheets and an offline IS based on commercial software) with a minor addition: the relevant information would be sent to the different stakeholders quarterly via email; (A2) creating live Business Intelligence (BI) dashboards on top of the current IS; and (A3) developing a tailor-made IS that would allow simple data access, have a user friendly interface, provide invoice auditing tools, and integrate with the payroll system. The alternatives, A1 to A3, are ordered by their richness of functionality, in ascending order. So, A3, if implemented, would further deliver participation values of efficiency, usability, flexibility and accessibility. However, A3 requires more resources than the other alternatives and calls for more willingness to adopt changes by the business units.

Note that business units adopt service alternatives with certain features in order to satisfy their business needs while improving their performance based on the value delivered from the features. In other words, features are needed by the business units at varying levels of priority (represented in the model as *PriF*). These priorities are subjective as discussed above. However, we assume that people belonging to the same business unit and thus having similar goals will assess these priorities similarly. For example, the finance division is mainly focused on auditing support from the service, while the corporate operations team and the employees are more interested in the quality of the user interface. In the future, we plan to conduct an empirical study to explore this hypothesis in the context of IT service adoption.

Each business unit is required to invest some effort in adopting a given alternative. This is quantified in the model by current value (V_0). For simplicity, we assume that the costs of developing and adopting alternatives occur in the present, i.e., in period zero (denoted by V_0); the future rewards of using the alternative are presented in period-one value (denoted by V_1), which takes into consideration the discounted values of all future periods, including maintenance costs. In our running example, the present value of A1 is the smallest and that of A3 is the largest.

2.3   A Value-Based Service Adoption Model

In our model, we aim at selecting the economically-preferred alternative and maximize its adoption by all business units. Hence, we express the impact (benefits) of the various service alternatives (different combinations of features). This can be used for estimating the future values of the service alternatives (V_1). We define two types of outcomes: IT-driven (the red/solid path in Fig. 1, involving mainly IT-related concepts) and BU-driven (the blue/dashed path in Fig. 1, involving mainly organizational concepts).

Definition 1. An *IT-driven outcome* represents the impact of the participation values of the proposed service alternatives on the enterprise performance indicators. It is computed as:

$$HasF \otimes Dlv \otimes VI$$

where $\otimes$ indicates matrix multiplication[2].

---
[2] We assume matrix representations of all mappings.

Definition 2. A *BU-driven outcome* represents the values offered by the proposed service alternatives to each business unit, taking into account the priorities of the business units for specific features and performance indicators. This is computed by:

$$HasF \otimes PriF^T \otimes PriPI$$

where $PriF^T$ is the transpose of $PriF$ and $\otimes$ indicates matrix multiplication.

Figure 2 exemplifies possible outcomes for our case study. They are represented as radial axis plots, where the radial axes represent the different performance indicators (PIs) and each proposed service alternative is represented as a polygon. The closer a vertex is to the origin, the lower the performance indicator value of that alternative is. The left figure (a) is IT-driven. It clearly shows that A3 (developing a new tailor-made IS) is superior in all examined performance indicators. However, the right figure (b), which considers the business units' preferences in terms of features (*PriF*) and performance indicators (*priPI*), shows that A2 (adding BI dashboards) may be more beneficial in

Fig. 2. Examples of possible outcomes: (a) IT-driven and (b) BU-driven

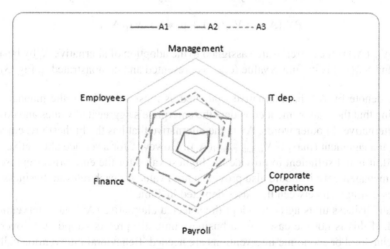

Fig. 3. A BU-driven view (HasF $\otimes$ PriF^T), highlighting the preferences of the individual business units

terms of cost, time, and resources. A2 also performs closely to the more expensive and desirable solution (A3) in terms of customer complaints.

Figure 3 shows another BU-driven view that mainly considers the business units' prioritization of features (*PriF*); here the radial axes represent the different business units. It is clear that while the management, payroll and finance divisions prefer the third alternative (A3), the IT department and the corporate operations team, who are central stakeholders, prefer alternative A2. The employees seem to be indifferent to alternatives A2 and A3. Note, however, that from a behavioral point of view, adopting A3 might be hampered due to people's tendency to resist changes and avoid adoption of new habits. Thus, we suggest employing behavioral economics strategies to support the process of selection and adoption of IT service alternatives.

3   Root-Cause Analysis of Economic Behavior

Our study illustrates the observation that the subjective values of the business units are not always aligned with the enterprise value. While the management evaluates the alternatives by discounting their future outcomes according to economic principles, the other units (in the current case study, mainly the corporate operations team and the IT department) assess them using subjective, behavioral discounting rates that represent the excess weight they assign to present-time outcomes.

The macroeconomic implications of present bias are very significant. To incorporate them into the understanding of the economy, Benchimol et al. [4] devised a theoretical framework for optimal monetary policy, acknowledging the time inconsistency characterizing intertemporal choices of consumers. Based on this work, we suggest the following definition for the present value of an alternative for a business unit.

Definition 3. Let δ be the (economic) discount factor and β_j – the present bias factor of business unit j. The *present value of alternative* A_i *for business unit* j is calculated as:

$$PV_j(A_i) = V_{0j}(A_i) + \beta_j * \delta * V_{1j}(A_i),$$

where $V_{0j}(A_i)$ is the current value assigned to the adoption of alternative A_i by business unit j and $V_{1j}(A_i)$ is its future value (e.g., as presented and demonstrated in Fig. 3).

We denote by A* the alternative evaluated as most valuable by the management, assuming that the management considers the enterprise's aggregated values and costs of each alternative. In other words, A* is the alternative that has the highest present value for the management ($\max_i (PV_{management}(A_i))$). However, for a service alternative to be adopted, it is not sufficient to provide the highest value for the enterprise (represented by the management); it should also provide a high value for each relevant business unit. We thus distinguish between the cases depicted in Table 2.

If all business units agree to adopt the selected alternative (A*), no intervention is needed. If this is not the case, i.e., a business unit still prefers adopting A_i over A*, then behavioral or economic interventions are needed. Behavioral intervention calls for applying nudges – positive reinforcement and indirect suggestions that aim to influence the behavior and decision-making of groups or individuals [24]. As the cost of most nudges is negligible, behavioral intervention should be always considered first. However, their effect is limited; they can increase the present bias factor of a business unit j to some extent, namely $\beta_j < \beta'_j \leq 1$, where β'_j is the original present bias factor of business unit j and β'_j is its new (maximal possible) value after performing behavioral interventions[3]. If behavioral interventions are not sufficient, economic interventions should also be considered.

Table 2. Possible interventions

#	Case	Intervention
1	All business units prefer A*; Formally expressed: $PV_j(A^*) < PV_j(A_i)$ for all i, j	No need
2	There is business unit j preferring alternative A_i, but may prefer alternative A* with some behavioral interventions; Formally expressed: There are i, j, β'_j such that $PV_j(A_i) < PV_j(A^*) < V_{0j}(A_i) + \beta'_j * \delta * V_{1j}(A_i)$	Behavioral intervention should be considered (to increase β to a higher value that will make A* more preferable than A_i for business unit j)
3	There is business unit j preferring alternative A_i, and behavioral interventions will not be sufficient to make it prefer alternative A*; Formally expressed: There are i, j such that for each β'_j $PV_j(A^*) \geq V_{0j}(A_i) + \beta'_j * \delta * V_{1j}(A_i)$	Both behavioral and economic intervention should be considered

4 Preliminary Results

To evaluate our model, we tested it based on a real situation at a multinational enterprise. This enterprise mainly designs and produces semi-conductors but also offers many other products and services. It has more than 50,000 employees around the globe, organized into dozens of business units. Based on the enterprise characteristics, we used a discount factor (δ) of 0.96.

As part of the employee compensation package, the employees may choose between additional salary and receiving a company vehicle. Currently, more than 3,000 employees choose the latter option. The vehicle program costs approximately $60M per year, including lease, fuel, maintenance, and insurance. The vehicle fleet is managed by the corporate operations team, but also involves the payroll division for gathering data, auditing and controlling the program, and the finance division for auditing and accounting for the benefit in the corporate budget.

---

[3] β'_i can be experimentally identified for each business unit. We plan to address this part in future research.

The enterprise currently uses a commercial software package to which most stakeholders have no direct access. The IT department suggested three alternatives: (A1) extending the current solution so that the relevant information will be sent to the different stakeholders quarterly, via email; (A2) creating live BI dashboards on top of the current solution; and (A3) developing a tailor-made information system.

Table 3 presents estimated values for our case study. We begin the analysis by depicting the current values assigned to the adoption of each alternative A_i by business unit j, i.e., $V_{0j}(A_i)$. To do so, we recorded the effort levels needed for the adoption of each solution by each of the business units, using a five-point Likert scale: 0.00 – no effort is needed; -0.20 – very low; -0.40 – low; -0.60 – medium; -0.80 –high; and -1.00 – extremely high. We denote the obtained values by $V^*_{0j}(A_i)$. Note that as these values represent effort, they are non-positive. Generally, for all business units, A3 requires a vast resource investment, and hence has the most negative value, while A1 requires very little effort. The corporate operations team and the IT department invest much more time and effort than the other groups of stakeholders and hence their effort levels are larger (more negative values).

Turning to the future-period values of the service alternatives, denoted $V^*_{1j}(A_i)$ for business unit j, we built on the BU-driven outcomes, as depicted in Fig. 3. Recall that these values include maintenance costs of the alternatives through financial performance indicators.

To assess the present bias (β) values of the business units, we incorporate behavioral principles. Working on the assumption that the farther away a business unit is from the management in the organizational hierarchy, the lower is its β value, we postulated β values as $1/(1 + d)$, where d measures the distance of the business unit from the management. The employees are the farthest from management, followed by the corporate operations team, the IT department, the payroll division, and the finance division, resulting in the β values appearing at the leftmost column of Table 3. We acknowledge that additional attributes affect the β values of the business units, for example, the extent to which their employees possess a tendency to make changes. Specifically, they may be willing to adopt changes, or may be unable to adjust to changes [14]. We leave the actual change-attitude modification of the β values for future research.

Table 3. The present values of the service alternatives in our case study

	β	A_1			A_2			A_3		
		V_0	V_1	PV	V_0	V_1	PV	V_0	V_1	PV
Management	1.00	0.00	0.07	0.06	-0.20	0.31	0.09	-0.40	0.58	0.15
Finance	0.83	0.00	0.29	0.22	-0.20	0.71	0.39	-0.20	1.00	0.61
Payroll	0.77	0.00	0.26	0.19	-0.20	0.58	0.26	-0.20	0.89	0.48
IT dep.	0.63	-0.20	0.20	-0.01	-0.40	0.51	0.06	-0.60	0.42	-0.12
Corporate Operations	0.56	-0.20	0.18	-0.02	-0.40	0.45	0.01	-0.80	0.33	-0.26
Employees	0.50	0.00	0.18	0.08	0.00	0.62	0.29	0.00	0.60	0.28

Figure 4 shows the present values of the three service alternatives, following Definition 3. It provides a tool for evaluating the effort required in order to persuade all business units to cooperate with the adoption of the alternative that is preferred from the enterprise viewpoint. The figure shows that the preferred alternative (A*) is A3. This is a consequence of the ranking of the outcomes by the management (which has a β value of 1). The figure also shows that the payroll and the finance divisions agree with the management on the preferred alternative (and the whole order of preference), while the IT department and the corporate operations team prefer A2, and the employees slightly prefer A2 over A3 (but can be considered as indifferent to those alternatives). Note that in this case there are no changes in alternative rankings when considering behavioral aspects (see Fig. 3 and Fig. 4), but the differences between the rankings of some business units decreased due to the expected adoption effort (as reflected in V_0 values) and the present bias (as reflected in β values), of these business units.

Having mapped the business units' preferences, we now know which business units should be the focus of persuasion efforts for the adoption of the preferred solution: mainly the IT department and the corporate operations team, and to a lesser extent the employees.

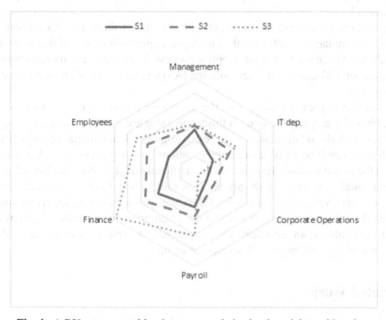

Fig. 4. A BU outcome, taking into account behavioral model considerations

Following the work in [23], we explored two families of nudges as behavioral interventions:

- *Framing:* Decisions depend on the way the information is presented. Thus, the management was advised to present the undesired alternatives (A1 and A2) as losses, compared to the desired alternative (A3). In particular, the management emphasized that if A1 or A2 are selected, the project will lose the possibility of integration with other systems, and much of the support for auditing activities.

- *Priming:* Priming effects are a result experience, preceding the decision at stake. Priming causes decisions to depend on the decision makers' conscious- and subconscious-associations with past events. To use this effect, the management was advised to present historical examples of features related to the desired alternative (A3) in a favorable light, and examples of features related to the undesired alternatives (A1 and A2) in an unfavorable light, prompting associations favoring adoption of the former.

While those interventions increased the present bias values of the business units, they were not sufficient to convince the IT department and the corporate operations team to prefer A3; they were still concerned that the investment would not pay off. Thus, we further recommended using classical economic incentives, in conjunction with the above nudges. Specifically, the management was advised to compensate all employees for the effort they would have to make in adopting alternative A3 (each employee got a bonus of 250$). In addition, some of the work, originally planned for the IT department and the corporate operations team, was reallocated to other business units; in particular, the finance and payroll units were responsible for the communication with the supplier of alternative A3.

The enterprise is currently seven months after adoption alternative A3. Although the old solution remained available for the employees, only a single use of that system was recorded after the completion of the adoption process. Moreover the corporate operations team reports on full usage of the new solution (A3) and reduction of support phone calls to almost zero.

Despite the impressive success of the adoption process, some threats to validity remain. First, the scope of the study is limited to a single enterprise and a single service. Further research should evaluate the suggested approach in additional settings. Second, we explored a small set of behavioral interventions and they seem to work to a certain degree in the examined case. Exploration of additional nudge families is planned, as well as experimental assessment of the present bias values (both β_j and β'_j). Third, we used a particular set of values (for calculating PV_j) and assumptions (e.g., for calculating β_j). Although the values were determined and the assumptions were verified by consulting relevant stakeholders, an empirical study is planned to explore these aspects and their impact on decision making and IT service adoption.

5   Related Work

In this section we briefly review works related to adoption challenges and solution selection, as well as to behavioral economics in information systems research.

5.1   IT Service Adoption Challenges and Solution Selection

Enterprises face challenges in the management of conflicting requirements and overcoming IT adoption barriers. The recent systematic review in [6] identified 18 barriers to IT adoption within small and medium enterprises. These are primarily divided into internal and external barriers. The internal barriers are further classified according to the involved entities/stakeholders and their roles in the organization. Top management faces barriers due to lack of commitment and engagement; lack of IT knowledge; competences, capacities, and expertise; lack of CEO interest, motivation and desire of growth; and lack of confidence and perception of IT benefits. End users, on the other hand, face barriers due to dissatisfaction and resistance to change; lack of participation and engagement; lack of knowledge and training on IT benefits; and lack of technical expertise and skills. One of the main findings in this review is that, to succeed in an IT adoption project and overcome the potential barriers, professionals must ensure the cooperation of all stakeholders of IT adoption and promote the acceptance of change throughout the organization. The enterprise must ensure the diffusion of information, IT knowledge and skills to the users, managers, external consultants and partners throughout the IT adoption process (preparation, planning, implementation, tests, maintenance, etc.). Our approach follows this finding and calls for involving all relevant stakeholders in a co-creation process.

Requirement prioritization [5] and multi-criteria decision making (MCDM) [24] techniques have been suggested to support solution selection, when more than one alternative exists. Many of them use fuzzy logic and machine learning algorithms to improve their performance. They all concentrate on finding the best alternatives in a static context. Our approach further recommends the use of behavioral and economic interventions in order to change the context and thus maximize IT service adoption by *all* relevant business units.

5.2 Behavioral Economics and Its Roles in Information Systems Research

A recent paper [3] contains a critical analysis of behavioral economics in information systems. It provides an intensive investigation of quality information-systems research, using bibliometric content analysis. The analysis shows that information systems researchers have a general understanding of behavioral economics, but their use of the theories has an ad-hoc feel, with only a narrow range of behavioral economics concepts and theories, forming the foundation of their research.

The papers [17] and [7] from the above study are the most relevant for our research. The first paper, by Lee and Joshi [17], examined the use of status-quo bias in information systems research, finding that researchers focus primarily on rational cost-and-benefit analysis, neglecting the phenomenon of status-quo bias prevalent in individuals' decision-making process, that manifests their cognitive limitations (and bounded rationality). They further highlighted and elaborated on the key tenets and components of status-quo bias that may be useful in advancing research on user acceptance/resistance to new information systems. Lee and Joshi also referred to the work of Kim and Kankanhalli [14] who study the issue of user-resistance to information systems and go beyond the status-quo bias to include other influencing factors from the technology acceptance literature: switching costs,[4] colleague opinion, self-efficacy for change, perceived value, and organizational support for change. They provide practical recommendations to management on how to alleviate user resistance to information system implementation, including fostering champions of the system, providing training, and emphasizing the benefits of switching, over its costs.

---

[4] An empirical analysis on the significant impact switching costs exert on behavior may be found at [15].

The other relevant paper from the bibliometric study, by Ferratt et al. [7], employs the taxonomy of fast and slow (a.k.a. system-1 and system-2) cognitive processes to develop a novel theory of IT adoption (cf. [12]). The three main insights from this theory are: (i) the cognitions that lead to a default response are not necessarily the cognitions found in extant theories of IT use; (ii) both system-1 (unconscious) and system-2 (conscious) processes are subject to bounded rationality; and (iii) the relationship between learning and the intervention potential for a system-2 response, although negative, may not be linear. The authors pointed to the need for further research on the cognitive control problem, exploring the effects of heuristics, nudges and bounded rationality on decisions to employ IT.

Overall, mainstream research in behavioral economics focuses on understanding the behavior of individuals. Arguably, behavioral economics may, and should, also be applied in the context of enterprises since the activities of business units are conducted by individuals. Thus, in this work, we examined how to operationalize behavioral economics for improving IT adoption decisions by the various stakeholders of the enterprise.

6 Summary and Future Research

We presented a behavioral model that conceptualizes the considerations that facilitate the selection of the economically-preferred IT service, from a list of alternatives. The approach assesses the present values of the alternatives from the viewpoints of the various stakeholders (business units in the enterprise). The approach was evaluated on a case study to demonstrate its abilities.

In the future, we intend to conduct empirical studies to devise and test behavioral and economic interventions that would help the enterprise achieve the support of all the business units in the implementation of the best service alternatives. We will start by refining the process of interviewing and surveying the business units' personnel in order to elicit the relevant values for the behavioral evaluation model. As part of this step, we will accommodate the work identity and dedication questionnaire to our project's needs. We will further suggest treatments and evaluate them in experiments, exploring different industries and different IT services. In particular, we intend to analyze additional treatments such as ambiguity, mood, attribution, and stress.

Acknowledgement. This research is supported by the Israel Science Foundation under grant agreements 1065/19.

References

1. Antlová, K.: Motivation and barriers of ICT adaptation in small and medium-size enterprises (2009)
2. Antony, J.: Six sigma for service processes. Bus. Process. Manag. J. **12**(2), 234–248 (2006)
3. Arnott, D., Gao, S.: Behavioral economics in information systems research: critical analysis and research strategies. J. Inf. Technol. 02683962211016000 (2021)
4. Benchimol, J., Bounader, L., Kliger, D.: Present-biased households and monetary policy. In: Proceedings of the 2022 Annual Meeting of the American Economic Association (2022)

5. Bukhsh, F.A., Bukhsh, Z.A., Daneva, M.: A systematic literature review on requirement prioritization techniques and their empirical evaluation. Comput. Stand. Interfaces **69**, 103389 (2020)
6. Chouki, M., Talea, M., Okar, C., Chroqui, R.: Barriers to information technology adoption within small and medium enterprises: a systematic literature review. Int. J. Innov. Technol. Manag. **17**(01), 2050007 (2020)
7. Ferratt, T.W., Prasad, J., Dunne, E.J.: Fast and slow processes underlying theories of information technology use. J. Assoc. Inf. Syst. **19**(1), 3 (2018)
8. Frederick, S., Loewenstein, G., O'donoghue, T.: Time discounting and time preference: a critical review. J. Econ. Lit. **40**(2), 351–401 (2002)
9. Garg, S.K., Versteeg, S., Buyya, R.: A framework for ranking of cloud computing services. Futur. Gener. Comput. Syst. **29**(4), 1012–1023 (2013)
10. Green, L., Myerson, J.: A discounting framework for choice with delayed and probabilistic rewards. Psychol. Bull. **130**(5), 769 (2004)
11. Jabarin, F., Hartman, A., Reinhartz-Berger, I., Kliger, D.: Towards improvement of IT service adoption in multi-business organizations. In: Ghose, A., Horkoff, J., Silva Souza, V.E., Parsons, J., Evermann, J. (eds.) ER 2021. LNCS, vol. 13011, pp. 210–223. Springer, Cham (2021). https://doi.org/10.1007/978-3-030-89022-3_18
12. Kahneman, D.: Thinking Fast and Slow. Farrar, Straus and Giroux ed. ISBN 978–0374275631 (2011)
13. Kang, K.C., Cohen, S.G., Hess, J.A., Novak, W.E., Peterson, A.S.: Feature-oriented domain analysis (FODA) feasibility study. Carnegie-Mellon Univ Pittsburgh Pa Software Engineering Inst (1990)
14. Kim, H.W., Kankanhalli, A.: Investigating user resistance to information systems implementation: a status quo bias perspective. MIS quarterly, pp. 567–582 (2009)
15. Kim, M., Kliger, D., Vale, B.: Estimating switching costs: the case of banking. J. Financ. Intermediation **12**(1), 25–56 (2003)
16. Laibson, D.: Golden eggs and hyperbolic discounting. Q. J. Econ. **112**(2), 443–478 (1997)
17. Lee, K., Joshi, K.: Examining the use of status quo bias perspective in IS research: need for re-conceptualizing and incorporating biases. Inf. Syst. J. **27**(6), 733–752 (2017)
18. Maglio, P.P., Vargo, S.L., Caswell, N., Spohrer, J.: The service system is the basic abstraction of service science. IseB **7**(4), 395–406 (2009)
19. Nardi, J.C., et al.: A commitment-based reference ontology for services. Inf. Syst. **54**, 263–288 (2015)
20. Rad, M.S., Nilashi, M., Dahlan, H.M.: Information technology adoption: a review of the literature and classification. Univ. Access Inf. Soc. **17**(2), 361–390 (2018). https://doi.org/10.1007/s10209-017-0534-z
21. Ruiz, D.M., Gremler, D.D., Washburn, J.H., Carrión, G.C.: Service value revisited: specifying a higher-order, formative measure. J. Bus. Res. **61**(12), 1278–1291 (2008)
22. Sales, T.P., Baião, F., Guizzardi, G., Almeida, J.P.A., Guarino, N., Mylopoulos, J.: The common ontology of value and risk. In: Trujillo, J.C., Davis, K.C., Du, X., Li, Z., Ling, T.W., Li, G., Lee, M.L. (eds.) ER 2018. LNCS, vol. 11157, pp. 121–135. Springer, Cham (2018). https://doi.org/10.1007/978-3-030-00847-5_11
23. Thaler, R.H., Benartzi, S.: Save more tomorrow™: using behavioral economics to increase employee saving. J. Polit. Econ. **112**(S1), S164–S187 (2004)
24. Thaler, R.H., Sunstein, C.R., Nudge: Improving Decisions about Health, Wealth, and Happiness. Yale University Press (2008)
25. Zavadskas, E.K., Turskis, Z.: Multiple criteria decision making (MCDM) methods in economics: an overview. Technol. Econ. Dev. Econ. **17**(2), 397–427 (2011)

Data Modeling and Analysis

Discovery of Spatial Association Rules from Fuzzy Spatial Data

Henrique P. da Silva[1], Thiago D. R. Felix[2], Pedro V. A. B. de Venâncio[3] (iD),
and Anderson C. Carniel[2(✉)] (iD)

[1] Federal University of Technology - Paraná, Dois Vizinhos, Brazil
`henriquepigozzo@gmail.com`
[2] Department of Computer Science, Federal University of São Carlos,
São Carlos, Brazil
`thiagofelix@estudante.ufscar.br`, `accarniel@ufscar.br`
[3] Grad. Program in Electrical Engineering, Federal University of Minas Gerais,
Belo Horizonte, Brazil
`pedrovinicius@ufmg.br`

Abstract. The discovery of *spatial association rules* is a core task in spatial data science projects and focuses on extracting useful and meaningful spatial patterns and relationships from spatial and geometric information. Many spatial phenomena have been modeled and represented by *fuzzy spatial objects*, which have blurred interiors, uncertain boundaries, and/or inexact locations. In this paper, we introduce a novel method for mining spatial association rules from fuzzy spatial data. By allowing users to represent spatial features of their applications as fuzzy spatial objects and by employing fuzzy topological relationships, our method discovers spatial association patterns between spatial objects of users' interest (e.g., tourist attractions) and such fuzzy spatial features (e.g., sanitary conditions of restaurants, number of reviews and price of accommodations). Further, this paper presents a case study based on real datasets that shows the applicability of our method.

Keywords: Spatial data science · Spatial association rule · Spatial fuzziness · Fuzzy spatial data · Fuzzy topological relationship

1 Introduction

Increasingly, applications have required specialized and sophisticated methods for exploring the special geometric and topological characteristics of spatial phenomena, such as location and spatial relationships. *Spatial data science* emerges as an important area that provides such methods [4]. The common assumption is that spatial phenomena are represented by instances of vector-based data types called *spatial data types* [15], such as *points*, *lines*, and *regions*. The locations, geometric shapes, and boundaries of such instances are precisely defined in space. Hence, these instances are denominated as *crisp spatial objects*. This also means

J. Ralyté et al. (Eds.): ER 2022, LNCS 13607, pp. 179–193, 2022.
https://doi.org/10.1007/978-3-031-17995-2_13

that the information extracted from these objects is exact. For instance, topological relationships (e.g., overlap) on crisp spatial objects yield exact results.

However, many spatial phenomena are characterized by *spatial fuzziness* [4]. Spatial objects with this feature have blurred interiors, uncertain boundaries, and/or inexact locations. Such objects cannot be adequately represented by crisp spatial objects. They are properly represented by instances of *fuzzy spatial data types*, such as *fuzzy points*, *fuzzy lines*, and *fuzzy regions*. Fuzzy set theory [16] is used to model such *fuzzy spatial objects*. The key idea is to assign a *membership degree* between 0 and 1 to each point of a fuzzy spatial object. This degree indicates to which extent a point belongs to the object. An example is a fuzzy region object that represents the coverage area of *expensive accommodations*. In this case, we represent areas with a particular characterization expressed by a *linguistic value* (i.e., *expensive*) in a given context denoted by a *linguistic variable* (i.e., *accommodations*). In this object, points with membership degree 1 represent certainly expensive locations. Points with degree 0 denote locations that are definitely not expensive. The remaining points (i.e., with degrees in $]0,1[$) characterize locations that are partially expensive (i.e., different degrees of truth). Spatial operations that handle fuzzy spatial objects are also fuzzy since they have to deal with the membership degrees of the objects. For instance, a *fuzzy topological relationship* (e.g., fuzzy overlap) [3] on fuzzy spatial objects yields a value in $[0,1]$ that indicates the degree of truth of the relationship.

The discovery of *spatial association rules* [11] is a core aspect of spatial data science applications. The focus is on extracting useful and meaningful spatial patterns from geometric information. That is, applications can express how frequently two or more spatial datasets are related by using *if-then* rules, which have associated values to measure their strength and significance. Usually, the interest is in mining *strong* rules, which are rules with large associated values (i.e., greater than minimum thresholds). For instance, we can mine strong spatial association rules that show how locations of tourist attractions are related to coverage areas of accommodations and restaurants.

Unfortunately, the available approaches that extract spatial association rules [7–14] face at least one of the following problems. First, their focus is on dealing with crisp spatial objects only. Second, they are incapable of processing fuzzy topological relationships. These problems seriously limit the representation of spatial fuzziness. The last problem refers to the non-use of linguistic variables and values to represent different fuzziness levels in objects and relationships.

In this paper, our goal is to solve the aforementioned problems by proposing a novel method for extracting spatial association rules from fuzzy spatial data. The central idea is to adequately deal with spatial fuzziness by representing spatial features of users' applications as fuzzy spatial objects and to compute fuzzy topological relationships between spatial information of users' interest (called *reference spatial dataset*) and such fuzzy spatial objects. Our method transforms the degrees returned by fuzzy topological relationships into linguistic values to intuitively express the meaning of the resulting relationships. Further, we represent concepts related to topological relationships, linguistic values, and reference spatial datasets in *hierarchies* to mine spatial association rules on multiple levels.

Table 1. Comparison of existing approaches with our work (last column).

Comparison Criteria	[11]	[14]	[13]	[7]	[8]	[9]	[10]	[12]	Our work
Crisp spatial datasets	✓	✓	✓	✓	✓	✓	✓	✓	✓
Fuzzy spatial datasets						✓*		✓*	✓
Crisp topological relationships	✓	✓	✓			✓			✓
Fuzzy topological relationships						✓*			✓
Hierarchies of concepts	✓	✓	✓			✓	✓	✓	✓
Linguistic variables and values								✓	✓
Multiple-level association rules	✓	✓	✓			✓	✓	✓	✓

*limited representation or handling of spatial fuzziness

The main contributions of this paper are:

- It introduces a novel method that solves the problem of discovering spatial association from spatial phenomena characterized by spatial fuzziness.
- It describes how to discover such rules by computing fuzzy topological relationships between a reference spatial dataset and fuzzy spatial features.
- It provides the possibility of mining multiple-level spatial association rules based on hierarchies of concepts.
- It shows the applicability of the proposed method by using a case study based on real spatial datasets.

The rest of this paper is organized as follows. Section 2 discusses related work. Section 3 introduces our case study. Sections 4 and 5 summarize basic concepts needed to understand the proposed method. Section 6 details the architecture of our method and shows its applicability by using our case study. Finally, Sect. 7 draws some conclusions and presents future work.

2   Related Work

Table 1 compares existing approaches that extract spatial association rules with our proposed approach. We check whether a given approach deals with different types of datasets and provides solutions to implementing specific concepts. We can group these existing approaches as follows: (i) approaches that deal with crisp spatial data, and (ii) approaches that apply concepts from fuzzy set theory.

With respect to the first group, we highlight the method proposed in [11]. To the best of our knowledge, it is the first method that extracts spatial association rules from crisp spatial datasets. It formally defines the concept of spatial association rules and employs key ideas from [1], such as the use of minimum thresholds for support and confidence when extracting rules. In addition, it presents *hierarchies of concepts* for spatial datasets and topological relationships. A hierarchy for a spatial dataset describes how spatial objects are organized based on their associated alphanumerical data, while a hierarchy of topological relationships groups similar relations into a coarser relation. Such hierarchies allow users to explore the extracted rules in different levels of aggregations (i.e., multiple-level

association rules). The approach in [14] applies similar concepts to extract spatial transactions, which are used to identify the rules. Other approaches mine
rules by using different strategies, such as inductive logic programming [13], cell
patterns [7], and Boolean matrix [8]. As shown in Table 1, the main limitation
of the previous approaches is that they do not consider spatial fuzziness.

The second group consists of approaches that incorporate fuzzy concepts to
the discovery of spatial association rules. The authors in [9] specify a method
to deal with fuzzy spatial data. They represent spatial fuzziness by using region
objects with *broad boundaries*. This means that an areal object has three disjoint
or adjacent parts: (i) exterior, which comprises all points that certainly do not
belong to the object, (ii) core, which contains all points that certainly belong
to the object, and (iii) broad boundary, which consists of all points possibly
belong to the object. The rules are based on the computation of topological
relationships for region objects with broad boundaries. As discussed in [3] and
shown in Table 1, this model limits the expressiveness of spatial fuzziness since
it is based on the three-valued logic only. The authors in [10] allow users to
specify fuzzy hierarchies in the sense that membership degrees represent to which
extent an item of a hierarchy belongs to its parent, allowing that an item has
multiple and different membership degrees. In [12], the authors consider the
resulting membership degrees of spatial relationships (e.g., distance relations)
when calculating the support and confidence of the rules. For this, they define a
membership function that determines to which extent a value belongs to a given
linguistic value that represents a spatial relationship, such as *near*. As shown in
Table 1, this approach deals with spatial fuzziness in a limited way. The reason
is that it maps alphanumerical attributes associated with spatial objects into
membership functions instead of using fuzzy spatial objects.

As previously discussed and shown in Table 1, we conclude that the aforementioned approaches face problems that negatively affect the task of discovering
spatial association rules from fuzzy spatial data. On the other hand, we introduce a novel method that adequately handles and manages spatial fuzziness
when extracting such rules. This method stores spatial features of an application (labeled with linguistic variables) by using fuzzy spatial objects (labeled
with linguistic values). By computing fuzzy topological relationships between
these features and a spatial dataset of interest, our method allows users to mine
multiple-level rules. In particular, the benefit of using linguistic variables and
values is that they allow users to intuitively interpret what a spatial object represents and the meaning of the topological relationships in the extracted rules.

3   Running Example

Our goal is to discover associations between tourist attractions and characteristics of accommodations and restaurants located in New York City. Hence, our
application is based on three real spatial datasets. The first one stores the tourist
attractions represented by crisp region objects. To build this dataset, we have
used OpenStreetMap data to extract crisp region objects inside New York City
that represent tourist attractions, such as culture, leisure, and historic areas.

As a result, this dataset contains 12,328 crisp region objects labeled with the category (e.g., *historic*) and type (e.g., *monument*) of the tourist attraction.

The other datasets are based on the application in [5]. The second dataset refers to the locations of Airbnb accommodations in New York City extracted from 2021-12-04 to 2021-12-05. The characteristics of interest are the price and number of reviews of accommodations. We have excluded the lines with missing data in these attributes from the dataset. The last dataset comprises the most recent graded inspection results of restaurants in New York City provided by the Department of Health and Mental Hygiene (DOHMH). To build this dataset, we have executed the R script supplied by the DOHMH, excluded the lines with negative scores and missing/invalid latitude and longitude coordinates, and guaranteed that the last inspection result occurred before the last extraction date of the Airbnb accommodations. As a result, we have obtained 38,277 Airbnb accommodations and 22,642 restaurants. By using them, we aim at representing the coverage area of each characteristic as fuzzy region objects (Sect. 5) to understand how such areas are associated with tourist attractions. The implementation of our running example is publicly available at https://github.com/accarniel/sarules-fuzzy.

4   Basic Concepts of Spatial Association Rules Mining

An association rule is expressed as $A \rightarrow B$ ($s\%, c\%$) where A and B are *itemsets*, i.e., they are sets of items or elements that appear together in a given transaction of a database [1]. Such a rule means that if the antecedent A occurs, then the consequent B also occurs with a *support* of $s\%$ and *confidence* of $c\%$. Support and confidence measure the strength and significance of rules. Support indicates how frequently the itemsets A and B appear in the transactions. Confidence denotes the percentage of transactions containing A that also contain B. Commonly, users define minimum values for support and confidence to get relevant rules.

A spatial association rule extends the meaning of a classical association rule by including spatial relationships in the itemsets A or B [11]. The key idea is to build transactions that store spatial relationships between a spatial dataset of the user interest and other spatial datasets that represent different characteristics of the application. Commonly, the employed spatial relationships are *topological relationships* (e.g., overlap, inside) [15], which express how two or more spatial objects are related with respect to their relative position. For instance, we can have a rule that expresses the strength and significance of the overlapping situation between the coverage area of cut-rate accommodations and regions representing tourist attractions. In this paper, we consider that the spatial datasets of the applications store fuzzy spatial objects and thus, we employ fuzzy topological relationships when mining spatial association rules.

5   Fuzzy Spatial Data Handling

5.1   Fuzzy Regions and Fuzzy Topological Relationships

In this paper, we deal with fuzzy regions, which are formally defined by using concepts from fuzzy set theory [16]. Fuzzy set theory extends and generalizes

Boolean set theory by allowing an element to have partial membership in the set. Let X be the *universe*. A fuzzy set $\tilde{A}$ uses a *membership function* $\mu_{\tilde{A}} : X \to [0, 1]$ to determine the *membership degree* of an element to $\tilde{A}$.

In the same way as crisp sets are extended to fuzzy sets, crisp spatial objects are generalized to fuzzy spatial objects. For a fuzzy region object $\tilde{R}$, this means that its geometric structure is the same as a *crisp* region object. $\tilde{R}$ consists of a finite set of disjoint fuzzy faces with special properties. A fuzzy face $\tilde{F}$ is a connected, bounded, and regular closed fuzzy set in $\mathbb{R}^2$ with a membership function $\mu_{\tilde{F}} : \mathbb{R}^2 \to]0, 1]$ that assigns a membership degree to each point in $\tilde{F}$. A crisp region object can be represented by a fuzzy region object that contains points with degree 1 only. Fuzzy regions are formally defined in [3].

A fuzzy region object is labeled with a *linguistic value* to characterize a specific instance of a spatial feature, which is represented by a *linguistic variable*. Commonly, linguistic variables are denoted by substantives, while linguistic values are denoted by adjectives. Our running example has three (fuzzy) spatial features denoted by the following linguistic variables and their corresponding linguistic values (in parentheses): *accommodation price* (*cut-rate, cheap, affordable, expensive, premium*), *accommodation notability* (*unknown, little-known, well-known, famous*), and *food safety* (*very low, low, medium, high, very high*).

Different types of fuzzy spatial operations have been defined to handle fuzzy region objects [4]. We are interested in applying *fuzzy topological relationships* [3] on fuzzy regions to discover spatial association rules. Differently from a classical topological relationship that yields a Boolean value, a fuzzy topological relationship yields a membership degree in $[0, 1]$ that expresses to which extent a relative position between two fuzzy region objects holds. In our running example, we employ the relationship *fuzzy overlap* to compute the *overlapping degree* of two fuzzy regions. The degree returned by a fuzzy topological relationship can be mapped to a *high-level linguistic value*, which provides the semantics of the relationship to the user. For instance, two fuzzy region objects can *quite* overlap.

5.2   Spatial Plateau Algebra and Its Implementation

The *Spatial Plateau Algebra* (SPA) [6] is a *executable type system* since it provides data structures for fuzzy spatial data types and specifications for fuzzy spatial operations. The SPA represents fuzzy spatial data types as *spatial plateau data types* where a spatial plateau object can be a *plateau point, plateau line*, or *plateau region*. A plateau region object consists of a list of pairs $\langle (r_1, m_1), \ldots, (r_n, m_n) \rangle$ where r_i is a crisp region object annotated with the membership degree $m_i \in]0, 1]$ with $i \le n$ for some $n \in \mathbb{N}$. The crisp region objects of all pairs must have different membership degrees and be disjoint or adjacent to each other. Further, the SPA specifies fuzzy spatial operations and fuzzy topological relationships as *spatial plateau operations* and *spatial plateau topological relationships*. The SPA's operations are specified by using well-defined concepts from crisp spatial algebras that are implemented by existing spatial libraries (e.g., GEOS).

The implementation of the SPA is given by the R package *fsr* [5], which provides all data types and operations specified by the SPA, including a two-

(a) *unknown*   (b) *little-known*   (c) *well-known*   (d) *famous*

Fig. 1. The plateau region objects for each linguistic value of the fuzzy spatial feature *accommodation notability* including New York City boundaries.

stage method for building plateau regions from point datasets. This method receives a point dataset as input, where each point represents the location of a phenomenon annotated with alphanumerical data. The first stage of the method, called *fuzzification stage*, uses a fuzzification policy to assign membership degrees to each point of the dataset according to the requirements of the application. Each membership degree indicates to which extent a point belongs to a particular linguistic value (e.g., *unknown*, *little-known*, *well-known*, *famous*) as a possible characterization of a linguistic variable (e.g., *accommodation notability*). The second stage called *construction stage* is responsible for geometrically grouping the points belonging to the same linguistic value into components of a plateau region object. This is performed according to a *construction policy*.

The two-stage method provided by *fsr* allows us to create the plateau region objects that characterize the linguistic values of each linguistic variable of our running example[1]. Similar to the application in [5], we have used the fuzzy set policy in the fuzzification stage. This policy requires the definition of membership functions to characterize the linguistic values according to the domain values of a numerical attribute (e.g., number of reviews) labeled with a linguistic variable (e.g., *accommodation notability*). Further, we have employed the construction policy based on Voronoi diagrams in the construction stage. In the end, five plateau region objects are built for representing the linguistic values of *accommodation price*, four plateau region objects for *accommodation notability*, and five plateau region objects for *food safety*. Figure 1 shows the built plateau region objects for the linguistic variable *accommodation notability*. In this figure, each point has a membership degree that indicates to which extent the point belongs to a specific linguistic value (as indicated by the sidebar).

6   Discovery of Spatial Association Rules from Fuzzy Spatial Objects

6.1   Architectural Overview

Figure 2 shows the architecture of our method, which extracts spatial association rules from fuzzy spatial datasets. The discovery is guided by the user's interest,

---

[1] Details can be found in the implementation of our running example.

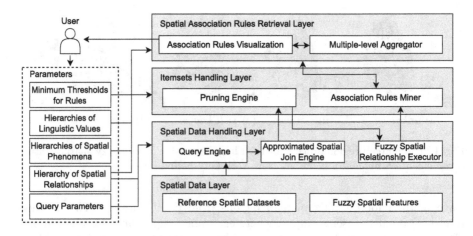

Fig. 2. The architecture of our method.

as indicated by a set of parameters (Sect. 6.2). They determine which subsets of the available datasets will be used in the extraction process, specify a set of hierarchies to describe how spatial relationships and the data itself are semantically organized, and set the minimum thresholds that rules must satisfy.

The layers of our architecture are: (i) Spatial Data Layer, (ii) Spatial Data Handling Layer, (iii) Itemsets Handling Layer, and (iv) Spatial Association Rules Retrieval Layer. As indicated in Fig. 2, each layer applies some specific user parameters to perform its processing. In summary, the Spatial Data Layer provides the datasets to be used in the extraction process. The Spatial Data Handling Layer fetches the relevant data from the Spatial Data Layer according to the user parameters. Further, this layer computes fuzzy spatial relationships on fuzzy spatial objects represented as spatial plateau objects. The goal of the Itemsets Handling Layer is twofold: (i) to organize the processed relationships into itemsets and filter them with respect to the minimum support indicated by the user, and (ii) to discover the spatial association rules by using a mining algorithm, such as the *Apriori* [1]. The extraction of rules is based on alphanumerical attributes of Reference Spatial Datasets and linguistic values that represent the results of fuzzy topological relationships and the characterizations of Fuzzy Spatial Features. Then, the Spatial Association Rules Retrieval Layer is responsible for interactively presenting the mined rules since they can be organized in multiple levels according to the definition of hierarchies. The layers of our architecture are detailed in Sects. 6.3 to 6.6, including examples in the context of our running example.

6.2 User Parameters

The parameters provided by the user play an important role in our method. As shown in Fig. 2, they consist of (i) Query Parameters, (ii) Hierarchy of Spatial

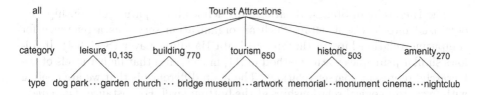

Fig. 3. The Hierarchy of Spatial Phenomena for our running example.

Relationships, (iii) Hierarchies of Spatial Phenomena, (iv) Hierarchies of Linguistic Values, and (v) Minimum Thresholds for Rules. The purpose of Query Parameters is to indicate (i) the relevant Reference Spatial Dataset of the application, (ii) the Fuzzy Spatial Features that will be considered in the mining process, (iii) the fuzzy topological relationship that should be employed when associating spatial data, and (iv) conditions applied to alphanumerical attributes that are associated with the chosen Reference Spatial Dataset. In our running example (Sect. 3), we are interested in finding spatial association rules based on the overlapping degree between tourist attractions and the fuzzy spatial features that represent coverage areas of distinct characteristics of accommodations and restaurants. For this, our Query Parameters are: (i) tourist attractions as the Reference Spatial Dataset, (ii) three Fuzzy Spatial Features containing fuzzy regions implemented as plateau region objects (Sect. 5), and (iii) fuzzy overlap as the fuzzy topological relationship.

The goal of defining hierarchies (parameters (ii)-(iv)) is to semantically organize concepts related to spatial relationships and characteristics of spatial data. Each hierarchy enables at least one of the following processes: (i) discovery and visualization of spatial association rules mining at distinct levels, (ii) pruning of fuzzy spatial features, and (iii) computation of approximated topological relationships. A hierarchy allows users to define how lower-level concepts are related to higher-level concepts. Given two attributes A and B where each attribute has its own domain of values (or concepts), A and B are related in a hierarchy if we can determine a value of B by aggregating a subset of values in A. In this case, we have $A \to B$, expressing that these attributes are levels of a hierarchy.

The Hierarchies of Spatial Phenomena are defined by using alphanumerical attributes that label crisp spatial objects stored in the Reference Spatial Datasets. It allows users to mine and visualize spatial association rules on different levels (as illustrated in Sect. 6.6). For instance, users can first identify rules containing itemsets of a more general level in a hierarchy. Then, they can mine rules on a more detailed level from a particular value of the previous level. Figure 3 depicts the Hierarchy of Spatial Phenomena built on the alphanumerical attributes of our Reference Spatial Dataset. It is defined by $type \to category$. Note that the upper level of this hierarchy (named all) aggregates all values from $category$ and as a result, consists of all tourist attractions. Further, this figure shows the number of members for each distinct value of $category$.

The Hierarchy of Spatial Relationships defines how spatial relationships are organized into levels of detail. Such an organization serves as a reference for computing relationships in the Spatial Data Handling Layer (Sect. 6.4). It follows similar principles as the method in [11] in the sense that higher levels of the hierarchy represent coarser relations. The main difference is that we are dealing with fuzzy topological relationships at the bottom level. For instance, *fuzzy overlap* and *fuzzy meet* can be grouped into a coarser relationship named *intersect*, which can be computed by using spatial approximations.

A Hierarchy of Linguistic Values describes how linguistic values of a Fuzzy Spatial Features are structured. This kind of hierarchy allows users to explore the discovered patterns at distinct grouping levels of linguistic values. For instance, we can specify a Hierarchy of Linguistic Values for the Fuzzy Spatial Feature representing the *accommodation notability* as *lvalues* → *class* where *lvalues* = {*unknown, little-known, well-known, famous*} and *class* = {*unpopular, popular*}. By grouping the values *unknown* and *little-known*, we obtain the class *unpopular*, whereas the aggregation of *well-known* and *famous* lead to the class *popular*.

Finally, the Minimum Thresholds for Rules determine the desired levels of strength and significance that the mined rules must satisfy. For instance, minimum values for support and confidence. The user can provide different minimum thresholds for each level of the hierarchy since the frequency of itemsets intrinsically decreases as we descend the levels of the hierarchy. In our running example and without loss of generality, we extract association rules by varying the levels in the Hierarchy of Spatial Phenomena only. For the level *category*, we use the support of 10% and minimum confidence of 30%. In the next level, we employ 5% and 20%, respectively.

6.3   Spatial Data Layer

The Spatial Data Layer is composed of two components: (i) Reference Spatial Datasets, and (ii) Fuzzy Spatial Features. The goal of the mining process is to discover associations between objects of a Spatial Reference Dataset and objects of Fuzzy Spatial Features. Hence, the first component consists of a collection of crisp spatial objects associated with alphanumerical attribute values that represent the users' interest. Let $n, m \in \mathbb{N}$. Let further $C = \{c_1, ..., c_n\}$ be a set of alphanumerical attributes where each $c \in C$ has a domain of values $cv_1, ..., cv_m$, i.e., $dom(c) = \{cv_1, ..., cv_m\}$. We define a Reference Spatial Dataset as a pair $\langle N, S \rangle$ where N provides its name and S is a set of tuples $(s, v_1, ..., v_n)$ such that $s \in \{point, line, region\}$ and $v_i \in dom(c_i)$ with $i \leq n$. By using the Query Parameters, the user picks one Reference Spatial Dataset that will be employed in the extraction of spatial association rules.

The second component refers to Fuzzy Spatial Features, where each feature is a fuzzy spatial dataset and represents a particular characteristic of the application. We define a Fuzzy Spatial Feature as a pair $\langle L, F \rangle$ such that (i) L is a linguistic variable with a domain of linguistic values $l_1, ..., l_k$ for some $k \in \mathbb{N}$, and (ii) F is a set of tuples (f, l) where $f \in \{fpoint, fline, fregion\}$ and $l \in dom(L)$.

Hence, a Fuzzy Spatial Feature is labeled with a linguistic variable and consists of one or more fuzzy spatial objects annotated by a linguistic value.

Recall that, as discussed in Sect. 6.2, the attributes in a Reference Spatial Dataset and linguistic values of the Fuzzy Spatial Features can be organized in hierarchical structures to represent different aggregation levels of concepts. Further, the user can also apply filters to the spatial datasets aiming to get a subset of tuples that will be used in the extraction process.

In our running example, we have one Reference Spatial Dataset that stores tourist attractions in New York City. In this case, $C = \{category, type\}$ and our Reference Spatial Dataset is given by $\langle Tourist\ Attractions, \{(s_1, leisure, dog\ park), ..., (s_{12,328}, tourism, museum)\}\rangle$ with $s_1, ..., s_{12,328} \in region$. Our Fuzzy Spatial Features represent the linguistic variables *food safety*, *accommodation notability*, and *accommodation price*. For instance, Fig. 1 shows the following Fuzzy Spatial Feature: $\langle Accommodation\ Notability, \{(f_1, unknown), (f_2, little\text{-}known), (f_3, well\text{-}known), (f_4, famous)\}\rangle$ where $f_1, ..., f_4$ are fuzzy regions implemented as plateau region objects respectively shown in Fig. 1a to d.

6.4   Spatial Data Handling Layer

This layer is responsible for handling the data loaded from the Spatial Data Layer and computing topological relationships. For this, it employs the following interacting components: (i) Query Engine, (ii) Approximated Spatial Join Engine, and (iii) Fuzzy Spatial Relationship Executor. The Query Engine captures the relevant subset of spatial objects from the Spatial Data Layer according to the Query Parameters provided by the user (Sect. 6.2).

Next, the Approximated Spatial Join Executor computes *approximated topological relationships* between the captured spatial objects from the Reference Spatial Dataset and the Fuzzy Spatial Features. The computation of an approximated relationship is based on *minimum bounding rectangles* (MBRs). MBR is a type of spatial approximation widely used in the literature [2] because MBRs allow fast computations of topological relations. We employ a function named *approx_rel* that yields a Boolean value to indicate whether the MBR of a crisp spatial object satisfies a given relationship (e.g., *intersect*) with respect to the crisp MBR of a fuzzy spatial object. Such a result can be a false positive since an MBR of a spatial object may include points that do not belong to the object. However, the use of MBRs allows us to quickly discover cases where two spatial objects are certainly not related and thus, identify those cases where an association does not exist. The approximated relationship is chosen based on the Hierarchy of Spatial Relationships provided by the user. For instance, the parent level of the fuzzy topological relationship *overlap* is the relationship *intersect*, which is a coarser relationship to be computed by using MBRs. Let RSD be a set of tuples containing the spatial objects of interest of a Reference Spatial Dataset and the pair $\langle L, F \rangle$ be a Fuzzy Spatial Feature with n tuples in F. Let also *ext* be a function that extracts the i-th fuzzy spatial object of F. The Approximated Spatial Join Executor computes the function *approx_rel* for each crisp spatial object in RSD with respect to each fuzzy spatial object in F. Hence, it yields a set of tuples $(s, a_1, ..., a_n)$ where s is a crisp spatial object belonging to RSD and $a_1, ..., a_n \in bool$ such that each element a_i is given by $approx\_rel(s, ext(F, i))$ with $1 \leq i \leq n$. The attribute name of a_i is a concatenation of the linguistic value of the $ext(F, i)$ and L. We compute this procedure for each Fuzzy Spatial Feature. In the end, we have a collection of sets where each set contains the results of how RSD is roughly related to each Fuzzy Spatial Feature. Since these sets share a common attribute (i.e., elements of the Reference Spatial Dataset), we join them to build a unique set of tuples. This set is then sent to the Pruning Engine of the Itemsets Handling Layer (Sect. 6.5).

Finally, the Fuzzy Spatial Relationship Executor computes fuzzy topological relationships between the crisp spatial objects of the Reference Spatial Dataset and the fuzzy spatial objects selected by the Pruning Engine. The main advantage of this strategy is that the number of required computations to process the costly relationships can be decreased since the Pruning Engine might identify some fuzzy spatial objects that do not have strong associations with the Reference Spatial Dataset. As discussed in Sect. 5.1, a fuzzy topological relationship yields a membership degree in $[0, 1]$ that indicates to which extent the given relationship occurs. Such a degree is then transformed into a linguistic value. Let ftr be a fuzzy topological relationship that returns a linguistic value in LT (e.g., as given in [3]). Let further $n' \in \mathbb{N}$ be the number of fuzzy spatial objects in a Fuzzy Spatial Feature $\langle L, F \rangle$ after processing the Pruning Engine. We obtain a set of tuples $(s, v_1, ..., v_m, tl_1, ..., tl_{n'})$ where s is a crisp spatial object annotated with a set of alphanumerical attributes $v_1, ..., v_m$, which are members of RSD, and $tl_1, ..., tl_{n'}$ are elements of LT such that tl_i is given by $ftr(s, ext(F, i))$ with $1 \leq i \leq n'$. Similar to the set of tuples returned by the Approximated Spatial Join Executor, the attribute name of tl_i is a combination of the linguistic value of the $ext(F, i)$ with L. As a result, we have a collection of sets of tuples that are joined and sent to the Itemset Handling Layer.

Due to space constraints, we show only one example of the result obtained by the Fuzzy Spatial Relationship Executor for our application. To compute the fuzzy overlap on spatial objects, we employ the fsr [5] with $LT = \{a\ little\ bit, somewhat, slightly, averagely, mostly, quite\}$. The set of tuples with the overlapping results between our Reference Spatial Dataset and the Fuzzy Spatial Feature representing the linguistic variable *accommodation price* (Sects. 5.1 and 6.3) is defined as $\{(s_1, leisure, dog\ park, a\ little\ bit, quite, a\ little\ bit), ..., (s_{12,328}, tourism, museum, quite, mostly, slightly)\}$. The attribute names respectively consists of *region_ obj, category, type, cheap accomm. price, affordable accomm. price*, and *expensive accomm. price* (*accom.* stands for *accommodation*). Note that the linguistics values *cut-rate* and *premium* are not included, which means that the fuzzy spatial objects representing these particular situations were not selected by the Pruning Engine. This set is then joined to the results for other Fuzzy Spatial Features. The resulting set of tuples is effectively used to extract the spatial association rules in our running example.

6.5   Itemsets Handling Layer

This layer is responsible for two key actions: (i) performing pruning operations, and (ii) mining the spatial association rules. The pruning operation takes place based on the set of tuples given by the Approximated Spatial Join Engine, named AT, and the minimum support for the highest level of the Spatial Phenomena Hierarchy. The goal is to identify the fuzzy spatial objects that are not frequently related to the crisp spatial objects of the Reference Spatial Dataset. Then, these fuzzy spatial objects are not used in the next step (i.e., the Fuzzy Spatial Relationship Executor). To accomplish this goal, the Pruning Engine first calculates the ratio of the number of times that the value *true* appears in each Boolean attribute of AT and the total number of tuples in AT. Then, it excludes all fuzzy spatial objects whose corresponding ratio values are lesser than a given minimum support. The non-excluded fuzzy spatial objects are sent to the Spatial Data Handling Layer.

The Association Rules Miner extracts rules by using the set of tuples returned by the Fuzzy Spatial Relationship Executor. This set is reshaped as a transactional dataset, which is given as input to the *Apriori* algorithm [1]. For each level of each hierarchy (e.g., the Hierarchy of Spatial Phenomena), we find itemsets with a frequency of appearance higher than the minimum support at that particular level. These itemsets are then frequent itemsets that will be used to form association rules. The strong rules (e.g., with confidence greater than the minimum threshold) are sent to the Spatial Association Rules Retrieval Layer.

In our running example, we employ the R package *arules* (https://cran.r-project.org/package=arules) to identify the frequent itemsets and association rules from the execution of the *Apriori* algorithm. An example of frequent itemset is $\{tourist\ attraction_{category=leisure}\}$ with support of 82.21%. This itemset refers to the number of transactions where the attribute *category* is equal to *leisure* in the Reference Spatial Dataset. Table 2 depicts examples of spatial association rules for our running example.

6.6   Spatial Association Rules Retrieval Layer

The purpose of this layer is to interactively present the knowledge discovered to the user. It consists of two components: (i) Association Rules Visualization, and (ii) Multiple-level Aggregator. The first one is a user interface that enables the general visualization and exploration of the strong spatial association rules extracted by the Association Rules Miner. The rules can be visualized in distinct formats, such as tables, graphs, scatter plots, and parallel coordinates. Table 2 shows six rules for our running example by using a formal tabular format inspired by the notation given in [14]. We also employed this component to get only rules that include attributes related to tourist attractions either on the antecedent or on the consequent.

The Multiple-level Aggregator allows users to identify rules at different levels of a hierarchy of concepts. This is mainly performed by selecting those rules that contain itemsets with the desired members of a given level. We employed this

Table 2. Some examples of rules for our running example.

Antecedent	Consequent	Support (%)	Confidence (%)
$\{tour.\ att._{category=leisure}\}$	$\{overlap_{quite},$ $accom.\ price_{affordable}\}$	30.89	37.57
$\{tour.\ att._{category=leisure}\}$	$\{overlap_{quite},$ $food\ safety_{high}\}$	30.31	36.87
$\{tour.\ att._{category=leisure}\}$ $\wedge\ \{overlap_{quite},$ $food\ safety_{high}\}$	$\{overlap_{quite},$ $accom.\ price_{affordable}\}$	12.49	41.21
$\{tour.\ att._{type=pitch}\}$	$\{overlap_{quite},$ $accom.\ notability_{famous}\}$	11.08	32.35
$\{tour.\ att._{type=pitch}\}$	$\{overlap_{quite},$ $accom.\ price_{cheap}\}$	9.15	26.69
$\{overlap_{quite},$ $accom.\ notability_{unknown}\}$	$\{tour.\ att._{type=pitch}\}$	7.89	27.10

tour. att. and *accom.* stand for *tourist attraction* and *accommodation*, respectively.

component in our running example to mine rules in each level of our Hierarchy of Spatial Phenomena (Fig. 3) by using the parameters given in Sect. 6.2. The first three rules in Table 2 are related to the highest level of this hierarchy (i.e., *category*), while the other rules refer to the lowest level (i.e., *type*). For instance, the first rule states that spatial objects representing *leisure* tourist attractions *quite* overlap coverage areas of accommodations with *affordable price*. This rule has support of 30.89% and confidence of 37.57%. By descending the hierarchy, the fourth rule shows that tourist attractions of type *pitch* quite overlap accommodations characterized by *famous notability* with the support of 11.08% and confidence of 32.35%. These results show that our method can effectively and adequately correlate distinct crisp and fuzzy spatial datasets by mining association rules according to minimum thresholds of strength and significance.

7   Conclusions and Future Work

In this paper, we have presented a novel method for extracting spatial association rules from fuzzy spatial data. We adequately deal with spatial fuzziness since we represent spatial features of an application as fuzzy spatial objects. The extracted spatial association rules are based on linguistic values that express the meaning of fuzzy topological relationships between such fuzzy spatial objects and crisp spatial objects representing the users' interests. We have shown the applicability of our method by using a case study based on real spatial datasets.

Future work will deal with two main topics. First, we aim to study automatic strategies to define hierarchies of concepts. Hence, we would not need such types of parameters from the user. Second, we intend to conduct experimental and qualitative evaluations and compare our method with other related approaches. In these evaluations, we plan to consider distinct application scenarios and employ different types of fuzzy spatial objects (e.g., fuzzy regions and fuzzy lines) and parameters. It will also allow us to characterize the runtime of our method.

Acknowledgments. This study was financed in part by the Coordenação de Aperfeiçoamento de Pessoal de Nível Superior - Brasil (CAPES) - Finance Code 001. Anderson C. Carniel was supported by Google as a recipient of the 2022 Google Research Scholar program.

References

1. Agrawal, R., Imieliński, T., Swami, A.: Mining association rules between sets of items in large databases. In: ACM SIGMOD International Conference on Management of Data, pp. 207–216 (1993)
2. Bertella, P.K., Lopes, Y.K., Oliveira, R.A.P., Carniel, A.C.: The application of spatial approximations to spatial query processing: a systematic review of literature. In: Brazilian Symposium on Databases, pp. 229–240 (2021)
3. Carniel, A.C., Schneider, M.: A conceptual model of fuzzy topological relationships for fuzzy regions. In: IEEE International Conference on Fuzzy Systems, pp. 2271–2278 (2016)
4. Carniel, A.C., Schneider, M.: A survey of fuzzy approaches in spatial data science. In: IEEE International Conference on Fuzzy Systems, pp. 1–6 (2021)
5. Carniel, A.C., Galdino, F., Philippsen, J.S., Schneider, M.: Handling fuzzy spatial data in R using the fsr package. In: ACM SIGSPATIAL Int. Conf. on Advances in Geographic Information Systems. pp. 526–535 (2021)
6. Carniel, A.C., Schneider, M.: Spatial plateau algebra: an executable type system for fuzzy spatial data types. In: IEEE International Conference on Fuzzy Systems, pp. 1–8 (2018)
7. Chen, J., Li, P., Fei, H., Wang, R.: An algorithm about spatial association rule mining based on cell pattern. In: Geoinformatics: Geospatial Information Science, pp. 662–671 (2006)
8. Chen, J., Lin, G., Yang, Z.: Extracting spatial association rules from the maximum frequent itemsets based on boolean matrix. In: International Conference on Geoinformatics, pp. 1–5 (2011)
9. Clementini, E., Felice, P.D., Koperski, K.: Mining multiple-level spatial association rules for objects with a broad boundary. Data Knowl. Eng. **34**(3), 251–270 (2000)
10. Kacar, E., Cicekli, N.K.: Discovering fuzzy spatial association rules. In: Data Mining and Knowledge Discovery: Theory, Tools, and Technology IV, pp. 94–102 (2002)
11. Koperski, K., Han, J.: Discovery of spatial association rules in geographic information databases. In: International Symposium on Spatial Databases, pp. 47–66 (1995)
12. Ladner, R., Petry, F.E., Cobb, M.A.: Fuzzy set approaches to spatial data mining of association rules. Trans. GIS **7**(1), 123–138 (2003)
13. Malerba, D., Lisi, F.A.: An ILP method for spatial association rule mining. In: First Workshop on Multi-Relational Data Mining, pp. 18–29 (2001)
14. Rinzivillo, S., Turini, F.: Extracting spatial association rules from spatial transactions. In: ACM Int. Workshop on Geographic Information Systems, pp. 79–86 (2005)
15. Schneider, M., Behr, T.: Topological relationships between complex spatial objects. ACM Trans. Database Syst. **31**(1), 39–81 (2006)
16. Zadeh, L.A.: Fuzzy sets. Inf. Control **8**(3), 338–353 (1965)

A Comprehensive Approach for the Conceptual Modeling of Genomic Data

Anna Bernasconi[1,2]([✉])[ID], Alberto García S.[1][ID], Stefano Ceri[2][ID], and Oscar Pastor[1][ID]

[1] PROS Research Center, VRAIN Research Institute,
Universitat Politècnica de València, Valencia, Spain
abernas@upvnet.upv.es, {algarsi3,opastor}@pros.upv.es
[2] Department of Electronics, Information, and Bioengineering, Politecnico di Milano,
Milan, Italy
{anna.bernasconi,stefano.ceri}@polimi.it

Abstract. The human genome is traditionally represented as a DNA sequence of three billion base pairs. However, its intricacies are captured by many more complex signals, representing DNA variations, the expression of gene activity, or DNA's structural rearrangements; a rich set of data formats is used to represent such signals. Different conceptual models explain such elaborate structure and behavior. Among them, the Conceptual Schema of the Human Genome (CSG) provides a *concept-oriented, top-down* representation of the genome behavior – independent of data formats. The Genomic Conceptual Model (GCM) instead provides a *data-oriented, bottom-up* representation, targeting a well-organized, unified description of these formats. We hereby propose to join these two approaches to achieve a more complete vision, linking (1) a *concepts layer*, describing genome elements and their conceptual connections, with (2) a *data layer*, describing datasets derived from genome sequencing with specific technologies. The link is established when specific genomic data types are chosen in the data layer, thereby triggering the selection of a view in the concepts layer. The benefit is mutual, as data records can be semantically described by high-level concepts and exploit their links. In turn, the continuously evolving abstract model can be extended thanks to the input provided by real datasets. As a result, it will be possible to express queries that employ a holistic conceptual perspective on the genome, directly translated onto data-oriented terms and organization. The approach is here exemplified using the DNA variation data type but is applicable to all genomic information.

Keywords: Conceptual modeling · Biological datasets · Genomics

---

A. Bernasconi and A. García S.—Should be regarded as Joint First Authors.

© The Author(s), under exclusive license to Springer Nature Switzerland AG 2022
J. Ralyté et al. (Eds.): ER 2022, LNCS 13607, pp. 194–208, 2022.
https://doi.org/10.1007/978-3-031-17995-2_14

1   Introduction

Representing the human genome DNA as a three billion base pairs' sequence is just a first attempt to capture the complex mechanisms of the life engine that is underlying all our characteristics and behaviors. Many other aspects, such as DNA mutations, the expression of gene activity, DNA's structural rearrangements, long distance contacts between DNA regions, and so on are now used to extract complex signals from the DNA, exploiting Next Generation Sequencing [30]; a rich set of data formats is used to represent such signals. The study of genomic information has practical implications on a number of fields such as cancer genomics, population genomics, and precision medicine. More importantly, being able to interoperate different signals in the context of a same analysis can provide insights and compute properties of the genome that remain otherwise hidden. Genomic data integration has so far been addressed mainly with operational approaches [1,18], whereas a holistic view – that encompasses the meaning of different genomic regions – has not been embraced yet. Conceptual models (CMs) have supported the effort of explaining such elaborate structure and behavior since 2000 [6,24]. However, genome data are frequently generated in practical lab settings without following any sound process of conceptual characterization. This creates a gap between "real" genome data CMs (that represent "genome data as it is") and pure genome CMs (that model "data as it should be"). Components obtained from the first kind of CMs must be connected with their corresponding components in the CMs that represent higher-level conceptual genome knowledge. We refer to the process of connecting concepts with their associated data as a "top-down" process, while we use the term "bottom-up" for connecting data to concepts.

A number of works, summarized by the Conceptual Schema of the Human Genome (CSG, [23]) produced by the PROS research center, provide a *concept-oriented, top-down* representation of the genome that is independent from the data formats, aiming to give a template of how the genome is supposed to behave. This perspective has contributed many valuable results devoted to building a general understanding of the language of life [12]. Another initiative, represented by the Genomic Conceptual Model (GCM, [5]) produced by the GeCo project [10], provides a *data-oriented, bottom-up* representation, targeting a high-level, abstract description of these formats, focusing on what data capture, how they capture it, to favour a joint use of the signals. With this approach, important achievements have been obtained in the area of data integration and search systems for genomics researchers [4,8].

By construction, the CSG model evolves according to upcoming requirements, while the GCM model evolves when new datasets arrive. In this work, we propose to join these two independent directions by explaining how, together, they can provide a more complete vision of the steps involved within the full-stack research that goes from the collection of data to the understanding of life mechanisms. On the one hand, we configure the CSG as the model that describes concepts, now renamed as the *concepts layer*, i.e., the template of the genome, where concepts are genome elements. On the other hand, we employ the GCM as the model that describes data, that is the *data layer*, where classes are real instances of datasets derived from tissues, cell lines, or individual cells that have undergone a sequencing process. The data layer is organized in DATASETS, each containing multiple SAMPLES. Samples may contain multiple SAMPLEREGIONS that are records representing fragments of the genome with specific measured properties. Each of these records can be linked to the corresponding concept in the concepts layer. New links are established when specific data types or experiments are chosen (in the data layer) triggering the selection of specific views (of the concepts layer). The benefit is two-fold: 1) the GCM is extended by the power of concepts, which enable high-level semantic-aware querying; 2) the CSG is empowered by its links to real-world data, that allow building computations on experimental instances and obtain biologically-relevant results.

In the following, we present how our background approaches to conceptual modeling in genomics deal with concepts and data (Sect. 2); we describe our vision of a unified conceptual model including a concepts and a data layer, and then illustrate our method for the linking of the two layers (Sect. 3); to exemplify the approach, we focus on the knowledge concerning DNA variation and we show how the two models can be pragmatically connected in this case (Sect. 4). This method is applicable to other genomic data types; in a more general framework, it will be possible to develop additional views and to use them together, towards a more encompassing conceptual perspective on the human genome (Sect. 5).

2   Background

As of today, two main approaches have tackled genomics from a conceptual modeling perspective, as briefly described in the following.

PROS: a Top-Down Approach. The Research Center on Software Production Methods (PROS) at the Universitat Politecnica de Valencia has invested many efforts in studying the genome from a conceptual modeling perspective, introducing the first Conceptual Schema of the Human Genome in 2011 [23] and producing several extensions since then [12,28]. The schema now results into a rich map of concepts and relationships that support the holistic understanding of different knowledge modules. The most recent version, called the Conceptual Schema of the Genome v3 (CSG) is reported in [13]. The employed method is considered top-down, as the main objective stands in identifying relevant concepts and their connections, independently on how datasets are really represented in available databases and sources.

GeCo: A Bottom-Up Approach. The approach devised within the data-driven Genomic Computing (GeCo) group, funded by the ERC AdG 693174 (2016–2021), has instead adopted a bottom-up approach, meaning that models are developed for representing existing data, with the purpose of making data more interoperable and ready for large-scale computations. Open data sources are analyzed and evaluated, understanding their underlying models; selected interesting datasets are imported within an integrative repository [4]. Information is divided between: region data (representing actual genomic elements, measured by experiments – using the Genomic Data Model, GDM [18]) and metadata (descriptions of genomic experiments – captured by the Genomic Conceptual Model, GCM [5]), which make data searchable [8]. Finally, the modeled datasets attempt to resolve data-level interoperability, thereby enabling powerful queries using, e.g., the GenoMetric Query Language (GMQL system [17]).

Fig. 1. Schematization of the two compared approaches.

Comparing the Two Approaches. We compare the two existing approaches under two perspectives: 1) how they deal with the concepts representing the knowledge of genomics; 2) how they manage their instantiation in the form of data. Genomic information can be interpreted as a dual system that is approached in two opposite directions, as observed in Fig. 1: on one side, the possibility to connect data to existing concepts that have been modeled in an abstract way (top-down approach), on the other side the possibility to build concepts based on already available data (bottom-up approach). Traditionally, PROS has adopted a top-down perspective, starting from modeling biological entities and only after checking if underlying data sources exist that represent such concepts, possibly unveiling problems in the quality of data structures definition and values. GeCo, instead, has adopted a bottom-up approach, starting from the observation of available data sources and only later building models to systematize, organize and interoperate such existing data, with the purpose of building easy-to-use systems that facilitate domain experts' work. With the intention of connecting these two perspectives, our work contributes a comprehensive approach that integrates them in order to facilitate genome data management by using a sound CM support.

3   Methodological Framework

We describe a general two-layer schema that contains:

- a concepts layer capturing the knowledge available about the human genome mechanisms (inspired by the CSG [13]);
- a data layer representing genomic data, with its types and experiments, captured by information structures and formats (inspired by the original GCM [5] for metadata and the Genomic Data Model [18] for region data).

Making an analogy with the triptych paradigm of Mayr and Thalheim [19], we can interpret our data layer as the one of "languages", enabling the narrative representation of our concepts layer (the "mental reasoning"). Written records (artifact world, our genomic data) stay on one level and – when instantiated – point directly to beliefs and perspectives (mental world, our genome concepts).

The Data Layer. The data layer (schematized in Fig. 2) is centered on the SAMPLE concept. It holds two metadata perspectives: the biological one contains the REPLICATE to which a sample belongs, part of a BIOSAMPLE, extracted from a DONOR; the organizational one has the CASESTUDY under which the sample was produced, which is contained in a greater PROJECT. Samples are built when an EXPERIMENTTYPE (e.g., DNA-Seq, RNA-Seq, or ChIP-Seq) is run, expressing information about the sequencing technology and representing a specific *genomic data type* (e.g., DNA variation, gene expression quantification, or binding sites of DNA-associated proteins). With respect to the original GCM, we also have that samples contain multiple SAMPLEREGIONS, typically a file row representing a fragment of the genome on a specific chromosome strand, with start and stop coordinates. All the regions in a sample follow the same SCHEMA. Note that these two classes were added to the data layer (w.r.t. the original GCM) as they are necessary to manage the linking between the two layers. Many samples are grouped into a DATASET, which is homogeneous in the schema and in the experiment type.

The Concepts Layer. The concepts layer is based on the last version of the CSG [13], including five modules, respectively describing i) the structure of the human genome; ii) protein synthesis; iii) changes in the sequence referring to a reference sequence (the "Variation module"); iv) information and sources related to the elements of the conceptual schema; and v) human metabolic pathways. The schema is manually-generated and incrementally enriched as new mechanisms are understood by a team of conceptual modelers or when new research findings are published. Genome knowledge is under continuous progress and understanding the human genome is an open big scientific challenge. For this reason, completeness is obviously not guaranteed and a mechanism to periodically handle needed extensions is employed. We consider this a "work-in-progress" model, where knowledge representation evolves, based on incoming requirements. While building the link with the data layer, it is likely that extensions to the CSG will be required, reinforcing the relevance of accomplishing the essential data-concepts genomic connection that this paper develops.

Data Type-Driven Linking of the Two Layers. Connections are built between the data and the concepts layers. By selecting specific genomic data types (based on the represented sequencing experiment type) we trigger a mechanism that invokes a specific portion of the concepts schema, as described by Fig. 2. In their previous description within the GCM [5], data types were forced into containers (i.e., SAMPLES) that flattened their semantics for integration and processing benefits; instead, here each data type is "freed" from its container, separately handled, analyzed, and mapped onto its explanation in conceptual terms.

The concepts layer and the data layer are connected by means of relations between concepts (i.e., a variation of DNA) and instances of data layer classes (i.e., the specific data record). For instance, a SAMPLEREGION measured through a DNA-Seq experiment, can be represented by its related concept, i.e., a variation at position 43,044,295–43,170,245 of the negative strand of chromosome 17.

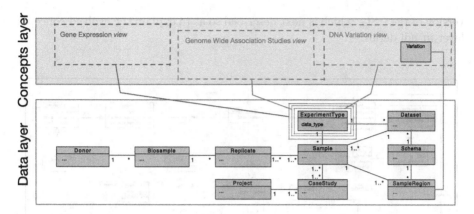

Fig. 2. Link between the concepts layer and the data layer by means of connections between sample regions and concepts.

Much in the spirit of Ontology-Based Data Access (OBDA [7]) approaches and in the fashion of ISGE [14], we envision the primary use mechanism of our two-layer schema as follows: 1) **Identification** of a *genomic data type* (EXPERIMENTTYPE in the data layer); 2) **Selection** of the related – possibly multiple – DATASETS, which have a corresponding SCHEMA that is followed by the SAMPLEREGIONS of the dataset (again, in the data layer); 3) **GEneration** of a *view* (in the concepts layer) built around a central concept that represents the SAMPLEREGION of the identified data type. Intuitively, the identification of a genomic data type (within an experiment type) triggers the generation of a specific view of interrelated concepts, comprising only entities and relationships that contribute to explain the content of that data type.

4 Method Application: Modeling DNA Variation

Many datasets are used in the daily practice of geneticists and computational biologists. These represent various types of information captured from the genome and the study of cohorts of patients, including information on the variation of DNA (population variation, its association with phenotype, somatic mutations, copy number variation, or structural rearrangements); the behavior of RNA (gene, miRNA, or isoform expression); or epigenetic signals (such as DNA methylation, DNA binding, or DNase I Hypersensitive sites).

For instantiating our method and describing it in more detail, we focus on one specific type of data, i.e., DNA variation, which includes both population variation and cancer-derived somatic mutations. We carefully considered the DNA variation module of CSG and applied appropriate changes to instantiate the related concepts layer *view*. The color code in Fig. 3 highlights which components have been added (green) or removed (red) with respect to the original model (blue classes) based on [13]; these changes are consolidated in an updated version of the CSG, which is next described so as to explain the evolved concepts layer in full detail.

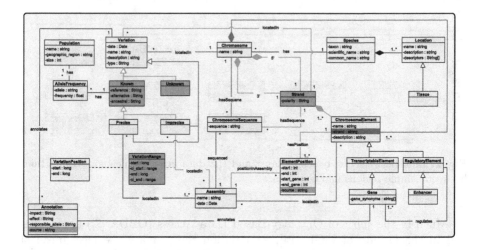

Fig. 3. Conceptual view dedicated to the DNA variation data type. Blue classes are derived from the CSG [28]; green classes, attributes, and relationships have been added here; red attributes and relationships are removed for the purpose of this effort. (Color figure online)

The obtained schema has 21 entity classes and 2 association classes, with six generalizations and three compositions (one of which is double). The most important class is the VARIATION one, with a *date*, *name*, *description*, and *type* (deletion, insertion or substitution); it is located on a specific STRAND (with positive or negative *polarity*), which contributes to compose a CHROMOSOME (with a *name*). Chromosomes are related to a SPECIES (with a taxonomy definition and scientific/common name), made of LOCATIONS (with *name*, *description*, and *descriptors*), such as TISSUES. On a strand, several CHROMOSOMEELEMENTS can be hosted (with their *name* and *description*). These include TRANSCRIPT-ABLEELEMENTS, such as GENES (with their alternative *gene_synonyms*) and REGULATORYELEMENTS that regulate genes, such as ENHANCERS. Elements present possibly multiple ELEMENTPOSITIONS (*start* and *end* positions on the chromosome, the genes on which they insist, and the information *source* from which the position has been obtained); these are measured with respect to an ASSEMBLY, i.e., a reference system based on a community-defined sequence (with a *name* and *date*). Each strand of the observed chromosome has a CHROMO-SOMESEQUENCE, which is also determined based on the assembly.

Variations may be specialized according to how their position is considered. If the position is not determined, we call the variation UNKNOWN; else it is KNOWN. Known variations have alleles called *reference* (the base reported by the reference sequence in that position), *alternative* (the mutated base), and *ancestral* alleles.

If the exact position is available, we call the variation PRECISE; if the position is reported within a range, we call it IMPRECISE. Precise variations record the VARIATIONPOSITION – with *start* and *end* coordinates – as an association class. Imprecise variations are also related to an assembly, but their association is characterized by a VARIATIONRANGE class that sets *start* and *end* positions within intervals of confidence (called *ci_start* and *ci_end*).

In the context of a POPULATION (with *name*, *geographic_region*, and *size*), a known variation has an ALLELEFREQUENCY, with a *frequency* indication reporting the percentage of presence of the *allele* within the considered population. Variations can alter the functionality of genes; we represent this with the ANNOTATION class, with an *impact*, *effect*, *responsible_allele*, and information *source*.

In Fig. 3, we applied notable additions (green elements) to the original CSG:

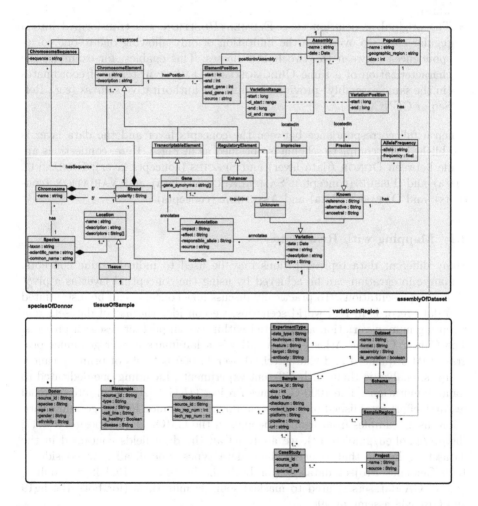

Fig. 4. Representation of the DNA variation information comprising the concepts view and related datasets.

- A STRAND class was added such that a chromosome is made of two strands and a VARIATION is exhibited only on one of them (i.e., variations can be read from 5' to 3' or from 3' to 5').
- The *ancestral* attribute was added in the KNOWN class to represent the allele of the last common ancestor of primates.
- The concept previously represented by the IMPRECISE class (i.e., variation for which coordinates were unknown) was updated to include variations with uncertain positions (within confidence intervals, represented by ranges), whereas the new UNKNOWN class was added to capture the original concept.
- The KNOWN variation class was added to generalize properties of both PRECISE and IMPRECISE variations.
- The *source* attribute was added in the ANNOTATION class to identify the origin of such assertion (e.g., a research group or automated annotation software).
- The original association class ELEMENTPOSITION was transformed into a regular class, to overcome the limitation of only allowing one-to-one correspondences between the two linked classes. This enables, for example, the characterization of a same CHROMOSOMEELEMENT in terms of coordinates (in the same assembly) provided by different authoritative *sources* (e.g., RefSeq or GENCODE).

When a full correspondence between the concepts layer and the data layer is established, the complete schema is obtained as in Fig. 4. Here, connections are made between DONOR (data layer) and SPECIES (concepts layer); BIOSAMPLE (data) and TISSUE (concepts): SAMPLEREGION (data) and VARIATION (concepts); and DATASET (data) and ASSEMBLY (concepts).

4.1   Mapping with Real Datasets

Many different data representations may be used to indicate same concepts. Semantic integration can be achieved by using the conceptual layer as a pivot of data representations. To practically discuss how concepts can be instantiated into data records in real world scenarios, we consider the use of datasets representing human variation as collected within two important research projects. The Cancer Genome Atlas (TCGA, [31]) is a landmark cancer genomics program that sequenced and characterized over 11,000 patients of primary cancer samples, analyzing them with different experiments, including one dedicated to somatic mutations. The 1000 Genomes Project (1KGP, [26]) is an international research effort established to create a catalogue of common human germline variation, using samples from healthy people. In the GMQL data repository [4,17] (http://gmql.eu/gmql-rest/), we analyzed all the data fields contained in the datasets' schemas that refer to these data types. Specifically, we considered 1000 Genomes Project datasets (for both the hg19 and GRCh38 assemblies) and TCGA datasets related to masked somatic mutations (for both the hg19 and GRCh38 assemblies [9]).

Table 1. Top part: relational schema of the data layer, with the 1000 Genomes Project population variation dataset and the TCGA masked somatic mutations dataset. Bottom part: examples of mapping rules for building the relational schema of the concepts layer; we assume POPULATION-ALLELEFREQUENCY to be a single table obtained as the join of tables derived from the POPULATION and ALLELEFREQUENCY classes.

Data.DONOR(source_id,species,age,gender,ethnicity)
Data.BIOSAMPLE(source_id,type,tissue,cell_line,is_healthy,disease)
...
Data.SAMPLE(source_id,size,date,checksum,content_type,platform,pipeline,url)
Data.SAMPLEREGION1KGP(chr,start,stop,strand,AL1,AL2,ref,alt,mut_type,length,id,quality,filter,DP,AF,AC,
    AFR_AF,AMR_AF,EUR_AF,EAS_AF,SAS_AF,AA,IMPRECISE,CIEND,CIPOS,"germline")
Data.SAMPLEREGIONTCGA(chrom,start,end,strand,gene_symbol,entrez_gene_id,variant_classification,
    variant_type, reference_allele, tumor_seq_allele1, tumor_seq_allele2, dbsnp_rs,"somatic")

Concept.VARIATION($gen()$,name,$gen()$,type)
　　　　　　　　　　⊇ Data.SAMPLEREGION1KGP(_,_,_,_,_,_,_,_,type,_,name,_,_,_,_,_,_,_,_,_,_,_,_,_,_)
Concept.VARIATION(date,name,description,type)
　　　　　　　　　　⊇ Data.SAMPLEREGIONTCGA(_,_,_,_,_,_,_,type,_,_,_,name,_)
Concept.KNOWN(reference,alternative,ancestral)
　　　　　　　　　　⊇ Data.SAMPLEREGION1KGP(_,_,_,_,_,_,reference,alternative,_,_,_,_,_,_,_,_,_,_,_,_,ancestral,_,_,_,_)
Concept.KNOWN(reference,f(allele1,allele2),null)
　　　　　　　　　　⊇ Data.SAMPLEREGIONTCGA(_,_,_,_,_,_,_,_,reference,allele1,allele2,_,_)
Concept.IMPRECISE()　　⊇ Data.SAMPLEREGION1KGP(_,**true**,_,_,_)
Concept.PRECISE()　　　⊇ Data.SAMPLEREGION1KGP(_,**false**,_,_,_)
Concept.VARIATIONRANGE(start,ci_start,end,ci_end)
　　　　　　　　　　⊇ Data.SAMPLEREGION1KGP(_,start,end,_,_,_,_,_,_,_,_,_,_,_,_,_,_,_,_,_,_,_,ci_end,ci_start,_)
Concept.VARIATIONPOSITION(start,end)
　　　　　　　　　　⊇ Data.SAMPLEREGION1KGP(_,start,end,_)
Concept.VARIATIONPOSITION(start,end)
　　　　　　　　　　⊇ Data.SAMPLEREGIONTCGA(_,start,end,_,_,_,_,_,_,_,_,_,_)
Concept.SPECIES(f(scientificName),scientificName,f(scientificName))
　　　　　　　　　　⊇ Data.DONOR(_,scientificName,_,_,_)
Concept.LOCATION(name, $gen()$, f(is_healthy,disease))
　　　　　　　　　　⊇ Data.BIOSAMPLE(_,"tissue",name,_,is_healthy,disease)
Concept.CHROMOSOME(name) ⊇ Data.SAMPLEREGION1KGP(name,_)
Concept.CHROMOSOME(name) ⊇ Data.SAMPLEREGIONTCGA(name,_,_,_,_,_,_,_,_,_,_,_,_)
Concept.STRAND(polarity)　⊇ Data.SAMPLEREGION1KGP(_,_,_,strand,_)
Concept.STRAND(polarity)　⊇ Data.SAMPLEREGIONTCGA(_,_,_,strand,_,_,_,_,_,_,_,_,_)
Concept.CHROMOSOMEELEMENT(name,$gen()$)
　　　　　　　　　　⊇ Data.SAMPLEREGIONTCGA(_,_,_,_,name,_,_,_,_,_,_,_,_)
Concept.GENE(geneSynonym) ⊇ Data.SAMPLEREGIONTCGA(_,_,_,_,_,geneSynonym,_,_,_,_,_,_,_)
Concept.ASSEMBLY(name,f(name))
　　　　　　　　　　⊇ Data.DATASET(_,_,_,name,_)
Concept.ALLELEFREQUENCY(allele,frequency)
　　　　　　　　　　⊇ Data.SAMPLEREGION1KGP(_,_,_,_,_,_,_,alt,_,_,_,_,_,_,AF,_,_,_,_,_,_,_,_,_,_)
Concept.ANNOTATION(effect,f(effect),f(ref,allele1,allele2))
　　　　　　　　　　⊇ Data.SAMPLEREGIONTCGA(_,_,_,_,_,_,effect,_,ref,allele1,allele2,_,_)
Concept.POPULATION-ALLELEFREQUENCY("African","Africa",1418,allele,frequency)
　　　　　　　　　　⊇ Data.SAMPLEREGION1KGP(_,_,_,_,_,_,_,_,allele,_,_,_,_,_,_,_,frequency,_,_,_,_,_,_,_,_)
...

To demonstrate a possible implementation of the proposed approach, we employ a relational database representation. The top part of Table 1 describes the schemas of the tables designed starting from the presented model. Note that most tables are directly derived from a translation from the class diagram into an RDBMS logical schema. The central SAMPLE class (a file in the repository) has one-to-many SAMPLEREGIONS, which correspond to a specific SCHEMA (an auxiliary table with a row for each dataset, in the example two rows for TCGA and two rows for 1KPG). For sample regions we employ one table for each different dataset. For simplicity, in this example we refer to SAMPLEREGIONTCGA and SAMPLEREGION1KGP (only considering their GRCh38 versions).

Mapping rules are used to describe how datasets information can be mapped into the concepts schema, considering the view that is specific for DNA variation.

The bottom part of Table 1 provides the mappings for the TCGA and 1KGP datasets. Each mapping rule is a logic formula (in Datalog-like syntax [11]) with variables in its left end side (LHS) that are computed from the variables in its right end side (RHS). The order of the variables follows the one indicated in the upper part of the table (e.g., the SAMPLEREGION1KGP table has 26 fields and the SAMPLEREGIONTCGA table has 13 fields). As an example, the entity VARIATION of the concepts schema is filled using data from the SAMPLERE-GION1KGP table, using the attributes in its 9th and 11th position (originally called *mut_type* and *id*) that map to the *type* and *name* attributes of the output VARIATION table. Similarly, the same VARIATION entity is filled using also data from the SAMPLEREGIONTCGA table, using the attributes in its 8th and 12th position (originally called *variant_type* and *dbsnp_rs*) that map to the *type* and *name* attributes of the output VARIATION table. Note that we wrote a different rule for each pair of output table (in the concepts layer) and input table (1KGP or TCGA in the data layer), when the mapping is meaningful.

In some cases, we need to derive new fields in the concepts layer schema as functions of original fields. One such example is in the KNOWN table: here, the second field *alternative* requires combining the values of three fields in the input table SAMPLEREGIONTCGA. For this, we use the notation *f(...)*. Moreover, names or descriptions are generated from the system admin (with *gen()*). A particular case is the one of POPULATION and ALLELEFREQUENCY tables: here the computation of the attributes of the second table (*allele* and *frequency*) depends on the values of the first. The values coming from the input table (e.g., AFR_AF from the SAMPLEREGION1KGP schema) denote the allele frequency only for a specific population. We thus represent this case using, as output table, the joined table that contains together the information of the population matching with its allele/frequency information. Here we did not report concepts layer's tables that could not be directly mapped to any field of the two data sources considered in this example; this is the case of CHROMOSOME, for instance, whose attribute *sequence* can be filled by inspecting authoritative sources such as RefSeq [22].

4.2 Examples of Applications

This section reports examples of queries that are enabled by concept-to-data linking, showing that: a) data improves the representation of genome concepts *within a specific view* (bottom-up); b) concepts and their connections improve the knowledge generation process allowing connections *across views* generated by different data types (top-down). Examples 1 and 2 demonstrate case (a) while examples 3 and 4 show case (b).

Ex 1. Extract positions of chromosome elements provided by different sources. Intuitively, one would expect that a specific gene was located in a uniquely defined range on a chromosome. However, its positions are identified by means of complex measurements which depend on the used technology or employed bioinformatics algorithm/parameters. Indeed, when such a query is posed to real data sources, we find multiple distinct positions. For instance, in the hg19 assembly, the PAQR6 gene is located in chromosome 1 at 156,213,111–156,217,908 according to RefSeq, whereas it is located at 156,213,205–156,217,881 according to GENCODE. The concepts layer adequately captures these aspects and it allows to pose a generic query while extracting heterogeneous definitions from the data.

Ex 2. Extract mutations whose position is not precisely identified. The concepts layer includes the possibility to represent known imprecise variations, which are commonly found in variation data sources such as the 1000 Genomes Project. For instance, a 297 bases-long variation could be located between position 14,477,084 (with a range of uncertainty that spans from 22 bases before, up to 18 bases after) and position 14,477,381 (with uncertainty between 12 and 32 bases).

Ex 3. Extract mutations located on enhancers associated to breast cancer. Let us consider the study of a patient genome targeting presence of mutations on BRCA1, i.e., a specific gene that is associated to breast cancer, located at position 43,044,295–43,170,245 of the negative strand of chromosome 17. From data, it can be observed that no relevant mutations are present in this range. However, in terms of clinical significance, in addition to genes, it is critical to consider also their regulatory elements. In this case, mutations should be tested also on the enhancers of BRCA1. Several data sources can provide this information. For example, the GH17J043124 enhancer is reported by GeneCards [29] at positions 43,123,800–43,127,201 and by ENCODE [27] at positions 43,124,247–43,126,961, being currently associated to breast cancer [2]. Note that mutation datasets (such as TCGA's ones) may sometimes report correspondence between variations and their enclosing genes; while this is a quite standard information, less studied elements, such as enhancers, are not typically considered. This connection, however, can be made by employing the concepts layer representation. The schema allows to make explicit a relation between positions and elements (including genes and enhancers) that remains instead hidden in the data.

Ex 4. Extract orthologous genes for humans and other species. By exploiting the connection between DONOR (data layer) and SPECIES (concepts layer) it would be possible to select genes of *Homo Sapiens* and genes of, e.g., canine models, which are orthologous (i.e., genes in different species that evolved from a common ancestral gene by speciation). Notably, over 58% of genetic diseases seen in the dogs closely depict the phenotype of human diseases caused by mutations in orthologous genes [15]. By exploiting the findings available for canine genes, candidates for gene-driven therapies may be found, e.g., for Duchenne muscular dystrophy [21].

5 Discussion and Conclusion

In this work we have described the concept-driven and data-driven approaches to conceptual modeling for genomics, that have guided the development of CSG and GCM. We then described a method for linking these models so as to generate an encompassing conceptual model that provides both the concept and data viewpoints. We applied our approach to the DNA variation case, showing that the new conceptual model can support interesting queries and applications, both acting on a single dataset and on several integrated datasets.

This work inspires future developments within the two projects and significant future joint activities that will integrate several available open data sources [3]. For what concerns the CSG model, the most substantial issue that will be addressed as future work is the inclusion of the notion of "individual". Indeed, DNA variation data, as well as many other genomic signals – here not discussed – do express information of this kind. Examples taken from the analyzed domain include 1) the person's genotype, which comprises the *allele1* and *allele2* attributes, concerning on which of the two chromosome copies the associated variant is located; 2) the *origin* (i.e., nature) of the variation, which could be somatic (occurring from damage to DNA in an individual cell during a person's life, not passed from parent to child) or germline (occurring in a sperm/egg cell, copied into every cell in the body, possibly passing from generation to generation). This may, for instance, enable studies on overlaps between variations that are recorded both as somatic and as germline in public databases [20]. The missing notion of "individual" is being investigated within the CSG working group and the upcoming results will be reported on this effort as well. For what concerns the GCM model, work has been so far driven by the requirement of creating a large repository (hosting, at the time of the writing, about 550 thousand files within a large database of 9 TB [17]). As a consequence of this initial choice, today GCM misses opportunities for conceptual data linking, that will drive its future extensions.

Regarding the joint effort described here, the most important challenge stands in generating views for all most relevant genomic data types, while carefully designing their links. In this paper, we show the variation-related information, but we will next take data types one by one and generate extensions of the concepts layer view by view. In this direction, we envision a holistic system that, based on the accurate view-specific contents, is able to provide a synergical perspective on the genome. The system will enable the combined use of multiple views, with selective mechanisms that activate one area or the other.

Users will then be allowed to ask questions that, for example, connect datasets on variation at the DNA level to variation at the amino acid level (i.e., proteins). More complex queries could compare somatic and germline variations (by means of "differential mutation analysis") to identify genes that are likely involved in a given disease [25] or identify susceptibility to tumorigenesis by exploiting genome-wide association studies [16]. More broadly, queries could span from mutations to their interaction with phenotype evidence, using their position within annotated genome elements, possibly also connecting it to interactions with the epigenome or the tridimensional organization of the genomic chain. All of these queries would benefit from the approach described in this work, facilitating in a natural way the interoperability between different data types connecting their corresponding views.

Acknowledgement. This research is funded by the ERC Advanced Grant 693174 GeCo (Data-Driven Genomic Computing), INNEST/2021/57, and MICIN/AEI/ 10.13039/501100011033.

References

1. Augustyn, D.R., et al.: Perspectives of using Cloud computing in integrative analysis of multi-omics data. Brief. Funct. Genomics **20**(4), 198–206 (2021)
2. Bass, J.I.F., et al.: Human gene-centered transcription factor networks for enhancers and disease variants. Cell **161**(3), 661–673 (2015)
3. Bernasconi, A., et al.: The road towards data integration in human genomics: players, steps and interactions. Brief. Bioinform. **22**(1), 30–44 (2021). https://doi. org/10.1093/bib/bbaa080
4. Bernasconi, A., et al.: META-BASE: a novel architecture for large-scale genomic metadata integration. IEEE/ACM Trans. Comput. Biol. Bioinf. **19**(1), 543–557 (2022)
5. Bernasconi, A., Ceri, S., Campi, A., Masseroli, M.: Conceptual modeling for genomics: building an integrated repository of open data. In: Mayr, H.C., Guizzardi, G., Ma, H., Pastor, O. (eds.) ER 2017. LNCS, vol. 10650, pp. 325–339. Springer, Cham (2017). https://doi.org/10.1007/978-3-319-69904-2_26
6. Bornberg-Bauer, E., et al.: Conceptual data modelling for bioinformatics. Brief. Bioinform. **3**(2), 166–180 (2002)
7. Calvanese, D., et al.: Ontology-based database access. In: SEBD, pp. 324–331 (2007)
8. Canakoglu, A., et al.: GenoSurf: metadata driven semantic search system for integrated genomic datasets. Database 2019 (2019)
9. Cappelli, E., et al.: OpenGDC: unifying, modeling, integrating cancer genomic data and clinical metadata. Appl. Sci. **10**(18), 6367 (2020)
10. Ceri, S., Bernasconi, A., Canakoglu, A., Gulino, A., Kaitoua, A., Masseroli, M., Nanni, L., Pinoli, P.: Overview of GeCo: a project for exploring and integrating signals from the genome. In: Kalinichenko, L., Manolopoulos, Y., Malkov, O., Skvortsov, N., Stupnikov, S., Sukhomlin, V. (eds.) DAMDID/RCDL 2017. CCIS, vol. 822, pp. 46–57. Springer, Cham (2018). https://doi.org/10.1007/978-3-319-96553-6_4
11. Ceri, S., et al.: What you always wanted to know about Datalog (and never dared to ask). IEEE Trans. Knowl. Data Eng. **1**(1), 146–166 (1989)
12. García, A., et al.: Towards the understanding of the human genome: a holistic conceptual modeling approach. IEEE Access **8**, 197111–197123 (2020)
13. García, A., et al.: A conceptual model-based approach to improve the representation and management of omics data in precision medicine. IEEE Access **9**, 154071–154085 (2021)
14. García S., A., Casamayor, J.C., Pastor, O.: ISGE: a conceptual model-based method to correctly manage genome data. In: Nurcan, S., Korthaus, A. (eds.) CAiSE 2021. LNBIP, vol. 424, pp. 47–54. Springer, Cham (2021). https://doi.org/ 10.1007/978-3-030-79108-7_6
15. Gopinath, C., et al.: Contemporary animal models for human gene therapy applications. Curr. Gene Ther. **15**(6), 531–540 (2015)
16. Mamidi, T.K.K., et al.: Integrating germline and somatic variation information using genomic data for the discovery of biomarkers in prostate cancer. BMC Cancer **19**(1), 1–12 (2019)

17. Masseroli, M., et al.: Processing of big heterogeneous genomic datasets for tertiary analysis of Next Generation Sequencing data. Bioinformatics **35**(5), 729–736 (2018)
18. Masseroli, M., et al.: Modeling and interoperability of heterogeneous genomic big data for integrative processing and querying. Methods **111**, 3–11 (2016)
19. Mayr, H.C., et al.: The triptych of conceptual modeling. Softw. Syst. Model. **20**(1), 7–24 (2021)
20. Meyerson, W., et al.: Origins and characterization of variants shared between databases of somatic and germline human mutations. BMC Bioinform. **21**(1), 1–22 (2020)
21. Nghiem, P.P., et al.: Gene therapies in canine models for duchenne muscular dystrophy. Hum. Genet. **138**(5), 483–489 (2019)
22. O'Leary, N.A., et al.: Reference sequence (refseq) database at ncbi: current status, taxonomic expansion, and functional annotation. Nucleic Acids Res. **44**(D1), D733–D745 (2016)
23. Pastor, O., et al.: Model-based engineering applied to the interpretation of the human genome. In: The Evolution of Conceptual Modeling, pp. 306–330. Springer (2011)
24. Paton, N.W., et al.: Conceptual modelling of genomic information. Bioinformatics **16**(6), 548–557 (2000)
25. Przytycki, P.F., et al.: Differential analysis between somatic mutation and germline variation profiles reveals cancer-related genes. Genome Med. **9**(1), 79 (2017)
26. 1000 Genomes Project Consortium: a global reference for human genetic variation. Nature **526**(7571), 68 (2015)
27. ENCODE Project Consortium: An integrated encyclopedia of DNA elements in the human genome. Nature **489**(7414), 57–74 (2012)
28. Reyes Román, J.F., Pastor, Ó., Casamayor, J.C., Valverde, F.: Applying conceptual modeling to better understand the human genome. In: Comyn-Wattiau, I., Tanaka, K., Song, I.-Y., Yamamoto, S., Saeki, M. (eds.) ER 2016. LNCS, vol. 9974, pp. 404–412. Springer, Cham (2016). https://doi.org/10.1007/978-3-319-46397-1_31
29. Safran, M., Rosen, N., Twik, M., BarShir, R., Stein, T.I., Dahary, D., Fishilevich, S., Lancet, D.: The GeneCards Suite. In: Abugessaisa, I., Kasukawa, T. (eds.) Practical Guide to Life Science Databases, pp. 27–56. Springer, Singapore (2021). https://doi.org/10.1007/978-981-16-5812-9_2
30. Schuster, S.C.: Next-generation sequencing transforms today's biology. Nat. Methods **5**(1), 16–18 (2008)
31. Weinstein, J.N., et al.: The cancer genome atlas pan-cancer analysis project. Nat. Genet. **45**(10), 1113–1120 (2013)

A Deep Learning Approach for Ideology Detection and Polarization Analysis Using COVID-19 Tweets

Md Yasin Kabir[ID] and Sanjay Madria[✉][ID]

Missouri University of Science and Technology, Rolla, USA
{mkabir,madrias}@mst.edu

Abstract. Polarization analysis is critical for effective policy and strategy implementation. Various aspects of the COVID-19 pandemic are discussed on social media platforms extensively. While social media are used to share factual information and official directives, there is also an abundance of misinformation and beliefs (both personal and political). Some of that misinformation and beliefs are driven by polarized opinions from different ideologies. Consequently, considerable polarization has been observed on widely discussed topics related to Covid-19 such as face masks and vaccines. The study of emotion is essential for polarization detection as positive or negative sentiment towards a topic might indicate favorability or hesitancy. While positive or negative sentiment indicates a polar view toward a subject matter, it is paramount to understand the fine-grained emotion (e.g. Happiness, Sad, Anger, Pessimism) for effective polarization detection. In this research work, we propose a deep learning model leveraging the pre-trained BERT-base to detect the political ideology from the tweets for political polarization analysis. The experimental results show a considerable improvement in the accuracy of ideology detection when we use emotion as a feature. Additionally, we develop a deep learning model accompanied by an adversarial sample generation module to detect the emotion in the tweets. The adversarial sample general module significantly improves the performance of the deep learning model. Finally, we explore the political polarization for the topics "mask" and "vaccine" in the different states of the USA throughout the pandemic.

Keywords: COVID-19 · Coronavirus · Polarization · Social media · Twitter · Emotion analysis · Data analysis · Machine learning

1 Introduction

COVID-19 pandemic forces people to stay at home which amplified the use of social media. The general population as well as officials leverage social media to disseminate information, and directives, and to create awareness. People became engaged in social media to express their opinions, beliefs, and political agenda

© The Author(s), under exclusive license to Springer Nature Switzerland AG 2022
J. Ralyté et al. (Eds.): ER 2022, LNCS 13607, pp. 209–223, 2022.
https://doi.org/10.1007/978-3-031-17995-2_15

along with different types of content. Various topics related to Covid-19 with great interest have emerged throughout the pandemic. "Mask, Vaccine, Stay at home" are some examples of the topics with higher engagement where people with different ideologies reacted differently on those topics. People actively decide their contents of interest which often brings the same ideology people together because of the recommendation system and followers network of the social media. During the pandemic, researchers have observed a concerning amount of bias and political polarization [9,11]. Moreover, the 2020 presidential election of the United States greatly influence people's opinions and beliefs related to Covid-19. Prior research works [1] show that such political events can reinforce beliefs through confirmation bias. Various research works have shown that social media is highly prone to echo chambers [4]. An echo chamber is a situation where certain beliefs or assumptions (both true/false) are reinforced by repeated communication and information sharing. Most of the prior works in polarization and echo chamber detection discuss mostly political topics. However, during the pandemic researchers have found polarization and conspiracies for general health directives such as masks and vaccines [3,19].

The use of face masks became highly polarized and a topic of debate because of different guidelines. There are various kinds of masks available and not all kinds of masks prevent COVID-19 infection at the same level. General types of masks such as surgical masks, reusable cloth masks, and face coverings do not prevent infections much while those reduce the transmission compared to professional N-95 masks. To prevent panic buying and hoarding, some official guidelines asked people not to buy masks stating that masks are not effective[1] After a few weeks, in April 2020, CDC urged all Americans to use a face mask. This kind of information created confusion among the general population which also instigates polarization.

Understanding polarization is very critical to motivating the mass population effectively and creating acceptable policies. A proper study of polarization for some topics can be useful for other topics that might arise in the future. It will also assist in sharing acceptable information across all demographic. While there are research works on COVID-19 polarization detection [6,10,19], most of those works use relatively small data sets or periods. In this work, we aim to study polarization using large-scale Twitter data collected from March 2020 to December 2021 regarding masks and vaccines. Our primary research contributions are:

– We leverage deep learning model and develop a transformer-based model to detect the partisanship from the tweeter data. We have also created a pipeline to semi-automatically annotate the political affiliation to create the data-set for the model. Instead of using high-level sentiments (positive, neutral, and negative), we have used many different emotion categories.
– To detect the emotion in a tweet, we propose a BiLSTM model with an adversarial sample generation module.

---

[1] Surgeon General Urges the Public to Stop Buying Face Masks - https://www.nytimes.com/2020/02/29/health/coronavirus-n95-face-masks.html.

- We have performed polarization analysis during the COVID-19 pandemic on "Mask" and "Vaccine" with respect to political ideology in the USA. We also explore the polarization in four states with different political ideology during the years 2020 and 2021.

2 Related Works

2.1 Polarization Detection Using Twitter

Twitter is becoming popular for anomaly detection, misinformation propagation and quantification, public response and communication monitoring during times of crisis. Polarization detection within social media content especially Twitter is a popular topic of research these days. To detect the polarization and political ideology in the tweets, researchers mostly take two approaches: content-based and network-based. User metadata, tags, tweet, location, and other information are used in content-based approaches. In this approach, authors use user metadata information and compared that information with seed users (verified profile with political affiliation) to infer the political ideology. While this method works well it also skews the result because of similarity in the shared content and the location. In the second approach, the user network is used to detect partisanship. The network is built using engagements, and followers [10]. Ideally the more interaction someone has with seed users with specific affiliation, it is more likely for that user to follow the same political ideology. Authors in [10] created an interaction network using retweets. The authors explore the echo chambers using the interaction network. While people who interact with each other might have a similar ideology, it is also possible for people to interact with someone who oppose the content. Topic-specific polarization exploration also became very popular during the COVID-19 pandemic. Yeung et al. [19] explore the polarization on personal face masks during the pandemic. The authors analyze the people with different demographic such as age, gender, geographic region, and household income. The authors use the valence-aware sentiment analysis to detect the polarity. The authors employ a content-based approach to detect the political ideology using a set of filtered keywords and follow networks. Jiang et al. [11] studied the polarization between different ideological groups on COVID-19 vaccine favorability and hesitancy. The authors use follower scores and expressions in the tweets to detect political affiliation. The authors examined whether and how people's opinions on the COVID-19 vaccine vary. While the above approaches can determine the political ideology those approaches are impacted by the considered sample data, sample size, and seed users. In this work, we take a content-based approach to detect political ideology. However, instead of using the profile meta-information or user network, we use the content in the tweet text and the emotion in the text to detect the political ideology. This method reduces the bias as instead of looking at user interaction network it focuses on the shared contents by a user.

2.2   Adversarial Sample Generation and Emotion Classification

Most of the traditional tweet emotional classification works treat the problem as a text classification problem and rely on a large amount of labeled data. Baziotis et al. [2] and Meisheri et al. [13] who hold the first and second place in the multi-label emotion classification task of SemEval-2018 Task1, developed classifiers using a biLSTM with an attention mechanism. However, none of those works perform emotion classification on a crisis dataset which might represent a wide variety of emotions with unbalanced data. Yang et al. [18] introduce a COVID-19 dataset and implemented XLNet, AraBert, and ERNIE for emotion classification. However, the authors did not attempt any adversarial approach or any other technique to make the model better context-aware.

Adversarial learning approaches are widely popular for computer vision problems. However, in recent years adversarial learning gaining popularity in the field of Natural Language Processing (NLP). In [14], a team of researchers from Google and OpenAi, introduce adversarial training methods for semi-supervised text classification. The authors introduced perturbations in the text embedding in a Recurrent Neural Network (RNN) and achieved a state-of-the-art result. In a recent work, Daniel et al. [7] explore domain adversarial training for low-resource text classification. The authors claimed that transfer learning from one language to another low-resource language using the adversarial technique is highly beneficial. The authors extended domain-adversarial neural network architecture to multiple source domains and evaluate the model performance to prove their claim. Authors in [5] used Generative Adversarial Learning to improve the BERT and make it robust for text classification. The authors found that adopting adversarial training to enable semi-supervised learning in Transformer-based architectures improves the model performance with fewer labeled examples. While research is scarce works on adversarial learning for emotion classification from text, the idea is gaining traction recently. In December 2020, Bo Peng et al. [15] proposed an adversarial learning method for sentiment word embedding to force a generator to create word embedding with high-quality utilizing the semantic and sentiment information. In [17], the authors utilize adversarial multi-task learning for Aggressive language detection (ALD) from tweets. The authors deploy a task discriminator for text normalization to improve the ALD. The adversarial framework uses the private and shared text encoder to learn the underlying common features across the labels and thus improve the performance. In [8], the authors developed a confrontation network and used transfer learning to achieve rapid theme classification and emotion detection from the text. The authors developed an adversarial network to extract the common features of different tasks to improve performance. In most of these works, authors are taking adversarial approaches for word embedding or transfer learning across the domains. However, due to the short text in social media contents (e.g. Tweets), the emotion can change by a single word where 80–90% of the words remain the same. In this work, we explore an adversarial learning approach to extract the common features across different emotions to improve emotion detection.

3 Data Preparation

Figure 1 represents the basic workflow of the data collection, processing, annotation, and manipulation. We have started collecting COVID-19-related tweets originating from the USA using Twitter Streaming API from March 5th, 2020. Since then we have collected over 800 million tweets until December 2021. During the filtering and pre-processing steps, we discarded non-English tweets and removed the duplicates and media-only tweets. Further, we process the user profile information to keep the essential information such as location, verified status, and profile description. To estimate the location of a user, we have used the Geo-information available with the tweets. However, less than 1% of tweets contain the geotag because of Twitter location privacy. In that case, we have used the user profile description and location meta information to estimate the location of the user. The pre-processed data is stored as CSV files. There was a total of $831M$ tweets. After processing the data there were $512M$ unique tweets. The total number of unique and verified users are $57,35,936$ and $59,883$ respectively.

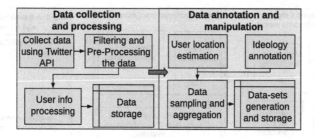

Fig. 1. Data processing, annotation, and manipulation

Data Annotation: For this work, we have annotated two sets of data. First, we manually annotate emotions using 10K tweets. Three annotators worked independently to annotate the emotion types using every single tweet. The detailed emotion annotation process is available in [12]. The tweets were annotated in 10 different emotion types (e.g. neutral, optimistic, happy, sad, surprise, fear, anger, denial, joking, pessimistic). To reduce the biases of the data annotation, we have added 4000 more emotion-labeled tweets publicly available at [18]. Further, we develop a semi-automatic annotation module to annotate the political ideology of a user. We have considered the members of the US Congress and self-claimed verified users with political ideology (Democratic, Republican) as the seed user. We annotated the tweets from those user profiles with the political affiliation. We only consider the original tweets by those users in the finalized data set which contains around 250K of tweets on masks and vaccines. We also identify the emotions in those tweets using the developed emotion detection model. We use this data set to train a transformer-based model, and further use that model to identify the political affiliation in the other tweets.

4   Emotion Classification

We develop a Deep Neural Network with adversarial sample generation and learning to classify the tweet text into a specific emotion category. The classification model comprises six primary components which are the input layer, embedding layer, Bidirectional Long-Short Term Memory (BiLSTM) layers, auxiliary features input, and output layers. A detailed description of each component is available in our previous research work [12]. In our prior work, the developed BiLSTM model outperforms other state of the arts in several metrics. To improve the proposed BiLSTM model for the minor emotion classes such as 'Jokes', we introduce a method for adversarial sample generation and learning which effectively increases the performance of the BiLSTM model while converging with fewer epochs of training. Figure 2 represents the basic idea of the proposed adversarial approach to detect the emotion labels. The process can be separated into 3 steps. The first step is adopted from our previous work and described in [12]. In the following subsections, we briefly describe steps two and three.

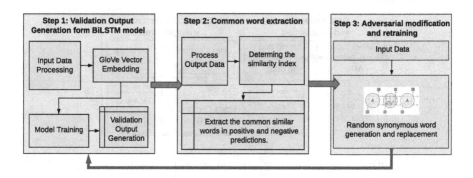

Fig. 2. Adversarial training steps

4.1   Common Word Extractor

The algorithm for common word determination from the text is presented in Algorithm 1. The algorithm takes the validation prediction outputs of the model during the training and calculates the similarity ratio and distance to determine the common words. We have used Normalized hamming similarity [16] to calculate the similarity. The algorithm compared the similarity ratio and distance between the positive and negative prediction to determine which words are critical and present across right and wrong predictions. It uses two threshold values α and δ to select the appropriate words that can be replaced to generate adversarial sample. During different training epochs, the model changes the values of α and δ to ensure different word selection, and hence, it maximizes the performance.

4.2   Adversarial Sample Generation

Let us denote the sequence of commons words across positive and negative labels as $\{W_d | d = 1, 2, 3, ..., N\}$. The module uses the pre-trained GloVe embedding vectors and seeks similar semantic words. It follows the steps in Algorithm 2. The algorithm initializes a probability value $P = 0.2$ and select a word randomly from the embedding space to replace the original word in the tweet. We have examined different probability values and found that 0.2 is the optimal one. After creating the adversarial sample this module forward those samples and combine those with the input data to create a new set of training data for the model.

Algorithm 1. Common Word Determination

Input: Validation Prediction P_v. Here [v = 1 to k]. Initial values for Similarity and Distance thresholds α, δ.

Output: Words dict W_d.

1: Initialization: Appends P_v with input text.
2: **for** $i = 1$ to len(P_v) **do**
3:     Calculate word frequency $W_f = [word, count]$.
4:     Calculate similarity index S_{idx} in the predictions.
5: **end for**
6: Determine the similarity ratio S_r and distance S_d between positive preds Pos_v and negative predes Neg_v.
7: **for** $i = 1$ to len(W_f) **do**
8:     **if** $S_r[i] > \alpha$ and $S_d[i] < \delta$ **then**
9:         W_d.append($W_f.word$);
10:     **end if**
11: **end for**
12: **return** W_d.

Algorithm 2. Adversarial Sample Generation

Input: Sample Tweets T, Common words dict W_d.

Output: Generated sample adversarial tweets T_{adv}, Probability vectors T_P.

Initialization: Define a initial probability $P = 0.2$.

2: **for** t in T **do**
    Iterate through the common words and find out the embedding vector for each word.
4:     With Probability P randomly select a similar word for respective common word.
    Replace the common words with similar world in t.
6:     Append the Probability P in T_P.
end for
8: **return** T_{adv}, T_P.

5   Political Ideology Detection

Figure 3 represents the architecture for political ideology detection using BERT-base transformer. BERT (Bidirectional Encoder Representations from Transformers) use transformers which is essentially an attention mechanism that learns contextual relations in the text. The model use encoders to learn the inputs and decoders to produce the output. In our work, we leverage a pre-trained BERT-base model and retrained it with the annotated political data-set. Along with the text, we also use the emotion class label as an input. We use a total of 150K annotated tweets for the training and validation. 80% of the data is used

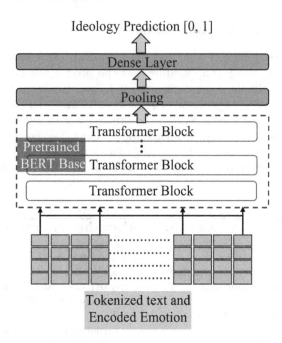

Fig. 3. BERT-based transformer model for ideology detection

during training and the rest of the data were used to evaluate the model performance. During the test, we have observed that the addition of the emotion label improves the performance of the model significantly.

6   Experimental Result and Analysis

All of the experiments of this project is performed using a machine comprises of Intel®Core™i9-9900K CPU, 64GB RAM and an Nvidia RTX-2080Ti GPU.

Table 1. Hyperparameter values for emotion classification model

Hyperparameters	Description
Text embedding	Dimension: 250
BLSTM Layer	2 layers; 250 hidden units in each
Dense Layer	2 layers; 150 and 75 units respectively
Drop-out rate	Word Embedding: 0.3; Dense layer: 0.2 each;
Activation function	ReLU; Output activation: Sigmoid;
Adam optimizer	Learning rate = 0.0001; $beta_1$ = 0.8;
Epochs and batch	Epochs = 25; batch size = 256;

6.1 Hyperparameters of the Models

We have performed rigorous hyper-parameters tuning and found that the values in Table 1 and Table 2 are ideal to reach the desired performance. The tables also presents the layers information that are used in both models. For emotion classification we have performed parameter tuning and optimize the model after the adversarial sample learning. We used the same set of parameters as presented in the tables for performance evaluation and model re-production. We have used 80/20 training and testing split for both of the models.

Table 2. Hyperparameter values of ideology detection model

Hyperparameters	Description
Pre-trained Model	BERT Base
Linear layer	768, Activation: ReLU;
Criterion	Cross entropy loss; Optimizer: Adam
Learning rate	0.0001; Drop-out rate: 0.5
Epochs and batch	Epochs = 25; batch size = 128;

6.2 Evaluation Metrics

To evaluate the classification model, we have used F1-Micro, F1-Macro, and Accuracy as metrics. Let L denotes the number of categories, TP denotes True Positive, FP denotes False Positive, and FN denotes False Negative. We can define the F1-micro average and F1-macro average score as follows:

$$Precision = \frac{TP}{TP + FP} \quad (1) \qquad F1 = \frac{2*Precision*Recall}{Precision+Recall} \quad (3)$$

$$Recall = \frac{TP}{TP + FN} \quad (2) \qquad F1_{macro} = \frac{1}{|L|} \sum_{k=1}^{L} F1_k \quad (4)$$

$$Precision_{micro} = \frac{\sum_{k=1}^{L} TP_k}{\sum_{k=1}^{L}(TP_k + FP_k)} \quad (5) \quad F1_{micro} = \frac{2*Precision_{micro}*Recall_{micro}}{Precision_{micro}+Recall_{micro}} \quad (7)$$

$$Recall_{micro} = \frac{\sum_{k=1}^{L} TP_k}{\sum_{k=1}^{L}(TP_k + FN_k)} \quad (6) \quad Accuracy = \frac{1}{T} \sum_{k=1}^{T} \sigma(Y_k == P_k) \quad (8)$$

Accuracy is used as a metric for model performance as it can give a better observation for imbalanced categories. Equation 8 defines the Accuracy score where $\sigma(Y_k == P_k)$ returns 1 if the prediction is correct, otherwise 0. To evaluate the performance of the political ideology detection model, we have used the accuracy score and ROC AUC(Area under the ROC Curve). ROC curve shows the performance of a classification model at all the given classification thresholds. We have used "sklearn" metrics package to calculate the ROC AUC score.

6.3 Experimental Results

Table 3a represents the primary experimental results. To test the adversarial approach, we have integrated the module with the above described BiLSTM network with auxiliary feature engineering. From the table, we can observe that the adversarial integration improved the performance considerably. The F1-Micro and F1-Macro scores are comparatively lower as we have some emotion categories with a very small number of labels (e.g. denial, joking, pessimistic). All of the models perform poorly for those classes. The performance evaluation for the different models for political ideology detection is present in Table 3b. We can see that the BERT with the addition of the emotion category outperforms other models. We have also evaluated RoBERTa with and without the the emotion labels. The performance of RoBERTa model is also very close to BERT models.

Table 3. Performace evaluation of the models

(a) Emotion Classification

Models	F1-Micro	F1-Macro	Accuracy
SVM-Unigrams	0.53	0.41	0.74
NTUA-SLP	0.60	0.49	0.85
BiLSTM$_{Aux}$	0.55	0.54	0.86
BiLSTM$_{Aux}$+ADV	0.64	0.61	0.91

(b) Ideology detection

Models	Accuracy	ROC AUC
SVM	0.73	0.70
CNN	0.79	0.76
RoBERTa	0.84	0.83
BERT	0.85	0.83
BERT$_{emot}$	0.88	0.87

6.4 COVID-19 Polarization Analysis

The primary aim of the polarization analysis is to find the polarized topics and explore the change in sentiment during the pandemic. Figure 4 depicts the word-clouds on the topics masks and vaccines using trigrams from the tweets by people with democratic and republican ideology, respectively. For each word cloud, a sample of 1 million tweets was used. We observe some polarized opinions across the demographics. For instance, trigrams "masks don't prevent" and "masks cant prevent" were prominent in the republication tweets. Similarly, we observe a different set of discussions on vaccines. In the republican tweets, "operation wrap speed" and "fake vaccine news" appears frequently compared to the democratic tweets.

Figure 5(a, b) represents the monthly polarity on the topics "Masks" and "Vaccines" in the USA, respectively. In the charts, the blue lines represent the polarization score for democratic ideology and the red lines represent republican ideology scores. To calculate the polarity values, one million tweets per month were selected from each ideology class. The polarity for each tweet is set as a positive one $(+1)$ for the positive emotion and negative one (-1) for the negative emotion. Further, we take the average of the polarity across all the tweets to calculate the polarization score. Therefore, the lower polarity score denotes the negative sentiment on the topics compared to the opposite ideology. We further

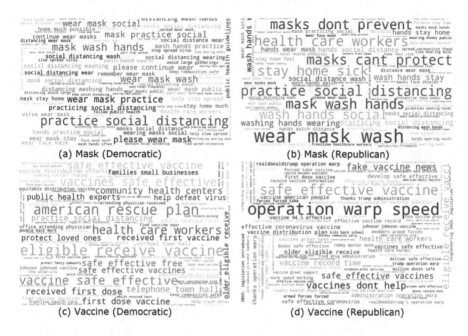

(a) Mask (Democratic)

(b) Mask (Republican)

(c) Vaccine (Democratic)

(d) Vaccine (Republican)

Fig. 4. Discussion on masks and vaccines since March 2020 to December 2021

explored the polarization in the four different states (e.g. NY - New York, CA - California, TX - Texas, and MO - Missouri) of the USA for the topic "Masks" and "Vaccines". In Fig. 5, we observe some interesting contrast in the polarity for each ideology before and after the year 2020 presidential election for both the topics. The score for the republican ideology significantly went down after the election in Texas and Missouri while the score was much higher before the election when compared to the democratic ideology. Figure 5(c) to 5(j) represents the polarization on "masks" and "vaccines" in the four states. While all the four states have a similar trend, we can see some distinct differences also. For instance, in Fig. 5(c), in April 2021 for the New York state, we see a higher polarity score for the republican ideology compared to the other three states. In the other states, the democratic polarity score on the topic "Masks" was much higher compared to the republication. We can see another interesting observation in Fig. 5(d) for May 2021 in California state. We can see that the republican sentiment went down significantly in May 2021. We present the topics of interest during the above-mentioned events in Fig. 6. We observe that the people in NY have considerably similar discussions and emotions on the masks in April 2021. Although there was a shift in the sentiment after the 2020 election, the people of NY decided to work together to contain the coronavirus. We observe a very

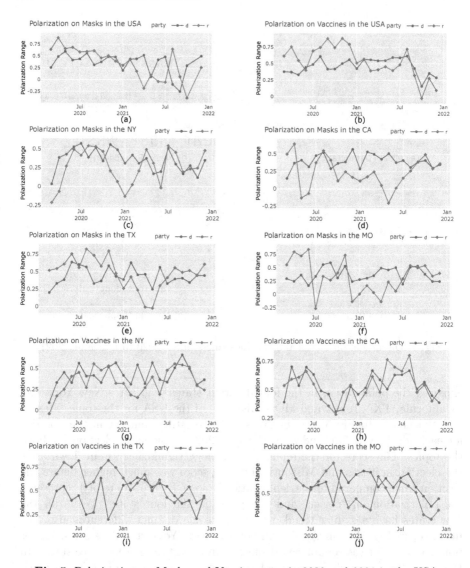

Fig. 5. Polarization on Masks and Vaccines over in 2020 and 2021 in the USA

different set of discussions and emotions among the democrats and republicans in California. While the Democrats want to enforce the use of masks, many republicans were strongly against it. We can see some trigrams such as 'hurts public confidence', 'forcing kids wear', and 'lift mask mandate' in the tweets, associated with the republican ideology.

Fig. 6. Discussion on Mask by people from New York and California

In Fig. 7, we can observe the contrast between the discussed topics related to "vaccines" by democrats and republicans during the years 2020 and 2021. People with the democratic ideology were strongly vocal about the vaccine development and affordable vaccines during the year 2020. They felt that the initiatives taken by the authorities are not enough. On the contrary, republicans were praising the operational speed of a safe and effective vaccine. In the year 2021, democrats discussed more American rescue plans and mass vaccination to encourage people to take the vaccine. However, the Republicans were vocal against the political spinning of vaccine success, and also vocal against forced vaccination policy by different authorities and employers. Due to the page limitation, we present a limited number of analyses in the paper. However, we plan to make more analyses publicly available along with our data and findings in the GitHub repository[2]. The repository will contain the interactive graphs which will be accessible through a GitHub website.

---

[2] https://github.com/mykabir/Covid-19-Polarization-Analysis.

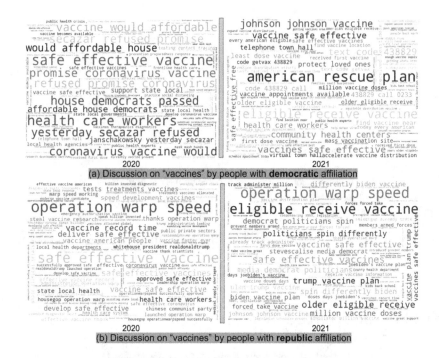

Fig. 7. Discussion on vaccines during 2020 and 2021

7   Conclusion and Future Work

In this work, we have extended our earlier emotion detection model and achieved higher scores compare to the state-of-the-art models for emotion classification. In addition, we also propose a BERT-based political ideology classification model where we use emotions as a feature for polarization detection using the tweets only. The performance evaluation shows that the proposed model outperformed other well-known models for the classification task. Further, we have used the classified ideology label to analyze the tweets and explored the polarization issues on the topics such as "mask" and "vaccine" during the COVID-19 pandemic. In the future, we plan to study the influence of the bias in our study and conduct experiments with different sample sizes for different periods.

References

1. Barberá, P., Jost, J.T., Nagler, J., Tucker, J.A., Bonneau, R.: Tweeting from left to right: Is online political communication more than an echo chamber? Psychol. Sci. **26**(10), 1531–1542 (2015)
2. Baziotis, C., et al.: Ntua-slp at semeval-2018 task 1: predicting affective content in tweets with deep attentive rnns and transfer learning. arXiv preprint arXiv:1804.06658 (2018)

3. Chen, E., Chang, H., Rao, A., Lerman, K., Cowan, G., Ferrara, E.: Covid-19 misinformation and the 2020 us presidential election. Harvard Kennedy School Misinformation Rev. (2021)
4. Colleoni, E., Rozza, A., Arvidsson, A.: Echo chamber or public sphere? predicting political orientation and measuring political homophily in twitter using big data. J. Commun. **64**(2), 317–332 (2014)
5. Croce, D., Castellucci, G., Basili, R.: GAN-Bert: generative adversarial learning for robust text classification with a bunch of labeled examples. In: Proceedings of the 58th Annual Meeting of the Association for Computational Linguistics, pp. 2114–2119 (2020)
6. Green, J., Edgerton, J., Naftel, D., Shoub, K., Cranmer, S.J.: Elusive consensus: polarization in elite communication on the covid-19 pandemic. Sci. Adv. **6**(28), eabc2717 (2020)
7. Grießhaber, D., Vu, N.T., Maucher, J.: Low-resource text classification using domain-adversarial learning. Comput. Speech Lang. **62**, 101056 (2020)
8. Haihong, E., Yingxi, H., Haipeng, P., Wen, Z., Siqi, X., Peiqing, N.: Theme and sentiment analysis model of public opinion dissemination based on generative adversarial network. Chaos, Solitons Fract. **121**, 160–167 (2019)
9. Jiang, J., Chen, E., Yan, S., Lerman, K., Ferrara, E.: Political polarization drives online conversations about covid-19 in the united states. Hum. Beh. Emerg. Technol. **2**(3), 200–211 (2020)
10. Jiang, J., Ren, X., Ferrara, E., et al.: Social media polarization and echo chambers in the context of covid-19: case study. JMIRx med **2**(3), e29570 (2021)
11. Jiang, X., et al.: Polarization over vaccination: Ideological differences in twitter expression about covid-19 vaccine favorability and specific hesitancy concerns. Social Media+ Society **7**(3), 20563051211048413 (2021)
12. Kabir, M.Y., Madria, S.: Emocov: machine learning for emotion detection, analysis and visualization using covid-19 tweets. Online Soc. Networks Media **23**, 100135 (2021)
13. Meisheri, H., Dey, L.: Tcs research at semeval-2018 task 1: learning robust representations using multi-attention architecture. In: Proceedings of The 12th International Workshop on Semantic Evaluation, pp. 291–299 (2018)
14. Miyato, T., Dai, A.M., Goodfellow, I.: Adversarial training methods for semi-supervised text classification. arXiv preprint arXiv:1605.07725 (2016)
15. Peng, B., Wang, J., Zhang, X.: Adversarial learning of sentiment word representations for sentiment analysis. Inf. Sci. **541**, 426–441 (2020)
16. Rajarajeswari, P., Uma, N.: Normalized hamming similarity measure for intuitionistic fuzzy multi sets and its application in medical diagnosis. Int. J. Math. Trends Technol. **5**(3), 219–225 (2014)
17. Wu, S., Fei, H., Ji, D.: Aggressive language detection with joint text normalization via adversarial multi-task learning. In: Zhu, X., Zhang, M., Hong, Yu., He, R. (eds.) NLPCC 2020. LNCS (LNAI), vol. 12430, pp. 683–696. Springer, Cham (2020). https://doi.org/10.1007/978-3-030-60450-9_54
18. Yang, Q., et al.: Senwave: monitoring the global sentiments under the covid-19 pandemic. arXiv preprint arXiv:2006.10842 (2020)
19. Yeung, N., Lai, J., Luo, J.: Face off: Polarized public opinions on personal face mask usage during the covid-19 pandemic. In: 2020 IEEE International Conference on Big Data (Big Data), pp. 4802–4810. IEEE (2020)

Effective Generation of Relational Schema from Multi-Model Data with Reinforcement Learning

Gongsheng Yuan[1,2(✉)], Jiaheng Lu[1], and Zhengtong Yan[1]

[1] Department of Computer Science, University of Helsinki, Helsinki, Finland
{gongsheng.yuan,jiaheng.lu,zhengtong.yan}@helsinki.fi
[2] School of Information, Renmin University of China, Beijing 100872, China

Abstract. To handle data variety in one project, some researchers proposed using multiple databases or one multi-model database to manage various data. However, considering that the predominated Relational Database Management Systems (RDBMSs) in the current market have powerful capabilities such as query optimization and transaction management, we propose using an RDBMS as a unified platform to store and query multi-model data. But the mismatch between the complexity of multi-model data structure and the simplicity of flat relational tables imposes a grand challenge. To address this challenge, we adopt the reinforcement learning method to design a workload-aware approach that could directly learn a relational schema to store multi-model data by interacting with an RDBMS with the given queries and data. To choose the right actions in the learning process, we propose a variant Q-learning algorithm (*Double Q-tables*) along with functions for updating the tables, which could reduce the dimension of the original Q-table and improve learning efficiency. Experimental results show that our approach could generate a relational schema with superior performance in terms of query response time and storage space cost over a multi-model storage schema.

Keywords: Multi-model data · Reinforcement learning · Relational schema · JSON · RDF · Relational data

1 Introduction

The current applications developed for processing different tasks in various scenarios are generating a tremendous amount of data. For those data, people could store them in tabular structures, unstructured object-like documents, or graph formats, etc. To manage those different data models, different databases are developed, such as RDBMSs and NoSQL databases. Unfortunately, using multiple databases instead of a unified platform may cause some possible problems [1]. Some people propose multi-model databases [6] to manage different data models with a unified query language. However, creating a mature multi-model data management system is rather time-consuming. Considering that RDBMSs

J. Ralyté et al. (Eds.): ER 2022, LNCS 13607, pp. 224–235, 2022.
https://doi.org/10.1007/978-3-031-17995-2_16

have powerful capabilities in handling security, user authentication, query optimization, etc., which have been hardened for decades by researchers, we propose using an RDBMS as a unified platform to store and query multi-model data.

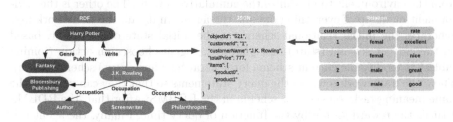

Fig. 1. An example of multi-model data.

To achieve this goal, we need to identify its main challenge - the mismatch between the complexity of multi-model data structure (see Fig. 1) and the simplicity of flat relational tables. Therefore, our main task in this paper is to design a relational schema to store multi-model data while having excellent query performance. To do this, we think that it is a great idea to make the proposed approach aware of queries, data, and the running environment. Considering this, we propose using the Reinforcement Learning (RL) method to address the problem of how to generate a relational schema with excellent query performance for the input data and queries [7,8]. This is because reinforcement learning could work with a dynamic environment and learn how to map different situations to corresponding actions so as to maximize the specific reward for achieving the final goals. Now, we summarize our contributions as follows:

1. Based on RL, we use Markov Decision Process to model the process of relational schema generation and attempt to obtain a relational schema to store and query multi-model data consisting of relational data, JSON documents, and RDF data in RDBMSs while having excellent query performance.
2. In this process, we design the initial state of the reinforcement learning, define the concept of actions, describe the representations of state observation, present the definition of rewards, and identify the final goal, which would make our approach work effectively.
3. Against our research problem, we propose a variant Q-learning algorithm (*Double Q-tables*) as a learning policy to help choose actions, which extremely reduces the dimensions of the original Q-table's action columns and makes our approach work efficiently.
4. Finally, we perform extensive empirical experiments that demonstrate our approaches could obtain a relational schema with excellent query performance and better than the state-of-the-art approach.

2   The Overview of Approach Framework

The framework (see Fig. 2) of learning a relational schema has two main components. One is the learner (i.e., the agent) that explores, interacts with, and learns from the environment to maximize the cumulative reward. The other is the environment made up of everything outside the agent. In detail, the framework first generates the initial relational schema as the initial state of RL. Next, based on the current schema (state) and policy, the agent chooses an action (joining tables) to modify the current schema for generating a new (next) schema (state). Then, the framework rewrites the query statements so that they can perform the same meaning tasks on the new schema in the RDBMS. After that, the RDBMS returns the reward gotten by the function of query time. Finally, the agent utilizes the learning algorithm to update the Q-tables with the information of the returned reward and observation state and then repeats the previous operations to continue exploring the potential relational schemas or collecting the most rewards that we already know about until the agent has tried all the actions in an episode (or the episode has reached the maximum number of iterations). Now, by collecting the generated states and comparing their executing time, we could obtain the best relational schema from the generated relational schemas for the input multi-model workload. Next, we will introduce the initial schema, states, actions, reward, goal, and policy in this framework separately.

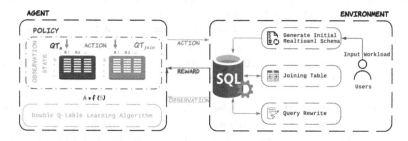

Fig. 2. The framework of generating schema for multi-model data based on RL. (Some icons are from https://www.iconfinder.com/)

2.1   Initial Relational Schema

We transform the input multi-model data into multiple narrow tables based on the fully decomposed storage model (DSM) [4]. Specifically, we decompose a JSON document including $(n + 1)$ keys into n two-column tables, where the JSON object id is regarded as the key of each two-column table (see Table 1). As for the name of each table, it is the same as its second-column attribute name. Besides, we design a fixed schema to preserve JSON arrays based on the model-based methods [3,5]. For example, Table 2 is used to store array elements that has string type. For the relational data, we split each table into multiple narrow tables whose amounts are equal to the number of attributes except the original table keys. For those narrow tables, their first several columns are the keys of the original table, and the following column holds the values of an attribute. For the RDF graph data, we divide the triples table into multiple two-column tables. Each two-column table consists of a subject and a predicate, and each tuple of this table is made up of the subjects having that specific predicate and object values corresponding to that predicate.

Table 1. customerName.

objectId	customerName
521	J.K. Rowling

Table 2. ArrayTableString.

objectId	Key	Index	valStr
521	Items	0	product0
521	Items	1	product1

2.2 Action

Based on the construction of the initial relational schema, we define our actions as joining operations. Specifically, we first collect and count all the keys of the JSON documents, all the predicates of the RDF data, and all the attributes of relation tables in the multi-model dataset. Next, we map those keywords into several numeric intervals (i.e., $[threshold_i + 1, threshold_i + m]$). With this mapping information, we could also use these numeric ids to represent the corresponding tables. Thus, if we choose a number id, we could use its corresponding table to do the joining operation. This means all these numeric ids form a set of actions A. For example, we could get $A = \{1, 2, 3, 101, 102, 103, 104, 201, 202\}$ from Fig. 1, where $\{1 : customerId\}$, $\{2 : customerName\}$, $\{3 : totalPrice\}$, $\{101 : Genre\}$, $\{102 : Write\}$, $\{103 : Publisher\}$, $\{104 : Occupation\}$, $\{201 : sex\}$, $\{202 : rate\}$ $threshold_1 = 1$, $threshold_2 = 100$, and $threshold_3 = 200$.

2.3 State

In this part, we will design an effective expression format for describing the relational schemas (states). We start with using a dictionary D to represent a relational schema. For example, we represent the initial relational schema as $d_0 = \{1:[1], 2:[2], 3:[3], 101:[101], 102:[102], 103:[103], 104:[104], 201:[201], 202:[202]\}$. In this dictionary, each key (numeric id) represents a table and its value consists of this table's attributes. The keys in d_0 represent the existing tables in the current relational schema. Next, we represent those relational schemas (states) as strings so that they can be identified in the MDP. For example, we could represent the initial state s_0 as a string "1 0 2 0 3 0 101 0 102 0 103 0 104 0 201 0 202", where we regard the reserved word "0" as an interval bit between different tables. Please note that we put these table ids in numerical order in this string. Even though a table consists of several attributes, there should be a numerical order for these ids in this sub-string.

2.4   Policy

To get a new state, we need the policy to help specify which action to take
in each state. Revisiting the definitions of states and actions in this paper, we
know that both of them are finite sets. Therefore, we propose a variant Q-learning
algorithm (*Double Q-tables*) to help the agent find an optimal policy maximizing
its total reward. The classic Q-learning is a model-free reinforcement learning
algorithm whose core idea is to generate a Q-table (QT_a) to store state-action
values. However, just with one Q-table, this would result in that we could not
make our action (joining operation) work except self-joins. This is because, so
far, we only have one table selected through the Q-table (QT_a), but we have
no idea which table should be chosen from the current schema to do joining
with that selected table. To complete our approach, we define another Q-table
QT_{join}, a ($n \times n$)-dimensional table. As shown in Fig. 3, rows (states) of the
Q-table QT_{join} are defined by action set A, columns (actions) are defined by
table ids. Its main idea is that when QT_a chooses an action a_i at state s_i, the
QT_{join} will decide which table (selected from the existing tables in the current
relational schema, i.e., keys in dictionary d_i) should be chosen to do joining with
a_i (QT_a) at the state a_i (QT_{join}). For example, if QT_a chooses an action a_3 (e.g.,
$a_3 = 3$) at the state s_0, then we will go to Q-table QT_{join} to choose another
table at the state a_3 of QT_{join}. Assume that QT_{join} chooses action a_1 at state
a_3, the new relational schema will be $d_1 = \{1:[1, 3], 2:[2], 101:[101], 102:[102],$
$103:[103], 104:[104], 201:[201], 202:[202]\}$ and the new state s_1 is "1 3 0 2 0 101
0 102 0 103 0 104 0 201 0 202". Since this process contains table joining, we set
a semantic constraint pool (including key and foreign key constraints, etc.) to
determine whether they could join. Next, we introduce how to update Q-tables.

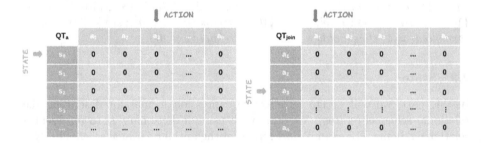

Fig. 3. Double Q-table.

Here, we use Eq. 1 [2] to update the first Q-table QT_a and use Eq. 2 to update
the second Q-table QT_{join}, where we use $\max_{a'} QT_a(s', a')$ as the maximum
expected value of QT_{join} at state a of QT_{join}. We use the previous example to
explain these equations, if QT_a chooses an action a (e.g., a_3) at the state s (e.g.,
s_0), then we will go to Q-table QT_{join} to choose another table at the state a (i.e.,
a_3) of QT_{join}. Assume that QT_{join} chooses action *tableID* (e.g., a_1) at state a

(i.e., a_3), we could get a new state s' (i.e., s_1). Next, we use these information to update two Q-tables.

$$QT_a(s,a) \leftarrow QT_a(s,a) + \alpha[r + \gamma \max_{a'} QT_a(s',a') - QT_a(s,a)] \qquad (1)$$

$$QT_{join}(a, tableID) \leftarrow QT_{join}(a, tableID) + \alpha[r + \\ \gamma \max_{a'} QT_a(s',a') - QT_{join}(a, tableID)] \qquad (2)$$

Algorithm 1. Double Q-table Algorithm

Input: The multi-model data and queries
Output: Relational schemas
1: Generate initial relational schema d_0 and initial state s_0
2: Initialize QT_a and QT_{join}
3: **for** each episode **do**
4:     $d = d_0$, $s = s_0$
5:     Initialize action space A
6:     **while** True **do**
7:         Choose a action a at state s by QT_a (ϵ-greedy)
8:         Remove the action a from the action space A
9:         Choose a $tableID$ at state a by QT_{join} (ϵ-greedy)
10:        Execute joining operation if possible, perform queries, and observe r, s'
11:        $QT_a(s,a) \leftarrow QT_a(s,a) + \alpha[r + \gamma \max_{a'} QT_a(s',a') - QT_a(s,a)]$
12:        $QT_{join}(a, tableID) \leftarrow QT_{join}(a, tableID) + \alpha[r + \gamma \max_{a'} QT_a(s',a') - QT_{join}(a, tableID)]$
13:        $s \leftarrow s'$
14:     **until** A is empty
15:     **end while**
16: **end for**

2.5 Reward and Goal

Considering that our goal is to find a relational schema having minimum query time, we first set the query time (gotten by performing a set of queries over the current relational schema with an RDBMS) as a negative value, denoted as $-t_{now}$. Next, we compare this value with the previous negative query time, denoted as $-t_{previous}$, and then get the reward by $R = t_{previous} - t_{now}$.

Based on the above concepts, we present Algorithm 1 to demonstrate the learning process of our RL method. According to the input multi-model data, it generates the initial relational schema and state in Line 1. Next, the algorithm initializes the Q-table QT_a and the Q-table AT_{join} in Line 2. After that, the algorithm runs the episodes as many as users want in Lines 3–16 to obtain the potential great relational schema (i.e., find an optimal policy maximizing the expected value of the total reward). For each episode, the algorithm first initializes the relational schema and resets the action space. Next, the algorithm chooses a action at state s though the Q-table QT_a with ϵ-greedy method in Line 7. Please note that action a will be removed from the action space once a is chosen, as Line 8 does. Then the algorithm uses the second Q-table QT_{join} to choose another table for preparing to join based on the ϵ-greedy method. If they could join, the agent could get a new state s' and reward given by the RDBMS. After that, the agent uses Eq. 1 and Eq. 2 to update two Q-tables, replace the current state with the new state, and repeat the whole process (Lines 6–15) until the action space A of QT_a is empty or the episode reaches the maximum number of iterations.

Table 3. The number of records/objects in different data models.

	Relational	JSON	RDF
Person	–	153 134	4 471 790
Film	–	84 322	522 800
UniBench	35 609	383 518	2 213 208

Table 4. Queries employed in the experiments.

ID	Queries
Q_1	Return the first element in normalized when pageid = "10867341"
Q_2	Return the colleges that George_Cowan attends
Q_3	Return the nationality, height, and birthYear of Sarah_Cawood
Q_4	Return the original and ns of Charles Phoenix
Q_5	Return the occupation and ns of Ron_Silver
Q_6	Return the plot of A.I. Artificial Intelligence
Q_7	Return the organizations that Ralf Little is affiliated to
Q_8	Return the academic advisor and the gender of Richard Griffiths
Q_9	Return the released time and IMDB rating of The Godfather
Q_{10}	Return the born place and the gender of director of E.T. the Extra-Terrestrial
Q_{11}	Return the titles of products which "8383" (person id) is interested in
Q_{12}	Return order "5099d82c-fea2-4f04-a3b7-f70af5e9e4fe"'s Orderline[0].brand
Q_{13}	Return the asin, price, and imgUrl of the product (product id = "11046")
Q_{14}	Return the total price of the order "cda31793-2809-4627-9c0a-f361dc5bdd1f"
Q_{15}	Return the order id of Delano (firstName) Muldaur (lastName)'s friends

3   Experiment

We use the datasets Person[1], Film[1] and UniBench[2] to compare the performance of our approach with ArangoDB [1] that is a multi-model database. After conducting the data clean, we list their statistics in Table 3. In Table 4, we use three groups of queries ($Q_1 - Q_5$ on Person, $Q_6 - Q_{10}$ on Film, and $Q_{11} - Q_{12}$ on UniBench) to evaluate our approaches, where each query involves one or more data models. For each Q_i, we write and execute the corresponding AQL statement in ArangoDB to collect its query time and answers for comparing them with our results. The experiments are implemented in Python and run on a laptop PC with a 2,6 GHz Intel Core i7 processor and 16 GB memory. The version of MySQL is 5.7.30, and ArangoDB is 3.7.1. Note that we perform all queries several times and use their median values in the experiments.

Table 5. Query time (s) of Q_i in the person dataset.

Approaches	Q_1	Q_2	Q_3	Q_4	Q_5	Total
Double Q-tables	1.005	0.005	0.102	0.078	0.300	1.490
ArangoDB	0.057	1.443	1.445	0.051	8.083	11.079

Table 6. Query time (s) of Q_i in the film dataset.

Approaches	Q_7	Q_7	Q_8	Q_9	Q_{10}	Total
Double Q-tables	0.042	0.0002	0.011	0.041	0.062	0.157
ArangoDB	0.045	0.168	0.224	0.048	1.818	2.303

Table 7. Query time (s) of Q_i in the UniBench dataset.

Approaches	Q_{11}	Q_{12}	Q_{13}	Q_{14}	Q_{15}	Total
Double Q-tables	0.394	4.343	0.016	0.222	1.089	6.064
ArangoDB	2.058	0.176	0.003	0.173	16.504	18.914

---

[1] https://www2.helsinki.fi/en/researchgroups/unified-database-management-systems-udbms/datasets.
[2] https://github.com/HY-UDBMS/UniBench_new/releases.

dataPerson.csv number value 0 1.6308557987213135 1 1.5574872493743896 2
1.5658411979675293 3 1.6000211238861084 4 1.5703368186950684 5 1.5866644382476807
6 1.6165239810943604 7 1.6253111362457275 8 1.6200993061065674 9 1.5524749755859375
10 1.5858750343322754 11 1.5762073993682861 12 1.594890832901001 13 1.6552848815917969
14 1.5513594150543213 15 1.6202647686004639 16 1.6136806011199951 17 1.611283540725708
18 1.6021888256072998 19 1.5925519466400146 20 1.5724148750305176 21 1.5179240703582764
22 1.6063611507415771 23 1.5931599140167236 24 1.5091149806976318 25 1.4896371364593506
26 1.5786502361297607 27 1.5069055557250977 28 1.5592091083526611 29 1.5059878826141357
30 1.6243464946746826 31 1.5681860446929932 32 1.5523219108581543 33 1.6178631782531738
34 1.6659140586853027 35 1.662156105041504 36 1.6138179302215576 37 1.5947730541229248
38 1.6182734966278076 39 1.6408576965332031 40 1.6108293533325195 41 1.6345841884613037
42 1.5953567028045654 43 1.61503005027771 44 1.61116361618042 45 1.5893759727478027
46 1.6439392566680908 47 1.5476438999176025 48 1.6152827739715576 49 1.5796737670898438
50 1.626760721206665 51 1.6371233463287354 52 1.591273546218872 53 1.6471381187438965
54 1.6558911800384521 55 1.6336548328399658 56 1.6371872425079346 57 1.6272952556610107
58 1.707350254058838 59 1.634063482284546 60 1.6615140438079834 61 1.6571168899536133
62 1.684919834136963 63 1.662580966949463 64 1.6489872932434082 65 1.6393580436706543
66 1.6368637084960938 67 1.6647536754608154 68 1.52919602394104 69 1.6468870639801025

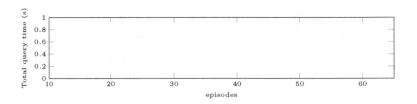

Fig. 4. The changes in query time as the increase of episodes.

dataFilm.csv number value 0 0.23364496231079102 1 0.23538804054260254 2
0.2819819450378418 3 0.28510522842407227 4 0.21438384056091309 5 0.2595701217651367
6 0.22042417526245117 7 0.27697062492370605 8 0.18156814575195312 9 0.22697877883911133
10 0.22908806800842285 11 0.2411055564880371 12 0.19133448600769043 13 0.24299001693725586
14 0.21609044075012207 15 0.280653715133667 16 0.26799678802490234 17 0.25737619400024414
18 0.27666783332824707 19 0.2296617031097412 20 0.17970681190490723 21 0.261854887008667
22 0.2569420337677002 23 0.2713689804077148 24 0.22025346755981445 25 0.2473621368408203
26 0.22237801551818848 27 0.22005844116210938 28 0.28400492668151855 29
0.2780940532684326 30 0.24843096733093262 31 0.24001312255859375 32 0.19508051872253418
33 0.2108228206634521 34 0.2204439640045166 35 0.2717950344085694 36 0.2568042278289795
37 0.1820704936981201 38 0.21265935897827148 39 0.2662839889526367 40 0.23563027381896973
41 0.2738637924194336 42 0.25235700607299805 43 0.2295215129852295 44 0.21104216575622559
45 0.20060849189758 46 0.2244570255279541 47 0.27466797828674316 48 0.2495348453521728
49 0.2795047760009756 50 0.2845191955566406 51 0.2174859046936035 52 0.2448613643646240
53 0.27667713165283203 54 0.23612594604492188 55 0.22630858421325684 56
0.2797186374664306 57 0.19123363494873047 58 0.20773077011108398 59 0.271579742431640
60 0.2677149772644043 61 0.18755412101745605 62 0.1766953468322754 63 0.20771002769470215
64 0.21070790290832 65 0.21358776092529297 66 0.1771376132965088 67 0.1908724308013916
68 0.22346735000610352 69 0.1565396785736084

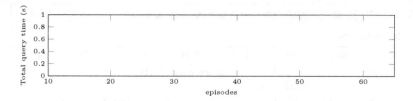

Fig. 5. The changes in query time as the increase of episodes.

dataUniBench.csv number value 0 6.5375590324401855 1 6.5007078647613525
2 6.5337114334106445 3 6.536458969116211 4 6.452621936798096 5 6.291561603546143
6 6.4155871868133545 7 6.3124213218688965 8 6.294771194458008 9 6.294673204421997
10 6.270218849182129 11 6.252112150192261 12 6.064265251159668 13 6.277676105499268
14 6.258821725845337 15 6.427833318710327 16 6.236349105834961 17 6.416132926940918
18 6.42907977104187 19 6.07938814163208 20 6.435817003250122 21 6.453512907028198
22 6.24445796012878 23 6.271257162094116 24 6.440478801727295 25 6.467978239059448
26 6.509033679962158 27 6.539574861526489 28 6.338322401046753 29 6.375007152557373
30 6.880248308181763 31 6.61084246635437 32 6.340642690658569 33 6.3280980587005615
34 6.456621170043945 35 6.2536537647247314 36 6.422722339630127 37 6.4283435344696045
38 6.418624401092529 40 6.393954038619995 41 6.401635408401489 42 6.448727607727051
43 6.355209827423096 44 6.0730061531066895 47 6.435367584228516 48 6.484595775604248
49 6.505710601806641 50 6.418363571166992 51 6.462645530700684 52 6.442893028259277
53 6.411004066467285 54 6.239349842071533 55 6.37992262840271 56 6.432523965835571
58 6.447792291641235 59 6.419814825057983 60 6.420297145843506 61 6.296583652496338
63 6.431811571121216 65 6.40365743637085 66 6.405707836151123 67 6.415660858154297
68 6.409823417663574 69 6.248623371124268

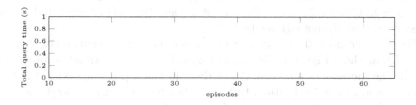

Fig. 6. The changes in query time as the increase of episodes.

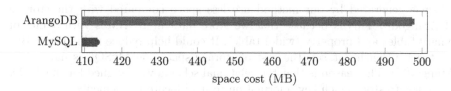

Fig. 7. The cost of storage spaces on MySQL and Arangodb.

Table 5, Table 6, and Table 7 present the executing time of queries on the
relational schema generated by our RL method and on ArangoDB. We can see

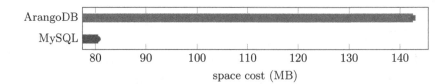

Fig. 8. The cost of storage spaces on MySQL and Arangodb.

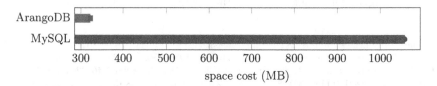

Fig. 9. The cost of storage spaces on MySQL and Arangodb.

that the execution time of queries like Q_1 and Q_{12} is less than that on our generated relational schema. This is because ArangoDB preserves data in document format, which is quite suitable for this kind of query. However, our method has its own benefits. For example, our method may generate a wide table that may include all attributes which one query needs. Thus, this could significantly reduce the query time. And users do not need to do many self-joins on the giant triples table (e.g., Q_3). Besides, for the queries involving multiple data models, our method could also reduce time consumption. The reason is that we could execute those queries just on the relevant attributes and ignore the useless information (e.g., Q_5 and Q_{15}). Finally, the total query time of our generated schema is less than that ArangoDB needs.

We set $\epsilon\_greedy = 0.5$ to attempt to balance the exploitation and exploration of our RL method. Figure 4, Fig. 5, and Fig. 6 show that the trend of total query time as the increase of episodes. All of them in the top few episodes, the total query time has some fluctuation. But in the last few episodes, it slowly becomes steady. Of course, we could set a small number for ϵ_greedy to make its best to explore different schema.

Figure 7, Fig. 8, and Fig. 9 demonstrate the consumption of storage spaces on MySQL and Arangodb. For the Person dataset and Film dataset, the relational schemas generated by our method use less space compared with the storage of Arangodb. This is because that we store data in RDBMSs with a mix of binary tables and property (wide) tables. It could help reduce redundancy. But for the UniBench dataset, the cost of storage spaces on MySQL is more than Arangodb's. The reason is that the relational schema we designed for the JSON array has to store much key information to help locate its elements.

4   Conclusion

In this paper, we proposed using RL to let the agent automatically learn a relational schema by interacting with the RDBMS. To this end, we modeled the process of generating a relational schema for multi-model data as an MDP. We also specified the state, action, reward, goal, etc., to complete our approach. Besides, we also presented a *Double-tables* algorithm to make the agent know how to choose actions at specific states and update the values in the Q-tables for helping the agent collect the most reward over time. Finally, we conducted extensive experiments on different datasets to show the performance of our methods. And these results show the performance advantage of our approach over multi-model data storage.

Acknowledgments. The work is partially supported by the China Scholarship Council and the Academy of Finland project (No. 310321). We would also like to thank all the reviewers for their valuable comments and helpful suggestions.

References

1. What is a multi-model database and why use it? [white paper]. ArangoDB (2020). www.arangodb.com/resources/white-paper/multi-model-database/
2. Bellman, R.E.: Dynamic programming (1957)
3. Chasseur, C., Li, Y., Patel, J.M.: Enabling json document stores in relational systems. In: WebDB, vol. 13, pp. 14–15 (2013)
4. Copeland, G.P., Khoshafian, S.N.: A decomposition storage model. ACM SIGMOD Rec. **14**(4), 268–279 (1985)
5. Florescu, D., Kossmann, D.: Storing and querying XML data using an RDMBS. IEEE Data Eng. Bull. **22**, 3 (1999)
6. Lu, J., Holubová, I.: Multi-model databases: a new journey to handle the variety of data. ACM Comput. Surv. (CSUR) **52**(3), 1–38 (2019)
7. Yuan, G., Lu, J.: MORTAL: a tool of automatically designing relational storage schemas for multi-model data through reinforcement learning. In: Proceedings of the ER Demos and Posters 2021, CEUR Workshop Proceedings, vol. 2958, pp. 7–12. CEUR-WS.org (2021)
8. Yuan, G., Lu, J., Zhang, S., Yan, Z.: Storing multi-model data in RDBMSs based on reinforcement learning. In: Proceedings of the 30th ACM International Conference on Information and Knowledge Management. ACM (2021)

Business Process

Ontology-Supported Modeling of Bots in Robotic Process Automation

Maximilian Völker[✉][iD] and Mathias Weske[iD]

Hasso Plattner Institute, University of Potsdam, Potsdam, Germany
{maximilian.voelker,mathias.weske}@hpi.de

Abstract. Despite omnipresent digitalization, the infrastructure for information processing in companies often lags years behind. As a result, employees have to compensate for the inadequacies of legacy software and spend their time collecting, copying, and reviewing data spread across multiple applications. Robotic Process Automation can help automate such structured and repetitive tasks by using software robots that mimic the worker's behavior. However, being mainly driven by industry, no modeling standard or possibilities for interoperability between different RPA vendors exist, which may lead to a vendor lock-in over time, for example. In this paper, we extend the ontology of RPA operations, that comprises conceptualizations for tasks that can be automated by RPA, and apply it for modeling RPA bots in a vendor-independent manner. To this end, a novel platform for modeling conceptual RPA bots and a corresponding prototype are presented, which open up new possibilities when creating and managing RPA bots.

Keywords: Semantic robotic process automation · RPA · Ontology · Modeling

1 Introduction

In recent times, companies see themselves confronted with an increasing amount of data, processes, and overall complexity. At the same time, the infrastructure for information processing in companies is often dated, leaving even more repetitive work to humans who must transfer and check data between computer systems. Robotic Process Automation (RPA) promises an automated and often also well scalable solution for handling the flood of data more intelligently, even in face of outdated systems [20].

To automate recurring, structured tasks performed on computer systems, RPA employs so-called software robots (bots) that mimic the behavior of a user and mainly operate on the user interface [1]. Thus, RPA can be applied on top of existing systems without requiring any changes to the current IT landscape [1,2]. It is therefore also considered as lightweight or non-invasive automation [7,18] and can easily be used, for example, to automate old legacy applications that do not provide an interface for programmatic access.

J. Ralyté et al. (Eds.): ER 2022, LNCS 13607, pp. 239–254, 2022.
https://doi.org/10.1007/978-3-031-17995-2_17

Driven by industry, the field of RPA has recently experienced a tremendous upswing, which is also inspiring more and more research in this area [7,27]. While a major focus has been on the automatic generation of bots based on observed behavior, less attention has been paid to the aspect of modeling bots. The lack of a common terminology [24] and modeling standard for RPA [4] results in very tool-specific languages and potential vendor lock-ins, leaving significant potential for improvement in this area.

In this paper, we present a novel approach for modeling RPA bots that are independent of a particular RPA vendor. This approach is based on the ontology of RPA operations (ORPAO) introduced in [24] and uses standardized modeling notations. The resulting vendor-independent bots can, due to the ontological foundation, later be translated into bots of different providers. In this regard, the ORPAO is extended to not only include individual operations but also common aspects of control flow in bots, such as triggers and decisions, and generic information on the role of these operations from a process perspective. We furthermore present a prototype that enables users to model RPA bots based on the extended ontology using the modeling standard BPMN and translate them into bots of two RPA vendors.

The remaining paper is structured as follows: In Sect. 2, the ontological foundations for this work are provided, including the ontology of RPA operations and a business process modeling ontology. The process aspects of RPA bots, such as control flow, are briefly motivated in Sect. 3 and subsequently explored in more detail in Sect. 4 for the purpose of extending the ontology of RPA operations. Section 5 describes a new platform for modeling vendor-independent, conceptual RPA bots and portrays a prototypical implementation of the platform. Before the paper is concluded with a discussion of limitations and opportunities for future work in Sect. 7, related work is addressed in Sect. 6.

2 Preliminaries

In this section, the ontology of RPA operations and a conceptualization of business process modeling languages from the literature are briefly introduced.

2.1 Ontology of RPA Operations

Robotic process automation relies on so-called RPA bots or software bots that mimic the behavior of a human to automatically perform a previously manual task, mainly by manipulating the user interfaces [1]. An RPA bot is a sequence of individual RPA operations which are, to a large extent, already predefined by RPA software vendors [13,24], like navigating to a given URL in the browser or clicking a certain button.

Since this technology emerged from a commercial context, there is no standard or common vocabulary for RPA robots yet [4]. To better understand this domain and to foster a vendor-independent exchange, the ontology of RPA operations was introduced and defined in [24]. As depicted in Fig. 1, it relates the concepts of *RPA operations*, the "building-blocks" of RPA bots; the *software* that can be automated; and *data* that can be operated on and with. Furthermore, it includes essential taxonomies for these concepts, such as a more detailed distinction between the different types of RPA operations. At the lowest level, the ontology contains abstract representations of RPA operations, like `read-cell` to represent the operation of reading the value of a cell in a spreadsheet application. Instances of these abstract operations in turn represent concrete operations that are implemented by RPA vendors, such as `excel-read-cell` as an instance of `read-cell`.

As also described in [24], the ontology of RPA operations can be extended to a knowledge base that links instances of conceptual operations included in the ontology to specific implementations by RPA vendors, such as *UiPath.Excel.ReadCell*. Such a knowledge base not only enables the translation of ontology concepts to concrete operations of different RPA providers, but also the translation of operations between providers.

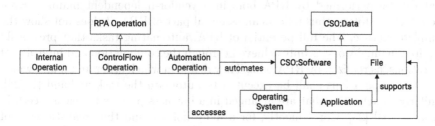

Fig. 1. Excerpt of main concepts from the RPA Ontology presented in [24]

2.2 Business Process Modeling Ontology

Various modeling languages for documenting business processes have been developed, such as event-driven process chains (EPC) or the Business Process Model and Notation (BPMN) [17], which is the de facto standard for modeling and also automating business processes [25].

Heidari et al. [10] introduced a meta-meta model that incorporates common concepts of business process modeling languages that was derived by analyzing seven different notations, including BPMN, EPC, and UML activity diagrams. As the concepts were extracted from multiple languages, the resulting ontology yields generic and language-independent concepts related to the modeling of processes. Nevertheless, it still allows linking those abstract concepts to the concrete realizations by the different notations, thus enabling a mapping between this conceptual level and specific models.

The main concepts present in the business process modeling ontology, referred to as BPMO in the following, encompass, among others, aspects related to behavior, such as *events* or *gateways*; functional aspects, such as *activities*; and informational aspects, like *messages* and *inputs* and *outputs* [10]. Figure 2 shows an overview of these concepts and their relations.

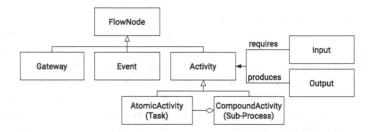

Fig. 2. Main concepts of the business process modeling ontology adapted from [10]

3 Motivation

Robotic process automation offers automation possibilities for various tasks that can be performed on a computer with only few to no human intervention. The ontology of RPA operations (cf. Section 2.1) captures and defines the operations that can be performed by RPA bots in a vendor-independent manner. Even though the ontology thus reflects an essential part of RPA, it does not show the complete picture. The full potential of RPA, automating tasks that previously required manual work, is only achieved through the combination and interplay of operations, as realized by RPA bots. They define in which order and under which conditions operations shall be executed to automate the task at hand [13,24], similarly to activities that are arranged in a business process to reach a certain business goal [25]. Consequently, for a more holistic and thus realistic view of RPA in the ontology, it is necessary to consider not only individual operations but also aspects of control flow [13], such as triggers, decisions, and sequence flow. In this regard, we introduce the notion of conceptual RPA bots in Definition 1.

Definition 1 (Conceptual RPA Bot). *A conceptual RPA bot is a vendor-independent representation of an RPA bot that is based on concepts of the ontology of RPA operations. It specifies the operations to be performed and their execution order.*

Figure 3 shows an example of a conceptual RPA bot in an arbitrary notation, as there is no modeling standard for RPA yet. The nodes each reference an RPA operation included in the ORPAO, and they are ordered by sequence flow indicated by arrows, defining their coordination during execution. Additionally, the control flow operator *IF* is used to represent a decision that influences this flow. It defines a point in the bot where only one of the outgoing branches can be activated during execution.

In the sense of Definition 1, conceptual RPA bots can serve as blueprints for vendor-specific RPA bots, provided that control flow elements are added to the ontology and the knowledge base (cf. Sect. 2.1). In other words, not only individual operations could be translated, but entire conceptual RPA bots could be modeled and translated into bots of specific vendors or even between them.

In the remaining paper, such an extension is described and subsequently used to design a platform for modeling conceptual RPA bots.

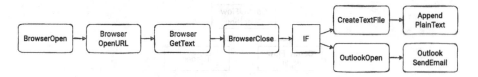

Fig. 3. An exemplary conceptual bot that retrieves text from a web page and either writes it to a new file or sends an email.

4   Extending the ORPAO by Process Aspects

To expand the focus from individual RPA operations to RPA bots, this section discusses an extension of the ontology of RPA operations by aspects of control flow, a more advanced modeling concept of RPA, and the process perspective of operations.

4.1   Steering the Control Flow of RPA Bots

So far, aspects related to control flow were not considered in detail in the ontology, apart from an abstract `ControlFlowOperation` concept. Control flow operations steer the sequence of operations within a bot, like pausing the execution until a certain event occurs or selecting the appropriate execution branch based on a decision. In the following, these aspects, triggers and decisions, will be examined in more detail. Basic sequence flow, which defines the temporal order of operations, and more advanced structural control flow constructs such as loops are not further addressed here as they have no active, RPA-specific characteristics.

Triggering RPA Bots. One important aspect of control flow is when to start or resume an execution based on external factors. In RPA, bots can mainly be triggered manually or via an API call. However, some vendors allow the use of more specific *triggers* that define when a certain RPA bot should be started. Prominent examples are to start a specific bot each time a new email arrives or following a defined time schedule. Similarly, bots may need to pause their execution to wait for something to happen, which could also be the arrival of a message, that a file was created, or simply that a certain timespan passed, before the execution can be resumed. To reflect this in the ontology, the concept of `ControlFlowOperations` is extended by the sub-concept `Triggers`. Triggers in this context are defined as the waiting for an external event before the execution of the bot is (re)commenced.

The main types of triggers, as shown in Fig. 4, are messages, such as emails; time-related; application-related, like the start or the termination of an application; file system-related, such as waiting for a file or folder to be created; or hotkeys, listening to a specific combination of key presses.

Although triggers are not yet comprehensively supported by existing RPA tools, they are nevertheless included in the ontology to reflect the full range of

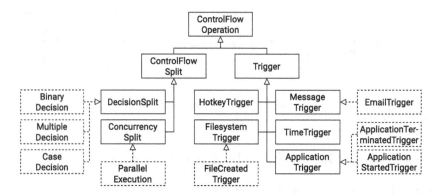

Fig. 4. Taxonomy of `ControlFlowOperation`. Terms with dashed borders are examples and not exhaustive.

RPA capabilities, not just the minimum supported by each tool. Ideas for dealing with the discrepancies in capabilities of different providers when working with the ontology are briefly discussed in Sect. 5.1.

Splitting the Control Flow. Almost every process notation supports some basic control flow elements, such as a *sequence*, and *split* and *join* of the control flow for parallel ("and") and alternative ("xor", "or") execution paths respectively [25]. RPA is no exception to this, even tough the support for such control flow elements varies from vendor to vendor. For example, parallel execution is not universally supported. In general, RPA bots, excelling at automating structured and repetitive tasks, often do not need complex structures for splitting the control flow, like they are necessary for complex, long-running business processes including multiple parties. Furthermore, as in the execution of RPA bots no human should be involved in the best case, elements influencing the control flow, e.g., decisions, must be well-defined to be automatically executable. Nevertheless, there are a few basic, commonly supported elements for making decisions and thus splitting the control flow, as observed in [23] and shown in Fig. 4. These include a simple binary ("if/else") split, chained conditions for multiple options ("if/elseif/else"), or splitting the control flow based on the value of a variable ("switch/case"). Additionally, the control flow can be split for parallel execution, although this often does not imply true concurrency of execution. Joins are not considered in detail here because, while important to the control flow itself, they have, like sequence flow, no RPA-specific meaning or implications.

4.2   Adding Context Containers

A distinctive, but disadvantageous, characteristic of RPA bot models is their complexity. Due to the atomic nature of RPA operations, RPA bot models tend to be very lengthy and thus difficult to understand. For example, in Fig. 3, the first two and the fourth operation do not directly contribute to the automation

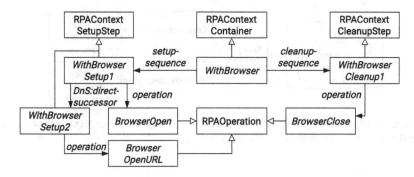

Fig. 5. Definition of the context container instance *WithBrowser* in the ontology

goal but are needed to manage the context the third operation requires. From a modeling perspective, it would be beneficial to aggregate such steps to reduce the overall model complexity. At the same time, grouping these related operations may improve clarity of which operations belong together and are executed in the same context from an application perspective.

There are RPA vendors that already offer "containers" for certain applications, that, e.g., automatically start the program and open the requested file, and save and terminate the program after the operations specified in the container were processed[1]. To be able to represent such constructs in the ontology as well, the concept of `ContextContainers` is introduced. Context containers include a sequence of operations that are needed to set up the context for the contained operations, as well as "cleanup" operations that must be executed afterwards.

In the ontology, the RPA context container is defined as a subtype of `OoP:SequentialTask`[2], which is a task that contains other tasks in a defined order. To be able to specify this order in the ontology, the auxiliary concept `RPAContextStep` with respective child concepts for setup and cleanup is introduced. Each `RPAContextStep` references a specific `RPAOperation` that should be performed in this step and, if applicable, also links to the subsequent step via the `DnS:direct-successor` relation. The `RPAContextContainer` only references the respective first step of its setup and cleanup sequence[3], as demonstrated in Fig. 5. The setup procedure for the context container *WithBrowser* consists of the `RPAOperations` *BrowserOpen* followed by *BrowserOpenURL*, while the cleanup involves only one step: closing the browser. Figure 6 shows the same conceptual bot introduced in Sect. 3 now using the newly introduced concept of context containers, notably reducing the amount of required elements.

---

[1] For example, in UiPath, there are *Application Scope* operations: https://docs.uipath.com/activities/docs/excel-application-scope (accessed 03.03.2022).

[2] OoP = Ontology of Plans. See [24] for information on the upper and foundational ontologies used in the ORPAO.

[3] This design is based on a recommendation for representing ordered lists: https://www.w3.org/TR/swbp-n-aryRelations/#pattern2 (accessed: 11.03.2022).

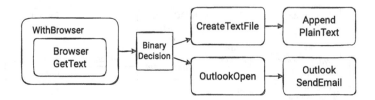

Fig. 6. Exemplary conceptual bot including the context container `WithBrowser` and a `BinaryDecision`, both defined in the ORPAO

4.3   Linking the Business Process Modeling Ontology

RPA is widely considered to be especially geared towards no-code or low-code development, i.e., so that bots can be created by non-technical users without any or only basic programming skills [2]. Thus, the major RPA vendors rely on graphical user interfaces for building RPA bots [7,13], which allow selecting RPA operations and arranging them in a process-like way [13]. Analogous to the modeling of traditional RPA bots, building conceptual RPA bots includes selecting and arranging concepts of the ontology in a certain order to define the bot's workflow to follow.

In the absence of an RPA modeling standard [4], various interfaces and thus modeling approaches emerged. Therefore, there is no common, general information on how to represent an RPA bot with its parts and their connections visually, which is, however, an essential aspect. The representation is not trivial, since bots are not only composed of homogeneous, atomic work instructions, but can also contain, for example, decision points that lead to a branching control flow or triggers that are waited for, as discussed in this section. Therefore, we decided to extend the ontology of RPA operations with suitable generic concepts from the business process modeling ontology presented in Sect. 2.2. With that, the ontology provides information not only about the building blocks of RPA, but also about their meaning from a process perspective. Furthermore, since the BPMO is notation-agnostic, the ontology remains on an conceptual level.

Table 1. Mapping of main concepts of the ORPAO to the BPMO, including examples for the concepts `Trigger` and `ControlFlowSplit`

Ontology of RPA Operations	BPMO
AutomationOperation	AtomicActivity
InternalOperation	AtomicActivity
ContextContainer	CompoundActivity
ControlFlowSplit	Gateway
DecisionSplit	*ExclusiveGateway*
Trigger	Event
MessageTrigger	*MessageEvent*

Table 1 presents an overview of the mapping between the ontology of RPA operations and the BPMO. The common building blocks, the operations, are mapped to `AtomicActitivies` which represent the smallest unit of work in a business process. The newly introduced context containers are linked to compound activities, as they may include several atomic operations and therefore form a kind of sub-process within the bot. `ControlFlowSplits` are associated with gateways in the BPMO as they are responsible for partitioning the control flow, and `Triggers` are mapped to events in the BPMO that represent a certain occurrence.

Sub-concepts can refer to more specific element accordingly, as demonstrated in Table 1. For example, a decision can have different results that are exclusive, leading to different execution paths. To express this behavior, `DecisionSplits` are mapped to `ExclusiveGateways`, which are defined in the BPMO.

With this extension, the concepts in the ontology of RPA operations are defined in respect to their semantic meaning from a process execution perspective and can also be visually represented in various process modeling languages.

5   A Platform for Modeling Conceptual RPA Bots

This section presents the architecture of a platform for visually modeling conceptual RPA bots based on the extension of the ontology presented in Sect. 4.

Figure 7 gives an overview of the required parts and resulting artifacts of the modeler. The platform consists of three main components: The *conceptual bot modeler* itself relies on the ontology of RPA operations to retrieve the elements available for modeling conceptual bots. Furthermore, it requires a mapping of the BPMO concepts that are referenced in the ORPAO (cf. Sect. 4.3) to a specific modeling language. Conceptual bot models that were created using the modeler are stored in the *conceptual bot model repository* and can be read and updated again. Taking advantage of the ontological foundation of conceptual bots, the *conceptual bot analyzer* offers various analyses for them. Finally, the *bot linker* enables the translation of conceptual bot models to vendor-specific bot models by using the knowledge base of RPA operations (see Sect. 2.1).

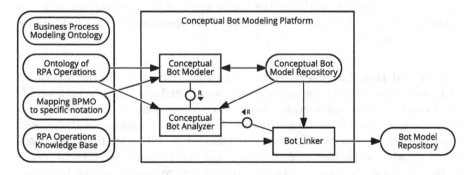

Fig. 7. Overview of the platform for modeling conceptual RPA bots

5.1   Components of the Modeling Platform

In the following, the main components of the outlined platform will be explained in more detail.

Conceptual Bot Modeler. The main component of the platform is the ontology-based modeler with its graphical user interface that enables users to build conceptual RPA bots. The ontology of RPA operations provides the information on the "building blocks" available for modeling and, with the previously described extension, also the type of these blocks from a process perspective. As the ontology only references abstract concepts of the business process modeling ontology, the modeler component additionally requires an (RPA-independent) mapping of the BPMO to a specific notation for business processes, like BPMN. For example, if the context container *WithBrowser*, as described in Sect. 4.2, is chosen by the user, the modeler component queries the ORPAO for the BPMO type of this concept which results in BPMO:CompoundActivity. Now, the mapping provides the information which notation-specific modeling element should be presented to the user for this concept, which in the case of BPMN is a sub-process. Additionally, the ontological foundation can provide the user with structured information, for example, which application can be automated and which data can be manipulated with a certain operation.

Conceptual Bot Model Repository. The repository stores and serves conceptual RPA bot models. To simplify the further use of created conceptual bots, the bot model repository stores them in a notation-agnostic format, using concepts like process trees [21] or refined process structure trees [22] that preserve the control flow information. While this requires more effort when saving and retrieving bots, as a conversion between the notation-specific model and the generic format is required, it also offers several advantages. Foremost, with a generic structure, a bot can be easily displayed and modified in different notations, similar to the concept described in [14]. Also, the translation process is simplified, as the linker does not need to understand a certain model language but only the generic, notation-independent format. Most important, such a generic structure also simplifies the performance of various analyses, as information related to the process structure and RPA operations are not hidden in a proprietary format.

Conceptual Bot Analyzer. As the conceptual bots stored in the repository are based on the ontology, various analyses can be conducted by searching for different concepts of the ontology, like applications, operations, or data, in the nodes of the generic, tree-based data structure. Compared to traditional RPA tools, where the bot repository might be searchable for specific operations, the ontological foundation enables more semantic and generic analyzes, e.g., to search for bots that modify Excel workbooks, or, even more generic, listing bots that handle spreadsheet data without specifying a certain type and software (any bot that includes `DataOperations` that `accesses Spreadsheets`). The analyzer also simplifies maintenance tasks. For example, if an application update includes breaking changes (e.g., to the UI), the repository can be scanned for bots that automate this application and thus need to be modified. But also more complex analyzes can be performed, e.g., to support replacing applications (cf. [24]), or to analyze if adjustments are necessary before translating to a concrete bot as discussed below.

Bot Linker. The bot linker component is responsible for converting conceptual bots to specific RPA bots of a certain vendor using the knowledge base of RPA operations. As the knowledge base links instances of RPA operations included in the ORPAO, such as `excel-read-cell`, to vendor-specific instances for each operation, like `UiPath.Excel.ReadCell`, the bot linker can translate each step in the conceptual bot to the individual implementation of this operation offered by the vendor chosen for linking.

A major issue that arises in this step is that the different RPA software programs do not all offer the exactly same set of operations. While the most common operations (core operations), e.g., related to office applications or the operating system, are usually supported by all vendors, there are also a few operations that are supported less often. Thus, when such special operations are used in a conceptual bot, it can no longer be translated to an arbitrary vendor. There are two different ways to mitigate this issue. Either the set of operations available for modeling is restricted in advance, e.g., so that only core operations or operations offered by a selected group of vendors can be used. Or, the bot analyzer is used to check the conceptual bot for such issues that need to be addressed before the translation.

An exception to this are the context containers introduced in Sect. 4.2. Even though they are not supported by all vendors, the described issue can be automatically resolved using the ontology. For RPA providers supporting containers, the conceptual bot can be directly translated. For the other vendors, the definition of the container in the ontology can be used to "flatten" the container, i.e., to replace the container in the linked bot by its included sequences of setup and cleanup operations.

The detailed internal process of generating bot source files for the respective vendors is beyond the scope of this paper, as it requires additional knowledge on the vendors' syntaxes, which is not part of the ontology or the knowledge base.

5.2 Prototype

To demonstrate the feasibility of the presented idea, we implemented an open-source prototype[4] that realizes the major parts of the platform.

The modeler component includes a mapping of the BPMO to BPMN, as this notation is widely used for modeling business processes in general and was also

---

[4] Demonstration of the prototype and its components: https://youtu.be/ Pq5FIS9KtqA. Source code: https://github.com/bptlab/conceptual-bot-platform.

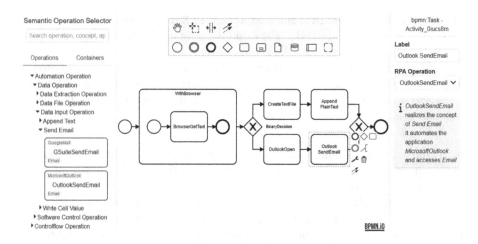

Fig. 8. A screenshot of the modeler component showing the exemplary conceptual bot. The sidebar on the left offers operations available for modeling based on the ontology.

already used for modeling RPA bots [14]. Figure 8 shows a screenshot of the prototype featuring the same bot as in Fig. 6. Conceptual bots are stored in a generic tree-like format, and a basic bot analyzer component enables the user to search for bots in the repository that automate a certain application or use a particular operation to simplify maintenance tasks. The included bot linker component, responsible for translating conceptual RPA bots to vendor-specific bots, can currently generate source files for RPA bots for the open-source RPA solutions Robot Framework[5] and taskt[6] from modeled conceptual bots. These can be opened and modified in the respective language and tool.

6   Related Work

Various topics are in focus of current RPA research [27], including different aspects of RPA methodology, such as synergies with business process management [8] or case studies (e.g., [2,15]), and more technical aspects, such as robotic process mining [6,16] or combinations with artificial intelligence [12]. Despite the strong focus of RPA on visual modeling, this aspect of RPA has barely been considered in research yet. Guidelines for user interfaces for interacting with RPA bots at run time are established in [26], but these do not address the interface for modeling bots. In [4], an RPA use case is described in a platform-independent, textual manner using controlled natural language and pseudocode. As the description is crafted manually and has no well-defined connection to RPA, it does not provide a systematic way for creating or translating RPA bots. In previous work, we have considered the visual representation and realization

---

[5] https://robotframework.org/.
[6] http://www.taskt.net/.

of decisions in RPA bots [23] and created an ontology of RPA operations [24], capturing the common types of RPA operations and their relationship to applications and data they can automate and access (cf. Sect. 2.1). This ontology is extended in this work to include various process aspects and, with the extension provided, is used as the basis for the platform introduced in this paper.

A tool for modeling RPA bots with BPMN and using a generic data structure was briefly demonstrated in [14]. However, that approach is not based on a defined, vendor-independent conceptualization, but focuses on different interfaces for a specific RPA provider. Moreover, it does not support more advanced concepts, like triggers or decisions.

In the field of business process management, the use of ontological knowledge to enable semantic business process modeling (SBPM) has already been studied (e.g., [5,9]). Here, business process models are annotated with concepts from domain ontologies to better specify the contained activities for a better understanding and also automation [11]. However, SBPM still lacks adaption in industry as it usually requires high initial effort [3]. Compared to business processes with their large number of different domains and thus possible types of activities, RPA with its predefined building blocks appears to be a prime candidate for semantic process modeling. Since the domain with its set of RPA operations is well-defined, the otherwise very time-consuming part of creating the domain ontology [3] is simplified or even eliminated as the ontology of RPA operations can be used as foundation as demonstrated in this work.

7   Conclusion

This work takes a first step towards semantic RPA by introducing a new approach for modeling RPA bots based on the ontology of RPA operations. For this, we first extended the ORPAO regarding different process-related aspects, such as control flow, and established a connection to an ontology of generic process elements which is independent of a specific modeling language. Subsequently, the ontology-based RPA modeling platform and its components were presented, including a prototypical implementation. The introduced platform not only facilitates modeling and managing bots in a visual, vendor-independent way, but also supports their evolution, e.g., by assisting in maintenance tasks, replacing software systems, or even using different RPA software.

The design decisions made in this paper also impose drawbacks and limitations. First, the limitations of the BPMO are inherited, that is, that the detailed semantics of concepts may differ slightly between specific notations and that only imperative process modeling is covered. Furthermore, the ontology and thus the platform in their current state do not include any configuration of operations that would be required to derive RPA bots that are directly executable. However, the ontology could be extended to include at least basic and common configuration options for operations to reduce the amount of required configurations after translation.

This work and the presented platform with its components provide the foundation for a variety of future extensions. For example, existing RPA bots could be translated to conceptual bots using the knowledge base, i.e., by reversing the conversion process conducted by the bot linker. Moreover, business process models could be analyzed to generate conceptual bots, e.g., by matching the activity labels with concepts in the ontology (similar to [19]). Regarding visualization, more emphasis could be placed on an adequate representation of data in the bot, as data plays a crucial role in RPA but is often not explicitly visualized. Another important aspect, both in traditional workflow management and in RPA, is exception handling for defining rules for how to detect and deal with erroneous executions. Future work should investigate what potential errors and common exception handling strategies of RPA are and how they can be incorporated in the ontology and modeling platform. Besides, the ontology could be extended to include other aspects, such as the automation goal or the context during execution.

References

1. van der Aalst, W.M.P., Bichler, M., Heinzl, A.: Robotic process automation. Bus. Inf. Syst. Eng. **60**(4), 269–272 (2018). https://doi.org/10.1007/s12599-018-0542-4
2. Aguirre, S., Rodriguez, A.: Automation of a business process using robotic process automation (RPA): a case study. In: Figueroa-García, J.C., López-Santana, E.R., Villa-Ramírez, J.L., Ferro-Escobar, R. (eds.) WEA 2017. CCIS, vol. 742, pp. 65–71. Springer, Cham (2017). https://doi.org/10.1007/978-3-319-66963-2_7
3. Corea, C., Fellmann, M., Delfmann, P.: Ontology-based process modelling - will we live to see it? In: Ghose, A., Horkoff, J., Silva Souza, V.E., Parsons, J., Evermann, J. (eds.) ER 2021. LNCS, vol. 13011, pp. 36–46. Springer, Cham (2021). https://doi.org/10.1007/978-3-030-89022-3_4
4. Correia, C., Da Silva, A.R.: Platform-independent specifications for robotic process automation applications. In: MODELSWARD 2022, pp. 379–386. SciTePress (2022). https://doi.org/10.5220/0010991200003119
5. Di Francescomarino, C., Ghidini, C., Rospocher, M., Serafini, L., Tonella, P.: Semantically-aided business process modeling. In: Bernstein, A., et al. (eds.) ISWC 2009. LNCS, vol. 5823, pp. 114–129. Springer, Heidelberg (2009). https://doi.org/10.1007/978-3-642-04930-9_8
6. Egger, A., ter Hofstede, A.H.M., Kratsch, W., Leemans, S.J.J., Röglinger, M., Wynn, M.T.: Bot log mining: using logs from robotic process automation for process mining. In: Dobbie, G., Frank, U., Kappel, G., Liddle, S.W., Mayr, H.C. (eds.) ER 2020. LNCS, vol. 12400, pp. 51–61. Springer, Cham (2020). https://doi.org/10.1007/978-3-030-62522-1_4
7. Enriquez, J.G., Jimenez-Ramirez, A., Dominguez-Mayo, F.J., Garcia-Garcia, J.A.: Robotic process automation: a scientific and industrial systematic mapping study. IEEE Access **8**, 39113–39129 (2020). https://doi.org/10.1109/ACCESS.2020.2974934
8. Flechsig, C., Lohmer, J., Lasch, R.: Realizing the full potential of robotic process automation through a combination with BPM. In: Bierwirth, C., Kirschstein, T., Sackmann, D. (eds.) Logistics Management. LNL, pp. 104–119. Springer, Cham (2019). https://doi.org/10.1007/978-3-030-29821-0_8

9. Greco, G., Guzzo, A., Pontieri, L., Saccà, D.: An ontology-driven process modeling framework. In: Galindo, F., Takizawa, M., Traunmüller, R. (eds.) DEXA 2004. LNCS, vol. 3180, pp. 13–23. Springer, Heidelberg (2004). https://doi.org/10.1007/978-3-540-30075-5_2

10. Heidari, F., Loucopoulos, P., Brazier, F., Barjis, J.: A meta-meta-model for seven business process modeling languages. In: 2013 IEEE 15th Conference on Business Informatics, pp. 216–221. IEEE (2013). https://doi.org/10.1109/CBI.2013.38

11. Hepp, M., Roman, D.: An ontology framework for semantic business process management. Wirtschaftsinformatik Proceedings 2007, 423–440 (2007)

12. Herm, L.-V., Janiesch, C., Reijers, H.A., Seubert, F.: From symbolic RPA to intelligent RPA: challenges for developing and operating intelligent software robots. In: Polyvyanyy, A., Wynn, M.T., Van Looy, A., Reichert, M. (eds.) BPM 2021. LNCS, vol. 12875, pp. 289–305. Springer, Cham (2021). https://doi.org/10.1007/978-3-030-85469-0_19

13. Hofmann, P., Samp, C., Urbach, N.: Robotic process automation. Electron. Mark. 30(1), 99–106 (2020). https://doi.org/10.1007/s12525-019-00365-8

14. Hüller, L., Jenß, K.E., Speh, S., Woelki, D., Völker, M., Weske, M.: Ark automate–an open-source platform for robotic process automation. In: BPM 2021 Demo Track, CEUR Workshop Proceedings, vol. 2973, pp. 126–130. CEUR-WS.org (2021)

15. Lacity, M., Willcocks, L., Craig, A.: Robotic process automation at Telefonica O2. MIS Q. Exec. 15(1) (2016)

16. Leno, V., Polyvyanyy, A., Dumas, M., La Rosa, M., Maggi, F.M.: Robotic process mining: vision and challenges. Bus. Inf. Syst. Eng. 63 (2020). https://doi.org/10.1007/s12599-020-00641-4

17. Object Management Group: Business Process Model and Notation (BPMN) (2014). www.omg.org/spec/BPMN/

18. Penttinen, E., Kasslin, H., Asatiani, A.: How to choose between robotic process automation and back-end system automation? In: ECIS 2018, AIS (2018)

19. Riehle, D.M., Jannaber, S., Delfmann, P., Thomas, O., Becker, J.: Automatically annotating business process models with ontology concepts at design-time. In: de Cesare, S., Frank, U. (eds.) ER 2017. LNCS, vol. 10651, pp. 177–186. Springer, Cham (2017). https://doi.org/10.1007/978-3-319-70625-2_17

20. Syed, R., et al.: Robotic process automation: contemporary themes and challenges. Comput. Ind. 115 (2020). https://doi.org/10.1016/j.compind.2019.103162

21. Van Zelst, S.J., Leemans, S.J.J.: Translating workflow nets to process trees: an algorithmic approach. Algorithms 13(11) (2020). https://doi.org/10.3390/a13110279

22. Vanhatalo, J., Völzer, H., Koehler, J.: The refined process structure tree. Data Knowl. Eng. 68(9), 793–818 (2009). https://doi.org/10.1016/j.datak.2009.02.015

23. Völker, M., Siegert, S., Weske, M.: Adding decision management to robotic process automation. In: González Enríquez, J., Debois, S., Fettke, P., Plebani, P., van de Weerd, I., Weber, I. (eds.) BPM 2021. LNBIP, vol. 428, pp. 23–37. Springer, Cham (2021). https://doi.org/10.1007/978-3-030-85867-4_3

24. Völker, M., Weske, M.: Conceptualizing bots in robotic process automation. In: Ghose, A., Horkoff, J., Silva Souza, V.E., Parsons, J., Evermann, J. (eds.) ER 2021. LNCS, vol. 13011, pp. 3–13. Springer, Cham (2021). https://doi.org/10.1007/978-3-030-89022-3_1

25. Weske, M.: Business Process Management: Concepts, Languages, Architectures, 3 edn. Springer, Berlin, Heidelberg (2019). https://doi.org/10.1007/978-3-662-59432-2

26. Wewerka, J., Micus, C., Reichert, M.: Seven guidelines for designing the user inter-face in robotic process automation. In: 2021 IEEE 25th EDOCW, pp. 157–165. IEEE (2021). https://doi.org/10.1109/EDOCW52865.2021.00045

27. Wewerka, J., Reichert, M.: Robotic process automation–a systematic mapping study and classification framework. Enterp. Inf. Syst. 1–38 (2021). https://doi.org/10.1080/17517575.2021.1986862

Stra2Bis: A Model-Driven Method for Aligning Business Strategy and Business Processes

Rene Noel[1,2](✉) , Jose Ignacio Panach[3] , Marcela Ruiz[4] ,
and Oscar Pastor[1]

[1] PROS-VRAIN: Valencian Research Institute for Artificial Intelligence, Universitat
Politècnica de València, València, Spain Valencia, Spain
rnoel@vrain.upv.es, opastor@dsic.upv.es
[2] Escuela de Ingeniería Informática, Universidad de Valparaíso, Valparaíso, Chile
[3] Escola Tècnica Superior d'Enginyeria, Universitat de València, València, Spain
joigpana@uv.es
[4] Zürich University of Applied Sciences, Winterthur, Switzerland
marcela.ruiz@zhaw.ch

Abstract. MDA-based initiatives for software development have
included computation-independent models to align information system
models with business knowledge which is important in the development
process. One source of business knowledge is the business strategy, which,
traditionally, has had a long-term perspective; changes in the organisational structure and their high-level ends and means were less frequent
and arguably not relevant for software development. However, organisations that aim to accelerate their software development cycles define
their business strategy and reconfigure their structure on a short-term,
continuous basis, fusing, splitting and creating as independent as possible
organisation units. These changes directly affect the business processes
and the design of software components of the organisation. Based on this
approach to business strategy, we propose Stra2Bis, a method for designing strategically aligned business processes in an MDA-based context.
Stra2Bis proposes a business strategy modelling step when redesigning
business processes and three transformation guidelines to support the
analysis of the alignment of processes with the organisational structure
and the measurement of the units' outcomes. We discussed the effect of
the guidelines on the software design with five professionals who supported the proposal's feasibility and usefulness.

Keywords: Model-driven architecture · Business process · Business
strategy

1 Introduction

The Model-Driven Architecture (MDA) [28] approach has been used for designing and developing information systems to ensure that the software products ful-

J. Ralyté et al. (Eds.): ER 2022, LNCS 13607, pp. 255–270, 2022.
https://doi.org/10.1007/978-3-031-17995-2_18

fil the business requirements. Computation-independent models (CIM) in MDA-based initiatives have been widely used to specify the system's business requirements, mainly in terms of stakeholder's goals, business processes and use cases [14]. Other high-level business concepts have been included less frequently at the CIM level [5], despite their usefulness for helping software developers make the most of the business knowledge.

One important source of business knowledge is business strategy, which addresses high-level organisational ends and the means to achieve them [21]. Traditionally, business strategy have had a long-term perspective. Suppose an organisation decides to fuse two business areas. In that case, it requires a considerable effort to re-design the organisational structure, processes, and systems and several years for implementation. This drives the need for analysing competing goals from different stakeholders across the organisation and aligning business processes and their supporting information systems, which has been addressed by goal modelling frameworks and included in MDA-based methods [1,5,19,22].

However, organisations whose value offer depends on software [11,16] (also called software-centric organisations or digital enterprises) have a different approach to business strategy and alignment. Forsgren et al. [11] found that independent, cross-disciplinary organisation units or teams yield loosely coupled systems, which improve software development performance and scalability. Most of the agile software development frameworks have adopted this approach [20,26], which is based on the principle that organisations replicate their communication structure to everything they design, following Conway's Law [4]. Inverse Conway Manoeuvre [11] is an approach for evolving the organisational structure, so business architecture matches the desired system architecture. Software-centric organisations continuously reconfigure their structure to foster the independence of their teams while carefully managing their dependencies [2]. The organisation structure design sets requirements for the design of business processes and the information systems that support them, which translates to more efficient software development delivery [11]. Since organisations need to adjust the strategy continuously, it is necessary to measure well-defined, customer-centred objectives [6,16], which also sets requirements for business processes and information systems. Also, broadly adopted software design techniques take a strategic approach for separating business domains [10] and for designing microservices [33].

From the above practices, we infer the need to include business strategy information in software development methods. Particularly, we focus on information about organisation units, their dependencies, and their associated strategic objectives. While most of the cited works also address other strategic level concerns such as portfolio managing, governance, and capability development, they arguably do not affect the software's requirements.

The scope of business strategy is broad, and has been mostly conceptualised by enterprise modelling frameworks. Archimate [30], through its strategy elements, supports defining the resources, capabilities, and courses of action to achieve the organisation's goals, while its motivation elements permit modelling the strategy drivers, goals, and outcomes. In the context of the alignment approach of our interest, one relevant concern that Archimate does not address is the organisational structure. Similarly, the Business Motivation Model (BMM) [29] addresses business strategy concepts but also lacks organisational structure concepts. Importantly, BMM coincides with agile operation models [16] in addressing the more dynamic aspects of business strategy, e.g., defining strategies, goals, and more detailed tactics and objectives to address external influences, leaving more long-term concerns such as capabilities and resources out of scope.

In previous work, we proposed LiteStrat, a business strategy modelling method designed for the specific requirements of capturing organisation structure and strategic ends and means jointly. LiteStrat provides a modelling language based on Archimate, BMM, and reuses and adapts concepts from i* to represent roles, organisation units, and participation relationships. LiteStrat follows a modelling approach similar to i*, which has been widely used for the strategic alignment in MDA-based methods [12,25,27]

This paper presents Stra2Bis, a method that integrates business strategy and business process models following the alignment approach of software-centric organisations. Stra2Bis proposes 1. Modelling a business strategy scenario before business process design, and 2. Three transformation guidelines from the business strategy model to the business process model, designed to enable the software-centric organisation's approach to alignment and, thus, to software design.

The expected benefits are to support the design of independent processes for organisational units and to explicitly address the success measurement requirements of the strategy at the business process level. These improvements at the CIM level are expected to help design loosely coupled and strategically aligned systems at the PIM level, improving the efficiency of the software development process. We conducted a first exploratory evaluation through a focus group with software development practitioners, who confirmed the proposal's value.

2 Related Work

Several initiatives that combine modelling languages have tackled the design of business processes aligned with strategy. Goal modelling languages have been used, for instance, to analyse whether business process activities (modelled using BPMN) support organisational goals (modelled with TROPOS) [13], or to study how business processes constraint business goals (modelled using KAOS) [22]. The Goal-Oriented Requirements Language (GRL) has been combined with Use Case Maps to model strategically aligned processes in the last two decades [1] and also to prioritise business processes [17]. MAP models (that define goals and the strategies to achieve them) have been mapped directly to the business processes elements that operationalise them [19] and also served to analyse the purpose behind the creation, modification, and deletion of business process elements [31]. I* models have been used for transforming social dependencies into interactions at the process level [25], validating the consistency of the process interactions [12], and checking whether the business processes have the elements needed to collect information to verify the goal achievement [27].

Besides goal modelling, other initiatives have combined frameworks addressing business strategy concerns. Business plans (modelled in Business Motivation Model [29]) have been used jointly with i* to add intentionality to the process of enterprise architecture construction [32]. Business value models (modelled using the e3Value method) have been used for generating performance requirements for an enterprise architecture [7]. In [3], organisational capabilities, modelled at the enterprise architecture level, are the starting point for the model-driven development of context-adapting software systems.

Enterprise architecture frameworks aim to provide strategic alignment for information systems. Archimate [30] covers several business strategy concepts, and its multi-viewpoint approach supports connecting strategy with process and information system concepts. However, it lacks organisational structure concepts, and the links between the concepts do not address specific alignment intentions.

The above initiatives show that integrating modelling methods is a powerful tool for strategic alignment. However, while stakeholders' strategic goals and actions have been the main driver of alignment, organisation units, their dependencies, and their associated strategic objectives have not been addressed by MDA approaches.

3   The Stra2Bis Method

Stra2Bis is a model-driven method for integrating business strategy information into MDA-based software development methods. Stra2Bis was designed following the Situational Method Engineering approach since it allows engineering methods to meet the requirements of a given situation [15]. Stra2Bis' requirements are inferred from the need to enable the software-centric organisations' approach to software design in MDA-based software development methods. Figure 1 presents the requirements map for the method, which are met by assembling method parts. Particularly, Stra2Bis assembles a business strategy and a business process modelling method. These methods are integrated by a model-to-model transformation that guides the analyst to design strategically aligned processes, following the approach of software-centric organisations.

The remainder of the section focuses on illustrating the method and the guidelines' design since the existing modelling methods are well documented. We describe Stra2Bis through a working example as a three-step business process improvement cycle in the following subsections. In Step 1, we present the working example. In Step 2, we present the business strategy model. Step 3 details the transformation guidelines and the re-designed business process model for the example. Even though the contribution of Stra2Bis is focused on the CIM level, we also comment on the effects of the business strategy information on the PIM level using a microservices refactoring example[1].

---

[1] https://microservices.io/refactoring/.

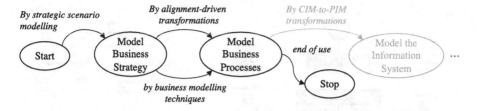

Fig. 1. Stra2Bis requirements map.

3.1 Step 1: Current Business Process Model (Working Example)

In this step, the current business process is modelled. The notation proposed is from the Communication Analysis (CA) method [8]. We choose this notation because CA, in the same way as BPMN's choreography diagram [24] is not focused on the work performed but on the information exchange between the process actors. Moreover, CA has been integrated into an MDA-based development process, having theoretical consistency and technical feasibility for generating information system models and software code [9].

Working Example: F-FOOD is a software-as-a-service company that allows **consumers** to order food from **restaurants**, for pickup or for delivery. After the restaurant confirms an order, the delivery orders are scheduled to the closest available **courier**. F-FOOD has had exponential growth since its foundation and most of its software development efforts have been focused on mobile applications. However, the back end is still a monolithic application.

Figure 2A presents the business process model for the current situation. In order to later discuss the effects of the Stra2Bis guidelines on the design of software components, we also present a class diagram of the current information system in Fig. 2B. Please note that there is no a `Delivery` class in the domain model and that `scheduledelivery` is a service offered by `OrderService`.

3.2 Step 2: Business Strategy Modelling by Strategic Scenario

This step proposes modelling the strategic scenario that drives the business process re-design. We define a strategic scenario as a model of the business strategy elements that are defined to react to a stimulus from the environment. Particularly, we refer to short-term definitions that affect the design of business processes and information systems: the strategic ends, the actions to achieve them, and the organisational structure needed to implement the strategy. The scenario does not consider other long-term strategic concerns such as capacity and resource development and portfolio management.

We propose using the LiteStrat method [23] to meet the business strategy modelling intention. LiteStrat is our previous work that proposes a business

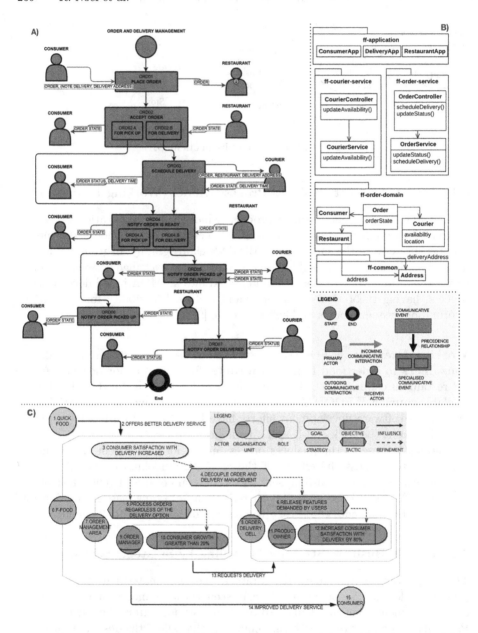

Fig. 2. Current situation models: A) Business process model. B) Class diagram of the Information System. C) Business strategy model.

strategy modelling language to represent the organisational structure and strategic ends and means jointly, as well as a modelling procedure to reduce the variability of models to improve their integration in MDA contexts.

LiteStrat addresses two organisational structure concepts: the organisation unit concept, which represents a group of social actors working together to achieve a goal (e.g. development teams, departments) and the role concept, which is an abstraction of a behaviour in an organisational context (similarly to Archimate and i*). The assignment relationship addresses the hierarchical dependencies. The influence relationship describes the dependency between a source element that performs an action that affects the target element for organisation units' dependencies representation. Regarding the organisational ends and means, LiteStrat uses concepts from the Business Motivation Model [29], providing two concepts for high-level definitions (goal and strategy) and the more specific tactic and objective concepts. The latter is a measurable and well-defined desired state of affairs used to measure the strategy's performance.

Other modelling methods can be used while they support representing: 1. The organisation units that are affected by the strategic definitions, 2. The dependencies between the organisation units generated in the strategic scenario, and 3. The measurable objectives to assess the strategy implementation. Figure 2C presents a LiteStrat model for the strategic scenario described below. The parenthesis indicates the model elements associated.

Strategic Scenario: In the last quarter, the growth of consumers in F-FOOD (0) has decreased. F-FOOD's finds out that a new competitor, QUICKFOOD (1), has a better order delivery service (2). Consumers claim that the F-FOOD app lacks several features for delivery tracking and has a slow response when putting delivery orders. F-FOOD discovers that the Order Management Area (7) constantly gives a lower priority to new delivery features and optimisations, favouring the order management functionality. F-FOOD management has decided that consumer satisfaction with the delivery is the top strategic goal for the next quarter (3). To achieve this goal, the strategy is to decouple the delivery service as an independent service (4), owned by a new cross-disciplinary team called Order Delivery Cell (8) that is meant to release all the features demanded by the customers (6). The Product Owner (11) will track the objective of increasing consumer satisfaction with delivery by 80% (12). The Order Management Area will have a leaner order processing, regardless of their delivery option (5) and will depend on the Order Delivery Cell for delivering the orders (13). New consumers are expected to increase by a 20% (10), which will be tracked by the Order Manager (9). The implementation of the strategy seeks to offer an improved delivery service (14) for the consumers (15).

3.3   Step 3: Business Process Modelling by Alignment-Driven Transformation

In this step, we take as input the business strategy model from Step 2 and apply three transformation guidelines to generate an initial version of the redesigned business process model. A guideline is a recommendation for designing parts of a business process model considering elements from business strategy.

Guideline 1 deals with designing independent organisation units, Guideline 2 with organisation units' dependencies, and Guideline 3 with measuring strategic objectives. As with other MDA transformations at the CIM level, the guidelines support a semi-automatic, skilled transformation process so that the analysts can change the mapped process parts according to the real-world context.

For each guideline, we describe its motivation by referencing an alignment practice from software-centric organisations, detailing the problem and the solution approach. Then, we describe the model-to-model transformation guideline according to the motivation; the mappings between the metamodel elements are shown in green in Fig. 3. Next, we describe the application of the guideline in the working example that produces the model depicted in Fig. 4A. Finally, we comment on the effects of the strategic scenario on the business process model, and provide recommendations to address some variations.

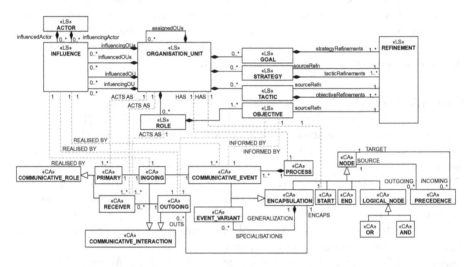

Fig. 3. Metamodel mappings for LiteStrat (LS stereotype) [23] and a simplified Communication Analysis (CA stereotype) [9] metamodels. Relationships for Guidelines 1, 2, and 3 are coloured in green, orange, and yellow, respectively. (Color figure online)

Guideline 1 - Organisation Units' Independence: *Design a single business process for each organisation unit.*

Motivation: This guideline is based on the research by Forsgren et al. [11], who found that the coupling between teams has been reported as a hindering factor for efficient software development. The problem addressed is that teams with multiple business processes or business processes addressed by multiple teams increase the need for communication and collaboration between teams, and, in the same way, the software design replicates the coupling. The solution proposed is to design processes that are as independent as possible for each team.

Transformation Description: For each organisation unit belonging to the overall organisation in the business strategy model, create a new process in the business process model. Add a start event with the unit's name to the new process to make the process visible in the model.

Example: In the business strategy model in Fig. 2C, "Order Management Area" and the new "Order Delivery Cell" units originate the "Order Management" and "Delivery Management" processes depicted as green start nodes in Fig. 4A. The start nodes are named following the names of their respective organisational units. The guideline proposes designing an independent business process for the delivery service, otherwise, the new team would still be coupled to the Order Management Area process. Although the example specifically regards the split of an existing unit, the guideline is also helpful in analysing the creation, fusion, or hiring of external teams for tackling new business opportunities.

Effects on the Business Process: Modelling a strategic scenario helps the analysts to reflect on designing separate processes for orders and delivery management. Failing to do this will traduce creating a new "agile" cell that will not be autonomous to manage their requirements at the process level and thus to design and evolve the information system. The generated elements in the business process model reflect the ideal separation of processes. The analyst should assess whether this separation is feasible considering the actual context of the problem.

Guideline 2 - Managed Strategic Dependencies: *Design the interactions between business processes to manage the organisation units' strategic dependencies.*

Motivation: This guideline is based on the need for managing and reducing the dependencies among development teams to foster their autonomy, which is a practice followed by operational models such as the Spotify Model [2] and also contributes to the design of autonomous teams [11,16]. Another motivation is the Domain-Driven Design approach [10], which states that the integration between different business contexts must be carefully designed at the information system level. The problem addressed is that new strategic scenarios could introduce new dependencies among units, which, if overlooked, could hinder the efficiency of the software delivery. The solution approach is to ensure that these dependencies are considered for designing business processes.

Transformation Description: For each influence dependency between organisation units in the business strategy model, add events to the source and target organisation units' processes to handle the dependency. In the source unit's process, add an event to provide the information to satisfy the dependency, and a receiver actor representing the target organisation units' process. Similarly, add an event and a primary actor to the target unit's process to receive information about the dependency from an actor representing the source organisation unit.

Example: The influence relationship "16.Requests Delivery" from the organisation unit "Order Management Area" to the "Order Delivery Cell" in Fig. 2C is mapped as the events depicted in orange in Fig. 4A: an event to perform the influencing behaviour (16.Requests Delivery), and an event to address the influence (DEL01-Handle Delivery Request). A new actor is introduced to handle the dependency, representing the target organisation unit of the dependency (Order Delivery Cell). The name of the events and actors follow the strategy diagram, but the analyst can change them according to the domain information.

Effects on the Business Process: The strategic scenario helps the analyst design the interface between the orders management area and the delivery cell based on strategic criteria. Since the delivery cell is affected by the requests of the order management area, the cell must provide a well-defined way to manage these requests at the process level, and the order management area must also consider this mechanism in its process. Failing to do this could result in designing ad-hoc interoperability mechanisms at the process and system levels. The guideline assumes that the information needed for the interaction between the processes is already known; otherwise, the analyst can add a primary actor to provide the required information.

Guideline 3 - Strategic Objectives Measurement: *Design business process elements to collect data to measure strategic objectives.*

Motivation: This guideline is based on the practice of a shared measurement of the success of strategic initiatives, which is enforced by frameworks for digital transformation such as EDGE [16] and Objectives and Key Results (OKR) [6]. The problem addressed is to consider in advance requirements to measure and share the status of strategic objectives in order to enable the assessment and continuous adjustment of the business strategy. The solution approach is ensuring that the strategic objectives are considered in business process design.

Transformation Description: For each business strategy objective, add an event to their respective organisation unit's process to collect information about the objective's status. Add a receiver actor following the name of the objective's role.

Example: In the strategy diagram in Fig. 2C, the objectives "10.Consumer growth greater than 20%" of the organisation unit "Order Management Area" is mapped to the event "ORD06.Report Consumer Growth" in Fig. 4A, depicted in yellow. Similarly, the objective "12.Increase consumer satisfaction with delivery by 80%" is mapped to the event "DEL06-Report Delivery Satisfaction". In both cases, the receiver actors are the roles assigned to the objectives in the strategy diagram (Order Manager and Product Owner).

Effects of the Business Process: Mapping the strategic scenario helps the analyst consider specifying requirements to measure consumer growth and satisfaction with the delivery service. Failing to consider these requirements may require adding them later on-demand of top executives, which may harm the system design and performance. Similarly to guideline 2, the transformation does not generate a primary actor to provide the information. It will not be needed if the information is already in the system; otherwise, the analyst can add a primary actor according to the problem domain.

3.4 Effects on the PIM Level in an MDA Context

The guidelines are expected to affect the information system model at the PIM level. Although the integration of the business process and the information system models is not part of this work (but has already been proposed in [9]), we exemplify in Fig. 4B. The effects of the guidelines on the initial information system model presented in Fig. 2B.

Regarding Guideline 1, since the two organisation units *Order Management Area* and *Order Delivery Cell* had their separated business processes *Order Management* and *Order Delivery Management*, the `Delivery` domain class and services must be disentangled in a different component. Figure 4B shows in green the components for both processes. The new component `ff-deliver-service` supports the Order Delivery Process. Some services are removed from the initial order management components (see Fig. 2B). The changes mainly consist of removing the delivery-related services that were initially located in the `ff-courier-service`, `ff-order-service` and `ff-order-domain` components and moving them to the new `ff-deliver-service` component.

Regarding Guideline 2, the interaction between the processes is mapped as an interface `ff-deliver-service-api` depicted in orange in Fig. 4B. The interface is implemented by the component supporting the delivery process `ff-delivery-service`. It allows the initial order management system to request the services that were moved to the new `ff-delivery-service`.

Finally, the effects of Guideline 3 are mapped into services and attributes to update the values for the strategic objectives collected through the process. As highlighted in yellow in Fig. 4Bs, the Order class has a new attribute `isNewConsumer` to identify whether the order is from a new consumer. This helps track the objective "10.Consumer growth greater than 20%" objective initially defined in the strategy model in Fig. 2C. Similarly, the `Delivery` class has the attribute `satisfactionLevel` of the objective "12.Increase consumer satisfaction with delivery by 80%".

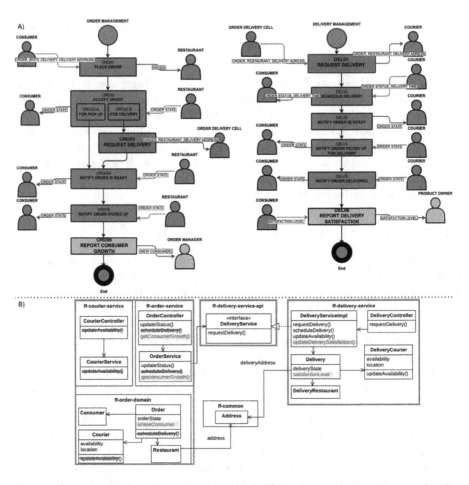

Fig. 4. A) Re-designed business process model. B) Re-designed class diagram for the information system model. (Color figure online)

4   Initial Evaluation and Discussion

We conducted an exploratory evaluation through a focus group since this technique is suitable for the *"initial evaluation of potential solutions, based on the practitioner or user feedback"* [18]. The research question was, "what information from the business strategy model is valuable for designing business processes?". The goal is to find whether practitioners' insights and experience match the Stra2Bis guidelines in terms of the information traceable from business strategy to business process and to the information system model. We wanted to contrast opinions from practitioners working in traditional consultancy services companies (CSC) and in Software-as-a-Service companies (SaaS), which main value offer is based on software. The participants were five volunteers having a technical leader or scrum master role, with between four and nine years of experience. Participants S1, S3 work in CSC, and participants S2, S4, S5 work in a SaaS.

The activity had two parts of 30 min each. First, we presented the working example from Fig. 2 and asked, "what information would be useful for redesigning business processes and why"?. The participants shared and agreed on a set of statements that the moderator publicly wrote down. In the second part, we presented the Stra2Bis guidelines and the models from Fig. 4, and asked the participants to comment on their usefulness and drawbacks. The analysis method was based on pattern-matching [18] the participant's ideas from the first part of the focus group with the guidelines and then looking for explanations in the discussion of the second part.

Insights for Guideline 1: In the first part, the respondents did not identify the organisation units as an important source of information for the business process design. After seeing the redesigned process and the guideline 1, all the participants agreed that independent units must have independent processes. All respondents recalled difficulties when business processes and software code of different units were entangled. Respondent S2, from a SaaS, stated that *"it is important for us to have an independent business flow because each cell can take the challenges and opportunities of their own process"*.

Insights for Guideline 2: In the first part, all the respondents identified as relevant the dependency among the organisation units. S1 and S2 agreed that *"the dependency must be clear in the business process flow"*. All the participants agreed on the value of the guideline for defining the dependency at the process level. It is worth noting that respondents S1 and S3, from CSCs, claimed that sometimes the flow interactions were not well defined by "business people", requiring *"several meeting between teams to define the flow"* (S1). On the other hand, S2, from a SaaS, declared that her unit was *"designed with a well-defined contract with other organisation units"* and never had this kind of problem.

Insights for Guideline 3: In the first part, just S1 identified as valuable the objectives and linked them with OKR, one of the frameworks on which the guideline is based on [6]. In the second part, all the respondents valued measuring strategic objectives in the business process. Participants S4 and S5 commented *we have code written to measure the NPS*[2]. However, for the rest of the participants, the effect on the software product was different to what we presented in Sect. 3.4, who stated that objectives measurement are solved using external tools such as Hotjar[3] (for measuring customer satisfaction) or Google Analytics.

Considering the above results, we discuss three topics: 1. The value added by the proposal, 2. The limitations of the method, and 3. The completeness and possible extensions of the method. On the first topic, we believe that the participants valued the proposal since it could help raise awareness of issues that

---

[2] Net Promoter Score, https://hbr.org/2003/12/the-one-number-you-need-to-grow.
[3] https://www.hotjar.com/.

affect their performance. As stated by S1, *"In my experience, when teams' processes are not independent, there is a chaotic development process."* and S5 *"It is problematic when business people have new ideas and assign them to existing cells with non-related business flows."*. This is consistent with the outcomes predicted by agile operation models [11,16]. On the second topic, we believe that the organisation's characteristics may limit the proposal's value; CSCs might not be able to participate in their customers' strategic definitions, as in the case of participant S1. However, this may also occur in SaaS organisations with many hierarchical levels: Participant S2 was part of a SaaS organisation inside a major retail company and declared that external business people designed the business process. These organisational characteristics are identified as problematic by one of the works that motivated the proposal [16]. Finally, considering the value perceived by the participants, we believe that the requirements of the method are fulfilled. However, participants S1, S2, and S4 raised another issue that is outside the proposal's scope but could be considered in a future extension. The issue regards mapping how the actions assigned to an organisation unit in the strategy model (tactics in Fig. 2C) are realised in the business process model. We believe that we could address this by adding a new method part to the proposal, such as the purpose analysis of the business process presented in [31].

5   Conclusions and Future Work

This article presented Stra2Bis, a method for designing strategically aligned business processes in an MDA context. Stra2Bis proposes to align business processes to the organisational units' structure, dependency and goals. Stra2Bis proposes adding a strategy modelling step to represent the organisational elements that drive the business process re-design and three guidelines to generate an initial version of the new business process model. We conducted an initial evaluation through a focus group with eight software development practitioners, who supported the proposals, however, some of the effects on software design could be different the predicted. Although the respondents' profile, experience, and non-model-driven context set threats to the evaluation's validity, the activity showed that the proposal was helpful for reasoning about the strategic alignment of business processes. Future work focuses on applying the proposal in an industrial case study and other focus groups and interviews with practitioners to foster the proposal's adoption.

Acknowledgments. This work has the financial support of the Spanish State Research Agency and the Generalitat Valenciana under the projects PID2021-123824OB-I00 and PDC2021-121243-I00 funded by MICIN/ AEI/ 10.13039/501100011033, INNEST/ 2021/57 and GV/ 2021/072, co-financed with ERDF and the European Union NextGenerationEU/PRTR, and the National Agency for Research and Development (ANID)/ Scholarship Program/ Doctorado Becas Chile/2020-72210494. Special thanks to Claudia Negri for her advice on the design of the focus group.

References

1. Amyot, D., et al.: Combining goal modelling with business process modelling. Enterp. Model. Inf. Syst. Architect. (EMISAJ) **17**, 1–2 (2022)
2. Atlassian: the spotify model. www.atlassian.com/agile/agile-at-scale/spotify. Accessed 31 May 2021
3. Bērziša, S., Bravos, G., Gonzalez, T., et al.: Capability driven development: an approach to designing digital enterprises. Bus. Inf. Syst. Eng. **57**(1), 15–25 (2015)
4. Conway, M.E.: How do committees invent. Datamation **14**(4), 28–31 (1968)
5. De Castro, V., Marcos, E., Vara, J.M.: Applying CIM-to-PIM model transformations for the service-oriented development of information systems. Inf. Softw. Technol. **53**(1), 87–105 (2011)
6. Doerr, J.: Measure what matters: how google, bono, and the gates foundation rock the world with OKRs. Penguin (2018)
7. Engelsman, W., Gordijn, J., Haaker, T., van Sinderen, M., Wieringa, R.: Quantitative alignment of enterprise architectures with the business model. In: Ghose, A., Horkoff, J., Silva Souza, V.E., Parsons, J., Evermann, J. (eds.) ER 2021. LNCS, vol. 13011, pp. 189–198. Springer, Cham (2021). https://doi.org/10.1007/978-3-030-89022-3_16
8. España, S., González, A., Pastor, Ó.: Communication analysis: a requirements engineering method for information systems. In: van Eck, P., Gordijn, J., Wieringa, R. (eds.) CAiSE 2009. LNCS, vol. 5565, pp. 530–545. Springer, Heidelberg (2009). https://doi.org/10.1007/978-3-642-02144-2_41
9. España, S.: Methodological Integration of Communication Analysis into a Model-Driven Software Development Framework, Ph. D. thesis, Universitat Politècnica de València, Valencia, Spain (2011)
10. Evans, E., Evans, E.J.: Domain-driven design: tackling complexity in the heart of software. Addison-Wesley Professional (2004)
11. Forsgren, N., Humbpotifle, J., Kim, G.: Accelerate: the science of lean software and devops building and scaling high performing technology organizations. IT Revolution Press (2018)
12. Gröner, G., Asadi, M., Mohabbati, B., Gašević, D., Bošković, M., Parreiras, F.S.: Validation of user intentions in process orchestration and choreography. Inf. Syst. **43**, 83–99 (2014)
13. Guizzardi, R., Reis, A.N.: A method to align goals and business processes. In: Johannesson, P., Lee, M.L., Liddle, S.W., Opdahl, A.L., López, Ó.P. (eds.) ER 2015. LNCS, vol. 9381, pp. 79–93. Springer, Cham (2015). https://doi.org/10.1007/978-3-319-25264-3_6
14. Habba, M., Fredj, M., Benabdellah Chaouni, S.: Alignment between business requirement, business process, and software system: a systematic literature review. J. Eng. **2019**, 6918105 (2019)
15. Henderson-Sellers, B., Ralyté, J., Ågerfalk, P.J., Rossi, M.: Situational method engineering, 1st Edn. Springer, Heidelberg (2014). https://doi.org/10.1007/978-3-642-41467-1
16. Highsmith, J., Luu, L., Robinson, D.: EDGE: value-driven digital transformation. Addison-Wesley Professional (2019)
17. Insfrán, E., Abrahão, S., de Oliveira, R.P., González-Ladrón-de Guevara, F., Fernández-Diego, M., Cano-Genoves, C.: Specifying value in GRL for guiding BPMN activities prioritization. In: Proceedings of the International Conference on Information Systems Development (2017)

18. Kontio, J., Lehtola, L., Bragge, J.: Using the focus group method in software engineering: obtaining practitioner and user experiences. In: Proceedings of the 2004 International Symposium on Empirical Software Engineering (2004)
19. Kraiem, N., Kaffela, H., Dimassi, J., Al Khanjari, Z.: Mapping from map models to BPMN processes. J. Soft. Eng. **8**(4), 252–264 (2014)
20. Larman, C., Vodde, B.: Large-scale scrum: more with LeSS. Addison-Wesley Professional (2016)
21. Mintzberg, H.: The strategy concept i: five PS for strategy. Calif. Manage. Rev. **30**(1), 11–24 (1987)
22. Nagel, B., Gerth, C., Engels, G., Post, J.: Ensuring consistency among business goals and business process models. In: 2013 17th IEEE International Enterprise Distributed Object Computing Conference, pp. 17–26. IEEE (2013)
23. Noel, R., Panach Navarrete, J.I., Ruiz, M., Pastor Lopez, O.: The LiteStrat method: towards strategic model-driven development. In: Proceedings of the International Conference on Information Systems Development (2021)
24. von Rosing, M., White, S., Cummins, F., de Man, H.: Business process model and notation-BPMN(2015)
25. Ruiz, M., Costal, D., España, S., Franch, X., Pastor, O.: GoBIS: an integrated framework to analyse the goal and business process perspectives in information systems. Inf. Syst. **53**, 330–345 (2015)
26. Scaled Agile, INC: Safe 5 for lean enterprises. www.scaledagileframework.com/. Accessed 10 Apr 2021
27. Sousa, H.P., do Prado Leite, J.C.S.: Modeling organizational alignment. In: Yu, E., Dobbie, G., Jarke, M., Purao, S. (eds.) ER 2014. LNCS, vol. 8824, pp. 407–414. Springer, Cham (2014). https://doi.org/10.1007/978-3-319-12206-9_34
28. The Object Management Group: Model driven architecture (MDA). www.omg. org/mda/. Accessed 14 Apr 2021
29. The object management group: business motivation model specification version 1.3 (2015). www.omg.org/spec/BMM/About-BMM/
30. The Open Group: Archimate®2.1 specification - motivation extension. https:// pubs.opengroup.org/architecture/archimate2-doc/chap10.html. Accessed 09 Nov 2020
31. de la Vara, J.L., Sánchez, J., Pastor, Ó.: Business process modelling and purpose analysis for requirements analysis of information systems. In: Bellahsène, Z., Léonard, M. (eds.) CAiSE 2008. LNCS, vol. 5074, pp. 213–227. Springer, Heidelberg (2008). https://doi.org/10.1007/978-3-540-69534-9_17
32. Yu, E., Strohmaier, M., Deng, X.: Exploring intentional modeling and analysis for enterprise architecture. In: 2006 10th IEEE International Enterprise Distributed Object Computing Conference Workshops (EDOCW2006), p. 32. IEEE (2006)
33. Zimmermann, O.: Microservices tenets. Comput. Sci. Res. Dev. **32**(3), 301–310 (2017)

Online Decision Mining and Monitoring in Process-Aware Information Systems

Beate Scheibel[1]([✉]) [iD] and Stefanie Rinderle-Ma[2] [iD]

[1] Research Group Workflow Systems and Technology, Faculty of Computer Science, University of Vienna, Vienna, Austria
beate.scheibel@univie.ac.at
[2] Chair of Information Systems and Business Process Management, Technical University of Munich, Garching, Germany
stefanie.rinderle-ma@tum.de

Abstract. Decision mining enables discovery of decision rules guiding the control flow in processes. Existing decision mining techniques deal with different kinds of decision rules, e.g., overlapping rules, or including data elements, for example, time series data. Though online process mining and monitoring are gaining traction, online decision mining algorithms are still missing. Decision rules can be, similarly to process models, subject to change during runtime due to, for example, changing regulations or customer requirements. In order to address these runtime challenges, this paper proposes an approach that i) discovers decision rules during runtime and ii) continuously monitors and adapts discovered rules to reflect changes. Furthermore, the concept of a decision rule history is proposed, enabling (manual) identification of change patterns. The feasibility and the applicability of the approach is evaluated based on three synthetic datasets, BPIC12, BPIC20 and sepsis data set.

Keywords: Online decision mining · Decision rule evolution · Decision rule monitoring · Process-aware information systems

1 Introduction

Process mining enables process discovery, conformance checking and process enhancement [1]. An important part of process discovery is decision mining, providing techniques to discover decision points in processes as well as the underlying decision rules guarding that decision based on event logs [6]. Process and decision mining are increasingly gaining traction as transparency and standardization become more and more important across different domains [5]. Existing decision mining approaches [7,8,11,14] operate in an ex-post way, i.e., by analyzing event logs after the process instances have been completed. Recent process mining research focuses on online process mining, for example, online process discovery [2], online sensor stream analysis [3] or online concept drift detection, i.e. detecting control flow changes during runtime, see for example [17]. However, to the best of our knowledge, neither runtime decision mining algorithms

J. Ralyté et al. (Eds.): ER 2022, LNCS 13607, pp. 271–280, 2022.
https://doi.org/10.1007/978-3-031-17995-2_19

nor algorithms to detect and monitor decision rule evolution, independent of control flow changes, exist. Hence, this work focuses on discovering decision rules during runtime and updating decision rules if changes occur in the process or the process environment. Such process or process environment changes include:

- *Available data:* Internal process data i.e., data attributes available in the event log such as patient age in a medical scenario, as well as external data, that can be mapped to process events, e.g. sensor data, has changed or additional data has become available. Examples comprise newly installed sensors and varying ranges of measured values in a workpiece within the specified tolerance range. Being able to adapt existing decision rules to additional information can lead to more comprehensive decision rules.
- *Seasonal or cyclical changes:* For example seasonal price adaptations in the tourism domain that are not specified as a data element.
- *Environmental changes:* Decision rules reflect business or objective rules based on, e.g., regulatory documents. The underlying rules might change over time, e.g., new regulations occur or customers change their requirements, resulting in an evolution of the corresponding decision rule.

If changes are not taken into account, outdated rules might drive decisions in running process instances, no longer reflecting, for example, state of the art parameters or current regulations.

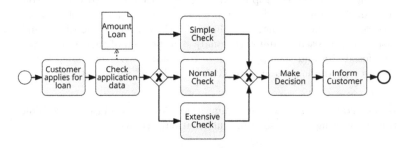

Fig. 1. Running example: loan application (modeled using Signavio©).

Consider the loan application process as depicted in Fig. 1. A customer applies for a loan. There are three levels of scrutiny: simple, normal, and extensive. Assume that the levels depend solely on the amount that is applied for as reflected by the following decision rule:

IF amount_loan <= 20.000 THEN Simple
IF amount_loan > 20.000 AND amount_loan <= 80.000 THEN Normal
IF amount_loan > 80.000 THEN Extensive

During execution, regulations might change, resulting in a lower limit for an extensive check, i.e., an amount greater than 50.000.

A comprehensive decision mining and monitoring approach would mean to i) discover the first version of the decision rule when the loan process starts to be instantiated and executed based on the event stream emitted during process execution ($\mapsto$ **RQ1**), ii) monitor and update the rule when the rule evolution comes into effect, again based on the event stream ($\mapsto$ **RQ2**). In order to tackle **RQ1** and **RQ2**, this paper proposes a novel algorithm to discover decision rules during runtime. It takes an event stream as input and determines the current decision rule as output. The algorithm uses windows that adapt according to the current performance measured by the F1 score. The different versions of a decision rule discovered during runtime are stored in a *decision rule history*. The decision rule history can be exploited for further analysis, e.g., to discover patterns in the decision rules such as seasonal variations. Three scenarios for decision rule evolution during runtime are described and the corresponding synthetic data sets are used for evaluating the feasibility of the approach. In addition, three real world data sets are used to evaluate the applicability of the approach.

Section 2 describes the decision mining and monitoring algorithm, which is evaluated in Sect. 3 and discussed in Sect. 4. An overview of related work is given in Sect. 5 and a conclusion is provided in Sect. 6.

2 Decision Rule Mining and Monitoring

During runtime, process instances are started and executed based on a process model that consists of control and data flow. The execution history is stored in the associated process event trace. Each trace is signified by a unique id and constitutes a sequence of events that reflect the execution of process tasks. The order of the activities is reflected by timestamps in the process event log. Events can hold additional information, i.e. data elements. An event stream contains the same elements as an event log. However, whereas an event log is finite (i.e., no more events are incoming) and complete (each trace has a start and end event), an event stream constitutes a continuous flow of events produced by process instances, with no specific start or end [17].

The *decision mining and monitoring algorithm (DMMA)* proposed in this work uses an event stream as input, with new instances being executed continually. We assume a predefined decision point DP in the underlying process model. DP could be discovered in a previous step using (online) process mining. At the start of the DMMA, no data and no decision rule are available. Hence, a grace period is implemented, where data is gathered, but not analyzed yet. As soon as the grace period has finished, a decision rule for DP is mined and added to the *decision rule history* which holds all discovered versions of a decision rule (cmp. process model history as proposed in [17]), formally:

Definition 1 (Decision rule history). *Let P be a process model with a decision point DP. The decision rule history $RH_{DP} := < R_0, R_1, \ldots R_k >$ for DP constitutes a list of discovered versions $R_i := (n_i, p_i, l_i)$ for the decision rule R connected to DP ($i \in \mathbb{N}$). n_i denotes the number of instances active at the point in time when R_i was discovered, p_i the performance of the algorithm for R_i, and l_i a link to the textual description of R_i. R_k denotes the current version of the decision rule for DP.*

The decision rule history RH_{DP} is updated continually, i.e., as soon as a new decision rule version is mined. In addition to the rules itself, the history includes the number of instances a specific rule was in place as well as the mean performance. We opt to store the decision rules textually to enable manual analysis. Note that in a process with multiple decisions, multiple decision rule histories might exist, each one covering decision rule versions for a specific decision point.

In the DMMA, a decision rule version R_k is mined and continually checked if it still aligns with new process instances. The window size determines the point in time to check the current rule. The alignment is assessed based on the performance, measured using the F1 Score, i.e., the ability of the rule to accurately classify new instances. If the rule is able to achieve a high performance, the window size is increased. If the performance drops below a certain threshold, i.e. the *remining criterion* is met, we assume that either the underlying data or the underlying rule has changed, and therefore the rule has to be remined which is then added to the decision rule history. If the remined rule is still not able to accurately classify new instances, the window size is decreased and increased in parallel for the next iterations to check which leads to more performant rule versions. The DMAA continues until no new process instances occur.

The pseudo code for DMAA is provided in Alg. 1. Input parameters are upper limit, lower limit, increase size, threshold, and step size (all parameter values in [0,1]). The upper limit *up* marks the point at which the performance of a rule version is seen as robust. On the contrary, the lower limit *low* is the threshold where the current version is not assumed to be robust anymore. The threshold t is used when deciding if the difference in F1 Score of the current (R_k) and the previous version (R_{k-1}) is significant. The increase i defines the percentage the window size is increased by if the rule version is robust, whereas the step size s defines the percentage by which the window is increased/decreased to find a new appropriate window size. In addition, a maximum window size can be set to avoid increasing the window to a size larger than the amount of incoming data, leading to no further performance checks. Similarly, a minimum size can be set. These mainly depend on the expected amount of data and the need to minimize computing resources, as smaller windows lead to more computational effort.

For rule mining a CART decision tree, a standard decision mining tool [6], is used. Any other decision mining implementation can also be used at this point, e.g. Incremental Decision Trees [10], which are optimized for runtime classification. Similarly, multiple metrics can be used to evaluate the performance of a decision rule, i.e., how accurately a rule classifies instances, such as accuracy, F1 Score, precision, recall, logloss, or AUROC. For DMAA, we choose the F1 Score, which is commonly used as performance metric for concept drift detection [15]. The F1 Score combines recall and precision. Precision is defined as all instances that are correctly labeled as class_x, divided by all instances of class_x, and recall as all instances that are correctly labeled as class_x, divided by all instances labeled class_x. Overall, an F1 Score close to 1 indicates high recall and precision values. The F1 Score is calculated for each class separately and then weighted according to the occurrence of the specific class in the data. For

---

Algorithm 1. DMAA

Input: start window size w, increase i, threshold t, upper limit up, lower limit low, step size s

Output: current rule version, decision rule history

1: *initial = True, robust = True, w_smaller = w, w_bigger = w*
2: create trace dictionary
3: **while** new event **do**
4:      add event to trace dictionary, counter $+=1$
5:      **if** initial mining AND grace period reached **then**   ▷ grace period default 200
6:          initial = false
7:          mine decision rule, store in *model*
8:          calculate F1 Score
9:          output decision rule, add rule to decision rule history
10:      **end if**
11:      **if** (*robust* AND *counter* $>= w$) OR not *robust* AND
12:          (*counter* $>= w\_bigger$ OR *counter* $>= w\_smaller$) **then**
13:          set *w_test* to appropriate size   ▷ depending on if condition
14:          F1 Score_old = F1 Score
15:          counter = 0   ▷ not for *w_smaller*
16:          calculate F1 Score for *w_test* and *model*
17:          **if** F1 Score < F1 Score_old*t **then**   ▷ t default 0.9
18:              remine decision rule, store in *model*
19:              calculate F1 Score
20:              output decision rule, add rule to decision rule history
21:          **end if**
22:          **if** F1 Score > up **then**   ▷ up default 0.98
23:              $w = w\_test$
24:              **if** robust **then**
25:                  increase w by i ▷ i default 1%
26:              **end if**
27:              $w\_smaller = w\_test, w\_bigger = w\_test, robust = True$
28:          **else if** F1 Score < low **then**   ▷ low default 0.90
29:              $robust = False$
30:              $w\_smaller = w\_smaller * (1 - s)$ ▷ s default 20%
31:              $w\_bigger = increase\_bigger * (1 + s)$
32:          **end if**
33:      **end if**
34:      **if** length dictionary > w_bigger **then**   ▷ set to biggest window size
35:          remove first dictionary entry   ▷ first in, first out
36:      **end if**
37: **end while**

DMMA, we calculate the F1 Score each time the window size is reached and when a new rule version is mined. We compare the current F1 Score to the last F1 Score. If the performance has significantly decreased, defined by a user-defined threshold t, the *remining criterion* is met, a new rule version is mined.

If a rule achieves an F1 Score of above the threshold *up*, we assume that it is robust, i.e. able to adequately classify the current instances.

Checking the remining criterion for each instance is computationally inefficient, in particular in connection with a large number of instances. Therefore, we use a window based technique, where only the most recent instances are kept in memory. The input, in form of a process stream, where new events arrive continually, is kept in an ordered dictionary and as soon as the window size is reached, the first instance with all respective events and data elements, is removed, i.e. the first in, first out principle is applied. This window also defines when the performance is checked, i.e., as soon as a complete turnover of stored instances has taken place, the performance is checked.

The optimal window size depends on the data, the underlying rules, as well as if and in what way the rule evolves and can impact the results significantly. Setting it too small might result in rules not being discovered, as the available data does not appropriately cover the rules. On the contrary, a too large size, might lead to the inability to discover a robust rule as multiple versions are present in the current window [15]. Therefore the goal is to find a balance discovering new versions as fast as possible and keeping the ability to mine robust and comprehensive rules, while minimizing computational complexity. The window size can be set statically or in an adaptive manner, i.e. the window size changes during the process. In related approaches it was shown that adaptive setting can lead to optimized results, reducing the impact of the initial size [9]. DMMA uses adaptive windows with a manually set starting size. If the last calculated F1 Score is above a fixed limit *up*, the window size is increased by i as we see the rule as robust. If the score is below lower limit *low*, the window size should be either increased, because the algorithm is not able to discover complex rules or the window size should be decreased to be able to discover rule changes. As we cannot know which is the case, two windows, *w_smaller* and *w_bigger*, are used in parallel, which are set by subtracting and adding a fixed step *s* to the current window size. Further incoming instances are checked and the rule remined if necessary for each of the different window sizes. If no robust rule is achieved, the windows are further decreased and increased. As soon as a robust rule is found, the current window size is set as *w*, and the process continues as described before until no more instances arrive.

3   Evaluation

The approach is implemented in Python, using the 'scikit-learn' module [13] as decision tree implementation. All data sets are preprocessed, simulating an event stream by reading in each event in the order of timestamps. In addition to the loan example, presented in Sect. 1, we provide a manufacturing and tourism use case with synthetic data sets, reflecting different decision rule evolutions. Data set characteristics are described together with the results in the following sections. The source code, the data sets as well as the full results are available online[1]. For the synthetic data sets, the exact point of change is known, therefore the results contain the mean number of instances from the point where the underlying rule change happened until a new robust rule version is mined (not including the grace period), as well as the number of *transition rules*, being defined as rules mined in between changes, where the resulting rule does not fully represent either the old or the new rule version. This is currently detected manually.

Use Case 1 - Loan Application: A synthetic data set according to the process shown in Fig. 1 is generated, containing 5000 instances in total. The rule change happens at instance number 2500. After the initial grace period, a rule was discovered that stayed consistent until the underlying rule changed at instance 2500. 241 instances later, a new rule version was successfully mined and stayed consistent until the process finished. The overall F1 Score is 97%.

Use Case 2 - Manufacturing: This scenario consists of a simplified manufacturing scenario where a workpiece is produced. The observed decision is whether the workpiece is OK or not (NOK). In the beginning the only available data are the diameter measurements. During production, a second data element, the temperature is made available. The synthetic data set contains about 5000 instances, the additional sensor is added from the $2500th$ instance on. Before the additional sensor was added, 16 rule versions, i.e. transition rules were mined indicating that no robust rule was found due to lack of data. As soon as the sensor was added it took 23 instances until a robust version, appropriately reflecting the underlying rule, was discovered. The mean F1 Score is at 0.93.

Use Case 3 - Tourism: This use case describes the process of calculating a room offer for hotel guests and can be seen in Fig. 2. The synthetic data set contains four seasons in total, each containing 2500 instances. Depending on the season and the occupancy rate, either a standard or a premium price is offered. Assuming that there are more guests in winter than in summer, the premium price is already offered at 60% capacity in winter, the summer rule version states that a premium is offered at 90% capacity. The seasons are not logged, therefore no respective data element exists. In total 6 rule versions are discovered during runtime, meaning that the four seasonal rules are discovered as well as two transition rules after changes occurred ($70 - 100$ instances later), containing old as well as new versions. However, if these rules are not taken into account the F1 Score is high with 98%, with those rules the mean F1 Score is at 0.95.

Real Life Data: The applicability is tested on three real life data sets, BPIC12[2], BPIC20[3], and a sepsis data set[4]. The BPIC12 contains a loan application

---

[1] https://github.com/bscheibel/dmma.

[2] https://data.4tu.nl/articles/dataset/BPI_Challenge_2012/12689204.

[3] https://doi.org/10.4121/uuid:52fb97d4-4588-43c9-9d04-3604d4613b51.

[4] https://data.4tu.nl/articles/dataset/Sepsis_Cases_-_Event_Log/12707639.

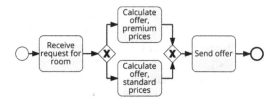

Fig. 2. Use Case 3: tourism.

process similar to the running example. The observed decision is whether a loan application was accepted or rejected. The only available data element is the requested amount. The decision rule history discovered by the DMMA contains 64 rule versions, i.e., after each window remining was necessary due to the low F1 scores between 0.28 and 0.59. However, the discovered rule versions are similar to the one described in [7], i.e. mostly loans are accepted when their amount is neither too high nor too low, e.g., one of the version states that the amount has to be between 5750 an 42000 to be accepted. The BPIC20 log contains permit applications and declarations from a travel expense reimbursement system. The analyzed decision determines whether an instance is marked as 'Overspent'. The discovered rule stays consistent over the entire runtime, with a mean F1 Score of 0.99, leading to the assumption that the underlying rule is robust and does not evolve. The sepsis data set contains event logs from a hospital. The decision point whether a patient is admitted to either "Normal Care" or "Intensive Care" is analyzed. Available data elements include lab values as well as other information such as patient age. In total, 7 decision rule versions are discovered by the DMMA with F1 Scores varying between 0.49 and 0.98 for the last discovered version. The last rule version states the lactic acid values as the decisive factor.

4   Discussion

The evaluation shows that the approach is feasible and able to discover decision rules and their evolution during runtime, enabling greater transparency of a process and its decision points. For the BPIC20 and the sepis data set we assume that not all necessary information is available to mine robust rules, leading to frequent remining. The extracted rule versions are stored in a decision rule history and can be used to manually analyze rule evolution, e.g., seasonal or alternating rules.

Limitations and Threats to Validity: Several parameters have to be set manually. In future work, guidelines on how to set these parameters based on process characteristics, e.g., amount of expected data or frequency of expected changes, will be developed. One window size is used to determine the amount of stored instances, the number of instances that are used to check a rule version as well as to the number of instances that are used to remine a rule version. Differing window sizes could be used for these values. However, this would increase the complexity of the approach without a clear benefit to it.

Computational complexity and runtime of DMAA depend on the underlying data, the window size (also depending on the underlying data) as well as the number of decision points in a given process. The computationally most expensive part is the rule (re)mining. If no underlying changes occur, rule mining happens only once. In contrast, if changes happen frequently and therefore the rule evolves continually, the computational complexity increases. The extreme case is that remining occurs for each window. An optimization with regards to computational complexity is part of future work.

5 Related Work

Decision mining was introduced as a way to discover data conditions that impact the routing of a specific instance at a decision point [14]. Multiple different decision mining algorithms exist, focusing on different aspects [6], e.g. aligning control flow and data flow to discover decision rules [7], discovering overlapping rules [11], incorporating linear relationships between variables [8], or mining decision rule based on time series data [16]. These algorithms are applied ex-post, i.e., after the process instances have finished. Recent work in online process mining focuses on process discovery [2], conformance checking [4], drift detection [17] and predictive process monitoring [12] during runtime. However, none of these works focus on online decision mining, especially with regards to the generation of textual decision rules, decision rule evolution and decision rule histories.

6 Conclusion

This paper presents DMMA, an algorithm for discovery and monitoring decision rule evolution during runtime. Decision rule evolution might become necessary due to newly available data and changes in environmental conditions. The DMMA algorithm takes as input an event stream and processes it as events occur. The output of the DMAA algorithm is the decision rule history for a decision point containing all versions of the decision rule connected with this decision point. The decision rule history enables the analysis of how decision rules evolve over time, i.e., lays the foundation for decision rule pattern analysis. In future work, we will investigate the potential of decision rule history analysis, together with root cause analysis why decision rules evolved. This provides insights into the evolution of the process and the decision structures behind. The decision pattern analysis will require the comparison of decision rule (versions) and similarity measures based on decision rules.

Acknowledgments. This work has been partially supported and funded by the Austrian Research Promotion Agency (FFG) via the Austrian Competence Center for Digital Production (CDP) under the contract number 881843.

References

1. van der Aalst, W.M.P.: Process Mining: Data Science in Action. Springer, Heidelberg (2016). https://doi.org/10.1007/978-3-662-49851-4
2. Burattin, A., Cimitile, M., Maggi, F.M., Sperduti, A.: Online discovery of declarative process models from event streams. IEEE Trans. Serv. Comput. 8(6), 833–846 (2015). https://doi.org/10.1109/TSC.2015.2459703
3. Ehrendorfer, M., Mangler, J., Rinderle-Ma, S.: Assessing the impact of context data on process outcomes during runtime. In: Service-Oriented Computing, pp. 3–18 (2021). https://doi.org/10.1007/978-3-030-91431-8_1
4. Koenig, P., Mangler, J., Rinderle-Ma, S.: Compliance monitoring on process event streams from multiple sources. In: Process Mining, pp. 113–120 (2019). https://doi.org/10.1109/ICPM.2019.00026
5. Leewis, S., Berkhout, M., Smit, K.: Future Challenges in Decision Mining at Governmental Institutions, p. 12 (2020)
6. de Leoni, M., Mannhardt, F.: Decision discovery in business processes. In: Encyclopedia of Big Data Technologies, pp. 1–12 (2018). https://doi.org/10.1007/978-3-319-63962-8_96-1
7. de Leoni, M., van der Aalst, W.M.P.: Data-aware process mining: discovering decisions in processes using alignments. In: Symposium on Applied Computing, p. 1454 (2013). https://doi.org/10.1145/2480362.2480633
8. de Leoni, M., Dumas, M., García-Bañuelos, L.: Discovering branching conditions from business process execution logs. In: Fundamental Approaches to Software Engineering, pp. 114–129 (2013). https://doi.org/10.1007/978-3-642-37057-1_9
9. Maaradji, A., Dumas, M., Rosa, M.L., Ostovar, A.: Detecting sudden and gradual drifts in business processes from execution traces. IEEE Trans. Knowl. Data Eng. (2017). https://doi.org/10.1109/TKDE.2017.2720601
10. Manapragada, C., Webb, G.I., Salehi, M.: Extremely fast decision tree. In: PKnowledge Discovery & Data Mining, pp. 1953–1962 (2018). https://doi.org/10.1145/3219819.3220005
11. Mannhardt, F., de Leoni, M., Reijers, H.A., van der Aalst, W.M.P.: Decision mining revisited - discovering overlapping rules. In: Nurcan, S., Soffer, P., Bajec, M., Eder, J. (eds.) CAiSE 2016. LNCS, vol. 9694, pp. 377–392. Springer, Cham (2016). https://doi.org/10.1007/978-3-319-39696-5_23
12. Pauwels, S., Calders, T.: Incremental predictive process monitoring: the next activity case. In: Business Process Management, pp. 123–140 (2021). https://doi.org/10.1007/978-3-030-85469-0_10
13. Pedregosa, F., et al.: Scikit-learn: machine learning in python. J. Mach. Learn. Res. 12, 2825–2830 (2011)
14. Rozinat, A., van der Aalst, W.M.P.: Decision mining in ProM. In: Business Process Management, pp. 420–425 (2006). https://doi.org/10.1007/11841760_33
15. Sato, D.M.V., de Freitas, S.C., Barddal, J.P., Scalabrin, E.E.: A survey on concept drift in process mining. ACM Comput. Surv. 54(9), 1–38 (2022). https://doi.org/10.1145/3472752
16. Scheibel, B., Rinderle-Ma, S.: Decision mining with time series data based on automatic feature generation. In: Conference on Advanced Information Systems Engineering (2022). https://doi.org/10.1007/978-3-031-07472-1_1
17. Stertz, F., Rinderle-Ma, S.: Process histories - detecting and representing concept drifts based on event streams. In: On the Move to Meaningful Internet Systems, pp. 318–335 (2018). https://doi.org/10.1007/978-3-030-02610-3_18

OPerA: Object-Centric Performance Analysis

Gyunam Park[✉][ID], Jan Niklas Adams[ID], and Wil M. P. van der Aalst[ID]

Process and Data Science Group (PADS), RWTH Aachen University,
Aachen, Germany
{gnpark,niklas.adams,wvdaalst}@pads.rwth-aachen.de

Abstract. Performance analysis in process mining aims to provide insights on the performance of a business process by using a process model as a formal representation of the process. Existing techniques for performance analysis assume that a single case notion exists in a business process (e.g., a patient in healthcare process). However, in reality, different objects might interact (e.g., order, delivery, and invoice in an O2C process). In such a setting, traditional techniques may yield misleading or even incorrect insights on performance metrics such as waiting time. More importantly, by considering the interaction between objects, we can define object-centric performance metrics such as synchronization time, pooling time, and lagging time. In this work, we propose a novel approach to performance analysis considering multiple case notions by using object-centric Petri nets as formal representations of business processes. The proposed approach correctly computes existing performance metrics, while supporting the derivation of newly-introduced object-centric performance metrics. We have implemented the approach as a web application and conducted a case study based on a real-life loan application process.

Keywords: Performance analysis · Object-centric process mining · Object-centric Petri net · Actionable insights · Process improvement

1 Introduction

Process mining provides techniques to extract insights from event data recorded by information systems, including process discovery, conformance checking, and performance analysis [1]. Especially performance analysis provides techniques to analyze the performance of a business process using process models as representations of the process [6].

Existing techniques for performance analysis have been developed, assuming that a single case notion exists in business processes, e.g., a patient in a

---

This work is supported by the Alexander von Humboldt (AvH) Stiftung. An extended version is available online: https://arxiv.org/abs/2204.10662.

J. Ralyté et al. (Eds.): ER 2022, LNCS 13607, pp. 281–292, 2022.
https://doi.org/10.1007/978-3-031-17995-2_20

healthcare process [5,6,8,11–14]. Such a case notion correlates events of a process instance and represents them as a single sequence, e.g., a sequence of events of a patient. However, in real-life business processes supported by ERP systems such as SAP and Oracle, multiple objects (i.e., multiple sequences of events) exist in a process instance [3,7] and they share events (i.e., sequences are overlapping). Figure 1(a) shows a process instance in a simple blood test process as multiple overlapping sequences. The red sequence represents the event sequence of test *T1*, whereas the blue sequences indicate the event sequences of samples *S1* and *S2*, respectively. The objects share *conduct test* event (*e4*), i.e., all the sequences overlap, and the samples share *transfer samples* event (*e6*), i.e., the sample sequences overlap.

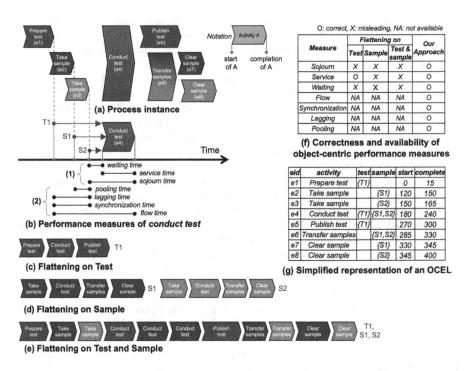

Fig. 1. A motivating example showing misleading insights from existing approaches to performance analysis and the proposed object-centric performance analysis (Color figure online)

The goal of object-centric performance analysis is to analyze performance in such "object-centric" processes with multiple overlapping sequences using 1) existing performance measures and 2) new performance measures considering the interaction between objects. Figure 1(b)(1) visualizes existing performance measures related to event *conduct test*. *Waiting time* of *conduct test* is the time spent before conducting the test after preparing test *T1* and samples *S1* and *S2*, while the *service time* is the time spent for conducting the test and *sojourn time* is the sum of *waiting time* and *service time*. Furthermore, Fig. 1(b)(2) shows new performance measures considering the interaction between objects. First, *synchronization time* is the time spent for synchronizing different objects, i.e., samples *S1* and *S2* with test *T1* to conduct the test. Next, *pooling time* is the time spent for pooling all objects of an object type, e.g., the pooling time of *conduct test* w.r.t. *sample* is the time taken to pool the second sample. Third, *lagging* time is the time spent due to the lag of an object type, e.g., the lagging time of *conduct test* w.r.t. *test* is the time taken due to the lag of the second sample. Finally, *flow time* is the sum of *sojourn time* and *synchronization time*.

A natural way to apply existing techniques to multiple overlapping sequences is to *flatten* them into a single sequence. To this end, we select an object type(s) as a case notion, removing events not having the object type and replicating events with multiple objects of the selected type [3]. For instance, Fig. 1(a) is flattened to Fig. 1(c) by using test as a case notion, to Fig. Figure 1(d) by using sample as a case notion, and Fig. 1(e) by using both test and sample as a case notion.

However, depending on the selection, flattening results in misleading insights. Figure 1(f) summarizes the correctness of object-centric performance analysis on flattened sequences. 1) Flattening on test provides a misleading waiting time, measured as the time difference between the complete time of *prepare test* and the start time of *conduct test*, and, thus, a misleading sojourn time. 2) Flattening on sample results in misleading insights on the service time since two service times are measured despite the single occurrence of the event. 3) By flattening on both test and sample, the waiting time for *take sample* is measured in relation to *prepare test* although they are independent events from different object types.

In this work, we suggest a novel approach to object-centric performance analysis. The approach uses an Object-Centric Event Log (OCEL) that store multiple overlapping sequences without flattening (cf. Fig. 1(g)) as an input. Moreover, we use Object-Centric Petri Nets (OCPNs) [3] as a formalism to represent process models, and the object-centric performance is analyzed in the context of process models. With formal semantics of OCPNs, we can reliably compute and interpret performance analysis results, considering the concurrency, loops, etc. [2].

More in detail, we first discover an OCPN that formally represents a process model from the OCEL. Next, we replay the OCEL on the discovered OCPN to produce *token visits* and *event occurrences*. Finally, we compute object-centric performance measures using the token visit and event occurrence. For instance, in the proposed approach, the waiting time of *Conduct test* is computed as the difference between $e4$'s start and $e1$'s complete. The synchronization time is computed as the time difference between $e3$'s complete and $e1$'s complete.

In summary, we provide the following contributions.

- Our approach correctly calculates existing performance measures in an object-centric setting.
- Our approach supports novel object-centric performance metrics taking the interaction between objects into account, such as synchronization time.

– The proposed approach has been implemented as a web application[1] and a case study with a real-life event log has been conducted to evaluate the effectiveness of the approach.

2   Related Work

Performance analysis has been widely studied in the context of process mining. Table 1 compares existing work and our proposed work in different criteria: 1) if formal semantics exist to analyze performance in the context of process models, 2) if aggregated measures, e.g., mean and median, are supported, 3) if frequency analysis is covered, 4) if time analysis is covered, and 5) if multiple case notions are allowed to consider the interactions of different objects. Existing algorithms/techniques assume a single case notion, not considering the interaction among different objects.

Table 1. Comparison of algorithms/techniques for performance analysis

Author	Technique	Form.	Agg.	Freq.	Perf.	Obj.
Maté et al. [13]	*Business Strategy Model*	-	✓	✓	✓	-
Denisov et al. [8]	*Performance Spectrum*	-	✓	✓	✓	-
Hornix [11]	*Petri Nets*	✓	✓	✓	✓	-
Rogge-Solti et al. [14]	*Stochastic Petri Nets*	✓	✓	-	✓	-
Leemans et al. [12]	*Directly Follows Model*	✓	✓	✓	✓	-
Adriansyah et al. [6]	*Robust Performance*	✓	✓	✓	✓	-
Adriansyah [5]	*Alignments*	✓	✓	✓	✓	-
Our work	***Object-Centric***	✓	✓	✓	✓	✓

Traditionally, methods in process mining have the assumption that each event is associated with exactly one case, viewing the event log as a set of isolated event sequences. Object-centric process mining breaks with this assumption, allowing one event to be associated with multiple cases and, thus, having shared events between event sequences. An event log format has been proposed to store object-centric event logs [10], as well as a discovery technique for OCPNs [3] and a conformance checking technique to determine precision and fitness of the net [4]. Furthermore, Esser and Fahland [9] propose a graph database as a storage format for object-centric event data, enabling a user to use queries to calculate different statistics. A study on performance analysis is, so far, missing in the literature, with only limited metrics being supported in [3] by flattening event logs and replaying them. However, object-centric performance metrics are needed to accurately assess performance in processes where multiple case notions occur.

---

[1] A demo video and manuals: https://github.com/gyunamister/OPerA.

3   Background

Defintion 1 (Universes). *Let* $\mathbb{U}_{ei}$ *be the universe of event identifiers,* $\mathbb{U}_{act}$ *the universe of activity names,* $\mathbb{U}_{time}$ *the universe of timestamps,* $\mathbb{U}_{ot}$ *the universe of object types, and* $\mathbb{U}_{oi}$ *the universe of object identifiers.* $type \in \mathbb{U}_{oi} \rightarrow \mathbb{U}_{ot}$ *assigns precisely one type to each object identifier.* $\mathbb{U}_{omap} = \{omap \in \mathbb{U}_{ot} \nrightarrow \mathcal{P}(\mathbb{U}_{oi}) \mid \forall_{ot \in dom(omap)} \forall_{oi \in omap(ot)} type(oi) = ot\}$ *is the universe of all object mappings indicating which object identifiers are included per type.* $\mathbb{U}_{event} = \mathbb{U}_{ei} \times \mathbb{U}_{act} \times \mathbb{U}_{time} \times \mathbb{U}_{time} \times \mathbb{U}_{omap}$ *is the universe of events.*

Given $e = (ei, act, st, ct, omap) \in \mathbb{U}_{event}$, $\pi_{ei}(e) = ei$, $\pi_{act}(e) = act$, $\pi_{st}(e) = st$, $\pi_{ct}(e) = ct$, *and* $\pi_{omap}(e) = omap$, *where* $\pi_{st}(e)$ *and* $\pi_{ct}(e)$ *denotes start and complete timestamps.*

Defintion 2 (Object-Centric Event Log (OCEL)). *An object-centric event log is a tuple* $L = (E, \prec_E)$, *where* $E \subseteq \mathbb{U}_{event}$ *is a set of events and* $\prec_E \subseteq E \times E$ *is a total order underlying* E. $\mathbb{U}_L$ *is the set of all possible object-centric event logs.*

Figure 1(b) describes a fraction of a simple OCEL with two types of objects. For the event in the fourth row, denoted as $e4$, $\pi_{ei}(e4) = e4$, $\pi_{act}(e4) = conduct\ test$, $\pi_{st}(e4) = 180$, $\pi_{ct}(e4) = 240$, $\pi_{omap}(e4)(test) = \{T1\}$, and $\pi_{omap}(e4)(sample) = \{S1, S2\}$. Note that the timestamp in the example is simplified using the relative scale.

Defintion 3 (Object-Centric Petri Net (OCPN)). *Let* $N = (P, T, F, l)$ *be a labeled Petri net with* P *the set of places,* T *the set of transitions,* $P \cap T = \emptyset$, $F \subseteq (P \times T) \cup (T \times P)$ *the flow relation, and* $l \in T \nrightarrow \mathbb{U}_{act}$ *a labeling function. An object-centric Petri net is a tuple* $ON = (N, pt, F_{var})$, $pt \in P \rightarrow \mathbb{U}_{ot}$ *maps places to object types, and* $F_{var} \subseteq F$ *is the subset of variable arcs.*

Figure 2(a) depicts an OCPN, $ON_1 = (N, pt, F_{var})$ with $N = (P, T, F, l)$ where $P = \{p1, \ldots, p9\}$, $T = \{t1, \ldots, t6\}$, $F = \{(p1, t1), (p2, t2), \ldots\}$, $l(t1) = prepare\ test$, etc., $pt(p1) = test$, $pt(p2) = sample$, etc., and $F_{var} = \{(p4, t3), (t3, p6), \ldots\}$.

A token consists of a place and an object, e.g., $(p3, T1)$ denotes a token of object $T1$ in $p3$. A marking of an OCPN is a multiset of tokens. For instance, marking $M_1 = [(p3, T1), (p4, S1), (p4, S2)]$ denotes three tokens, among which place $p3$ has one token of object $T1$ and $p4$ has two tokens of objects $S1$ and $S2$.

A binding describes the execution of a transition consuming objects from its input places and producing objects for its output places. A binding (t, b) is a tuple of transition t and function b mapping the object types of the surrounding places to sets of object identifiers. For instance, $(t3, b1)$ describes the execution of transition $t3$ with $b1$ where $b1(test) = \{T1\}$ and $b1(sample) = \{S1, S2\}$, where *test* and *sample* are the object types of its surrounding places (i.e., $p3$, $p4$, $p5$, and $p6$).

A binding (t, b) is *enabled* in marking M if all the objects specified by b exist in the input places of t. For instance, $(t3, b1)$ is enabled in marking M_1 since $T1$, $S1$, and $S2$ exist in its input places, i.e., $p3$ and $p4$. A new marking is reached by *executing* enabled binding (t, b) at M. For instance, as a result of executing $(t1, b1)$, $T1$ is removed from $p3$ and added to $p5$. Besides, $S1$ and $S2$ are removed from $p4$ and added to $p6$, resulting in new marking $M' = [(p5, T1), (p6, S1), (p6, S2)]$.

4   Object-Centric Performance Analysis

This section introduces an approach to object-centric performance analysis. In the approach, we first discover an OCPN based on an OCEL. Next, we replay the OCEL with timestamps on the discovered OCPN to connect events in the OCEL to the elements of OCPN and compute *event occurrences* and *token visits*. Finally, we measure various object-centric performance metrics based on the event occurrence and token visit. The discovery follows the general approach presented in [3]. In the following subsections, we focus on explaining the rest.

4.1   Replaying OCELs on OCPNs

We couple events in an OCEL to an OCPN by "playing the token game" using the formal semantics of OCPNs. As a result, a set of *event occurrences* are annotated to each visible transition, and a set of *token visits* are recorded for each place. First, an event occurrence represents the occurrence of an event in relation to a transition.

Defintion 4 (Event Occurrence). *Let* $ON = (N, pt, F_{var})$ *be an object-centric Petri net, where* $N = (P, T, F, l)$. *An event occurrence* $eo \in T \times \mathbb{U}_{event}$ *is a tuple of a transition and an event.* O_{ON} *is the set of possible event occurrences of* ON.

For instance, $(t3, e4) \in O_{ON_1}$ indicates that transition $t3$ of ON_1 shown in Fig. 2(a) is associated with event $e4$.

A token visit describes "visit" of a token to the corresponding place with the begin time of the visit, i.e., the timestamp when the token is produced, and the end time of the visit, i.e., the timestamp when the token is consumed.

Defintion 5 (Token Visit). *Let* $ON = (N, pt, F_{var})$ *be an object-centric Petri net, where* $N = (P, T, F, l)$. $Q_{ON} = \{(p, oi) \in P \times \mathbb{U}_{oi} \mid type(oi) = pt(p)\}$ *is the set of possible tokens. A token visit* $tv \in Q_{ON} \times \mathbb{U}_{time} \times \mathbb{U}_{time}$ *is a tuple of a token, a begin time, and an end time.* V_{ON} *is the set of possible token visits of* ON.

Given token visit $tv = ((p, oi), bt, et)$, $\pi_p(tv) = p$, $\pi_{oi}(tv) = oi$, $\pi_{bt}(tv) = bt$, and $\pi_{et}(tv) = et$. For instance, $((p3, T1), 15, 180) \in V_{ON_1}$ represents that token $(p3, T1) \in Q_{ON_1}$ is produced in place $p3$ at 15 and consumed at 180.

Given an OCEL, a replay function produces event occurrences and token visits of an OCPN, connecting events in the log to the model.

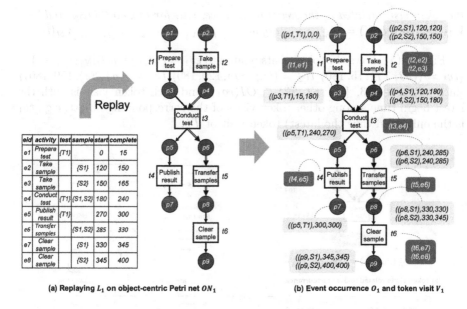

(a) Replaying L_1 on object-centric Petri net ON_1 (b) Event occurrence O_1 and token visit V_1

Fig. 2. An example of replaying object-centric event logs on an object-centric Petri net

Defintion 6 (Replay). *Let ON be an object-centric Petri net. A replay function* $replay_{ON} \in \mathbb{U}_L \to \mathcal{P}(O_{ON}) \times \mathcal{P}(V_{ON})$ *maps an event log to a set of event occurrences and a set of token visits.*

Figure 2(b) shows the result of replaying the events in L_1 shown in Fig. 2(a) on model ON_1 depicted in Fig. 2(a). The dark gray boxes represent event occurrences O_1 and the light gray boxes represent token visits V_1, where $replay_{ON_1}(L_1)$ = (O_1, V_1). For instance, replaying event $e1$ and $e4$ in L_1 produces event occurrences, $(t1, e1)$ and $(t3, e4)$, respectively, and token visit $((p3, T1), 15, 180)$ where 15 is the time when $e1$ completes and 180 is the time when $e4$ starts.

4.2   Measuring Object-Centric Performance Measures

We compute object-centric performance measures per event occurrence. For instance, we compute *synchronization, pooling, lagging,* and *waiting* time of $(t3, e4)$ that analyzes an event of *conduct test*. To this end, we first relate an event occurrence to the token visits 1) associated with the event occurrence's transition and 2) involving the objects linked to the event occurrence's event.

Defintion 7 (Relating An Event Occurrence to Token Visits). *Let L be an object-centric event log and ON an object-centric Petri net. Let eo = (t, e) ∈ O be an event occurrence.* $OI(eo) = \bigcup_{ot \in dom(\pi_{omap}(e))} \pi_{omap}(e)(ot)$ *denotes the set of objects related to the event occurrence.* $rel_{ON} \in O_{ON} \times \mathcal{P}(V_{ON}) \to \mathcal{P}(V_{ON})$ *is a function mapping an event occurrence and a set of token visits to the set of* *the token visits related to the event occurrence, s.t., for any eo ∈ O_{ON} and $V \subseteq V_{ON}$, $rel_{ON}(eo, V) = \bigcup_{oi \in OI(eo)} argmax_{tv \in \{tv' \in V | \pi_p(tv') \in \bullet t \wedge \pi_{oi}(tv')=oi\}} \pi_{bt}(tv).*

Figure 3(a) shows the token visits related to $eo_1 = (t3, e4)$. $rel_{ON_1}(eo_1, V_1) = \{tv_1 = ((p3, T1), 15, 180), tv_2 = ((p4, S1), 120, 180), tv_3 = ((p4, S2), 150, 180)\}$ since $p3, p4 \in \bullet t3$, $\{T1, S1, S2\} \subseteq OI(eo_1)$, and each token visit is with the latest begin time among other token visits of the corresponding object, e.g., tv_1 is the only (and thus the latest) token visit of $T1$.

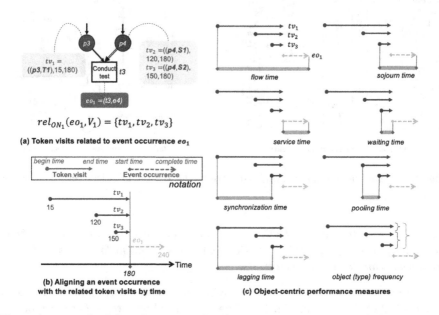

Fig. 3. An example of the token visits related to an event occurrence and object-centric performance measures of the event occurrence.

A measurement function computes a performance measure of an event occurrence by using the related token visits.

Defintion 8 (Measurement). *Let ON be an object-centric Petri net. measure ∈ $O_{ON} \times \mathcal{P}(V_{ON}) \to \mathbb{R}$ is a function mapping an event occurrence and its related token visits to a performance value. $\mathbb{U}_m$ denotes the set of all such functions.*

In this paper, we introduce seven functions to compute object-centric performance measures as shown in Fig. 3(c). With L an OCEL, ON an OCPN, and $(O, V) = replay_{ON}(L)$, we introduce the functions with formal definitions and examples as below:

– *flow ∈ $\mathbb{U}_m$ computes flow time. Formally, for any $eo = (t, e) \in O$, $flow(eo, V)$ $= \pi_{ct}(e) - min(T)$ with $T = \{\pi_{bt}(tv) \mid tv \in rel_{ON}(eo, V)\}$.*

- $sojourn \in \mathbb{U}_m$ computes *sojourn time*. Formally, for any $eo = (t, e) \in O$, $sojourn(eo, V) = \pi_{ct}(e) - max(T)$ with $T = \{\pi_{bt}(tv) \mid tv \in rel_{ON}(eo, V)\}$.
- $wait \in \mathbb{U}_m$ computes *waiting time*. Formally, for any $eo = (t, e) \in O$, $wait(eo, V) = \pi_{st}(e) - max(T)$ with $T = \{\pi_{bt}(tv) \mid tv \in rel_{ON}(eo, V)\}$.
- $service \in \mathbb{U}_m$ computes *service time*. Formally, for any $eo = (t, e) \in O$, $service(eo, V) = \pi_{ct}(e) - \pi_{st}(e)$.
- $sync \in \mathbb{U}_m$ computes *synchronization time*. Formally, for any $eo = (t, e) \in O$, $sync(eo, V) = max(T) - min(T)$ with $T = \{\pi_{bt}(tv) \mid tv \in rel_{ON}(eo, V)\}$.
- $pool_{ot} \in \mathbb{U}_m$ computes *pooling time* w.r.t. object type ot. Formally, for any $eo = (t, e) \in O$, $pool_{ot}(eo, V) = max(T) - min(T)$ with $T = \{\pi_{bt}(tv) \mid tv \in rel_{ON}(eo, V) \wedge type(\pi_{oi}(tv)) = ot\}$.
- $lag_{ot} \in \mathbb{U}_m$ computes *lagging time* w.r.t. object type ot. Formally, for any $eo=(t, e) \in O$, $lag_{ot}(eo, V) = max(T') - min(T)$ with $T = \{\pi_{bt}(tv) \mid tv \in rel_{ON}(eo, V)\}$ and $T' = \{\pi_{bt}(tv) \mid tv \in rel_{ON}(eo, V) \wedge type(\pi_{oi}(tv)) \neq ot\}$ if $max(T') > min(T)$. 0 otherwise.

5   Case Study

The approach discussed in Sect. 4 has been fully implemented as a web application with a dedicated user interface. Using the implementation, we conduct a case study on a real-life loan application process of a Dutch Financial Institute[2]. Two object types exist in the process: *application* and *offer*. An application can have one or more offers. First, a customer creates an application by visiting the bank or using an online system. In the former case, *submit* activity is skipped. After the completion and acceptance of the application, the bank offers loans to the customer by sending the offer to the customer and making a call. An offer is either accepted or canceled.

In this case study, we focus on the offers canceled due to various reasons. We filter infrequent behaviors by selecting the ten most frequent types of process executions. Moreover, we remove redundant activities, e.g., status updates such as *Completed* after *Complete application*. The resulting event log, available at Github repository, contains $20,478$ events by $1,682$ applications and $3,573$ offers.

First, we compare our approach to a traditional technique for performance analysis based on alignments [5]. To apply the traditional technique, we first flatten the log using the application and offer as a case notion. Figure 4(a) shows the performance analysis results from *Inductive Visual Miner* in *ProM* framework. As shown in ①, $1,799$ applications repeat activity *Send*. In reality, as shown in $\boxed{1}$, no repetition occurs while the activity is conducted once for each offer except 92 offers skipping it. Furthermore, the average sojourn time for the activity is computed as around 2 days and 23 h, whereas, in reality, it is around 15 minutes as shown in $\boxed{1}$.

---

[2] doi.org/10.4121/uuid:3926db30-f712-4394-aebc-75976070e91f.

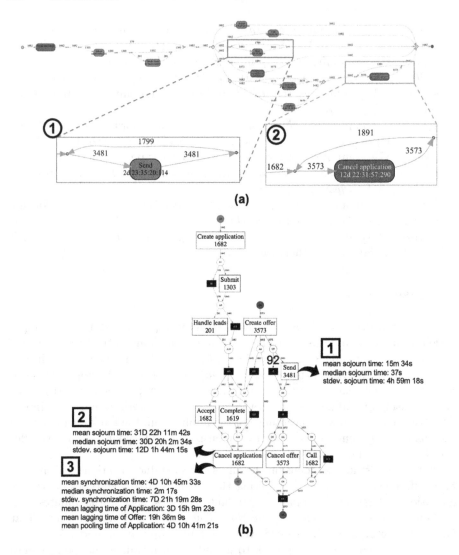

Fig. 4. (a) Performance analysis results based on *Inductive Visual Miner* in *ProM* framework and (b) Performance analysis results based on our proposed approach.

Furthermore, ② shows that activity *Cancel application* is repeated 1891 times, but it occurs, in reality, 1,682 times for each application, as depicted in ②. In addition, the average sojourn time for the activity is measured as around 12 days and 22 h, but in fact, it is around 31 days and 22 h, as shown in ②.

Next, we analyze the newly-introduced object-centric performance measures, including synchronization, lagging, and pooling time. As described in ③, the average synchronization time of activity *Cancel application* is around 4 days and 11 h. Moreover, the average lagging time of *applications* is 3 days and 15 h and the lagging time of *offers* is 19 h, i.e., *offers* are more severely lagging *applications*. Furthermore, the pooling time of *offers* is almost the same as the synchronization time, indicating that the application is ready to be cancelled almost at the same time as the first offer, and the second offer is ready in around 4 days and 11 h.

6 Conclusion

In this paper, we proposed an approach to object-centric performance analysis. To that end, we first replay OCELs on OCPNs to couple events to process models, producing event occurrences and token visits. Next, we measure object-centric performance metrics per event occurrence by using the corresponding token visits of the event occurrence. We have implemented the approach as a web application and conducted a case study using a real-life loan application process.

The proposed approach has several limitations. First, our approach relies on the quality of the discovered process model. Discovering process models that can be easily interpreted and comprehensively reflect the reality is a remaining challenge. Second, non-conforming behavior in event data w.r.t. a process model can lead to misleading insights. As future work, we plan to extend the approach to support reliable performance analysis of non-conforming event logs. Moreover, we plan to develop an approach to object-centric performance analysis based on event data independently from process models.

References

1. van der Aalst, W.M.P.: Process Mining, 2nd edn. Springer, Heidelberg (2016). https://doi.org/10.1007/978-3-662-49851-4
2. van der Aalst, W.M.P., Adriansyah, A., van Dongen, B.F.: Replaying history on process models for conformance checking and performance analysis. WIREs Data Mining Knowl. Discov. **2**(2), 182–192 (2012)
3. van der Aalst, W.M.P., Berti, A.: Discovering object-centric petri nets. Fundam. Informaticae **175**(1–4), 1–40 (2020)
4. Adams, J.N., van der Aalst, W.M.P.: Precision and fitness in object-centric process mining. In: ICPM 2021, pp. 128–135 (2021)
5. Adriansyah, A.: Aligning observed and modeled behavior. Ph.D. thesis, Mathematics and Computer Science (2014)
6. Adriansyah, A., van Dongen, B., Piessens, D., Wynn, M., Adams, M.: Robust performance analysis on YAWL process models with advanced constructs. J. Inf. Technol. Theory Appl. **12**(3), 5–26 (2011)
7. Bayomie, D., Ciccio, C.D., Rosa, M.L., Mendling, J.: A probabilistic approach to event-case correlation for process mining. In: ER 2019, pp. 136–152 (2019)
8. Denisov, V., Fahland, D., van der Aalst, W.M.P.: Unbiased, fine-grained description of processes performance from event data. In: Weske, M., Montali, M., Weber, I., vom Brocke, J. (eds.) BPM 2018. LNCS, vol. 11080, pp. 139–157. Springer, Cham (2018). https://doi.org/10.1007/978-3-319-98648-7_9

9. Esser, S., Fahland, D.: Multi-dimensional event data in graph databases. J. Data Semant. **10**(1–2), 109–141 (2021)
10. Ghahfarokhi, A.F., Park, G., Berti, A., van der Aalst, W.M.P.: OCEL. In: Bellatreche, L., et al. (eds.) SIMPDA 2021, pp. 169–175 (2021)
11. Hornix, P.T.: Performance analysis of business processes through process mining. Master's thesis, Mathematics and Computer Science (2007)
12. Leemans, S.J.J., Poppe, E., Wynn, M.T.: Directly follows-based process mining: exploration & a case study. In: ICPM 2019, pp. 25–32 (2019)
13. Maté, A., Trujillo, J., Mylopoulos, J.: Conceptualizing and specifying key performance indicators in business strategy models. In: ER 2012, pp. 282–291 (2012)
14. Rogge-Solti, A., Weske, M.: Prediction of remaining service execution time using stochastic petri nets with arbitrary firing delays. In: ICSOC, pp. 389–403 (2013)

Quality and Performance

Bidirectional Relation Attention for Entity Alignment Based on Graph Convolutional Network

Yayao Zuo$^{(\boxtimes)}$, Minghao Zhan, Yang Zhou, and Peilin Zhan

Guangdong University of Technology, Guangzhou, China
yyzuo@gdut.edu.cn

Abstract. Entity alignment is an effective solution to integrate resources from different knowledge graphs (KGs). It aims to establish link between entities in different KGs that refer to the same object in the real world. Most of the existing embedding-based methods embed entities and relations into the same vector space or utilize a graph neural network (GNN) for nodes aggregation to learn the topology of the KG. However, these approaches do not sufficiently distinguish the effects of different relations on node features and ignore the dependencies between relations and entities. Some latent semantic information hidden in the relations is underutilized. This paper proposes a bidirectional relation attention mechanism to jointly learn entity and relation embeddings. We employ a graph convolutional network (GCN) to obtain the structure embedding for the KGs, then the attention mechanism used in relation embeddings facilitates the flow of information from entities to relations and strengthen the dependency between them. Finally the relation attention exploited in the aggregation stage integrates both direction information and connected relation semantics of neighborhoods that capture different impacts of relation on the neighborhood nodes. Experiments conducted on the DBP15K dataset validate the effectiveness of our proposed model and show that our model outperforms the baseline methods.

Keywords: Knowledge graph · Entity alignment · Graph convolutional neural network · Relation attention

1 Introduction

Knowledge graph (KG) is a large-scale semantic network which was first proposed by Google in 2012 of which original intention is to improve the ability of search engines. Due to the powerful semantic expression ability, it has been also applied to the field of conceptual modeling where KG is used to assist users in semantic search to obtain entity information [1]. However, because the data for constructing KGs derives from different resources, the same entity may have different representations in different KGs. Entity alignment provides a solution to the problem above. It aims to discovery entity pairs that refer to the same

J. Ralyté et al. (Eds.): ER 2022, LNCS 13607, pp. 295–309, 2022.
https://doi.org/10.1007/978-3-031-17995-2_21

object in two knowledge graphs based on heterogeneous resources and establish links between them.

In recent years, methods based on representation learning have been widely used in entity alignment researches. It embeds entities into a low-dimensional vector space and retains rich semantic information between entities at the same time. These methods are divided into translation models and graph neural network based models. Among them, most of the translation models rely on TransE [2]. However, the limitation in dealing with complex relations restrains the efficiency of TransE. To this end, based on TransE, some extended models such as TransH [19], TransD [5], and TransR [6] have been subsequently proposed to exploit complex relation information between entities from multiple perspectives.

In contrast, methods based on graph convolutional network (GCN) embed an entity by aggregating the neighborhood information and utilize propagation rules to capture the structure of the entire graph. However, GCN-based embedding methods merely consider the topology of the knowledge graph while ignore the semantic information of relations between entities, so the relation embeddings make little progress to entity representations. Some GCN-based models [15, 16, 21, 22, 24, 25] have tried a bunch of different approaches to represent relations, but GCN still lacks in dealing with multi-relational graphs and these methods fail to capture the dependencies between entities and relations. On the other hand, GCN employs a shared parameter matrix in the unified feature transformation for all nodes, so it cannot distinguish the importance of different relations on entity features during the neighborhood nodes aggregation. Graph attention network (GAT) [18] boosts GCN in neighborhood information aggregation to some extent. It assigns different weights to one-hot neighbors to aggregate information, but the calculation of attention weight is dependent on the characteristics of each node. GAT ignores the relation edges that are directly connected between nodes. In addition, the existing relation representation methods have poor ability to deal with 1-to-N or N-to-N relationships. As shown in Fig. 1 (a), in a 1-to-N or N-to-N relationship, an entity may have the same relation with different entities. We cannot directly predict the tail entity according to the head entity and the relation. Therefore, when we represent a relation, we should not simply average the representations of head entities and tail entities related to it but should assign different weights to the triples under the same relation. In this case, a pair of head and tail entity that are more closely related under the same relation will have a higher weight in the relation representation. At the same time, most of the existing GCN-based methods for KGs alignment focus on embedding nodes and relations in a simple undirected graph, so they cannot capture the effect of the transmitting direction of the relation on entity features.

However, the Knowledge Graph is a graph structure with complex relations. As shown in Fig. 1(b), each entity is connected to several neighbor nodes through different relation edges. The information of the neighbor nodes is transmitted along the direction from the head entity to the tail entity. In order to make full use of relational information to improve the representation of an entity, we need to not only learn the relation types, but also leverage the contextual information hidden in the direction of relations. For example, in Fig. 1, there is a 'succession' relation between 'Trump' and 'Biden'. We can infer that there is also a 'predecessor' relation between them (labeled with dashed lines in the figure). For the same relation triple, its contextual semantics for the head entity and the tail entity are different.

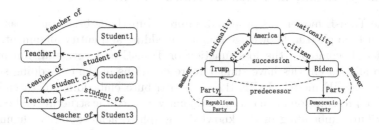

(a) 1-to-N and N-to-N relations   (b) bidirectional relation example in KG

Fig. 1. Relation examples in KG

In this paper, we put forward a novel entity alignment model BiRA-GCN (Bidirectional Relation Attention GCN) that applies an attention mechanism in relation edges to enhance the semantic representation of entities. Each relation embedding is the weighted summary of the attention weights of the triples associated with it. At the same time, we improve the general GAT in which semantic information of relation is put into the calculation of attention weight in the neighbor nodes aggregation stage. Therefore, the feature of an entity not only aggregates the characteristic of its neighbor nodes, but also integrates the relation information connected to its neighbors. To extract the importance of relational direction information in entity alignment, inspired by compGCN [17], we introduce inverse edges to extend the relations in the KGs, which distinguishes the relation edges with direction features during aggregation. The main contributions of this paper are as follows:

- Proposes a relation attention mechanism to jointly learn entity and relation embeddings based on GCN. Enhanced dependency between entities and relations applied with relation attention in relation embedding and neighbor aggregation improves the representations of 1-to-N or N-to-N relations and strengthens the relation information in entity representation. Each entity not only aggregates the features of its neighbor nodes but also directly captures the relation semantics.
- Extends the relation attention from an undirected graph to a directed graph, which enhances the ability of GCN to learn directional features of relations and actually enriches the representation of an entity.

– Experiments on the benchmark datasets validate the effectiveness of our proposed model and show that our model outperforms the baselines in multiple metrics including MRR and Hits@K.

2   Related Work

2.1   Entity Alignment Based on Translation Models

Since the TransE model was proposed, improved methods based on it has been continuously applied in knowledge graph embedding and entity alignment. The JE model [4] combines the loss function of TransE and entity alignment, so that two aligned entities have similar representations in the embedding space. Based on the JE model, JAPE [12] adds attribute embedding to extend the semantic representation of an entity, and jointly learned the structure embedding and attribute embedding of the knowledge graph to achieve entity alignment. MtransE [3] embeds the structures of two knowledge graphs in different spaces and establishes a mapping between the two embeddings. IPTransE [11] employs a shared parameters approach to embed entities and relations in two KGs into the same vector space, and adopts an iterative training strategy for entity alignment. BootEA [13] proposes a bootstrapping iterative strategy to add possible aligned entities to the training data for further optimizing knowledge graph embedding.

2.2   Entity Alignment Based on GCN

Benefiting from the excellent performance in modeling graph data, graph convolutional neural networks (GCN) and its extensions have been widely used in recent entity alignment research. GCN-Align [20] first proposes to apply GCN for entity alignment technique, assuming that the equivalent entities may have similar neighborhood structures so their embeddings are closed to each other. NAEA [26] combines with neighborhood subgraph-level information of entities and employs an attention mechanism to exploit different impacts of their neighbors' representations. NMN [23] also learns the neighborhood structure of entities on the basis of GCN, then uses a sampling strategy for neighbor nodes to calculate the similarity of neighbor subgraphs so that the similarity between two entities can be transformed into the similarity of their neighbor subgraphs. Wu et al. [21] proposes a relation-sensitive dual graph convolutional neural networks (RDGCN) that integrates relation information through the close interaction between the original graph and its dual relational graph and further captures adjacent structures to learn a better entity representation. RAGA [27] takes account of multiple relations between two entities, which inspires us to explore the representations of 1-to-N and N-to-N relations and further improve the representations of complex relations in different situations. But it does not exploit the latent direction information hidden in an inverse relation. RE-GCN [25] considers the direction of relations. It constructs a triadic graph that represents the primal relation triples in KGs. But RE-GCN ignores the reverse relations in primal KGs so that the direction information only deliver from the primal head entity to the tail. HGCN [22] proposes a joint relation embedding and entity embedding learning framework for entity alignment. It firstly approximates the representation of each relation by the head and tail entity in the triple, and then employs a set of joint pre-aligned entities and relations to optimize the embedding of an entity. MRAEA [8] designs a meta relation aware representation to exploit the meta semantics of relations for entities, which inspires us to incorporate relation semantics in the neighborhood information aggregation.

3 Methodology

In this section, we introduce our proposed BiRA-GCN model. We will first define the problem formulation of knowledge graph and then illustrate the component of BiRA-GCN in detail. The framework of BiRA-GCN is shown in Fig. 2.

3.1 Problem Formulation

The knowledge graph can be defined as $G = (E, R, T)$ and E, R, T represent entity set, relation set and triple set respectively. Each triple can be described as $\{(u, r, v)|u, v \in E, r \in R, (u, r, v) \in T\}$, where u and v represent the head entity and tail entity respectively, and r is the relation between u and v. To introduce an inverse relation, we need to extend the triples in G. For each triple (u, r, v) in G, there is a reverse relation r^{-1} and a reverse triple (v, u, r^{-1}), we respectively expand R and T to R' and T', where $R' = R \cup R^{-1}$, $R^{-1} = \{r^{-1}|r \in R\}$, $T' = T \cup \{(u, r^{-1}, v)|(u, r, v) \in T\}$.

For two different knowledge graphs $G_1 = (E_1, R_1, T_1)$ and $G_2 = (E_2, R_2, T_2)$, we define some already aligned entities as seed set $S = \{(e_1, e_2)|e_1 \in E_1, e_2 \in E_2\}$, where (e_1, e_2) is a pair of equivalent entities that represent the same object in the real world. The task of entity alignment is to find more equivalent entity pairs in G_1 and G_2 given a pre-aligned entity seed set S.

3.2 Model Architecture

Based on GCN, the BiRA-GCN model incorporates bidirectional relation attention to learn the representation of relations and entities, which makes full use of the dependency between entities and relations to enhance their feature representations. As shown in Fig. 2, our model from left to right are GCN-based structure embedding module, relation embedding module, bidirectional relation-attention-based aggregation module and entity alignment module respectively.

First, we input the knowledge graph into GCN to learn the neighborhood structure of nodes. Then BiRA-GCN employs the attention mechanism to calculate the attention weight of each triple (u, r, v) about r and generate the final relation representation. After introducing the inverse relation r^{-1}, aggregation module employs the relation attention mechanism to focus on the incoming and outgoing directions of the relation and calculates the attention weight for each edge which is connected to the entity. The joint embedding based on bidirectional relation attention not only aggregates local relation semantics at the neighborhood level, but also learns the latent contextual information from relational directions. Finally, the entity features aggregated with relation information are used as the final vector representation and are input to the entity alignment module for training.

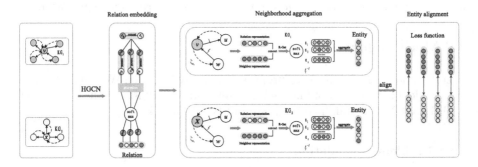

Fig. 2. The components of BiRA-GCN from left to right are respectively the KG structure embedding module, the relation embedding module, the aggregation module and the alignment module.

3.3   KG Structure Embedding Based on GCN

For the basic neighborhood structure of each node in the knowledge graph, we firstly initialize the entity representation with pre-trained word embeddings, and then input all triples in the two KGs into GCN to obtain the structural features. This module consists of multiple GCN layers that utilize a forward propagation to update the node features. The input of each layer of GCN is a representation matrix $X^{init} = \{x_1, x_2, ..., x_n | x_i \in R^d\}$, where d represents the embedding dimension of the entity. The forward propagation between GCN layers is shown in Eq. (1):

$$X^{(l+1)} = \sigma(\tilde{D}^{-\frac{1}{2}} \tilde{A} \tilde{D}^{-\frac{1}{2}} X^{(l)} W^{(l)}) \tag{1}$$

where $\tilde{A}$ represents the Laplacian matrix converted from the adjacency matrix of knowledge graph G and $\tilde{D}$ is the degree matrix.

In order to reduce the influence of noise propagation between layers of GCN on the neighborhood information aggregation, similar to the previous work [9, 22], we apply a highway gates mechanism [10] in the GCN, as shown in (2) and (3):

$$T(X^{(l)}) = \sigma(X^{(l)} W_T^{(l)} + b_T^{(l)})) \tag{2}$$

$$X^{(l+1)} = T(X^{(l)}) \cdot X^{(l+1)} + X^{(l)} \cdot (1 - T(X^{(l)})) \tag{3}$$

where $X^{(l)}$ is the input of the $l+1$ layer; σ is the sigmoid function; $\cdot$ represents element-wise multiplication; $W_T^{(l)}$ and $b_T^{(l)}$ respectively represent the bias vector of the weight matrix and the transform gate $T(X^{(l)})$.

3.4   Relation Embedding

In a knowledge graph, the relation between entities is represented by triples, but GCN is insensitive to relation information. In order to improve the representation of 1-to-N or N-to-N relations, we introduce an attention mechanism to assign different weights to each triple associated with the same relation, so we can exploit those pairs of head and tail entities that are more closely related under the same relation.

For each relation r_k, this module takes the set $S_k = \{(e_{h1}, e_{t1}), ..., (e_{hn}, e_{tn})\}$ as input, which includes the head and tail entities of triples associated with the relation r_k, where n is the number of triples corresponding to r_k. We first take r_k^0, the average summation of the head entity and the tail entity, as the initial vector representation of the relation r_k. Then the attention mechanism is introduced to focus on the head entity e_h and the tail entity e_t connected by r_k. Since the feature dimensions of entities and relations are different, it is necessary to operate a linear transformation for the feature vectors after concatenating the head entity and the tail entity. The concatenating feature vector will be operated with the attention to calculate the attention weight for each triple (e_i, r_k, e_j) with respect to r_k. So the output vector r_k^{out} of relation r_k can be represented as an attention weighted summation of the triples:

$$r_k^0 = \frac{\sum_{i=1}^{n} e_{hi} + e_{ti}}{n} \tag{4}$$

$$m_{h,t} = LeakyRelu(v^T[r_k^0, W^r[x_i, x_j]]) \tag{5}$$

$$\alpha_{ijk} = soft\max(m_{ij}) = \frac{\exp(m_{ij})}{\sum_{e_i, r_k, e_j) \in T_k} \exp(m_{ij})} \tag{6}$$

$$r_k^{out} = Relu(r_k^0 + \sum_{(e_i, r_k, e_j) \in T_k} \alpha_{ijk} W^r[x_i, x_j]) \tag{7}$$

where T_k represents the triple set of relation r_k; $v^T \in R^{2d_r}$ is a specific shared weight vector; $W^r \in R^{2d_e \times d_r}$ is a linear transfer matrix that maps head and tail entities from entity feature space to relation feature space; $[,]$ indicates the concatenating operation for the vectors.

3.5   Bidirectional Relation Aggregation

In the graph neural network (GNN), the representation of each node is implemented by the aggregation operation. But GNN is not able to distinguish the importance of different neighborhoods to the nodes. Although the graph attention network (GAT) pays attention to the neighbors' characteristics to calculate the attention coefficient, it ignores the useful relation information. So we propose that in the aggregation stage, neighborhood features should be combined with those relative relations that expand the latent semantic information for entities.

We utilize the relation embeddings learned in Sect. 4.4 to compute the attention coefficients of each relation r_k for the entity e_i through relation attention mechanism, so the relation features of r_k and its corresponding neighbor nodes e_j would be aggregated into the entity representation of e_i. Taking into account the direction of the relation edge, we introduce the directional weight matrix $W(dir)$ of the relation r during aggregation, which is used to learn the incoming and outcoming relation direction:

$$\alpha_{ijk} = \frac{\exp(Leak\,\mathrm{Re}\,lu(a^T[W_{dir(r)}r_k, x_j]))}{\sum_{r_k \in R_{ij}} \exp(Leak\,\mathrm{Re}\,lu(a^T[W_{dir(r)}r_k, x_j]))} \tag{8}$$

$$x_i^{out} = \mathrm{Re}\,lu(\sum_{r_k \in R_{ij}} \alpha_{ijk}[W_{dir}r_k, x_j]) \tag{9}$$

$$W_{dir(r)} = \begin{cases} W_{out}, r \in r_{out} \\ W_{in}, r \in r_{in} \end{cases} \tag{10}$$

α_{ijk} represents the attention weight of neighbor node e_j connected to the entity e_i through the relation r_k; $v'^T \in R^{d_r+d_e}$ is another specific shared vector for attention weight; R_{ij} represents the set of relations between e_i and neighbor nodes and x_j is the representation of neighbor node e_j corresponding to the relation r_k. For each entity e_i, its relation in the knowledge graph can be divided into two types according to the direction. When e_i is the head entity, it is interpreted as active relation r_{out} and the connected node e_j is called the outgoing neighbor; otherwise, when e_i is the tail entity, it is interpreted as passive relation r_{in} and the corresponding neighbor node is called the incoming neighbor. Therefore, we can choose different direction weight matrices $W(dir)$ according to the direction of r_k.

3.6   Entity Alignment

After aggregating the neighborhood information, the final output feature matrix of the nodes can be represented as $X^{out} = \{x_1^{out}, x_2^{out}, ..., x_n^{out} | x_i^{out} \in R^d\}$. Then entity alignment is implemented by measuring the distance between the two entities in the embedding space. The distance for two entities e_i and e_j is computed as follows:

$$dis(e_i, e_j) = ||x_i^{out} - x_j^{out}||_{L_1} \tag{11}$$

In the training stage, the entities and relations in the two knowledge graphs have been embedded into the same continuous low-dimensional vector space, and a set of pre-aligned entity seeds are input as training data. The training goal of entity alignment is to force the embedding distance between two equivalent entities to be as close as possible while those non-equivalent entities should be far away from each other. Therefore, this paper uses a loss function based on edge ranking for training:

$$\sum_{(p,q)\in S} \sum_{(p',q')\in S'} \max\{0, d(p,q) - d(p',q') + \gamma\} \tag{12}$$

$\gamma > 0$ represents the margin hyperparameter; S represents the pre-aligned seed set, and S' is the set of negative sample entities selected according to the nearest neighbor sampling method.

4   Experiments

4.1   Datasets

We conduct experiment on the DBP15K [12] dataset. DBP15K is a cross-lingual entity alignment dataset constructed from DBpedia that refers to four languages: Chinese, English, Japanese and French. It contains three subsets including zh-en (Chinese-English), ja-en (Japanese-English) and fr-en (French-English). Each subset contains 15000 pairs of pre-aligned entities. The statistics in the three datasets are shown in Table 1. For experiments, we follow the previous researches and use 30% of the pre-aligned entity pairs as training data and 70% for testing.

Table 1. Statistic of DBP15K Dataset.

Dataset		Ents	Rels	Triples
zh-en	Chinese	66,469	2,830	153,929
	English	98,125	2,317	237,674
ja-en	Japanese	65,744	2,043	164,373
	English	95,680	2,096	233,319
fr-en	French	66,858	1,379	192,191
	English	105,889	2,209	278,590

4.2   Experimental Settings

Evaluation Metrics. In accordance with the previous researches, Hits@k and mean reciprocal rank (MRR) are used for the evaluation metrics in our experiment. Hits@k represents the proportion of correctly aligned entities appearing in the top k list. MRR calculates the mean of the reciprocal rank values of all correctly aligned entities. The higher Hits@k and MRR, the better performance of the entity alignment model.

Parameter Settings. The hyper-parameters used in our experiments are set as followed: the depth of GCNs $l = 2$, the dimension of relation $d_r = 100$, margin $\gamma = 3$, the learning rate is 0.001 and we sample $K = 10$ negative pairs every 10 epochs.

Baselines. For comparable models, our experiments choose some classical and recent methods as the baselines, which can be divided into the following two categories:

- translation-based methods: MTransE [3] embeds the structure of two KGs in different spaces and learns a transition. IPTransE [11] utilizes the sharing parameters to encode entities and relations in the two KGs into the same vector space. JAPE [12] adds attribute embedding to extend the semantic representation of entities. BootEA [13] uses a bootstrapping strategy in training. TransEdge [14] proposes an edge-centric embedding model to capture fine-grained relation semantics.
- GCN-based methods: GCN-Align [20] combines entity and relation embedding with additional attribute embedding. RDGCN [21] constructs a dual relation graph for interactive learning of entity and relation embeddings. HGCN-JE [22] integrates entity alignment with relation alignment during the training process. NMN [23] utilizes a graph sampling method to extract a discriminative neighborhood for each entity. MRAEA [8] models the meta semantics embedded in relations. AttrGNN [7] uses an attributed value encoder to model the various types of attribute triples for enhanced entity representations.

4.3 Main Results

As can be seen from Table 2, compared with other methods, our model BiRA-GCN that integrates bidirectional relation attention mechanism gets a performance improvement on the ja-en and fr-en datasets. Specifically, on those two datasets BiRA-GCN achieves at least 5.15% and 1.23% respectively on Hits@1. Although on the zh-en dataset our model is merely 0.2% higher on Hits@1 than AttrGCN, it still outperforms the rest of the comparable models.

In Table 2, the models are divided into two categories according to their embedding fashions. We conclude that there is no obvious difference between the two methods in learning knowledge graph embeddings. GCN has advantages in learning the global structure of KG while variant TransE models are proficient in capturing local semantics so some of them have comparable performances. Among translation-based methods, TransEdge obtains the best performance on Hits@1 and Hits@10. That is because TransEdge represents relations with contextualized embeddings and interprets the edge embeddings as translations between entities to preserve KG structure. This enables it to have superiority in modeling complex relational structures and outperform other translaiton-based methods. BootEA's performance ranks second among the translaiton-based methods, which explains the effectiveness of the bootstrapping strategy to add possible pre-aligned entities for training.

Table 2. Comparatie experiment results

	zh-en			ja-en			fr-en		
	H@1	H@10	MRR	H@1	H@10	MRR	H@1	H@10	MRR
MTransE	30.83	61.41	0.364	27.86	57.45	0.349	24.41	55.55	0.335
IPTransE	40.60	73.50	0.516	36.70	69.30	0.474	33.30	68.50	0.451
JAPE	41.18	74.46	0.490	36.25	68.50	0.476	32.39	66.68	0.430
BootEA	62.94	84.75	0.703	62.23	85.39	0.701	65.30	87.44	0.731
TransEdge	73.50	91.90	0.801	71.90	93.20	0.795	71.0	94.10	0.796
GCN-Align	41.25	74.38	0.549	39.31	74.46	0.546	37.29	74.49	0.532
RDGCN	70.75	84.55	0.746	76.74	89.54	0.813	88.64	95.72	0.917
HGCN-JE	72.03	85.70	0.768	76.62	89.73	0.813	89.16	96.11	0.917
NMN	73.30	86.90	0.781	78.50	91.20	0.827	90.20	96.70	0.924
MRAEA	75,70	**92.98**	0.827	75.78	93.38	0.826	78.04	94.81	0.849
AttrGNN	79.60	92.93	**0.845**	78.33	92.08	0.834	91.85	97.77	0.910
Ours	**79.70**	91.45	0.841	**83.65**	**93.97**	**0.875**	**93.08**	**97.85**	**0.949**

Among GCN-based methods, AttrGNN obtains the best results on DBP15K dataset. The primary reason for its performance is the usage of additional attributes and values that partition the KG into subgraphs according to different types of attribute triples. Nevertheless, we find that the remaining GCN-based methods (RDGCN, HGCN-JE, NMN and MRAEA) which ignore the additional attribute information also obtain good results. All of them outperform the translation-based methods except TransEdge on Hits@1, Hits@10 and MRR. Their competitive performances demonstrate neighborhood features is essential for the entity alignment accuracy.

Although the current GCN-based methods have made significant progress compared with those classical methods above, our model still represents a more competitive performance. In the same case of without extra attribute information, our model obtains remarkable improvement on the DBP15K with an average increase of 4.14% on Hits@1 and 3.40% on MRR compared with other GCN-based models(RDGCN, HGCN-JE, NMN and MRAEA). Even compared to the AttrGNN model, our model outperforms it on the ja-en and fr-en dataset with a higher alignment accuracy. We believe that is because our bidirectional realtion attention that has never been used in other GCN-based methods plays a vital role in the neighborhood informaiton aggregation. This enables the GCN to overcome the weakness in learning semantic information in relations and enables our model to preserve global structure and local semantic information of KGs, which exactly strengthens the representaion of an entity and improve the alignment accuracy.

4.4   Ablation Experiment

In order to verify the effect of incorporating the bidirectional relational attention mechanism on the representation of entity features, we conduct ablation experiments based on HGCN, and design different model configurations to verify the effectiveness of the method proposed in this paper. The results of the ablation experiments are shown in Table 3.

Table 3. Ablation experiment results

	zh-en			ja-en			fr-en		
	H@1	H@10	MRR	H@1	H@10	MRR	H@1	H@10	MRR
HGCN-Based	67.21	80.33	0.719	73.87	85.69	0.782	88.24	94.32	0.905
HGCN-GAT	77.28	89.75	0.818	81.55	92.56	0.856	91.85	97.27	0.940
HGCN-RGAT	79.14	91.17	0.836	83.48	93.57	0.873	92.71	97.72	0.946
BiRA-GCN	**79.70**	**91.45**	**0.841**	**83.65**	**93.97**	**0.875**	**93.08**	**97.85**	**0.949**

Model Variants. We design the following model variants for the ablation experiments:

- HGCN-Based: Representing the initial structure embedding model designed in Sect. 3.3, which adds a highway gate mechanism on the basic of GCN layer.
- HGCN-GAT: Integrating the ordinary graph attention network to aggregate neighborhood information on the basic of HGCN-Based. Notice that in order to distinguish from relation attention mechanism, the HGCN-GAT here does not aggregate the relation semantics between entities and their neighborhood nodes.
- HGCN–RGAT: The ordinary graph attention network is replaced with relation attention and the semantics of relations from neighborhood nodes are integrated into the entity features.
- BiRA-GCN: Expanding the edges in the KGs to bidirectional and integrating the directional features of the edges during aggregation.

As illustrated in the Table 3, on the basis of HGCN, all the metrics(Hits@1, Hits@10 and MRR) of entity alignment have been consistently improved after incorporating graph attention, relation attention and bidirectional relation attention in turn. Among them, the BiRA-GCN achieves the best result on the three metrics.

Compared with HGCN-Based, HGCN-GAT has an average increase of 7.12% on Hits@1 and 6.41% on Hits@10 in the DBP15K dataset, which obviously demonstrates the advantages of the graph attention network in aggregating the entity neighborhood structure. After replacing the ordinary graph attention with the relation attention, the performance of entity alignment further improves as the Hit@1 and Hit@10 increase by an average of 1.55% and 0.96% respectively. The improvement of HGCN-RGAT verifies the effectiveness of relational semantics in the neighborhood information aggregation. BiRA-GCN further expands the direction of relations in KGs so that it achieves an average increase of 0.37% on Hits@1 and 0.27% on Hits@10 compared with HGCN-GAT. Although the improvement is not significant, we find that all the metrics of BIRA-GCN are always higher than those of HGCN-GAT on the three datasets. This indicates that in addition to the type of relations, the direction information also plays a certain role in modeling relation semantics for entity alignment.

5   Conclusion

This paper proposes a graph convolutional network (GCN) entity alignment model cooperated with bidirectional relation attention mechanism. The model uses graph convolutional neural network to embed entities and relations in knowledge graph to learn the global structure of KGs. In order to enhance the ability of GCN to learn relational semantics, we enrich the neighborhood features of entities by introducing relation attention mechanism to focus on the edges connected among entities. The model also extends the direction of the edges in KGs thus incorporating the relations with directional characteristics and expanding the hidden semantic expression in relations. Experiments on the DBP15K dataset demonstrates the model proposed in this paper represents a more competitive performance than the current entity alignment methods and different model variants designed in the ablation experiments validate the effectiveness of bidirectional relation attention mechanism.

Acknowledgements. The research is supported by The Natural Science Foundation of Guangdong Province (No.2018A030313934).

References

1. Bernasconi, A., Canakoglu, A., Ceri, S.: From a conceptual model to a knowledge graph for genomic datasets. In: Laender, A.H.F., Pernici, B., Lim, E.-P., de Oliveira, J.P.M. (eds.) ER 2019. LNCS, vol. 11788, pp. 352–360. Springer, Cham (2019). https://doi.org/10.1007/978-3-030-33223-5_29
2. Bordes, A., Usunier, N., Garcia-Duran, A., Weston, J., Yakhnenko, O.: Translating embeddings for modeling multi-relational data. Adv. Neural Inf. Process. Syst. **26** (2013)
3. Chen, M., Tian, Y., Yang, M., Zaniolo, C.: Multilingual knowledge graph embeddings for cross-lingual knowledge alignment. arXiv preprint arXiv:1611.03954 (2016)
4. Hao, Y., Zhang, Y., He, S., Liu, K., Zhao, J.: A joint embedding method for entity alignment of knowledge bases. In: Chen, H., Ji, H., Sun, L., Wang, H., Qian, T., Ruan, T. (eds.) CCKS 2016. CCIS, vol. 650, pp. 3–14. Springer, Singapore (2016). https://doi.org/10.1007/978-981-10-3168-7_1

5. Ji, G., He, S., Xu, L., Liu, K., Zhao, J.: Knowledge graph embedding via dynamic mapping matrix. In: Proceedings of the 53rd Annual Meeting of the Association for Computational Linguistics and the 7th International Joint Conference on Natural Language Processing, vol. 1: Long Papers, pp. 687–696 (2015)

6. Lin, Y., Liu, Z., Sun, M., Liu, Y., Zhu, X.: Learning entity and relation embeddings for knowledge graph completion. In: Twenty-Ninth AAAI Conference on Artificial Intelligence (2015)

7. Liu, Z., Cao, Y., Pan, L., Li, J., Chua, T.S.: Exploring and evaluating attributes, values, and structures for entity alignment. arXiv preprint arXiv:2010.03249 (2020)

8. Mao, X., Wang, W., Xu, H., Lan, M., Wu, Y.: MRAEA: an efficient and robust entity alignment approach for cross-lingual knowledge graph. In: Proceedings of the 13th International Conference on Web Search and Data Mining, pp. 420–428 (2020)

9. Rahimi, A., Cohn, T., Baldwin, T.: Semi-supervised user geolocation via graph convolutional networks. arXiv preprint arXiv:1804.08049 (2018)

10. Srivastava, R.K., Greff, K., Schmidhuber, J.: Highway networks. arXiv preprint arXiv:1505.00387 (2015)

11. Sun, M., Zhu, H., Xie, R., Liu, Z.: Iterative entity alignment via joint knowledge embeddings. In: International Joint Conference on Artificial Intelligence. AAAI Press (2017)

12. Sun, Z., Hu, W., Li, C.: Cross-lingual entity alignment via joint attribute-preserving embedding. In: d'Amato, C., et al. (eds.) ISWC 2017. LNCS, vol. 10587, pp. 628–644. Springer, Cham (2017). https://doi.org/10.1007/978-3-319-68288-4_37

13. Sun, Z., Hu, W., Zhang, Q., Qu, Y.: Bootstrapping entity alignment with knowledge graph embedding. In: IJCAI, vol. 18, pp. 4396–4402 (2018)

14. Sun, Z., Huang, J., Hu, W., Chen, M., Guo, L., Qu, Y.: TransEdge: translating relation-contextualized embeddings for knowledge graphs. In: Ghidini, C., et al. (eds.) ISWC 2019. LNCS, vol. 11778, pp. 612–629. Springer, Cham (2019). https://doi.org/10.1007/978-3-030-30793-6_35

15. Sun, Z., et al.: Knowledge graph alignment network with gated multi-hop neighborhood aggregation. In: Proceedings of the AAAI Conference on Artificial Intelligence, vol. 34, pp. 222–229 (2020)

16. Tian, J., Li, X., Qiang, C.: Cross-lingual knowledge graph alignment via neighborhood reconstruction network. In: 2021 4th International Conference on Artificial Intelligence and Pattern Recognition, pp. 338–345 (2021)

17. Vashishth, S., Sanyal, S., Nitin, V., Talukdar, P.: Composition-based multi-relational graph convolutional networks. arXiv preprint arXiv:1911.03082 (2019)

18. Veličković, P., Cucurull, G., Casanova, A., Romero, A., Lio, P., Bengio, Y.: Graph attention networks. arXiv preprint arXiv:1710.10903 (2017)

19. Wang, Z., Zhang, J., Feng, J., Chen, Z.: Knowledge graph embedding by translating on hyperplanes. In: Proceedings of the AAAI Conference on Artificial Intelligence, vol. 28 (2014)

20. Wang, Z., Lv, Q., Lan, X., Zhang, Y.: Cross-lingual knowledge graph alignment via graph convolutional networks. In: Proceedings of the 2018 Conference on Empirical Methods in Natural Language Processing, pp. 349–357 (2018)

21. Wu, Y., Liu, X., Feng, Y., Wang, Z., Yan, R., Zhao, D.: Relation-aware entity alignment for heterogeneous knowledge graphs. arXiv preprint arXiv:1908.08210 (2019)

22. Wu, Y., Liu, X., Feng, Y., Wang, Z., Zhao, D.: Jointly learning entity and relation representations for entity alignment. arXiv preprint arXiv:1909.09317 (2019)

23. Wu, Y., Liu, X., Feng, Y., Wang, Z., Zhao, D.: Neighborhood matching network for entity alignment. arXiv preprint arXiv:2005.05607 (2020)
24. Yan, Z., Peng, R., Wang, Y., Li, W.: Soft-self and hard-cross graph attention network for knowledge graph entity alignment. Knowl.-Based Syst. **231**, 107415 (2021)
25. Yang, J., Zhou, W., Wei, L., Lin, J., Han, J., Hu, S.: RE-GCN: relation enhanced graph convolutional network for entity alignment in heterogeneous knowledge graphs. In: Nah, Y., Cui, B., Lee, S.-W., Yu, J.X., Moon, Y.-S., Whang, S.E. (eds.) DASFAA 2020. LNCS, vol. 12113, pp. 432–447. Springer, Cham (2020). https://doi.org/10.1007/978-3-030-59416-9_26
26. Zhu, Q., Zhou, X., Wu, J., Tan, J., Guo, L.: Neighborhood-aware attentional representation for multilingual knowledge graphs. In: IJCAI, pp. 1943–1949 (2019)
27. Zhu, R., Ma, M., Wang, P.: RAGA: relation-aware graph attention networks for global entity alignment. In: Karlapalem, K., et al. (eds.) PAKDD 2021. LNCS (LNAI), vol. 12712, pp. 501–513. Springer, Cham (2021). https://doi.org/10.1007/978-3-030-75762-5_40

A Behavioural Analysis of Metadata Use in Evaluating the Quality of Repurposed Data

Hui Zhou[1]([✉]) [iD], Lei Han[1] [iD], Gianluca Dermatini[1] [iD], Marta Indulska[2] [iD], and Shazia Sadiq[1] [iD]

[1] School of Information Technology and Electrical Engineering, The University of Queensland, Brisbane, QLD, Australia
hui.zhou1@uq.net.au, {l.han,g.demartini}@uq.edu.au, shazia@itee.uq.edu.au
[2] Business School, The University of Queensland, Brisbane, QLD, Australia
m.indulska@business.uq.edu.au

Abstract. Existing approaches for evaluating data quality were established for settings where user requirements regarding data use could be explicitly gathered. Currently, however, users are often faced with new, unfamiliar, and repurposed datasets where they have not been involved in the data collection and creation processes. Furthermore, there is evidence that despite various standardisation initiatives, supporting information or metadata for such datasets is provided in a variety of ways or even lacking altogether. Yet, users need to evaluate the quality of such data to determine if it is suitable for their intended purposes. In this regard, there is limited understanding of the role of metadata in evaluating the quality of repurposed datasets. Thus, in this paper, we aim to investigate how users engage with metadata during data repurposing tasks. In particular, we gather multi-modal user behaviour data through a lab experiment, using eye-tracking techniques and cued-retrospective think-aloud analysis to explore when, how and why users use metadata in such tasks. The results of our study shed light on the critical role metadata plays in evaluating repurposed data, highlight the existence of relationships between data quality error type and metadata, and identify a number of metadata usage patterns relative to the task. This bears implications for the design of systems or tools related to data quality discovery and evaluation.

Keywords: Metadata · Data repurposing · Data quality assessment · Eye-tracking · Think-aloud

1 Introduction

Data is recognised as a valuable asset for governments and organisations [1]. However, poor data quality is detrimental to business and decision-making [2]. Naturally, the study of data quality has gained substantial attention from the industry and academic community [3], within which data quality assessment is a large subset due to the extensive need to evaluate data quality and prepare data for subsequent analytical purposes [4].

© The Author(s), under exclusive license to Springer Nature Switzerland AG 2022
J. Ralyté et al. (Eds.): ER 2022, LNCS 13607, pp. 310–324, 2022.
https://doi.org/10.1007/978-3-031-17995-2_22

Data quality (DQ) assessment follows a top-down approach in the most general case, which includes determining user requirements, data quality measurement, data cleaning, and continuous quality monitoring [5]. However, as data accessibility and sharing increase, these existing DQ assessment approaches are being challenged. This challenge is in particular evident in the context of *data repurposing*, which refers to when data originally collected for a purpose, is used by different users for a different purpose. In this case, the new users have no or little knowledge of the data and its quality characteristics. Existing DQ assessment approaches require metadata, e.g. in the form of conceptual models, data catalogues or database schemas, as a prerequisite, which is often unavailable or at least incomplete for repurposed datasets [5]. As a result, predetermined user requirements and traditional DQ assessment approaches are not sufficient to address the challenge.

Indeed, there is a critical research gap in assessing the quality of repurposed data [6], and recent studies have begun to respond to this need. For instance, [7] proposed a "bottom-up" approach to discover DQ problems for repurposed datasets. Machine learning techniques have also been exploited to conduct data profiling and data preparation tasks at scale [8]. However, full automation of DQ assessment for repurposed data is not feasible because human judgement plays an essential role in monitoring and managing various fitness-for-purpose issues, as well as issues relating to bias, transparency and fairness [9]. To assist human judgement, metadata has been studied and integrated in DQ assessment as a fundamental artifact, often in the form of a conceptual model, to support the evaluation of the quality and fitness of a dataset [10]. For example, prior studies on metadata usage in DQ assessment have shown that metadata can change the outcomes and efficiency in the decision of data usage [11]. Although integrating metadata into the decision process requires additional cognitive load from users, providing relevant and timely metadata generally outweighs these negative impacts [12].

Accordingly, there is a need to understand how users engage with metadata when evaluating repurposed datasets. Understanding this phenomenon is central to developing design guidelines for tools that assist the effective use of repurposed data. For example, open data portals often display minimal metadata (e.g., the creator, number of downloads), which does not effectively support data users' understanding towards the fitness-for-(re)purpose of such a dataset. As a result, data users may spend excessive amounts of time analysing the data only to find that the quality is insufficient and not fit for their purpose. To provide an in-depth understanding of how data users engage with metadata when evaluating the quality of repurposed datasets, this exploratory study adopts an empirical lens. Specifically, we carry out an empirical study assisted by eye-tracking technology and a cued retrospective think-aloud protocol [13] to:

1. Observe user attention on the metadata artefact considering diverse groups of users, different data quality issues and different analytical tasks.
2. Gather insights on the performance, benefits and challenges associated with the metadata artifact in a data repurposing setting.
3. Identify common strategies of metadata use in data quality evaluation tasks.

In the remainder of this paper, we first provide prior studies on the role of metadata in data quality evaluation. We subsequently illustrate the study design and results of our experiment. We conclude the paper with a summary of contributions and an outlook for future research.

2 Related Work

Data quality has been extensively studied for more than four decades [14] by various research communities, including Information Systems, Computer Science, Statistics, etc. To enable measurement and management of data quality, substantial effort has gone into classifying DQ dimensions, which can be used as a basis to assess data quality and discover data quality problems. Recent research offers a consolidation of the various classifications of DQ dimensions and identifies eight classes, namely: Completeness, Accuracy, Validity, Consistency, Currency, Availability and Accessibility, Reliability and Credibility, and Usability and Interpretability and 33 dimensions overall [15].

A variety of DQ assessment methodologies exist, such as Total Data Quality Management Methodology (TDQM) [16], and Data Quality Assessment Framework (DQAF) [17]. Common activities in data quality assessment include data analysis, measurement and profiling, DQ requirements analysis, and identification of priorities [18]. Data profiling is extensively used in practice as it can produce metadata in the form of measurements for various DQ dimensions, that can in turn be used to evaluate the quality and fitness of data [19]. For example, data users make judgements about data quality by reviewing the percentage of null values in their target columns, the number of distinct values in a column, or the most frequent patterns of data values [19]. Metadata is broadly recognised as a fundamental artifact in supporting the human judgement in evaluating the quality and fitness of a dataset for a given purpose [20].

Historically, metadata is known as "data about data" and is generally classified into three types: descriptive, structural and administrative [21]. In our work, we adopt this classification on the basis of the following understanding: a) Descriptive metadata: describes data related to discovery purposes; b) Administrative metadata: describes the collection, licence, and access for data, such as statistics produced from data profiling; c) Structural metadata: describes the storage, conceptual model, and structure information of data.

Researchers have highlighted the benefits of having high-quality and well-documented metadata in helping data users evaluate data [18]. Whereas this may be the case in traditional Information System settings, through the availability of data catalogues and dictionaries, such metadata is generally lacking in *data repurposing* settings [7] (e.g. current (big) data analytics settings), where users are often repurposing the data and are confronted with datasets that they have little or no knowledge of. In these settings, a lack of high-quality metadata, or even any metadata, is a common problem.

Despite notable recent works to automate data profiling [10], DQ assessment currently cannot be fully automated due to its highly contextual nature and the need for human judgement [9]. Current practice is predominantly manual and ad-hoc in nature [25], causing inefficiencies and redundancy in the data evaluation processes as well as the potential of the creation of analytics solutions and decision making based on flawed data. In our previous study [23], we conducted a qualitative study with data practitioners to understand the role of metadata in human judgement in evaluating the quality of repurposed data, which reveals key challenges, preferences and approaches in practice. The study confirmed that metadata is a fundamental artefact to support human judgement in evaluating the quality of repurposed data and that metadata has been commonly used as a proxy to evaluate data quality in practice. Yet, there is a paucity of research on when, how, and why metadata is used to evaluate the quality of repurposed data. In this paper, we address this gap through a study conducted to understand the behaviour of users in metadata use during data repurposing tasks.

3   Study Design

Given the aims of our study, our study design is based on a lab experiment with a purpose-designed platform to understand the impact of metadata on the participants' performance and behaviour while evaluating the quality of repurposed datasets. During the experiment, we collect behaviour log data, eye-tracking data (using Tobii Pro TX300 eye tracker[1]) and qualitative verbal data through a cued-retrospective think-aloud method. Prior research has shown the value of these methods in gaining an understanding of users' interaction behaviour [24]. Eye-tracking allows direct collection of eye movement data and measurement of objective metrics such as fixation[2] durations [25] on a specific area of interest (AOI), that can identify the exact area that draws the attention of the participant, allowing researchers to track users' eye gaze and movement while interacting with external stimuli. To gain a deeper understanding of user behaviour, i.e., how users perceive and why they interact with the metadata, we adopt cued-retrospective think-aloud method. Specifically, participants are instructed to report retrospectively based on a recording replay of their eye movements during the problem-solving process. This method allows us to overcome a shortcoming of concurrent think-aloud methods, which may limit users' ability to report their thoughts in high-demand situations [13]. The combination of eye-tracking and the think-aloud method is commonly used to observe and gain an understanding of humans' cognitive processes [26].

The participants are students from two Australian universities. There is no prior knowledge required, given that data users can be the general public without specific data analytics experience. Participation is voluntary, with a $45 voucher offered for attendance. In total, 20 students participated in this experiment, resulting in 19 usable responses (one unusable due to a poor level of eye tracker data), which is considered an adequate sample size in similar studies [26]. On average, the experiment lasted 81 min, within which 41 min were taken on average to complete the tasks.

The overall experiment design is summarised in Fig. 1. In the preparation stage, each participant was asked to complete a pre-experiment questionnaire about their background information and prior knowledge of data quality. An eye-tracking calibration was implemented to ensure the correctness of the eye-tracking data collection. Afterwards, a tutorial was conducted to provide explanations and examples of data quality issues: *missing, inconsistent, non-unique*, the web-based platform and the overall experiment process. There was no time limit on the tutorial and the practice, and participants could start the experiment at their discretion.

---

[1] For more specifications of the eye tracker, please visit: https://www.tobiipro.com/product-lis ting/tobii-pro-tx300/, last accessed 2022/04/19.

[2] A fixation is the time span when the eye remains still at a specific position of the stimulus.

The Execution Stage commences when participants begin work on the first task in the experiment. Participants received three tasks (see Sect. 3.2), presented in a random order to each participant to ensure robustness and to mitigate potential learning effects. Eye movement and log data (i.e., mouse clicks and keyboard strokes) were collected during the experiment to understand the interaction with the platform interface (see Sect. 3.1). Upon completion of our experiment, each participant was asked to complete a post-experiment survey where we used NASA-TLX [27] to ask about perceived cognitive load. Finally, we conducted a cued-retrospective think-aloud session with each participant, during which we replayed the recording of the task completion process, showing eye gaze movement, and asked the following questions to better understand their reasoning in line with our objectives of the study: (1) Did you use the information in the Detailed Information panel to help you complete this task? Which specific information did you use? (2) When and for what reason did you look at the Detailed Information panel? Did you find it helpful to complete the task?

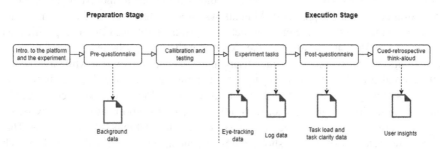

Fig. 1. Experiment process

3.1 Platform Design

Given that data users generally view data profiling as a common strategy to estimate data quality and that they prefer to see important metadata elements without having to switch contexts [23, 28], we designed our platform by incorporating both aspects in the same interface window. Inspired by existing data quality exploration platforms (e.g., Ataccama One[3]), open data portals (e.g., U.S. Government's open data portal[4]), and data analytics software (e.g., RapidMiner[5]) that display metadata on the right side [28], we designed our platform UI as three panels (Fig. 2): on the left panel, we allow participants to select the dataset among different versions; on the middle panel, the participants undertake the experiment task, and on the right panel, we provide various forms of metadata. The metadata shown on the right panel is grouped into *basic information* and *detailed information*, which is shown in two tabs. In the *basic information* tab, participants can obtain administrative information, such as creation date and sample data (first ten rows

---

[3] https://www.ataccama.com/platform/data-quality, last accessed 2022/04/19.
[4] https://data.gov/, last accessed 2022/04/19.
[5] https://rapidminer.com, last accessed 2022/04/19.

in the dataset), etc. In the *detailed information* tab, we provide statistical metadata for both table-level and column-level. The choice of the displayed metadata elements was based on a mapping between data quality issues and metadata in the context of data quality assessment extracted from [29]. This includes missing values and distinct values at table-level, and missing, distinct, common value patterns at column-level. Participants can click the tabs to switch and view the information they are interested in. They can also download the raw data (i.e., spreadsheet) from the platform if they want to explore information in the source data file.

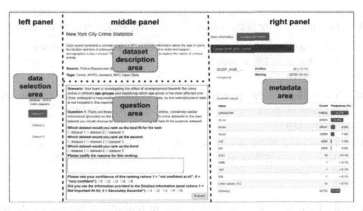

Fig. 2. Experiment platform with three panels. Note the annotation of areas of interest (AOIs) is relevant to the eye-tracking software.

3.2 Task Design

The dataset used in our experiment is the New York City Crime dataset that can be publicly downloaded from the New York City Open Data Portal, which is treated as the original version of the working dataset. It includes all valid felony, misdemeanour, and violation crimes reported to the New York City Police Department (NYPD), containing more than 320,000 rows and 36 columns, and has been used for various (re)purposes such as studying the relationship between obesity and a set of neighbourhood factors including NYC crime statistics [30]. We used all records (323,817 rows) and ten columns (with irrelevant and administrative columns excluded).

In our experiment, we focus on these three types of errors based on their high prevalence [31], namely *Missing* (The value of a specific attribute does not contain a valid value, including invalid semantic information), *Inconsistent* (Data values are not consistent, or data formats are not consistently used), and *Non-unique* (Different records identified by the same key). These errors can also be found in the source dataset as shown in Fig. 3, e.g., missing values shown as NULL or UNKNOWN. For each type of error, we create three variations of the original dataset by systematically injecting errors (e.g., by removing or changing values – see Table 1 for an example). The variation is set at 5% to allow for version discernability based on our pilot studies as well as typical error distributions in open datasets such as the NYC Crime dataset.

CMPLNT_NUM	BORO_NM	LAW_CAT_CD	LOC_OF_OCCUR_DESC	RPT_DT	SUSP_AGE_GROUP
100000410	BRONX	FELONY		03/22/2021	45-64
100002576	BRONX	VIOLATION	INSIDE	09/18/2021	45-64
100007253	BROOKLYN	MISDEMEANOR		6/01/2021	25-44
100008256	MANHATTAN	MISDEMEANOR	OPPOSITE OF	09/30/2021	UNKNOWN
100010900	STATEN ISLAND	MISDEMEANOR		08/14/2021	18-24

Fig. 3. Sample of the NYC crime dataset. Source: https://data.cityofnewyork.us/Public-Safety/
NYPD-Complaint-Data-Current-Year-To-Date-/5uac-w243, last accessed 2022/01/10

Table 1. Data quality errors in three variations in column "SUSP_AGE_GROUP"

Dataset #	Data quality error in this column	Compared to the original dataset
Dataset #1	The value of 19.4% records is empty, the value of 36.7% records is "UNKNOWN"	This is the original dataset
Dataset #2	The value of 24.4% records is empty, the value of 36.7% records is "UNKNOWN"	5% increase of empty cells, no change to value "UNKNOWN"
Dataset #3	The value of 29.4% records is empty, the value of 36.7% records is "UNKNOWN"	10% increase of empty cells, no change to value "UNKNOWN"

Because data quality issues generally exist in multiple columns, we design three tasks in total to mitigate learning effects. In our design, participants are faced with a different analytical purpose in each task. Each task is focused on one DQ issue: missing, inconsistent or non-unique. Users are then presented with three versions of a given dataset, each with a different level of errors that exist not just in the relevant column(s) but also in other columns (i.e., 5 percent tweak in each variation). During the experiment, the order of the tasks, and the order of dataset variations within each task is randomized to reduce any learning effects and maintain robustness in the design.

An example of the analytical task that participants see is:

> *Your team is investigating the effect of unemployment on the crime status in different age groups and identifying which age group is the most affected. There are three NYPD datasets found online (provided on the left panel), containing similar information. Which one of the NYPD crime datasets is the best dataset you would choose for this task? (Rank 1 being the best fit-for-purpose dataset)*

Participants can use the metadata on the platform to decide the most desired dataset and provide their answers on the platform, i.e., the ranking of the datasets, justification for the ranking, the level of confidence (on a scale of 1–10) and the level of importance on the use of metadata in their decision making (on a scale of 1–10).

Due to space limitations, the full protocol of the experiment task design is omitted from the paper and is available online[6], together with related dataset variations and data quality errors injection procedures.

---

[6] https://www.dropbox.com/sh/5417f2qdcwelngw/AABsU9JdbMgrA6pKDQF1xSM5a?dl=0.

4 Results

In this section, we report on our findings from the analysis of the five datasets we collected in the experiment, namely pre/post-questionnaires, eye-tracking, log, and think-aloud data. We first provide an analysis of task performance and identify three groups, i.e., high, medium, and low performers. We then present further analysis of the behaviour within and between these groups on the role of metadata and respective strategies, with the support of the insights extracted from the think-aloud data[7].

4.1 Task Performance

The ranking of the datasets provides the measure of the correctness of participants' answers. We use Kendall's τ correlation coefficient [33] to measure the ranking correlation between the rankings produced by the participants and the ground truth. The value of τ ranges from -1 (perfect negative correlation) through 0 (un-correlated) to 1 (perfect positive correlation). We average this score across all tasks for each participant as their overall performance in our experiment and subsequently use the K-means clustering algorithm [34] to cluster participants based on their performance. To determine the optimal value of k, we apply the popular Elbow method [35] to conduct clustering analysis with different k ranging from 2 to 15. The results show the optimal value being $k = 3$, and thus, we cluster the participants into three groups: *high performers* (6 participants, mean $\tau = 1.00$), *medium performers* (9 participants, mean $\tau = 0.76$), *low performers* (4 participants, mean $\tau = 0.46$). Further one-way analysis of variance (ANOVA) confirmed the differences between groups are indeed significant ($p < 0.05$ for each pair of the three groups).

The data collected from the pre-experiment questionnaire allows us to partition participants' backgrounds into various levels of data quality awareness. We follow [36] to measure DQ awareness based on participants' responses to four DQ related questions[8], by which we defined participants as having full data quality awareness if they answered four questions correctly, medium quality awareness if answered 2 or 3 questions correctly, otherwise no prior data quality awareness. By running the Kruskal-Wallis test, we conclude that there is no significant difference in the level of prior data quality awareness across high, medium and low performers, and thus prior DQ knowledge does not imply a higher level of performance. Similarly, we did not find differences in time efficiency, i.e. spending more time does not guarantee better performance or self-reported confidence ($p > 0.05$). We further investigated the performance relative to the type of data quality error, as displayed in Table 2. For *missing*, the correctness of both high (mean = 1) and medium performers (mean = 1) is significantly higher than low performers group (mean = 0.63), with $p = 0.001$ and $p = 0.000$. For *inconsistent*, the correctness of both high (mean = 1) and medium performers (mean = 0.27) is significantly higher

---

[7] We extracted the subjective insights from the transcripts using Nvivo 12, following a methodology to develop recurring aspects and group them into categories [32].

[8] 1). How do you define missing data in the data quality context? 2). Can you please give one example of missing data? 3). Can you please mention some data quality dimensions/attributes? 4). Can you please explain what is meant by data quality dimensions/attributes?

than low performers group (mean = 0.04), with p = 0.000 and p = 0.004. However, the difference across three clusters for non-unique is not significant.

Table 2. Mean correctness for tasks (missing, inconsistent, non-unique) across three performance groups: high, medium, and low performers

Group	Task: missing	Task: inconsistent	Task: non-unique
High	Mean = 1.00, SD = 0.00	Mean = 1.00, SD = 0.00	Mean = 1.00, SD = 0.00
Medium	Mean = 1.00, SD = 0.00	Mean = 0.28, SD = 0.22	Mean = 1.00, SD = 0.00
Low	Mean = 0.64, SD = 0.06	Mean = 0.04, SD = 0.08	Mean = 0.75, SD = 0.50

4.2 Metadata and Task Performance

To investigate the role metadata played with regard to participants' performance, we examine the eye fixation duration on the platform. To this end, we analyse the time duration that each participant spent fixated on a particular AOI on the platform.

Experiment-Level Analysis. Attention to the metadata AOI throughout the experiment is determined by the percentage of fixation on metadata compared to the overall fixation on the platform for all the tasks. In this way, we were able to use this normalised fixation as the measure of reflecting the attention on the *metadata* AOI. We observe high performers (mean = 0.621) spent more time looking at the *metadata* AOI compared to medium (0.468), and low performers (mean = 0.363). We conclude that the normalised fixation on metadata of high performers is significantly higher than medium and low performers (using ANOVA, p = 0.043, p = 0.006). This indicates that time focusing on metadata is a possible indicator of better performance.

The think-aloud data also confirms this observation, as our participants recognised the importance of metadata, and they made decisions by relying on the metadata provided. As P1 (from the high performers group) mentioned, "*I can find information in the detailed information panel to answer the question, if the dataset has a higher rate of missing, then it means they don't have enough information. So, I rank them based on the ratio of the missing values*".

Task-Level Analysis. Next, we break down the fixation duration data by each type of data quality error (i.e., missing, inconsistent, non-unique). Our results show that the normalised fixation duration on *metadata* AOI of high performers is significantly higher than the low performers in each of the three tasks, using ANOVA with p = 0.049 for *missing*, p = 0.033 for *inconsistent*, and p = 0.032 for *non-unique*. Thus, consistent with experiment-level analysis, high performers spent significantly more time focusing on metadata than low performers in each task. We can also see that the means of the durations are consistently higher across the performance levels (Fig. 4).

We note that the correctness of *non-unique* for low performers is not significantly lower than high performers (as shown in Fig. 4.), despite low performers spending

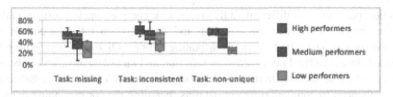

Fig. 4. Normalised fixation duration on metadata area AOI in three tasks (missing, inconsistent, non-unique) across three clusters: high, medium and low performers

significantly less time on metadata. In fact, the correctness of non-unique is the highest of the three issues among low performers, indicating this is the most straightforward question for them. However, this result is not consistent with earlier findings [28] that indicate non-unique is one of the most challenging data quality errors to identify. A possible explanation from the qualitative analysis for the think-aloud data indicates that participants relied on knowledge from the tutorial and obtained vital information to evaluate the data quality from the platform: "*I think the first column should be the primary key for this table, and as the tutorial mentioned, it should contain unique values. Then I choose the dataset with the least duplication on this column to be the first rank.*" (P13, clustered in low performers). This is consistent with existing research showing that data quality education and training is essential to assist people with the full benefits of integrating metadata in their decision-making processes [11].

Additionally, we observe normalised fixation on metadata for task *inconsistent* shares similar trends compared to the other two tasks; however, the correctness of this task is the lowest across three tasks for medium and low performers (see Sect. 4.1 and Table 2), indicating *inconsistent* is the most challenging task in this experiment, despite participants having used a similar processing strategy to focus on metadata. For the *inconsistent* task, participants are expected to use the common values provided for each column to identify there are inconsistency errors (i.e., there are two values for the same district: "BKLYN", and "Brooklyn") under column "BORO_NM" which is describing the district where the crime originally occurred. The statistical information of the number of distinct values and the table displaying common values with their corresponding frequency are the metadata provided for this data quality error. However, some participants were unable to see the relevance of the metadata provided, and thus were unable to provide the correct answer for this task. As reported by P8 (clustered in the low performers group), who has spent time looking at the metadata area but was unable to identify the useful information: "*I didn't notice any useful information regarding the format inconsistency error in this task, I couldn't find the information to help me answer this task.*" Data inconsistency is a challenging problem [37], and our findings shed further light on the importance and the need of relevance mapping between data quality errors and associated metadata.

4.3 Strategies of Metadata Use

To understand the patterns and common strategies of metadata usage in our experiment, we investigate eye-tracking data to extract participants' information scanning behaviour. We aggregate the gaze positions based on each AOI (see Fig. 2) as we focus on high-level interaction patterns with different AOIs during task completion. We further analysed transition frequency between different AOIs and identified two dominant gaze position transition patterns (i.e., the behaviour of fixating at one AOI and then switching fixation to a different AOI): 1) between *data selection* and *metadata* area, and 2) between *question* and *metadata* area. In the transition between *data selection* and *metadata* area, participants need to compare different datasets regarding the corresponding metadata. The think-aloud data shows that most participants mentioned this pattern, for instance, P5:*"When I notice some errors in one dataset, I will go back and forth to check each dataset on the same column in order to identify the difference in this error, so I can make the decision which dataset is the best to use"*. In the transition between *question* and *metadata* area, participants need to either refer to the given question or provide their answers by looking at metadata. P6 elaborated on this experience: *"I will carefully look at the Detailed Information panel to find some errors such as missing values, and the statistical information there can help me decide which dataset is the best to use for the task"*.

Given this observation, we focus on these two types of gaze transition behaviours and study how these transition patterns change over time. To this end, we normalise the frequency of transitions for each participant. Figure 5(a)(b) shows the (mean) relative frequency of the two transitions divided by all transitions that have been made by each participant, and Fig. 5(c) shows the (mean) frequency of all transitions for three groups respectively. We find that high performers make more gaze transitions between the *data selection* and the *metadata* AOIs when they perform the first task (Fig. 5a and 5c). This shows that high performers exhibit a good interaction with the metadata to assist them in making comparisons between different datasets. Furthermore, we observed an increased number of transitions between the *question* and *metadata* area for high performers as they progress in tasks, while medium and low performers do not exhibit such a clear trend of the increased transitions between these two areas (see Fig. 5b). Additionally, medium and low performers have more interactions between *data selection* and *metadata* area, while high performers do not necessarily increase such interactions when they perform their last task in the experiment (Fig. 5a). One possible explanation is that high performers have developed task completion strategies of searching relevant information from the *metadata* area to assist them in tasks, and thus, they can be more focused on which part or metadata to look at and reduce the unnecessary transitions, among other AOIs. P12 (clustered in the high performer group) shared this experience of performing the same procedure throughout the experiment: *"I generally use a similar procedure; I will check the question first and go through all the information from Basic Information and Detailed Information and see if there's any information about some data quality issues … And after the first question, I directly look at Detailed Information to look for missing or duplication."*

By contrast, medium and low performers have increased the number of transitions between the data selection and metadata AOIs as they progress in tasks. This shows a learning effect - they perform more interactions with the metadata and more comparisons between different datasets as they answer more questions. Too many interactions, however, may also suggest that they may have difficulties in identifying useful information. The think-aloud data confirms that some participants appreciate the detailed metadata but also find that too much information makes it difficult for them. For example, P14 (clustered in the low performer group) shared: the opinion that the metadata provided is causing a mental overload, *"I was paying attention to the Detailed Information panel, and I can find some support there to answer some of the tasks, but sometimes I am not really sure about some of the number (metadata) provided the Detailed Information panel ... I am not sure about the actual meaning of some statistics, and I become frustrated at some point".*

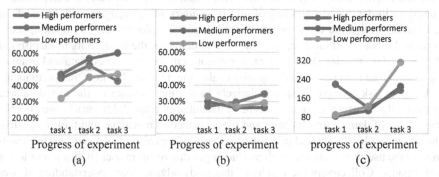

Progress of experiment (a)   Progress of experiment (b)   progress of experiment (c)

Fig. 5. The two most frequent transitions relating to the progress of the experiment are (a) transition frequency between *data selection* and *metadata* area relating to time, and (b) transition frequency between *question* and *metadata* area relating to time. The total number of transitions between different AOIs: (c) Total count of transitions between different AOIs relating to time.

5 Limitations

While our study is an initial step to understand metadata use when evaluating the quality of repurposed data, a topic that suffers from a paucity of empirical evidence, it is not without limitations. In the following, we discuss the main threats to validity.

Our study involved twenty participants, which is in line with the number of participants in other similar studies [26]. While we controlled for background homogeneity in the recruitment, as with any human study, the background knowledge of participants may have a confounding effect on the study results, and a study with more participants might also lead to the identification of further insights. In addition, the participant group in our study consisted of university students as a proxy for data users in the general public. While using students as proxies is an accepted practise, it remains the focus of research. In our case, because we were not focused on studying experienced professionals using repurposed data, we consider a student cohort acceptable.

We also acknowledge that a different setting for the task, dataset, or type/level of errors may provide different results. For this reason, our choice and design of the repurposing tasks and dataset was based on input of data practitioners with experience in repurposing data [23]. The measures used to analyse the results can cause a threat to validity if not correctly implemented. To reduce this threat, the findings from the eye-tracking data analysis were supported by the think-aloud qualitative data collection to offer triangulation and deeper insight. The inclusion of the think-aloud aspect of our study exposed it to limitations inherent to analysing think-aloud datasets in that the qualitative analysis may be impacted by subjectivity. To reduce this effect, we have followed well-accepted mitigation strategies based on dual coder approaches [38].

6 Conclusions

Metadata is a foundational form of conceptual models [39]. This study is a step towards gaining an in-depth understanding of user behaviours when engaging with metadata in data quality evaluation tasks for repurposed data. By exploiting the eye-tracking technique and think-aloud method, we were able to delineate the behaviours in identifying DQ errors (i.e., missing, inconsistent, non-unique) in the repurposed data and evaluating multiple datasets based on the quality evaluation. Our results show that participants with higher task correctness spent relatively more time focusing on the metadata area on the platform, irrespective of the type of data quality error. Additionally, we note the importance of data quality training and the relevance of metadata, and their respective impact on user behaviour and performance. Our findings also identify successful strategies for the use of metadata as well as challenges that result in user frustration or lower performance. Collectively the results of this study advance our understanding of user behaviour, perceptions, and strategies for the effective use of metadata during analytical tasks on repurposed data, thereby contributing to the body of knowledge on the role of conceptual models in these new settings. Additionally, the findings can assist in the improved design of DQ assessment tools or data curation systems, and in particular on how and when metadata is presented in such tools and systems.

Overall, the insights of this exploratory study contribute to the current research on the role metadata played in evaluating repurposed data. We also foresee a number of future extensions of this work. In this study, we studied three common DQ errors; however, there are several additional problematic DQ issues. Metadata is critical to assessing the DQ issues, and we hope to conduct more comprehensive studies on other DQ errors. We also recognise that mental workload is a critical factor in such tasks. Further studies can help decide the right amount of information (i.e., metadata) provided to adequately undertake the tasks while avoiding the information overload effect, including the study of design strategies, such as cues and flags, to reduce cognitive load.

Acknowledgements. This study was supported by the Australian Research Council through ARC Discovery Grant DP190102141.

References

1. Fisher, T.: The Data Asset: How Smart Companies Govern their Data for Business Success. John Wiley & Sons (2009)
2. Redman, T.C.: If your data is bad, your machine learning tools are useless. Harvard Business Review **2**, (2018)
3. Jaya, I., Sidi, F., Affendey, L., Jabar, M., Ishak, I.: Systematic review of data quality research. J. Theor. Appl. Inf. Technol. **97**, 3043 (2019)

4. Krishnan, S., Haas, D., Franklin, M.J., Wu, E.: Towards reliable interactive data cleaning: A user survey and recommendations. In: Proceedings of the Workshop on Human-In-the-Loop Data Analytics, pp. 1–5 (2016)
5. Borek, A., Woodall, P., Oberhofer, M., Parlikad, A.K.: A classification of data quality assessment methods. In: Proceedings of the 16th International Conference on Information Quality Presented at the ICIQ 2011, January 1 (2011)
6. Belkin, R., Patil, D.: Everything we wish we'd known about building data products (2018)
7. Zhang, R., Indulska, M., Sadiq, S.: Discovering data quality problems. Bus. Inf. Syst. Eng. 61(5), 575–593 (2019). https://doi.org/10.1007/s12599-019-00608-0
8. Stonebraker, M., et al.: Data curation at scale: the data tamer system. In: CIDR. Citeseer (2013)
9. Cichy, C., Rass, S.: An overview of data quality frameworks. IEEE Access 7, 24634–24648 (2019). https://doi.org/10.1109/ACCESS.2019.2899751
10. Lee, Y.W., Pipino, L., Funk, J.D., Wang, R.Y.: Journey to Data Quality. MIT Press, Cambridge (2006)
11. Fisher, C.W., Chengalur-Smith, I., Ballou, D.P.: The impact of experience and time on the use of data quality information in decision making. Inf. Syst. Res. 14, 170–188 (2003). https://doi.org/10.1287/isre.14.2.170.16017
12. Shankaranarayanan, G., Even, A., Watts, S.: The role of process metadata and data quality perceptions in decision making: an empirical framework and investigation. J. Inf. Technol. Manage. 17, 50–67 (2006)
13. Van Gog, T., Paas, F., Van Merriënboer, J.J., Witte, P.: Uncovering the problem-solving process: cued retrospective reporting versus concurrent and retrospective reporting. J. Exp. Psychol. Appl. 11, 237 (2005)
14. Sadiq, S., Indulska, M.: Open data: quality over quantity. Int. J. Inf. Manage. 37, 150–154 (2017). https://doi.org/10.1016/j.ijinfomgt.2017.01.003
15. Jayawardene, V., Sadiq, S., Indulska, M.: An analysis of data quality dimensions (2015)
16. Wang, R.Y.: A product perspective on total data quality management. Commun. ACM 41, 58–65 (1998)
17. Sebastian-Coleman, L.: Measuring data quality for ongoing improvement: a data quality assessment framework. Newnes (2012)
18. Batini, C., Cappiello, C., Francalanci, C., Maurino, A.: Methodologies for data quality assessment and improvement. ACM Comput. Surv. (CSUR). 41, 1–52 (2009)
19. Abedjan, Z., Golab, L., Naumann, F.: Profiling relational data: a survey. VLDB J. 24(4), 557–581 (2015). https://doi.org/10.1007/s00778-015-0389-y
20. Aljumaili, M., Karim, R., Tretten, P.: Metadata-based data quality assessment. VINE J. Inf. Knowl. Manage. Syst. 46, 232–250 (2016). https://doi.org/10.1108/VJIKMS-11-2015-0059
21. Méndez, E., van Hooland, S.: Metadata typology and metadata uses. In: Handbook of Metadata, Semantics and Ontologies, pp. 9–39. World Scientific (2014)
22. Clarke, R.: Big data, big risks. Inf. Syst. J. 26, 77–90 (2016). https://doi.org/10.1111/isj.12088
23. Zhou, H., Demartini, G., Indulska, M., Sadiq, S.: Evaluating the Quality of Repurposed Data–The Role of Metadata. (2021)
24. Bera, P., Soffer, P., Parsons, J.: Using eye tracking to expose cognitive processes in understanding conceptual models. MIS Q. 43, 1105–1126 (2019)
25. Chen, F., Zhou, J., Wang, Y., Yu, K., Arshad, S.Z., Khawaji, A., Conway, D.: Robust Multimodal Cognitive Load Measurement. Springer (2016) https://doi.org/10.1007/978-3-319-31700-7
26. Abbad Andaloussi, A., Zerbato, F., Burattin, A., Slaats, T., Hildebrandt, T.T., Weber, B.: Exploring how users engage with hybrid process artifacts based on declarative process models: a behavioral analysis based on eye-tracking and think-aloud. Softw. Syst. Model. 20(5), 1437–1464 (2020). https://doi.org/10.1007/s10270-020-00811-8

27. Hart, S.G., Staveland, L.E.: Development of NASA-TLX (task load index): results of empirical and theoretical research. Adv. Psychol. **52**, 139–183 (1988)

28. Han, L., Chen, T., Demartini, G., Indulska, M., Sadiq, S.: On understanding data worker interaction behaviors. In: Proceedings of the 43rd International ACM SIGIR Conference on Research and Development in Information Retrieval, pp. 269–278. Association for Computing Machinery, New York, NY, USA (2020)

29. Visengeriyeva, L., Abedjan, Z.: Anatomy of metadata for data curation. J. Data Inf. Qual. (JDIQ). **12**, 1–30 (2020)

30. Black, J.L., Macinko, J., Dixon, L.B., Fryer, G.E., Jr.: Neighborhoods and obesity in New York City. Health Place **16**, 489–499 (2010). https://doi.org/10.1016/j.healthplace.2009.12.007

31. Scannapieco, M., Catarci, T.: Data quality under a computer science perspective. J. ACM **2** (2002)

32. Charmaz, K.: Constructing Grounded Theory. Sage (2014)

33. Kendall, M.G.: A new measure of rank correlation. Biometrika **30**, 81–93 (1938)

34. Ray, S., Turi, R.H.: Determination of number of clusters in k-means clustering and application in colour image segmentation. In: Proceedings of the 4th International Conference on Advances in Pattern Recognition and Digital Techniques, pp. 137–143. Citeseer (1999)

35. Syakur, M.A., Khotimah, B.K., Rochman, E.M.S., Satoto, B.D.: Integration k-means clustering method and elbow method for identification of the best customer profile cluster. In: IOP Conference Series: Materials Science and Engineering, p. 012017. IOP Publishing (2018)

36. Moges, H.-T., Vlasselaer, V.V., Lemahieu, W., Baesens, B.: Determining the use of data quality metadata (DQM) for decision making purposes and its impact on decision outcomes — An exploratory study. Decis. Support Syst. **83**, 32–46 (2016). https://doi.org/10.1016/j.dss.2015.12.006

37. Guo, A., Liu, X., Sun, T.: Research on key problems of data quality in large industrial data environment. In: Proceedings of the 3rd International Conference on Robotics, Control and Automation - ICRCA 2018, pp. 245–248. ACM Press, Chengdu, China (2018)

38. Miles, M.B., Huberman, A.M.: Qualitative Data Analysis: An Expanded Sourcebook. Sage (1994)

39. Gartner, R.: What metadata is and why it matters. In: Metadata, pp. 1–13. Springer, Cham (2016). https://doi.org/10.1007/978-3-319-40893-4_1

Modeling Context for Data Quality Management

Flavia Serra[1,2]([✉]) [iD], Verónika Peralta[2] [iD], Adriana Marotta[1] [iD],
and Patrick Marcel[2] [iD]

[1] Universidad de la República, Montevideo, Uruguay
{fserra,amarotta}@fing.edu.uy
[2] Université de Tours, Blois, France
{veronika.peralta,Patrick.Marcel}@univ-tours.fr

Abstract. The importance of context for data quality (DQ) has been shown decades ago and is widely accepted. Early approaches and surveys defined DQ as fitness for use and showed the influence of context on DQ. However, very few proposals for context modeling can be found in DQ literature. This paper reviews many context components suggested in the literature and proposes a context model tailored for DQ management. Through a running example, and relying on the literature reviewed, we illustrate the applicability of the model.

Keywords: Data quality · Context model · Context components

1 Introduction

Taking into account the *fitness for use* concept [15], for studying the quality of a specific dataset, it is necessary to consider the context of such dataset. The notions of good or poor quality of data cannot be separated from the context in which the data is produced or used [2]. However, there is no consensus on a single definition of context for Data Quality Management (DQM). According to the Systematic Literature Review (SLR) carried out in [11], there are some convergences about what components make up the context of data (such as the task at hand or DQ requirements) [12]. In fact, there are very few works that propose a context definition and formalize it.

DQM deal with the monitoring and improvement of data quality, performing activities such as analysis of DQ requirements, data profiling, DQ model definition (where DQ metrics are defined to assess how well DQ requirements are satisfied), DQ measurement, DQ evaluation and DQ improvement. In these activities context is generally considered as an abstract element. In despite of this lack, many authors claim that context includes several components [11]. Therefore, defining context implies determining such components, which are the ones that actually influence DQ. This means that context components influence the design of DQ models, when selecting DQ dimensions and DQ factors, as well

J. Ralyté et al. (Eds.): ER 2022, LNCS 13607, pp. 325–335, 2022.
https://doi.org/10.1007/978-3-031-17995-2_23

as when defining DQ metrics. The proposed context model is intended for DQM, especially for the three DQ activities most addressed by literature: DQ model definition, DQ measurement, and DQ evaluation.

DQ experts need more than a definition of context. A model of the context (and of its components) is necessary, since a DQ expert needs conceptual tools to consider or manipulate data context, not only to design a DQ model but also throughout the DQM process. In addition, as we mentioned before, DQ literature presents the need to standardize the concept of context and its components.

Our contribution is a context model that gives support to the DQ expert throughout the different activities involved by the DQM process. Additionally, the proposed model is generic, since the set of context components can be adapted to the application domain. For instance, in a domain of Health, clinical histories, medical records or standards of the area such as snomed ct[1], can be taken into account as components of the context. Finally, we emphasize that this context model is consensual since it is created based on the needs and proposals present in the most relevant bibliography reported by the DQ community.

The paper is organized as follows: Sect. 2 analyzes related work. Section 3 presents the context model for DQM and illustrates it with. At the end, in Sect. 4, we conclude and present our future work.

2   Related Work

The influence of context on DQM have been stated decades ago [15] and still attracts attention in the DQ community. Indeed, a SLR [11] brought out 58 recent papers dealing with the use of context in DQM, and in a variety of application domains. Most of them describe some context components, while half of them propose a representation for such components, and only 6 formalize it. However, and despite the existence of operational definitions of context and context-aware computing [4], context representation is neglected in DQM. In particular, the literature only offers partial representations of context, each proposal dealing with very few context components, and having few intersections with other proposals. In this section, we review the context components that have been highlighted as relevant for DQM, mentioning the main works that describe them.

Many articles suggest that *DQ requirements* must be considered for an efficient DQM. In particular, DQ evaluation is carried out based on DQ requirements. For instance, in [16] the authors point out that a DQ framework needs to be capable of representing user DQ requirements (e.g. the level of precision or the rate of syntactic errors). *Data filtering needs* are also requirements on data that are stated, generally implied or obligatory [6], and these typically express concrete data needs for a specific task. *System requirements* should also be considered, especially in domains with special characteristics. For instance, traditional activities and concerns of DQ assurance do not take into account

---

[1] https://www.snomed.org/.

the characteristics of Big Data Systems, so their special network and storage requirements should be considered [3].

Data at hand are conditioned by the *application domain*, one of the main context components. In fact, each application domain may pose specific requirements, either in terms of quality, data or system (as we pointed out before for the Big Data domain). *Business rules* (constraints defined over data) also give context to data [9], by typically expressing conditions that data must satisfy in order to ensure consistency [6]. In turn, the task performed by the user plays an important role when defining the context. It is strongly domain-dependent and determines the usage of data at hand. Wang and Strong [15] underline that DQ must be considered within the context of the *task at hand*. Some works go further and not only consider the user's task, but also *users characteristics*, for example user profile [1,13] or user demographic characteristics [10].

Often the quality of the contextualized data is evaluated based on *other data* [2,8], i.e. data disjoint to the contextualized data. For example, in healthcare, contextualized data could be a patient's data, while other data could be a health standard. This standard would give context to the patient's data and support DQ experts in decision making. *DQ metadata* are a special metadata type that are also proposed to contextualize other DQ values [7]. In turn, *other metadata* are considered context components too. In particular, the connection between this kind of metadata (count of rows, count of nulls, or count of value patterns) and DQ problems is investigated in [14].

According to the literature review [11], context components, and the relationship among them, vary depending on how data are used, who uses them, and for what purpose. Furthermore, there is no global proposal considering the various perspectives of context for DQM, let alone a conceptual model describing them together and highlighting their relationship. We claim that context defined in terms of the different identified components and their inter-relationships will help the development of efficient DQM solutions, supporting DQ experts in the DQM process.

3 Context Model for Data Quality Management

In this section we propose a conceptual model representing context- and data quality-related concepts and their relationships. Firstly, we introduce a running example that allows us to represent each of the proposed concepts. Later, we describe separately some model parts, concerning specifically the proposed context and DQ models. Finally, we highlight how the context model influences DQ modeling.

3.1 Running Example

This example is inspired by a real case study proposed for the Digital Government domain[2]. We consider the Citizen Complaints System (CCS), over a

---

[2] Research project for the e-Government Agency and Information and Knowledge Society (AGESIC) in Uruguay, https://www.gub.uy/agencia-gobierno-electronico-sociedad-informacion-conocimiento/.

Table 1. Work scenario for the running example.

Element types	Elements identified
Business processes	Complaints Management
Organizations	Municipality of the city of Montevideo, in Uruguay
	Directorate of Civil Identification of Montevideo
Data collections	Relational database of Municipality of Montevideo
	Relational database of the Directorate of Civil Identification
Users roles	Citizen, Public official
Business rule	BR: Complaints must be done by citizens with legal age
DQ Requirement	RQ: Names of citizens must be real

relational database, where citizens, who are the end users of the CCS, register complaints, and public officials manage these complaints.

Table 1 presents the most relevant elements for our running example. We consider two data collections, the database of the Municipality and the database of the Directorate of Civil Identification. The former contains data about the citizens who register complaints (*Complaints table*). The latter contains information on the entire population of Uruguay (*Population table*).

3.2   Context

We present the context defined as a set of components, their representation (green classes) and the relationships among them are shown in the Fig. 1. We consider as a starting point the ten context components identified in the SLR [11] and briefly described in Sect. 2.

Some components are generalized. Firstly, we identify three disjoint subtypes of requirements: DQ, data filtering and system ones. Second, for metadata we distinguish DQ metadata from other metadata. Indeed, as argued in Sect. 2, DQ metadata have a particular role, as DQ measures (e.g. for data accuracy, completeness or freshness) can be aggregated to generate new DQ values. On the other hand, other metadata specifically represent data profile. In addition, we represent relationships among components. In particular, the task at hand and business rules are strongly linked to the application domain. All types of requirements (DQ, data filtering or system ones) and business rules are also generally established according to the application domain.

We remark that non-contextualized data (i.e. other data that are not the evaluated data) are of interest as context components. For example, in the health domain, we could verify the correctness of patient data using data from the civil identification area as part of the context. Finally, we underline that, for a specific work scenario, all these components may not be necessary. Contrarily, the user may choose and instantiate the ones that are considered relevant.

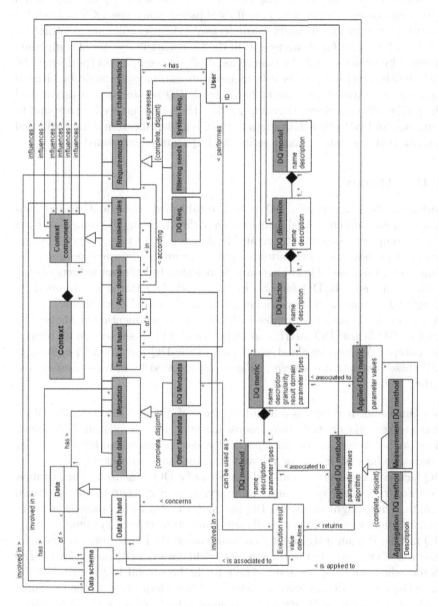

Fig. 1. Influence of the context model on DQ modeling.

Identifying the Context in the Running Example. According to the system described in Subsect. 3.1 and the Table 1, we define the context of the *data at hand* (i.e. data in the Municipality database). The context components identified (highlighted in italics) in the CCS are the following: (i) the *application domain*, this context component is well established, since the CCS is intended for Digital Government, (ii) *users characteristics*, the user roles are identified by the CCS, (iii) *tasks at hand* carried out in the CCS are the register of complaints (performed by citizens) and the management of such complaints (performed by public officials), (iv) a *business rule* (complaints can only be made by citizens of legal age) conditions the data at hand, (v) a *DQ requirement* is established by the public officials. Since, they require that the names entered correspond to real citizens, and (vi) *other data* (data in the Civil Identification database), used to validate that the data at hand verify the DQ requirement called *RQ*.

3.3 Data Quality

Historically "data accuracy", DQ is well established as a multifaceted concept, for which different DQ dimensions are defined. Some DQ dimensions are accuracy, completeness, consistency and freshness [15]. In turn, DQ dimensions address DQ problems such as outdated data, incomplete information, inconsistent data, etc. Possible DQ problems are represented by different aspects of each DQ dimension, namely DQ factors. In turn, each DQ factor is measured by applying DQ metrics, and they are implemented through DQ methods.

A DQ model is mainly composed of the 4 concepts mentioned above: DQ dimension, DQ factor, DQ metric and DQ method. In this subsection we present these concepts. We consider and adapt part of the DQ metamodel proposed in [5]. All these concepts are shown in Fig. 1 (represented by orange classes), and described below:

- DQ dimension: It captures a high-level facet of quality. Traditionally, DQ is characterized via multiple dimensions, however, not all existing DQ dimensions are of interest. Since, for a particular work scenario and for a particular dataset we have to select the relevant ones (as many as necessary).
- DQ factor: It represents a particular aspect of a DQ dimension. For instance, data accuracy involves semantic accuracy, syntactic accuracy and precision of data. There might be several DQ factors for the same DQ dimension, since each DQ factor best suites a particular problem or type of system.
- DQ metric: It is an instrument to measure a certain DQ factor. For example, the ratio of system data that match real-world data is a DQ metric for the DQ factor called semantic accuracy. There might be several DQ metrics for the same DQ factor. Metrics have an associated granularity (e.g. in the relational model, it could be table, attribute, tuple or value) and a result domain (e.g. Boolean or [0,1]). Types of parameters can also be specified (e.g. a consistency metric, checking the satisfaction of a functional dependency, should take a dependency as input).

Table 2. DQ metric and DQ method for measuring syntactic accuracy.

DQ metric	
Metric name	**SynAcc_dictionary_check**
Description	It evaluates if a data item is syntactically correct by checking against a dictionary.
<influenced by> Ctx. comp.	RQ (Names of citizens must be real)
<influenced by> Ctx. comp.	Other metadata (data collection type)
Granularity	Value
Result domain	{0, 1}
Parameter types	attribute, dictionary
Applied DQ metric	
<influenced by> Ctx. comp.	Other metadata (data collection type)
Parameter values	citizenName, attribute of the Population table
DQ method	
Method name	**Check_value**
Description	It evaluates the syntactic accuracy of a string <data> by checking against a set of correct value
<influenced by> Ctx. comp.	Other metadata (data collection type)
Parameter types	string <data>, attribute of a relational table
(Meas.) Applied DQ method	
<influenced by> Ctx. comp.	Other data (Population table)
Parameter values	data of the citizenName attribute, attribute of the Population table
Algorithm	Check_value(data, attribute) { Return isInCollection(data, attribute) }

- Applied DQ metric: Metrics can be applied for assessing the quality of different datasets, by providing appropriate names, and parameters. For example, the consistency metric checking the satisfaction of a functional dependency, when applied to geographical data, could check that *city_code* determines *state*.
- DQ method: It is a process that implements a DQ metric. In this case, types of parameters can also be specified. There might be several DQ methods to implement the same DQ metric.
- Applied DQ method: Methods can be applied for assessing the quality of different datasets, by providing appropriate names, parameters and algorithms. In addition, two types of applied DQ methods are defined: (i) *measurement DQ methods*, which compute the quality of an object by directly measuring it (e.g. counting the number of null values in a tuple), and (ii) *aggregation DQ methods*, which compute the quality of a composed object by aggregating quality values of object parts (e.g. computing precision of a table by averaging the precision of its tuples). In this case, a description of the semantics of the aggregation is recorded.

Defining a DQ Model in the Running Example: In this subsection we focus on the DQ model definition, while in the next subsection we will delve into the influence of the context on this DQ model. We illustrate the model for a single dimension, *accuracy*, and one of their DQ factors, *syntactic accuracy*. According to this, in Table 2 we present the definition of a DQ metric and a DQ method that implements it. The former is associated to several applied DQ metrics (we illustrate only one), and the latter is associated to several applied DQ methods (we illustrate only one, in this case, measurement type). We present each of the concepts used in the definitions, considering the model in Fig. 1:

- DQ metric defined for the selected DQ factor: the granularity of this DQ metric is *value*, because we measure the quality of a data item. The domain of each obtained result in the measurement is *0* or *1*. In addition, the DQ metric receives two parameters of type *attribute* and *dictionary*.
- Applied DQ metric associated to the DQ metric: the parameters values are the attribute *citizenName* of the Complaints table, and the dictionary represented by the *attribute with people names* of the Population table, i.e. the set of syntactically correct names.
- DQ method that implements the DQ metric: the type of the parameters that it receives is a *string*, because each evaluated name is a sequence of characters (i.e. a data), and a *attribute of a relational table*.
- Applied DQ method associated to the DQ method: it receives the values for these parameters: a *citizen* name and a *attribute of the Population table*. The algorithm seeks the citizen name among the dictionary entries and returns *1* whether it founds it, otherwise it returns *0*. These are all its attributes, because it is a measurement DQ method type.

3.4   Influence of the Context Model on DQ Modeling

DQ model definition is influenced by the context components. We present the relationships between the context components and the DQ model in Fig. 1. Firstly, when defining a specific DQ model, the selection of DQ dimensions, and their respective DQ factors, is influenced by the context components. For instance, the existence of business rules in the context of data suggests the analysis of data consistency. Moreover, the context components influence and support the definition of the DQ metrics and DQ methods. For example, the granularity of DQ metrics could be set based on DQ requirements (e.g. DQ requirements for a relational table or for a tuple), and parameter types of DQ methods could be set differently depending on the task at hand (e.g. a task requires alphanumeric codes, while another task requires numeric codes).

Regarding applied DQ metrics and applied DQ methods, they are also influenced by context components. For instance, applied DQ metrics may take parameters values from filtering needs (e.g. data recorded from the year 2000), business rules (e.g. all clients of legal age) or metadata (e.g. amount of null values). In turn, applied DQ methods could include (in the algorithm) conditions given by quality thresholds imposed by DQ requirements (e.g. 90% of names must be syntactically correct), or temporal limits (e.g. data are recent if they were recorded after today noon) required by the application domain or the task at hand. Also DQ metadata obtained in preliminary measurements, can be used for defining aggregation DQ methods, while in the case of other metadata, such as the amount of nulls in a relational table, they can be used for analyzing data completeness. In our conceptual model (see Fig. 1), we include other classes (white colored) that, although not belonging to context nor DQ models, are relevant for the interaction between them. For example, users have characteristics that are part of the context, express requirements and perform the task at hand. In turn, DQ metrics are applied on data schemas, which have metadata and involve business rules and requirements. We assess the quality of the data at hand, through the execution of applied DQ methods (aggregation or measurement DQ method). Execution results containing a DQ value, the date and time in which they were obtained, can be used as DQ metadata. Moreover, this information allows to analyze the evolution of DQ and supports decision-making.

DQ Influenced by the Context in the Running Example. According to the Table 2, we describe which context components influence DQ modeling:

- Context components that influence the DQ metric: they are *RQ* and *metadata* (in particular, other metadata) about the data collection. The former implies syntactic accuracy assessment of the citizens names, and the latter provides information about the type of the database containing the evaluated data. In Table 1, the database of the Municipality is relational, and this conditions the type of one of the parameters, that it is an attribute.
- Context components that influence the applied DQ metric: *metadata* also influences the applied DQ metric because the dictionary proposed in the DQ metric is implemented using an attribute of the relational table called Population.
- Context components that influence the DQ method: *metadata* about the data collection also influences the DQ method. The dictionary is implemented by an attribute in a relational table. In this case, it is not necessary to specify any particular relational table, since the defined DQ method could receive any attribute.
- Context components that influence the applied DQ metric: *other data* (in the Civil Identification database), influence the returned results by the algorithm in the measurement DQ method, because if the dictionary (i.e. the attribute of the Population table) changes, the results of the measurement could change.

In an indirect way, user characteristics (user role) also influence the DQ model, since *RQ* is expressed by the public officials. Therefore, if we were considering another user role (instead of public officials), the DQ requirement could change. For instance, a user with a department manager role might be more interested in complete data, rather than exact data. Then, the entire DQ model would change, since instead (or in addition to) of considering data accuracy, we would consider data completeness.

4   Conclusions

Literature demonstrates the importance of data context in DQ activities, especially in DQ model definition, DQ measurement and DQ assessment. The latter is carried out based on DQ metadata, and it is totally subjective, since such DQ metadata might be acceptable for one task but not for another. Interestingly, while many works point out the importance of the context in DQ, this concept is rarely formally specified and no consensual definition has yet been proposed.

In this paper, we address this lack and give a definition of context in terms of context components. We propose a consensual and generic context model for DQM, and show its impact on the definition of a DQ model. This context model is consensual in the sense that it follows from a comprehensive and systematic literature review. Moreover, the model is generic because the set of context components can be adapted to the application domain. This context model supports DQ experts not only in the specification of the DQ model, but also in the development of different DQ activities present in the DQM process. Additionally, we showcase the model usefulness thought a running example.

As future work, we will apply the context model in a whole DQM process. This will allow us to make an evaluation of the proposed model in a complete and real case study, obtaining feedback of the application domain experts, which will allow us to validate the modeling decisions.

References

1. Akram, M., Malik, A.: Evaluating citizens' readiness to embrace e-government services. In: Proceedings of the 13th Annual International Conference on Digital Government Research, pp. 58–67 (2012)
2. Bertossi, L., Rizzolo, F., Jiang, L.: Data quality is context dependent. In: Castellanos, M., Dayal, U., Markl, V. (eds.) BIRTE 2010. LNBIP, vol. 84, pp. 52–67. Springer, Heidelberg (2011). https://doi.org/10.1007/978-3-642-22970-1_5
3. Davoudian, A., Liu, M.: Big data systems: a software engineering perspective. ACM **53**(5), 1–39 (2020)
4. Dey, A.: Understanding and using context. PUC **5**(1), 4–7 (2001)
5. Etcheverry, L., et al.: Qbox-foundation: a metadata platform for quality measurement. In: Proceeding of the 4th Workshop on Data and Knowledge Quality (2008)
6. Fürber, C.: Data Quality Management with Semantic Technologies, chap. Data Quality. Springer, Heidelberg (2016). https://doi.org/10.1007/978-3-658-12225-6
7. Görz, Q., Kaiser, M.: An indicator function for insufficient data quality – a contribution to data accuracy. In: Rahman, H., Mesquita, A., Ramos, I., Pernici, B. (eds.) MCIS 2012. LNBIP, vol. 129, pp. 169–184. Springer, Heidelberg (2012). https://doi.org/10.1007/978-3-642-33244-9_12
8. Marotta, A., Vaisman, A.: Rule-based multidimensional data quality assessment using contexts. In: Madria, S., Hara, T. (eds.) DaWaK 2016. LNCS, vol. 9829, pp. 299–313. Springer, Cham (2016). https://doi.org/10.1007/978-3-319-43946-4_20
9. Merino, J., et al.: A data quality in use model for big data. FGCS **63**, 123–130 (2016)

10. Serra, F., Marotta, A.: Data warehouse quality assessment using contexts. In: Cellary, W., Mokbel, M.F., Wang, J., Wang, H., Zhou, R., Zhang, Y. (eds.) WISE 2016. LNCS, vol. 10042, pp. 436–448. Springer, Cham (2016). https://doi.org/10.1007/978-3-319-48743-4_36

11. Serra, F., et al.: Use of context in data quality management: a systematic literature review (2022). arxiv.org/abs/2204.10655

12. Strong, D., et al.: Data quality in context. CACM **40**(5), 103–110 (1997)

13. Todoran, I., et al.: A methodology to evaluate important dimensions of information quality in systems. JDIQ **6**(2-3), 1–23 (2015)

14. Visengeriyeva, L., Abedjan, Z.: Anatomy of metadata for data curation. JDIQ **12**(3) (2020)

15. Wang, R., Strong, D.: Beyond accuracy: what data quality means to data consumers. JMIS **12**(4), 5–33 (1996)

16. Wang, J., et al.: An ontology-based quality framework for data integration. In: Workshops on Business Informatics Research, pp. 196–208 (2012)

A Modeling Rule for Improving the Performance of Graph Models

Dietrich Steinmetz[1], Felix Merz[1], Gerrit Burmester[1], Hui Ma[2],
and Sven Hartmann[1(✉)]

[1] Clausthal University of Technology, Clausthal-Zellerfeld, Germany
sven.hartmann@tu-clausthal.de
[2] Victoria University of Wellington, Wellington, New Zealand

Abstract. Graph databases are an emerging technology with the potential to support complex data-intensive applications. Existing works on designing graph models often take an intuitive approach. In this paper, we discuss why this can easily lead to performance degradation for application-specific queries, and illustrate this with the example of dynamic taxi ride-sharing. Our findings call for more sophisticated data modeling approaches. We propose a new filter-based graph model for dynamic taxi ride-sharing based on a thorough analysis of an existing intuitive graph model. In particular, we suggest a new modeling rule using filter nodes to improve the performance of mission-critical queries. We evaluate our proposed graph model using simulations with real-world data. The results demonstrate that our proposed filter-based model outperforms the intuitive graph model in terms of query performance.

Keywords: Graph database · Data modeling · Taxi ride sharing

1 Introduction

In the era of big data, data-intensive applications are used in various domains to solve complex data-intensive problems. To effectively solve such problems we need to manage not only a big volume of data but also information about relationships among the data. With the increasing volume of data in data-intensive problems, the relationships among data are getting more and more complex. A typical example is dynamic taxi ride-sharing [8] where customers are allocated to taxis and taxi routes are determined to serve customers best possible, while the cost for operating the taxis as well as customer inconvenience caused by the waiting time or detours from the shortest possible route should be minimized [1]. Dynamic taxi ride-sharing is NP-hard [15]. A major challenge in practice is that solutions must be determined in real-time, so that a trade-off between the solution quality and computation time is needed.

To efficiently find solutions for data-intensive problems, the quality of the database schema used for storing and managing data and relationships plays a crucial role to met quality requirements in practice like performance or scalability [6,16]. Though relational databases are still most widely used for data-intensive

J. Ralyté et al. (Eds.): ER 2022, LNCS 13607, pp. 336–346, 2022.
https://doi.org/10.1007/978-3-031-17995-2_24

applications, they are not efficient for evaluating queries that involve expensive joins on interconnected data. To avoid expensive joins, graph databases can be used to store interconnected data, which can then be efficiently retrieved. A graph database consists of nodes representing objects and relationships representing relations between objects. Retrieving related objects from a graph database is more efficient since native support is provided not only for data but also for relationships between data [14,18].

To take advantage of graph databases an adequate modeling of interconnected data plays an important role to design a high-quality database schema for evaluating queries efficiently. However, since the emergence of graph databases, there is limited research work on data modeling for graph databases [2]. In practice, data is often modeled in an ad hoc way or based on best practice recommendations [16]. There are no common rules regarding how to model interconnected data and abstract them as nodes and edges in a graph database. An intuitive graph model is proposed in [17] for dynamic taxi ride-sharing. However, it may not be able to handle complex queries efficiently when there is a large number of requests and the size of the road network is too big. Further, dynamic taxi ride-sharing is a dynamic problem for which the current state of the relevant application data are changing dynamically. To find solutions in real-time, it is inefficient to search the entire data stored about the current state.

The overall aim of this paper is to investigate the modeling of data for dynamic taxi ride-sharing so that mission-critical application-specific queries can be answered efficiently. The major contributions of this paper are the following:

- We propose a filter-based graph model, for dynamic taxi ride-sharing that provides more efficient support of mission-critical tasks such as finding taxi routes, and allocating customers to taxis.
- We evaluate the efficiency of our proposed graph model using simulations with real-world data of dynamic taxi ride-sharing.
- We generalize our approach for improving graph models and propose a general modeling rule that helps database designers to increase the performance of answering mission-critical queries in a graph database.

Organization. This paper is organized as follows. Section 2 outlines current data modeling approaches for graph databases, and recalls mission-critical application-specific queries and an intuitive graph model for dynamic taxi ride-sharing. In Sect. 3, we critically discuss this model with respect to the performance of answering the mission-critical queries. In Sect. 4, we propose a modification of the intuitive graph model, and apply it to obtain a filter-based graph model. In Sect. 5, we report on the simulations conducted to compare the new graph model against the intuitive one. Section 6 discusses related work, and Sect. 7 gives conclusions and an outlook on future work.

2   Preliminaries

A graph model is a data model for graph database. In this paper, we use the labeled property graph model. Data modeling for graph databases has not yet attracted the same attention in research and practice as data modeling for relational databases. Most often an **intuitive modeling approach** was taken, i.e., based on intuitions about the objects in the application domain, cf. [16]. This is quite natural since the data to be managed in the database often already exists in some graph-like structure which is often the motivation for using a graph database. On their website, Neo4j gives some examples for data modeling in the so-called GraphGists list [11], and provides a few more complicated examples for popular use cases [10]. Intuitive graph modeling was utilized in application domains such as healthcare [12], biology [7], security [5], or transportation [17].

Dynamic Taxi Ride-sharing has attracted much interest, see [8,9,15] for a survey. Customers can call a taxi to pick them up from their origin and take them to their destination. Travel requests from customers are serviced by a number of taxis that are available in a city or some other area of interest. Taxis usually have multiple seats so that they can be shared by customers. The overall goal is to satisfy the travel requests in best possible quality (which is measured by the travel request execution time) while at the same time restricting the cost of operation (which is measured by the travel distance of the taxis). The workload of travel requests to be executed is dynamic and unknown beforehand, i.e., requests occur on the fly and must be executed in real-time. It is common to proceed in two steps: 1) customers are allocated to taxis, and 2) the driving schedule for the individual taxis is sequenced. When a customer issues a travel request, then a nearby taxi is identified that can serve the customer, i.e., there must be a spare seat, the requirements of the customer must be satisfied as well as the requirements of other customers served by the same taxi. If this is positively assessed, the request is allocated to this taxi, and the taxi's schedule is updated to reflect the detour and waiting time needed to pick up the new customer. Note that identifying the best candidate taxi for a customer depends on which updates of the taxi route it causes, i.e., the allocation of customers to taxis and the sequencing of taxi schedules are not independent.

In [17], an **intuitive graph model for dynamic taxi ride-sharing** was proposed, see Fig. 1. It was designed solely with the goal to meet the data needs of the following queries that are fundamental for the allocation of customers to taxis and the sequencing of taxi schedules, cf. [8,9,15].

Task 1. *Retrieve the minimum travel time between the pickup and dropoff location for a specified travel request.*

Task 2. *Retrieve suitable candidate taxis that can reach the pickup location of a request in a specified timeframe.*

Task 3. *Retrieve the remaining capacity and the remaining slack time at a specified point in the taxi schedule.*

As explained in [17], these tasks are mission-critical for dynamic taxi ride-sharing. Task 1 evaluates the graph database to determine the minimum travel time of a request. This is the basis of calculating the maximum detour time for this request. Using the minimum travel time together with the time when a request is issued and the maximum detour time, the latest arrival time of a

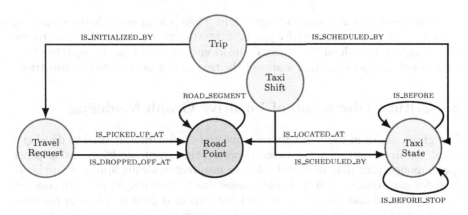

Fig. 1. An intuitive graph model for dynamic taxi ride-sharing [17].

request is determined. This is essential to determine whether a candidate taxi can arrive in time at the pickup location. Task 2 evaluates the graph database to determine suitable taxis for a travel request which is essential for allocating customers to taxis. Task 3 evaluates the graph database to determine the maximum slack time of involved trips and the empty seats in a taxi are used when checking if a request can be inserted into the schedule of a taxi. Then the best candidate taxi is determined, i.e., with smallest increase of the overall travel distance.

Travel requests from customers are shown as nodes with label *TravelRequest*. Their properties are *datetime, passenger count* and *maximum slack time*. Relationships with types IS_PICKED_UP_AT and IS_DROPPED_OFF_AT connect them to two road points for the pickup and dropoff location, respectively. Road points are shown as nodes with label *RoadPoint*. Their properties are *latitude* and *longitude*. Relationships with type ROAD_SEGMENT connect a road point to the subsequent one in the road network. Road segments have property *travel time*. Taxis are shown as nodes with the label *TaxiShift* representing the shift of a taxi driver. Their properties are *passenger capacity, shift start* and *shift end*. The schedule of a taxi is modeled as a set of taxi states. Relationships with type IS_SCHEDULED_BY connect a taxi to its taxi states. Taxi states are shown as nodes with label *TaxiState* representing the stay of a taxi in a road point. Their properties are the *number of passengers, period start, period end* and *is_stop*. A relationship with type IS_LOCATED_AT connects a taxi state to its road point. A relationships with type IS_BEFORE connects a taxi state to the previous taxi state (if existent) in the same taxi shift. The period start of a taxi state and the period end of the previous taxi state just differ by the travel time between the respective road points. The property is_stop indicates whether this taxi state is a taxi stop where a customer is picked up or dropped off. Taxi stops have higher relevance than other taxi states since they must be passed while other taxi states connecting the stops can be replaced by different routes. Relationships with type IS_BEFORE_STOP connect a taxi stop to the previous stop (if existent).

Trips are shown as nodes with label *Trip*. Their sole property is the *remaining slack time*. A relationship with type IS_INITIALIZED_BY connects a trip to the travel request for which it occurred. Relationships with type IS_SCHEDULED_BY connect a trip to the taxi states of the taxi that was allocated to this trip.

3 Critical Discussion of Intuitive Graph Modeling

The graph model in Fig. 1 is very intuitive and can be directly used to develop a graph database and solve the tasks. However, this graph model as well as other graph models that were designed using an intuitive modeling approach are likely to suffer performance and scalability issues due to the complexity of the queries to be evaluated and the way how the interconnected data is stored in the data structures of the graph database. That is, it may take a long execution time to select the best taxi and compute its new schedule after receiving a travel request. It depends on how efficient the mission-critical tasks can be solved, which again depends on how well they are supported by the graph database.

The **technical implementation of graph traversals** depends on the graph database implementation. Native graph databases [13, p. 149] are defined as graph databases with index-free adjacency, i.e., each node maintains direct references to its adjacent nodes. Thus, each node acts as a microindex of its neighbors. Therefore, query times are independent of the total size of the graph, but depend on the valency of the nodes, i.e., the number of neighbors.

Neo4j uses separate files to store nodes, relationships, and other information. The file stores for nodes and relationships use a fixed-length record structure, which enables fast lookup. Figure 2 illustrates the record structure used for nodes and relationships. For node traversals, the identifier *nextRelId* of each node is essential. When searching for a relationship, this identifier is the first to look up.

Relationships are connected with one another by two doubly-linked lists. Figure 2 illustrates the essential identifiers between nodes and relationships with dashed lines. The first list maintains the relationships for the starting node through the identifiers *firstPrevRelId* and *firstNextRelId*. The second list maintains the relationships for the ending node through the identifiers *secondPrevRelId* and *secondNextRelId*. The identifier *relationshipType* refers to an entry in the relationship type store. Thus, relationships can be filtered by their type. However, the entire list of relationships must be parsed.

Hence, all outgoing and incoming relationships of a node are stored together in a doubly-linked list. To retrieve a part of this list with any specific characteristic, the entire list must be scanned. This has implications for the complexity.

(a) Node store record structure (id for the first relationship highlighted)

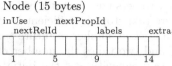

Node (15 bytes)

inUse   nextPropId
    nextRelId   labels   extra

1   5   9   14

(b) Relationship store record structure (id's linking to other relationships highlighted)

Relationship (34 bytes)

inUse   secondNode   firstPrevRelId   secondPrevRelId   nextPropId
   firstNode   relationshipType   firstNextRelId   secondNextRelId   firstInChainMarker

1   5   9   13   17   21   25   29   33

(c) Dashed arrows illustrating id's that connect nodes and relationships

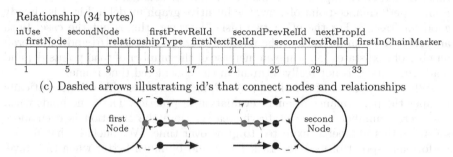

Fig. 2. Node and relationship store record structure used in Neo4j [13, p. 153]. Essential identifiers for the list of relationships at each node are highlighted.

Theorem 1. *When using the intuitive graph model in Fig. 1, the worst-case complexity for Task 1 is* $\mathcal{O}(|E|+|S|+|R|+(|V|+|S|+|R|)\cdot\log(|V|+|S|+|R|))$.

The same holds for Task 2. For Task 3, however, it is only almost $\mathcal{O}(1)$. *In summary, the travel request execution time (which involves all three tasks) is* $\mathcal{O}(|E|+|S|+|R|+(|V|+|S|+|R|)\cdot\log(|V|+|S|+|R|))$.

Sketch of proof. Firstly, let us look at Task 1. Every request node has three adjacent nodes. Thus, finding the pickup and dropoff road points of a request takes constant time. The computation of the shortest path depends on the particular algorithm used, but can be approximated by the complexity of Dijkstra's algorithm which is $\mathcal{O}(|E'|+|V'|\log(|V'|))$, cf. [3]. Herein, V' and E' denote the sets of considered nodes and relationships, respectively. These are not only road points and segments, *but each node or relationship in the graph database that is looked at during the search, including taxi states and travel requests.*

Secondly, let us look at Task 2. For finding the taxi states nearby to the pickup location of the customer, it is efficient to use Dijkstra's algorithm with a maximum path weight instead of a single destination.

Thirdly, let us look at Task 3. To compute the remaining seat capacity only the taxi state node itself and the respective taxi node must be accessed. The current passenger number is stored as an aggregated property in the taxi state node, while the total capacity is stored as a property in the taxi node. This needs constant time. The number of adjacent nodes of a taxi state is limited, since with at least one customer per request the number of connected trips is not larger than the taxi capacity. The current maximum slack time of a given taxi state, however, is dependent on the trips that are connected to this state or any future state. Any delay at this state affects the remaining schedule. Trips connected to any future taxi state are also connected to at least one future taxi stop. This is because the customers have to enter or leave the taxi at some point. Hence, iterating over future taxi stops is sufficient to collect trips affecting the current maximum slack time. The number of future taxi stops is at most equal to the number of current and two times the number of future connected trips. These are limited by the taxi capacity and the initial maximum request slack time. Hence, the complexity of this task is almost constant.   □

From a performance-point of view, the intuitive graph model in Fig. 1 is already good for Task 3. For the other two tasks, however, this is not the case. Both are sensitive to an increase of the number of travel requests $|R|$ and the overall number of taxi states $|S|$, while an increase of the number of road points $|V|$ and road segments E is not really a threat in the considered time frame.

When the number of travel requests $|R|$ increases, then this will dramatically hamper the performance of query evaluation in practice. The same holds when the overall number of taxi states increases. Here the situation is even more severe as this number is expected to grow over time. We conclude that from a performance-point of view for Task 1 it would be much better when the travel requests and the taxi states are not *directly* connected to the road points.

Moreover, we also observe that future taxi states $\sigma_h \in S$ that are connected to those road points scanned by Dijkstra's algorithm are taken into account to find candidate taxis for Task 2. Hence, additionally to addressing the issue about the connection to travel requests and taxi states, we can infer that a separation of past and future taxi states in respect to the current time would be better.

We can conclude that Tasks 1 and 2 cannot be performed efficiently using the intuitive graph model in Fig. 1. This is only possible for Task 3. As all three tasks are mission-critical, the travel request execution time will be high when using the intuitive graph model.

4   Towards a Filter-Based Graph Model

The discussion above motivates a modification of the graph model in Fig. 1. A weakness for Task 2 was the missing distinction between past and future taxi states. Intuitively, taxi states can be separated by two different relationship types, say WAS_LOCATED_AT and WILL_LOCATED_AT. However, it becomes clear that this is not very effective because the graph database stores all outgoing and incoming relationships of a node together in a doubly-linked list, see Sect. 3. It would be necessary to scan through all (!) WAS_LOCATED_AT relationships when looking for WILL_LOCATED_AT relationships to get future schedule states at a road point. The separation by relationship type only prevents the loading of past taxi states, but nothing more.

To ensure the scalability of Dijkstra's algorithm used for Tasks 1 and 2, it is crucial to enforce a limited number of relationships at each road point. Using the intuitive graph model in Fig. 1, however, this aim cannot be achieved. At each road point there is a potentially unlimited number of past and future taxi states. To overcome this concern we propose a modification of the graph model: we introduce two additional nodes that collect and encapsulate past and future schedules, respectively. We give these two auxiliary nodes the labels *TaxiHistory*

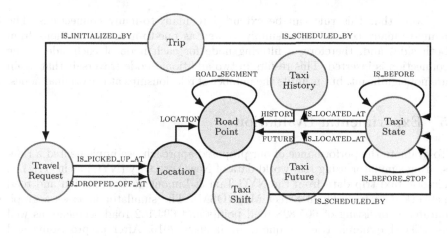

Fig. 3. Filter-based graph model obtained by applying our proposed modification.

and *TaxiFuture*, respectively. Their purpose is to "hide" the taxi states from the road point behind a single (!) relationship. Therefore, we call them *filtering nodes*. Using this modification, the major advantage is that there is only one additional node traversal from the road point to the taxi future to retrieve all future taxi states. This single extra traversal can be neglected, as it is easily accessed. Every past taxi state hidden behind the taxi history is completely ignored and the two relationships for the new nodes at each road point are not significantly affecting the performance when looking for the shortest path in Task 1.

We apply our proposed modification to the road points in the intuitive graph model in Fig. 1. Both, travel requests and taxi states should be hidden behind filtering nodes. Because we also want to distinguish taxi states between past and future states, one filtering node for each of both sets of states is inserted.

When running Dijkstra's algorithm for Tasks 1 and 2, travel requests should not be accessed from a road point. Therefore we group them behind a single filtering node. We give this auxiliary node the label *Location*. Figure 3 shows the graph model after inserting the new filtering nodes. We call this the *filter-based graph model*. Only road segments and relationships to filtering nodes remain at each road point in this model. Thus, the number of relationships is limited, which greatly improves the performance of Dijkstra's algorithm.

Our proposed modeling technique can be generalized to a **new modeling rule**: *Consider a node v_A with label A that has a one-to-many connection to a set of n nodes $v_1, \ldots, v_n$ with label B while also maintaining connections to other nodes. If there is an important task that utilizes the later connection, there needs to be a new node v_C with label C connected to node v_A and to all nodes $v_1, \ldots, v_n$ replacing the connections between v_A and nodes $v_1, \ldots, v_n$.*

Note, that this rule can be extended to many-to-many connections. The many-to-many connection is simply viewed as one-to-many connections from both sides and, therefore, a filtering node for each node of each side of the connection is inserted. This results in two additional node traversals that again are not significant, but it limits the number of relationships at the original nodes.

5   Experimental Evaluation

To evaluate the performance of our proposed approach, we implemented a ride-sharing simulator using real-world data of New York City (NYC) as in [17], i.e., historic taxi trip data from the NYC Taxi & Limousine Commission and road network data from Open Street Map (OSM). The simulator accesses a graph database consisting of 605,828 road points and 694,102 road segments as well as 319,081 dynamic travel requests in January 2016. After preprocessing and cleaning the data, 328,643 travel requests were generated from the original taxi trips. Following the discussion in [17], we used 500 taxis for our simulation.

We evaluated the performance (in terms of the travel request execution time) of finding solutions using our proposed filter-based graph model in comparison to the intuitive one [17]. That is, two graph databases were implemented, with one based on our proposed filter-based model and the other based on the intuitive graph model in [17]. Two simulations were conducted on each of the two graph databases. Since real-world datasets were considered, the number of travel requests will naturally vary throughout the day and week and, consequently, the workload of the taxis. This may lead to increased execution time for a single travel request in those hours with a higher number of requests due to e.g. the possibly higher number of future taxi states to be considered. To produce a comparable output, we look at the *average request execution time*. It displays the average time of handling a single request of a customer in the respective hour.

Figure 4 shows the average request execution time on the filter-based graph model compared to the intuitive one. It indicates that the average request execution time on the filter-based graph model is near constant and depends primarily on the respective workload of the taxis. For the intuitive graph model, however, it suggests that the average request execution time increases linearly.

The average request execution time on the filter-based model is consistently lower after the first hour. The higher execution time on the filter-based graph model during the first hour can be explained by the difference in the data structure. Using filter nodes comes with a very small overhead because there are a few extra nodes that need to be traversed. However, these filter nodes are the reason that the execution time is dramatically smaller later on and stays almost stable. The payoff of using filter nodes increases considerably over time.

In summary, it can be stated that the filter-based data model is obviously more suitable for the application-specific requirements.

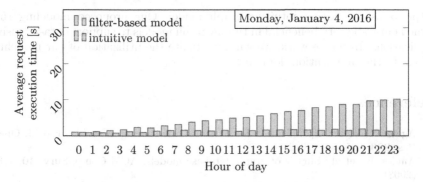

Fig. 4. Average request execution times for our filter-based graph model versus the intuitive graph model for each of the hours of January 4, 2016. (*The lower the better.*)

6 Related Work

Research work on data modeling for graph databases is limited and often for a specific domain. To support efficient query processing, query optimization techniques on graph databases were proposed. For example, [7] proposes a query tuning method by using the *explain* and *profile* commands to analyze the query execution plan. There are very few works on a design methodology for graph databases. In [4] a model-driven methodology for the design of graph databases based on an Entity-Relationship (ER) schema is proposed, to minimize the number of data accesses and therefore to improve the efficiency of data retrieval. However, the proposed methodology does not consider any application-specific requirements and therefore cannot work well for dynamic taxi ride-sharing. To incorporate domain-specific requirements [19] introduces a scenario-based design, which first designs a domain model using common strategies of object-oriented design for scenarios of the domain. The domain model is transformed into a graph model based on some rules. Evaluations are conducted by applying the modeling approach to the problem of route tracking in a criminal network analysis system. However, the graph model cannot be used to capture the domain-specific requirements of dynamic taxi ride-sharing. [16] proposes a process to convert a ER schema into a logical schema for a graph database. A set of mapping rules is defined for conceptual-to-logical scheme conversion. However, there is neither a discussion on how to design the ER schema nor attention to query performance.

In summary, research on data modeling for graph databases is still in its early stages. There is very limited work on data modeling of graph databases to support efficient queries by incorporating application-specific requirements.

7 Conclusions and Future Work

In this paper, we proposed a filter-based graph model for dynamic taxi ride-sharing so that mission-critical tasks can be performed efficiently. Simulations using real-world data demonstrate that our proposed filter-based graph model outperforms an exiting intuitive graph model. Our proposed modeling rule turned out to be very beneficial in tuning graph models to support data-intensive applications. In future work, we will investigate the utilization of our modeling rule in further application domains.

References

1. Agatz, N., et al.: Optimization for dynamic ride-sharing: a review. Eur. J. Oper. Res. **223**, 295–303 (2012)
2. Angles, R., et al.: Survey of graph database models. ACM Comp. Surv. **40**, 1–39 (2008)
3. Barbehenn, M.: A note on the complexity of Dijkstra's algorithm for graphs with weighted vertices. IEEE Trans. Comp. **47**, 263 (1998)
4. De Virgilio, R., Maccioni, A., Torlone, R.: Model-driven design of graph databases. In: Yu, E., Dobbie, G., Jarke, M., Purao, S. (eds.) ER 2014. LNCS, vol. 8824, pp. 172–185. Springer, Cham (2014). https://doi.org/10.1007/978-3-319-12206-9_14
5. Joslyn, C., et al.: Massive scale cyber traffic analysis: a driver for graph database research. In: ACM International Workshop Graph Data Management Experiences Systems (2013)
6. de Lima, C., dos Santos Mello, R.: A workload-driven logical design approach for NoSQL document databases. In: iiWAS, pp. 1–10 (2015)
7. Lysenko, A., et al.: Representing and querying disease networks using graph databases. BioData Min. **9**, 23 (2016)
8. Ma, S., et al.: T-share: a large-scale dynamic taxi ridesharing service. In: IEEE ICDE, pp. 410–421 (2013)
9. Ma, S., et al.: Real-time city-scale taxi ridesharing. IEEE Trans. Knowl. Data Eng. **27**, 1782–1795 (2015)
10. Neo4j: Graph database use cases. https://neo4j.com/use-cases/
11. Neo4j: Neo4j GraphGists. https://neo4j.com/graphgists/
12. Park, Y., et al.: Graph databases for large-scale healthcare systems. In: IEEE ICDE Workshops, pp. 12–19 (2014)
13. Robinson, I., et al.: Graph Databases. O'Reilly (2013)
14. Sahu, S., et al.: The ubiquity of large graphs and surprising challenges of graph processing. In: Proceedings VLDB , vol. 11, pp. 420–431 (2017)
15. Santos, D.O., et al.: Dynamic taxi and ridesharing: a framework and heuristics for the optimization problem. In: IJCAI, vol. 13 (2013)
16. de Sousa, V.M., Cura, L.M.d.V.: Logical design of graph databases from an entity-relationship conceptual model. In: iiWAS, pp. 183–189 (2018)
17. Steinmetz, D., Merz, F., Ma, H., Hartmann, S.: A graph model for taxi ride sharing supported by graph databases. In: Laender, A.H.F., Pernici, B., Lim, E.-P., de Oliveira, J.P.M. (eds.) ER 2019. LNCS, vol. 11788, pp. 108–116. Springer, Cham (2019). https://doi.org/10.1007/978-3-030-33223-5_10
18. Vicknair, C., et al.: A comparison of a graph database and a relational database. In: ACM SE Conference, p. 42 (2010)
19. Zhao, M., Liu, Y., Zhou, P.: Towards a systematic approach to graph data modeling: scenario-based design and experiences. In: SEKE, pp. 634–637 (2016)

Security, Privacy and Risk Management

Object Normal Form, Fourth Normal Form and Their Application to Database Security

Sebastian Link[✉] [ID]

School of Computer Science, The University of Auckland, Auckland 1010, New Zealand
s.link@auckland.ac.nz

Abstract. An important question in database schema design concerns the effort required to maintain data consistency under updates. Similarly, an important question in database security concerns the effort required to maintain data confidentiality under inference attacks. Previous work has addressed these questions for the popular class of functional dependencies. In this paper, we will extend solutions to the more expressive class of multivalued dependencies. In particular, we will show that schemata in Fourth Normal Form with a unique minimal key require very little effort to maintain data consistency, and can guarantee confidentiality under inference attacks by access control only.

Keywords: Access control · Boyce-Codd Normal Form · Confidentiality · Fourth Normal Form · Functional dependency · Independence · Inference control · Key · Multivalued dependency · Object normal form · Uniqueness

1 Introduction

The design of relational databases is a classical topic in database research. The overarching goal is to organize data in tables on which future update and query operations can be performed effectively and efficiently. In particular, schema normalization is concerned with minimizing the effort required to maintain consistency while processing update operations. Data redundancy, as caused by integrity constraints such as functional, multivalued and join dependencies (FDs, MVDs, JDs), slows down updates since redundant values need to be updated wherever they occur in the relation. Hence, during normalization tables are decomposed by transforming redundancy-causing data dependencies into keys that prevent data redundancy. For example, schemata in Boyce-Codd Normal Form (BCNF) only exhibit relations in which no data redundancy caused by FDs can ever occur [12,33]. Fourth and Fifth Normal Form (4NF, 5NF) achieve the same but for MVDs and JDs, respectively [16,32]. Since JDs extend MVDs and MVDs extend FDs, schemata in 5NF are also in 4NF, and schemata in 4NF are also in BCNF, but not vice versa [17]. There is evidence that schemata in practice are often in BCNF, but not in higher normal forms, such as 4NF [37].

Biskup showed [2] that BCNF is equivalent to schemata in weak object normal form, where the left-hand side of any left-reduced FD of the schema forms a so-called weak object. The latter are attribute sets that are unique and weakly independent. That

J. Ralyté et al. (Eds.): ER 2022, LNCS 13607, pp. 349–364, 2022.
https://doi.org/10.1007/978-3-031-17995-2_25

is, any relation has unique projections to weak objects, and inserting new combinations of values on attributes of the weak object ensures that these values can be completed with *some* values on the remaining attributes such that the updated relation will satisfy all constraints. Biskup also introduced objects as attribute subsets that are unique and strongly independent. Here, inserting new combinations of values on attributes of the object ensures that these values can be completed with *any* values on the remaining attributes such that the updated relation will satisfy all constraints. Object Normal Form (ONF) means that the left-hand sides of any left-reduced FD of the schema are objects, and Biskup showed that schemata are in ONF if and only if they are in BCNF with a unique minimal key [2] (there is only one key that is minimal with respect to set inclusion of attribute subsets). BCNF ensures that one will never need to worry about any non-key values when updating records in the database. However, one still needs to worry about the uniqueness of value combinations on all minimal keys. In ONF, one only needs to worry about the uniqueness of value combinations on *the* minimal key.

The theory of object normal forms has been limited to functional, inclusion and exclusion dependencies so far [2,7]. As the following example illustrates, it would be interesting to extend the theory to more expressive dependencies, in particular tuple-generating dependencies such as multivalued dependencies.

Example 1. Consider the simple example where relation schema MEET collects information about project meetings, where members of projects meet on a date. An example relation over MEET is given as follows.

Project	Date	Member
Green Goddess	19/12/2021	Clyde
Green Goddess	19/12/2021	Bonnie

Since all project members should be present during all meetings of the same project, we specify the MVD $P \twoheadrightarrow M$. In addition, team members can only attend one project meeting on any given day, and therefore we have the FD $DM \rightarrow P$. It follows that $R = PDM$ with $P \twoheadrightarrow M$ and $DM \rightarrow P$ has the unique minimal key DM. This means that the schema is in BCNF and has only one minimal key. That is, the schema is in ONF for the given FDs. However, the schema is not in 4NF since $P \twoheadrightarrow M$ is a non-trivial MVD where P is not a key.

In fact, the left-hand side attribute P of the MVD $P \twoheadrightarrow M$ does not satisfy the uniqueness property: the relation r satisfies the constraints, but the two different tuples of r have the same value on P. While DM is strongly independent with respect to the FD, it is not strongly independent with respect to the MVD. Indeed, while tuple $t = (P{:}\text{Green Goddess}, D{:}02/12/2021, M{:}\text{Bonnie})$ has a projection on DM that does not occur in r, $r \cup \{t\}$ violates the MVD $P \twoheadrightarrow M$.   □

Hence, our first objective is to generalize the concept of Object Normal Form from FDs to MVDs. We will show that 4NF is equivalent to Weak Object Normal Form, and Object Normal Form is equivalent to 4NF with a unique minimal key.

As a second contribution, we will show an application of our new results in database security. An important goal of security is *confidentiality*. In general, enforcing confidentiality requires costly dynamic inference control. In practice, security administrators often only use efficient access control based on static access rights. This, however, lays the burden on administrators to properly set access rights such that access to data must never allow users to infer information that is meant to be confidential. We illustrate the intrinsic difficulty of inference control on our example from before.

Example 2. Consider the relation r from Example 1. Suppose a user wants to keep the following combination of specific values confidential: (D:19/12/2021,M:Bonnie). That is, an answer to a query such as $(\exists P)\text{MEET}(P, 19/12/2021, \text{Bonnie})$ must be refused since it would reveal the confidential combination of values. This appears to be no problem at first glance. However, given the constraints from Example 1, a user may bypass access control by issuing the queries $(\exists M)\text{MEET}(\text{Green Goddess}, 19/12/2021, M)$ and $(\exists D)\text{MEET}(\text{Green Goddess}, D, \text{Bonnie})$. None of the two queries reveals the confidential combination of values. However, applying the MVD $P \twoheadrightarrow M$ to the answers of the two queries results in the inferred tuple (P:Green Goddess, D:19/12/2021, M: Bonnie), which reveals the confidential combination of values. Such an inference is not possible with the given FD only.   □

As we will show, combining schemata in Object Normal Form with a restriction of potential secrets to attribute sets that are so-called facts, ensures that costly inference control can be reduced to efficient access control while retaining confidentiality. Since facts are based on the constraints of the schema, an extension to MVDs ensures that administrators can declare a richer set of potential secrets as well.

Main Contributions. (1) We generalize object normal forms from the single class of FDs to the combined class of FDs and MVDs. For such constraints sets, we show that i) schemata are in weak ONF if and only if they are in 4NF, and ii) schemata are in ONF if and only if they are in 4NF and exhibit a unique minimal key. (2) For potential secrets that are defined over facts, we show that confidentiality can be guaranteed efficiently by access control whenever the underlying schemata are in ONF. Hence, we do not only provide insight on the effort required to retain data consistency under updates, but also on the effort required to guarantee confidentiality under inference attacks. Next we illustrate how the problems from Examples 1 and 2 are resolved by schemata in ONF.

Example 3. Consider the following relation over the schema MEET from Example 1.

Project	Date	Member
Green Goddess	19/12/2021	Clyde
Green Goddess	02/12/2021	Bonnie
Green Goddess	19/12/2021	Bonnie
Green Goddess	02/12/2021	Clyde

We may decompose MEET into the three schemata $(PD, \{PD\})$, $(PM, \{PM\})$ and $(DM, \{DM\})$ without loss of information. This is done following a 4NF decomposition with respect to the MVD $P \twoheadrightarrow M$ resulting in $(PD, \{PD\})$ and $(PM, \{PM\})$. The final schema $(DM, \{DM\})$ is added to preserve the minimal key DM and therefore the FD $DM \rightarrow P$. Indeed, each of the schemata is in Object Normal Form with respect to the input set of FDs and MVDs. Using the decomposition, the relation above is decomposed into the following relations as well.

Project	Date	Project	Member	Date	Member
Green Goddess	19/12/2021	Green Goddess	Clyde	19/12/2021	Clyde
Green Goddess	02/12/2021	Green Goddess	Bonnie	02/12/2021	Bonnie
				19/12/2021	Bonnie
				02/12/2021	Clyde

Potential secrets over these schemata are restricted to entire tuples in each of the three relations. Access control is sufficient to guarantee confidentiality under inferences. □

Outline. We discuss previous work in Sect. 2. Preliminary definitions are given in Sect. 3. Weak objects, weak ONF, and its equivalence to 4NF are discussed in Sects. 4 and 5, respectively. Objects, ONF, and its equivalence to 4NF with a unique minimal key are established in Sects. 6 and 7, respectively. The application to database security is detailed in Sect. 8. Section 9 concludes and discusses future work.

2   Related Work

Logical schema design for relational databases has been studied in great depth. Indeed, normal forms and database schema normalization are classical topics of introductory database textbooks [15]. Third [6], Boyce-Codd [12], and Fourth Normal Form [16] are well-known, and their achievements and limitations have been surveyed [3]. Biskup introduced Object Normal Forms for functional dependencies [2], and generalized them later to inclusion and exclusion dependencies [7]. Hence, the first contribution of the current paper addresses a shortcoming of relational database theory by extending Object Normal Form to MVDs. This is important since MVDs provide a sufficient and necessary condition for relations to be decomposable into two of its projections without loss of information, providing a strong basis for database normalization [16,23]. Many database schemata in practice that are in BCNF actually violate 4NF [37].

Likewise, the guarantee of confidentiality is a fundamental topic in information security [18,30]. Here, inference control is necessary to guarantee confidentiality but costly to implement, while access control is easy to implement but cannot guarantee confidentiality under inference attacks. Many textbooks on computer security [19] explain the main concepts of access control. Farkas and Jajodia give a general overview of the inference problem in databases [18]. Lunt et al. [26] propose a formal security model for mandatory access control in the context of relational databases. Subsequent work studies how to consistently declare the classifications of structured objects that are bound to constraints, in order to prevent unwanted inferences, e.g., see Olivier and von Solms [29], Cuppens and Gabillon [13], Dawson et al. [14], Wang and Liu [35], and Brodsky et al. [10]. Controlled query evaluation is rooted in the papers of Sicherman et al. [30] and Bonatti et al. [9]. Biskup and Bonatti propose a unified framework and analyze controlled query evaluation for closed queries in complete databases [4,5]. Biskup et al. [8] have shown that inference control reduces to access control for schemata in Object Normal Form when potential secrets are specified on attribute sets that form left-hand side reduced functional dependencies with a singleton right-hand side attribute. Our second contribution extends these results to Object Normal Forms for multivalued dependencies, and even more expressive classes of constraints.

Schema design is essential to every data model, which means that the work on schema design in the context of relational databases influences schema design on any extensions of the relational model. It is therefore no surprise that schema design has been deeply investigated in other data models as well, including conceptual models [11], SQL data models [20,22], nested data models [28,34], object-relational models [31], temporal models [21], Web models such as XML and JSON [1,27], and models for uncertain data [24]. No matter which data model is used, the design of a database schema will always determine how well updates and queries can be processed on database instances [25]. In view of data quality, normalization reduces data redundancy which is the source of data inconsistency and update inefficiency. Hence, eliminating data redundancy can lead to better data quality and make data-driven decision making more effective. Recent work has also started to extend classical database normalization to design for data quality [36].

3   Preliminaries

In the real world we ascribe two properties to an object: 1) It is unique within its domain, and 2) It can emerge and exist independently of the current environment. We will formalize these properties for relational databases with different classes of data dependencies, including functional and multivalued dependencies.

A relation schema R is a finite set of attributes that denote the column names of a table. Every attribute $A \in R$ is associate with a domain $dom(A)$ that contains the set of possible values that may occur in column A. A tuple t over R assigns to every attribute $A \in r$ some value $t(A) \in dom(A)$. A relation r over R is a finite set of tuples over R. For an attribute subset $X \subseteq R$, we use $t(X)$ to denote the projection of tuple t over R onto the attribute set X.

A relation schema R typically comes with a set Σ of data dependencies from a given class, such as the class of functional dependencies or multivalued dependencies. A functional dependency (FD) is a statement $X \to Y$ with $X, Y \subseteq R$, and a multivalued dependency (MVD) is a statement $X \twoheadrightarrow Y$ with $X, Y \subseteq R$. The FD $X \to Y$ is satisfied by a relation r over R whenever every pair of tuples with matching values on all the attributes of X have also matching values on all the attributes of Y. The MVD $X \twoheadrightarrow Y$ is satisfied by a relation r over R whenever for every pair of tuples in r that has matching values on all the attributes of X there is some tuple in r that has matching values with the first tuple on all the attributes in XY and matching values with the second tuple on all the attributes in $R - XY$, respectively. For a given class of data dependencies, and for a given set Σ of data dependencies from that class, we denote by Σ^+ the set of dependencies from that class implied by Σ, that is, the set of all dependencies from that class that are satisfied by every relation that already satisfies all the dependencies in Σ. For example, every FD $X \to Y$ implies the MVD $X \twoheadrightarrow Y$, but not vice versa. Trivial dependencies are those satisfied by every relation. For instance, an FD $X \to Y$ is trivial iff $Y \subseteq X$, and an MVD $X \twoheadrightarrow Y$ is trivial iff $Y \subseteq X$ or $XY = R$.

We say that (R, Σ) is in *Boyce-Codd Normal Form* (BCNF) if and only if for every non-trivial FD $X \to Y \in \Sigma^+$, $X \to R \in \Sigma^+$ holds. That is, every left-hand side X of a non-trivial FD functionally determines all the attributes of the schema. In other words, X is a key. That means no relation that satisfies a key X can have different tuples with matching values on all the attributes of X.

Similarly, we say that (R, Σ) is in *Fourth Normal Form* (4NF) if and only if for every non-trivial MVD $X \twoheadrightarrow Y \in \Sigma^+$, $X \to R \in \Sigma^+$ holds.

Example 1 shows a relation that satisfies the set $\Sigma = \{P \twoheadrightarrow M, DM \to P\}$. While (MEET, Σ) is in BCNF, it is not in 4NF. For example, the given relation violates the FD $P \to D$, which means that P is not a key. Consequently, for the MVD $P \twoheadrightarrow M \in \Sigma^+$, $P \to R \notin \Sigma^+$.

4   Weak Objects

The aim of the next two sections is to recall the concepts of weak objects and weak ONF, and to show that schemata are in weak ONF if and only if they are in 4NF.

We recall the definition of weak objects. While Biskup [2] only considered FDs, we assume Σ may contain other types of data dependencies as well, such as MVDs.

Definition 1 (weak object). *Let (R, Σ) denote a relation schema R together with a set Σ of data dependencies over R. An attribute subset X of R is said to be a weak object if and only if the following hold:*

- *(Uniqueness) For all relations r over R that satisfy Σ, for all $t \in r$, $t(X)$ is unique. That is, there is no $t' \in r - \{t\}$ such that $t(X) = t'(X)$.*
- *(Weak independence) For all R-relations r that satisfy Σ, for all $\mu \in dom(X)$ such that $\mu \notin r(X)$, there is some $\nu \in dom(R - X)$ such that $r \cup \{\mu\nu\}$ satisfies Σ.*   □

In Example 1, the attribute set DM is a weak object while P is not. The first property shows that keys satisfying weak independence are actually minimal keys.

Proposition 1. *Let X be a key over (R, Σ). If weak independence holds for X, then $Y \to R \notin \Sigma^+$ for all $Y \subset X$.*

Proof. Let t denote a tuple over R. The relation $r = \{t\}$ satisfies Σ. Now, let t' be a tuple over R such that $t'(Y) = t(Y)$ and $t'(X - Y) \neq t(X - Y)$. It follows that $\mu := t'(X) \notin r(X)$. Due to weak independence there is some $\nu \in dom(R - X)$ such that $r' = r \cup \{\mu\nu\}$ satisfies Σ. It follows that r' does not satisfy $Y \to R$.   □

The second property shows that minimal keys of schemata in 4NF satisfy weak independence.

Proposition 2. *Let X be a key over (R, Σ). If X is a minimal key and (R, Σ) is in Fourth Normal Form, then the weak independence property holds for X.*

Proof. Let r denote a relation over R that satisfies Σ. Let $\mu \in dom(X)$ such that $\mu \notin r(X)$. As there are infinitely many constants, we can find a tuple $\nu \in dom(R-X)$ such that $\nu(A) \notin r(A)$ for all $A \in R-X$, that is, ν is composed of values not occurring in the projection of r onto $R - X$. We claim that $r \cup \{\mu_i\nu\}$ is a relation over R that satisfies Σ. For consider $Y \twoheadrightarrow Z \in \Sigma^+$ with $Z \not\subseteq Y$ and $Z \not\subseteq R - Y$ and assume $t' := \mu\nu$ and some $t \in r$ violates $Y \twoheadrightarrow Z$. In particular, $t'(Y) = t(Y)$ must hold and, by the construction of ν, $Y \subset X$ (Y is a proper subset of X). Due to the minimality of the key X for R, we have $Y \rightarrow R \notin \Sigma^+$. This, however, violates the hypothesis that (R, Σ) is in 4NF. Consequently, our assumption that $r \cup \{\mu\nu\}$ violates $Y \twoheadrightarrow Z$ must have been wrong. This shows that the weak independence property for X. $\qquad \square$

5   Weak Object Normal Form

We will now define when a schema is in weak ONF, and prove that weak ONF and 4NF are equivalent. Here we extend the previous definition [2] from FDs to MVDs.

Definition 2. *Let (R, Σ) be a relation schema and*

$$LHS = \{X \subseteq R \mid \exists Y \subseteq R(Y \not\subseteq X \wedge XY \neq R \wedge (X \twoheadrightarrow Y \in \Sigma^+))$$
$$\text{with minimal } X \text{ or minimal key } X \text{ for } (R, \Sigma)\}.$$

The relation schema (R, Σ) is in Weak Object Normal Form *if and only if for every left-hand side $X \in$ LHS, X is a weak object over (R, Σ).* $\qquad \square$

In Example 1, $P \in LHS$ but P is not a weak object. Consequently, (Meet, Σ) is not in weak ONF. Evidently, it is also not in 4NF.

Theorem 1. *Let Σ denote a set of FDs over relation schema R. Then (R, Σ) is in Weak Object Normal Form if and only if (R, Σ) is in Fourth Normal Form.*

Proof. *(If).* Let $X \in LHS$. Since (R, Σ) is in 4NF, X must satisfy the uniqueness property. Proposition 2 implies the weak independence property. Consequently, X is a weak object, and (R, Σ) is in Weak Object Normal Form.

(Only if). Let $Y \twoheadrightarrow V \in \Sigma^+$ such that $V \not\subseteq Y$ and $YV \neq R$. Consider any minimal $Z \subseteq Y$ such that $Z \twoheadrightarrow U \in \Sigma^+$ where $U \not\subseteq V$ and $ZU \neq R$. Then $Z \in LHS$, and thus, by assumption, Z is a weak object. It follows that $Z \rightarrow R \in \Sigma^+$, and, in particular, $Y \rightarrow R \in \Sigma^+$. Hence, (R, Σ) is in Fourth Normal Form. $\qquad \square$

6   Objects

We will now recall the concepts of objects and ONF, and prove that ONF is equivalent to 4NF with a unique minimal key.

Definition 3 (object). *Let (R, Σ) denote a relation schema R together with a set Σ of FDs and MVDs over R. An attribute subset X of R is an* object *iff the following hold:*

- *(Uniqueness) For all relations r over R that satisfy Σ, for all $t \in r$, $t(X)$ is unique. That is, there is no $t' \in r - \{t\}$ such that $t(X) = t'(X)$.*

– *(Independence) For all relations r over R that satisfy Σ, for all $\mu \in dom(X)$ such that $\mu \notin r(X)$, for all $\nu \in dom(R - X)$, $r \cup \{\mu\nu\}$ satisfies Σ.* □

Our running example illustrates the definition of independence.

Example 4. Let $\Sigma = \{P \twoheadrightarrow D, DM \to P\}$ be a set of FDs and MVDs over $R = PDM$. In particular, (R, Σ) is not in 4NF since the only minimal key is DM. For instance, consider the following relation $r = \{t, t'\}$.

Project	Date	Member
Green Goddess	19/12/2021	Clyde
Green Goddess	19/12/2021	Bonnie

P is not an object since the relation satisfies Σ but violates uniqueness on P since $t(P) = t'(P)$. Indeed, the attribute subset DM is also not an object since it does not satisfy independence as we show now. Let $t'' := (\text{Green Goddess}, 02/12/2021, \text{Bonnie})$ where $(02/12/2021, \text{Bonnie}) \notin r[DM]$. Then $r \cup \{t''\}$ does not satisfy $P \twoheadrightarrow D$. Hence, DM is not an object. □

Example 5. Let $\Sigma = \{P \twoheadrightarrow D, PD \to L, PL \to D\}$ be a set of FDs and MVDs over $\text{MEET-LEAD} = PDL$ where L denotes the lead for the project on the day. In particular, (R, Σ) is in 4NF with the unique minimal key P. For instance, consider the following relation $r = \{t\}$.

Project	Date	Lead
Green Goddess	19/12/2021	Bonnie

Let $t' := (\text{Passion Pop}, 19/12/2021, \text{Bonnie})$ where *Passion Pop* $\notin r(P)$. Then $r \cup \{t'\}$ satisfies Σ. In fact, P is an object. □

The next result shows that a key satisfies the independence property if and only if the underlying schema is in 4NF and the key is the only minimal key.

Proposition 3. *Let X denote some key over (R, Σ). Then X satisfies the independence property if and only if all of the following hold:*

1. *X is a minimal key for (R, Σ).*
2. *If Z denotes some minimal key for (R, Σ), then $Z = X$.*
3. *(R, Σ) is in Fourth Normal Form.*

Proof. We show first that the three conditions are sufficient for the independence property for X to hold.

Let r denote a relation over R that satisfies Σ, let $\mu \in dom(X)$ such that $\mu \notin r(X)$. Let $\nu \in dom(R - X)$. We claim that $r' = r \cup \{t'\}$ satisfies Σ for $t' = \mu\nu$. For consider $Y \twoheadrightarrow V \in \Sigma^+$ such that $V \not\subseteq Y$ and $YV \neq R$, and assume that r' violates $Y \twoheadrightarrow V$. In particular, $t(Y) = t'(Y)$ for some $t \in r$. The 4NF condition (3) implies that $Y \rightarrow R \in \Sigma^+$. Hence, Y is a key for (R, Σ). If Y is even a minimal key, then by (1) and (2), $Y = X$. If Y is not a minimal key, then Y is a superset of some minimal key, and by (1) and (2), $X \subseteq Y$. Consequently, $t'(X) = t(X) \in r[X]$, which is a contradiction. That means our assumption that r' violates $Y \twoheadrightarrow V$ must have been wrong, which means that r' satisfies Σ. This proves the independence property for X.

We show now that the independence property for X is sufficient for (1), (2), and (3) to hold.

Firstly, since the independence property for X implies the weak independence property for X, Proposition 1 implies (1).

We are now going to show that (2) holds as well. Assume there is some other minimal key Z, different from X. We then know that $X - Z \neq \emptyset$ and $Z - X \neq \emptyset$ holds. Let $r := \{t\}$ with any tuple t over R. It follows that r satisfies Σ. We now define a tuple t' over R such that $t'(X - Z) \neq t(X - Z)$ and $t'(Z - X) = t(Z - X)$, and $t'(R - X) = t(R - X)$. In particular, we have $t'(X) \notin r(X)$. Due to the independence property for X it follows that $r' := r \cup \{t'\}$ satisfies Σ. However, it follows that $t'(Z) = t(Z)$, which means that r does not satisfy $Z \rightarrow R \in \Sigma^+$, a contradiction to the assumption that Z is another minimal key. Consequently, (2) must hold.

It remains to show (3). For consider $Y \twoheadrightarrow V \in \Sigma^+$ such that $V \not\subseteq Y$ and $YV \neq R$. We distinguish between two cases.

Case 1: $X \subseteq Y$. Since X is a key for (R, Σ) we have $Y \rightarrow R \in \Sigma^+$.

Case 2: There is some $A \in X - Y$. We will show that this case cannot occur. Indeed, let $r := \{t\}$ be some relation over R. Then r satisfies Σ. Define a tuple t' over R such that, $t'(Y \cap X) := t(Y \cap X)$, $t'(Y - X) := t(Y - X)$, for all $B \in X - Y$, $t'(B) \neq t(B)$, and for all $B \in R - Y$, $t'(B) \neq t(B)$. It follows that $t'(X) \notin r(X)$. By the independence property for X we conclude that $r' := r \cup \{t'\}$ satisfies Σ. However, by construction of t', we have $t'(Y) = t(Y)$ and, since $V - Y \neq \emptyset$ and $R - VY \neq \emptyset$, r' does not satisfy $Y \twoheadrightarrow V$ since there is no $t'' \in r$ such that $t''(YV) = t(YV)$ and $t''(R - YV) = t'(R - YV)$. This is a contradiction, and Case 2 cannot occur. $\square$

7 Object Normal Form

We can now recall the definition of ONF and show that it is equivalent to 4NF with a unique minimal key.

Definition 4. *The relation schema* (R, Σ) *is in* object normal form *if and only if for every left-hand side* $X \in$ LHS, X *is an object over* (R, Σ). $\square$

Theorem 2. *Let* Σ *denote a set of FDs and MVDs over relation schema* R. (R, Σ) *is in Object Normal Form if and only if* (R, Σ) *is in Fourth Normal Form and there is one minimal key.*

Proof. (If). Let $X \in LHS$. Since (R, Σ) is in 4NF, X must satisfy the uniqueness property. Due to Proposition 3, X satisfies the independence property and is, therefore, an object. Consequently, (R, Σ) is in Object Normal Form.

(Only if). Let $X \twoheadrightarrow Y \in \Sigma^+$ such that $Y \not\subseteq X$ and $XY \neq R$. Since (R, Σ) is in object normal form, it follows that there is some minimal key Z for (R, Σ) such that $Z \subseteq X$ and Z is an object. Proposition 3 then yields the assertion that (R, Σ) is in Fourth Normal Form and Z is the only minimal key.   □

Our running example illustrates the difference between 4NF and ONF.

Example 6. Let $\Sigma = \{P \twoheadrightarrow D, D \twoheadrightarrow P, PD \rightarrow L, PL \rightarrow D, DL \rightarrow P\}$ be a set of FDs and MVDs over $R = PDL$. In particular, (R, Σ) is in 4NF with minimal key P and minimal key D. For instance, consider the following relation $r = \{t\}$.

Project	Date	Lead
Green Goddess	19/12/2021	Bonnie

Let $t' := (Passion\ Pop, 19/12/2021, Clyde)$ where $Passion\ Pop \notin r[P]$. Then $r \cup \{t'\}$ violates $D \twoheadrightarrow P$. Hence, P is not an object. However, for $\bar{t}' := (Passion\ Pop, 02/12/2021, Clyde)$ where $Passion\ Pop \notin r[P]$, $r \cup \{\bar{t}'\}$ does satisfy Σ. Indeed, P is a weak object.

Similarly, let $t'' := (Green\ Goddess, 02/12/2021, Clyde)$ where $02/12/2021 \notin r[D]$. Then $r \cup \{t''\}$ violates $P \twoheadrightarrow D$. Hence, D is not an object. However, for $\bar{t}' := (Passion\ Pop, 02/12/2021, Clyde)$ where $02/12/2021 \notin r[D]$, $r \cup \{\bar{t}'\}$ does satisfy Σ. Indeed, D is a weak object.

We conclude that the schema is in weak ONF but not in ONF.   □

8   Application to Database Security

We report on a showcase of our new results in the area of database security, in particular the ability to reduce inference control to access control for schemata that are in object normal form.

8.1   Motivating Example

An important goal of security in information systems is *confidentiality*. In general, enforcing confidentiality requires costly dynamic inference control. In practice, security administrators often only use efficient access control based on static access rights. This, however, lays the burden on the administrator to properly set access rights so that permitted data accesses may never allow users to infer information to be kept secret.

Illustrating the difficulties arising in this context, imagine an application that associates the fee for some insurance policy and the name of some beneficiary.

Policy	Name	Fee
JF759	James Muller	125.60

Now assume the beneficiary wants to keep the combination of his name with the fee confidential. Consequently, a security administrator will need to protect the combination *(James Muller, 125.60)* by specifying access rights appropriately. Without further consideration, protecting only the critical information itself suffices to preserve unwanted disclosures. However, suppose that the data is governed by the functional dependencies *Policy* $\rightarrow$ *Name, Policy* $\rightarrow$ *Fee, Name* $\rightarrow$ *Policy* and *Name* $\rightarrow$ *Fee*. In this case, the protection can be bypassed by querying the combinations *(P:JFY759,F:125.60)* and *(P:JFY759,N:James Muller)*, both unprotected, and joining the results to associate *James Muller* with the fee *125.60*.

In response, Biskup et al. [8] identified a common situation guaranteed to meet, for any discretionary assignment of access rights, the goals of inference control. Essentially, this situation is given by a relational database schema in Object Normal Form with respect to a given set of FDs, and restricting the confidentiality policy to the protection of certain parts of a tuple, called facts. Hence, when a security administrator can declare access rights in a content-dependent way, the system can guarantee confidentiality and easily perform inspections by a simple lookup of access rights.

8.2 Reducing Inference to Access Control on Schemata in ONF

In the context of [8], queries are expressed in a fragment of relational calculus. Let *Var* denote a set of variables. The query language $\mathcal{L}_Q$ is the set of all closed formulae of the form $(\exists X_1) \cdots (\exists X_l) R(v_1, \ldots, v_n)$ with $0 \leq l \leq n$, $X_i \in Var$, $v_i \in Const \cup Var$, $\{X_1, \ldots, X_n\} \subseteq \{v_1, \ldots, v_n\}$, and $v_i, v_j \in Var$ and $i \neq j$. Let $\Phi \in \mathcal{L}_Q$ be a query and r a relation over R. The *ordinary evaluation* of closed queries is defined by

$$eval(\Phi)(r) := \texttt{if} \ \models_r \Phi \ \texttt{then} \ \Phi \ \texttt{else} \ \neg\Phi.$$

Biskup and Bonatti [4] developed *controlled query evaluation* (CQE). We briefly outline their approach in terms of our framework. A *potential secret* Ψ is a formula of a given language. If $\not\models_r \Psi$ for a relation r, the database user may learn that Ψ is false in the relation; however, if $\models_r \Psi$, it needs to be kept secret that Ψ is actually true. The set $pot\_sec \subseteq \mathcal{L}_Q$ denotes a confidentiality policy being *known* to the database user, and $log_0 \subseteq \mathcal{L}_Q \cup \Sigma$ is the a priori user knowledge with $\models_r log_0$ and $log_0 \not\models \Psi$ for every $\Psi \in pot\_sec$, that is, log_0 is actually true and none of the potential secrets is known to the user in advance. Finally, let a query sequence be given by $\mathcal{Q} = \langle \Phi_1, \Phi_2, \ldots \rangle$ with $\phi_i \in \mathcal{L}_Q$. The CQE for known potential secrets enforced by refusal (that is, the answer is refused by returning the constant *mum*) is defined by

$$cqe(Q, log_0)(r, pot\_sec) := \langle (ans_1, log_1), (ans_2, log_2), \ldots \rangle.$$

The values of the returned answers ans_i and the representation of the current user knowledge log_i are determined subject to a *censor function* [5]:

$$censor(pot\_sec, log, \Phi) := (\exists \Psi)[\Psi \in pot\_sec \wedge$$
$$((log \cup \{\Phi\} \models \Psi) \vee (log \cup \{\neg\Phi\} \models \Psi))]$$

$ans_i :=$ if $log_i \models eval(\Phi_i)(r)$ then $eval(\Phi_i)(r)$ else
      if $censor(pot\_sec, log_{i-1}, \Phi_i)$ then mum else
      $eval(\Phi_i)(r)$

$log_i :=$ if $censor(pot\_sec, log_{i-1}, \Phi_i)$ then log_{i-1} else
      $log_{i-1} \cup \{ans_i\}$.

A CQE is *secure for pot_sec* if for every finite prefix Q' of Q the following holds: For every $\Psi \in pot\_sec$, for every relation r_1, and for every log_0 with $\models_{r_1} log_0$ there is some relation r_2 with $\models_{r_1} log_0$ and (1) $cqe(Q', log_0)(r_1, pot\_sec) = cqe(Q', log_0)(r_2, pot\_sec)$ and (2) $eval(\Psi)(r_2) = \neg\Psi$. A CQE is *secure* if it is secure for all possible confidentiality policies, and *cqe* is secure in the sense of this definition.

Biskup et al. [8] showed how schemata in ONF with respect to FDs alone, in combination with restricting the confidentiality policy *pot_sec* to so-called facts avoids non-trivial inferences. Let $lhs(\sigma)$ denote the set of attributes that appears on the left-hand side of an FD $\sigma \in \Sigma$, which we have assumed to be a minimal cover. Given a schema in Boyce-Codd Normal Form, we are interested in those attribute sets that might be considered as domains of basic meaningful subtuples. We call these *facts*. Formally, we define the set of facts of a BCNF schema by

$$fact(R) := \{X \subseteq R \mid \exists \sigma \in \Sigma(lhs(\sigma) = X) \cup \{XA \mid A \in R \wedge \exists \sigma \in \Sigma(lhs(\sigma) = X)\}.$$

For example, when $R = PNF$ and $\Sigma = \{P \rightarrow N, P \rightarrow F, N \rightarrow P, N \rightarrow F\}$, then $fact(R) = \{P, N, PF, PN, NF\}$. A confidentiality policy *pot_sec* is restricted to the facts of R if for every potential secret $\Psi \in pot\_sec$ the set of attributes instantiated with some constants in Ψ is an element of $fact(R)$.

Biskup et al. [8][Theorem 3] were then able to show the following.

Theorem 3. *Let (R, Σ) denote a relation schema that is in Object Normal Form for the given set of FDs over R and pot_sec be restricted to the facts of R. Consider a query Φ_i and the user knowledge log_{i-1} and assume that $log_{i-1} \not\models eval(\Phi_i)(r)$[1]. Then the censor of cqe returns* true *if and only if Φ directly implies a potential secret Ψ, that is, if $\Phi_i \models \Psi$.*

Consequently, the answer needs to be refused only if the user asks for a formula directly implying a potential secret. In this case, however, there is no more need for inference control, but access control is sufficient to preserve confidentiality by protecting exactly the elements from *pot_sec*. This leads to access control mechanisms generating a single label per potential secret (for each of them there can be at most one tuple).

---

[1] Note that the censor function is not computed at all whenever $log_{i-1} \models eval(\Phi)(r)$.

8.3 Tigthness of the Conditions

Note that the conditions in Theorem 3 cannot be easily generalized.

Example 7. In our motivating example, the relation schema R consists of the attributes P, N, and F, and the set Σ of FDs consists of $P \to N$, $P \to F$, $N \to P$ and $N \to F$. Consequently, (R, Σ) is in BCNF but not in ONF since it has two minimal keys P and N. Indeed, access to the potential secret $(\exists P)R(P, \text{James Muller}, 125.60)$ can be bypassed by the queries

$$(\exists N)R(\text{JFY759}, N, 125.60) \text{ and } (\exists F)R(\text{JFY759}, \text{James Muller}, F).$$

Note that the potential secret is limited to the fact $\{N, F\}$.   □

Example 8. Similarly, suppose that $\Sigma' = \{P \to N, P \to F\}$. Then (R, Σ') is in Object Normal Form. Suppose we want to protect the potential secret

$$(\exists P)R(P, \text{James Muller}, 125.60),$$

which is not a fact of (R, Σ'). We can issue the queries $(\exists N)R(\text{JFY759}, N, 125.60)$ and $(\exists F)R(\text{JFY759}, \text{James Muller}, F)$, allowing inference of (JFY279, James Muller, 125.60).   □

Example 9. Finally, suppose that $\Sigma'' = \{P \to N, N \to F\}$ such that R has the unique minimal key P but is not in BCNF. Suppose we want to protect the potential secret $(\exists P)R(P, \text{James Muller}, 125.60)$, which is a fact of (R, Σ''). Here, we can issue the queries $(\exists N)R(\text{JFY759}, N, 125.60)$ and $(\exists F)R(\text{JFY759}, \text{James Muller}, F)$, allowing inference of (JFY279, James Muller, 125.60) which uncovers the potential secret.   □

8.4 Extension to Multivalued Dependencies

Multivalued dependencies occur frequently in database practice. Indeed, FDs $X \to Y$ that are satisfied by a relation r, provide a sufficient condition for r to be the lossless join of $r[XY]$ and $r[X(R - Y)]$. However, MVDs $X \twoheadrightarrow Y$ that are satisfied by a relation r, provide a sufficient and necessary condition for r to be the lossless join of $r[XY]$ and $r[X(R - Y)]$. Wu [37] conducted a practical study identifying that approximately 20% of database schemata in practice satisfy BCNF, but not 4NF. Hence, it is important to consider MVDs.

Theorem 3 can be generalized to schemata that are in ONF for a given set of FDs and MVDs. The reason is that every FD and MVD in a given set over a schema in 4NF are implied by some minimal key.

Proposition 4. *For a schema (R, Σ) that is in 4NF there is an FD set Σ' that is a minimal cover of Σ and where (R, Σ') is in BCNF.*

Proof. Since (R, Σ) is in 4NF, every constraint implied by Σ is implied by a minimal key. Let $K_1, \ldots, K_n$ denote the set of minimal keys for (R, Σ). Then the set $\Sigma' = \{K_i \to R - K_i\}_{i=1}^n$ forms a minimal cover of Σ, which is obviously in BCNF.   □

Consequently, we can guarantee confidentiality by access control for schemata in ONF, even if the constraint set includes multivalued dependencies.

Theorem 4. *In a relation schema in ONF, controlled query evaluation with pot_sec protecting only facts can be replaced by access control generating a single label per element of pot_sec. The resulting system is still secure.*

Proof. For a given schema (R, Σ) that is in ONF for a set of FDs and MVDs, there is a minimal cover Σ' of Σ that consists of FDs only. Consequently, (R, Σ') is in ONF for the FD set Σ'. The theorem follows from Theorem 3.   □

Similar to Theorem 3, the conditions of Theorem 4 cannot be easily generalized. In Example 7 the minimal FD cover Σ might be represented in the form $\Sigma_m = \{P \twoheadrightarrow N, N \twoheadrightarrow P, PN \rightarrow F, PF \rightarrow N, NF \rightarrow P\}$. Then (PNF, Σ_m) is in 4NF and has the minimal keys P and N. Indeed, $P \twoheadrightarrow N$ implies $P \twoheadrightarrow PN$, and $P \twoheadrightarrow PN$ and $PN \rightarrow F$ imply $P \rightarrow F$. Similarly, $P \twoheadrightarrow N$ implies $P \twoheadrightarrow F$ and $P \twoheadrightarrow PF$, and $P \twoheadrightarrow PF$ and $PF \rightarrow N$ imply $P \rightarrow N$. Similarly, we can infer $N \rightarrow P$ and $N \rightarrow F$. Vice versa, all elements of Σ_m are implied by Σ. Consequently, Example 7 shows how access control based on Σ_m can be bypassed.

In Example 8 the minimal FD cover Σ' might be represented in the form $\Sigma'_m = \{P \twoheadrightarrow N, PN \rightarrow F, PF \rightarrow N\}$. Then (PNF, Σ'_m) is in 4NF and has the minimal key P. Consequently, Example 8 shows how access control based on Σ'_m can be bypassed.

In Example 9 the minimal FD cover Σ'' might be represented in the form $\Sigma''_m = \{P \twoheadrightarrow N, N \twoheadrightarrow F, PN \rightarrow F, PF \rightarrow N\}$. Then (PNF, Σ''_m) has the minimal key P, but is not in 4NF. Consequently, Example 9 shows how access control based on Σ''_m can be bypassed.

9   Conclusion and Future Work

We have provided further insight into the effort required to i) maintain data consistency under updates, and ii) guarantee data confidentiality under inference attacks. Firstly, we found that updates over schemata in 4NF with a unique minimal key only require attention to values on attributes of the key when inserts happen. Secondly, we found that schemata in 4NF with a unique minimal key can guarantee confidentiality by simple means of access control, as long as potential secrets are declared over facts.

In future work it would be interesting to understand the effort required for data consistency and confidentiality when schemata are in less restrictive normal forms, such as 3NF, BCNF, or 4NF with a fixed number of keys. The properties of uniqueness and independence appear to be interesting subjects of study in richer data models, including incomplete, inaccurate, and uncertain data.

References

1. Arenas, M.: Normalization theory for XML. SIGMOD Rec. **35**(4), 57–64 (2006)
2. Biskup, J.: Boyce-Codd normal form and object normal forms. Inf. Process. Lett. **32**(1), 29–33 (1989)

3. Biskup, J.: Achievements of relational database schema design theory revisited. In: Thalheim, B., Libkin, L. (eds.) SiD 1995. LNCS, vol. 1358, pp. 29–54. Springer, Heidelberg (1998). https://doi.org/10.1007/BFb0035004

4. Biskup, J., Bonatti, P.: Controlled query evaluation for enforcing confidentiality in complete information systems. Int. J. Inf. Secur. **3**(1), 14–27 (2004). https://doi.org/10.1007/s10207-004-0032-1

5. Biskup, J., Bonatti, P.A.: Controlled query evaluation for known policies by combining lying and refusal. Ann. Math. Artif. Intell. **40**(1–2), 37–62 (2004)

6. Biskup, J., Dayal, U., Bernstein, P.A.: Synthesizing independent database schemas. In: Proceedings of the 1979 ACM SIGMOD International Conference on Management of Data, Boston, Massachusetts, USA, May 30–June 1, pp. 143–151 (1979)

7. Biskup, J., Dublish, P.: Objects in relational database schemes with functional, inclusion, and exclusion dependencies. RAIRO Theor. Inf. Appl. **27**(3), 183–219 (1993)

8. Biskup, J., Embley, D.W., Lochner, J.: Reducing inference control to access control for normalized database schemas. Inf. Process. Lett. **106**(1), 8–12 (2008)

9. Bonatti, P.A., Kraus, S., Subrahmanian, V.S.: Foundations of secure deductive databases. IEEE Trans. Knowl. Data Eng. **7**(3), 406–422 (1995)

10. Brodsky, A., Farkas, C., Jajodia, S.: Secure databases: constraints, inference channels, and monitoring disclosures. IEEE Trans. Knowl. Data Eng. **12**(6), 900–919 (2000)

11. Chen, P.P.: The entity-relationship model - toward a unified view of data. ACM Trans. Database Syst. **1**(1), 9–36 (1976)

12. Codd, E.F.: Recent investigations in relational data base systems. In: Information Processing, Proceedings of the 6th IFIP Congress 1974, Stockholm, Sweden, August 5–10, 1974, pp. 1017–1021 (1974)

13. Cuppens, F., Gabillon, A.: Logical foundations of multilevel databases. Data Knowl. Eng. **29**(3), 259–291 (1999)

14. Dawson, S., di Vimercati, S.D.C., Lincoln, P., Samarati, P.: Minimal data upgrading to prevent inference and association. In: Proceedings of the Eighteenth ACM SIGACT-SIGMOD-SIGART Symposium on Principles of Database Systems, May 31–June 2, 1999, Philadelphia, Pennsylvania, USA, pp. 114–125 (1999)

15. Elmasri, R., Navathe, S.B.: Fundamentals of Database Systems, 3rd Edn. Addison-Wesley-Longman, Boca Raton (2000)

16. Fagin, R.: Multivalued dependencies and a new normal form for relational databases. ACM Trans. Database Syst. **2**(3), 262–278 (1977)

17. Fagin, R.: A normal form for relational databases that is based on domains and keys. ACM Trans. Database Syst. **6**(3), 387–415 (1981)

18. Farkas, C., Jajodia, S.: The inference problem: a survey. SIGKDD Explor. **4**(2), 6–11 (2002)

19. Gollmann, D.: Computer Security (3 edn.) Wiley, New York (2011)

20. Hartmann, S., Link, S.: The implication problem of data dependencies over SQL table definitions: axiomatic, algorithmic and logical characterizations. ACM Trans. Database Syst. **37**(2), 1–40 (2012)

21. Jensen, C.S., Snodgrass, R.T., Soo, M.D.: Extending existing dependency theory to temporal databases. IEEE Trans. Knowl. Data Eng. **8**(4), 563–582 (1996)

22. Köhler, H., Link, S.: SQL schema design: foundations, normal forms, and normalization. Inf. Syst. **76**, 88–113 (2018)

23. Link, S.: Characterisations of multivalued dependency implication over undetermined universes. J. Comput. Syst. Sci. **78**(4), 1026–1044 (2012)

24. Link, S., Prade, H.: Relational database schema design for uncertain data. Inf. Syst. **84**, 88–110 (2019)

25. Link, S., Wei, Z.: Logical schema design that quantifies update inefficiency and join effi-ciency. In: SIGMOD 2021: International Conference on Management of Data, Virtual Event, China, 20–25 June 2021, pp. 1169–1181 (2021)
26. Lunt, T.F., Denning, D.E., Schell, R.R., Heckman, M.R., Shockley, W.R.: The Seaview secu-rity model. IEEE Trans. Softw. Eng. **16**(6), 593–607 (1990)
27. Mok, W.Y.: Utilizing nested normal form to design redundancy free JSON schemas. iJES. **4**(4), 21–25 (2016)
28. Mok, W.Y., Ng, Y., Embley, D.W.: A normal form for precisely characterizing redundancy in nested relations. ACM Trans. Database Syst. **21**(1), 77–106 (1996)
29. Olivier, M.S., von Solms, S.H.: A taxonomy for secure object-oriented databases. ACM Trans. Database Syst. **19**(1), 3–46 (1994)
30. Sicherman, G.L., de Jonge, W., van de Riet, R.P.: Answering queries without revealing secrets. ACM Trans. Database Syst. **8**(1), 41–59 (1983)
31. Tari, Z., Stokes, J., Spaccapietra, S.: Object normal forms and dependency constraints for object-oriented schemata. ACM Trans. Database Syst. **22**(4), 513–569 (1997)
32. Vincent, M.W.: A corrected 5NF definition for relational database design. Theor. Comput. Sci. **185**(2), 379–391 (1997)
33. Vincent, M.W.: Semantic foundations of 4nf in relational database design. Acta Inform. **36**(3), 173–213 (1999)
34. Vincent, M.W., Levene, M.: Restructuring partitioned normal form relations without infor-mation loss. SIAM J. Comput. **29**(5), 1550–1567 (2000)
35. Wang, H.W., Liu, R.: Privacy-preserving publishing data with full functional dependencies. In: Kitagawa, H., Ishikawa, Y., Li, Q., Watanabe, C. (eds.) DASFAA 2010. LNCS, vol. 5982, pp. 176–183. Springer, Heidelberg (2010). https://doi.org/10.1007/978-3-642-12098-5_14
36. Wei, Z., Link, S.: Embedded functional dependencies and data-completeness tailored database design. ACM Trans. Database Syst. **46**(2), 7:1–7:46 (2021)
37. Wu, M.S.: The practical need for fourth normal form. In: Proceedings of the 23rd SIGCSE Technical Symposium on Computer Science Education, SIGCSE 1992, Kansas City, Mis-souri, USA, 5–6 March 1992, pp. 19–23 (1992)

An Ontology of Security from a Risk Treatment Perspective

Ítalo Oliveira[1]([✉]), Tiago Prince Sales[1], Riccardo Baratella[1],
Mattia Fumagalli[1], and Giancarlo Guizzardi[1,2]

[1] Conceptual and Cognitive Modeling Research Group (CORE),
Free University of Bozen-Bolzano, Bolzano, Italy
`{idasilvaoliveira,tprincesales,rbaratella,mfumagalli,gguizzardi}@unibz.it`
[2] Services and Cybersecurity Group, University of Twente,
Enschede, The Netherlands

Abstract. In Risk Management, security issues arise from complex relations among objects and agents, their capabilities and vulnerabilities, the events they are involved in, and the value and risk they ensue to the stakeholders at hand. Further, there are patterns involving these relations that crosscut many domains, ranging from information security to public safety. Understanding and forming a shared conceptualization and vocabulary about these notions and their relations is fundamental for modeling the corresponding scenarios, so that proper security countermeasures can be devised. Ontologies are instruments developed to address these conceptual clarification and terminological systematization issues. Over the years, several ontologies have been proposed in Risk Management and Security Engineering. However, as shown in recent literature, they fall short in many respects, including generality and expressivity - the latter impacting on their interoperability with related models. We propose a *Reference Ontology for Security Engineering (ROSE)* from a Risk Treatment perspective. Our proposal leverages on two existing Reference Ontologies: the *Common Ontology of Value and Risk* and a *Reference Ontology of Prevention*, both of which are grounded on the *Unified Foundational Ontology* (UFO). ROSE is employed for modeling and analysing some cases, in particular providing clarification to the semantically overloaded notion of Security Mechanism.

Keywords: Risk Management · Security Engineering · Ontology

1 Introduction

In Risk Management, security issues arise from complex relations among objects and agents, their capabilities and vulnerabilities, the events they participate in, and the value and risk they ensue to the stakeholders at hand. Moreover, there

---

Work supported by Accenture Israel Cybersecurity Labs.

J. Ralyté et al. (Eds.): ER 2022, LNCS 13607, pp. 365–379, 2022.
https://doi.org/10.1007/978-3-031-17995-2_26

are patterns involving these relations that crosscut many domains, including aviation, information systems, chemical industry, public safety, and national defence [16]. Understanding the details and having a shared conceptualization and vocabulary about those notions and their relations is fundamental for modeling and analysing the corresponding scenarios, so that proper security countermeasures can be devised. Once this conceptualization task is done in a proper way, it is possible to model and reason about actual and possible scenarios to assess and counter the risks through security mechanisms.

Models representing risk and security scenarios play an important role in the understanding, analysis, communication, and training in Risk Management. They provide guidance regarding what questions should be asked, and the type of data that should be collected; they establish relations between pieces of information and help giving meaning to data; they define the ways risks can be treated; they provide a shared conceptual framework among stakeholders which support communication and training [19]. Ontologies are instruments developed in many domains to address the tasks related to conceptual clarification and terminological systematization. Indeed, the need of a general security ontology was already noticed in [9] as a way of rigorously organizing the knowledge about security of information systems, helping to report incidents more effectively, share data and information across organizations. Then, several ontologies have been proposed in Risk Management and Security Engineering to offer support for many conceptual problems and applications. For example, risk and security assessment [23]; data integration and interoperability [7]; simulation of threats to corporate assets [11]. In parallel, domain-specific modeling languages, such as CORAS [20], Bowtie Diagrams [27], and the risk and security overlay of the ArchiMate language [3], implicitly assume an ontology of risk and security in their modeling constructs. An adequate reference ontology of this domain would be able to analyse, (re)design, and integrate languages like these, improving their modeling capabilities, in way analogous to how the *Common Ontology of Value and Risk* (COVER) [24] has been used to redesign Archimate w.r.t. risk and value modeling (e.g., [25]).

Existing proposals for conceptualizing risk and security - counting current security core ontologies and the metamodels of domain-specific modeling languages - fall short in many respects, including generality (e.g., they tend to suffer from premature domain optimization) and expressivity (e.g., they tend to be represented through ontologically neutral modeling languages, missing ontological distinctions) - the latter impacting on their interoperability with related models. Often, these problems come from the fact that these models are designed as lightweight ontologies (i.e., focused on computational aspects) as opposed to Reference ontologies (i.e., focused on ontological precision and conceptual adequacy). For example, although CORAS language, Bowtie diagrams and ArchiMate language show an appropriate degree of generality for representing different scenarios, they are informal languages which, in ontological terms, conflate the *object*, its *capability*, and the associated *event* and *situation* with regard to security mechanisms. On the other hand, security core ontologies presented in computational logic languages, such as OWL, are often narrow by having specific applications in mind, missing at least the desirable generality. In fact, these core ontologies of security even fall short w.r.t. the *FAIR principles*, i.e., basic management standards for scientific artifacts (as shown by [22]).

To address these limitations, we employ an Ontology-Driven Conceptual Modeling approach [28] to propose a *Reference Ontology for Security Engineering (ROSE)* from a Risk Management perspective. The primary purpose of ROSE is to support activities related to ISO 31000 so-calls *Risk Treatment* process [16]. Alternatively, one could refer to this as *security engineering of cybersocial systems*, because of the nature and pervasiveness of the problem of devising mechanisms for controlling and preventing the risks in cyber-physical and social systems (e.g., woody gates, circuit breakers, antivirus software, lockdown norms). Our proposal leverages on two existing Reference Ontologies, namely, the *Common Ontology of Value and Risk* and a *Reference Ontology of Prevention*, both of which are grounded on the *Unified Foundational Ontology* (UFO). ROSE is employed for modeling and analysing some cases, in particular providing clarification to the semantically overloaded notion of Security Mechanism.

In what follows, Sect. 2 presents the requirements we expect ROSE to fulfil. Section 3 presents the foundations on which our proposal is based, that is, the Unified Foundational Ontology, in particular its conceptualization of the phenomenon of prevention. Section 4 presents our main contribution, the reference ontology of security termed ROSE, reusing an extended and reinterpreted version of COVER. Section 5 shows how ROSE satisfies the proposed requirements. Section 6 discusses the main related works. Section 7 marks our final considerations.

2   Requirements for a Reference Ontology of Security

ISO 31000 [16] defines that the process of Risk Management involves communication and consultation about the risks, risk assessment, risk treatment, recording and reporting, and monitoring and review. In this view, the purpose of risk treatment is to select and implement options for addressing risk. Risk treatment involves an iterative process of: "(a) formulating and selecting risk treatment options; (b) planning and implementing risk treatment; (c) assessing the effectiveness of that treatment; (d) deciding whether the remaining risk is acceptable; (e) if not acceptable, taking further treatment" [16]. ISO 31000 states that selecting the most appropriate risk treatment option(s) involves balancing the potential benefits derived in relation to the achievement of the objectives against costs, effort or disadvantages of implementation. Risk treatment options include: "(a) avoiding the risk by deciding not to start or continue with the activity that gives rise to the risk; (b) taking or increasing the risk in order to pursue an opportunity; (c) removing the risk source; (d) changing the likelihood; (e) changing the consequences; (f) sharing the risk with another party or parties (including contracts and risk financing); and (g) retaining the risk by informed decision" [16]. ROSE can be seen as a way of *ontologically unpacking* [15] this notion of risk treatment, according to the risk treatment options, through an ontological analysis based on the Unified Foundational Ontology (UFO) and its general-purpose conceptual modeling language OntoUML [12].

Taking these tasks into account, we distinguish three types of requirements that ROSE shall satisfy:

Analysis Requirements (AR): domain-specific capabilities associated to the tasks the ontology should help to realize:

1. Since security engineering requires risk assessment as a previous step in the risk management process, ROSE shall support the identification and assessment of risks;
2. ROSE shall support activities associated with security engineering in multiple domains.

Ontological Requirements (OR): domain-specific concepts and relations the ontology should have in order to realistically represent its domain of interest and thus support what it is intended to support:

1. ROSE shall support the task of representing the risk treatment options (a)–(g), which are directly connected to the AR2;
2. ROSE shall include both risk and security concepts, explaining explicitly how they interact with one another, including the ones mapped in [22] as the most common in security core ontologies: Vulnerability, Risk, Asset, Attacker, Threat, Control, Countermeasure, Stakeholder, Attack, Consequence;
3. ROSE shall be able to distinguish intentional and non-intentional threats, because this distinction impacts the risk treatment options.

Quality Requirements (QR): domain-independent characteristics the ontology is expected to possess, so it becomes a better artifact:

1. *Domain appropriateness* [12] - ROSE shall capture the relevant entities and relations of the domain through an ontological analysis;
2. *Generality* - Since security crosses multiple different areas, a security reference ontology should represent the most general concepts of the domain;
3. *FAIR principles* - ROSE should be Findable, Acessible, Interoperable and Reusable [17].

3   Ontological Foundations of Prevention

Our strategy to address the requirements described in Sect. 2 is to employ the Unified Foundational Ontology (UFO) - in particular, a module that covers the phenomenon of prevention. ROSE will be represented through the UFO-based modeling language OntoUML [12]. We are interested in UFO's conceptualization of prevention (presented in [4]), which involves multiple ways of stopping or forestalling certain types of events, because this sort of dynamics plays a fundamental role in the domain of security. In Sect. 4, we build ROSE as an extension and rein-terpretation of the Common Ontology of Value and Risk (COVER), applying the theory of prevention. COVER was chosen, because it includes several concepts and relations about value and risk that are crucial for a reference ontology of security. Indeed, COVER was used to evaluate and redesign ArchiMate language regarding to value and risk [25,26]. Additionally, COVER has been successfully applied for modeling different domains, such as trust [2], software anomalies [10], among others. However, COVER assumes specific future events are entities of its domain of discourse [24], an assumption that is inconsistent with UFO the-ory of events, which claims that particular events are immutable entities in the past or that are happening [14]. We adopt UFO assumption with the support of higher-order types to represent future events as types of events, and review some cardinality constraints in COVER.

UFO [12] distinguishes individuals and types: objects, dispositions, events, situations instantiate object types, disposition types, event types, and situation types, respectively. The same type-token distinction applies to relations. Types can be more or less saturated, depending on the presence of individual concepts in the type definition, provided the type can be instantiated by multiple individuals. A fully unsaturated type is defined only by general properties (e.g., the type "Physical Object" is defined by general properties such as spatial extension, weight, color). Individual concepts (e.g., the concept of "Facebook"), on the other hand, are fully saturated, i.e., they are instantiated by only one individual and always the same individual. A semi-saturated type is defined by general properties as well as individual concepts. For instance, the type "cyberattack against Facebook" includes the general type "cyberattack" and the individual concept "Facebook", but it can be instantiated by multiple events.

According to UFO [4,14], events are manifestations of interacting objects' dispositions, which are activated by certain situations. For example, the event of a lion attack on customers in a given zoo is the result of manifestations of capa-bilities of the lion and the vulnerabilities of customers, when these dispositions meet each other in the right situations that activate them. In this example, the vulnerabilities and the capabilities bear a *mutual activation partnership* relation among each other. If an event E_1 brings about a situation S that activates the dispositions that are manifested as event E_2, then we say that S *triggers* E_2, and that E_1 *directly_causes* E_2; if E_1 *directly_causes* E_2, and E_2 *directly_causes* E_3, then E_1 *causes* E_3, where *causes* is a strict partial order relation [14]. So *causes* is the transitive closure of *directly_causes*. Furthermore, likelihood or probability can be ascribed to events of certain types, as described in [24] and incorporated in UFO theory of prevention [4] in the following way: TRIGGERING LIKELIHOOD inheres in a Situation Type, and it refers to how likely a Situation Type will trig-ger an Event Type once a situation of this type is brought about by an event; the CAUSAL LIKELIHOOD inheres in an Event Type, and it means the chances of an event causing, directly or indirectly, another one of a certain type.

This theory about the relations between situations, objects, their disposi-tions, and events implies that certain types of events can prevent other types of events due to some effect on dispositions, their partner dispositions, or the situ-ation that could activate the dispositions. For instance, caging the lion prevents

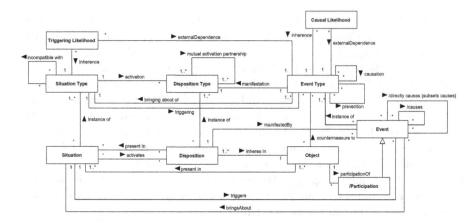

Fig. 1. Theory of prevention in UFO (adapted from [4]). Notice we added the relations *incompatible with*, *triggering*, and *causation* to the original diagram.

the formation of a situation in which capacities of the lion and the vulnerabilities of the customers could meet; sedating the lion would remove some of its threatening capabilities; in both cases, the (semi-saturated) type of event of the lion attack in the zoo would be prevented. In general, prevention of events of type E_T that are manifestations of dispositions of type D_T occurs when an event of type E'_T brings about a situation of a type S'_T that is incompatible with the situations required to activate instances of D_T [4]. This incompatibility means these situations cannot obtain concurrently, and, on the type-level, *incompatible*(S_T,S'_T) implies that there are no two instances of these two types that obtain in overlapping time intervals. These situation types are semi-saturated, that is, they must share some relevant dispositions or objects. E.g., a situation with updated software is compatible with a situation that contains a different outdated software, even if the two situations temporally overlap, though they would be incompatible if the referred software was the same individual in both situations.

Prevention can then be defined as a relation between two types of events: *prevention*(E_T,E'_T) implies that the occurrence of events of type E_T brings about situations that are incompatible with the conditions required for the occurrence of events of type E'_T. Again, these event and situation types are semi-saturated in the proper way, i.e., guaranteeing the presence (co-reference) of the same disposition and bearer. For example, it is the event of *Humidifying object x* that prevents an event of *Catching on Fire of object x*. Obviously, humidifying flammable objects, in general, does not prevent other flammable objects from catching on fire. Besides, notice an event (or a type of event) cannot hold a prevention relation with a specific event, which is always an immutable existing entity, but an event can prevent a type of event, therefore precluding the occurrence of instances of this type.

Given this definition, there is a sense in drawing a distinction between two types of *indirect prevention*. One way of producing indirect prevention is if an event e causes an event e', and e' prevents events of type E_T, so we say e indirectly prevents E_T. Another way of producing indirect prevention is if an event e prevents events of type E_T, which is causally connected to E_T', so we say e indirectly prevents E_T'. For example, an event *my car engine failure* causes the event *my car stops in the traffic*, which prevents the events of (semi-saturated) type *me attending the job interview*; if I had attended the job interview, *I would have gotten the job* - a type of event that is historically dependent on the events of type *me attending the job interview*. Indirect prevention plays an important role in security engineering, because Security Mechanisms (a) may produce a chain of events that eventually prevents directly the desired type of event or (b) may block a causal chain of undesired types of events.

UFO theory of prevention also defines a concept of *Countermeasures* [4]. In general, given a disposition d whose manifestations are of type E_T, countermeasures are designed interventions that endow a setting containing d with other dispositions $\{d_1, ..., d_n\}$, whose manifestations prevent any instance of E_T. More specifically, *Countermeasure Mechanisms* are designed such that: they contain dispositions of type D_T, and given the situations of type S_T that would trigger events that would (directly or indirectly) cause instances of E_T, the instances of S_T instead activate the instances D_T whose associated event type prevent E_T. For example, a circuit break contains a disposition to close the circuit in a situation where there is a current above a certain threshold. The manifestation of that disposition of the circuit breaker thus prevents the event of an overcurrent.

This analysis makes explicit several ways in which countermeasures can be designed [4]: (i) removing the disposition d whose manifestation we want to avoid (this can be done by removing the object with that disposition from the setting at hand); (ii) removing from the scene required activation partners (e.g., produce a vacuum to prevent fires); (iii) including in that setting a disposition that is incompatible with a mutual activation partner (e.g., humidifying a flammable object, removing dryness as a required property); (iv) designing countermeasure mechanisms surrounding the bearer of d, which have the capacity of preventing the manifestation of d. The theory of prevention is summarized in Fig. 1.

4   A Reference Ontology for Security Engineering (ROSE)

Our approach is to understand the domain of security as the *intersection* between the domain of value and risk, understood under the terms of COVER [24], and the theory of prevention [4]. In this sense, security mechanism creates value protecting certain goals from risk events. In COVER, Value is a relational property that emerges from the relations between capacities of certain objects and the goals of an agent. The manifestations of these capacities are events that bring about a situation that impacts or satisfies the goal of a given agent - the goal is simply the propositional content of an intention [13]. Risk is the anti-value: risk events are the manifestations of capacities, vulnerabilities and, sometimes, intentions that inhere in an agent; these events bring about a situation that hurts the goal of a given agent. Like value, security is a relational property that emerges from the relations between capabilities of objects and goals of an agent; the manifestations of these capabilities bring about a situation that impacts the goal of an agent in a very specific way: preventing risk events. In what follows we develop this conceptualization, firstly by extending COVER, then by presenting an ontology of security.

4.1 Extending the Common Ontology of Value and Risk

In COVER, RISK EVENT is the result of the manifestations of THREAT CAPA-BILITY of THREAT OBJECT and VULNERABILITY of OBJECT AT RISK or of RISK ENABLER. A THREAT EVENT is one with the potential of causing a LOSS EVENT, which brings about a LOSS SITUATION that hurts an INTENTION of an AGENT called RISK SUBJECT [24].

The assumption that a THREAT EVENT can be intentional is implicit in COVER, so we make it explicit specializing it through the class ATTACK, an ACTION caused by an INTENTION of an AGENT called ATTACKER, which specializes THREAT OBJECT. Traditionally, the presence or not of intention in a THREAT EVENT is raised to set the difference between security and safety, respectively [5], though in both cases the goal is the prevention of the LOSS EVENT.

An important addition to COVER is the understanding that THREAT CAPA-BILITY, VULNERABILITY and, sometimes, INTENTION are dispositions associated to types whose instances maintain a mutual activation partnership to each other: a THREAT OBJECT can only manifest its THREAT CAPABILITY if a VULNERA-BILITY can be exploited; if the THREAT OBJECT creates an ATTACK, then the INTENTION is also required. Analogously, a VULNERABILITY is only manifested in the presence of a THREAT CAPABILITY. This *generic dependence* relation among these entities determines some ways by which Security Measures can work: the removal of any of them from the situation that could activate them all together implies the prevention of the associated RISK EVENT.

We need to mention briefly the notions of VALUE ASCRIPTION and RISK ASSESSMENT in COVER, because they are able to represent the quantification of value and risk [24]. In a nutshell, an AGENT, called VALUE ASSESSOR or RISK ASSESSOR, evaluates her value and risk experience, considering the satisfaction or dissatisfaction of her goals by the manifestation of dispositions of certain objects. This judgment is then a reified relational entity to which a *quality* can be assigned - for example, like in the severity scale of risk matrix with discrete or continuous values (e.g., ⟨*Low,Medium,High*⟩).

Our extension of COVER is represented in OntoUML language in Fig. 2. The colors used signal the corresponding UFO categories: object types are represented in pink, intrinsic aspect types in light blue, situation types in orange, event types in yellow, higher-order types in a darker blue.

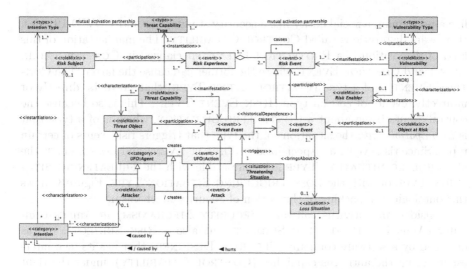

Fig. 2. COVER extension concerning risk concepts and relations.

4.2   Unpacking the Notion of Security Mechanism

A SECURITY MECHANISM is always designed by an AGENT called the SECU-
RITY DESIGNER to be a *countermeasure to* events of certain type (RISK EVENT
TYPE). The AGENT creating a SECURITY MECHANISM is not necessarily the
one who is protected by its proper functioning, i.e., the PROTECTED SUBJECT.
Both agents, nonetheless, have INTENTIONS that are positively impacted by
this proper functioning. For example, the government designs policies for public
safety, the functioning of such policies satisfies some goal the government had
when it designed them, but also satisfies the goal of people who want to be safe.
Sometimes, the PROTECTED SUBJECT is the same AGENT as the SECURITY
DESIGNER, like when a person builds a wall for their own house.

An INTENTION can be generic or specific, according to how specific the situation that satisfies it is. For example, in aerospace domain some goals related to
the costs of the mission are generic, because they can be satisfied by more funding or an assurance; even goals related to replaceable engineering parts can be
satisfied by other parts of the same type. However, the completion of the mission
is a specific goal that can only be satisfied by a specific situation. This distinction
is important, because certain security mechanisms only work for generic goals.
For instance, a space company that transfers some of its risks to an insurance
company can be protected from financial loss, but not from the losses cased
by the explosion of a space shuttle. Ultimately, GENERIC INTENTION can only
be impacted by a setting with generic VALUE OBJECTS (money, for example),
but the SPECIFIC INTENTION may be satisfied by a specific setting with generic
VALUE OBJECTS (say, the need for money under a deadline of bankruptcy).

A SECURITY MECHANISM is an object, which may be a simple physical object
like a wall, a high-tech air defense system like the Israeli Iron Dome, an AGENT

like a policeman, a social entity like a security standard or anti-COVID-19 rules, that bears dispositions called CONTROL CAPABILITY. The manifestation of this kind of disposition is a PROTECTION EVENT, specialized in CONTROL CHAIN EVENT and CONTROL EVENT, where the former can cause the latter. The CONTROL EVENT is of a type (CONTROL EVENT TYPE) that prevents, directly or indirectly, events of certain type (RISK EVENT TYPE). This is so because the control events bring about a CONTROLLED SITUATION, which is of a type that is *incompatible with* the situations of the type that triggers risk events of certain types. Since risk events are specialized in THREAT EVENT and LOSS EVENT, the CONTROLLED SITUATION TYPE is incompatible with the THREATENING SITUATION TYPE or with the LOSS TRIGGERING SITUATION TYPE. Figure 3 shows this ontological unpacking of the notion of Security Mechanism.

Consider an antivirus software (SECURITY MECHANISM) in Anna's computer (Anna is a PROTECTED SUBJECT, but also a RISK SUBJECT). It was designed by a software company (SECURITY DESIGNER) that has its own interest in seeing the antivirus capability (CONTROL CAPABILITY), under the right settings (PROTECTION TRIGGER), working properly (manifesting the PROTECTION EVENT). Under the right settings (PROTECTION TRIGGER), the antivirus searches for malware (the very search can be considered a CONTROL CHAIN EVENT of the causal chain, while the malware as a software is a THREAT OBJECT). Suppose Anna's computer is infected by a malware, which was a THREAT EVENT in the process of causing a LOSS EVENT (say, erasing Anna's files in her computer, where her files are the OBJECT AT RISK). This event of infection (an ATTACK) was only possible due to the conjunction of malicious INTENTION of someone (an ATTACKER), the THREAT CAPABILITY of this person, and the VULNERABILITY of Anna or her computer (RISK ENABLER). However, before the manifestation of the LOSS EVENT, as the antivirus software is running, an event in the control chain causes a CONTROL EVENT of a type that is incompatible with the LOSS TRIGGERING SITUATION TYPE (say, the situations that activate the execution of malware's code to delete Anna's files), therefore preventing the LOSS EVENT of certain type (the loss of Anna's files) that would have hurt Anna's goals. Instead, a CONTROLLED SITUATION (say, Anna's computer free from the referred malware) became a fact brought about by the CONTROL EVENT (say, interrupting the malware running process and deleting it), impacting positively Anna's goals.

Notice that both kinds of indirect prevention play an important role in security: (1) when a CONTROL CHAIN EVENT indirectly prevents a RISK EVENT TYPE through the causation of a CONTROL EVENT, which prevents directly a RISK EVENT TYPE; and (2) when the CONTROL EVENT prevents indirectly the LOSS EVENT TYPE that is causally connected to the directly prevented THREAT EVENT TYPE. In the next section we show how ROSE, which includes the extended ontology of value and risk from COVER as well as the ontology of security represented in Fig. 3, satisfies the requirements proposed in Sect. 2.

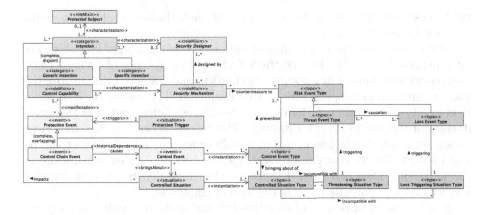

Fig. 3. Unfolding security mechanism.

5   Evaluation

ROSE incorporates a modified extended version of COVER, hence capturing risk and value concepts that are necessary for supporting the activity of risk identification and assessment. Indeed, by the notions of TRIGGERING LIKELIHOOD and CAUSAL LIKELIHOOD ascribed to types of situations and events, ROSE is able to support probabilistic assessment of value, risk, and security happenings. By the VALUE ASCRIPTION and RISK ASSESSMENT inherited from COVER, ROSE is able to support comparison of choices involving values, risks, and security, so supporting decision-making process, since in Risk Management the chances as well as the impact of risky and valuable options should be considered. This machinery allows for the representation of risk treatment options (a) and (b) of ISO 31000: the first case regards to the case that, from the point of view of the experience of the same AGENT that is VALUE ASSESSOR and RISK ASSESSOR, the risk is assessed as higher than the expected ascribed value; in this scenario, considering the chances of the respective events, the AGENT may choose not to start or to continue the activity; the second case is the opposite, when all things considered, the possible success of the endeavor is assessed by the AGENT as more valuable than its associated risks; in this scenario, the AGENT may choose to pursue an opportunity, despite of the risks.

ROSE shows the ambiguity of the risk treatment option (c) "removing the risk source" of ISO 31000, since there are multiple interacting entities that can be considered the "risk source": instances of THREAT OBJECT, OBJECT AT RISK, RISK ENABLER, THREAT CAPABILITY, INTENTION, and VULNERABILITY. It is possible to remove the THREAT CAPABILITY without removing the THREAT OBJECT, though removing the latter implies the removal of the former due to the existential dependence of dispositions on their bearers. For example, a caged lion in a zoo is in such a situation, brought about by a caging event, such that its THREAT CAPABILITY and the VULNERABILITY of the visitors cannot be present in the same situation, though both dispositions remain untouched. However, if the lion escapes and it is sedated by a dart gun shot, the lion, while unconscious, loses its THREAT CAPABILITY.

ROSE also shows the risk treatment options (c), (d) and (e) of ISO 31000 are interconnected. Since the PROTECTION EVENT is an instance of EVENT TYPE that has its associated TRIGGERING LIKELIHOOD and CAUSAL LIKELIHOOD, the effect of prevention happens with a given likelihood. This means the chances of risks events of a certain type happening are different before and after the introduction of the SECURITY MECHANISM. The "consequences" of risk treatment option (e) is simply the loss events of certain types, but a LOSS EVENT can be the THREAT EVENT that causes another LOSS EVENT - for example, a fire in the university office is a LOSS EVENT for the university, but it is a THREAT EVENT that can potentially harm the lives of employees.

Risk treatment option (f) of ISO 31000, "sharing the risk with another party or parties (including contracts and risk financing)", was already described as a SECURITY MECHANISM that is only applicable to protect GENERIC INTENTION by the dispositions of interchangeable VALUE OBJECTS. In this case, the money or the replaceable object may be lost, but, once the equivalent reposition takes place, the events of the type associated to the initial loss are prevented. So the initial loss is both a LOSS EVENT (the loss of money) and a THREAT EVENT for future losses (the consequences of that).

The last risk treatment option of ISO 31000 concerns to retaining the risk by informed decision, that is, the decision to be taken about *residual risks* [18], the risks left after the treatments. This option is a combination of the previous ones: it says that, once options (c), (d), (e), and (f) are implemented, we return to the options (a) and (b) in an iterative decision process, as described in the standard [16]. Again, ROSE can inform such decision-making process by representing scenarios involving value, risk, and security. Residual risks is known to be difficult to assess [18], but ROSE offers a precise picture about the scenario before and after the security mechanism implementation.

ROSE includes all concepts mapped in [22] as the most common in security core ontologies, as requested by OR2. Indeed, ROSE ontologically unpacks them and explains their interactions in details, also distinguishing between intentional and non-intentional threats, and how this matters for security. It is worth noting that ROSE allows for the representation of *redundancy* and multiple layers of protection in security engineering, as different security mechanisms can be designed to be countermeasures of the same type of RISK EVENT.

Concerning the quality requirements, ROSE has shown a rich set of ontological distinctions, thanks to the support of UFO and COVER, maintaining generality, which is noted, for example, by the fact the SECURITY MECHANISM can be an object of different kinds, including physical and social objects. ROSE reuses COVER with some modifications, showing a level of interoperability with a close domain (value and risk), which can be further exploited through connection to other UFO-based ontologies. As UFO and OntoUML are formally defined in First-Order Logic, having support for an OWL implementation[1] , ROSE ben-

---

[1] See: https://purl.org/nemo/gufo.

efits from that, in terms of formality and capacities, since it is expressed in OntoUML, making the use of ROSE for supporting formal reasoning easier. Finally, to make ROSE findable and accessible [17], we provide it publicly in a repository with related information[2].

6 Related Work

The closest related works to ours are proposals of reference ontologies of security based on some foundational ontology. In a recent literature review [22], only four with this approach were found, while nearly all the 57 selected security core ontologies miss every FAIR principle. In [6] the authors propose an ISO-based information security domain ontology, represented in OWL and designed under the principles of the Basic Formal Ontology (BFO), to facilitate the management of standards-related documents and compliance in an Information Security Management System. [21] uses the upper ontology DOLCE to combine two other ontologies to support the activity of modeling security requirements, representing the proposed ontology in the Extended Backus-Naur Format. In [23], based on DOLCE, the authors continue a previous work presenting human factors in this ontology for cyber security operations. To the best of our knowledge, none of them is publicly available besides what can be found inside each corresponding paper. Moreover, they present a limited scope concerning security, given their respective specific aims.

There exist UFO-based ontologies addressing security or related concepts. In [29], the authors propose an ontology to support hazard identification using some UFO categories, though presenting the ontology in UML, instead of OntoUML. Specific security aspects are not addressed therein. The proposal of [1] is more related to ours: based on UFO, but represented in UML, a "Combined Security Ontology" (CSO) that could be aligned with other ontologies. In CSO, countermeasure is an ACTION and asset is a Kind. In ROSE, we take a different ontological interpretation of these notions. Regarding the former, an ACTION may be the manifestation of a CONTROL CAPABILITY of a SECURITY MECHANISM, countermeasures are OBJECTS, not necessarily AGENTS, e.g., a software firewall. Regarding the latter, the type Asset cannot be a Kind, because being an asset depends on the relations the object has with other entities: firstly, nothing is necessarily an asset, but only to the extent the thing's dispositions, when manifested, satisfy someone's goals; moreover, entities of different kinds can be assets. Thus, this notion would be better modelled as role mixin in OntoUML/UFO. So CSO does not seem to commit to UFO in its full extent. The Dysfunctional Analysis Ontology (DAO) [8] continues the Goal-Oriented Safety Management Ontology (GOSMO) and aims at providing a systematization of the goal-oriented dysfunctional analysis through a terminological clarification in order to prevent hazards. They are represented in UML and OWL, making the same (in our view, mistaken) choice of interpreting SAFETY MEASURES as an ACTIONS.

---

[2] See: https://github.com/unibz-core/security-ontology.

7   Final Considerations

We have presented an ontological analysis of security mechanism, making explicit the relations among objects and agents, their capabilities and vulnerabilities, the events they participate and that affect them, and the value and risk they ensue to the stakeholders at hand. The result of this analysis was a concrete artifact called *Reference Ontology of Security Engineering* (ROSE), filling a gap left by the Common Ontology of Value and Risk (COVER) that lacked security-related concepts. With the support of the theory of prevention from the Unified Foundational Ontology, our ontology shows the different generals ways by which a security mechanism works. In the future, we intend to combine ROSE with other UFO-based ontologies, in particular to address legal aspects, and to employ ROSE in the process of evaluating and (re)designing ArchiMate language.

References

1. Adach, M., et al.: A combined security ontology based on the unified foundational ontology. In: International Conference on Semantic Computing, pp. 187–194 (2022)
2. Amaral, G., Sales, T.P., Guizzardi, G., Porello, D.: Towards a reference ontology of trust. In: Panetto, H., et al. (eds.) OTM 2019. LNCS, vol. 11877, pp. 3–21. Springer, Cham (2019). https://doi.org/10.1007/978-3-030-33246-4_1
3. Band, I., Engelsman, W., Feltus, C., Paredes, S.G., Diligens, D.: Modeling enterprise risk management and security with the ArchiMate language (2015)
4. Baratella, R., Fumagalli, M., Oliveira, Í., Guizzardi, G.: Understanding and modeling prevention. In: Guizzardi, R., Ralyte, J., Franch, X. (eds.) Research Challenges in Information Science. RCIS 2022. LNBIP, vol. 446, pp. 389–405. Springer, Cham (2022). https://doi.org/10.1007/978-3-031-05760-1_23
5. van den Berg, B., Hutten, P., Prins, R.: Security and safety: an integrative perspective. In: Jacobs, G., Suojanen, I., Horton, K.E., Bayerl, P.S. (eds.) International Security Management. ASTSA, pp. 13–27. Springer, Cham (2021). https://doi.org/10.1007/978-3-030-42523-4_2
6. Casola, V., et al.: A first step towards an ISO-based information security domain ontology. In: International Conference on Enabling Technologies, pp. 334–339 (2019)
7. Chen, B., et al.: Research on ontology-based network security knowledge map. In: International Conference on Cloud Computing, Big Data and Blockchain, pp. 1–7 (2018)
8. Debbech, S., et al.: An ontological approach to support dysfunctional analysis for railway systems design. J. Univers. Comput. Sci. **26**(5), 549–582 (2020)
9. Donner, M.: Toward a security ontology. IEEE Secur. Priv. **1**(03), 6–7 (2003)
10. Duarte, B.B., de Almeida Falbo, R., Guizzardi, G., Guizzardi, R., Souza, V.E.S.: An ontological analysis of software system anomalies and their associated risks. Data Knowl. Eng. **134**, 101892 (2021)
11. Ekelhart, A., Fenz, S., Klemen, M.D., Weippl, E.R.: Security ontology: simulating threats to corporate assets. In: Bagchi, A., Atluri, V. (eds.) ICISS 2006. LNCS, vol. 4332, pp. 249–259. Springer, Heidelberg (2006). https://doi.org/10.1007/11961635_17
12. Guizzardi, G.: Ontological foundations for structural conceptual models (2005)

13. Guizzardi, G., et al.: Grounding software domain ontologies in the unified foundational ontology (UFO): The case of the ODE software process ontology. In: Ibero-American Conference on Software Engineering, pp. 127–140 (2008)
14. Guizzardi, G., Wagner, G., de Almeida Falbo, R., Guizzardi, R.S.S., Almeida, J.P.A.: Towards ontological foundations for the conceptual modeling of events. In: Ng, W., Storey, V.C., Trujillo, J.C. (eds.) ER 2013. LNCS, vol. 8217, pp. 327–341. Springer, Heidelberg (2013). https://doi.org/10.1007/978-3-642-41924-9_27
15. Guizzardi, G., Bernasconi, A., Pastor, O., Storey, V.C.: Ontological unpacking as explanation: the case of the viral conceptual model. In: Ghose, A., Horkoff, J., Silva Souza, V.E., Parsons, J., Evermann, J. (eds.) ER 2021. LNCS, vol. 13011, pp. 356–366. Springer, Cham (2021). https://doi.org/10.1007/978-3-030-89022-3_28
16. ISO: ISO 31000:2018 - Risk management - Guidelines (2018)
17. Jacobsen, A., et al.: FAIR principles: interpretations and implementation considerations. Data Intell. 2(1–2), 10–29 (2020)
18. Katsikas, S.K.: Risk management. In: Vacca, J.R. (ed.) Computer and Information Security Handbook, pp. 507–527. Morgan Kaufmann, 3 edn. (2013)
19. Kjellén, U.: Prevention of Accidents Through Experience Feedback. CRC Press, Boca Raton (2000)
20. Lund, M.S., Solhaug, B., Stølen, K.: Model-Driven Risk Analysis: The Coras Approach. Springer, Heidelberg (2010)
21. Massacci, F., Mylopoulos, J., Paci, F., Tun, T.T., Yu, Y.: An extended ontology for security requirements. In: Salinesi, C., Pastor, O. (eds.) CAiSE 2011. LNBIP, vol. 83, pp. 622–636. Springer, Heidelberg (2011). https://doi.org/10.1007/978-3-642-22056-2_64
22. Oliveira, Í., et al.: How FAIR are security core ontologies? A systematic mapping study. In: Research Challenges in Information Science, pp. 107–123 (2021)
23. Oltramari, A., et al.: Towards a human factors ontology for cyber security. Semant. Technol. Intell. Def. Secur. 2015, 26–33 (2015)
24. Sales, T.P., Baião, F., Guizzardi, G., Almeida, J.P.A., Guarino, N., Mylopoulos, J.: The common ontology of value and risk. In: Trujillo, J.C., et al. (eds.) ER 2018. LNCS, vol. 11157, pp. 121–135. Springer, Cham (2018). https://doi.org/10.1007/978-3-030-00847-5_11
25. Sales, T.P., et al.: Ontological analysis and redesign of risk modeling in ArchiMate. In: International Enterprise Distributed Object Computing Conference, pp. 154–163 (2018)
26. Sales, T.P., Roelens, B., Poels, G., Guizzardi, G., Guarino, N., Mylopoulos, J.: A pattern language for value modeling in ArchiMate. In: Giorgini, P., Weber, B. (eds.) CAiSE 2019. LNCS, vol. 11483, pp. 230–245. Springer, Cham (2019). https://doi.org/10.1007/978-3-030-21290-2_15
27. Saud, Y.E., Israni, K., Goddard, J.: Bow-tie diagrams in downstream hazard identification and risk assessment. Process Saf. Prog. 33(1), 26–35 (2014)
28. Verdonck, M., et al.: Ontology-driven conceptual modeling: a systematic literature mapping and review. Appl. Ontol. 10(3–4), 197–227 (2015)
29. Zhou, J., et al.: An ontological approach to identify the causes of hazards for safety-critical systems. In: System Reliability and Safety, pp. 405–413 (2017)

Modeling Cybercrime with UFO: An Ontological Analysis of Non-Consensual Pornography Cases

Mattia Falduti$^{(\boxtimes)}$ and Cristine Griffo$^{(\boxtimes)}$

Free University of Bozen-Bolzano Faculty of Computer Science, Piazza Domenicani 3, 39100 Bolzano, Italy
{mattia.falduti,cristine.griffo}@unibz.it

Abstract. The legal domain has challenging aspects. One is that legislation is written to regulate an unpredictable number of cases and, therefore, the language of the law is made of open texture and ambiguous terms. Another peculiarity is that each country has its own legislation, often using the common legal expressions but with different meanings. This results in difficulty in understanding supranational cases and in the interoperability of knowledge bases as well. For example, cybercrimes, in particular, image-based sexual abuses (also known as "revenge porn" or non-consensual pornography) are on the rise globally. Several countries are responding to this social issue by adopting dedicated regulations. However, these regulations are still fragmented, do not share a common conceptualization. In this work, we face these challenges by proposing the application of an ontology-based conceptual modeling to represent a set of concepts and legal relations in cybercrime law. To evaluate the model built, we analyzed the subdomain of cybercrimes, in particular, cases of non-consensual pornography on digital platforms. The result is a conceptualization capable of being shared with other models, increasing the interoperability and clarity of the meaning of common terms and relations found in the various laws studied.

Keywords: Cybercrime · Non-consensual pornography · Legal knowledge representation · UFO-L · Legal ontology

1 Introduction

Non-consensual pornography is a recent crime[1]. It consists of sharing in digital platforms nude photos or videos without the consent of the individuals depicted

---

[1] We point out that, even if the terms "non-consensual pornography" and "revenge pornography" have been used in the literature, official documents, and news, the term *pornography* appears not properly used, because it refers to a particular adult content, legitimate and for mass consumption [32]. We encourage the use of the following terms *Non-Consensual Intimate Images* (NCII) abuse [29] and *Image-based Sexual Abuse* [12] notwithstanding the general public's unfamiliarity with these terms. In this paper, we use the cited terms interchangeably in order to make the content of the article as accessible as possible to all readers.

© The Author(s), under exclusive license to Springer Nature Switzerland AG 2022
J. Ralyté et al. (Eds.): ER 2022, LNCS 13607, pp. 380–394, 2022.
https://doi.org/10.1007/978-3-031-17995-2_27

or recorded [9]. Colloquially, this phenomenon is known as "revenge porn", a highly misleading expression, usually used in the news, with many stigmatising implications for the victim. Sharing intimate images without the consent of the person depicted aims at shaming and humiliating someone, while publicly exposing the most intimate and private sphere of life, obtained in several ways, or digitally generated (deepfake).

Unfortunately, data confirms the global reach of the phenomenon and the urgency for providing effective solutions. According to the Italian law enforcement agency [24], only last year there were more than 500 complaints with over 1.400 people accused. This represents an increase of almost 80% as compared to the previous year. Northern countries display even more dramatic figures. According to the UK Police data, in the same year there were 1,185 cases of private multimedia content illegally shared online, while in Germany, the crime of violation of the personal realm by pictures counted 9.233 cases only in 2020 [4]. The UK press suggests that, due to the current pandemic, cases of revenge pornography raised by 329% only in London [34].

Although non-consensual pornography phenomenon is a global concern and several countries have regulated this conduct in their legal systems as crime (e.g. Italy, Germany, France, Denmark, Spain, UK, Australia, Canada, Japan), a shared and portable common knowledge has not been formalized yet. In fact, the phenomenon *per se* is well defined, but semantic differences arise from different legislation.

A possible solution to the semantic problem in different legislations is the ontological analysis of each one of them and its representation using a common well-founded ontological modeling language. A next step would be the application of some approach of ontology matching, alignment, or correspondence [35]. In this paper, we present the beginning of this process by proposing an ontological conceptualization of the crime. We analyzed the main concepts and relations existing in the non-consensual pornography struggled by legislation of different countries. Then, we applied a well-grounded legal core ontology (UFO-L) [15] to build a domain ontology for the phenomenon of non-consensual pornography.

Once the effects of cybercrimes go beyond the jurisdiction of a country, it is appropriate that information systems of different countries can interact and use the same set of concepts and relations to represent the same phenomenon. This work contributes to extending the body of knowledge by proposing a common conceptualization for the mentioned phenomenon. We believe that this is the first step towards enabling the interoperability of information systems in cybercrime cases.

The paper is organized as follows: Sect. 2 presents a brief summary of the main works on legal ontologies found in the literature; Sect. 3 presents the ontological analysis of the selected cybercrime, emphasizing fragments of legislation from five countries. Based on this ontological analysis, it is presented the ontological representation of the scenario of the non-consensual pornography crime, from the content generation phase, passing through the preparatory actions, and culminating with the crime realization. The preliminary results are presented in

Sect. 5 with the application of the model to three real cases. In Sect. 6, we discuss the main results and limitations followed by the final considerations and future works.

2   Related Work

Legal knowledge is usually modeled using ontologies. As reported in [21], ontologies can be seen as explicit specifications of conceptualisations and as representations of terminological legal knowledge. As any other domain, the legal knowledge can also be represented at different levels of abstraction. For instance, *Core* legal ontologies are devoted to formalizing the general aspects of the legal domain, with the main aim of reasoning and inference on general legal concepts. As pointed out in [14], over the previous decades, the field of legal ontologies had seen an increase in the number of papers. The literature on legal ontologies now covers a wide variety of topics and research approaches. One of these topics is represented by legal core ontologies, which had received significant attention since the 1990s.s. However, the heterogeneity of the legal domain has led to the construction of content description models of miscellaneous ontological types. Indeed, at a lower level of abstraction, we find several *domain* legal ontologies. These are devoted at formalizing concepts and relations featuring a single domain such as civil law, commercial law, data protection and copyrights, international law, European law, public law and criminal law. Legal domain ontologies aim mainly at i) understanding the domain [16], ii) organizing and structuring information for applications/system [6], iii) semantic indexing and information search [7]. The criminal domain has been modeled in several ontologies, but usually with only a national-based and domestic point of view [10].

2.1   National Criminal Law Ontologies in the Literature

Regarding the criminal domain, several works have been proposed in different countries. Further details about the mentioned works are described in [10].

The Netherlands. In [2], the authors present the use of various ontologies for the information management of documents produced inside the criminal trial hearings. These ontologies are used in the e-COURT project and cover the Dutch criminal law by following the structure of the LRI-Core ontology [3]. The main aim of this work is to support information retrieval by tagging and annotating the hearing documents.

India. A semantic web-based recommendation system is presented in [30]. The proposed OWL ontology helps legal expert users in extracting court decisions from a case law repository with respect to similar cases. The authors report that the ontology is designed exclusively for that purpose. Indeed, the knowledge represented derives from the Indian Penal Code and an application on murder cases is proposed.

Lebanon. In [13] a criminal ontology defining Lebanese criminal law is formalized in Semantic Web Rule Language (SWRL). Authors modeled this ontology for constructing a legal rule-based decision support system for the criminal domain named CORBS. The system supports legal decision-making with the use of a rule-based reasoning approach. The rule-based decision system contains a set of logic rules composed of atoms, which are defined based on the ontology elements and formalized using SWRL. Authors report that SWRL is used because it is better suited to express deductive knowledge by rules composed of atoms.

USA. [11] presents an ontology engineering methodology and a semi-automated approach of legal ontology generation, both derived from a collection of legal documents. Their model represents semantic information about the USA criminal law. The generation approach also includes legal rules to provide reasoning support to an automatic legal question answering system.

Italy. In [1] an Italian criminal law ontology is described. A UML ontology, based on the Italian crime law, used as a support tool for the judges' activity in the criminal field, is here presented. The ontology formalizes the difference between the criminal behaviours with respect to the offences and to the interests protected by the law, presenting the crime structure as follows: an offender, a behaviour, a penalty and optionally, an event and a coercion.

Tunisia. In [22], the CrimAr ontology for Arabic criminal law is presented. CrimAr is based on the top-levels of LRI-Core ontology [3] and represents all the relevant knowledge in the Arabic legal domain, especially in the criminal matter.

South Korea. [31] presents an ontology for the South Korean criminal law. In particular, this work discusses an ontology-based legal knowledge representation first, and then a logic-based legal rule design methodology, with an application tested on the Korean anti-graft act.

3   Ontological Analysis

The ontological analysis started with the study of legislation, followed by the study of real cases. In general, diffusion of personal data is forbidden by data protection regulations. However, these regulations do not always introduce a criminal punishment. Differently, to consider non-consensual pornography as a criminal activity, the introduction of a dedicated criminal law is necessary.

From real-cases, we noticed that media object are usually i) self-taken, i.e. created or shared between partners during a relationship, or ii) stealth-taken, i.e. stolen, obtained without authorization or extorted. The criminal action consists in uploading - and making public - these media on one or more digital platforms, with the intention of diffusing the intimate imagery and abusing the victim.

Analysing the existing criminal legislation we identified three main phases, namely, 1) *Content Generation*, i.e., the creation of the intimate private media object; 2) *Preparatory Action,* i.e., the uploading of the intimate private media object; and 3) *Crime Realization,* i.e., the visualization of these media objects by third parties. This last phase is when the crime is consummated To be more precise, uploading intimate content online, for example, in a chat group, could already be relevant from a criminal perspective. Indeed, this fact can be recognized as an offensive preparation for the crime. On the contrary, uploading an intimate media content on an empty chat group or on a deprecated website, might be realized only a potential offence, maybe irrelevant from a (pure) criminal perspective, but possibly sanctioned with civil law remedies.

According to the European Network of Legal Experts on Gender Equality and Non-discrimination of the European Commission, in 2021 eleven states (Belgium, France, Ireland, Italy, Malta, Netherlands, Poland, Portugal, Spain, Sweden, United Kingdom) have specifically criminalised the non-consensual dissemination/publication/disclosure of intimate/private/sexual images [28]. In the USA, according to a study of the Center for Internet and Society, most of the states have a dedicated legislation. Moreover, Canada, Australia, Israel, New Zealand and Japan have also specifically criminalised the phenomenon. For the sake of space, we mention here some excerpts from the legislation collected[2].

Belgium. The Article 371/1 of the Belgian Criminal Code, as reported in [25] states that *whoever [...] made or caused to be made a visual or audio recording of a person: (i) directly or by technical or other means; (ii) without that* **person**'s *authorization or without his or her knowledge; (iii) while the person was* **nude** *or engaged in* **explicit sexual activity***; and (iv) in circumstances in which the person could reasonably be expected not to* **invade his or her privacy** *showed,* **made accessible** *or disseminated* **images or the visual or audio** *recording of a person who is nude or engaged in explicit sexual activity, without his or her consent or without his or her knowledge, even if that person has consented to their production will be punished [...].*

Brazil. 218-C of the Penal Code [26] establishes that it is a crime to *offer, exchange, make available, transmit, sell or exhibit for sale, distribute,* **publish or disseminate,** *by any means, including through mass communication or computer or telematics system,* **photography, video or other audiovisual record** *that contains a scene of rape or rape of a vulnerable person or that makes incitement or induces its practice, or,* **without the consent of the victim, sex scene, nudity or pornography,** *setting the penalty of imprisonment from one to five years.*

Italy. As pointed out in [5] the Article 612 ter of the Italian Criminal Code states that *[...] a* **person** *who, after having made or stolen them,* **sends, delivers, transfers, publishes or disseminates images** *or* videos *containing* **sexually explicit materials,** *intended to remain* **private,** *without the consent of the* **persons depicted,** *is liable to be punished [...].*

---

[2] The full content can be accessed at the link https://github.com/mf-thesquare/ NCP_legislation.

Malta. Article 208E of the Maltese Criminal Code was introduced in 2016 and it punishes *whoever, with an intent to cause distress, emotional harm or harm of any nature,* **discloses a private sexual photograph or film** *without the consent of the person or* **persons displayed or depicted** *in such photograph or film shall on conviction be liable to imprisonment [...]* [8].

3.1 Problem Statement

Even if many states have attempted to use existing statutes or created new ones to combat non-consensual pornography, there is no consistent approach, which has led to variable results among states [27]. The legal literature confirms that, for protecting victims efficiently and response with efficacy to this vicious phenomenon, *"the need for a consistent approach is obvious, especially given the borderless nature of the crime"*. To move direction consistency, we noticed that legislators are using different terms to express very similar or identical concepts. Examples are the terms *photography, video, audiovisual, image, visual, audio, film, recordings* for expressing a media content, or *nude, explicit sexual activity, pornographic, sexually explicit material, private sexual, sex scene* to express the concept of intimate media content. With our knowledge model, we try to systematize the criminal knowledge.

4 Model

Analysing the legislation and real-case applications emerging in the literature and in the news, we identified concepts, roles, events and relations. Some concepts were named following the legal literature or the text of the studied laws (e.g. *Depicted Person, Perpetrator, Private Intimate Media Object*). Others, however, we harmonize to converge the different terms found in the analyzed laws (e.g. *Depicter Person, Publisher, Content Consumer*). Finally, following the UFO-L patterns, we elaborated four main relations, namely i) Right to Privacy of an Intimate Media and ii) Uploading of the Private Media Object, iii) Accessing of the Private Intimate Media and iv) Violation of the Right to Privacy of an Intimate Media. To model these relations, we applied UFO/OntoUML [17] and UFO-L P1-RD-LR legal relator pattern [15]. As we used the OntoUML plugin for Visual Paradigm, colours are set by default according to the stereotypes. For instance, the colour rose for *role*; green for *relator*; blue for *mode*.

4.1 Legal Roles

We identified several legal roles modeling non-consensual pornography phenomenon. Usually, in sex offenses, the involved subjects are natural persons (see Fig. 1).

Depicted Person in Intimacy: is a person depicted in an intimate media (e.g. photo, video), recognizable from the face or other unique characteristics.

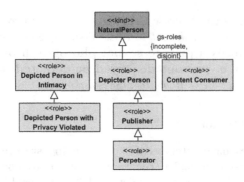

Fig. 1. Legal Roles Taxonomy

Depicted Person with Privacy Violated: is a natural person who has his/her privacy violated by means of the uploading or publishing of the media in which s/he is in intimacy.

   Constraint 1:Depicted Person with Privacy Violated may not play the role of *Depicter Person* in the same relation because, in this case, it would be a self-action and, hence, no crime would have occurred.

Depicter Person: is a person able to upload and publish an intimate media. *Depicter Person* has the duty to keep the privacy of the *Depicted Person's* intimate media.

   Constraint 2: Depicter Person may not play the role of *Depicted Person with Privacy Violated* in the same relation.

Publisher: the *Depicter Person*, being in possession of intimate media, becomes a *Publisher* after uploading it to an *Accessible Digital Platform.*

Perpetrator: Publisher becomes a *Perpetrator* with the access to private media by the *Content Consumer* and the violation of the depicted person's right to privacy.
Constraint 3: In a same relation of Right-Duty to Keep the Intimate Media Object Privately, Perpetrator may not be *Depicted Person in Intimacy.*

Content Consumer: is one or more third-parties accessing and consuming the private, intimate media content uploaded. If one or more *Content Consumer(s)* re-upload the private intimate media content, they may become publisher(s) and potentially perpetrator(s).

   Constraint 4: in a same relation, *Content Consumer* may not be *Depicted Person with Privacy Violated.*

4.2   Right to Privacy of an Intimate Media

The legal position *right to privacy* is represented by applying the legal relator pattern *right-duty to an action* between *Depicted Person in Intimacy* and

Depicter Person after the *publication and entry into force of the criminal law.* In the model, *Depicted Person in Intimacy* is entitled with the right to privacy after the effective publication of the criminal law as well as *Depicter Person* has the duty to keep *Intimate Media Object Privately* (see Fig. 2).

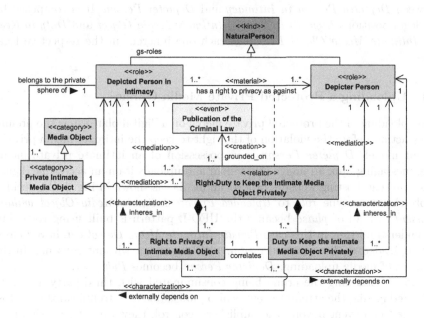

Fig. 2. Right-Duty to Privacy

Effective Publication of the Criminal Law: is the event, (usually the date) when the legislation that criminalizes the conducts of non-consensual diffusion of intimate imagery is officially published and entries into force. We precise that before the introduction of the criminal law, in some countries, the non-consensual publication of intimate imagery could be forbidden or sanctioned by non-criminal legislation or case law.

Private Intimate Media Object: is any image, videos, or audio with intimate content, both self-created by or stealth-obtained, representing sexual activities, genital regions or female breast. This subkind specializes *Media object* in terms of content.

Right to Privacy of Intimate Media Object: is the right that *Depicted Person in Intimacy* may exercise against *Depicter Person.* Even if there exists a general right to privacy, recognized by various data protection legislation, proper criminal protection against illicit publication comes to light with the *Publication of the Criminal Law.*

Duty to Keep the Intimate Media Object Privately: is the duty of *Depicter Person* to keep an intimate media private. This duty comes to light with the *Publication of the Criminal Law.*

Right-duty to Keep the Intimate Media Object Privately: is the legal relation between *Depicted Person in Intimacy* and *Depicter Person.* It is composed by the legal positions *Right to Privacy of Intimate Media Object* and *Duty to Keep the Intimate Media Object Privately,* each one inherent in the respective legal roles.

4.3   Uploading a Protected Private Media Online

The uploading of the protected private media on a digital platform is the preliminary action before the violation of the right to keep the intimate media private. In our model, *Depicter Person* is in possession of an intimate private media (e.g. messaging app, an image or a video) and uploads it on an accessible digital platform (e.g. hosting website, or a social media) as shown in Fig. 3. We decided apply the stereotype *role* to *Uploaded Private Intimate Media Object without Consent* instead of *phase* because the UFO-L pattern is built using roles, but we understand that in this case *Private Intimate Media Object* can have phases (e.g. uploaded media, accessed media, with consent or without consent). In the moment of media uploading, *Depicter Person* becomes *Publisher.*

Notwithstanding the crime being consummated with third-party access to uploaded media, the attempt event is also punishable (e.g. to upload the photos, but due to an event beyond the publisher's control, they are not accessible).

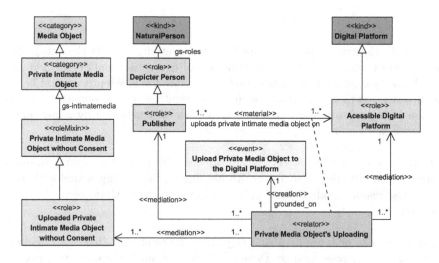

Fig. 3. Uploading of a private intimate media online

Accessible Digital Platform: is the *Digital Platform* where the media content can be uploaded or posted and accessed, such as messaging apps, social media, image or video hosting websites and forums.

Private Media Object's Uploading: is the ternary relation between Publisher, Accessible Digital Platform, and the intimate media uploaded without the consent of the Depicted Person. The event *Upload Private Media Object to the Digital Platform* is run by Publisher and grounds the described relation.

Uploaded Private Intimate Media Object without Consent: is the *Private Intimate Media Object without Consent* after the end of the uploading event made by *Publisher* on a *Accessible Digital Platform.*

4.4   Violation of Depicted Person's Right to Privacy

After the uploading, the private intimate media is potentially accessible and visualized by one or more content consumers. This is the first moment when the realization of the crime of non-consensual pornography is complete and, consequently, the right to privacy of the depicted person is violated according to criminal law (Fig. 4). At this moment, *Publisher* becomes *Perpetrator.*

Private Intimate Media Accessing: is the intimate media accessed by third-parties on an *Accessible Digital Platform.*

Violation of the Depicted Person's Right to Privacy: when an intimate media has been uploaded and accessed/visualized, the privacy of *Depicted Person* is violated. Therefore, there is a relation between a person, who had the duty to keep private the intimate media and violated it; and the person, who had the right to privacy violated. Both *Violated Right to Privacy of an Intimate Media* and *Violated Duty to Keep Private an Intimate Media,* are aspects inherent in *Depicted Person with Privacy Violated* and *Perpetrator* respectively.

Accessed Private Intimate Media Object: is the *Uploaded Private Intimate Media Object without Consent* accessed and visualized by one or more *Content Consumer* on an *Accessible Digital Platform.*

5   Preliminary Evaluation

We evaluate our model with real cases reported in the news and literature. More in particular, involving two criminal law experts, we ask them to analyse cases and classify the facts. We tested the instantiation of these cases in our model, and we compare the facts' classification performed by the expert and by the model.

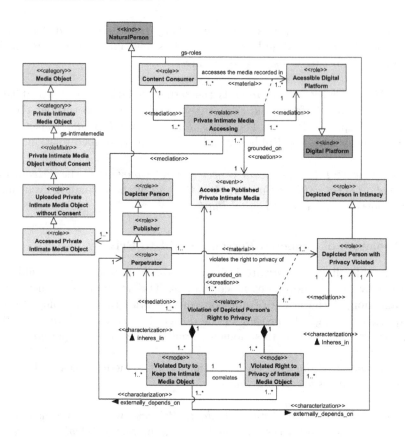

Fig. 4. Violation of Depicted Person Right to Privacy

5.1 Real Cases

Tiziana Cantone. This case was extensively reported in the Italian news [33] and in the criminal literature [5]. The 31-year-old woman caught the public attention due to the viral dissemination of videos of her performing sexual acts, found online from April 2015 on several porn websites, and circulated on the messaging application like WhatsApp. There were also dedicated Facebook pages and groups, and a phrase recorded in the video became a so-called "meme". Non-consensual pornography became a specific criminal offence in Italy in August 2019.

Chrissy Chambers. This case has also been largely reported in the UK news [20] and in the literature [36]. Chrissy Chambers, a famous YouTuber and activist, discovered that people around her received a message saying literally "Did you know that Chrissy has a porn video on RedTube? [...]" Chambers googled herself and discovered that her ex-boyfriend uploaded between December 2009 and January 2012 seven videos of them having sex to dozens of porn sites, and people had left comments underneath the video. Non-consensual pornography became a specific criminal offence in England in Wales in April 2015.

John Duffin. This case has also been reported in several UK news [18] and discussed in the literature [19]. As described and reported, the John Duffin in 2015 saved an intimate picture of his ex-girlfriend and set it as his WhatsApp profile picture, which allowed all his contacts to view it. Non-consensual pornography became a specific criminal offence in England in Wales in April 2015.

5.2 Experts Analysis

The criminal law experts analysed the narratives of the facts. They report that the cases have many facts in common, namely, a female victim, a broken relationship, a perpetrator, an intimate video of the victim, the publication of this video committed by the ex-boyfriend, and the access of these videos by an undefined set of people. However, the first two cases are not relevant from a pure criminal perspective because they occurred before the introduction of criminal legislation. In contrast, the last case occurred after the publication of the legislation criminalizing non-consensual pornography in the UK and therefore, it is recognizable as a crime. Having this expert-based facts classification, we aim at making legal interpretation machine-readable by instantiating roles, concepts and relations, performing a preliminary model classification and comparing it with the expert-based classification.

5.3 Model Instantiation and Facts Classification

We instantiated our model with the information extracted (see a fragment in Fig. 5). Considering that the crime of non-consensual pornography is consummated if all events and the roles modeled occur, we first instantiate the events and roles, and then we compared the model and the expert classification of the facts. More in particular, as presented in Fig. 1, the crime phases present different roles of the *Natural Person*. For example, if the crime is consumed and the ex-partner 1) has taken the picture (is the *Depicter Person*), 2) has published the picture online (is the *Publisher*) and 3) has made it available for the public (is the *Perpetrator*), following the path of the crime, it is possible to instantiate each role with the ex-partner. Differently, if the crime does not reach its last phase or the three action described above are committed by different agents, it is possible to instantiate the model accordingly. Similarly, *Private Intimate Media Object* assumes the last role of *Accessed Private Intimate Media Object* (see Fig. 4) when the crime is consumed. With this approach, it is possible to formalize the different phases of the crime and identify each legal roles during the crime evolution, which is mapped through the events.

6 Final Considerations

In this paper, we presented a preliminary ontological analysis of non-consensual pornography cases. With this work, we aim at presenting the first step for the

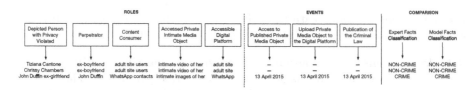

Fig. 5. Model Instantiation and Facts Classification (fragment)

process of interoperability of information systems on cybercrimes, in particular, on non-consensual pornography crime. With the proposed conceptualization, we aim also at encouraging effective multinational solutions and cooperation.

The benefits of our approach range from the possibility of representing the dynamics of roles and their respective interactions over time. Also, it is possible with this approach to clearly identify the intrinsic aspects of each role in each relation, making it possible to identify the legal positions of each person in each role during the path of crime. This is relevant in the criminal law, as the penalty dosimetry depends on the role each agent played in the crime.

At the same time, we recognize the limits of our approach. Our model does not represent the geographical and temporal evolution of the law. We decided to leave the model temporal and national-agnostic, but we also plan to model the dynamic aspects of the criminal evolution in future works. Furthermore, non-consensual pornography evolves with different and new conducts, such as *sextortion*, i.e. the threat to distribute intimate materials unless a victim complies with specific demands [23] and *cyberflashing*, i.e. the act of sending non-requested obscene images or videos [12]. These conducts present peculiarities that have not been modeled in this preliminary formalization and will also be part of our future work. Moreover, we plan to add to this first representation the knowledge concerning the initial steps of the access to justice, such as victims reports, police investigations, and formal allegations.

References

1. Asaro, C., Biasiotti, M., Guidotti, P., Papini, M., Sagri, M.T., Tiscornia, D.: A domain ontology: Italian crime ontology. In: Proceedings of the Workshop on Legal Ontologies and Web Based Legal Information Management (LegOnt 2003), pp. 1–7. Edinburgh, UK (2003)
2. Breuker, J.: The construction and use of ontologies of criminal law in the e-Court European project. In: Proceedings of Means of Electronic Communication in Court Administration, pp. 15–40 (2003)
3. Breuker, J., Hoekstra, R.: Core concepts of law: Taking common-sense seriously. In: Proceedings of the 3rd International Conference on Formal Ontologies in Information Systems (FOIS 2004), pp. 210–221. Torino, Italy (2004)
4. Bundeskriminalamt: BKA - Police Crime Statistics. https://www.bka.de/EN/CurrentInformation/PoliceCrimeStatistics (2022)

5. Caletti, G.M.: Can affirmative consent save "Revenge Porn" Laws? Lessons from the Italian criminalization of non-consensual pornography. Virginia J. Law Technol. **25**(3), 112–174 (2021)
6. Castano, S., Falduti, M., Ferrara, A., Montanelli, S.: Crime knowledge extraction: an ontology-driven approach for detecting abstract terms in case law decisions. In: Proceedings of the 17th International Conference on Artificial Intelligence and Law (ICAIL19), pp. 179–183. Montreal, Canada (2019)
7. Castano, S., Falduti, M., Ferrara, A., Montanelli, S.: A knowledge-centered framework for exploration and retrieval of legal documents. Inf. Syst. **106**, 101842 (2021). https://doi.org/10.1016/j.is.2021.101842
8. Degiorgio, E.: Criminalising Revenge Porn. Ph.D. thesis, University of Malta (2016)
9. European Institute for Gender Equality: Cyber Violence against Women and Girls. Vilnius, European Institute for Gender Equality (EIGE) (2017)
10. Falduti, M.: Law and Data Science: Knowledge Modeling and Extraction from Court Decisions. Ph.D. thesis, Università degli Studi di Milano (2021)
11. Fawei, B., Pan, J.Z., Kollingbaum, M.J., Wyner, A.Z.: A semi-automated ontology construction for legal question answering. N. Gener. Comput. **37**(4), 453–478 (2019)
12. Fido, D., Harper, C.A.: An introduction to image-based sexual abuse. In: Nonconsensual Image-based Sexual Offending. PSC, pp. 1–26. Springer, Cham (2020). https://doi.org/10.1007/978-3-030-59284-4_1
13. Ghosh, M.E., Naja, H., Abdulrab, H., Khalil, M.: Towards a legal rule-based system grounded on the integration of criminal domain ontology and rules. Proc. Comput. Sci. **112**, 632–642 (2017)
14. Griffo, C., Almeida, J.P.A., Guizzardi, G.: A systematic mapping of the literature on legal core ontologies. In: Proceedings of the 7th Brazilian Symposium on Ontology Research (ONTOBRAS 2015), pp. 79–90, Sao Paolo, Brazil (2015)
15. Griffo, C., Almeida, J.P.A., Guizzardi, G.: Conceptual modeling of legal relations. In: Trujillo, J.C., Davis, K.C., Du, X., Li, Z., Ling, T.W., Li, G., Lee, M.L. (eds.) Conceptual Modeling. LNCS, vol. 11157, pp. 169–183. Springe, Cham (2018). https://doi.org/10.1007/978-3-030-00847-5-14
16. Griffo, C., Almeida, J.P.A., Guizzardi, G., Nardi, J.C.: Service contract modeling in enterprise architecture: an ontology-based approach. Inf. Syst. **101**, 101454 (2021). https://doi.org/10.1016/j.is.2019.101454
17. Guizzardi, G.: Ontological foundations for structural conceptual models. Ph.D. thesis, University of Twente, October 2005
18. Harriet Thurley: Bristol man found guilty of revenge porn against his ex – via WhatsApp. Cosmopolitan (2015)
19. Haynes, J.: Legislative approaches to combating 'revenge porn': a multijurisdictional perspective. Statut. Law Rev. **3**(39), 319–336 (2018)
20. Kleeman, J.: The YouTube star who fought back against revenge porn – and won. The Guardian (2018)
21. Benjamins, V.R., Casanovas, P., Breuker, J., Gangemi, A.: Law and the Semantic Web. Legal Ontologies, Methodologies, Legal Information Retrieval, and Applications. LNCS (LNAI), vol. 3369. Springer, Heidelberg (2005). https://doi.org/10.1007/b106624
22. Mezghanni, I., Gargouri, F.: CrimAr: A criminal Arabic ontology for a benchmark based evaluation. In: Proceedings of the 21st International Conference on Knowledge-Based and Intelligent Information & Engineering Systems (KES 2017), pp. 653–662. Procedia Computer Science, Marseille, France (2017). https://doi.org/10.1016/j.procs.2017.08.113

23. O'Malley, R.L., Holt, K.M.: Cyber sextortion: an exploratory analysis of different perpetrators engaging in a similar crime. J. Interpers. Violence. 37, 258–283 (2020). https://doi.org/10.1177/0886260520909186
24. Postale, P.: I dati 2021 della Polizia postale. https://www.poliziadistato.it/articolo/23393
25. Resourcehub: Fighting Domestic Violence - Belgium. Technical report, Bakermckenzie (2021)
26. Rocha, R.L.M., Pedrinha, R.D., de Oliveira, M.H.B.: O tratamento da pornografia de vingança pelo ordenamento jurídico brasileiro. Saúde em Debate 43(spe4), 178–189 (2019). https://doi.org/10.1590/0103-11042019s415
27. Roffer, J.: Nonconsensual pornography: an old crime updates its software. Fordham Intellect. Prop. Media Entertain. Law J. **27**(4), 935 (2017)
28. Sara De Vido, Sosa, L.: Criminalisation of gender-based violence against women in European States, including ICT-facilitated violence. Technical report, European network of legal experts in gender equality and non-discrimination, European Commission (2021)
29. Semenzin, S., Bainotti, L.: The use of telegram for non-consensual dissemination of intimate images: gendered affordances and the construction of Masculinities. Soc. Media + Soc. **6**(4), 205630512098445 (2020). https://doi.org/10.1177/2056305120984453
30. Shankhdhar, G.K., Singh, V.K., Darbari, M.: Legal semantic web - a recommendation system. Int. J. Appl. Inf. Syst. **7**(3), 21–27 (2014)
31. Pagallo, U., Palmirani, M., Casanovas, P., Sartor, G., Villata, S.: AI Approaches to the Complexity of Legal Systems. AICOL 2015-2017. LNCS (LNAI), vol. 10791. Springer, Cham (2018). https://doi.org/10.1007/978-3-030-00178-0
32. Maddocks, S.: "Revenge Porn": 5 Important Reasons Why We Should Not Call It By That Name. GenderIt.org (2019)
33. Stephanie Kirchgaessner: Tiziana Cantone: Seeking justice for woman who killed herself over sex tape. The Guardian (2016)
34. Terry, K.: Pandemic fuels 329% rise in revenge porn offences in London: Met Police records 1,185 cases of private snaps and videos illegally shared online in last year - with victims as young as TEN. https://www.dailymail.co.uk/news/article-10303961/Pandemic-fuels-329-rise-revenge-porn-offences-London-victims-young-TEN.html (2021)
35. Trojahn, C., Vieira, R., Schmidt, D., Pease, A., Guizzardi, G.: Foundational ontologies meet ontology matching: a survey. Semant. Web. 1–20 (2021). https://doi.org/10.3233/SW-210447
36. Véliz, C.: The internet and privacy. In: Edmonds, D. (ed.) Ethics and the Contemporary World, pp. 149–159. Abingdon, UK (2019)

Goals and Requirements

Modeling Rates of Change and Aggregations in Runtime Goal Models

Rebecca Morgan[1]($\boxtimes$) (iD), Simon Pulawski[2] (iD), Matt Selway[1] (iD),
Wolfgang Mayer[1] (iD), Georg Grossmann[1] (iD), Markus Stumptner[1] (iD),
Aditya Ghose[2] (iD), and Ross Kyprianou[3] (iD)

[1] Industrial AI Research Centre, UniSA STEM, University of South Australia,
Adelaide, SA 5000, Australia
{rebecca.morgan,matt.selway,wolfgang.mayer,georg.grossmann,
markus.stumptner}@unisa.edu.au
[2] Decision Systems Lab, University of Wollongong, Wollongong, NSW 2500, Australia
{spp701,aditya}@uow.edu.au
[3] Defence Science and Technology Group, Edinburgh, SA 5111, Australia
ross.kyprianou@defence.gov.au
https://www.unisa.edu.au/research/industrial-ai/

Abstract. Achieving real-time agility and adaptation with respect to changing requirements in existing IT infrastructure can pose a complex challenge. We explore a goal-oriented approach to managing this complexity. We argue that a goal-oriented perspective can form an effective basis for devising and deploying responses to changed requirements in real-time. We offer an extended vocabulary of goal types, specifically by presenting two novel conceptions: differential goals and integral goals, which we formalize in both linear-time and branching-time settings. We then illustrate the working of the approach by presenting a detailed scenario of adaptation in a Kubernetes setting, in the face of a DDoS attack.

Keywords: Goal-modeling · Self-adaptive systems · Micro-services · Context-awareness

1 Introduction

Managing complex information systems deployed on cloud platforms remains a challenge in dynamic environments where systems must respond to changes in demand, failures, attacks, or evolving organizational requirements. Despite automated monitoring and adaptation mechanisms provided by cloud platforms such as Kubernetes, oversight of the adaptation remains a human responsibility necessitating a high degree of situational awareness [13].

Situational awareness [10] is an emergent property resulting from system interactions with the environment and provides the environmental context for making optimal decisions regarding system adaptations to meet operational

© The Author(s), under exclusive license to Springer Nature Switzerland AG 2022
J. Ralyté et al. (Eds.): ER 2022, LNCS 13607, pp. 397–412, 2022.
https://doi.org/10.1007/978-3-031-17995-2_28

goals. Similarly, the human operator's situational awareness arises from knowing how the system's automated adaptations to the changing environment are performing with respect to goals. This is often impeded by the overwhelming volume of detail collected in dashboards visualizing sensor information, such as resource utilization and event statistics. Enhancing situational awareness of both autonomous agents and human operators to support effective decision-making requires an understanding of how changes in the environment (manifested in low-level sensor readings) impact higher-level system goals.

We hypothesize that a goal-oriented lens provides the appropriate set of abstractions to improve situational awareness and resulting human/computer decision making that can be layered over the top of existing complex systems, for example, to facilitate the management of monitoring and adaptation of complex IT infrastructure deployments. We offer a goal-oriented approach to presenting system state and controlling system adaptation, offering the advantage that goals are well-suited for human understanding while leveraging well-established reasoning mechanisms to transform higher-level goals into executable adaptation plans [1,17]. We use goals in two modes: goal-level sensing, i.e., using goal-based abstractions (probes) for building situation awareness models; and goal-based actuation planning, i.e., refining overall adaptation goals into executable plans for achieving the targeted adaptation (via effectors). To this end, we extend the repertoire of available goal types discussed in the literature with two new categories (differential and integral goals) and show how goals can be refined into executable adaptations using probes and effectors as abstractions to the underlying Kubernetes platform. The resulting goal-driven approach is illustrated on a case study drawn from the cybersecurity domain.

This paper is organized as follows. The motivating case study on cybersecurity is introduced in Sect. 2. A discussion of related work is provided in Sect. 3, followed by the introduction of differential and integral goals in Sect. 4. The case study exemplifying the goal model and reasoning is presented in Sect. 5, and we conclude in Sect. 6.

2   Case Study: Cybersecurity

In this paper, we use the cybersecurity context to illustrate goal-based adaptation with proactive situational awareness. For example, consider an aim to be providing responsive and reliable web services to as many users as possible, without making unnecessary or expensive demands on resources.

Ideally, these goals are achieved by applying a management policy that dynamically scales (up or down) the services in response to actual or predicted demand. To maintain reliability, new instances are created or services are restarted in response to failures, and requests are rerouted to alternatives during the fail-over period. Under normal usage conditions, such a policy would appear to meet our goals, where demand scales predictably and failures are infrequent. However, during anomalous events such as a Distributed Denial of Service (DDoS) attack, the scale-up response to the increased load could become detrimental to the system. Since resources are finite, the scale-up will eventually stop, the DDoS having overwhelmed the available capacity, ultimately leading to total system failure. Such a scenario may incur a pair of undesirable possibilities: uncontrolled scale-up may put additional load on infrastructure resources as new service instances are created, hampering the ability of existing instances to respond to requests and leading to catastrophic failure, while a sudden return to "business as usual" may be difficult to monitor and would not allow system administrators to investigate if any systems, data, etc., were compromised during the attack. Both situations require constraints over time to support 'gradual' adjustments.

Additionally, we desire the system to have the capability to recognize the anomalous event and autonomously change its policies in response. That is, once an attack is detected, the policy change prioritizes the goal of protecting the integrity of the system over the goal of reliably serving users' requests. This may be achieved by the system adapting to filter some of the adversarial requests aiming to compromise the system (e.g., by changing network policies to block regions, sequester services, etc.). While services are being restored, other policies allow the systems to gradually return to "business as usual".

3   Related Work

Goal-modeling is used in a variety of frameworks for different purposes, such as requirements engineering. However, we are particularly interested in goal-modeling for runtime frameworks such as those used by self-adaptive systems, as the proposed goal types are particularly applicable in such situations.

Goal-Oriented Frameworks: There have been many goal-oriented frameworks and methodologies proposed in the past. Notably, most of the goal-related work assumes that goals are used for requirements specification and are mainly design-time artifacts, with the Tropos4AS and GoalD approaches being the exception. Like these two approaches, our approach retains goal models and instances in the runtime environment.

Tropos for Adaptive Systems (Tropos4AS) is an agent-oriented framework for engineering adaptive systems based on i* and following the Tropos engineering methodology [15]. The Tropos4AS modeling language features an extended *goal model* with runtime satisfaction criteria, an *environment model* representing external elements which affect goal satisfaction, and a *failure model*, representing unwanted states and associated recovery plans. While our approach shares many modeling similarities, unlike Tropos4AS, we do not use an explicit separate category of failure models, instead dealing with failure as an outcome of goal reasoning. In particular, we define new types of differential and integral goals supported by *contexts*, which generalize the notion of failure models. Also, the Tropos4AS implementation focuses on code generation for prototype implementation while we are aiming at a service interface to provide adaptive capabilities to an existing deployed system.

The KAOS goal-driven specification methodology has been extended with runtime event-monitoring for reconciling system requirements and runtime behavior [11]. Similar to our approach, a goal modeling language is proposed which allows specifying reconciliation tactics like shifting to an alternative system design. However, this is a design-time approach, whereas our approach is applicable at runtime to an existing system such as Kubernetes. Later work [12] applied a goal-driven approach for system reliability and security which is closely related to our example, though still looking at a design-time perspective. In the latest iteration [5], goals have been extended to operating as runtime entities that are monitored, predicting goal satisfaction rates, and adapting the goal model to adjust to the varying obstacle probabilities to maximize these success rates. Detailed probabilistic obstacle models in a formalism mirroring the goal models are used for success estimates and applying countermeasures for improving the overall success rate. Our notion of contexts can also capture obstacles in addition to modeling other situations that are considered part of typical system operations; while the monitoring aspects could be applied, mutatis mutandis, to our approach.

Dalpiaz et al. [7] address adaptation challenges in open systems through emphasizing interactions between agents, and modeling agent interactions in terms of commitments. This approach focuses on agent interactions, selection, and operationalization of adaptation strategies. Our approach instead aims at reasoning about adaptation strategies in response to variability in requirements. GAAM [18] assumes self-adaptive software using a goal-based model, but focuses specifically on the decision-making problem of action selection at runtime, whereas our approach focuses on the capability enhancement of goal models to help in effectively abstracting and characterising the behavior of a system.

Similar principles have been applied to so-called Awareness Requirements in the body of work leading to [3,4,19]. Our approach also considers adaptations as a response to variability in requirements. In our approach, the new differential and integral goal types are used to represent variability as a requirement similar to fuzzy goals as described in [4], rather than variation parameters applied to requirements as in [19]. In the Awareness Requirements approaches, adaptation strategies are enacted through reactive changes made to a live goal model based on current operating conditions [4], through the application of rules generated from qualitative models based on user experience [19], or quantitative models generated from previous system behavior [3]. In comparison, we use a unified goal model to enable adaptation even within a single highly structured domain process that may be subject to multiple iterations of goal and action adaptations within a single problem instance. As such, we extend the kinds of goals that can be expressed. While there is overlap between what can be expressed in our two approaches, neither subsumes the other, and our approach could be combined with such goal success/adaptation monitoring approaches described above. Our approach provides the capacity for explicit representation of the runtime environment through the introduction of contexts, goal probes and goal effectors, variability requirements in the form of the new goal types, and potential adaptation strategies as part of a single live goal model.

Applications in Service Environments: Pereira et al. [16] proposed the ATMOSPHERE/TMA platform implementing the MAPE-K control loop for cloud systems and supported by a distributed monitoring system. The MAPE-K components are designed as microservices deployable in container-based systems, e.g., Kubernetes. The usage example focuses on maintaining trustworthiness w.r.t. system/service performance scores, but mention is made that TMA can be used with other metrics, such as dependability, privacy, and security. In contrast to our work, it does not address how goals are incorporated or can evolve over time to address a changing environment. Alkhabbas et al.'s [2] work on deploying self-adaptive IoT systems focuses on environments which are (partly) unknown, e.g., it could be a cloud, edge, or hybrid edge-cloud model. It is not clear to which extent the work can deal with changes at runtime.

Other Goal-Driven Adaptation Frameworks: Sykes et al. [20] proposed a 3-layer model for adaptable software architecture which focuses on task synthesis from high-level goals. In the *Goal Management* layer, reactive plans are generated from domain models and goals expressed in temporal logic. These plans are interpreted and component configurations are generated in the *Change Management* layer, with the configuration changes applied in the *Component* layer. This approach is limited in the ability to express structural constraints, e.g., resource competition, and did not support dynamic replanning or feedback loops. Mendonça et al. [14] propose a modeling and analysis framework for contextual failures and dependable system requirements, aligning concepts of dependability and failure classification to the requirements of a Contextual Goal Model (CGM). This approach can be coupled with self-adaptation mechanisms at design time to support the use of dependability criteria. Rodrigues et al. [17] describe *GoalD*, a goal-driven framework for autonomous resource deployment in heterogeneous computing environments, operating in two stages: offline activities performed in preparation for deployment, and online deployment adaptation activities for the runtime environment. The latter are performed by a MAPE-K based manager. GoalD incorporates a runtime framework and algorithms for synthesizing and updating system goal models. In contrast to our approach, GoalD does not support the reconfiguration of already deployed systems.

4   Goals for Change and Aggregation

The Kubernetes use case motivates a novel taxonomy of goals. These new goal types are not currently supported even in sophisticated temporal logics such as CTL and LTL or by the most sophisticated model checkers on offer (including probabilistic model checkers such as PRISM). The two new goal types are *Differential goals* and *Integral goals*.

Differential Goals. A number of the use case scenarios involve goals that involve gradual ramping down or ramping up provisioning. All of these are statements about *differentials* or rates of change. In terms of the underlying semantics of this extension to the goal language, on every path, between some specified lower and upper bound (specified using the UNTIL and UNLESS temporal operators, as one possibility), the rate of change of some numeric variable should be equal to, no more than, or no less than some value. This will permit the specification of the *rate* at which we want to ramp up or ramp down provisioning. In other words, we are making the notion of "gradually" changing something concrete by qualifying it with numbers.

We use $D(F, start, end)$ op k to denote that the rate of change of function F satisfies the inequality op with constant k at the end of the interval between the first state where the condition *start* is true and the first state where condition *end* is true. Furthermore, if the rate of change of F holds unconditionally, we omit references to *start* and *end*. As an example, consider the requirement that storage capacity is restored at a rate no faster than 2 GB per min. This would be formalized as:

$$D(StorageCapacity, attackMitigated \wedge reducedStorage \wedge now - 2min, now) \leq 2$$

Integral Goals. In a similar spirit to specifying goals in terms of differentials, we will also want to specify goals in terms of definite integrals, e.g., the total duration of downtime between some lower and upper bound, should be equal to (or no less than or no greater than) some value. The semantics over paths would be similar, i.e., we would count the number of states satisfying a given property.

We use $I(F, start, end)$ op k to denote that the definite integral of the function F satisfies the inequality op with constant k in all states between the first state where the condition *start* is true and the first state where condition *end* is true. As an example, consider the requirement that the total downtime for the IP-Telephony service should not exceed 2 h between the point when a DOS attack is detected and the point where full restoration of normal operations occurs. We use the boolean state variable $notAvailable(IPTelephony)$ to denote the non-availability of the IP-Telephony service. We assume that state transitions are uniformly spaced over time. The *start* condition is denoted by *attackDetected*. The *end* condition is denoted by *operationsRestored*. The property would then be formalized as:

$$I(notAvailable(IPTelephony), attackDetected, operationsRestored) \leq 2$$

Extensions. In the following, we present an intuitive formalization in a linear time setting as an extension to LTL (henceforth referred to as Ext-LTL), and then a formalization in a branching time setting as an extension to CTL (henceforth referred to as Ext-CTL). We consider Ext-LTL first. Let H be the state history. Given s_i in H, let s_m and s_n be states in that history such that $m \leq i \leq n$ such that s_m is the first state where *start* is true, s_n is the first state after s_i where *end* is true. Then $(H, s_i) \models D(F, start, end)$ *op* k iff $| F_n - F_m | / | n - m |$ *op* k. (Here we use F_j to denote the value of F at state s_j, for any j.)

Also, $(H, s_i) \models I(F, start, end)$ *op* k iff $\#S_F$ *op* k where $\#S_F$ represents the count of the number of states between the *start* and *end* conditions where F is *true*. Alternatively $\#S_F = |\{s_j \in H \mid m \leq j \leq n, s_j \models F\}|$

Note that, for simplicity, this considers only boolean variables, states are observed at each time increment, and the constraints are defined with a corresponding time unit. If there is not a one-to-one correspondence then the formalization is more involved but, ultimately, straightforward. Similarly, the formalization can be extended to non-boolean variables.

Ext-CTL expressions for integral and differential goals would involve appending A and E in front of the corresponding Ext-LTL expressions, with the usual semantics involving universal and existential quantification over paths. Variations on the general categories of differential and integral goals can also be posed. One variation of the general formulation of the differential and integral goals discussed above is the category of *sliding-window* differential and integral goals. Building on the integral goal example above, consider a goal where we want to ensure that the total service downtime should not exceed 2 h in the preceding 24 h. The property would then be formalized as $I^-(notAvailable(IPTelephony), 24) \leq 2$ (where the dash superscript denotes the sliding window version of the integral goal and here we are counting the number of times when *notAvailable(IPTelephony)* is true). In general, a sliding-window integral goal is written as $I^-(F, w)$ *op* k and is equivalent to the integral goal $I(F, t_0 - w, t_0)$ *op* k where the sliding window has width w time units ending at time t_0 (often taken to be now). Here, we have extended the concept of *condition* from being only associated with system states to also include events, including the passage of time. Sliding differential goals are defined similarly: $D^-(F, w)$ *op* k means $D(F, t_0 - w, t_0)$ *op* k.

For simplicity, we assume the window width is given in integer units of time - in our example, hours - matching the state interval; again, if there is not a 1-to-1 correspondence then the formalization is more involved but straightforward.

5   Cybersecurity Use Case and Goal Model

We now return to the cybersecurity use case. The basic policies, such as those provided by Kubernetes, for dynamically scaling (up or down) services in response to actual or predicted demand are suitable only for normal conditions. During anomalous events, such as Distributed Denial of Service (DDoS) attacks, the same policies are no longer appropriate. In our example application of IT infrastructure deployments, we apply goal-based management on top of existing systems like Kubernetes to enhance their capabilities in dealing with such anomalous situations and improve their resilience. We first discuss the Kubernetes environment, the setting for the example. The concrete goals and other entities making up the goal model will be described in Sect. 5.2.

5.1 The Kubernetes Framework

Kubernetes manages *clusters* of *nodes* on which applications are deployed and run[1]. Nodes may be physical or virtual machines and comprise several *pods* that it manages. Each pod is a collection of *containers*, where each container is a running application defined by a *container image* providing the packaged software, its dependencies, and core configuration – i.e., everything necessary for the application to run. Containers within a pod can communicate with one another via a loopback network, but cannot communicate with containers in other pods (unless enabled through configuration).

Kubernetes supports basic self-healing, i.e., restarting failed containers and rescheduling pods on new nodes if a node fails, manual and automatic (resource-based) scaling, managed upgrades and rollbacks of applications/containers. However, the information and decision-making is low-level, so we raise the basic functionality into a goal-based framework through probes that can query Kubernetes state, monitoring, etc., and effectors, which can take actions on the Kubernetes configuration. Raising the information and decision-making to the goal level provides additional control over the framework based on the higher-level goals and situational awareness.

5.2 Goal Model

The goal model is based on well-established notions of goal decomposition following the i* framework [21], complemented by dependency and inhibition relationships among goals as defined in Tropos4AS [15]. To account for situational goals which may apply in one context but not another, we employ and extend the notion of a goal life cycle, introduced in [9], with the goal model providing an explicit context structure. Three major categories of goals are available. *Achieve-goals* are satisfied once, in specified conditions, *Maintain-goals* are satisfied when specified conditions are maintained over a period of time, while *Perform-goals* (or Manual Goals) are satisfied through execution of associated activities. Goal relationships are expressed in terms of goal *sequence* and *inhibition*, expressing runtime precedence between goals.

The goal life cycle we have chosen, which differs somewhat from [9], centers on the *Active* state, with the *Suspended* state permitting the goal to be temporarily removed from consideration to be later reactivated, and the *Dropped*

---

[1] https://kubernetes.io/docs/.

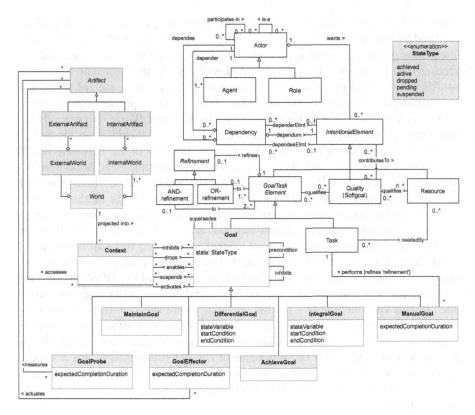

Fig. 1. Goal Meta-model: core i* in white, Tropos4AS extensions in blue, and this work's extensions including Contexts, Differential and Integral Goals at the bottom in orange. (Color figure online)

state represents the goal being discarded. The *trigger* relationship results in the achievement of a goal initiating the transition to a different context. In each context, a different set of goals may apply. Upon transition, goals can be re-activated, suspended, or dropped, and maintenance goals can be carried over to the target context (unless they are dropped). Goals can be equipped with domain-specific attributes representing, e.g., costs and delays associated with the goal. For clarity of presentation, we omit the details of cost and temporal consideration in the goal reasoning of the following scenario. We rely on the notion of *probes* for sensing system state and *effectors* for manipulating system state [6]. Probes and effectors at the goal level facilitate the reasoning process, while their concrete implementation is conceptually represented by the invocation of platform services.

A sketch of the goal meta-model is shown in Fig. 1 in the context of i* concepts (specifically iStar 2.0 [8]), shown in white, and which incorporates aspects of the Tropos4AS methodology which relate to the environmental context (shown in blue). The proposed extensions (shown in orange) are predominantly refinements of the i* goal concept, covering the three major categories of goal as described in the previous section. In addition, *Goal Probes* and *Goal Effectors*, which measure properties of or actuate behaviors in the internal world and the external world, respectively, are associated with the *Artifact* concept from Tropos4AS, which represents the non-autonomous things, states, etc., of the world that do not possess autonomous behavior. *Artifacts* are separated into *internal* and *external* artifacts, the latter comprising the *External World*. We extend this representation with a general representation of *Internal World*, vis-á-vis *External World*, and an overall *World* being the composition of an *External World* and a multitude of *Internal Worlds* (possibly representing each Actor's internal state, for example). It is the totality of the world that is then projected onto the environmental *Context* under which the goals operate as the contexts required for situational awareness and adaptation of decision making may cross boundaries, factoring in not only the external state but also the internal states of autonomous agents (at minimum, the agent performing the goal reasoning).

We show the use of the novel differential- and integral goals in a cyber-situational awareness scenario where a system is affected by a DDoS attack and must respond. The response is governed by general cybersecurity response plans, which in this case include five phases: normal, where the system performs normally; analysis, where the nature and effects of a detected attack are analyzed; mitigation, where the response measures are taken to mitigate the effects of the attack; learning, where the outcomes of the defense measures are assessed; and restoration, where the system attack has been mitigated and the system is returned to normal operations. The different phases map directly to contexts in the goal model.

In each context, different goals are relevant, which is shown in Fig. 2 including the goals, their decomposition, and relations. Table 1 lists the goals in brief. Achievement and maintenance goals are represented as green shapes: optional adornments identify differential and integral goals. Probes and effectors are purple subgoals. Subgoals whose achievement establishes the preconditions for their parent goals are annotated with a yellow precondition symbol.

In the *normal operations context*, the system is concerned with monitoring and maintaining its ability to deliver services (goal G1). This integral goal measures the services functioning as expected (as assessed by probing or measuring service response times) over a period and takes remedial action if services are thought to be affected in terms of their ability to respond within a set time threshold, in which case the system can restart failed instances or spawn additional instances to increase the capacity of the system. At the same time, goal G2 ensures that costs are maintained within a pre-set budget profile by reducing provisioned resources and preventing the spawning of new instances. This integral goal aggregates the resource usage over a period and takes remedial action if the number (or equivalently, cost) of resources exceeds acceptable thresholds. Differential goal G3 ensures that the rate of change in resource provisioning remains at acceptable levels to avoid catastrophic downscaling and undesirable upscaling due to mispredictions of resource demand. This goal constrains the

Table 1. Goal Summary (excl. manual goals)

ID	Type	Goal description
G1	Int.	Services shall be available for no less than 1425 min in any 24 hr interval (i.e., 99%)
G1.1	Maint.	Monitor availability of services
G1.2	Achieve.	Establish availability of a service
G2	Int.	Limit number of pod allocation events to no more than 5 over the baseline (e.g., 3) while we have 2 nodes
G2.1	Achieve.	Reduce resource usage (to prevent need to allocate a new pod)
G3	Diff.	Planning constraint limits resource alloc. change (no. pods) to within 35% (i.e., 2 pods) per 5min
G4	Achieve.	Detect DDoS attack; indicated by monitoring events
G6	Achieve.	Mitigate attack
G6.1	Achieve.	Filter attack
G6.2	Maint.	Prevent restart of failed services
G6.3	Maint.	Monitor logs for suspicious activity
G8	Achieve.	Restore normal operations
G8.1	Diff.	Redirect requests to original; no more than 20% of service instances (i.e., 1 instance) per 5 mins
P1	Probe	Active Probing of service accessibility every 5 min (performed by Kubernetes)
P2	Probe	Monitor Response Times (monitoring and recording by Kubernetes components)
E1	Effector	Restart Failed Instance (triggered in Kubernetes based on restart policy)
E2	Effector	Spawn Instance (triggered in Kubernetes based on configuration change)
P3/P4	Probe	Monitor Resources (as for P2)
E3	Effector	Stop Instance; (temporarily) stops a container instance using Kubernetes API
P5/P6	Probe	(D)DoS Alert raised by IDS
E4	Effector	Redirect Routes (updates network for pods/containers via Kubernetes configuration)
E5	Effector	Restore Route; as E4 only undoes filtering

Note: The manual goals G5 and G7 are not listed for brevity.

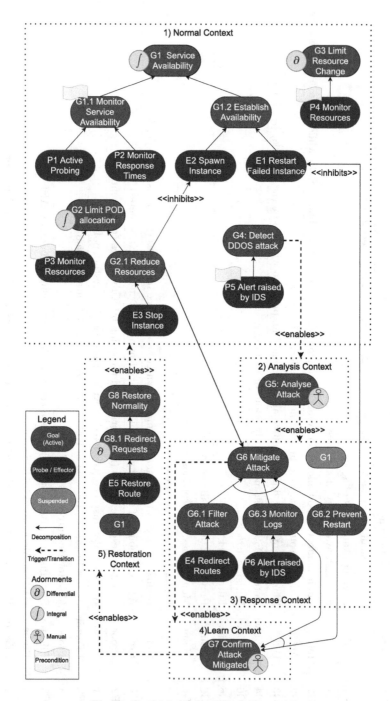

Fig. 2. Goal Model for DDoS Scenario

actions triggered by G1 and G2. The system shall detect DDoS attacks and trigger an appropriate response (goal G4). We abstract from the details of the detection mechanisms for G4 and instead rely on intrusion detection and monitoring systems (IDSs) to detect potential attacks. Once an attack has been detected, the response is initiated, and the system exits the normal context and enters the analysis context.

In the *Analysis Context*, the goal of analyzing the nature of the attack (G5) is added to the active goals. These activities are predominantly manual tasks aiming to identify the nature of the attack, its sources, and its impacts on the system. Here, the goal model can provide situational awareness about the progress of these tasks to the team, and support activities through collecting and extracting relevant information. These technical support tasks are not shown in the goal model for brevity. Once the nature of the attack is understood, the response context is triggered. For discussion purposes, it is assumed that the attack is a request flood, where the system is overloaded by a huge number of requests from external sources.

Upon entering the *Response Context*, goal G1 is suspended to prevent uncontrolled growth of resources to serve the spurious requests. Goal G6 is initiated, which aims to implement measures to mitigate the effects of the attack. We consider three possible measures: implementing network-level filters to remove as many bogus requests as possible (G6.1), disabling automatic fail-over mechanisms that can degrade the system performance further due to many restarts of assumed failed services (G6.2), and implementing monitoring tasks to assess if any other attacks may be masked by the DDoS attack (G6.3). Once mitigation activities are implemented, the learning phase of the response protocol begins.

The *Learning Context* involves predominantly manually controlled activities to assess the success of the response measures and to confirm that the attack has been mitigated (G7). Akin to the analysis phase, the technical monitoring and information collection tasks initiated by the goal model are omitted for brevity. Once the attack has subsided, the system enters the restoration phase to return it to normal operations.

In the *Restoration Context*, goal G1 is reinstated, and the actions taken during mitigation must be undone. Goal G8 is activated to govern the gradual return to normality. This differential goal ensures that parts of the system are made available incrementally (for example by service, by data center, or by zone) by controlling the rate at which services are reinstated. As services need to return to normal operation, goals G6.2 and G6.3 are dropped, preventing goal conflicts and allowing G6 to be achieved—Goals G6 and G6.1 were already achieved upon executing the filtering with the maintenance of G6.2 and G6.3 transferring to G7. Once G8 is achieved, the system reenters the normal context and resumes operation.

5.3   Goal Reasoner Implementation

To demonstrate our approach we have developed a prototype implementation of a goal reasoner that utilizes the novel differential and integral goals to reason about the new goal states of our automated system. The goal reasoner takes as input an *instantiated goal model*, i.e. a goal model for which goal states have been assigned to each goal, and a *state history*, a set of *state variables* and their corresponding values at particular points in time. The values of state variables are extracted from the environment using *probes*, which are an element in the goal model. The goal reasoner returns a new instance of the goal model for which the goal states and the active contexts have been updated given the state histories. The implementation has been made available.[2]

The new goal model also encodes information on which *effectors* to activate or suspend, consequently providing information on how the automated system utilizing the goal reasoner should act on the environment in which it is operating. The model similarly provides information on which probes to activate or suspend so that state variable measurements can be recorded for the subsequent reasoning cycle.

In the implementation, the values of state variables at particular points in time take the form of logical predicates $at(Predicate, Time)$ where $Predicate$ is the predicate containing the state variable and its value, and $Time$ is the time at which the predicate was recorded.

For each differential or integral goal, several attributes must be provided to define the goal within the goal reasoner: `stateVar` specifies the predicate which contains a goal's relevant state variable. `start` specifies the starting time at which the state variable's value becomes relevant to the goal (setting this to `-inf` specifies that the values are relevant immediately). `finish` specifies the final time which a value is relevant to the goal (this can be set to `inf` to specify that it is a maintenance goal going on forever). `intervalSize` specifies the window size for summing states or measuring rates of change (this can be set to `inf` to specify a goal that has a static window). `atLeast` specifies the lower bound on the rate of change or aggregation value being computed. `atMost` specifies the upper bound on the computed value, `frequency` specifies how often the value of a state variable must be known. In this paper, we have assumed evenly distributed time steps and assume that state variable values are known in each state, so frequency does not affect our example in this paper; we have included it for generality.

Each time the goal reasoner is called, it checks each goal to see if its satisfaction of failure condition has been reached given the known values of state variables at each time step. This information is used to update the goal states of each goal, which then triggers the context phase. The context phase determines which contexts should be activated given the new goal states in the goal model. Once new contexts have been activated, goal states are updated again given the new contexts. Finally, the new goal model is returned.

---

[2] https://github.com/DSL-UOW/ER2022-Differential-Integral-Goal-Reasoner.

6   Conclusions

We presented a goal-oriented approach to IT infrastructure agility in the context of the Kubernetes cloud platform and showed that the goal-based approach can help maintain situational awareness of intended and actual system operations through high-level goals aligned with human abstractions. We introduced differential and integral goals to capture goals related to the rate of evolution and aggregate measurements derived from the system operations over time and showed how these goals can inform the goal reasoning and goal refinement process. Mappings of elements in the goal models to elements in the underlying execution platform facilitated the synthesis of concrete executable adaptation and monitoring activities. For future work, we intend to study the characteristics of the approach in more detail in additional case studies on the Kubernetes platform. This will involve the abstraction of requirements of a real-world system into a goal model which utilizes our novel differential and integral goals to reason about how the system states change over time and how this impacts goal fulfillment. We will extend the prototype implementation through the development of an integrated goal modeling environment that can probe the environment, reason about goals, and act on the environment autonomously. This implementation will be executed on a real system to provide a basis for end-user evaluation.

Acknowledgements. This research is supported by the Commonwealth of Australia as represented by the Defence Science and Technology Group of the Department of Defence and the Defence Artificial Intelligence Research Network (DAIRNet), an initiative of the Department of Defence and the Next Generation Technologies Fund (NGTF).

References

1. Ali, R., Dalpiaz, F., Giorgini, P.: A goal-based framework for contextual requirements modeling and analysis. Requir. Eng. **15**(4), 439–458 (2010)
2. Alkhabbas, F., Murturi, I., Spalazzese, R., Davidsson, P., Dustdar, S.: A goal-driven approach for deploying self-adaptive IoT systems. In: Proceedings ICSA2020, pp. 146–156. IEEE (2020)
3. Angelopoulos, K., Papadopoulos, A.V., Souza, V.E.S., Mylopoulos, J.: Engineering self-adaptive software systems: from requirements to model predictive control. ACM Trans. Auton. Adapt. Syst. **13**(1), 1–27 (2018)
4. Baresi, L., Pasquale, L., Spoletini, P.: Fuzzy goals for requirements-driven adaptation. In: Proceedings RE2010, pp. 125–134. IEEE (2010)
5. Cailliau, A., van Lamsweerde, A.: Runtime monitoring and resolution of probabilistic obstacles to system goals. ACM Trans. Auton. Adapt. Syst. **14**(1), 1–40 (2019)
6. Cheng, S.W.: Rainbow: cost-effective software architecture-based self-adaptation, Ph. D. thesis, CMU School of Computer Science, CMU-ISR-08-113 (2008)
7. Dalpiaz, F., Chopra, A.K., Giorgini, P., Mylopoulos, J.: Adaptation in open systems: giving interaction its rightful place. In: Parsons, J., Saeki, M., Shoval, P., Woo, C., Wand, Y. (eds.) ER 2010. LNCS, vol. 6412, pp. 31–45. Springer, Heidelberg (2010). https://doi.org/10.1007/978-3-642-16373-9_3

8. Dalpiaz, F., Franch, X., Horkoff, J.: iStar 2.0 language guide, v3 (2016)
9. Dastani, M., Riemsdijk, M., Winikoff, M.: Rich goal types in agent programming. In: Proceedings AAMAS2011, pp. 405–412. IFAAMAS (2011)
10. Endsley, M.R.: Toward a theory of situation awareness in dynamic systems. Hum. Factors **37**, 32–64 (1995)
11. Feather, M., Fickas, S., van Lamsweerde, A., Ponsard, C.: Reconciling system requirements and runtime behavior. In: Proceedings International Workshop on Software Specification and Design (IWSSD), pp. 50–59. IEEE (1998)
12. van Lamsweerde, A.: Engineering requirements for system reliability and security. In: Software Systems Reliability and Security, vol. 9, pp. 196–238. IOS Press (2007)
13. Li, N., Cámara, J., Garlan, D., Schmerl, B.R., Jin, Z.: Hey! preparing humans to do tasks in self-adaptive systems. In: Proceedings SEAMS2021, pp. 48–58. IEEE (2021)
14. Mendonça, D.F., Ali, R., Rodrigues, G.N.: Modelling and analysing contextual failures for dependability requirements. In: Proceedings SEAMS2014, pp. 55–64. ACM (2014)
15. Morandini, M., Penserini, L., Perini, A., Marchetto, A.: Engineering requirements for adaptive systems. Requirements Eng. **22**(1), 77–103 (2015). https://doi.org/10.1007/s00766-015-0236-0
16. Pereira, J.D., et al.: A platform to enable self-adaptive cloud applications using trustworthiness properties. In: Proceedings SEAMS2020, pp. 71–77. ACM (2020)
17. Rodrigues, G.S., et al.: GoalD: a goal-driven deployment framework for dynamic and heterogeneous computing environments. Inf. Softw. Technol. **111**, 159–176 (2019)
18. Salehie, M., Tahvildari, L.: Towards a goal-driven approach to action selection in self-adaptive software. Soft. Pract. Exp. **42**(2), 211–233 (2012)
19. Souza, V.E.S., Mylopoulos, J.: Designing an adaptive computer-aided ambulance dispatch system with Zanshin: an experience report. Softw. Pract. Exp. **45**(5), 689–725 (2015)
20. Sykes, D., Heaven, W., Magee, J., Kramer, J.: From goals to components: a combined approach to self-management. In: Proceedings SEAMS2008, pp. 1–8. ACM (2008)
21. Yu, E.: Modelling strategic relationships for process reengineering, Ph. D. thesis, University of Toronto (1995)

Trying to Elicit and Assign Goals to the Right Actors

Anouck Chan(✉) ⓘ, Anthony Fernandes Pires(✉) ⓘ, and Thomas Polacsek(✉) ⓘ

ONERA, Toulouse, France
{anouck.chan,anthony.fernandes_pires,thomas.polacsek}@onera.fr

Abstract. At the beginning of a project, an organisation may define very abstract goals. These high-level goals describe organisation characteristics that all projects must fulfil. Due to the very generic and abstract nature of these goals, it is sometimes not easy to break them down into more concrete goals and to decide who should be responsible for what. For many years, goal modelling approaches have proposed frameworks for eliciting and defining stakeholders' goals in an organisation. In the context of an aeronautical company, we conducted an application on a case of study of a goal modelling method. From high-level goals, we have supported business experts in eliciting more concrete goals, assigning them to the right actors and identifying possible organisational needs. For this, we started from an existing method that we have adapted to fit our purposes.

Keywords: Goal modeling · Requirements engineering

1 Introduction

Goals are widely studied in the context of Goal-Oriented Requirements Engineering (GORE) [8,10,14]. Unlike a requirement, a goal is not mandatory, it is more a prescriptive statement. Goals express the objectives that the system should achieve [9]. Interactions between goals and interactions among goals and other elements like actors or resources are finely studied in GORE frameworks such as *Non-Functional Requirements* (NFR) [3,13], iStar [4,16] or KAOS [5].

Goals are generally quite concrete objectives whose responsibilities are clearly defined, even if they are used in the preliminary phases of projects. Knowing which goal is under whose responsibility is a crucial organisational element. In practice, a growing number of organisations are incorporating very abstract goals, namely *high-level goals*, whose assignment and translation into requirements are not trivial. Moreover, these high-level goals are often derived from the activity the company wants to conduct and the value the company is driven by and wants to convey in its products. Take the basic example of a watch manufacturer, whose activity is to create watches and who may choose to reflect the value of modernity or, on the contrary, of tradition. In one case, the creation of the watches will be driven by goals to show that they are at the cutting edge of

J. Ralyté et al. (Eds.): ER 2022, LNCS 13607, pp. 413–422, 2022.
https://doi.org/10.1007/978-3-031-17995-2_29

innovation, while in the other the emphasis will be on historical continuity or a heritage of craftsmanship.

We were approached by an industrial firm, an aircraft manufacturer, who has developed a value repository. These values are not only applied to aircraft, but also to the company itself, whether it is on manufacturing, operational services or maintenance operations. The notion of value used here is the same as the one used in psychology, as it is generally the case for companies [7,12]: values are *"concepts or beliefs, about desirable end states or behaviors, that transcend specific situations, guide selection or evaluation of behavior and events, and are ordered by relative importance"* [15]. When the aircraft manufacturer contacted us, high-level goals were already derived from the company values and its activity[1]. The problem for the company was how to elicit more concrete goals from these high-level goals and assigning these concrete goals to the right actor who has the skills to ensure their satisfaction.

The contribution of this article is to present an adaptation of an existing GORE methodology to address a real industrial problem. As presented in Sect. 2, we have searched through the research literature an existing methodology using refinement and delegation through actors to obtain a satisfying set of goals from a global objective. Then, we introduce an adaptation of an existing method to suit our problem in Sect. 3. Section 4 is dedicated to the application of our approach to three aircraft manufacturer high-level goals. Based on this, we draw some observations and conclude in Sect. 5.

2   Looking for a Methodology

Several works address the problem of goal elicitation and goal refinement. However, very few focus on the refinement of very abstract goals into more concrete goals assigned to actors.

The refinement calculus CaRE proposes a tool to build a consistent, complete and realisable set of requirements (specifications) from an initial and incomplete one given by stakeholders [6]. Each requirement can be discarded or modified as long as there is an acceptable chain of arguments for this. The chain consists in an alternation between defects of the requirements and proposals for their resolution in the form of requirements refinement named operators. This method is mainly oriented to obtain a coherent set of requirements, avoiding conflicting or inconsistent ones. Finding a solution to satisfy the initial set of goals is therefore not a priority, nor defining a set of actors who can satisfy the refined goals. This is why the method is not completely suited to our study situation.

The method presented in [11] allows to elicit satisfiable subgoals from an initial goal and to distribute them to agents able to satisfy them. Goals are expressed with modal logic and each agent can control and monitor some variables. An agent can satisfy a goal only if it has control on the goal variables. Because some goals may not be realisable, the authors present *tactics* (*i.e.*

---

[1] How high-level goals are derived from values and activities is a point that deserves much investigation, but this is out of the scope of this article.

schemes) for refining them into satisfiable subgoals. These tactics consist in a guideline to resolve the issue for each condition for which a goal is unrealisable. In our context, the main restriction for applying this method is the fact that goals are expressed with variables and temporal operators. The high-level goals we use cannot be described in such details, either because they are too abstract or because their description would involve too many variables. Moreover, we are not interested in how each goal is satisfied but only in who is responsible for its satisfaction.

Bryl, Giorgini and Mylopoulos present a method to find an optimal set of actors' actions that satisfy an initial set of goals [1,2]. They use predicate logic to describe goals, actors' properties, and relations between actors. The actors have some autonomy and personal objectives. As the defection of one actor could be prejudicial to the achievement of the initial objectives, the method tries to ensure actors' collaboration by computing *stable* solutions.

Each actor is described through its capacities to execute actions and their assumption about the other actors' capacities.

A special actor, namely the *manager*, starts the process. It refines high-level objectives into subgoals and delegates them to other actors. Then, steps are iterated until a *stop-criterion* is reached (*e.g.* time limit). At each step, actors explore alternatives to achieve all goals that have been assigned to them and select the best alternative according to their criteria. For each goal, an actor can choose between three actions: *satisfy* it, *refine* it into subgoals or *delegate* it to another actor. Refinement can be *AND*-type, to divide goals in simpler ones, or *OR*-type, to elicit then choose the favourite alternative. Delegating allows an actor who has a goal it cannot, or decide to not, satisfy itself, to give it to another actor. A stable solution is reached when no actor is willing or able to change any of its actions.

3   Our Approach

Several elements of Bryl *et al.* approach are close to our problem while others need adjustments.

Firstly, the combination of refining and delegating actions are a way for actors to work together to achieve a global goal and to ensure their collaboration. The whole process is based on the knowledge of the actors on how to meet a goal. This is particularly relevant in situations where the actors have specific and dedicated know-how as ours. Therefore, we keep the refining and delegating actions. Actors personal objectives are out of scope of our problem, *i.e.* we only consider the company's high-level goals satisfaction. Thus, we are no longer looking for a stable solution from which the actors do not want to deviate, but a solution in which each goal is assigned to an actor that can satisfy it.

Secondly, goals refinement can be stopped as soon as an actor is able to satisfy the goal. Thus, actors may have a great autonomy on how achieve their goals without harming the global objectives. However, the solution obtained is dependent on actors initial description, in particular of how they can refine and to whom they can delegate, which makes the first method step, *i.e.* the manager step, quite crucial. In that respect, the method could end in a final situation where an actor can neither satisfy a goal assigned to it, nor delegate it to another actor. In order to avoid this issue, we add a set of unsatisfiable goals named *Unknown*. As detailed later, this set is made up of goals that the company does not yet know how to satisfy or to assign to.

Finally, in Bryl *et al.*, actors choose the actions they perform. We focus on elicitation and not a multi-agent decision elicitation system. So, we use a common pool of knowledge (who can satisfy what) and allow all possible delegations. A central entity decides what actions are performed. This is made possible by the fact that no actor wants to deviate from the solution and by the addition of the *Unknown* set that models all potential new ways to satisfy unsatisfiable goals.

Key Concepts. The key concepts of our adaptation can be described as follows. *High-level goals* are the main input of our approach. They correspond to abstract objectives, whose achievement is not obvious. High-level goals are linked to a *value* and an *activity*, which are out of the scope of our method. Actors we consider can be a person or a group of persons (seen as a single entity). A *goal* is an objective that should be satisfied and can be assigned to an actor. In the first step of the method, a goal is derived from each high-level goal. All actors have *skills* and skills are required to satisfy goals. If an actor possesses all the skills required to satisfy a goal assigned to it, the latter is a *satisfiable goal*. If no actor possesses -even partially- the required skills to satisfy the goal, it is an *unsatisfiable goal*. Otherwise, the goal can be *refined* into subgoals or can be *delegated* to another actor. A goal is satisfied if it is a satisfiable goal or if all its subgoals are satisfied. The concept of *Unknown* set corresponds to a set where unsatisfiable goals are stored. Therefore, all *unsatisfiable goals* are *de facto* delegated to the *Unknown set*.

Method. The inputs of our algorithm are the company's high-level goals HG and the set of actors $\mathcal{A}$. The set of goals handled by the approach is denoted $\mathcal{G}$ and the set of skills required for satisfying a goal $g \in \mathcal{G}$ is denoted $skills(g)$. Note that set $\mathcal{G}$ is built iteratively by the algorithm. For each actor $a \in \mathcal{A}$, $skills(a)$ denotes the set of skills of a. We also consider three functions, *satisfy*, *delegate* and *refine*, that correspond to actions that can be performed by actors. The result of applying the *refine* function on an actor $a \in \mathcal{A}$ and a goal $g \in \mathcal{G}$ is a pair of goals (g', g'') such that: 1. the satisfaction of subgoals g' and g'' implies the satisfaction g, 2. g' is satisfiable by a ($skills(g') = skills(g) \cap skills(a)$) and 3. g'' is not satisfiable by a, even partially ($skills(g'') = skills(g) \backslash skills(a)$).

The output of our algorithm is, for each actor $a \in \mathcal{A}$, the set of its satisfiable goals $\mathcal{G}^a$ and the *Unknown* set of unsatisfiable goals $\mathcal{U}$.

At the beginning of our algorithm, $\mathcal{U}$ is empty. Each high-level goal in HG is refined into a goal g that is assigned to an actor a such that a can, even partially, satisfy it ($skills(a) \cap skills(g) \neq \emptyset$). We assume that this initialisation is always possible.

Our algorithm is then a loop that ends when all goals are either satisfied or assigned to $\mathcal{U}$. As long as there exists an actor a with a goal g assigned to it and that is not satisfied yet, if $skills(g) \subseteq skills(a)$ then g is satisfied and added to the set of satisfiable goals of a ($\mathcal{G}^a$ becomes $\{g\} \cup \mathcal{G}^a$). Otherwise, the function *refine* is performed to obtain the subgoals g' and g'' as described earlier, and g' is satisfied and added to $\mathcal{G}^a$. Regarding g'', if there exists an actor a' in $\mathcal{A}$ that can, even partially satisfy it ($\exists a' \in \mathcal{A}, skills(a') \cap skills(g'') \neq \emptyset$) then g'' is assigned to a' else g' is added to $\mathcal{U}$.

4   Application to Our Industrial Problem

In this section we present the application of our method in an industrial context and give the lessons learned from our case of study application.

4.1   Modus Operandi

We have worked with an aircraft manufacturer who has developed a value repository, along with their associated high-level goals. During the whole case study application, we have worked with three company high-level goals.

First, we have the high-level goal *Aircraft Deliverability* derived from the value *Deliverability* and the activity *Producing the aircraft*. The value *Deliverability* means the capacity of the system to deliver as expected. So this high-level goal is the ability to deliver the aircraft to customers when they are needed at the desired rate. Second, we have the high-level goal *Industrial System Deliverability* derived from the value *Deliverability* and the activity *Producing the industrial system*. This high-level goal is the ability to produce the factories, assembly lines and infrastructures needed to manufacture the aircraft. Third, we have the high-level goal *Industrial System Performance* derived from the value *Performance* and the activity *Producing the industrial system*. The value *Performance* means the capacity of the system to work as expected. So this high-level goal is the ability of the industrial system to perform according to production criteria.

The application was conducted with two aircraft manufacturer experts. The first one is specialised in the architecture aircraft design, the second in methods and digital solutions for design and manufacturing. Both of them have been involved for many years in company projects aiming at linking the design of the aircraft with the design of the means of production. Prior to our work, the two experts had some notions in goal modelling, especially concerning the notion of actors and goals, but had never used any refinement methods.

We have first organised a three-hours long session dedicated to our method presentation. To do so, we worked on a simple example of high-level goals refinement and actor assignment. Then, for each high-level goal, we have worked with the experts during two three-hour sessions. The objective of the first session was to apply the method. At the beginning of the session, we identified a set of potential actors and then applied our algorithm. As there were some actors that we had not thought of until we reached a certain stage in the process, we repeated algorithm application several times. At the end of the session, a first model was obtained. The second session took place a week later and its purpose was to amend and improve the model collectively. Between the two sessions, we reviewed the model and identified issues to be fixed with the experts. An issue could be, for example, that we did not understand the description of a goal, or that a goal delegated once to an actor, was delegated again to the initial actor without being refined.

Finally, two months later, three one hour long sessions allowed us to finalise the model by working on specific issues like language issues or actor description.

4.2   Goal Elicitation and Assignation

Figure 1 describes the application of our method to the high-level goals *Aircraft Deliverability* and *Industrial System Deliverability*. These two high-level goals become respectively the goals D1 and D2 and were assigned by the experts to two actors: the *Industrial System Operator*, in charge of operating the industrial system to produce aircrafts on a daily basis, and the *Industrial System Developer*, in charge of the design of the industrial system and its development.

The *Industrial System Operator* cannot completely satisfy the goal D1 , so the goal is refined into two goals: one related to the supply chain (goal D1a), the other related to the line balancing (goal D1b). Because this actor is in charge of logistics, the D1a goal is her responsibility. Goal D1b, on the other hand, is not her competence. Line balancing consists of scheduling the assembly tasks in order to obtain the best production rate. D1b is therefore not a goal that depends on the operational aspect, but on the design of the assembly line. So D1b is delegated to the *Assembly Line Developer* actor. D1b is in turn refined into four goals. Two are not in the actor competence scope: D1bc which is a goal for the daily operations and D1ba which aims at setting the assembly tasks. Goal D1ba is the responsibility of a new actor the *Aircraft Architect*, the actor who is in charge of the aircraft design. Indeed, the assembly actions depend directly on the design choices made by the *Aircraft Architect* and therefore they can influence these choices depending on the complexity of the tasks to be performed. However, the tasks at the architectural level are too abstract, they need to be refined to a more basic level, the actions performed by the workers. Therefore, D1ba cannot be completely satisfied by the *Aircraft Architect*, so the goal is refined into two goals: one is to provide the aircraft design (goal D1baa), which implies defining the assembly tasks at the architectural level, and another one is to define the detailed assembly tasks (goal D1bab). Because it belongs to the work of the line workers, this latter goal is assigned to the *Industrial System Operator* actor.

Now let's look at the goal D2. Through the refinements of this goal, we see three goals that belong to the actor, D2cb, D2ab and D2ac, and two goals that are transferred to the *Assembly Line Developer* actor. In fact, goals D2cb, D2ab and D2ac deal with the ability to build and evolve infrastructures such as buildings, roads, etc., while goals D2ca and D2b deal with assembly line tools and their possible evolution. Goal *Design the aircraft parts transport infrastructure* (goal

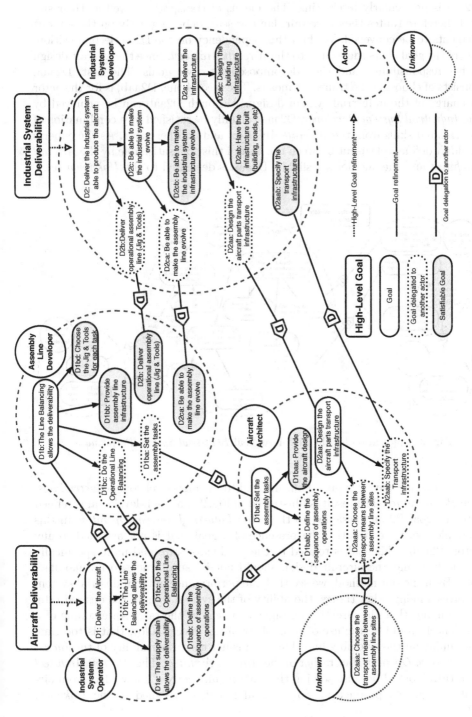

Fig. 1. Application for the high-level goals *Aircraft Deliverability* and *Industrial System Deliverability*

D2aa) is particularly interesting. The means of transport, as well as their size and therefore routes they take (air, land or sea), depend greatly on the aircraft elements to be conveyed. We find this dependency on the D2aa decomposition, where the goal is first delegated to the *Aircraft Architect*, since the aircraft design is her responsibility, and then decomposed into two goals. The first, D2aaa, consists of choosing the transport means. The second one, D2aab, is for the actor in charge of the industrial system design. Although D2aab can be achieved by the *Industrial System Developer*, D2aaa can only be satisfied by a combination of interrelated skills from the *Aircraft Architect* and another actor. As the experts couldn't define a clear-cut between the part of this goal satisfiable by the *Aircraft Architect* and the one not satisfiable, D2aaa is delegated to the *Unknown* set.

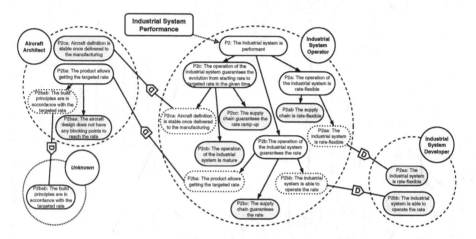

Fig. 2. Application for the high-level goal *Industrial System Performance*

In the same way, we applied our method to the high-level goal *Industrial System Performance*. The result is illustrated in Fig. 2. The high-level goal is refined into the goal P2 and assigned to the actor *Industrial System Operator*. In this example too, we can notice the presence of a goal that is not assigned to any actor: P2bab. This goal is related to the production rate and more specifically to the fact that the aircraft design should not be an obstacle to its manufacture. By using our method, we see that the performance of the industrial system involves, among other things, the ability of the system to hold the desired rate. This implies that the aircraft is designed to achieve the rate. An example of a bottleneck would be the use of technology, like a special alloy, that is too time consuming on the assembly line. This goal is not the responsibility of the *Industrial System Operator*, but rather of the *Aircraft Architect*. The *Aircraft Architect* is in turn blocked because solving this goal requires mixed knowledge, from aircraft design and production. So the goal P2bab is assigned to the *Unknown* set.

5   Conclusion

Following this work, we have discussed our results with the two experts and with a third architect specialist in product/production relationships. The methodology was well received. They particularly appreciated having a precise and reproducible method to clearly set everyone's goals, and the ability to bring out the need to create new actors to manage the goals derived from the high-level goals. From this first experiment, we can draw some observation.

Firstly, in our algorithm, the refinement of one goal leads to two goals, not more. In our use case, we frequently violated this rule. It is not clear whether this deviation comes from our method being too restrictive or whether we skipped intermediate steps in the refinement during the experiment. Secondly, sometimes we had an abundance of information and it was difficult to capture all of it. We sometimes got lost in the rich expert knowledge: they know so many details about their domains that we had a hard time going back to an abstract level. Thirdly, it was also difficult to express the goals in terms of wording directly from the first session. Even if the experts had a good vision of what needed to be done to achieve a goal, it was often in the form of actions or process (i.e. sequences of actions) which was very difficult to formulate as goals. A rewording of the goals often happened in the second session. Finally, some goals are indeed delegated to the *Unknown* set. In this use case, they are nobody's responsibility because the experts could not decide which actor could satisfy them. Practically speaking, such goals require an indivisible combination of different actors skills, who therefore have to actively cooperate. This raises the question of creating within the company these new actors able to act as a bridge among the different actors.

Regarding future work, we plan to investigate further the preliminary lessons learned in order to improve the method. Then, we need to extend it in order to give solutions to the user for the goals delegated to the *Unknown* set. It could be a way to identify missing important actors in the company or to define the need for strong cooperation between existing actors. We also need to examine goals of the actors which are not elicited through the method but still important for the actors and the company. We will have to understand the meaning of their absence from any high-level goal refinements for the company. In addition, we would like to join this method with traditional GORE approaches. The idea would be to use the resulting elicitation of goals and actors as an input for further goals refinement and dependencies elicitation. Finally, we could also investigate the derivation of high-level goals from values, in order to procure traceability between company values and goals assigned to actors.

Acknowledgements. We want to warmly thank François Bouissière, Claude Cuiller and Pierre-Éric Dereux, who allowed us to work on this case study, and Stéphanie Roussel for her support. Their encouragement, their availability and their comments were invaluable in the development of this work.

References

1. Bryl, V., Giorgini, P., Mylopoulos, J.: Designing cooperative IS: exploring and evaluating alternatives. In: Meersman, R., Tari, Z. (eds.) OTM 2006. LNCS, vol. 4275, pp. 533–550. Springer, Heidelberg (2006). https://doi.org/10.1007/11914853_32
2. Bryl, V., Giorgini, P., Mylopoulos, J.: Designing socio-technical systems: from stakeholder goals to social networks. Requir. Eng. **14**, 47–70 (2008)
3. Chung, L., Nixon, B.A., Yu, E., Mylopoulos, J.: Non-Functional Requirements in Software Engineering. International Series in Software Engineering, vol. 5. Springer, New York (2000). https://doi.org/10.1007/978-1-4615-5269-7
4. Dalpiaz, F., Franch, X., Horkoff, J.: iStar 2.0 language guide. CoRR abs/1605.07767 (2016)
5. Dardenne, A., van Lamsweerde, A., Fickas, S.: Goal-directed requirements acquisition. Sci. Comput. Progr. **20**(1–2), 3–50 (1993)
6. ElRakaiby, Y., Borgida, A., Ferrari, A., Mylopoulos, J.: A refinement calculus for requirements engineering based on argumentation theory. In: Dobbie, G., Frank, U., Kappel, G., Liddle, S.W., Mayr, H.C. (eds.) ER 2020. LNCS, vol. 12400, pp. 3–18. Springer, Cham (2020). https://doi.org/10.1007/978-3-030-62522-1_1
7. Ferrario, M.A., Simm, W., Forshaw, S., Gradinar, A., Smith, M.T., Smith, I.C.: Values-first SE: research principles in practice. In: IEEE/ACM 38th International Conference on Software Engineering Companion (ICSE-C), pp. 553–562. ACM (2016)
8. Horkoff, J., et al.: Goal-oriented requirements engineering: a systematic literature map. In: 24th IEEE International Requirements Engineering Conference (RE), pp. 106–115. IEEE (2016)
9. van Lamsweerde, A.: Requirements engineering in the year 00: a research perspective. In: Proceedings of the 22nd International Conference on on Software Engineering, ICSE, pp. 5–19. ACM (2000)
10. van Lamsweerde, A.: Goal-oriented requirements engineering: a guided tour. In: 5th IEEE International Symposium on Requirements Engineering (RE), p. 249. IEEE (2001)
11. Letier, E., van Lamsweerde, A.: Agent-based tactics for goal-oriented requirements elaboration. In: Proceedings of the 24th International Conference on Software Engineering (ICSE), pp. 83–93 (2002)
12. Mougouei, D., Perera, H., Hussain, W., Shams, R.A., Whittle, J.: Operationalizing human values in software: a research roadmap. In: Proceedings of the ACM Joint Meeting on European Software Engineering Conference and Symposium on the Foundations of Software Engineering, ESEC/SIGSOFT FSE, pp. 780–784. ACM (2018)
13. Mylopoulos, J., Chung, L., Nixon, B.A.: Representing and using nonfunctional requirements: a process-oriented approach. IEEE Trans. Softw. Eng. **18**(6), 483–497 (1992)
14. Mylopoulos, J., Chung, L., Yu, E.S.K.: From object-oriented to goal-oriented requirements analysis. Commun. ACM **42**(1), 31–37 (1999)
15. Schwartz, S.H., Bilsky, W.: Toward a psychological structure of human values. J. Personal. Soc. Psychol. **53**, 550–562 (1987)
16. Yu, E.S.: Towards modelling and reasoning support for early-phase requirements engineering. In: Proceedings of the 3rd IEEE International Symposium on Requirements Engineering (ISRE), pp. 226–235. IEEE (1997)

Law Modeling for Fairness Requirements Elicitation in Artificial Intelligence Systems

Ana Lavalle[✉][ID], Alejandro Maté[ID], Juan Trujillo[ID],
and Jorge García-Carrasco[ID]

Software and Computing Systems, University of Alicante, Carretera San Vicente del
Raspeig s/n, 03690 San Vicente del Raspeig, Alicante, Spain
{alavalle,amate,jtrujillo}@dlsi.ua.es, jorge.g@ua.es

Abstract. As Artificial Intelligence (AI) algorithms become
widespread, concerns rise regarding their potential discrimination using
protected attributes such as race, sex, or age among others. Fairness is
a quality highly desired by society, however, it can be really difficult to
achieve. Identifying protected attributes and trying to maintain fairness
is both an important as well as a challenging task. In this paper, we propose a dynamic framework that considers the project context together
with law modeling in order to identify protected attributes that threaten
the fairness of AI models. This leads to a conscious evaluation of both
the accuracy and fairness of the AI solutions developed. To this aim, we
propose to model legal requirements by using Nòmos 3, which allows us
to capture the legal requirements that should be fulfilled into legal contexts that can be loaded into our framework. By following our proposal
we (i) map the duties in legal requirements to attributes in the used
dataset, identifying protected attributes and providing traceability, (ii)
help users in the selection of the definition of fairness that best suits the
context at hand, (iii) represent the output of AI models visually in order
to allow users to interpret how correct and fair are the decisions achieved
by the model. To show the applicability of our proposal, we exemplify
its application through a illustrative use case.

Keywords: Artificial Intelligence · Fairness · Legal requirements ·
Law modeling · Machine learning

1 Introduction

The use of Artificial Intelligence (AI) algorithms has become widespread, with
multiple predictive applications such as credit grant, recidivism, or employabil-
ity among others. At the same time Artificial Intelligence becomes a common
practice, multiple scandals derived from racist, sexist. In general, biased Artificial Intelligence outputs demand a closer analysis of the process involved in the
definition and training of AI algorithms.

© The Author(s), under exclusive license to Springer Nature Switzerland AG 2022
J. Ralyté et al. (Eds.): ER 2022, LNCS 13607, pp. 423–432, 2022.
https://doi.org/10.1007/978-3-031-17995-2_30

AI systems learn primarily from observing data. If that data is laden with stereotypical concepts of gender, the resulting application of the technology will perpetuate this bias [12]. The same situation applies to biases derived from race, religion, or any other sensitive aspect of individuals (we will refer to these aspects as protected attributes). As [2] asserts, testing for whether there is bias in AI applications is an absolutely relevant and challenging topic, not only for practitioners and researchers, but also for the benefit of having a fairer society.

Given the potential severity of the situation, the European Commission has presented ethical guidelines for a trustworthy AI [1], which describes how a trustworthy AI should be: lawful, ethical and robust Therefore, it is essential to ensure that the decisions made by AI solutions do not reflect discriminatory behavior and comply with the norms established in laws.

However, although fairness is a quality highly desired by society, it can be really difficult to achieve in practice [13]. Multiple definitions of fairness exist and there is no clear agreement on which one apply in each situation [17]. Moreover, the detailed differences between multiple definitions are difficult to grasp. The underneath question in order to guarantee the fairness in AI processes is to be able to clearly locate the main variables that may cause unfairness, and therefore, to properly manage them throughout the whole learning process.

Thereby, in this paper, we propose a dynamic framework that identifies protected attributes which threaten the fairness of AI models by considering the project context together with law modeling. The main advantage of our proposal is that it helps to discover protected attributes that are present in legal requirements and it should be taken into account. Furthermore, it helps to choose and measure fairness of Artificial Intelligence systems decisions in an easy manner and from different perspectives.

2   Related Work

Bias can appear in many forms. Depending in which phase we find the bias, different techniques will be applied. Authors in [14] groups them into three categories: (1) Understanding bias: Helping to understand how bias is created in the society and how it forms the input of our technological systems. (2) Mitigating bias: Addressing bias at different stages of Artificial Intelligence decision-making systems (3) Accounting for bias: Realizing bias proactively, through bias-aware data collection, or retroactively, by explaining AI decisions in human terms.

Several works have focused on a try to identify biases in the data. In [10] an approach is proposed to automatically detect the existence of biases in datasets through an algorithm and generates a series of visualizations to represent the bias. In [16] a transparent model distillation approach is presented to detect bias in Black-box risk scoring models.

Other works are focused on the explainability of machine learning models [4], this could be linked to our work as it provides a way to assess the degree of fairness that a model has in the context of Law.

On the other hand, several techniques are focused in modifying the dataset according to protected data in order to mitigate bias, mainly based on rebalancing techniques [11, 15]. [9] try to identify bias in the labels and proposes a method based on the re-weighting of the elements in the dataset to mitigate such bias.

However, even if bias was detected and mitigated, fairness can be really difficult to achieve in practice [13]. As [17] argues, there is no clear agreement on which definition to apply in each situation. Moreover, the detailed differences between multiple definitions are difficult to grasp. Therefore, it can be complicated to choose the most appropriate fairness definition for each particular case.

Additionally, different contexts may arise containing different protected attributes which may be affected by fairness. Frameworks such as Nòmos 3 [6] help us to represent legal knowledge in requirements engineering. However, to the best of our knowledge, none of the approaches provide a way to extract protected attributes from Legal Requirements and assist in the definition and interpretation of Fairness in AI models.

Therefore, we propose a dynamic framework that considers the project context together with law modeling to identify protected attributes that threaten the fairness of AI models. Moreover, it helps to choose and measure fairness definitions of AI systems in an easy manner and from different perspectives.

3   How Fairly Meet Legal Requirements in Artificial Intelligence Algorithms

As previously-argued, Artificial Intelligence algorithms are being used in high-risk decisions where they can show discriminatory behavior towards certain groups. However, identifying protected attributes and trying to maintain fairness is both an important as well as a challenging task.

Figure 1 represents an overview of our framework, the left side represents the Legal Requirements Modeling by using Nòmos 3 [6], while the right side represents the Fairness Elicitation and Interpretation Process. The users involved in our framework will be AI experts, who will extract information from the company's personnel to define its requirements.

On the left side, we can see as our framework supports several Requirements Models where requirements from AI projects are modeled. These models should follow different laws established in the context of an application. Therefore, by following our proposal, it is possible to reuse a set of the legal components (Legal Models) since different contexts may be affected by the same laws.

In order to formalize the laws we have follow Nòmos 3 [6], a framework aimed to ensure compliance of requirements to a given law. Once the laws have been established and the norms that each law should follow have been specified, it is possible discover protected attributes that may be presented in legal requirements and it should be taken into account.

Following the Fairness Elicitation and Interpretation Process (right side), it will be possible to match if the dataset contains any of the protected attributes exacted from the laws. In case that the dataset contains protected attributes, we provide a set of guidelines to help users to choose and measure fairness of AI systems decisions in an easy manner and from different perspectives.

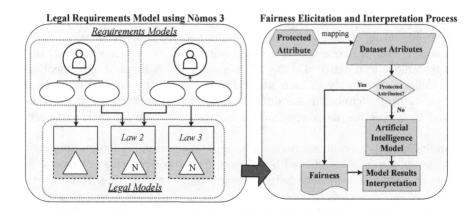

Fig. 1. Proposed framework overview.

In the following sections, we further describe the different steps of our proposal. Our proposal is applicable to any AI system, however it is important to take it into account in systems related to public services, selection systems, bank loans, access to education, etc. For the sake of the comprehension, we describe every step by applying it in a illustrative use case based on a German bank's credit granting. We assume that this bank must follow the "Organic Law 3/2007, of March 22, for the effective equality of women and men [8]".

3.1 Dataset Description

The dataset that we have chosen in order to apply our approach is Statlog (German Credit Data) dataset published in the UCI Machine Learning Repository [5]. This dataset is related to credit risk assessment; it contains information about 1000 loan applicants, including if they were suitable for a credit or not, i.e., whether the individual will be able to return the credit correctly or not.

3.2 Modeling Legal Requirements by Using Nòmos 3

The first step of our proposal is to capture the legal requirements that should be fulfilled into our use case. To this aim, we have used Nòmos 3 [6], a framework widely accepted for representing legal knowledge in requirements engineering.

Figure 2 represents the Legal Requirements Model associated to the Role of a Bank operating in Germany that must follow the "Organic Law 3/2007, of March 22 [8]". The concepts and relationships used to model laws were proposed in [6,7]. **Concepts** are briefly described as: ***Goal:*** a requirement that the Social Role wants to achieve. ***Norm (Duty):*** the conditions, which are given by laws or other regulations, that the system should comply with. ***Situation:*** the conditions that make a Norm applicable/satisfied. ***Role:*** two types of roles. *Legal Role* is responsible for make happen the Duties, is the role that the law

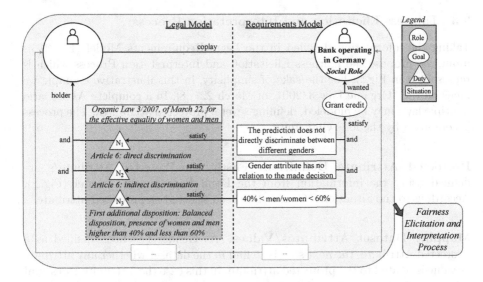

Fig. 2. Legal requirements model using Nòmos 3.

addresses as being the holder of the duty and *Social Role*, who wants to achieve the Goals defined in the requirements model.

The **relationships** are defined as: ***Coplay***: Social Roles have to comply with the Norms for whom the Legal Role is responsible. ***Hold***: relation from Legal Role to Norms. It represents that the Role is responsible for the Situations in the consequent of those Norms. ***Satisfy***: relationships between Situations and Norms, when the Situation is satisfied the Norm is satisfied. ***Want***: represents the Goals that a Role want to achieve. ***And***: something is fulfilled if all the sources of the relationships fulfills it.

In this case, the model (Fig. 2) is used to evaluate the compliance of the Bank goals following certain duties established in the "Organic Law 3/2007, of March 22 [8]". As seen in Fig. 2, the model is discomposed into two models. The left side represents the legal duties that should be complied with, while the right side represents the system goals and requirements.

Starting from the right side of Fig. 2, the Social Role of the Bank wants to grant credit. To satisfy this goal it should comply with the situations "The prediction does not directly discriminate between different genders", "Gender attribute has no relation to the made decision" and "The distribution between men and women should be between 40% and 60%". This specific Situations help us to detect which are the protected attributes that arise in this context. The Duties established in the "Organic Law 3/2007, of March 22 [8]" are grouped. This will help users to reuse this package of duties when the same law affect them in another context. Moreover, other laws can be decomposed into Duties in order to take into account all the laws that affects the Legal Role.

3.3   Fairness Elicitation and Interpretation Process

Taking the information detailed in the Legal Requirements Model (Fig. 2) as input, we propose the Fairness Elicitation and Interpretation Process which is represented in Fig. 3. For the sake of simplicity, in this illustrative example we focus on the "Organic Law 3/2007, of March 22" [8]. In a complete AI scenario multiple laws may be modeled, defining several protected attributes. The process is composed by the following steps:

Protected Attribute Definition. Firstly, the Protected Attribute/s are defined using the information from the Legal Requirements Model (Fig. 2). According to the Situations, Gender has been selected as protected attribute.

Mapping Dataset Attributes/Values. As Gender has been defined as a Protected Attribute, the next step is to find in the dataset whether any attribute or value is related to the protected attribute. In this case the, attribute **Personal status and sex** have been detected.

Fairness. Since protected attributes have been detected in the dataset, the next step in our process is to establish how to measure the fairness. In this case, as detailed in the Legal Requirements Model (Fig. 2), there are two roles, the Legal Role and Social Role, and they may pursue different definitions of fairness.

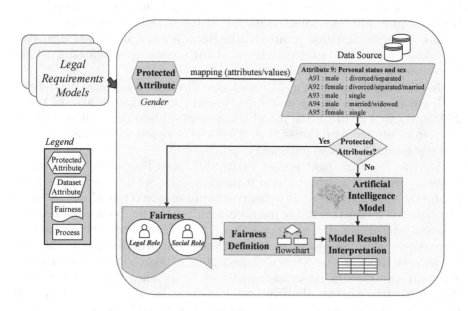

Fig. 3. Fairness elicitation and interpretation process.

Multiple definitions of fairness exist and it can be unclear which is the most appropriate for each particular case. Hence, with the aim of making the fairness definitions more understandable and help users in the selection of the best metrics for each particular case, we have proposed Table 1. It contains the definitions of the most common group fairness metrics, along with a brief description in a language that the different roles could understand. There are more specific metrics related to fairness at individual or subgroup level [17], but the metrics presented in the Table are already enough to quantify the degree of fairness, so they are omitted.

In the case of the bank acting as Legal Role, it should hold the "Organic Law 3/2007, of March 22 [8]" and its Duties established in Fig. 2. For this reason, it choose Equal Opportunity to measure the fairness. According to the Law, it should be maximized the grant of credit to worthy individuals.

On the other hand, the bank acting as Social Role has the goal of grant credit. However it should minimize the granting of credit to non-worthy individuals as the bank always wishes to minimize the number of individuals that will not return the credit. For this reason, it choose Predictive Equality.

Artificial Intelligence Model Training. In order to predict whether an individual is worthy of a grant or not, the *CatBoost* classifier [3] with default hyperparameters will be used. 80% of the data will be used for training, and the

Table 1. Group fairness definitions.

Equalized odds	Worthy and non-worthy individuals should be treated equally independently of its sex	Groups within protected attributes have the same rate of true and false positives	Equal Opportunity + Predictive Equality
Equal opportunity	The frequency of classifying a worthy individual as worthy should be maximized and equal for both sexes	Same true positive (or false positive) rates	$TPR = \dfrac{TP}{TP + FN}$
Predictive equality	The frequency of incorrectly classifying a non-worthy individual as worthy should be minimized and equal for both sexes	Same false positive (or true negative) rates	$FPR = \dfrac{FP}{TN + FP}$
Predictive parity	The ratio of correctly predicted worthy individuals by the model should be the same for both sexes	Same precision across all groups	$Pr = \dfrac{TP}{TP + FP}$
Conditional demographic parity	If two individuals have the same creditability level, treat them equally, independently of its sex	Given a set of legitimate factors L, the probability is the same across all groups within protected attributes	$P(Y\|L = l, A = 0) = P(Y\|L = l, A = 1)$

remaining 20% will be used for evaluation purposes. An accuracy of 77.5% was obtained, i.e. it has enough performance to continue with the framework. For further details, code and dataset can be found at: https://gitlab.com/lucentia/bias-in-ai/-/tree/main/ER2022.

Model Results Interpretation. Finally, the last step of the framework is to assess the fairness of the model according to the fairness metrics chosen from Table 1, namely Equal Opportunity (from the Legal Role standpoint) and Predictive Equality (from the Social Role standpoint). The confusion matrices can be seen in Fig. 4, which contains all the information that will be used to compute the chosen fairness metrics, i.e. the True Negatives (TN), False Positives (FP), False Negatives (FN) and True Positives (TP), reading the matrix left-to-right then top-to-bottom, separated by the different values of the protected attribute, in this case, the sex. By using the confusion matrices and the formulas of Table 1, we can quantify the degree of Equal Opportunity and Predictive Equality as the difference in absolute value of the TPR and FPR of both sexes, respectively. Therefore, a value closer to zero means a higher degree of fairness.

The results are presented in Table 2. As it can be seen, the TPRs for both sexes are considerably high, i.e., the majority of worthy individuals for both sexes will receive grants. As the TPRs are also similar, the value of Equal Opportunity is 0.020, close to zero, so it can be affirmed that fairness is achieved from the Legal role standpoint, as the fairness metric selected following Table 1 is achieved.

On the other side, the FPRs differ considerably between both sexes: 61% for men, while women is around 38%, resulting in a 22.3% deviation from the perfect predictive equality. In other words, it is more likely to give a grant to a non-worthy male than to a non-worthy female, thus Predictive Equality is not achieved and fairness is not completely achieved from the Social role standpoint.

Regarding the Situation "the distribution between men and women should be between 40% and 60%" indicated in Fig. 2, it can also be shown that, of all individuals predicted by the algorithm as worthy of a grant, only the 28.3% are women, so this Situation is not satisfied.

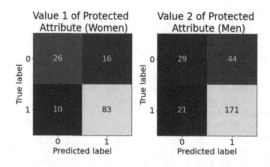

Fig. 4. Confusion matrices of the predictions given by the model for both sexes.

Table 2. Values obtained for the chosen fairness metrics, less is better, except on TPR.

	TPR	Equal opportunity	FPR	Predictive equality
Men	0.907	0.020	0.610	0.223
Women	0.927		0.381	

4 Conclusions and Future Work

Throughout the paper, we have described the relevance of guaranteeing the fairness of Artificial Intelligence (AI) systems. One of the main difficulties for achieving fairness is to detect critical variables that may affect the fairness, choose the fairness type more suitable for each context and measure it.

Thus, in this paper we have presented a dynamic framework that considers the project context together with law modeling in order to identify protected attributes that threaten the fairness of AI models. Our proposal (i) maps legal requirements to dataset attributes identifying protected attributes, (ii) helps users to choose the most appropriate fairness definition and (iii) represents the output of AI models visually in order to interpret how correct and fair are the decisions achieved by the model.

To show the applicability of our proposal, we have exemplified its application through an illustrative use case based on a German bank credit grant. We have shown that the model trained treats worthy individuals equally disregarding their sex. However, it tends to overestimate non-worthy men in comparison to non-worthy women when predicting their creditability for a grant. Furthermore, we have also shown that of all individuals predicted by the algorithm as worthy of a grant, only the 28.3% were women.

As part of our future work we are studying how to link protected attributes through semantic analysis and taking into account the user feedback. Furthermore, we are trying to define how to deal with conflicting laws, rules that depend on other rules and changing requirements.

Acknowledgements. This work has been co-funded by the AETHER-UA project (PID 2020-112540RB-C43), funded by Spanish Ministry of Science and Innovation. And the BALLADEER (PROMETEO/2021/088) project, funded by the Conselleria de Innovación, Universidades, Ciencia y Sociedad Digital (Generalitat Valenciana).

References

1. Commission, E.: Ethics guidelines for trustworthy AI (2021). https://digital-strategy.ec.europa.eu/en/library/ethics-guidelines-trustworthy-ai
2. Davenport, T., Guha, A., Grewal, D., Bressgott, T.: How artificial intelligence will change the future of marketing. J. Acad. Mark. Sci. **48**(1), 24–42 (2019). https://doi.org/10.1007/s11747-019-00696-0
3. Dorogush, A.V., Ershov, V., Gulin, A.: Catboost: gradient boosting with categorical features support. arXiv preprint arXiv:1810.11363 (2018)

4. Došilović, F.K., Brčić, M., Hlupić, N.: Explainable artificial intelligence: a survey. In: 2018 41st International Convention on Information and Communication Technology, Electronics and Microelectronics (MIPRO), pp. 0210–0215. IEEE (2018)

5. Hofmann, H.: UCI Machine Learning Repository–Statlog (German Credit Data) (1994). https://archive.ics.uci.edu/ml/datasets/Statlog+%28German+Credit+Data%29. Accessed 10 Apr 2022

6. Ingolfo, S., Jureta, I., Siena, A., Perini, A., Susi, A.: Nòmos 3: legal compliance of roles and requirements. In: Yu, E., Dobbie, G., Jarke, M., Purao, S. (eds.) ER 2014. LNCS, vol. 8824, pp. 275–288. Springer, Cham (2014). https://doi.org/10.1007/978-3-319-12206-9_22

7. Ingolfo, S., Siena, A., Mylopoulos, J.: Goals and compliance in nomos 3. In: iStar (2014). http://ceur-ws.org/Vol-1157/paper8.pdf

8. Jefatura del Estado Español: Ley Orgánica 3/2007, de 22 de marzo, para la igualdad efectiva de mujeres y hombres (2007). https://www.boe.es/buscar/act.php?id=BOE-A-2007-6115. Accessed 10 Apr 2022

9. Jiang, H., Nachum, O.: Identifying and correcting label bias in machine learning. In: International Conference on Artificial Intelligence and Statistics, pp. 702–712. PMLR (2020)

10. Lavalle, A., Maté, A., Trujillo, J.: An approach to automatically detect and visualize bias in data analytics. In: Proceedings of the 22nd International Workshop on Design, Optimization, Languages and Analytical Processing of Big Data, DOLAP@EDBT/ICDT 2020. CEUR Workshop Proceedings, vol. 2572, pp. 84–88. CEUR-WS.org (2020). http://ceur-ws.org/Vol-2572/short11.pdf

11. Lavalle, A., Maté, A., Trujillo, J., García, J.: A methodology based on rebalancing techniques to measure and improve fairness in artificial intelligence algorithms. In: Proceedings of the 24nd International Workshop on Design, Optimization, Languages and Analytical Processing of Big Data DOLAP@EDBT/ICDT 2022. CEUR Workshop Proceedings, vol. 3130, pp. 81–85. CEUR-WS.org (2022). http://ceur-ws.org/Vol-3130/paper9.pdf

12. Leavy, S.: Gender bias in artificial intelligence: the need for diversity and gender theory in machine learning. In: 2018 IEEE/ACM 1st International Workshop on Gender Equality in Software Engineering, GE@ICSE, pp. 14–16. ACM (2018). https://doi.org/10.1145/3195570.3195580

13. Mehrabi, N., Morstatter, F., Saxena, N., Lerman, K., Galstyan, A.: A survey on bias and fairness in machine learning. ACM Comput. Surv. (CSUR) 54(6), 1–35 (2021). https://doi.org/10.1145/3457607

14. Ntoutsi, E., et al.: Bias in data-driven artificial intelligence systems-an introductory survey. Wiley Interdiscip. Rev. Data Min. Knowl. Discov. 10(3), e1356 (2020). https://doi.org/10.1002/widm.1356

15. Peng, K., Chakraborty, J., Menzies, T.: xFAIR: better fairness via model-based rebalancing of protected attributes. arXiv preprint arXiv:2110.01109 (2021)

16. Tan, S., Caruana, R., Hooker, G., Lou, Y.: Detecting bias in black-box models using transparent model distillation. CoRR abs/1710.06169 (2017). http://arxiv.org/abs/1710.06169

17. Verma, S., Rubin, J.: Fairness definitions explained. In: Proceedings of the International Workshop on Software Fairness, FairWare@ICSE, pp. 1–7. ACM (2018). https://doi.org/10.1145/3194770.3194776

Author Index

Printed in the United States
by Baker & Taylor Publisher Services